PROFESSIONAL PHOTOGRAPHER'S SURVIVAL GUIDE

Charles Rotkin

Writer's Digest Books

Cincinnati, Ohio

About the Author

Charles E. Rotkin has been concerned for a lifetime about the care and feeding of all artists, especially those in photography, his profession for five decades. He firmly believes the old news photography maxim: "f/8 and be there." And he has been there. For fifty years he was a photographer and writer for nearly every major publication group. He has achieved prominence worldwide, won many awards, and has led a lifelong fight for the rights of his colleagues. He has written and lectured extensively, and teaches photography and photographic book-making at several institutions. He was an early president of the American Society of Magazine Photographers. He is a life member of the National Press Photographer's Association, member emeritus of the Picture Agency Council, and is active in many press and writing groups.

Charlie is editor and publisher of *The Rotkin Review*, a photographic book reviewing journal. His other books include *The USA — An Aerial Close-up, Europe — An Aerial Close-up*, and *Puerto Rico — Caribbean Crossroads*. Of the two books of aerial photography Cornell Capa (Executive Director of the International Center of Photography) has written, "frustrated by military photo missions that caused him to fly too high to photograph the land below, he perfected a low-level technique that made his books a priceless collection of views that ordinary mortals could never see in any other way than in these volumes."

He is now working on a novel about his five decades in photography. His friends and co-workers need not head for the storm cellars. He loves the people he writes about and has no desire to write a *kiss and tell*, he just wants to tell about a wonderful world.

Professional Photographer's Survival Guide. Copyright © 1992, 1982 by Charles E. Rotkin. Printed and bound in the United States of America. All rights reserved. No part of this book may be reproduced in any form or by any electronic or mechanical means including information storage and retrieval systems without permission in writing from the publisher, except by a reviewer, who may quote brief passages in a review. Published by Writer's Digest Books, an imprint of F&W Publications, Inc., 1507 Dana Avenue, Cincinnati, Ohio 45207; 1(800)289-0963. First edition.

96 95 94 93 92   5 4 3 2 1

This book was originally published by American Photographic Book Publishing, an imprint of Watson-Guptill Publications, a division of Billboard Publications, Inc., 1515 Broadway, New York, NY 10036.

Library of Congress Cataloging-in-Publication Data

Rotkin, Charles E.
    Professional photographer's survival guide / Charles E. Rotkin.
        p.   cm.
    Includes index.
    ISBN 0-89879-554-0 (paper)
        1. Commercial photography. 2. Photography — Business methods.
    I. Title.
    TR690.R67 1992
    770'.23'2 — dc20   92-26691
                                                                                                    CIP

Designed by Paul Neff

Table of Contents

Preface and Acknowledgements

To distill a lifetime of my experience, and that of my friends and colleagues in photography, into one small book is not only a monumental task but a near impossibility as well. Something is certain to be left out, someone will surely be misquoted, some will applaud and others may rise to anger or insult, however honorable my intentions. Yet I want to impart as much knowledge as I can to my readers about this marvelous, exciting, and sometimes perplexing method of communication called photography. I want them to enjoy it as much as I have.

Perhaps because I grew up in a working-class environment that, fortunately, included an appreciation of the arts, I have always been aware of the problems that artists (hereafter called photographers) have had in surviving. Because if they don't survive, how can they produce their body of work? I don't believe in the "starving artist" theory and prefer to think that a photographer can better practice his craft if he does not have to spend an inordinate amount of time just scrounging for the necessities of life.

In order to accomplish both objectives — art and survival — the photographer has to learn to act as an intelligent businessman. Can this be done? Let's put it this way — if it can't, both are in trouble.

My two-term presidency of the ASMP and subsequent twelve years on the Board of Governors did not seem to do a lot for me professionally, as I frequently found myself in the dubious position of working on assignment with the very editors I often had to do battle with on questions involving the care, feeding and rights of the photographers. If nothing else, it was a learning experience.

So, many years later, after the twentieth phone call from former Picture Editor of *Audubon Magazine*, book packager, editor, friend and colleague, Ann Guilfoyle (see pages 59-61) asking me how I would deal with Photographer X or Editor Y on various questions, plus calls from other purveyors and users of photography with similar questions, I began wondering just what the photographer did look like from the other side of the desk. More importantly, I thought about ways of developing a mutual working ground rather than a battleground in the arena of photography.

Again it was Guilfoyle who not only talked me into doing this book, but assisted mightily in the preparation of its outline, and for this I offer her a very special thanks. Other editor-friends including Robert Rahtz, former Editor in Chief of Macmillan's School Division, threw life preservers to me when I was drowning in a sea of verbiage, proving that the blue pencil is indeed mightier than the sword. Often my day would be made when I would find a terse marginal note in the manuscript that simply said "yucch" or offered some other comment that would forcibly restrain me from wandering off course when recollecting some memorable kiting of an expense account or nutty behavior by a photographer, editor or client.

My deep thanks is also reserved for all those who sat patiently for me while I interviewed them and who so graciously shared their feelings and philosophies about photography and their roles in it. I am especially touched by (and grateful to) Alfred Eisenstaedt and Gordon Parks, who not only took the time to tell mc how they got started and survived in photography, but also how they "blew" their first assignments, survived, and lived (professionally) to tell the tale. There are others who always had time for a phone call with some useful and pertinent advice about a host of things.

Unlike the movie Oscar winners who usually credit their mothers, mothers-in-law and agents with everything leading up to the Oscar award, I do want to thank my wife Adele for giving up her personal fight with the computer to assist in the preparation of this manuscript, and as a former picture editor, art director and book designer herself, for raging at my syntax that, like the symbol for infinity (∞), is often difficult to comprehend. And thanks too, to the many others not listed here who were responsive and caring. They know who they are, and they know my appreciation.

Also, my computerized thesaurus has no synonym for the word "photographer," and I refuse to use some of the terms bandied about, i.e., "shooter" (ugh); "camera bug" (we are not insects!); "lensmen" or "lenswomen" (terible); or to adopt what some old city-desk types might roar across the room: "Send out a camera!"

A writer, who is also a good friend, warned me before I wrote a single word of this book that I had to be careful of the his/her, he/she designations. I want to assure my readers that I am totally aware of this problem in the language, but I found no better solution than the traditional one. So I did not encumber this book by adding the feminine counterpart of "he" or "him" in each sentence where it arose. To paraphrase a famous reporter, "I have seen the future (in writing) and it doesn't work."

So there are no he/she's, men/women or other dual designations in the book, and I have kept the generic *he* to a minimum.

So I salute every photographer, editor, picture user, or other contributor to our craft, be they male or female.

Charles E. Rotkin

Introduction

What this book will do is tell you how to conduct yourself as a professional photographer. It will not tell you how to make a photograph. Presumably, you know that by now or you wouldn't be reading this. Nor are you going to be told how to develop a roll of film or make a print or a transparency. You should have mastered these skills by now. Making the picture is only the tip of the iceberg, and what lies beneath those cold waters determines whether you sink or swim. This book will tell you what is important after the photograph is made, as well as give you some insight about what to do before a camera is unlimbered.

The book you hold in your hands is a guide to survival in the complex field of professional photography. It concerns itself not only with getting you ready for a shooting or an assignment but with what happens to those pictures after the shutter is released. How do you market, store, retrieve, and perhaps resell them, time and time again? What follows here will tell you how to protect not only your rights but your skin as well. This is a guide to getting a career launched as a professional — and keeping it going.

Sixteen special interviews are interspersed between the chapters of this book. If you perceive an emphasis on interviews with "older" and more seasoned photographers (after all they are the ones who have survived) and less time spent on younger ones, there is a good reason for it. As this book is a manual for survival, I want to bring you the thinking and experience of fine photographers who have indeed "survived" and managed to stay in business, leading full and productive lives over a long period of time. Accordingly, I have concentrated on talking more with photographers whose professional careers have extended beyond the minimum of ten or fifteen years of activity that I feel are necessary for a photographer to be considered "established."

But we have not neglected younger contemporary photographers who by the strength of their talent, drive and devotion to craft have begun carving impressive niches in their own right. Many of these newer talents have succeeded by using tools and techniques that did not exist beyond the experimental laboratories a dozen years ago. My total concern is with photographers who have consistently produced a fine body of work over the years, and who continue to function well despite the ravages of time and age.

Side by side with giants like Alfred Eisenstaedt, Carl Mydans, Arnold Newman, Gordon Parks and Berenice Abbott, are their much younger contemporaries, Peter and David Turnley, twin-brother journalists from the Midwest, one of whom has won a Pulitzer Prize. As a team they have won numerous other national and international awards. Mary Ellen Mark's magnificent and sensitive photographs continue to grace the pages of many major magazines. Ebullient and bouncy Jade Albert leads both her nearly-infant models and assistants a merry chase down the halls of her spacious studio in New York's photo district to produce sparkling, lively commercial photography. Greg Heisler, who couples his already incisive photography with electronic imaging, gives a new meaning to the art of photojournalism.

Sadly, since this book was first written, some of the towers of photography are gone. Berenice Abbott, who had just celebrated her ninety-third birthday, Arthur Rothstein, and Philippe Halsman are no longer with us, but their images will live forever. All were friends of mine, had spoken freely with me, and passed their photographic philosophies forward. Their thoughts had no time frame and so I call to your attention their very real attitudes which were strong then and are still valid today.

Too few photographers understand that professionalism is as important as ability. All of you who wish to follow in the footsteps of Henri Cartier-Bresson, David Douglas Duncan or W. Eugene Smith must remember that these photographic giants would never have achieved the success they did if they had not been thoroughgoing professionals in the first place.

In this book I am attempting to cover as many problems as possible that the new professional may face and give seasoned advice as to how he should deal with them. But what about the problems of the *picture buyer* or user in dealing with and respecting the needs of the photographer? How does the man or woman on the other side of the desk perceive *you*, the photographer?

A good part of the behavior of the picture buyer toward the photographer stems from his personal attitudes toward creativity, productivity, honesty and dependability. Not a little of this is based on the first contact with the photographer and how the latter's personality comes through. Not an inconsiderable part of all these perceptions arise from the needs of the buyer and whether the photographer can supply them. If the editor or picture buyer (your client) is insecure and uncertain of the requirements of the picture request, these insecurities will be transmitted to the photographer. Thus, the client may be dependent on the judgment and ability of the photographer, and if that judgment is also lacking, both parties are in trouble. The clients' training and experience will, in great measure, reflect on their dealings with the photographer, and that may be the critical factor as to whether a job is a success or failure.

While gathering the material for this book, I spoke with a broad spectrum of picture users, editors, researchers, art directors, art buyers, and electronic-imaging experts. They included the managing editors of some of the great picture publications through associate editors, ad agency art buyers, advertising and editorial art directors, picture editors, educators, electronic-imaging and conventional laboratory managers, museum and gallery directors, and others concerned with photography, its production, sale and use. I asked for a brief rundown on their professional backgrounds, how they saw the photographers they dealt with, what responses they received, and if relevant, if they received what they wanted from the photographers. I also asked them what the photographer had to do to reach them, not so much physically, but in the acceptance of their work.

Too often today, I hear moans about the demise of the great photomagazines that were published from the 1930s to the 1970s and the so-called loss of markets created by their death. Actually, there are more magazines being published than ever before, and we look back with pleasure to the big picture magazines that set the style and pace of honest photojournalism. They remain in our minds as beacons, for they taught us lessons that left indelible marks on all of us. We should never forget them as we move on to the new technologies that permit us to make even greater photographs, move them faster and distribute them to millions of people who never had the chance to see many of those great and historic images. But they'll see others of equal importance and each new generation of photographers will add to the luster of the stalwarts and pioneers of the first 150 years of the era of the silver halide image.

Years ago, when sound motion pictures began, there seemed to be a disproportionate number of Hungarian directors, so much so that it was rumored there was a sign in the director's lounge of one of the major studios that read: "It is not enough to be a Hungarian; one must have talent as well." Maybe true, maybe not, but we borrow from the principle and remember that it is not enough to be just a good photographer—one must have professionalism as well.

Even the term "professional photographer" is an ambiguity. Take a sampling of the nearly 5,000 photographers in the American Society of Magazine Photographers (ASMP) or the more than 8,000 in the National Press Photographers Association (NPPA) and you will find that only a small number ever had formal photographic schooling. Doctors, lawyers and architects, among others, call themselves "professionals" and have degrees to prove it. But a degree is only one way to defining a professional. Others point to "a whole body of work" or use the measurement of being able to *sell* as a definition of what makes a professional. I define it in other ways, drawing a little from all the existing definitions. If you are being paid to make or sell a photograph, then do it in a way that will bring credit to you and your colleagues. If you can deliver what is asked of you on time, in a direct nononsense way, treat your colleagues and clients with respect, demand and receive the same respect from them, keep from tripping over your own ego or from getting caught up in phony romanticism or macho complexes, and still produce fine photography, then by my definition you are a professional.

"Professionalism" is not a label to be taken lightly. Nor is the word "artist." The old arguments about whether photography is art have been trampled into the dust. Yet this wasn't always so. It took many years before photography was accorded art status. Even today there are skeptics who still want to consider photography a cold, mechanical science. Perhaps it is, in some highly technical fields of fully automated, computer-controlled (but not electronically imaged) photographs, but I consider photography a graphic art and a magnificent one at that. And while the computer may indeed help to produce images that no human can possibly do alone, it still takes a creative human to direct those computers. Nor should we forget that while it takes a human to start a machine, it also requires a human to run it, stop it and utilize well what it has produced.

How does the professional photographer balance these extremes? Only by proving he can be at one time both artist and businessman. The terms are not mutually exclusive. Can the artist survive *without* being a businessman? Probably not, and that is the real reason for this book. The photographers presented here are indeed both. Otherwise they could not have survived long enough in the marketplace to be able to make it to the top.

Chapter One
The Professional Photographer and His Markets

What Is a Professional Photographer?

The professional photographer is one who earns a living (or attempts to do so) by producing and selling photography. Sadly, the operative word here may be 'attempts.' Although frequently, it is not a *lack* of markets that frustrates the beginning professional, but a lack of knowing where the markets are and how to get one's foot in the door so that his or her craft may be shown.

Professional photographers vary widely. They may work in a small-town studio that supplies graduation, confirmation, bar mitzvah, wedding photographs; or in a high-tech studio that photographs fashion, food and other illustration for glossy paper, magazine advertising. They may also be artists creating sensitive, introspective portraits. Photographers also make sophisticated, and in some cases highly complex, photographic forays into forensic science and micro-photography. And now, with the advent of the computer that can digitalize images, the photographer's output may be headed for a satellite dish for transmission to a printing plant halfway around the world as well as to a fine-arts gallery around the corner.

There are at least one and perhaps many categories for each letter of the alphabet: A for architecture or art, X for Xerography, Y for youth, and Z for zoology. But whatever your category, there are basic needs that apply to all photographers: the need for a subject, the need for some (and I use the word *some* advisedly) mastery of technique, and the need for a market.

Photographs can be as varied as the locales in which they are taken. They come from those same small-town studios or from high-fashion emporiums ringed by thousands of dollars of expensive lighting gear and multi-speaker stereo systems. Pictures also flow out of labs, studios and on-site locations of photographers who make their photographs on the streets, on farms, in fields, or in forests—in any geographic location from outer space to Outer Mongolia. Any place that a camera can be transported to and operated, whether by hand, remote control or robot, offers photographic possibilities. An image is only that until it can be transferred to some reproducible medium and brought to the attention of a viewer or viewers.

What is the common denominator? It is the photographer. Much has been written about the multiple roles the photographer must play in order to function—teacher, counselor, chemist, seeing-eye dog, plumber, psychologist, stage manager, coffee runner, computer hacker, whatever—and much of it is true. The photographer, after all, has to bring together a variety of talents, skills, and approaches toward one final goal . . . a goal that requires him to use every sense or sensation available. In one way specialists have advantages. They can limit their coverage to one particular kind of photography. But most photographers are not so specialized, and, it seems, there has been a sharp reversal in the trends toward specialization.

Photographers are creative persons, and like creative persons everywhere, they tend to become restless and unhappy when they are confined to one branch of the art. They yearn to do something else, enter a new world, explore different facets of their own and others' lives. They look for a challenge, or perhaps a way to relieve boredom, or a means to augment their income.

Cornell Capa, long-time photojournalist, ex-*LIFE* staffer, creator and Executive Director of the International Center for Photography in New York, summed up the requirements of the photojournalist well. Capa said, "What will obviously make the difference between a successful and an unsuccessful photographer is the intellectual 'baggage' he brings with him. He should have a heightened sense of curiosity and be able to foresee and predict sequences of events. He should have the right equipment, preset and ready, so that when an event does occur, he is in the right position at the right time to take that sequence very quickly. I think the old-fashioned statement, 'f/8 and be there!' is true even today. The ability of the photographer to 'get in' to shoot is 99 percent of the battle and requires that he be 'trusted.' "

Trust is an intangible but very critical part of the photographer's "baggage," for unless the photographer can engender a feeling of trust within those he is photographing, it is likely that the pictures will fail. Capa gave the example of photographer John Bryson, a former magazine editor and now a much sought after photographer of theatrical personalities, who was permitted to photograph Katherine Hepburn only because Miss Hepburn trusted him. Capa related another example where trust was vital in the relationship between a photographer and his subject. Famed *LIFE* photographer Gordon Parks (see page 146) was put to a test of trust when he had to photograph his own good friend Mohammed Ali. Parks was admitted to the dressing room after Ali had taken a particularly savage beating at the hands of Joe Frazier in the ring. But because Ali was his friend and trusted him, Parks did not photograph Ali's condition even though he knew this was the picture his editors were looking for. Capa said about Parks, "He knew what he didn't take! But this can also be good and bad, because as a truth-telling, hard-hitting photojournalist, he missed the picture. But in not making the picture he retained Ali's trust as a friend. The editors were impressed, as it turned out, not angry at all, and wrote a sensitive piece about the situation. And it also ensured Parks's relationship with Ali for future pictures."

"The basic rule," said Capa, "is for the photographer to use intelligence and sensitivity as a primary part of his photographic skill. The photographer's ability to gain the confidence of his subjects is important. Unfortunately, he can also use his abilities the other way—he can betray a confidence and create all sorts of havoc in the name of news or a feature story. Gaining people's confidence can be either a short-term or a long-term endeavor. Even if a photographer takes a long time to build people's confidence, he eventually will capitalize on it. But if he uses his position in a hit-and-run manner and betrays confidences or trusts, he will suffer from it. If he develops a hit-and-run reputation, it won't be long before everyone guards against him, and he will find many closed doors. "Eventually," Capa said with irony, "he will get the job his reputation has brought him, what he is known for."

What Are a Professional Photographer's Qualities?

Here is what a number of noted photographers and others have had to say about the subject.

The late Philippe Halsman, one of the finest photographers of all time, said that a photographer was essentially a voyeur. He didn't mean that the photographer is a "Peeping Tom," but merely that he or she is an intensely curious person. A picture book published in France at the time of the Paris Commune (1871) said that the photographer was a "faithful witness." Susan Sontag, in her book *On Photography*, implies that photographers are people who seem to have been robbed of their past and thus become avid photographers so that they can "steal," by the "taking" of an image, the very thing that they are photographing. Perhaps, but since I have always felt that a photographer is "making" (or creating) an image rather than "taking" one, I disagree with her.

In my opinion, the photographer has all these qualities, plus a lot more, such as the ones Roy Stryker, former director of the landmark Farm Security Administration (FSA) photographic project, has listed. He said that a photographer needs "rectangular or square eyeballs and horse blinders to frame and focus the vision of what is seen." Among some of the other attributes required, at least for the photojournalist or field photographer, are copper kidneys, a cast-iron stomach and legs and arms of steel to drag equipment and to climb ladders and stairs. The photographer cannot suffer from airsickness, vertigo, or shyness, and probably needs a skin as tough as that of an armadillo or rhinoceros. But, most of all, photographers need sensitivity and visual awareness of what is around, whether the view is restricted to the four walls of a studio or is as open as a vast urban complex or rural plain. Moreover, they have to keep up-to-date on technology and techniques, and be alert to social and economic changes. It's not easy.

A photographer also needs to be unobtrusive. Dorothea Lange, the noted FSA photographer, had an uncanny ability to blend with the background. The pictures she made were evidence of her intuitive ability to "get inside" a situation. Her craft was the highest example of the photographer's role in recording events rather than creating them, as so many photographers do by their very often intrusive presence. The photographer's mission is to create and retain an image. The attribute the photographer needs most to carry out this mission is the ability to interpret the subject of that image. The interpretation is what makes the difference between a good and a bad photograph.

How Much Do You Need to Know in Order to Handle an Assignment?

In your rush to get enough work, and your desire to accept new challenges, it is understandable if you say "yes" to everything, even if you have little or no experience in a particular area. Sometimes (we shall see later), no expertise is necessary if there are other compensating factors. But your acceptance as a photographer by picture buyers, whether in the book, magazine or corporate fields, may well depend on how much you need to know about the subject to be photographed. Let's look at several situations and then you can draw some conclusions.

Must a photographer of industry understand a process, a machine or an end product in order to do a better job of photographing it? Should he or she know medicine or science when photographing doctors or scientists? Should the photographer be politically sophisticated in order to photograph a politician? Is it necessary to know in intimate detail the personality or the lifestyle of the person being portrayed? Or should the photographer operate by gut reaction to the subject, tempered by aesthetic considerations?

These are difficult questions, and after more than fifty years of experience I still have mixed feelings about the answers. Is a little knowledge helpful or dangerous? One answer can be, "Let the photographer learn." Really?

Yes, we all can learn. A friend who teaches film-making at a well-known school was approached by a noted brain surgeon who wanted a private two-week crash course in film-making because he wanted to make a film on a medical procedure. "Okay," my friend said, "but I won't charge you for the course if you'll swap me a two-week course in brain surgery. That's something I've always wanted to do."

Another time, a picture editor (and friend) at a national magazine showed me a story on mining they had just run. The photographs were a mixed collection of good and bad, and the credit line had been inadvertently omitted. I asked who had made the pictures, and my friend mentioned someone I did not know.

"Why him?" I asked. "Did he have an industrial or mining background?" "No," she replied, "but my editors wanted an 'arty' approach, so we assigned him on the basis of his portfolio."

Did their decision pay off? No, because of the overall poor quality of the photographs. The lead photograph was the best. It was a picture of a conveyor traveling over rugged terrain. The "establishing shot" was acceptable. It showed the general site and was well composed. But the underground pictures of the miners at work were a disaster.

What happened? My friend really did not seem to know, but I had certain hunches. Having worked underground in many different kinds of mines (which was why she had asked my opinion), I suspect the problem was that the photographer, basically skilled in that he knew form, color and composition, apparently knew nothing about mining and was terrified of working underground. Perhaps he was confused by the darkness, noise, dirt and dust, and the always-present explosion hazard, so he literally "snapshot" his pictures and got out of there as fast as he could. If so, I don't blame him. The first time I photographed underground I had the same reactions, as have others who were subjected to such stressful conditions. The temptation to rush through the take as fast as one can is understandable. This may be an extreme example of why a photographer should have an understanding of what it is he is photographing, but it is an appropriate one.

And one may ask, "How many times does a general assignment photographer have to go into a coal mine or shoot a huge factory that makes three-level widgets? Is experience really important? Or should he simply have sound knowledge of his craft and adapt to each situation as it arises?" In situations such as the one above, the answer is clear. The lives of others and himself may well depend on what he does, the lighting he uses, his way of dealing with the host of other problems that arise under miserable conditions, where nothing works because of dampness, impossible terrain, dust, extremes of temperature, etc. Technical problems begin to transcend the more creative, and there probably is not much room for both when one is underground in waist-deep water in a coal mine.

How about other, less physically demanding situations? Once one of the great European photographers, noted for his extraordinary photographs of people, was invited to photograph the legislature of a midwestern state. He made many excellent individual pictures, but the story was a failure. Why? Because he simply did not understand the American political system with its nuances and shadings. He missed the backroom deals, the cloakroom politicking, the wheeling and dealing, the high jinks and low comedy that are the hallmarks of such a session. He didn't understand these things, and his pictures showed it, so the story missed.

Another time I was called upon to do a complicated semi-technical story on a medical research lab for a medical magazine. Should I have been a medical expert? In this case a good scientific background was useful, but not mandatory. My own photographic skills enabled me to photograph something as minute as a live mosquito and earlier experiences helped me cope with working in a highly controlled, sterile atmosphere. Thus I was able to relate well to scientists and technicians in the lab. The assignment was successful, thanks to prior experience in this kind of situation.

There are times, however, when a lack of knowledge can be an asset. Gordon Parks, 'on loan' to *Sports Illustrated* from *LIFE*, was assigned to photograph a lacrosse game. He came back with a great set of pictures and, as he turned in his story, he said to the editor, "What did you say the name of that game was?"

I mentioned the dichotomy to Melvin Van Peebles, a multi-talented writer, director and composer, who said, "Ah, but Parks brought with him his *own* sense of beauty and movement that transcended his knowledge of sports." Without such extraordinary qualities, I am afraid the photographer who knows little about his subject will be unable to do the best job possible.

Insiders: Edward K. Thompson, Roy Rowan and Arnold Drapkin

There is always more for a photographer to learn. This may not be apparent to someone who is starting out after a long educational or apprenticeship training and presumably has his instruction days behind him. But it was corroborated in a conversation I had with Edward K. Thompson, *LIFE* magazine's famous managing editor from 1949 to 1967, and editor and publisher of *Smithsonian* magazine for ten years after that.

I asked Thompson to appraise the current American photographer and to comment on what he sees or doesn't see. He stated, "What I don't see is the photographer who has learned basic skills beyond the casual use of the 35mm camera." He was equally concerned about the lack of photographers who can straighten up lines, who know their lighting and who in general are craftsmen. He misses photographers who do know their trade. "It's like a musician learning the scales or a skater doing the 'school figures'," he said. "Doing exercises is very boring, but you can then use the knowledge of them as a take-off point."

Roy Rowan, a former assistant managing editor for *LIFE* magazine and Senior Writer and member of the Board of Editors at *FORTUNE*, has had a strong influence on the directions of photojournalism. New photographers will be fascinated not only by his professional background (see interview page 185) but by his close associations with photographers, his respect for them and how they fit into the team pattern that's so necessary in high-level photojournalism.

He told me, "I have always had a very close relationship with photographers. I understand them and their thinking. I guess as a writer and editor, I have spent more time in the field with photographers than anyone else I can think of. I always liked being with them on an assignment and always thought that a story was a two-person proposition. And even when you are out on a story you envision lay-outs and help plan the shooting. You don't go out and just randomly shoot pictures. You think of openers and closers, sequences and scene setters, different perspectives. I think that goes back to my interest in drawing and painting. My strongest forte I know is visual. The best parts of my writing are 'scenes' which are really visual. I really like thinking visually. Right now I'm writing a major article but I'm thinking visually about it and I've got scenes in this thing too.

"I think photography has really changed. There are entirely different concepts about the relationship between pictures and copy. Editors really want stories personalized, and want to see them through the eyes of an individual rather than seeing them objectively as a journalist. The key is to find an individual through whose eyes you can tell the story photographically or in words.

"For young photographers today, it's darn hard to make a living, doing just editorial assignments. It's very important to be flexible, keep an open mind and be willing to try anything, even if it's very unusual and takes a lot of effort to create a unique opening picture. Even magazines which are really not picture magazines such as *Vanity Fair* and *Esquire* are putting a lot of effort into their cover images, such as Annie Liebovitz's cover photo of a nude pregnant actress. So to repeat, I think you must be very open-minded and susceptible to new ideas."

I asked Arnold Drapkin, former picture editor at *TIME* magazine and now Consulting Picture Editor, what his feelings are about the photographers he comes in contact with. He said, "One of the problems with the younger photographers today is that they have not learned their craft the way the old-timers did. There have been enormous technical advances but the young kids think they can pick up a 35mm, load it with 400-1200 ASA film and shoot available light. They do not know how to light a subject or how to use other equipment. The old-timers started out with a Speed Graphic with one holder and two pieces of film. The knew how to wait for that precise moment, or peak of action, and bring back the picture. Today's kids come in with motor drives, and they're taking movies. But," he said, "there are many exceptions; there are many good young photographers who really do know what they're doing.

"With the proliferation of the single-lens-reflex cameras, motors, fast film, etc., the vast majority think they have to know nothing more. It's very difficult to find someone who can photograph a painting on an 8″ × 10″, with color bars and gray scales, and not have it 'keystone' or have any reflections and produce a good, well-exposed photograph of a painting. It's akin to artists learning to draw first from plaster casts and then studying the great masters and composition. I often tell young photographers to put their cameras away for a while and go to the Metropolitan Museum of Art to study some of these masters to see how they composed and 'lit' their paintings."

Drapkin added, "They know nothing about perspective, color balance and color meters. There are also very few photographers who know, or bother to know, how to properly develop their own film. I still have photographers who prefer to develop and print their own work, good as our lab is. Too many photographers today simply do not have a good grounding in their craft."

I asked Drapkin how he accounted for the lack of basic photographic skills in the young and where the responsibility lay. He believes that it clearly lies with the schools. He said the schools should put a greater emphasis on the uses of the enormous number of tools available in the photo industry, especially the new computer techniques in addition to electronic imaging, and the great variety of improved film.

He re-emphasized the need to know how to properly develop and print both black and white and color. He added, "Professionals may not often get to do their own printing, but when they are out shooting, they will have a much better understanding of what it means to have to deliver a bad negative. When they produce bad negatives, it is usually because they don't know any better. The labs lose enormous amounts of time trying to salvage the images for printing. There is not enough grounding in basics in the schools and too much emphasis on 'creativity,' which is becoming a trite expression in our world.

"Real creativity comes from experience and good basic grounding in the craft. Creativity will come when the photographer can look at something and, instead of shooting it with a 35mm, will say, 'Gee, this ought to be shot with a 4″ × 5″.' Too many photographers use the 35mm for everything from sporting events to architecture," Drapkin continued. "Then they come in and show me a 35mm and tell me how it can be blown up to reproduce to full-page size. They cannot see that the 35mm they shot doesn't have good quality, wasn't filtered properly or was shot on the wrong kind of film. It's shocking!"

"Where is their thinking coming from?" I asked, and cited a statement made by Eliane Laffont, director of the New York office of the Sygma Agency, who requires their photographers to have a deep awareness of world politics and the politics of the area in which they are working, and hopefully to be able to speak the language of that area.

Drapkin answered, "The most important attribute a photographer can have is enthusiasm. The people I respect and like the most as photographers are those who have enthusiasm for the task, and that statement does not restrict itself to young photographers. There are some photographers on our staff who have been around here longer than I have, and whose enthusiasm constantly amazes me. In every assignment you give them, they are really enthusiastic and come up with new ideas or new ways of doing it. Look at the Turnley brothers (see page 68) who do not wait for assignments to come over the transom, but are an endless source of both visual and text ideas to editors. They got started by knocking on doors and telephoning people they never knew but whose work stimulated them, and they learned more this way than any other way I can think of.

"Photographers, as other graphic artists, go through styles," Drapkin continued, "and while a style may have been created twenty or so years ago and may have gone out of vogue, it may now be coming back. The photographer should know what's been photographed and how. He should not try to reinvent the wheel but concentrate on producing superior photography in the best and most innovative way he can."

Drapkin spoke of his own training in graphic arts and its relationship to photography. He feels strongly that a photographer should know about printing production. He said, "Young photographers, if they are going to be photojournalists, must understand that a beautiful original print is useless to us, even if it's the best print in the world, unless it will reproduce for our magazine's 4.5 million subscribers. They must know how to print (or how their negatives will print) for our kind of reproduction. They must realize that a print made for salon purposes is very different from a print made for halftone engraving."

He also reminded us that the need for the best printing possible is not restricted to black and white and that color pictures made for projection are not going to print as brilliantly as on an opaque (conventional) press. "When we did a piece on Ansel Adams," he continued, "Adams himself, one of the greatest printers in contemporary photography, wanted to know exactly what kind of process we were going to use in the reproduction of his work. He then printed his pictures so that they would receive the maximum quality our presses could provide."

Drapkin closed his remarks by saying that the best photographers get that way because they are the best businessmen. "Unless the business side of their lives parallels their creative, they cannot last long enough to achieve greatness," he said.

Following Arnold Drapkin to *TIME* magazine's picture desk was Michele Stephenson, who carried on the tradition of expert picture editing that never lost sight of the human factors in dealing with world-ranging photojournalists.

Insider: Michele Stephenson, Picture Editor, *TIME* magazine

"I was a journalism major at the University of Arizona," she said, "where my supervising professor had been a city editor at *The New York Times*, and realized early on that I was more interested in magazine than newspaper journalism. I worked briefly on my college newspaper and some small community papers, but I knew I really wanted to be in New York and especially at *TIME* magazine. I came cold, though I did have an introduction through a family friend which in turn led me to joining the staff. After moving around I was assigned to the picture department and have been there for some twenty years. I was deputy picture editor to Arnold Drapkin (see pages 8-11), and became picture editor in 1987.

"What I want from photographers beyond the basics of technical skills, which I expect, is the ability to work with people, being able to grasp the point of a story quickly, get themselves together rapidly, move around easily, and understand deadlines.

"All of these attributes are present in the experienced photographers I deal with and it gets better and better. But for the new person it's tougher because I also want experience. With the new photographer I look for style and a sense of composition. It's nice to see a photographer take an ordinary situation and give me something I haven't seen before. You don't always see that in someone brand new, but usually by the time they come here, they've been published elsewhere, at least in newspapers and perhaps in magazines as well.

"I also see a lot of students' work and portfolios. What I look for at that level is an understanding of what to put in a portfolio, how to show a broad range of work without boring the viewer, and someone who shows an understanding of who he is coming to see, which seldom happens. They rarely do their homework. Of course, you can't put together a different portfolio for every editor you're going to see, but you certainly can vary it. Or you can say, 'You'll be most interested in this part.' I find it would make such a difference to these photographers if they would spend just a few minutes looking at the publication they are going to see."

What separates the photographers who "make it" and those who don't is style. "Style" is the word I have heard many times from several people interviewed for this book, and I asked Stephenson to speak to that subject.

"Style," she said, "is the way a photographer uses the ability to compose a picture to make a statement, to express a point of view. For a news magazine we can't always use a particularly stylistic picture; we have to use a news picture, and there are photographers who can accomplish that, who can just find the way he or she looks at a situation, sees it, and frames it. You get a different perception of the subject and see it in a way that best suits the story. For example, in Arnold Newman's famous photograph of Alfried Krupp, although that was a very controlled situation, and definitely not a news event, Newman brought out the essence of what he wanted to say in an exceptionally strong, provocative manner. In a news situation these opportunities do not always exist. But the photographer still has to be alert and do the most interesting work he can. This is why we choose certain photographers to do innovative and original concepts of even the most ordinary hard-news events. You want that interpretation and you want their input into the process. At least I do, I want that kind of input.

"When we assign a photographer, we have a general idea of what we are looking for. It has to have certain elements if it's news; it needs to complement the text we're planning, hopefully not literally repeated but adding to the understanding of what the words are saying. So you give the photographer the basics, the five W's and all of that, and expect him to come back with what he's been sent to get and optimistically more. We expect in the early part of the assignment the photographer will get the picture you've asked for, and then experiment and try something on their own and surprise you. I think we're all looking for surprises. And when it's there it makes all the difference.

"As for the dichotomy of the old *LIFE*'s procedure of the photographer and the reporter working as a team and *Fortune*'s preference to keep them apart, and where *TIME* fits, we're in between; we do some of each, but more often than not they work fairly independently. They may communicate verbally but they are often not traveling as a team. Whenever two people are covering a candidate, the writers are looking for different things than the photographer. They might get together after work and discuss the assignment but they are not joined at the hip.

"Because we are a news magazine and it takes longer to put a photograph onto a page, we have to decide ahead of the text department as to what we are going to cover. For instance, this week because we are talking about Armenia, which is a long distance off, we have to dispatch our photographers ahead of the writers, even though the story editors have not even decided if we will actually do the story or even send a reporter, but we have to be prepared for it. Sometimes it's the reverse, where our photographers are already out and happen on a story and call in to advise us of it.

"We work with the production news agencies a great deal but most of the work for *TIME* is assigned to contract photographers who have been with us for a long time. We also work a lot with freelance, both agency and nonagency. We go with the photographer who we feel is best for the story and it doesn't matter who they are with. So most of the work you see in the magazine is shot for us, and the credits reflect that.

"For a new photographer to see us, all it takes is a phone call or a letter, depending on where the photographer lives. And according to what kind of pictures they shoot they will be directed to the editor of that department. If they specialize in portraiture or celebrities, politics or world affairs, they are directed to that editor. I have one other editor who screens work in general and actually sees the better-known photographers who haven't worked with us very much and directs them to the appropriate editor or to me. But someone sees every book that comes in, and we respond. If one of our editors is very impressed with the work, they'll ask me to come in and look at it.

"We usually have books dropped off early in the week but most often people are seen with their books when we can handle the volume. I like to meet the photographer. How can you assign someone if you don't know the person? It's not that you don't know the subject, but you need to have a feel for who you're sending out there and the kind of presence and command they have. This is the kind of person you put with a reporter, or is this someone who has a studio and does his work there. How do you know if you don't talk to them? You can tell a certain amount from a portfolio, but I think it really helps to meet the photographer.

"An important difference between assigning advertising work and editorial work is that in advertising the photographer usually has complete control over the situation, whereas in news, editorial people have to work into a situation, and get people to cooperate. We want somebody who is persuasive and gets along well with people.

"Because we are a news magazine, we seldom have room for outside stories that are not hard-news driven. Our contract people, both writers and photographers, will come in with ideas that we will assign and run. But with suggestions coming in from correspondents in the field, senior editors and writers, it's hard to find room for other outside ideas. If one of our contract photographers says he's going to a certain place and I think it's going to be a great story, we will discuss it among ourselves. We ask senior editors if they are interested in it, and possibly take a 'first look' position and offer the photographer some financial help or other support.

"Occasionally when a large and possibly undefined story is suggested, which may have national or international implications, though we may not have room for that story, we might still be interested enough to see how we can use part of it and also offer some advance help. But the story has to have a focus; it can't be a fact-finding mission. We have done this in the past. We did one last year that turned into a cover story in the International edition and a smaller story for domestic. Often International will do wholly separate stories you never see in the domestic edition. We handle both from this office, and that includes photo essays which sometimes run to six pages, which we call 'Views'. We run any number of those that are seen overseas and are never seen here.

"I would like to suggest to young photographers that they need to be absolutely dedicated, that this is what they love. I talk to a lot of young photographers and ask them questions: Why do you care about doing this?, What do you want your pictures to say?, etc. I'm not sure they understand that this is no easy life and although it sounds glamorous, with the travel, being published, becoming well known, meeting famous people, being a part of history, we all know it's a very tough life, especially for a freelance photojournalist who does want to travel the world.

"So I recommend that they really search their souls about the kind of commitment they have. We know it's not particularly lucrative, but it can be very rewarding in terms of what you can do for people and the kind of effect you can have. I think the best place to get started is a newspaper, a small one. I've been talking to students, have seen a lot of portfolios and talked to many editors of small newspapers who have one or two staff photographers. They give the photographers the run of the place, the chance to shoot a photo essay a week, help lay it out, to pitch subjects they are interested in, work with correspondents, reporters or writers, and experience a whole range of work in a microcosm that you can't find elsewhere.

"And what better place to learn, because I don't think they're learning it in school. I don't think schools can provide on-the-job training. I think this is symptomatic of education in general and not a practical application. It's an academic view of things; we may be turning out photographers who appreciate fine art or even photojournalism but they don't know how to get a job. It's not that I want vocational schools exactly but I think colleges can be doing better in preparing students for jobs in that area. I encourage internships or to work assisting professional photographers. You just can't beat that kind of experience. I agree with Arnold Drapkin's earlier statement about art appreciation and it can only help in terms of their own work. I might also add that it helps for editors, too, to have the same kind of art appreciation when they're looking at work. Photographers just have to get out there and keep shooting and show work to everybody they can.

"When a photographer comes in I don't want to see a lot of work—just a handful of great pictures and a cohesive story. Even though we can't always publish it as a photo essay, photographers want to shoot it and I encourage them to do so. And for us of course you have to be able to tell a story in just one or two pictures, which is another talent. We don't demand writing ability but photographers must be able to communicate the facts about the story with accuracy and detail."

Choosing a Direction

Making the leap from amateur to professional photography, while seemingly a simple and evolutionary step, is actually quite complex and often happens before the photographer is truly ready for it. Sometimes the photographer gets into it by sheer drive which starts at the soles of the feet and grows into a burning desire in his lifestyle until it becomes an all-consuming way of life.

When one compares how amateur photographers outnumber professionals by a hundredfold or more, it seems unlikely that professional photography could have been the first, and only, choice of working pros. Often they began in other ways with an interest in art and graphic expression and dexterity in using the camera as a tool of visual communication. Schools began teaching advanced courses in photography, some good, some poor, but all combined to fuel a new and continuing interest in photography as a profession. And, of course, sheer happenstance was sometimes the deciding factor.

Serious photography can begin in many ways. There has always been a certain amount of glamour and romance associated with the dashing correspondent, whether it was Roger Fenton (the first war correspondent in the Crimean War) or a modern-day Dave Duncan, Robert Capa or Jim Nachtwey, who carried the torch of tradition. Artists for years have used photography to make photographic notes of what they want to paint and draw, and some went on to become first-rate photographers. The late great American artist Ben Shahn was gifted both as photographer and artist. There has always been a great cachet about carrying a camera under one's arm, a la Henri Cartier-Bresson. But it is no longer a five-dollar box Brownie, but a sophisticated 35mm SLR along with a collection of expensive lenses.

The omnipresence of the large picture magazines, *LIFE* and *Look*, the growing use of editorial photography by mid-sized publications and books, and certainly the rise of "girlie" magazines, all contributed to the mystique of the camera and what it could produce. And when some lucky amateur shot a fast-breaking news item and made a lot of money with it, the rumors of the heaps of money paid for these pictures stimulated hundreds of others to try to find markets for their pictures. Even today there is always the glamour of the big buck for a newsbreak photo. The tragic shooting of singer/composer John Lennon was a bizarre coincidence for an amateur photographer who made a picture of the accused murderer while Lennon autographed his record album. This coincidence thrust the photographer into the limelight and accorded him television interviews and a rumored $10,000 for a quick sale to a local newspaper, with probably little if any more for wire service distribution. At first glance this seemed like a lot of money, but the manager of one of the big picture agencies told me later that she could have probably obtained as much as $250,000 for that picture with proper syndication.

Today, with the proliferation of almost foolproof automated cameras, there are growing numbers of people becoming entranced with photography but without much technical understanding. So it appears the necessity of knowing technique is decreasing as automatic capability increases.

The World War II babies who came of age in the 1960s became fascinated with the 35mm camera as a means of recording the human condition, influenced by their predecessors who used the camera as an instrument to document serious aspects of life, social injustice and anything else that was "real" to them and capable of being photographed. Many stayed with the medium and developed into fine amateur photographers. It is what they have to do to support their interest that usually sparks the jump from amateur to professional status.

There are other circumstances that influence photography careers, some of them odd indeed. In the advertising world there seems to be a constant parade of art directors turning photographer. Having been an art director is certainly a plus, as they understand the basics of composition and other factors involved in the production of acceptable photographs, and knowing fellow ADs doesn't hurt either.

Then there are the engineers and the technical people who have to document problems in their own fields. They learn to make pictures of broken parts or of factories in remote areas and ask themselves, "Why can't I sell these pictures to *Business Week* or *Fortune*?" There are reverse situations where companies and publications have thrust cameras into the hands of their field people and made photographers out of them. But whether by design or accident, the desire to become a professional photographer *can* be strong, and with it comes the problem of developing a marketing strategy.

If commercial photography seems and, indeed, may be a lot less glamorous than photojournalism, there is no less a standard for quality and professionalism. A still life of a ketchup bottle or a local fashion spread should be produced as competently as a portrait of a company president or a picture of a roaring fire in an oil refinery.

But perhaps "glamorous" is the wrong word to use because it is so over-worked in photography—we speak of glamorous women, glamorous locations and glamorous personalities. Photography can be a profitable means of self-expression and personal fulfillment even without glamour, especially in these days of electronic imaging when the photographer may not even have to leave the computer terminal. The creation of a fine portrait or a first-rate (and visually interesting) industrial photograph, or taking an exciting photo of an incident that might be parlayed into a news event or be used ultimately in some educational medium—all of these are daily grist for the mill of the commercial photographer.

How does the work of the studio photographer differ from that of the photojournalist? Both must deal with many of the same technical problems, but the photojournalist's main function often ends when the last roll of film is turned in to the darkroom and the last caption written.

The photojournalist's mission is, thus, more direct—to record visually something that has actually happened. Much of his success depends on split-second timing or an instinctive interpretation of what may happen to a mood or a situation. Sometimes in hard-news situations, photographs of the same event are taken by clusters of photographers standing shoulder to shoulder, using virtually identical equipment, turning out pictures that are exactly the same. Or are they? A hairline move to the left or right, a split-second difference in timing, the blink of an eye, the twist of a mouth or the movement of a hand—all result in a different image. Photojournalism, in its purest sense, is truth.

By and large the photojournalist is apt to be nonstaff. Today the bulk of the ASMP membership tends to be made up of freelancers or small-studio based operators. It isn't that staffers have refused to join the society; it is simply that there aren't that many staffers around. The old *LIFE* magazine had a regular staff of about thirty-five photographers, many of whom were already in the Newspaper Guild, with almost double that number either under contract or working as stringers or in other forms of employment. Today the new *LIFE* has three picture editors and no staffers. *Look* is gone, after an abortive attempt at resurrection, and so are many other magazines. Specialized magazines and books have proliferated, but their publishers, too, rarely use staff people. They use freelance photographers or work with production agencies (page 249) or standard stock agencies (page 251). And while there are still a handful of staffers or contract photographers asociated with various national magazines, the numbers have diminished.

The membership of the National Press Photographers Association (NPPA) is, on the other hand, mostly staff, particularly from the smaller papers which use one or two photographers. Happily this is a growing rather than a declining market.

Photojournalists, unlike studio owners, need not possess darkroom space, though in many cases they do. But if budding photojournalists expect to tap the resale market, they should have some sort of accessible storage and retrieval system, or they should work out a deal with a stock agency so that their pictures don't become moldy in their files, unloved and unwanted.

Photojournalists and fixed-base commercial photographers differ also in the markets they serve. The local commercial photographer tends to draw from the community, and his task can be as exciting or as dull as he makes it. The photojournalist often must travel when an assignment is received. No, photojournalists do not have routine jobs, but neither do they have routine incomes. The local commercial photographer, furthermore, has an almost built-in repeat business, whereas the photojournalist does not.

Both photojournalism and local commercial photography have compensations and pitfalls, and often the fields overlap. As for capital investment, while there are differences there are also similarities. Field cameras and equipment may be an infinitely more expensive, fragile and complex investment for the photojournalist, but the fixed-base operator has overhead expenses and other costs not dealt with by the journalist, especially if electronic imaging hardware and software is involved.

My point here is to discuss the direction the new photographer can take — to settle into the comfortable routine of working in the community and building a reliable business or to answer the call of adventure and risk what photojournalism promises. This is a decision I cannot make for others, but this book will try to help in whatever direction you take.

The development of the picture magazine concept that started in Germany after World War I and traveled here in the 1930s, brought with it wonderful European photographers who had tremendous influences on modern-day photojournalism. Among them were Philippe Halsman (below) and Alfred Eisenstaedt (page 30).

Insider: Philippe Halsman, Photographer

Ask almost any qualified judge of contemporary photography — photographer, editor, art director, or museum curator — to compile a list of the five most important, prolific, and most talented photographers, and it's almost a certainty it will contain the name of Philippe Halsman, who died in 1980 at the age of seventy-three. Though my friend Philippe is gone, the impact of his humanistic and deft approach, his images will last forever; his subtle sense of humor was recorded on countless printed pages.

Halsman, who amassed a staggering 101 covers for *LIFE* magazine, was one of the great portrait photographers of all time, and it is hard to imagine any other photographer reaching the stature that this quiet, gentle man attained. His understanding of humanity, coupled with his great photographic skill, produced some of the most incisive portraits of the famous and near-famous. Halsman's great wit was probably best exemplified by his famous series of "jump" photographs. Somehow early in his career he got into the habit of asking those who posed for him to jump in the air in front of his camera, and most of his famous clients complied. So many did, in fact, that a most wonderful book emerged from this collection, among them the spectacular photograph of Salvador Dali leaping in the air accompanied by a bucket of water and a flying cat. I asked Yvonne Halsman (his widow) how many "takes" Halsman had made of that scene and she said it took twenty-six buckets of water and three cats, twenty-six times!

Yet Halsman was by no means a saint. He had an iron will and could demolish (verbally) anyone who took him on in any cause he espoused, though more often than not his weapon was the sword of wit rather than a blunderbuss.

He was born in Latvia, and his father, a dentist, had hopes of his son following in the profession. But Halsman, fascinated with mathematics, went to Dresden, Germany, to study electrical engineering. It was training he used later when dealing with cameras, optics, lights, and other photo equipment.

While still a student, he went to Paris to attend his sister's wedding and became so enamored of the city that he never returned to Germany, continuing his engineering studies in France. It was difficult because he knew little French, especially the technical jargon needed for his engineering studies.

Yvonne Halsman said with a twinkle in her eye, "Philippe, as a young modern man in Paris, had a girlfriend who wanted to learn photography, and asked him to explain things. In order to do so, he dropped engineering and concentrated on photography to the dismay of his parents and teachers.

"Philippe," she said, "had a great interest in faces; he loved human beings and enjoyed making portraits of them. He opened his first studio, without a bath or running water, in Montparnasse in 1932.

"He was an omnivorous reader, fascinated by the great writers of the time and wanted to photograph them. He started with Andre Gide, and over a long period of photographing artists and writers, he began to develop a reputation for unusual portraits of them." By the time he was ready to leave Paris ten years later, ahead of the oncoming Nazi occupation, one news magazine said he was the best portrait photographer in Paris. Halsman's escape to the United States was not easy. Not being a French national he couldn't get an exit visa, and as he had already begun to make a name for himself with his photographs of prominent anti-Nazis, it was obvious that his days in Paris were numbered. Fortunately, because of his mathematical interest, he had already established communication with Albert Einstein, who by then was in the United States and who in turn interceded with Eleanor Roosevelt. With her assistance, the International Rescue Committee was able to get a visa for Halsman to leave France.

His first job was on a retainer with a draw against sales of his work for the Black Star Agency (see page 265). After the first year he asked how much he had made and was told that he owed them $2,000. After that he felt he couldn't do any worse, so he struck out on his own and began contacting publishers. He maintained friendly relations with Black Star, however, and they suggested that he photograph Salvador Dali, the Spanish surrealist painter. This was Halsman's first real break. Black Star sent the picture to *LIFE* magazine, who published it in their feature section then called Picture of the Week. Another important break for Halsman came when Simon & Schuster commissioned him to illustrate a book on Wendell Wilkie that sold over 100,000 copies, a large amount even today.

Halsman never forgot the early struggles he endured as a photographer. By the end of the decade he had become the first president of the fledgling ASMP, and was to spearhead their fight for the dignity and rights of the professional photographer. He fought for the right of a photographer to own his work, for the protection of the copyright law, and until he died he was an outspoken leader in helping the photographer survive. He always had time for the new photographers, always a word of encouragement for them.

Halsman was the quintessential magazine portrait photographer, but did not restrict himself to portraits. He loved general journalism and many of his covers were backed up by pages of fine photo coverage. Nor did he limit himself just to known personalities. He photographed several Presidents, and paid the same careful attention to corporate executives. He did not care much for fashion, never having worked for a big fashion magazine. However he did do fashion multi-page stories for *LIFE*.

Halsman's philosophy was to learn as much as he could about the person or situation he was about to photograph. Much of his work involved famous personalities and he studied them as well before the shooting so he would be confident in bringing out their strong points.

He loved teaching and always urged his students to learn, read, go to museums, watch films — in fact, watch anything, including television, and absorb everything they saw. He worried that too many photographers lacked understanding of their subject matter and did not take time to research personalities.

He never allowed his thinking to be delegated to others. He designed cameras and lighting systems to fit his particular needs and, like Berenice Abbott, refused to accept standards set by equipment manufacturers as a limiting factor to his creativity.

If Halsman saw talent in a young photographer, he would call an editor he knew to tell him of the photographer's work, suggesting the editor give the young hopeful assignments. Often such assignments became important steppingstones to young photographers' careers. This was certainly the case of a then young *LIFE* editor named John Bryson (see page 5). Halsman saw a great deal of potential talent as a photographer in him and worked closely with him. Bryson is now a highly regarded and sucessful photographer, and noted for his photographs of theatrical personalities.

Developing a Market Strategy: How to Select Your Market and/or Audience

Advising the new professional on how to single out his markets is tough because there are no two photographers who think or work alike; just as in every other form of the arts, interests vary widely. Basic likes and dislikes are the keys to what a new photographer should specialize in. But beyond the knowledge that you are interested and have some competency in photography, now is the time to sit down and take an introspective look and ask yourself, "What do I really *want* to photograph? Can I make a living from it, and if I can make a living from it, will *I enjoy* myself?"

I really believe deep thinking is required here, some research, and if you are young, capable, and just coming out into the world of self-sufficiency, a little advice might be useful. It doesn't have to be very profound or, for that matter, expensive. College advisors or professors can be a starting point. If you have graduated from photographic school, talk with your instructors and even with your fellow students.

What *excites* you in the way of photography? Think about it a bit and forget the so-called glamour, high pay or other fancied benefits. Are you really an observer of what is happening around you? Do you really care? Do politics, news and community affairs hold a fascination for you? Then perhaps photojournalism is the way you should go. Or are you more interested in lifestyles, food, fashion? If so, then the journalism route may not be for you and you should investigate the studio world. Your interests are the best way to determine an area of specialization. One of the best architectural photographers in the country actually trained as an architect. However, another trained architect became one of the leading photographers of nature, flora and fauna. There are no hard rules and I can only suggest that you be excited and love what you're doing, and you'll bring drama to your photographs. If you look at photography as just a way of earning a living, you may well do that, but it's going to be pretty dull potatoes (and so will your pictures).

There has been a radical change in photographic philosophy in the past dozen years. When we were in an age of specialty and if you were the expert in steamrollers, then that was what you would invariably be called upon to photograph. It's different today. Now it's important for you to not only have a specialty, but you must have a solid background in general photography as well, and be capable of handling most assignments that come your way. There is too much cross-over work, and art directors, picture editors and other photographic buyers expect more flexibility in the people they hire, especially in the areas of electronic imaging which often requires combining photographs of all sorts into a single final image. So with cost-containment becoming a dominating factor, it is obvious that a buyer will prefer to deal with one photographer who can be flexible rather than several specialists.

Give serious thought to the bare requirements of making a living, but try also to come to a conclusion about the kind of photography that not only will provide a living but also be enjoyable and emotionally satisfying. Make no mistake—happiness in photography is more than a good checkbook balance and a fast f/stop. If you cannot imagine professional photography as a way of life that is emotionally satisfying, try something else.

Who Will Be Interested in Seeing Your Work?

Those who are simply interested in *seeing* your work should not be written off as a nonproductive audience. Often those who may have no reason to buy a picture may be sufficiently impressed with what they see to recommend purchase by someone else. So that brings up the questions of whom to reach and how.

Those around you are often those who are most immediately interested: your family, friends and associates—and it will be their encouragement that may spark you to higher aspirations. When you make pictures of family events, school activities or local community and political happenings, don't hesitate to send free prints or even spare transparencies to some of the people involved. A print sent out of sheer courtesy may bring back a wealth of remembrance later that could be translated into working dollars, and also be a way of establishing new friendships.

Learn your lessons early. Even at first crack, protect your pictures. It may seem pompous and officious for a new photographer to start putting copyright notices on the free pictures he or she sends out to friends or acquaintances, but it is important to do so. Photographs dispatched on innocent missions sometimes develop a life of their own and can wind up in some strange and unforseen places.

Who else will want to see your pictures? Show them outside the immediate circle of your personal life. Show them to your local community leaders, politicians, office holders—they might very well be interested in the subject matter, and while they may not buy any of them, they will remember you. As for remembrance, well, that too is an important factor. It is part of establishing a professional identity.

Join local camera clubs. True, you may run into a lot of competition among other members, some of whom will be trying to carve out their own niches, but at least you will be in touch with those around you who share common interests. Most camera clubs have exhibition programs, critiques, talks and slide shows. All of these will add to your potential of seeing and being seen.

If you go on a trip and do a lot of shooting, it is probably easy enough to arrange free slide shows in your community at churches, recreation centers and senior citizens homes. Exposure of this type is worth pursuing in the beginning of your career.

All of the above activities are directed at what I would call a *non-revenue-producing* audience. Do you need it? Emphatically yes! A number of prominent photographers would agree. One of them, probably among the most famous in the world, has for years exhibited his photographs free, or at most charged a small door fee to cover the cost of hall rental. His interest in increasing his exposure as a photographer may have been geared to attracting new customers, but I doubt it since he was already world famous. Ego? Perhaps, but I doubt that. He simply enjoyed sharing his work with others.

Who Will Be Interested in Buying Your Work?

This is the moment of the quantum leap: the day you really consider yourself a *professional* and try to make some money at photography. This could be the day you graduate from a journalism or technical school or the day you decide you are bored with what you are doing and are going to devote yourself more to professional photography.

If you have attended a photography school with a view toward opening a local business in portrait, wedding, school or other community photography, the next step is to go out and find a studio to work from — or perhaps you might choose to buy into an existing business and hang out your shingle. With a reasonable amount of effort and promotion the work should come to you.

However, if you are interested in freelancing or in a studio operation devoted to either editorial or commercial work, then you have to track down your own market rather than wait for it to come beating on your door.

In order to find a buyer for your work, you must first decide what you are going to sell in the way of photography — journalism, fashion, food, still lifes, hard news, architecture or industrials? Now is the time for you to start zeroing in on appropriate market areas. After determining a market area, you next must address yourself to finding the right people to approach. In the editorial world there are editors, picture editors, designers, art directors, layout and makeup people and assistants of all kinds; promotion directors, advertising managers and their advertising agencies; public relations directors and their public relations agencies. All of these people and organizations and more have an *interest* in using photography, but the authority to buy may be vested in someone other than the contacts mentioned. You have to determine who the right person is in each case, and contact that person.

When we get into the world of advertising, it's a whole new ball game, and an ever-changing one at that (see page 76). Here you will come up against account executives, media buyers, group heads, art buyers, art directors, promotion and display art directors and market researchers, just to name a few of the people concerned with buying pictures.

Then consider those in the corporate area: chief executive officers (CEOs), corporate presidents, vice presidents — sometimes not just one or two but often groups of them who may be assigned to some particular endeavor that involves photography. There are also the secretary and/or the treasurer of a corporation. Not interested, you might think? Don't you believe it. These may very well be the people who are responsible for the production of the annual report, stock offering literature and product promotion. Next in the pecking order lie the public relations people, the house advertising managers and inside copywriters and their various production and promotion people including, in some larger organizations, complete photographic and printing departments.

And after shaking your head a few times to clear the confusion, you start down "Publishers' Row" to run into a heap of new titles in the book-publishing world. You will find the usual listings of presidents and corporate officers, but also some wondrous titles such as rights and permissions, fiction and nonfiction, sales managers, editors and editors in chief, department editors, division editors, publicity, vice presidents in charge of customer relations, picture editors (photo), picture editors (art) and art editors for pictures. And, in recent years, book packagers. (See page 59.)

But the list doesn't stop there. In the fine arts field you will find curators, museum directors, gallery owners (both private and public), acquisitionists, designers, catalogers, and sponsors of collections and foundations that offer grants.

This overview only begins to scratch the surface in the search for those interested in buying photography. There are also the fields of audiovisual multimedia for both educational and commercial applications; interior decorators who purchase photographs for private residences and corporate adornment; printers and graphic specialists who buy photography for client use; and travel organizations that publish their own brochures, guidebooks, etc. There are gift and display manufacturers who make calendars, posters and postcards and reproduce photographs for wall decoration in homes and public buildings and limited public places such as hotel rooms. The outlets are enormous and the photographer must make basic choices about what direction he will take.

You should try to sell your photos in the medium that can best use them. Now is the time to identify those markets.

Publications That Can Help You Choose Paying Markets

There are a growing number of publications that purport to be accurate market listings telling where to sell your photographs, quoting the names of the publications, their addresses and the prices they pay (or in many cases the prices they don't pay!). Some of these publications are reliable and try to be as truthful as possible, but others, unfortunately, do little more than pick up other publications' listings and imitate much of their information. When using or buying any reference book, pay particular attention to both the original dates of publication and the current copyright dates, or you might be misled about what is current and what isn't.

There are only about a dozen basic information guides covering important aspects of photographic marketing, and while they can be found in libraries, I am also listing the publishers and current costs for those who wish to buy any of them. Included are reference works of value in certain specialty areas, though much of this information exists in the primary publications listed.

General Publication Directories (Books and Magazines)

The most important directory is published by the R.R. Bowker Company, 121 Chanlon Rd., New Providence, NJ 07974. Tel. (800)521-8110. Bowker is the major producer of reference works in the publishing world. You should be aware of the many services this unusual company offers in the way of research materials on all aspects of publishing, but for the moment let us concentrate on:

Literary Market Place (LMP) ($134.95), R.R. Bowker. *LMP* is the "bible" of the publishing industry and carries detailed listings of every book publishing house in the country, as well as many magazine and periodical publishers. (It also publishes a worldwide foreign edition.) Here you will find the names, addresses and telephone numbers (including toll-free numbers in separate listings) of everyone in an important capacity in publishing and ancillary services such as printing, binding, mailing lists, government agencies, literary agents, editorial and research services, etc. Publications are classified by specialty, from textbooks and trade books to encyclopedias.

Other useful directories are: *Photo Marketing Handbook* ($21.95), *Photographer's Market* ($21.95) and *1993 Guide To Literary Agents & Art/Photo Reps*. All are published by Writer's Digest Books, 1507 Dana Ave., Cincinnati, OH 45207; 1(800)289-0963; and are targeted at specific genres.

Newspaper Directories

In the newspaper field there are several volumes (some of which are enormous) that are important because they identify in great detail most of the key people in newspaper publishing. They are highly specialized and it is doubtful they will be of enough use to the young professional to be worth the expenditure of large sums of money. They are all available in decent-sized libraries, but are listed here so that you are aware of this source material. The most prominent are: *Editor and Publisher Market Guide* ($80), Editor and Publisher Company Inc., 11 W. 19th St., New York, NY 10011. Tel. (212)675-4380. *Ulrich's International Periodicals Directory* ($339.95), R.R. Bowker (above). *Gebbie Press-All-in-One Directory* ($80 ppd., disks available 3 sets @ $105), Gebbie Press Inc., P.O. Box 1000, New Paltz, NY 12561. Tel. (914)255-7560. *Gale Directory of Publications & Broadcast Media* ($265), Gale Research, Inc., 835 Penobscot Bldg., Detroit, MI 48226. Tel. (800)877-GALE.

Corporate and Advertising Directories

There are many listings of corporations throughout the United States, but viable markets for new photographers are in the companies large enough to have significant advertising budgets for their products or services. The best of the publications listing this level of company is *The Standard Directory of Advertisers* ($497), National Register Publishing Company, Macmillan Directory Division, 3004 Glenview Rd., Wilmette, IL 60091.

This is a most useful volume, published in two editions, one organized alphabetically by specialty or industry, and the other geographically by state. The latter is more useful for traveling photographers as it gives them information on markets in specific regions, enabling them to line up assignments on home ground or to pick a group of companies to contact before a trip to a different area. The directory includes the names of the companies' advertising agencies and often identifies the account executives (AEs) who handle their work. Useful, also, is the media breakdown of where a given company spends its money—newspapers, radio, television, magazines, trade magazines, etc. This is important because you should be aware of what media the company uses. Paired with this publication is: *The Standard Directory of*

Advertising Agencies ($517.00), better known as the "Red Book" or the "Agency List," which appears three times a year. Macmillan also publishes *Consumer Magazine and Agri-Media Rates & Data* ($447/year), but for those wanting to do advertising photography the Red Book is invaluable. Arranged alphabetically by name, it lists every advertising agency in the United States, and provides not only their addresses, telephone numbers and names of key personnel, but also lists the clients the agencies serve. This is helpful when a photographer is in contact with a particular agency on one account, and perhaps can make a pitch to its other clients as well.

Agency listings can be confusing, however, especially with the larger companies. Sometimes there will be literally column after column of account supervisors, TV and art directors, group vice presidents, media buyers and all sorts of other people who may or may not be interested in purchasing still photography. Frequently, as in the corporate directory, these listings also give some breakdowns of where the money is being spent in the media. You can then make a judgment about whether a particular account is worth pursuing. For example, there isn't much of a market for still photography in an agency concentrating on radio and television advertising.

Public Relations Directories

While most major corporations have their own internal public relations departments, a large segment of the industry uses the services of outside public relations companies or consultants, not only for annual report production but for other media programs as well. Often there is a corporate director of public relations to whom the outside house is responsible. The public relations company will try to place material in the media, and this requires a lot of expertise not only in its preparation but in its media positioning as well. The history of public relations has many examples of how "news" was created rather than reported.

Since the main purpose of public relations is to bring a message to the public, and because advertising in its way has many of the same goals, I think it is time to say that they are, nonetheless, *different*. Unfortunately, even some dictionaries' definitions are remarkably vague, and in some cases lump public relations in with advertising and vice versa, adding to the general confusion about the dissimilarities of these areas.

The outside public relations house is often deeply concerned with photography, whether it is for a simple product photo or a deep, well-thought-out and well-produced photographic essay strategically placed in a major magazine. Public relations work doesn't always go to such lengths, however; sometimes simple one-shot pictures are used with news releases. Public relations photos need not be of a product or service necessarily; picture needs in this area can extend to publicity photos for a new book or author, entertainer or politician. Or entire corporate programs of public information can be conceived, arranged and executed by a public relations staff.

I feel that the public relations market is a strong one for the new photographer and as much attention should be paid to it as to the markets for hard news, advertising or any other form of photography. This field also has some important journals, and they should be studied closely as a source of contacts. Directories of interest are:

The Public Relations Journal-Service Section, Public Relations Society of America, PRSA, 33 Irving Pl., New York, NY 10003. Tel. (212)228-7228. Free if requested on business stationery. This is the membership list of the

Public Relations Society of America, a trade organization made up of active public relations people. It is also broken down into geographic and organizational listings. Most PR agencies have people who are members, or their agencies themselves have membership accounts, so it should not be too difficult to find someone who will lend you a copy of the list if you cannot qualify for a free one.

O'Dwyer's Directory of Public Relations Firms and *O'Dwyer's Directory of Corporate Communications* ($110 ea.), J.R. O'Dwyer Co., Inc., 271 Madison Ave., New York, NY 10016. Tel. (212)679-2471.

With the larger directories being so costly, on occasion I have been given previous editions by AD friends who normally would discard them. While there is always movement of personnel within a given agency or corporation, directories which are only six months or a year old are usually accurate enough for a new photographer's use.

Graphic Designers and Art Directors Directories

Graphic designers, industrial designers and art directors, be they in editorial or advertising, are important markets. All have membership organizations and publish annual rosters. The Art Directors Club membership is limited to art directors working in the field, but the AIGA (American Institute of Graphic Arts, 1059 Third Ave., New York, NY 10021, Tel. (212)752-0813) does welcome membership by photographers as well as art directors. Check for current dues. Membership could be useful because part of the membership package is the annual roster of 2,000 members of the AIGA, most of whom work in the graphic arts field. They might be valuable contacts for photographers. Both organizations publish annuals and other lists, but it may be that a friendly contact with a member of either group could result in the opportunity to borrow the lists.

Miscellaneous Additional Directories

There are many other books that would certainly be of interest to the professional, but not all of them are necessarily up to date and many have material already incorporated in the publications mentioned earlier. Some are listed here for photographers interested in the specialized areas these publications cover:

Audio Visual Market Place ($85), R.R. Bowker, 121 Chanlon Rd., New Providence, NJ 07974. Tel. (800)521-8110.

Business Publications/Audit of Circulation, Inc., 360 Park Ave. S., New York, NY 10010. Tel. (212)532-6880.

Standard Rate and Data, 3004 Glenview Rd., Wilmette, IL 60091. Tel. (800)323-4588. Single copy $228.00, subscription $497.00. This is useful for photographers who wish to try to peg their fees to a percentage of media rates for regional magazines or newspapers.

This list of reference sources is limited because many of the available lists of markets are duplicative, and the photographer may have difficulty deciding which to buy and which to pass up. It is much wiser for the photographer to carefully go over the major publications recommended in the local library. Study them carefully before buying, or borrow copies when possible. Also, there are many mailing list companies that sell lists especially geared to the advertising market. (See page 248.) But only after a detailed study should any real thought be given by the new photographer to actual purchase.

Some directories seem so remotely connected with the business at hand that it is not evident why they should be purchased at all, but occasionally they make more sense than meets the eye. I know of one photographer who travels extensively and seemingly has suffered more than his share of fouled-up airline reservations, as well as near-misses on many air freight and express shipments of film and equipment. He went so far as to order a subscription to the Pocket Guide (monthly) of the *Official Airline Guides* (OAG), 888 Seventh Ave., New York, NY 10019. Tel. (800)323-3537. He told me that once one of his clients stared in disbelief when he opened his briefcase at a meeting and the only visible things were: one small camera with a 35-200mm zoom lens and a small strobe flash unit and six rolls of film (two each of three emulsions); a toothbrush, razor, one clean shirt and a pair of socks; and the *OAG* pocket edition. He assured me that he has made more than one deadline by literally chopping minutes off his connection times at airports and that the *OAG* was the most useful list he could carry with him on an assignment. So think about what you should invest your money in when it comes to reference works.

Excluded from the list is a new type of publication that is essentially listings of promotion and self-advertising for photographers, studios and services. These books are aimed at some of the same markets that the young new professional is trying to reach but are paid for and subsidized by more established photographers in the form of advertisements about themselves or their studios. Do not confuse these books with the corporate directories mentioned previously. Among these directories are the following:

American Showcase, 915 Broadway, New York, NY 10010. Tel. (212)673-6600. (They also publish *Corporate Showcase*.)

Adweek Portfolio, 49 E. 21st St., New York, NY 10010. Tel. (212)529-5500.

The Creative Black Book, 115 Fifth Ave., New York, NY 10003. Tel. (212)254-1330.

The 1992 Workbook (LA) ($85), Scott & Daughters, Inc., 940 N. Highland, Los Angeles, CA 90099. Tel. (800)547-2688.

The Guilfoyle Report AG Editions, 142 Bank Street, New York, NY 10014. Tel. (212)929-0959. Fax. (212)924-4796. ($68 p/a.) This unusual quarterly publication is designed for nature photographers and users, but it is a gold mine for freelance photographers because it carries much general photographic information that can be used by the non-nature photographer. In it are valuable listings by editors seeking unusual and hard-to-find nature photographs and related subjects. *AG Editions* also sponsors a photographer's source guide, *The Green Book*, for nature editors; similar, but far less expensive and lavish than the costly "work books" above. Write or call for information.

Professional Organizations

Photography is part of the communications business, yet I am often amazed at how little communication there is among practitioners of the craft. Much professional information does come, however, from exchange and interchange with both colleagues and competitors, and new photographers are not alone in wanting this exchange. There are many professional associations that provide such opportunities and new photographers should consider joining some of them as a means of keeping up with current trends and developments.

Not all organizations are for all photographers, of course. Many are specialized groups that operate only within their own economic framework. But many are broadly based organizations that cut across a range of specialties. All have the welfare of the photographer as a common denominator.

Probably the two most important groups of working professional photographers in the journalism field are the American Society of Magazine Photographers (ASMP) and the National Press Photographers Association (NPPA). The ASMP is made up of mostly freelance photographers, although there are a handful of staffers among its membership. The NPPA deals essentially with the staff newspaper photographer, but it, too, cuts across some lines and admits freelance photographers whose output is essentially press directed. The ASMP has about 5,000 members nationwide with local chapters in the United States and some representation abroad. The NPPA, with eight regions nationwide, has many more members, about 8,000 in all, most of whom are on newspaper staffs, though a large percentage are in TV news production.

Both organizations have extensive educational programs that are of immense value to their memberships. The NPPA, for example, sponsors a well-known "Flying Short Course," during which it flies a planeload of photographers and editors on cross-country trips, holding seminars for working photographers. The ASMP has regional programs that gather the photographers in their own chapter areas for seminars and discussions. Both organizations have active publications programs. *News Photographer* is the NPPA's principal periodical. The ASMP publishes its *Bulletin* and specialized "white papers," and booklets on business practices, copyright laws, stock picture sales and tax guides. The ASMP has a medical insurance program that is most useful to the freelancer, but the NPPA members usually rely on their own employer-sponsored programs for health and accident coverage. Depending upon the nature of your work, you should consider joining one or both organizations:

American Society of Magazine Photographers (ASMP), 419 Park Ave. S., New York, NY 10016. Tel. (212)889-9144.

National Press Photographers Association (NPPA), #306, 3200 Croasdaile Dr., Durham, NC 27705. Tel. (800)289-6772.

Advertising Photographers of America (APA), 27 W. 20th St., New York, NY 10011. Tel. (212)807-0399.

American Society of Picture Professionals, P.O. Box 2401, Nashville, TN 37202 (or local chapters).

There are other specialized or regional photographic organizations that the new photographer should also be aware of. These range from local special groups such as the Industrial Photographers Association of New York (IPANY) to the International Association of Theatrical and Stage Employees (IATSE), which is essentially a union of motion-picture people but includes still photographers working in the motion-picture field.

Photographers interested in the field of education might investigate the Society for Photographic Education (SPE), which is largely a group of photography teachers in schools and colleges. Other special associations include the Professional Photographers of America (PP of A), Society of Photographers and Artists Representatives (SPAR), highly technical groups such as the Society of Scientists and Engineers in Washington, D.C., and organizations devoted to photogrammetry, biological photography in the Federal government, and photography related to the forensic sciences. The list is long. There is also the primary association of some 130 picture agencies, The

Picture Agency Council of America (PACA). To get further information and a catalog contact the H. Armstrong Roberts Agency, 4203 Locust Street, Philadelphia, PA 10104.

Besides professional organizations, there are press clubs, which include writers, editors, public-relations people, ad agency members, literary agents and so on. There are about thirty such clubs in this country and as many abroad. All can be useful as meeting places for the interchange of ideas and information. Most have exchange privileges. Some have exhibit areas.

Photo researchers and editors have a highly respected group of their own, the American Society of Picture Professionals (ASPP). Its membership consists mostly of art and picture editors and picture researchers, but a sizable number of photographers and some writers are also represented in this group.

Major museums that exhibit photography as a fine art are worthy of your support and participation, too, because the material they exhibit and their publications are of importance to you. The best known is the International Center for Photography (ICP), with two fine centers in New York. The main one is at 1130 Fifth Ave., New York 10128, and there is a beautiful and impressive center (ICP-Midtown) at the Eastman Kodak Building at 43rd St. and Avenue of the Americas, New York 10036. Also check out The Museum of Modern Art (MOMA), 11 W. 53rd St., New York 10019; The Metropolitan Museum of Art, 1000 Fifth Ave., New York 10028; and major museums and art centers in California including the Getty Center in Los Angeles, Chicago Art Museum in Chicago, Woodruff Art Center in Atlanta, and other museums in Philadelphia, Providence, Boston and elsewhere. All will answer mail inquiries about membership and benefits.

Can You Get Rich in Photography?

Some photographers can but most probably cannot. There are some rich photographers but their wealth in many cases comes from their families. Some photographers have earned large amounts of money through their photography, particularly in advertising, and individual stock sales and assignment fees can be impressive indeed. Taking the statements of some of the news (production) agencies at face value, if they have a total sale of one story for $300,000 and the agency takes half, even allowing for the highest of expenses that are jointly shared by agency and photographer, a photographer can obviously come out with some $100,000 or more on that single story. (See interview with Howard Chapnick, page 265.)

A large studio operation billing in the millions of dollars annually may cover the expenses of transporting as many as twenty models, actors, technicians, etc., on a single shoot. How much money does the studio or the studio photographer make out of it? It's hard to say. Only the IRS knows, but in discussing this with colleagues I find that a high-level advertising photographer can net more than $250,000 annually.

What about the small studio or local photographer? What can he expect? I asked Arnold Newman, one of the leading portrait photographers in the country (see page 93) and role-model for many younger photographers today. While he would not be specific in terms of dollars and cents, he made it clear that he felt a good photographer who worked regularly could earn a very comfortable living indeed. How comfortable is that? Well, I can only say that Newman himself lives well, has raised a family, is much respected, and works frequently at the highest level. Is this possible in the small city studio? Newman cites a former assistant of his who opened a studio in the South and now has over twenty assistants and is probably running a much larger dollar volume than Newman himself. Or think about the huge capital investment in electronic imaging equipment by Meteor Photo Company in Atlanta, Georgia and Troy, Michigan (see page 322). Granted they are serving a growing advertising agency market, but advertising agencies in order to effectively utilize the services of laboratories and services such as these, must hire photographers to produce photographs they need. And advertising fees can be sizable (see page 82).

On the editorial side, I know of a number of top-rated photographers who, judging by their lifestyles, homes and furnishings, have to be earning more than $250,000 per year. But I also know of one very promising and talented photographer who is driving a cab when he is not working (or looking for work), and a talented young woman who has to supplement her income by uninspiring work as a waitress or secretary.

There are other ways to attain wealth, but none guaranteed. One photographer I know, as a young man, photographed a lot of equally struggling young artists of his own age. He often swapped his pictures for some of their early artwork. Some of these artists are today among the country's most renowned, and this photographer in effect has amassed a priceless collection of fine art that, if liquidated, would bring an enormous amount of money to him or his estate. I also know of several photographers who, while getting started, were canny about investment opportunities and selectively and knowledgeably made investments in securities and slowly built up their portfolios. After twenty years they now have sizable holdings that add considerably to their financial worth. (See interview with Don Underwood, pages 355-357.) So it can be done — a photographer can get rich, but probably at no higher a statistical rate than his nonphotographic artistic counterparts.

Interview

Alfred Eisenstaedt

Photographer

In Germany in the 1920s, Alfred Eisenstaedt's spectacular photographic career was launched via the newspaper route, and now ninety-four years old, he is still active. In recent years there has been an ongoing flow of books, exhibitions, slide shows and lectures by this talented and prolific man, who, since he is one of the surviving original four photographers at *LIFE* magazine, should probably be declared a national monument.

"Eisie," as he is affectionately known the world over, began his photographic career in Germany as a twelve-year-old when an uncle gave him his first camera, an Eastman Folding Kodak #3 using roll film. As a teenager Eisenstaedt became avidly interested in photography and drove his parents wild by preempting the bathroom of their Berlin home for his darkroom. His output, however amateurish, fascinated him, and he kept at it until he was drafted into the German army during World War I. Eisie was wounded, survived and returned to Berlin after the war to work in the button business where, by his own admission, he was a poor salesman.

On a family vacation trip, he made a picture of a woman playing tennis and sold it to the *Weltspiegel* of the *Berliner Tageblatt*, the German equivalent of the Sunday *New York Times Magazine*. It was his first sale. He received twelve German marks, then worth about three U.S. dollars. But he was hooked when the editor wanted more pictures from him.

He related a fateful conversation with the editor, who said, "Why don't you become a photographer? You should be doing what Dr. Erich Salomon is doing." Salomon, long credited as the father of candid photography, was a pioneer in the use of the Leica, although at that time he used a small German camera called the Erminox. Eisie also acquired an Erminox, and a Plaubel Makina, another fine camera of its time.

His pictures began to "move," and he sold his first story on the Berlin chapter of the Salvation Army to an early version of the Associated Press. Always fascinated with art, theater and society, he found to his amazement that no one was covering those events. He began doing so and had the field to himself. He began meeting celebrities and during this period made his now famous picture of Marlene Dietrich. His boss in the button business pointedly suggested that Eisie make up his mind whether he wanted to remain in the business or become a full-time photographer and gave him three days to decide. After the grace period, Eisie said he would become a photographer. He relates, "The man looked at me as if I had dug my own grave." When he announced this career change to his friends and family they too felt he was committing suicide.

His photos began appearing regularly in many German publications and he did his first AP assignment, covering a Nobel Prize ceremony in Stockholm. He tells an amusing story of how he "blew" his second AP job. "My second assignment was a disaster. I had to go to Assisi in Italy to cover the wedding of Sophia, the youngest daughter of King Victor Emmanuel. I carried 240 pounds of baggage, all glass plates and other heavy equipment. I was supposed to do the wedding but I was fascinated by the choir boys, by the pageantry. I saw King Ferdinand of Bulgaria, who had the longest nose of all royalty, strutting by with Mussolini. I photographed everything and when I came back the AP developed my pictures and asked me, "Where are the bride and groom?" I answered, "What bride and groom? I didn't see them." The boss of the AP Bureau in London said, 'Fire that man immediately!' But they couldn't, because I wasn't employed by them."

That fiasco taught him a lesson that, he says, was underscored time and time again when he went to *LIFE*. It was the necessity of doing the background pictures first, then concentrating only on the purpose of the assignment. In other words, Eisie says, "Do the overall scene first. If you are sent out to do a story on a politician or well-known figure, do all the less important pictures first — the man's house, lifestyle, and what he looks like, before zeroing in on the details that are the most important part of the story."

He started traveling over Europe on political stories where he covered the rise of Adolf Hitler and made the famous picture of Hitler's meeting with Mussolini. Even though Eisenstaedt had met and worked with Dr. Salomon, he had never seen a Leica until about 1932, when he was introduced to it by another photographer. Eisie was fascinated with the camera and its incredible flexibility compared to the glass-plate cameras most other photographers were using. After he acquired his first Leica he continued using them, and still has his first one.

In 1935 Eisenstaedt emigrated to the United States. He began working almost immediately and found assignments with *Harper's Bazaar* and *Vogue*. Thereafter he was introduced to publisher Henry Luce by Kurt Korff, another photojournalism pioneer and then editor of *The Berlinger Illustrated Zeitung*, a prominent German publication using documentary photography well. Lucc, who was beginning to formulate *LIFE* magazine, and already producing pilot editions, was impressed with the young immigrant. Eisie had already helped establish *Pix*, one of the news photo agencies similar to *Black Star* (see page 265) that was to have a strong influence on the fledgling *LIFE*.

His assignment for the experimental *LIFE* was to go to Hollywood to do an essay on California, photographing everyone and everything, from Clark Gable and Shirley Temple to the orange groves. Back in New York, Luce saw the pictures and instantly promised Eisie a berth on the new magazine. The promise was kept and he became one of the original four staff photographers along with Margaret Bourke-White, Tom McAvoy and Peter Stackpole, to be joined shortly by Carl Mydans (see page 215). From the beginning of his *LIFE* staff association, Eisie began making photographic history. He ranged the world covering presidents, kings, emperors, dictators, master politicians, and many other prominent people. One of his many books is called *Witness to Our Time*, an apt title indeed. But he did not concentrate only on the VIPs. His work included splendid essays on nature and the elements, including a masterful coverage of a savage hurricane on his beloved Martha's Vineyard, where he has vacationed for forty-odd years. An acquaintance, who was heavier and stronger, tells of hanging on to him so he wouldn't blow away in the gale.

How did Eisenstaedt achieve his monumental position in photography? Part of the answer lies in the times and availablity of the tremendous show-case that the weekly *LIFE* was. But the real answer comes from his incredible care and attention to detail in whatever he photographed, and the unflagging enthusiasm he put into his work. "I am still crazy about taking pictures," he told me after his eightieth birthday. And he said that if he were younger he would do different things and keep experimenting. A few years ago he announced proudly that two cataract operations had fully restored his vision to what it was when he was a much younger man. His last book, *EISENSTAEDT: Remembrances*, 1990, is proof of his continuing vitality.

Eisenstaedt says the pictures coming from the younger photographers now are "terrific," but he thinks if he were just starting out, he would not make it in photography. He puts himself in the hypothetical position Johann Strauss might be in if he were alive now trying to write waltzes and sell them in a rock and country music market.

Asked about craftsmanship, he said, "Craftsmanship, as I see it, is not the way it used to be. What's missing is the more intimate feeling. Today, photographers are much more interested in doing technical things. To me, both then and now, technique is not that important." He does not consider "technique" part of craftsmanship and thinks that picture content is lacking because of preoccupation with technical perfection. Not enough time is spent, as he puts it, on being the person behind the camera. He believes that his style of photography is dying out. He feels that the lack of craftsmanship is caused by both audience and editors failing to demand it from photographers, accepting instead almost anything handed to them.

I asked Eisie, as the unquestioned dean of American photography, what advice he had to offer the up-coming photographer. His immediate answer was, "He should never become conceited just because he has something published. It can go away tomorrow and then he has to try again and again. Whatever I have accomplished over the years, whatever I am, I am not egotistical, and a big ego in a young photographer will only hold him back."

He echoed what many of his colleagues have said, that there is much more at stake than the money, and with tongue in cheek added, "We did it for God, and Luce." There was great satisfaction in working for the big magazines, and sadly, because many do not exist today, much of the team spirit this type of photography engendered is gone too. The great still-photo coverages of major events, catastrophes and funerals of heads of state don't command the space they once did. Their immediacy and news value has been preempted by television and the speed of world-wide satellite transmissions of journalism. So the photographer has to seek other outlets. New showcases are here, perhaps in book form, but they do exist.

He spoke of the resurgence of the personal essay, citing outstanding work by Mary Ellen Mark, the Turnley brothers, Sebastiao Salgado and others. He was excited over the "New ways of seeing," by electronic imaging in news, fashion and art photography, saying this is the future way for the young photographer. And he feels the versatile photographer is more useful to an editor than the specialist. Versatility is an attribute that every new photographer should have as basic stock in trade. The ability to work well in many genres is an important quality of professionalism.

Chapter Two

Analyzing Specific Markets: The Editorial World

Now let's direct our attention to selecting, investigating and evaluating the needs of specific markets. Doing preliminary work before proceeding with your selling strategy is essential for getting your work into the markets where it will sell best.

Let's start with the editorial world. In this major group are hundreds, probably thousands, of newspapers, magazines, city weeklies and monthlies, trade publications and all manner of corporate publications, not to mention the thousands of hard and soft cover books which are printed by the millions every year. Add to this calendars, posters, special editions and government reports, and you have a fair idea of the demand for photography.

In this chapter we analyze these markets and their products, show how to contact appropriate people in the organizations, and how to evaluate their particular picture needs.

Newspapers

Daily Newspapers: As a rule, newspapers use black-and-white photographs of news events, including accidents, fires, personalities; features on homemaking, travel, books, sports, politicians and other public officials, local business developments, construction and weather (extremes of heat, cold or the elements); and pictures of people in the news, including marriages, births, deaths, funerals and other public events and happenings. In reality there is almost nothing that is not of some photographic interest to newspapers, provided they have the space and budget for the pictures. Photos are frequently used with only brief captions and no text at all. Generally, little color is used in daily newspapers, but it is increasing and ROP (run of press) color is becoming more frequent. But it is still expensive and usually reserved for front page news. However, the increased use of electronic imaging and its applications to the color separation process via the Scitex and similar systems (see page 322) will probably lower the cost of color printing in daily newspapers, and we should see an increase in color use throughout the average daily newspaper.

Sunday Newspapers: Most big city and many small town daily papers also have Sunday editions that are often a bigger market for local photographers than the dailies. Sunday editions tend to use more color and run more household features. They frequently have enlarged special sections or departments. Many of the big city daily Sunday sections are themselves almost national magazines, such as the Sunday *New York Times Magazine* and *Washington Post Sunday* magazine. In addition, a great many smaller and medium-size papers buy complete newspaper magazine packages. *Parade* magazine services over one hundred papers with a 22,000,000 + circulation nationwide and has the largest Sunday circulation of any newspaper magazine in the country. There are also other publishing groups putting out preprinted packages, among them *Family Weekly* and Metro Sunday Newspapers, plus numerous feature syndicates that supply picture stories, photo columns, etc., to be inserted into local papers. Many of the latter are associated with the larger wire and news services. *Literary Market Place* lists over one hundred syndicated services, many that buy and use photography. They should not be ignored and careful study of the information given will show who the editors are, the kind of material they are interested in, and where and how to contact them.

Also, many of the large metropolitan papers run special sections in connection with their regular Sunday magazine sections. They may be devoted to food, fashion, travel, or other special subjects. They frequently pay well. The big problem there is the obvious one. In order to crack a special section, the photographer usually needs a strong track record in the field. Sometimes it can be too strong, however. I know of one well-known fashion photographer who acted so obnoxiously on location with his demeaning behavior and holier-than-thou attitude with the studio crew that he barely made it through the shoot. When he left the last picture to his assistant to finish up, the editor of the issue, who was present throughout the shoot, calmly made a paper airplane of a publicity photo of the photographer and set fire to it before she sailed it across the studio floor. No, he was not called back to do the special issue for the following year.

Weekly Newspapers: These are usually rural, and circulation is for the most part via direct mail. Frankly, these publications are less promising markets for the up-and-coming photographer, except for those interested in acquiring tearsheets rather than remuneration. These papers will undoubtedly take free pictures or, if they do pay, the fees may be less than the cost of paper and chemicals used to make the prints. However, it is a showcase of sorts, but after a few placements, I suggest that the new photographer move to greener pastures.

There is another type of weekly paper that does use photographs frequently: the weekly personality-oriented tabloids sold at supermarket checkout counters. Some pay extremely well, but working for them may result in unforeseen complications. Whether a photographer who supplies this sort of photography could be a party to a lawsuit is being debated, though the consensus at present seems to be that photographers are not liable as long as they do not violate privacy, copyright or libel statutes in providing material to the publisher.

I had an amusing call from such a weekly recently. The editor apologized profusely for even calling me to supply some clearly intrusive photographs of a popular personality. When I told her I did not stock such photographs in my files, she breathed a sigh of relief and said, "Thank God, I can't locate any anywhere and I don't want to be a part of insulting and smearing the person whose pictures we were looking for."

There are other weekly papers that fall between both payment extremes. They use pictures well and frequently pay more than the ASMP pricing recommendations. The *Village Voice* in New York is typical, and although they don't set hard guidelines, their pay scales range widely from a few dollars to $300 per photo, depending on its importance, use and position.

By and large, the average small town paper, be it daily, weekly, biweekly or monthly, is probably not much of a paying market, though it can be a stepping-stone to better opportunities, even staff jobs at larger papers.

Locating a Picture Buyer at a Newspaper

Newspapers usually print the names of their important editorial personnel in front of the magazine or on the editorial pages in a time-honored format called the "masthead." Magazine mastheads are usually more precise than their newspaper counterparts, which are somewhat limited, though there is a wealth of information that can be gained from both.

Newspaper mastheads are different from those in the national magazines even though their working structures are very similar. The mastheads of the big city papers and many mid-sized ones usually carry only the names of corporate officers and top editorial management. *The New York Times*, for instance, shows only twenty-one management people ranging from the publisher, the executive and magazine editor, five assistant managing editors and ending with three vice presidents, the controller and circulation and production officials. Yet we know there is a vast editorial staff and a large photographic department, including several photo and assignment editors, and a sizable staff of photographers, supporting studio and darkroom people. Was photography being downgraded in the corporate hierarchy? No, because one of the five assistant managing editors was the picture editor.

How are new photographers supposed to know that? They can't, unless they simply pick up the phone and ask the switchboard operator for the picture desk. Eventually the caller will probably be directed to the right person, but it's not simple.

This organizational pattern is followed by most newspapers, though the staffs will be proportionally smaller. Yet newspapers are a unique editorial market because most are dailies with tight closing times. The handling of the photographs is apt to be highly departmentalized, with the department editors being more or less responsible for the pictures that appear in their sections. Most dailies have their own photo departments, usually complete with staff photographers, assignment and/or picture editors, lab personnel, etc., and when a department editor calls for a photographer, it will be the picture editor, assignments editor or chief photographer (depending on the title) who makes the actual assignment. Once a picture is made, it then starts back up the chain of command from the picture editor to the department editor, national or city desks. The larger dailies with the bigger staffs tend to group their photographers by specialty, so it is rare that general news will be covered by the sports department photographer and vice versa, yet the versatility needed in most newspaper photography will often require that the photographer jump the barrier from one specialty to another to cover for someone on vacation or sick leave, or when a major news story breaks, requiring every available hand.

With the exception of the lucky happenstance of a nonstaffer running across a hard news event, most of the photographs appearing in a daily newspaper will have been photographed by staff photographers or supplied by a news service or agency. But this does not necessarily apply to the Sunday editions, which are treated more as magazines than daily papers.

Does that mean the new photographer should give up on the newspaper market? Certainly not. There are many independent freelance situations that probably won't bring in much money at the beginning, but a steady effort in these areas can eventually lead to regular acceptance, frequent calls, or stringer status and ultimately a staff association. It can start on any level. (See pages 16 and 213.)

There are countless stories of successes that have come about because of sheer perseverance. I know of one man who even before graduation from high school in a small midwestern town installed a radio scanner in his car and began chasing police cars, fire engines, state troopers' cars and ambulances. Prior to graduation he had been submitting pictures to his hometown daily where he was hired after graduation. He learned to edit as well as shoot news photos and quickly became adept at feature stories as well as "one-shots." For a while he was doing both editing and photographing, and even sweeping out the darkroom occasionally, and at that stage those activities complemented each other. He moved on to a daily in a nearby bigger city and became a feature photographer-writer-editor. Eventually he came to New York and has made a fine name for himself as the editor of one of the most prestigious nature/picture magazines around. He still has the time to produce excellent photographic stories and makes a fair amount of extra money from his continuing love of his work. Horatio Alger stuff? No, he simply demonstrates the time-proven tradition of starting small.

This is not an isolated occurrence. In fact, it is the norm rather than the exception. Many photographers have made it by "starting small" at the local level and moving up the ladder, more by perseverance than anything else. In fact, there are some photographers who, in my opinion, are much better salesmen than photographers and who appear regularly in some of the most important magazines.

Magazines and Related Markets

Consumer Magazines: There are about 1,500 publications with national circulation in this group. They are usually more selective in their photographic requirements, often using complete picture stories, though they may restrict themselves to one editorial photograph that sets the tone for an entire article. With most of the larger magazines the accompanying text is an important part in which the photographer plays no contributory role, except to provide information for captions. Captions themselves may be fairly brief or elongated to function as short text peices. On the smaller publications, particularly those where budgets are tight, the photographer may often be called on to write not only the captions but the text of the article as well.

Magazines can be a very big market for new photographers because they need vast amounts of photographic material and most of them will buy only one-time reproduction rights for their particular publication, thus leaving the field open to multiple sales in different regional publications or noncompetitive areas. Although some publications have staff photographers, the majority use freelancers. Color is also more prevalent in magazines than in newspapers. Magazines, too, are more often keyed to specific audiences than newspapers. There are many authoritative directories of newspaper, magazine and book publishers. For a detailed listing of names, addresses and prices, please see the special directories section (pages 22-26).

Interwoven through the list of general consumer periodicals is a new and growing field of city and city/metro magazines. Some of these are large-scale, slick, modern publications which, though directed at a precise group, have in fact grown to considerable national circulation. *New York* magazine, *Arizona Highways*, *Sunset* and *Washingtonian* are good examples. There is probably at least one so-called "city magazine" for every large city in the country and for many smaller ones as well. They are all excellent markets for photographers.

Airline magazines: Although these magazines at first proliferated, the actual number of original publications was reduced with many published by one company with different covers for different airlines, and with some of the same stories used in several editions. Also, these magazines have had as many ups and downs as a student pilot making test landings because of the mergers, consolidations and failures of so many airlines. There are, however, a number of substantial airline publications that are still individually published by the airlines or special groups concentrating on this field. Some are of extremely high caliber and should be explored as a market for regional photography. These magazines are not considered "specialized" magazines because their subject matter is general, not aviation oriented. However, some of the remaining airline books continue multiple use of stories with different covers.

Trade and specialized publications: There are a large number of trade and specialized publications in business, law, medicine, health, religion, science, aviation and many other areas of interest. These specialized publications deal directly with a specific subject, industry or trade, and range from *Advertising Techniques* through *Yard and Garden*. Many of them are well produced, use photography effectively, and have pay scales beginning to approach national standards. The trend is that quality magazines are demanding and paying for quality photography. Color covers are becoming standard and more color is being used inside the publication as well. Many trade magazines are indeed industry-wide publications and often have clout comparable to the big national magazines, even though their focus of inquiry is narrowed to a specialized area.

Because of traditionally low budgets, the trade magazines frequently are more amenable to photographers also functioning as authors, provided the photographer knows enough about the industry being photographed and has the ability to write. Such magazines often permit, and in fact encourage, the more experienced and capable photographers to write the captions and text pieces that accompany photographs. Unfortunately, this is rare among the major consumer magazines which are, for the most part, managed and edited by people who frequently are more word than picture conscious. These editors often take the position of "let the photographer photograph and the writer write, and never the twain shall meet." Some of these same editors also fall prey to an attitude known as "typecasting" and wait until they are desperate before they permit a photographer expert in one particular area to cross the line into another specialization.

Once photographer Dan Weiner and I wound up in the same Illinois town at the same time to photograph different aspects of the same corporate story for a large magazine. Weiner was assigned to do the executive portraits and I the heavy machinery, and both of us were bored to tears by being stuck in these niches by this magazine's constantly assigning us to covering "heads or tails." It didn't take but a few martinis at the hotel bar to plot an exchange in roles. The unexpected arrival of the writer quickly put a crimp in those plans, though we were both certain that the editorial office would have never known the difference.

Ironically, many of these same magazines that express opposition to using photographers as writers seem to have little hesitation about their writers acting as photographers, and have gone to great lengths to provide writers with cameras saying, "While you're at it, knock off a few pictures for us."

Versatility is particularly important for young photographers trying to sell themselves. But the "I can photograph anything, anywhere, anytime" attitude is equally dangerous and if pushed too far can give an editor a feeling of "Jack of all trades, master of none." So the new photographer has to determine a workable compromise and be able to handle a variety of situations without alienating editors or buyers. When the situation arises and he is called upon to write a piece as well as make the photographs, he is responsible for double craftsmanship. So while a skill in writing is often called for, it must be used carefully. If the photographer must pay extra attention to the copy, he should not do so at the expense of the photographs. The best way to handle this is to concentrate wholly on the pictures until the shooting is completed and then, and only then, consider the words. An editor can alter or improve copy—but there is little that can be done to improve a poor photograph.

In general, the magazine field is an excellent market for new photographers, particularly those who are alert, creative and sensitive to the needs of the publications they are trying to serve.

One-Shot Publications

One-shot publications can also provide a good outlet for the photographer. These publications can be carefully researched educational or government projects or "quickie" magazine productions on a specialized and popular subject such as auto racing, skiing or energy-saving. They are usually published in softcover format, use many photographs and are reproduced by the most inexpensive form of offset lithography. They hit the magazine newsstands for a quick one-time distribution, and unsold copies go off to the pulp mills. The reason this type of publication is of interest to the photographer, aside from the quick money, is that this type of "how-to" or specialized subject matter usually provides a good file of photographs for secondary use. As always, care must be exercised to specify in writing who owns the rights to the photographs if they are to be sold again for other uses.

Special Reports

This is a smaller but no less active field for editorial photography. Thousands of special reports and projects are published every year utilizing photography. What are these reports? Who publishes them?

The prime originators of this type of publication are engineering and construction companies that need background material on city planning, urban redevelopment and housing organizations, conservation (or the lack of it), land use and impact reports. Many of these are published by private firms and many by hundreds of government bureaus on all levels, from federal government departments to state commissions, as well as local interest groups. City, county and state legislators frequently make use of area studies, aerial photographs and street scenes to prove some political point. It is not always easy to find out what's going on and how to make contacts in these fields, but many of the groups involved in a publishing venture will seek out the sources of photography, using professional or trade lists and many classified listings including telephone books. Specialized picture research groups have come to know the sources of photographs, as do many art production houses specializing in corporate annual reports and other company publications.

Another area of the special report lies in the field of consumer testing and technical analysis. Public interest groups frequently need photographs of environmental conditions. Unfortunately, most of them have little money to buy such photography, but frequently there are public funds and grants available for such purposes.

Other Market Opportunities for Selling Photographs

We are now getting down to smaller (but not necessarily less lucrative) outlets for editorial photography, such as posters, postcards, calendars and other promotional items. The use of photographs in postcards goes back as far as when photography became a reproducible medium. As in most other publishing ventures, there are the giants and the small operators. The giants have nationwide promotional plans to acquire material for postcards but invariably pay little for the pictures. I have a handful of cheery letters from postcard printers from all over the country offering to buy my photographs almost by the pound, with no mention of distribution or royalties. My advice? Stay away from them unless they offer a system of clear (CPA) accounting procedures and rights acquisition, not to mention a fair price.

On the other hand, this is also the kind of business a photographer can go into in his hometown without any great capital outlay, provided he works out some sort of distribution system in *advance* of getting involved in expensive four-color reproduction. I knew of a good amateur photographer who by profession was an inn-keeper in a small but popular resort area. He made his own photographs, had them well reproduced in postcard format, and sold them literally by the thousands in the area where he lived. Even after his death, his cards continue to sell and his estate has a steady income from them.

After a little research I found that, surprisingly enough, even though there is a good deal of competition, especially from the large printing companies, the postcard and poster markets are so localized that photographers can easily arrange distribution of their work in this form without great cash outlays. The same is also true of slide shows and audiovisual corporate promotions.

So much for the editorial market. As you can see, there is a potential for vast usage of photography and for some substantial returns, provided the photographs are well marketed and the clients competently serviced.

The First Placement: Breaking Into Print via Low-Budget and Free Publication

This is your moment of truth. But sometimes one doesn't recognize it when it happens. I didn't when I sold a photograph of a string of bagels to the *New York Sun* in 1941 for $10. Ten bucks? Why would anyone want to pay me for something I enjoyed doing so much? But there it was, a two-column cut with byline, and a couple of weeks later a check for $10. And the circulation of the *Sun* went up that day by fifty copies.

This is not what caused me to turn professional, but it was the first photograph I sold, although I had been dabbling in photography for a couple of years while holding down another job at night so that I could learn to photograph during the day. Most of my dabbling seemed to be in the direction of dragging carrying cases for established professionals and doing other "gofer" chores. This is the classic way of getting started for many a photographer, even now. There are many who advise that the best way to become a photographer is to get a job as an assistant in a studio. For those who are interested in studio work, I agree that while it may not be the best way, certainly it is a good way. But after three or four years of photojournalism school or an equal amount of amateur shooting with other jobs paying the rent, finally making that first sale is a joy indeed.

How do you actually break into print or make that very first sale? I spoke earlier of young people chasing emergency vehicles to find a newsworthy occurrence. There is also the high school yearbook routine, using portraits of your fellow students or shooting some small sports photo feature from your school days. When you produce those photographs, do not be ashamed of them. Take the better ones to your local paper and show some enthusiasm over the opportunity to photograph your peers. The local editors may see news value in some of them that you do not.

Breaking into print, especially if it's of no cost to the user, is not particularly difficult. There will always be someone who can use a photograph. Selling your work is tough, but becomes a way of life if you are to be a professional photographer. In any business or professional art form, starting at the bottom is traditional, and probably the first photographic markets to be explored are the so-called free markets. They have their value to you. The up and coming photographer needs a showcase, needs to build a portfolio, and while a portfolio made up of prints or transparencies is fine, one that is made up in part of actually reproduced photographs is even better, provided the reproduction quality is good and the display meaningful.

The fact that a photograph has been published is a plus. It means that someone else thought enough of it to print it—to pay for the cost of the engravings or separations and the resulting paper and presswork costs.

What are these so-called free markets that are important to the new photographers, and should they be exploited? The latter answer is yes, exploit them, but not for long! Try them perhaps just long enough to earn some reasonable credit lines.

Probably the easiest publications to reach are the small-town or rural "give-away" publications that carry enough advertising to cover production and distribution costs and whose audiences are strictly limited to their immediate areas. There are also the close relatives, the local county or village weeklies or monthlies. They will probably offer five to ten dollars per photo, which for them might seem like a lot, but you will probably spend an equal amount to shoot, process and print.

Times are changing very rapidly, however, and with the wider use of cold type, cathode-ray tubes (CRT), video-display terminals (VDT), and with the fast-developing electronic imaging, other electronic and computer technology, and faster total offset reproduction, the smaller papers are proliferating. They are spending more proportionately on original photography. Why? Even though this new equipment is expensive to purchase, the unit cost per picture drops considerably. Thanks to this new technology, there is not much difference in cost between reproducing a page of pictures or a page of type.

These newer papers are one step removed from the "free" market and are a stepping-stone for the new photographer. They probably will be grateful for pictures of local news interest that they can get for very little. After the photographer has made his contacts with the editors, has proved that he or she can produce the kind of photography they can use, then it's time to ask for remuneration. This will not hurt you in the eyes of the editors, because they know what a young photographer must do to get started.

So, after a reasonable amount of low-cost service, you should either move up the ladder or out the door. And by the time you have appeared in a fair number of issues you should also be developing some expertise as to how pictures are used in these types of publications, and you will begin to develop a sense of what is worth printing and what isn't. Perhaps, too, you are beginning to approach the time for making the decision about whether to specialize or not, and you should be getting ready to explore wider markets and broader horizons of specialization.

Where you direct your pictures is then your next major move. The directories listed in chapter one have many pages of current listings of publications classified by areas of interest. Many of the publications are probably low budget and need low-cost photographs. For instance, if you were to approach a labor newspaper or magazine with a story on some part of a local labor situation, the chances are the editors would be most happy to publish the piece (provided it reflected their point of view on the story) and probably would pay a small fee for both the pictures and the text, if necessary.

But be realistic. Don't approach a labor paper with a Chamber of Commerce position on a local labor story, or vice versa. And be sure of your facts and information before you try to sell a story. This is also "professionalism" and it pays to learn it from the beginning of your career. Bear in mind that even if you allow your photographs to be printed without a fee or for a very small one, it does not mean that you should give up your rights to them. Make sure your pictures are protected by copyright (see chapter ten). It is simple to do, not costly, and it may save you a lot of grief later.

Government and State Publications, Small Local Papers and Newsletters

Another source of placement for the new photographer is with government publications, on all levels from federal down to the smallest municipality or county organizations. There is always a need for photographers here, but frequently little or no money to pay for them. Other sources (non-governmental) are agricultural organizations, conservation and land development groups, and private natural resource, pollution control and environmental violation review groups.

On the federal level, the General Services Administration, the watchdog and procurement arm of the U.S. government, will put you on a list for possible bids on things photographic. The U.S. Government Printing Office has lists of U.S. government publications that use photographs. Virtually every branch of the government has some publications, from the smallest department to some large cabinet-level bureaus. Much photography on the state and municipal level is done by open bidding. Write your own state, city or local procurement offices to be placed on their bidding lists. Not only can these lists be strong pointers to revenue sources for yourself in finding local jobs (or even big ones), they might well lead you to some larger outfit that may have outbid you, but who themselves can use your services. Remember, when you are starting small and your overhead is minimal, chances are you can beat the bids of many larger and more experienced organizations and thus land some substantial contracts or parts of contracts. But be careful when making your photographs available to the government for little or no fee, as pictures made under these circumstances can fall into the public domain. If you are hired as a government photographer, even on a temporary basis, you can lose your copyright protection, but you do not have to as there are ways of protecting your work, even work you do for the government. Read up on your copyright law. It's something you are going to be concerned with all of your photographic life. So you may as well start now. Check these aspects thoroughly before you offer a picture to a government publication. The pictures you lose, like your life, can be your own.

Locating a Picture Buyer at a Magazine

In a recent issue of *LIFE* magazine, there are thirty-four titles on the masthead, beginnning with Founder (Henry Luce, who died in 1967) and six other top listings: Editor in Chief, Chairman of the Board, President, Editorial Director, Group Vice President—Magazines, and Vice Chairman. None of these six executives will ordinarily be interested in seeing your work, as their roles are corporate management rather than involvement with the specifics of the structure of the magazine.

Next are the top working group and here there are four titles: Managing Editor, Assistant Managing Editor, Senior Editor and Picture Editor. Technically all four would be interested in your pictures since *LIFE* is essentially a picture magazine. Of these four editors, the picture editor would, in theory, most certainly be the person to see, and he or she will be available to as many photographers as he has time for, but he is probably very busy because he has responsibility for many stories in all stages of production. But don't rule the picture editor out as unreachable, because part of his job is to see and find new talent. Yet you should be extremely thoughtful about making demands on a picture editor's time and be selective in what you show.

Next on the list is the art director. It is unlikely you will have any contact with an editorial art director because, unlike ad agency art directors, he is mainly concerned with dealing with the photographs prepared for him by the editors.

Then comes the articles editor, followed by the news editor. These are people with whom story ideas should be discussed, but even they are not the ones who make the final judgment about whether you get an assignment or not. If they do like a story idea, they will probably present it at a story conference or to a senior editor who will have more to say on the subject.

Still reading the masthead, you will come to an echelon of assistant editors, all of them aides to those already listed. This is the group you will probably start with. Here you will find other important personnel: the staff writers, reporters, researchers and many who provide liaison service with the rest of the corporation's available facilities—darkroom, studio, if any, and the picture collection ("morgue" in newspaper jargon).

The editorial market is the one that is receptive to outside ideas, unlike the advertising world, where it is extremely rare that an "outside" idea is ever accepted. But in the editorial world the situation is different. With the high percentage of freelancers competing for assignments and the relatively small staffs (if any) at most magazines, it is only natural that editors will look outside for ideas.

Pass this philosophy down to the freelance level and you can see why magazines have always welcomed outside story suggestions. One freelancer who had a long association with the managing editor on a publication before he moved over to another asked, "How many years do I have to have under my belt before I get a direct assignment from you without my originating it?" The editor replied, "Look, I have twelve issues a year with space for about four or five stories per issue. That makes fifty to sixty stories a year, and I have two hundred photographers clamoring for work, including the thirty-five or forty I know from my earlier years, who are top producers and whom I want to help keep alive. The only way I can deal with this is to select the photographer who comes in with an idea we can use."

This all ties in with the approach made by the new freelancer to the magazine world and why he has to be careful not only about the selection of story material he presents but also to whom it is shown. For now let us consider that the assistant picture editor of this particular type of magazine will probably be your point of first contact, but bear in mind that proving photographic ability alone is not enough.

Newsweek, a general news weekly, has even more precise divisions of responsibility than a monthly magazine like *LIFE* because it publishes more frequently, requiring a more specialized staff. *Newsweek* and its competitor, *TIME*, are similar in structure. They have vast staffs, while *LIFE* is put out by some thirty staffers along with the contributions of numerous freelancers. The two major weekly news magazines have permanent staffs of several hundred, including those at the various bureaus nationwide and worldwide. Each magazine has a battery of picture editors and department editors, many of whom deal with just one section. Each has a stable of photographers whose names appear on the masthead, although they are usually photographers under contract who are located in major cities and news centers. They also use many freelance photographers and buy heavily from picture agencies specializing in news coverage. Because of the short deadline time and the need for weekly news material, the big photo essay is very hard to come by, and though these magazines may devote four to eight color pages per issue to a major picture story, it is usually a news-oriented piece produced more often than not by several photographers rather than one.

An important point for the new photographer to remember is that each of these magazine publishing groups, as well as some of their smaller and more business-oriented competitors such as *Forbes, Business Week* and *U.S. News and World Report*, all have bureaus both in this country and abroad, from which many stories originate. In dealing with these magazines it may be easier to work with the local bureau chief on a one-to-one level.

Not all magazines, however, are as tough to contend with as the news weeklies and bimonthlies. The monthly magazines usually have a slower pace, are more specific in their focus of interest, and are less gargantuan in scope, yet many may be termed "general interest" magazines.

Even the city/metro weekly magazines, while caught up in fast closings, are a little more controlled because the staffs are smaller and they use fewer stories per issue. Usually one story per department is the norm, and it may have taken weeks to put together. Here is a better opportunity for the young photographer to get a foot in the editorial door, as the subject material is often a home-grown topic and the editors are less concerned with national issues.

The men's and women's fashion, house, shelter and lifestyle magazines are departmentalized, too, and the contact people are easier to locate because their jobs are generally better defined on the masthead. A food editor is usually just that. Ditto the book reviewer, sports editor and the editors for new products and services. At some magazines where the staffs are small and the jobs varied, the term "editorial assistant" is the catch-all phrase for people who are moved around from department to department and who may be involved in anything from the crossword pages to eight-page color photo essays. On these smaller publications where there is no picture editor, photography is usually handled by the art director—a title that is really an anachronism, a throwback to the days preceding reproduction of photos when all illustration in any publication was considered "art."

Let's look at the masthead of *Smithsonian*, certainly one of the finest magazines using photographs. *Smithsonian*, with a circulation of approximately 1,850,000, has only thirty-five names on the masthead. Of these names, twenty are directly involved in editorial matters, with only five or six of them interested in picture buying, and the rest handling circulation, advertising, production and the like. How do they handle their photographic coverages? With freelancers only. The standards are incredibly high, the reproduction excellent and it is magazine journalism at its best. On the masthead there is no picture editor listed *per se*, but included in the listing of "Board of Editors" is a person with "Pictures" added to her title, as well as her assistant's title of Associate Editor, Pictures. Actually, these are the picture editor and assistant picture editor respectively. They are the people the new photographer should contact. At this magazine, photographers with story ideas that might normally go directly to a story or department editor at another magazine should channel their ideas through the picture department. The picture people take the idea to the editorial group, which makes the decision about whether a story is of interest or not. Then one of the picture editors gets back to you for the "yes," "no" or "maybe."

You can see, then, that the masthead is an all-important clue about whom to see or contact. While the terminology may change, the job responsibilities are usually easily spotted, although sometimes it may be hard to discern who to see.

If there seems to be no one identified as responsible for pictures, particularly occurring at smaller magazines, the next step is to contact the art director or assistant art director. Even these jobs may not be too well defined, or the titles may be obscured by fancy verbiage, such as "Graphics Editor" or "Design Director," or, the magazine may be so small that the job of art director could be combined with production. But perseverance is the answer, and if all else fails, the solution is to pick up the phone and ask the publication's switchboard operator, "Who is responsible for pictures, what's his or her name, and how is it spelled?" Don't laugh at the question of spelling. There is nothing that will turn people off more than to have their names and titles misspelled or misrepresented.

Turning to a different kind of magazine, let's look at *Family Circle*. This is a large-circulation, family/home-oriented publication with a wide distribution through newsstands, stores and supermarkets and subscriptions. This is not a small, independent magazine, but a major one, published nationally and internationally by the New York Times Company.

Family Circle's corporate officers appear on the contents page. At the top of the masthead are six titles. Judging from the bylines, these people are active in the editorial content of the magazine rather than just concerned with corporate management, as in the case of those on the *LIFE* masthead. On this masthead each department is clearly identified and there is a large group of senior editors and other editorial service personnel. But note here that the art director is listed as one of the top editorial people, with no picture editor identified at all. One person carries the classification of "Photography" after his name. Is this the picture editor we are looking for? Probably not, because he appears as a photographer in the credits. In a situation like this you can go directly to the story (specialization) editor, and if that person is not the right one, he or she can redirect you.

What we are really saying is that while the job listings are apparently defined, precision must be used in pinpointing your first contact; the photographer must make a careful study of the masthead before considering who is to be approached with what sort of material.

We have looked at the monthlies, news weeklies, the home/lifestyle and the general-interest magazines. All are national in scope. Are the regionals or the city/metros any different?

Let's look at *New York* magazine. It is set up similarly to the national magazines except that, as a weekly, the staff is smaller than that of the major news weeklies such as *TIME* or *Newsweek*. At *New York* the "Design Director" occupies the third position on the masthead and the picture editor is almost at the bottom of the list after a large block of senior editors who really do the bulk of the editorial work. After the senior editor listing is another large group of "contributing editors" who usually supply columns in specialty areas such as theater or film, books, shopping, restaurant critiques, and the like. Photographers will have a tough time approaching contributing editors because most of them are not "in residence" at the magazine. So in this case it's back to the picture editor, though on first contact he may suggest speaking directly with one of the senior or contributing editors to see if there is an area of mutual interest that could be turned into a picture story. As in most of the other magazines discussed, the pattern is to funnel most picture assignments through the picture editor rather than the art director. So, in summation, on most magazines where a picture editor is clearly indicated, that is the person to see rather than an art director, senior editor or news editor.

Editorial art directors are generally less visible to the working photographer than their counterparts at advertising agencies. The reason for this is that an editorial assignment is usually conceived by the editors of a publication, a freelance writer, sometimes a photographer, and occasionally a combination of them. The story script or outline may go first to a researcher, department editor or picture editor before being assigned to a photographer, and rarely does a publication bring its art director in beforehand except to get a general idea of how much editorial space is available.

It has become almost automatic not to preplan the makeup of a major national publication until the last minute because of the possibility of late-breaking news that will throw the whole magazine out of kilter and the art director's plans and layouts out the window. Two pungent remarks, one by a famous managing editor and the other by an equally famous art director, illustrate this best. The editor, when being pressed to guarantee the running of a specific story by someone with clout and a vested interest in the piece, is reported to have said, "I wouldn't guarantee to run a four-color spread on the Second Coming of Christ unless I knew what was in the book the week before and what we were planning for the week after." And the art director, on hearing of the assassination of a head of state, exclaimed, "What a thing to happen on the day after we closed!" Though the pressures of timing and deadlines are crucial in the editorial world, this is less true of advertising layouts that are sometimes prepared six months or a year in advance.

The impact of the editorial art director on the shooting of a story by a photographer is great, however. Even though he may not have been in contact with the photographer, it is the art director's influence and talent that definitely will affect how a story is shot, laid out and printed.

Insider: John Loengard, Picture Editor

Attitudes toward photographers at the level of the picture editors or assignment editors at magazines or newspapers are critical, because these are the people the photographers will generally be dealing with on a day-by-day basis. John Loengard, who was a *LIFE* staff photographer for many years and formerly the picture editor of the new edition of *LIFE*, is typical of the new breed of knowledgeable and responsive editors. In his former staff position, he was aware of the problems of photographers as well as the needs of his publication and was responsible for the production of most of the photography that went into the magazine.

Loengard started as a photographer at the age of eleven when he borrowed a camera from his parents. He started taking pictures as a student in a prep school in New Hampshire, and later in college he photographed for the college newspaper. He went on to taking photographs for his college alumni magazine, his first paid assignments. This was important, because the magazine was influenced by the photography in the big, picture magazines of that time, and it was a very good training ground for Loengard. He joined *LIFE*'s staff in 1961, remaining with them until it folded in 1972. He was then attached to a special team called the Magazine Development Group which put out ten special issues of *LIFE*, keeping *LIFE*'s format alive and its name before the public until it started publishing again. He was the first picture editor of *People* magazine and worked on several other experimental publications in 1979. Loengard has certainly paid his dues as both photographer and editor and understands the needs and interests of both.

When Loengard was still at *LIFE* I asked him how he viewed the photographers who come to see him, how he feels about them, his attitudes toward them. He replied, "We at *LIFE* have an appreciation of what they are doing because we are in a very privileged position. Those who come here feel that this is the very best, and they take us seriously. We know they are going to give us the best they possibly can. We think it's a wonderful attitude and we try to be as sympathetic to them as they are to us. We have a special interest in photographers under thirty. Not that we don't use the older ones. We do, and are happy to use them, but the future is going to come from those younger photographers under thirty. I think we can offer them an opportunity to do something that no other publication can today.

"Because so much material was needed on the weekly *LIFE*, it used to be much more common for editors to take a chance on a story and a photographer, but there is not as much leeway for this now. However, it is still done, they benefit from it, and the young photographer does as well.

"If I were going to generalize, I would guess photographers come from two places—the New York (or other big-city) studio that is entirely commercially oriented, where one learns technique and develops photographic abilities, and from newspapers, where one learns the editorial sense. Both kinds of photographers are invaluable.

"*LIFE* magazine looks for people who not only have an interest in photography but also are concerned about the sense and structure of the story, who have an interest in what's going on and a feeling for a rough dramatic structure. I am talking here about the photographer who wants to know what's different and has the ability to go out and see what's special about a subject, not just what's going to make a nice picture."

I asked him how a young photographer gets to do work for *LIFE*. He was both candid and sympathetic, citing the literally hundreds of photographers he and assistant picture editors have seen since the inception of the new magazine. That function has now largely been taken over by one assistant picture editor, who will see new photographers, but it will take time.

Loengard said, "*LIFE* is always interested in somebody who is different, who is good. But there are lots of people who are good, so we look for somebody who makes something seem a little larger than what other people are doing. The funny thing is that most things we ask people to go and photograph are dull, and most of the pictures we print are (hopefully) interesting. Something happens between the subject and the picture, and that's what the photographer is doing. I think what we are looking for is not how *good* a photographer is, but how *interesting* he can be with a camera and how interesting he can be about subjects. I think that's a rare quality and a rare ability."

Loengard feels that in journalism the photographer should find what's distinctive about a subject as compared with advertising or industrial photography, which tries to avoid the peculiar and depicts the generality.

LIFE magazine, both the old weekly and the current monthly, has always been perceived as a standard of excellence for the industry and a goal to be aimed at by the new photographer. But almost as important has been its influence on photojournalism, in general, as the current masthead of almost any important magazine using pictures well will attest. Somewhere on those long lists will be many who learned their skills on this unique publication or its sister magazines.

Insider: Caroline Despard, Associate Editor, Pictures

Typical of these competent and caring people is Caroline Despard, now on the Board of Editors of *Smithsonian* magazine. Despard, in the course of assigning and editing photography for *Smithsonian*, deals with photographers every working day and probably many nonworking days as well. She is totally dedicated to her craft and intensely desirous of seeing good photography. She has a deep feeling for, and understanding of, photographers and is sympathetic to their problems.

Professionally, she started in the text department of a book publisher. After a few years at standard publishing houses, she joined the TIME, Inc. staff in Paris, partly because of her fluency in Italian and French. Even though she had been developing an interest in photography, she was suddenly thrust into it at TIME's Paris bureau by being assigned to work with photographers. After an apprenticeship there, she went on to join the new *Smithsonian* magazine in Washington then being formed by Ed Thompson.

As with all new magazines under development, the planning and test issues were produced with a minimum of staff, and Despard got a very intensive education in the production of a quality picture magazine.

She feels that the significant differences apparent in photojournalism today stem from radical changes in equipment and the technical simplification of the problems of obtaining good images on film. She does not minimize the need for craftsmanship, but underscores the fact that with so many technical aids on hand, there is more room for the photographer to concern himself with content.

"Too many photographers come into my office," she says, "with pictures that all look as if they were shot by the same person." She looks for a photographer with an "individual, exceptional eye." She feels that there are really very few photographers around with that exceptional approach and guesses that there are no more today than there were thirty years ago.

She thinks the attitudes of editors toward photographers have changed radically over the years, probably due to the change in markets. There is not as much "baby-sitting," as she puts it (sending out researchers or reporters with the photographers) as there used to be.

"What we're looking for," she said, "is to be able to trust the photographer completely. I want to give him all the information I have, and let him take it from there, knowing I'll get a good story back. That's the guy I love. I want a good job; I don't want to have to send him back, and I want him to understand that the story is for *Smithsonian* and not for *LIFE*, *Paris MATCH* or anyone else.

"But the basic attribute has to be intelligence. Not only must he understand what the story is about, but he must have the initiative to go where the story is and often transform a nonvisual story into a highly visual one. At *Smithsonian* I think we do that a lot more than *LIFE* or *Look* did in the old days, because they often chose their stories visually and for their news value. Today we often run hi-tech, hard-science stories that don't lend themselves easily to human interest or evocative pictures, yet the photographer has to find them."

Photographer-originated stories are not as much in demand at *Smithsonian* as at other magazines because many of their stories start as text pieces already in house. Despard does not want to discourage photographers from submitting ideas, however, as she confirms that for new photographers at least it is by far the best way of getting into a magazine. She also suggests that one possibility of presenting an idea is for the photographer to team up with a writer so the presentation will be even more complete and be easier for the magazine to assess as an entire package. This does not mean that a finished story has to be submitted. Far from it, because editors will view with suspicion anything they are locked into in the way of a finished product.

Insider: Renee Bruns, Managing Editor

Up to now we have been concerned with the opinions of the editors of the big popular and prestigious magazines. But how about the editorial viewpoint of the smaller and more specialized publications? Numerically there are many more with not inconsiderable circulations, cumulatively far exceeding those of the big publications.

I talked with Renee Bruns, *Popular Photography*'s managing editor, and her thoughts paralleled many of her contemporaries'. There seems to be far too much talent for the number of pages available. In spite of the magazine's orientation toward the amateur photographer, professional photographers have demonstrated that they like *Popular Photography* as a showcase, particularly in new areas of work. She told us that what they look for in a photographer is technical competence and professional behavior in general.

She alluded briefly to *Popular Photography*'s sister magazine, *American Photo*, as another market for fine arts photography, but did make it clear that her magazine wants to see, and often uses, photographs with high artistic merit. Their real desire is to run pictures that can be used to illustrate an aesthetic question or how-to-do-it story. She is amazed at how many photographers cannot really present a well-thought-out story of this type. She said, "It is a most useful ability for the photographer to acquire and would certainly help those who are trying to sell us not only pictures but stories that go along with them."

Contrary to some editors who prefer to separate writing from photography, Bruns thinks writing ability is a plus, as the photographer will be able to communicate better with her. She said, "The photographer will make a heck of a good impression when he comes here if he can discuss his work intelligently and suggest how we might be able to use it." She feels that, while it is rare for the pictures and stories to be equally good, when it happens, it is an exceptional combination and the photographer benefits from it, not just financially but also because there is a better chance of getting published if a strong message goes along with the photographs.

On other editorial projects *Popular Photography* works with combined editor-writer-photographer teams, particularly when testing new products. Usually the photographer adds a great deal of verbal input that enhances the story and this results in an editorial style the magazine is proud of. They also issue general assignments to photographers and then will either look for a writer in house or use freelancers. Usually the photographer fills out detailed data sheets when the magazine holds pictures for consideration in order to have material for the writers to work with.

She admitted that about half the time the photographers fill these sheets out haphazardly and often don't remember how the pictures were taken. I asked her if they would reject a set of pictures because of poor caption material. She sighed and said that if the pictures are really that good, they will try to use them somehow. There have been times also when a story was delayed because of inadequate information.

Picture Researchers

Photographers have to deal with editorial people on many levels below the rank of managing editor and picture editor at large-circulation magazines. Frequently they are dealing closely with staff or freelance picture researchers from book publishing houses whose photographic needs are quite different from those of the major magazines. The latter more often use assigned stories; book publishers work more frequently with stock photographs. Because it is rare that a photographer will have "in stock" exactly what the researcher is looking for, it then comes down to a compromise as to what is available and also useful. This is why an understanding of the picture researcher is important.

Photographic editing and research specifically are not usually taught in colleges. As a result, the majority of picture researchers seem to be art history or fine arts majors, and almost none have photographic backgrounds. True, experience on the job fills many formal educational gaps, but there is often a communications gap between the photographer and researcher, so that frequently it is up to the photographer to do more than simply pull a picture out of his file. He may well have to question the researcher closely as to what is really needed and go beyond the specifics of the original request. This, in turn, may put a strain on the relationship between the photographer and researcher, so an understanding of the photographer by the researcher is vitally important and vice versa.

A classic example of this problem arose when I received a call from a textbook researcher who asked: "Do you have pictures of oil wells gushing?"

I told her I did not, because oil wells no longer gushed and probably had not done so for the past thirty or forty years except in cases of accidents at the wellhead. If those accidents did happen, it's probable that the foreman would be fired for wasting oil, and it's doubtful that any photographers would be permitted to make pictures of the "blow-out."

But to me it was unlikely that she was really looking for photographs of oil spilling on the ground, so I asked what was she really after—oil production? industrial accidents? or something historic like the old wooden derrick in Titusville, Pennsylvania, which was photographed before the turn of the century and was indeed spewing oil from its head?

Her answer surprised me. She was not looking for any of the above, but for photographs of steel tower construction and thought if she could get some pictures of the steel towers that oil rigs are made of, she could enhance the drama of the picture by showing a gushing oil well.

So it was my job to put her back on course, to explain the actualities of the situation, and better translate the photo request into realistic pictures. Some other agencies or photographers might have simply said they did not have any pictures of gushing wells and let it go at that. But by probing the request more deeply, I was eventually able to come up with a salable photograph.

But there is more to this than merely probing an odd request. There has to be clarity in what the researcher is really asking for and, if for any number of reasons that clarity is lacking, then the photo source must "back into" the situation by asking what the article is about, and what the author is trying to say. Then the researcher and the photo source can work together a lot more efficiently.

Insider: Margaret Mathews, Book Picture Researcher

Reader's Digest Books is typical of a large publishing house that prints handsome picture books. To get the views of one of their staff picture researchers, I turned to Margaret Mathews, who worked for *Reader's Digest* for many years. She went into photography research because of her interest in art, after attending Knox College in Illinois, one of the few places that at that time offered a liberal arts education as well as a major in the arts. After graduation she worked at the Philadelphia Art Museum, and her first job working with photography was in the New York Metropolitan Museum of Art's department of prints and photographs.

At *Reader's Digest*, her initial training came from her picture editor who, besides showing her the whys and the wherefores of obtaining photographs, was quite concerned about how picture researchers dealt with photographers on a personal level. He taught her how to defuse situations in which photographers felt "threatened" by the picture researcher.

I asked Mathews to outline the procedures followed by her publication in producing a picture book with emphasis on obtaining the photographs. She told us that the basic ideas for new books often come out of meetings that include the entire editorial staff, who are invited to present them in concise memo form. Those ideas that interest the editorial board are then pretested, without photographs or copy, and if the response is favorable, an expanded outline is prepared and presented to management. If they feel an idea is salable, it goes to the brochure stage, a full four-color mailer that is sent out as a wide-range test of the market, and if this test response is good, the project is put in the works.

These test brochures are by no means small efforts. They are complete with sample pages, sections of copy, and lavish use of color photographs. I asked her where the photographs for the sample mailers came from and she said that the list they use for the brochure is the same they use for source material for the book itself. A book project staff is then broken into two groups: the copy group and the art group, and this is where the researchers and art editors have to do their most intensive work in bringing together the needed visual material.

Some of these projects take as long as nine months or longer to research and two years to produce, so it is understandable why pictures have to be held for long periods of time. To reduce the strain on the photographer in this long gestation period, Reader's Digest Books sets up a slide-copying system by which a photograph is copied in nonreproducible form, such as a dupe slide with a line etched across it, the data is noted, and the originals are returned to the photographers for recall when needed. This is expensive for the publisher, and most do not do this, as sometimes thousands of pictures are brought in for a single project. It was done at *Reader's Digest* when the photographer felt he needed the pictures back in his files quickly and could not wait out the long production period. *Reader's Digest* is responsive to holding fees and service charges for pictures held for a long period of time, although there are differences of opinion over what is a reasonable holding period. Therefore, they leave it to the photographer to state how long his pictures can be held, as this publication group generally exceeds the average two-week free time specified on most delivery memos.

Because of the large number of pictures moving through their system, they have by now developed long lists of photographers and their specialties or regional coverages, and turn to them when pictures are needed.

Mathews emphasized the importance of proper captioning and valid information accompanying each photograph submitted to Reader's Digest Books. They want every photograph to carry the name, address, and telephone number of the photographer and/or the agency, as well as the copyright symbol and date. Each photograph should be captioned on the mount, if possible, or at least on an accompanying delivery memo sheet.

Mathews also reiterated her colleagues' advice about protecting the transparencies submitted with sturdy, chemically inert slide or transparency envelopes. One of the "beefs" she has against photographers is that "some don't have the proper respect for their own work. They don't properly identify, protect or mark it. This is a total lack of professionalism."

On professionalism, Mathews said that they try to deal with established professionals who do their job properly. When they occasionally have to turn to an amateur or young professional without much experience, because he or she happens to have specific material from some exotic locale, they often find it is difficult to get correct captions and other identification, which is a time-consuming process.

Mathews is critical of photographers or agents who submit a vast number of virtually unedited photographs from one particular "take"; she then is unable to properly discern the quality of the individual photographer due to lack of time. Mathews sees many pictures she would like to buy personally if she were a potential collector and suggests the photographer sign such images to increase their value when sold. These are the photographers she is stimulated by because their pictures show devotion to craft, thought to composition, care in printing, pride of workmanship and, above all, sensitivity to the subject matter. She feels strongly about photographers who take the time to do their own printing, because to her it shows a mastery of technique and that the photographer is serious about his or her work.

She says, "To me it's completely subjective. I respond because I am me, and if I think a picture is beautiful, it's because there is something in me that says I like the beauty of that, whether it's abstract, realistic or powerful or whatever. But on the other hand I get turned off by blatancy."

Evaluating the Needs of a Magazine

What to sell to whom? To determine this you must take more than a passing glance at a magazine you think might be interested in your work. You should study several issues of the publication in depth because a type of story seen in a particular issue may never have appeared previously or may never be needed again.

Studying a publication as a potential market is easy to do. Most libraries carry back issues of many national publications, as well as more specialized ones. The out-of-town bureaus of national magazines all have bound copies of every issue they have ever published. College and university libraries have many publications, and you can even go to stores selling used books and magazines and find some for a few cents per copy.

But it is important, when picking a market, to know exactly what the particular publication is interested in. For instance, studying a big batch of issues of the same house/shelter magazine will show a definite pattern of how many building stories are in an issue. Studying a general consumer magazine through several issues will indicate how many food pieces are part of the editorial plan, how much space is devoted to fashion trends or medical problems or whatever.

Knowing the *type of readership* is also essential. I remember an agonized telephone call from an editor of a shelter magazine to a photographer saying, "Please. No more stories of barbecues on highrise balconies. Our audience is made up almost entirely of small homeowners with their own backyards."

Most major publication groups print indexes of what they have already published, and these can be found in their main offices or at their out-of-town bureaus. Some also are available in the public libraries, so when you are overwhelmed by the big story idea and feel it's perfect for a certain magazine or paper, it might be wise to check the index first to see if it has already run. Can't get hold of an index? Then phone the publication, and their index department will tell you the date and issue of anything they've printed on the subject. For the cost of a telephone call you might save yourself a lot of embarrassment. If the publication's index shows there was a story on the subject, get the date and issue of the magazine in which it appeared, locate a copy, and see if your story is a duplication or a whole new approach. One simple source of information on whether a particular idea has been previously published is *Ulrich's International Periodicals Directory*, available at most public libraries.

Evaluating the policy of any publication is always tricky but is, in the long run, often rewarding. Much of this evaluation can be accomplished by a continued study of successive issues of a magazine or by analyzing editorial page opinions. You are not going to get much of a favorable response to a story on migrant farm workers and their problems and poverty from a trade magazine in the fruit and vegetable business, but you might come up with an eight-pager from a medical magazine interested in the health aspects of food workers.

The medical trade magazines, by the way, offer a most unusual opportunity for photographers in the general-interest field. There are a great many medical magazines that are technically oriented, to be sure, but many are not. "General interest" specifically refers to stories that are nontechnical, and one editor told me that she was interested in stories that doctors would *like to read*. This can be interpreted in two ways and often is. She was referring to stories that had medical overtones, such as one about the health problems of migratory farm workers, or a profile of a doctor in an Ohio River community who looks after the health of the passing rivermen, and also to "general interest" stories such as one on Rome, simply because doctors travel on their vacations.

One interesting sidelight unique to the medical magazine group is that several of these magazines are prosperous because they have such a clearly defined audience that they publish several editions—European, South American, etc.,—and pay secondary publication fees for the extra editions.

Knowing the policy and the types of photography used by the national consumer and trade magazines is comparatively easy. After all, the magazines come out regularly, and after watching them over the period of an editorial year, you should not find it too hard to understand what they are looking for. It is then up to you to think out the kind of stories you can do which they would be interested in seeing. In assessing the photographer from the other side of the desk, consideration must be given to the personal feelings of the editor concerning photography and photographers in general. It is evident from those I interviewed that if there are biases, they are usually in favor of the photographer, although there are exceptions, and frequently the biases are not against the photographer himself but against the material he submits. Ed Thompson, former managing editor of *LIFE* and editor and publisher of *Smithsonian* magazine, in an amusing letter to a photographer who had suggested that *Smithsonian* do a certain kind of story on railroads (he turned the idea down), wrote (referring to himself in the third person), "Because he was working late on a Saturday, his then boss, John Shaw Billings [first managing editor of *LIFE*], spotted him and sent him on a railroad story. He worked hard and was assigned to every rail story that came along. He got so sick of railroads that they lost their journalistic appeal for him. Perhaps we should say he rises to a point of personal prejudice— Billings always used to say that an editor was no good unless he had unreasonable prejudices." Here we have a case of two biases. Thompson against, and Billings for, railroad stories. In either case, however, there was no bias or prejudice against the photographer.

When personal prejudice against a photographer does exist, it usually is based on behavioral problems in the field, failure to deliver what is asked of him, or the editor may perceive him to be insensitive to the needs of the publication. On one recent shooting for a national magazine, a photographer with a big name and monumental ego behaved so obnoxiously on location that in a very short time he had everyone against him and, by transference, against the publication as well. This situation became so difficult that it was carried back to the editorial directors of the magazine, and it is doubtful if that photographer will ever work for them again. The photographer in this case had some talent, but his talent was not so unique that the client would tolerate that kind of outrageous behavior.

Book Publishing

Books are a major source of activity for the photographer, whether he is new or experienced. The number of new titles published each year is in the tens of thousands, and there are literally thousands of publishing houses all over the world. *Literary Market Place (LMP)*, and the other guides noted previously list more than ten thousand publishers in the United States alone, and almost twelve hundred "selected major publishers." There are basically three major classifications of book publishing: trade, text and specialized. *Trade books* as a rule are sold in bookstores or book departments of other stores. *Textbooks* speak for themselves, and *specialized books* can fall in several areas, such as instruction, direct mail or promotional ventures for premiums and almost any other method of book marketing. Many books overlap in classification and are sold in multiple markets—some of these books are identical in every respect and others have changes in binding (hardcover, softcover, library edition, etc.). Some are re-edited for special markets or produced in different (often cheaper) ways for mass distribution. Some publications can be highly specialized and selective, with press runs ranging from the millions to a few hand-printed copies. Many use photographs, both color and black-and-white; many do not. There are almost as many different types of books as there are publishers.

For the photographer to enter this market, careful and detailed analysis is required. Money can indeed be made in substantial sums by the photographer who authors a major picture book that sells well or supplies publishing houses with pictures that fill their specific needs. Unfortunately, most large, handsome, all-photographic books rarely make a great deal of money, so probably the best-paying market for the photographer is the textbook houses that use many photographs and frequently reuse them in secondary editions or other publications.

Insider: Marilyn Bridges, Book Photographer

Marilyn Bridges is one of the most unusual and dedicated photographers I have met. Before ever meeeting her I had seen some of her aerial work and was instantly drawn to it because of my own life-long interest in the medium. But why her? There were other fine photographers who have made wonderful and evocative images from the air, Margaret Bourke-White, Bradford Washburn, William Garnett, Georg Gerster, among others.

Bridges is different. She, like I, loved working close to the ground, using the plane as a mobile stepladder, whereas most other aerial photographers seemed more fascinated with magnificent ground patterns from high altitude, snowcapped mountains and cityscapes. We both agreed that flying low gave us points of view that could not be obtained in any other way. So much can be learned about a farm when you can see details of a barn or tracks in the snow in winter, or about lone shepherds in Utah and oil rig roughnecks in a swamp in Louisiana.

"I received a Bachelor of Fine Arts at Rochester Institute of Technology (RIT) and my MFA also from RIT in 1981," Bridges said. "My thesis was on aerial photography and I did my graduate work in aerial photography as an art form. I also went to the Art Students League before I entered RIT and studied drawing. Immediately after RIT, I received a Guggenheim Fellowship for additional work in aerial photography. This was encouraging. I had a friend in upstate New York who owned a plane, so I hired him to fly me to the Yucatan and be my pilot for the photography I wanted to do.

"I realized then that if I was going to do aerial photography as a project for many years it was time for me to get my pilot's license. I had learned a little about piloting on the trip down and was forced to do some in the Yucatan because we got lost. So I flew the plane while the pilot navigated from the charts. It was then that I learned how much I really loved flying and how important it was to know how to use the plane as a tool to do my work. I learned how slow I could go before stalling, what the plane could do in turning and banking, how far I could push the plane to get what I needed; reading air charts, learning about altitude restrictions, and everything else directly concerned with flying.

"I do not find it comfortable to fly and photograph simultaneously because I do very low altitude work, only a few hundred feet above the ground where we have to almost stall the plane to get the picture. So I knew if I tried to fly and photograph, I'd be sacrificing something, that edge, and possibly my life. So I decided to put 100 percent of my effort into the photography and hired pilots when I was shooting. But being a pilot myself enabled me to control what I wanted to do.

"I've worked from helicopters but avoid them because of the high expense, and frequent lack of availability. And as I'm not a helicopter pilot I cannot take the controls in an emergency, something I can do with a fixed-wing aircraft.

"The majority of my photographs have been of ancient ritual sites in different parts of the world and I have done it because I am personally interested in them. I am spiritually and mystically inclined and being around these sites has always been an energy boost.

"Also so many of the lines and markings such as the one at Nazca in Peru can be seen only from the air as described in Erich van Daniken's book *Chariots of the Gods*. That's where he started talking about extra-terrestrials coming down and using these as landing strips. I began to concentrate on aerial photography, professionally. I was really hooked, and also not a little bit frightened by the hazards of shooting from a plane.

"Up to then I had been interested in ground photography and all my undergraduate study at RIT was in ground photography. I was a bit of a photojournalist, interested in journalism, and I also liked fine arts photography. I loved studio work and the way I could rearrange things, work with lighting, and it was very meditative to be able to go to a studio and spend all day there. It's the opposite of what I do now, because I work in the sky and am outdoors all the time. And yet in a way I treat the landscape as a studio, in the way a photographer will treat a still life. That's one of my secrets. I look at the landscape, I look at the lighting, and the subject matter: front-lit, back-lit, side-lighted, I circle it, just to find the right light as if it were on a tabletop. Lighting is everything to me.

"For the present I am staying in aerial work. This year I will be doing some new projects and that takes all my energy. As for what I may be doing five years down the line, I do not know. There are lots of things I'm interested in but I don't think I've exhausted aerial photography by any means.

I've seen my work change over the years, especially my print quality, which has improved.

"Also my ability to find new objects, not only on ancient sites, but markings contemporary man is making on the terrain. Those are things I'm finding for myself out there, and it's intriguing. I don't have a definite subject matter all the time but I often find it in the landscape.

"My work has social value. It's important to show people the environment. There are a lot of messages we're leaving on the landscape that can tell us about the way we treat the planet. This is the view that man does not ordinarily get to see from the customary high altitude of commercial planes. In commercial flying you cannot see the details, you cannot feel intimate with the land and the subjects below. At 20,000-30,000 feet everything is abstract, so when you are closer to the earth things have more meaning.

"I prefer the medium size (6cm × 7cm) format and shoot in black and white only. With this size negative I am able to make very sharp prints, as big as 30" × 40". I like dealing with the landscape in black and white because of the sculptural effects that can be created. When I fly over the land I tend to see colors that are not that attractive to me, so I feel it's not necessary to use these colors in my work. I prefer just painting with light; color can be a distraction for me.

"In black and white I can create the feelings I have for a lost past. My pictures are not always pretty, they are more dramatic, and the black-and-white medium suits that best. I don't think a photographer can be good in both black and white and color at the same time. I feel that color is a whole different way of thinking as far as light is concerned and the messages you want to get across. I don't believe I can do both at the same time. I've tried it but it doesn't work for me because my mind thinks in black and white, and to switch to color is a whole different way of thinking, so I have to totally separate them.

"In general I've been fortunate in being able to create my own work and selling it afterward. No one has ever dictated to me what to shoot so I've had a lot of freedom. Luckily I received many grants and sponsorship, such as the last one from Eastman Kodak, and I have used these to create my own projects. I've also had three books published from this work: *Markings*, *Planet Peru*, and the catalog from the ICP exhibit which is essentially a book called *The Sacred and Secular*. I've done a few small commissions, but most of it is of my own origination.

"As for my point of view, I truly believe that in every photograph, a photographer makes a self-portrait that says something about himself. I'm thinking of a photograph I made of Machu Picchu, not the close-up but the distant one with the peaks of the Andes in the background. There is something mysterious about it, something that's quiet, something that's luminous, and I think those are some qualities I see in myself.

"Being a woman in photography hasn't made too much difference, but sometimes it has. It all depends on where I am, where I'm photographing, or who I'm showing my work to. Sometimes I've felt a lot of jealousy from men, I'm pretty much in a man's world in aviation and even photography has been male dominated for many years. If a woman is doing well in it, there are some men who are very happy about it, but there are other men who have a hard time with it, especially if it's competitive, although I'm not talking about job competition because I rarely work that way. I guess because I'm an attractive woman that makes a difference too. Sometimes it can be very helpful and sometimes it can be a real problem. Some people can see me on a purely professional level, others can't get past an exterior, and some just look at my work. Sometimes that attention doesn't mean a thing either unless you have strong work to back it up with.

"I don't know if there is a growing or declining market for aerial photography, particularly the kind that I do, but for young photographers in general I would say you really must have a love for what you are doing, you have to believe in yourself, you have to learn how to talk about your work, you have to learn how to take criticism, you have to learn ways to let your ego go, and you have to stick to it. You should not take offense over what someone might say to you about your work. When it stops you from being able to see, or creates a wall that can't be penetrated, that's dangerous and it usually happens when people are afraid of failure. They don't want to hear anything that might be negative. I always listen, I always let it come in. I love advice and criticism as it makes me stop and think. I may accept the criticism or reject it and make my decisions based on it, but I do listen and I do hear it.

"Let's take my prints, for instance. They've changed considerably over the years. At first they were very contrasty but now I'm putting more tone into them, and I think the prints are much more beautiful now. But this came from a bit of criticism from my peers and I paid attention. I learned also to become aware of the printing processes that a particular publisher uses and print accordingly. This is especially true for my books because I want the maximum quality possible. Making books has taught me a lot. I go to the printing plants and watch the whole process."

Trade Books

The trade book market probably offers the most tantalizing, but not necessarily the most lucrative, opportunity for the photographer in book publishing. How wonderful it is to see a large and handsome book, well reproduced, selling well and with a jacket bearing the magical phrase "Photographs by — — —," or better, "Photographs and Text by — — —." Well, it can happen and does, but not nearly so often as most photographers would like. In order to get published in the "monograph" category, a photographer has to spend many years, perhaps a lifetime, before his name becomes sufficiently familiar to book purchasers. Only that fame will open a publisher's door to the photographer or agent, and that is only half the battle. Photographic books are infinitely more expensive to publish than general trade books; furthermore, they cannot compete with the sexy blockbuster novel in the marketplace. The publisher's interest in warehousing beautiful but unsold books (or flat unbound sheets) over a period of years has been squelched by a recent ruling by the IRS against a large machine tool manufacturer (Thor Mfg. Co.) who wanted to write down unsold assets for tax purposes. The fallout for publishers came when they started refusing to print books they could not sell immediately for fear they would be taxed as unsold assets that could not be written down as amortized inventory. Application of this ruling makes the publisher's warehouse a wayside stop enroute to the pulp mills or recycling plants.

The prospect of selling that beautiful photographic book for a big advance and a steady flow of royalties is fast becoming a fading dream. Yet all is not lost, as there remain a few publishers who continue to publish beautiful picture books.

There is, however, more to the trade book market than monographs.

Almost every trade book uses a picture of the author on the flap if not on the back cover. Some photographers, particularly those in big publishing centers, get a good return on their author photos, especially because there is a growing trend to send authors out on nationwide book-promotion tours and local publications need pictures of these traveling celebrities. True, many of these pictures do originate in the big cities where the books are published or where the author lives, but in many cases the newer author, who may be on the way up the ladder, can very well be a market for the younger photographer.

Another outlet in the trade book field is sociological coverage — housing, adventure, exploration, even news and disasters, theater and drama. Books dealing with these and similar subjects often use many photographs and are for the most part over-the-counter books, though they may be sold in college bookstores, for example.

In book publishing there is also something called the "vanity press" (see page 339). This is *not* the name of a publishing house but is publishing jargon for companies that profit from the vanity and egos of those who feel that they must be published and have the money to pay for the printing and distribution of their own books. Occasionally, if an author is lucky enough to have a bookstore sell a few copies, he may get perhaps a 5 percent return on the initial investment. But it is in essence an expensive ego trip, and no matter how much talent the photographer thinks can be displayed, sales are too often nil. Unless you are very rich or egotistical or both, it is wisest to avoid this route of publication.

There is, however, a smaller and more "legitimate" form of publishing that can provide a good deal of recognition and a small financial return. This is the publication of limited, unpretentious editions by small houses that can distribute and sell three thousand copies or less of a decent picture book. But in order to get even this type of book on press with a legitimate house, the costs have to be tightly controlled, with the author (i.e., the photographer) supplying virtually everything in the way of finished prints, layouts and text, and in some cases absorbing other costs with little or no advance against royalties.

There are about ten thousand general trade bookstores in the U.S., but not all of them will take every book offered, nor does the small publisher always have ready access to the more remote stores, so it is obvious that distribution is always limited, and consequently so are sales. Therefore the photographer-author should have some knowledge about manufacturing costs. A conversation with a quality printer can result in an approximate determination of the costs of typesetting, paper, printing, binding, etc. There is an old rule of thumb for most picture books, that the list price should be about five or six times the bare manufacturing cost in black and white and about eight or ten times for color. With that in mind, the author can project the maximum potential royalties on a picture book.

So, if the busy photographer-author can come up with a fine picture book in an economical format and is lucky, he can sell five thousand copies; after the year and a half or so that has been spent on putting the project together, there may be a gross profit of about $15,000, before deducting the cost of materials, travel, processing and prints, all of which are rarely covered in nonreturnable advances. An experienced photographer might earn from this a standard royalty of 10 to 15 percent of list price, but there has been a disturbing trend to tying royalties to the wholesale price, which in reality means a 50 percent cut in royalties to the author. If a book should prove successful, requiring additional printings, the author and the publisher can both make money, because once the initial plate and type costs are recovered, the manufacturing costs drop, and frequently the schedule of royalties increases as the sales go up.

At first glance the budding photographer-author might say, "Swell, there is a market." But not to be overlooked are the costs of distribution, warehousing, selling and promotion, not to mention the publisher's profit, all of which have to come out of the 50 to 60 percent of list price that the publishers get to keep from the sale, providing they don't have to refund part of that to the bookseller for the unsold copies returned for full credit *before* royalties are paid. Another indignity being foisted on new or inexperienced authors is the withholding of royalty payments against *future* returns. This is unconscionable, especially when the average royalty payments are not made until three to six months *after* sales periods close.

What can the new photographer/author do about this? Very little unless he is supported by a tough agent, or if the author is willing to forgo publication with that particular house. So back to the primary question. Are photographic books a high-income market for the photographer? Not really.

There is no question about the personal satisfaction received from the authorship of a fine picture book, and the expectation that the attention drawn to it will lead to valuable new markets. But the author should not be misled. It's a difficult market to break into.

How-To Books

One growing field for the use of photography in books is the so-called "how-to" book, or what some publishers call "self-help." Their subjects range from installing weatherstripping in a house to auto mechanics and even do-it-yourself head-shrinking. Books of this nature are usually commissioned and are sometimes purchased on a "buy-out" basis, paying little if any royalties in return for a flat fee.

Insider: Ann Guilfoyle, Book Packager and Publisher

My long-time friend and colleague (and occasional burr under the saddle since she was the primary impetus to my creating *Professional Photographer's Survival Guide*), Ann Guilfoyle, has had a lifelong relationship with photography and photography reproduction processes. I have always felt that Ann, a product of New York's lower west side, has more asphalt and/or printer's ink in her veins than blood. Her father, George Hornby, was a prominent book designer and packager. Though I believe she never saw a tree until she was fourteen years old [not true], she became a fine nature picture editor and for nine years was picture editor at *Audubon Magazine*, and was instrumental in helping it attain the visual quality it now has.

She left *Audubon* to become a book packager and has been responsible for many excellent nature books including *The Peaceable Kingdom*/Macmillan (1979), *The Nesting Season*/Viking (1979), *Amiable Little Beasts*/Macmillan (1980), and *Wildlife Photography*/Amphoto (1982 — and still in print). She is now editor and publisher of *The Guilfoyle Report*, a quarterly nature publication linking photographers and picture users.

Though she is no longer actively book packaging, she is in close enough touch with the industry to be both knowledgeable and objective about it. I interviewed her especially for this book and pass her thoughts on to you.

"Book packagers are useful in getting photographic books done," Guilfoyle said. "More and more publishers do not have facilities to handle illustrated books, so what they do in one way or another is to farm out an entire project to one person. It might be a freeperson, a studio, or a design and production house. No matter what you call them, they are book packagers.

"It may be a work-for-hire project or it may be a totally creative process originated by the packager or the author. Sometimes it is financed by the packager, but more often than not it is done under a guarantee from the publisher for the packager to deliver X-number of copies at a specified price. The book packager handles the entire project, including the supervision of printing until the books are shipped to the publisher's warehouse.

"Numerous big photo books, some very impressive ones, have been packaged. Generally these are the work of first-rate photographers, are produced with great care, and can sell very well.

"To interest a packager you have to have something to offer. The days when picture books are produced solely because they offer striking images are going. Fine pictures are now a given in business, and content has become the deciding factor. Today's visually oriented reading public wants photo books to say something. Besides telling a story, they have to contain information. A book is an educational tool; it has a beginning, an end and a middle, and the reader expects to learn something in the process by going from one end to the other.

"Most photographers do not understand photo books and they often make proposals that are meaningless. Creating a photo book is an art or at least a high craft. Production requires an enormous investment on the part of the publisher and a huge amount of effort on the part of the photographers, artists, writers and designers.

"If a photographer expects a proposal to be seriously considered, he or she must spend time learning what the field is all about before they approach the packager or publisher. The libraries, including those of the great museums, have magnificent photo book collections. Sometimes it takes an effort to see these collections but when you do, and spend time there, you can get an idea of what has been done in the entire field of photographic books, and perhaps come to some understanding of how your idea can fit in.

"The first step is to find out if it has been done before. If it has been done well within the past ten years and with some success, then it's not probably worth doing again. If it hasn't been done before or you think it should be redone, go to the next step. Come up with an outline, an introduction, a sample text chapter (not the introduction) to show you can write (or if there is a co-author involved who is going to do the writing, a sample of his or her work). The text chapter should be long enough to show how the author thinks. The outline should not exceed a page, and the introduction should not exceed a page. The material has to show why this book should be published. It is also almost a given that the photographer must do enough market research to show to whom the book will sell and what circulation can be expected.

"It's hard to convince a publisher that there is a viable market for a picture book, and in order to do this the research must be thorough and honest. Part of what you have to do in thinking through an idea is finding out if there are people out there who are going to want to see it. And to get that picture book published you have to convince the publisher that enough copies will be sold to cover the cost of make-ready, production, sales, overhead, and show a profit. This means 10,000-15,000 copies.

"If, for instance, you want to do a book on a national park which will be a point of interest for sales of that book, find out how many bookstores are in that area, how many people visit that park every year, if there are book shops there, and what in general can be sold. If the numbers are insignificant, no publisher is going to be interested. It's as simple as that. This is true of almost any subject for a photographic book. *There is* information out there, and you have to find it. In the process of doing this, not only will you be getting the necessary information for the publisher, but the book concept will become more real to you. And if indeed you do get a contract, you will have a much better idea of what to produce. All books are vehicles of communication, and the more you know who it is you are trying to communicate with, the better your book will be.

"The final selling of the concept to a publisher is done by the packager. If you can pre-sell the book there's no point in going to a packager because the packager is going to take a large part of the profit. There are trade book publishers who specialize in picture books, for example, Chronicle Books in San Francisco, and Aperture, Abrams, Abbeville and Knopf in New York. There is a whole list of them and you can find them in *LMP*. Packagers will approach them, and so can you. The author must make the choice. However, if you are inexperienced in the book field, the packager will prepare a dummy that is more presentable and may help you solve the problems of putting a picture book together in such a fashion that a publisher will take it seriously.

"Before making a commitment be very sure that a packager is experienced and competent to do the kind of book you want, because if they go under, you have little redress. Your money comes from them, not the publisher. Even though the packager signs a contract with the publisher, it is still the packager who is liable and this is what you have to watch out for. And while the packager may be well meaning, if he or she is not efficient in producing what the publisher needs on time, it's the photographer who gets hurt when a book comes out too late and thus loses its market.

"If you decide to forego a packager, consider working with an agent, but only if you can find one who knows how to work with picture books. There are only a few such agents out there. So if your concept is worthy of being a book, and if you can make a strong presentation yourself to the publisher, you can probably make the sale yourself. But in the event an agreement to publish is received, then I would have a lawyer knowledgeable in publishing law check the contract."

Textbooks

Textbooks requiring a good deal of specialized photography can be a fine market in the same manner that many of the "how-to" books can make money, but they too should be approached with caution. Unless the photographer is highly specialized in a single subject, it is unusual to find any one photographer who can completely supply the average textbook with stock photographs. More frequently the photographer can fill only a few of such specific needs, but if the photographer is a member of a picture agency that receives a picture request, it may be that the agency as a group can supply a larger share of the requirements of the publisher, and that may accrue some added advantage for the photographer.

However, being an agency member may not be that advantageous financially, as the commission taken by the agency could offset the higher return per picture to the individual photographer. Sometimes a royalty arrangement can be worked out if large numbers of photographs on a single subject can be supplied by one photographer (or in some cases by one photo source such as an agency). Textbook royalties are usually much lower than royalties for trade books, though this can be offset because of the larger press runs of textbooks. Here again caution must be exercised because some royalties will have to be shared with the author or co-authors.

Another way of dealing with textbook publishers reluctant to go the royalty route is to try to work out some sort of total package deal, basing picture production costs on a time-spent rather than a per-picture basis. But this can work only when a photographer can supply most of the illustration needed and the subject matter is concentrated in one field. However, if it means trying to supply a wide variety of material for a 250-page textbook, then cost factors will probably put it out of reach.

These contracts are rare because publishers are not eager to give out assignments. Traditionally, textbook publishers prefer to play it safe and buy only what they can see in front of them, rather than take a chance and commission a work or even part of it. Some publishers have gone so far as to set up staff photo systems, but for the most part these have proven unsatisfactory, because the broad scope of material needed in an average illustrated textbook makes it virtually impossible to spread staff people so thin as to be in all places at all times.

There are some special problems regarding textbook photography that the photographer must be aware of. For the most part, textbooks are relatively small in format, usually not over 7" × 9½", often 6" × 9" in size. Also, textbook publishers rarely give a photograph much space except in chapter openers, frontispieces or occasionally as end papers, covers and/or dustjackets. Often several photographs run on one page, so the average photograph occupies a quarter of a page or less.

The size of photographs in textbooks poses problems other than content. Scenics and landscapes are usually ineffectual unless there is some prominent object in the foreground to indicate scale and depth. Content should be restricted to a single theme. In other words, simplicity is the key. Robert Rahtz, formerly Vice President and Editor in Chief of Macmillan's School Division, says, "Arty and moody photographs are not likely to be accepted for textbooks where the emphasis is on hard facts."

Racial equality is an important element in the content of pictures used in school books. Ethnic mixes are now extremely important, and in many cases photographs will not be accepted unless there is a racial mix of blacks, Orientals, Hispanics and Native Americans. Part of these specifications come from pressures by local and state educational departments, as well as from federal statutes. Another trend is to show minorities and women in what Rahtz calls "positive approaches." "Don't," he says, "show them in the so-called traditional roles—women as secretaries or nurses, blacks and Hispanics as porters or maids. Find female professionals, black and Hispanic scientists, computer programmers and educators. Show handicapped people working in average situations. The federal aid to education laws mandate this, and even if the photographer's picture is perfect in all other respects, unless it meets these criteria it will be rejected. Strangely enough," he continues, "when this program started some years ago there were indeed few people fitting these 'positive' categories, but the increasing number of photographs coming through now show that it is no longer a rarity to find people in these jobs. Perhaps this type of illustration has really forced the level of minority employment upward toward the more positive."

You must know what you want to photograph in the textbook world. Is it science, biology, anthropology, home economics, fashion, design or carpentry? Go to your library and dig out books from competing publishers and see just what interests you. Note the publishers and their addresses. If the books in your library are relatively current, they might give you the clue you are looking for. If you do not have enough on hand to make a selection, then get the catalog or catalogs of publishers who interest you. Many of the directories described previously are an excellent source of complete addresses and the names of the people to contact for catalogs and sales lists. A study of these catalogs could show, for example, that this year a particular house is publishing a book on biology with 200 pictures or one on anthropology with 150 pictures. By going through earlier editions, you will get a pretty good idea of not only the kind of pictures they are interested in but how they may handle their new or revised books on biology or anthropology.

If they use a great many photographs in a very specialized area, you have to decide whether you are qualified to do that work. And remember, more than specialization in high technology is involved here. I am not talking only about photographing laser beams or micro-chip processors or liquid-quartz crystals. I am talking about a general understanding of the work to be done and an appreciation of the problems from the *client's* point of view.

How to Locate a Picture Buyer in a Book Company

Having touched briefly on textbooks and their potential for photographers, let's look at them a little more closely in terms of the photographer evaluating them as a market. I talked at length with the head manager of research at one of the large textbook houses, an established publisher of college textbooks. She agreed that the photographer must know something about the publishing house he pursues as an avenue of picture sales.

If approaching the picture editor of a magazine requires a great deal of thought and consideration, contacting the picture editor of a textbook house is just as involved. Possibly even more so, because the magazine editor is apt to have more experience in dealing with seasoned journalists who have already worked in the magazine world. The textbook editor, however, appears to get more calls from young and inexperienced photographers who are trying to turn professional. Often they fail before they even get a foot in the door.

"This is very sad," she said, "because they sometimes have terrific material, though it may take a crowbar to pry it out of them."

She also gets annoyed when she gets letters from photographers enclosing a list of vague generalities. "These lists," she says, "may have some value to an art director who needs a picture of a bluebird or even a tractor to possibly copy from, but a list that states, 'We have pictures of airplanes, bicycles, children, dogs,' and includes Wyoming in the *W*'s is of no value to me whatsoever. There is not one *detail about what kind of* airplanes or dogs or whatever, or what they are doing or where they are, or any information of genuine use to the editor."

Another type of communication she gets which is guaranteed to raise her hackles is best epitomized by a postcard she received which simply said,

"Please send me your wants." Her immediate reaction was to write back and say, "How about someone six feet tall with a half million bucks who owns a liquor store?" But on second thought she filed it in the wastebasket.

She emphasized that the material she looks for has to be germane to the books she is working on or will be considering. That is why studying the publisher's catalog is so important to the photographer who wants to enter this market.

She related an example where this paid off. "I got a list recently from a photographer who said, 'I have photographed in these countries,' adding a list of them and their cities and a small description of what each coverage entailed and where the photo emphasis was. The letter also had an introductory paragraph that stated, 'I think the material below would be of use to you in your upcoming volume on sociology.' This letter grabbed my attention," she remarked, "because the photographer had taken the trouble to find out what kind of material we were looking for. His list, while not perfect, nevertheless showed his understanding of the picture buyer's needs and reflected the thinking he had put into the situation." This photographer is now on her list for future calls when those subjects he mentioned are required.

Corporate Publications

Annual Reports

Corporate publications are a fertile field for editorial photography, with the annual report as the flagship publication of most companies. Required by law when a company's stock is publicly held, there have been impressive changes in these publications, particularly over the past two decades.

Prior to World War II, the annual report was the bastion of frozen-faced members of boards of directors. Corporate art directors were unheard of, and the design of the publication was usually left to the nearest print-shop operator, who may or may not have known the difference between a pica rule and a print proportional scale. No one on the corporate level cared so long as the financial tables were readable (particularly if a profit was to be shown for that year).

After World War II a new awareness of corporate images developed, and a new breed of company executive came forward. This was the public relations director (or some other fancy title bestowed on them such as Corporate Information Manager, Public Information Coordinator, etc.) While large corporations have always had some sort of public relations person, they invariably had been ex-newspapermen who had paid their dues on the financial pages of the local newspapers and probably knew the location of the "watering holes" of the local press. Their function was to maintain a *low profile* for the company: play down accidents, tout acquisitions or mergers, and publicize community service activities such as contributions to worthy organizations.

The "new look" to corporate communications changed all this. Corporations started to polish their images. Management had begun to realize that the sale of stock (and thus the public acceptance of the company and its product) was no longer entirely controlled by a small number of financial institutions. There was a large market of people who were interested in buying not only the company's products but their stock as well. For this, an image of modernity was needed, and the influence of the big picture magazines' direct (and presumably honest) journalism began to be felt.

Farsighted public relations people began to turn to magazines such as *LIFE, Fortune, Business Week* and *Look* as a source of talent. Photographers with strong magazine credentials, most of whom were freelancers, began to appear on the open-hearth floors and in the aluminum plant pot rooms, and as some of the smoke-stack industries began fading, in the computer and electronic laboratories, plants and factories in Silicon Valley, California and in Texas and New England. The annual report began to look better, and corporate public relations departments found that it became an impressive showcase not only for required annual statements but for general information as well.

With the growth of these elaborate annual reports, company treasurers were willing to allocate substantial sums for production, not only for good printing and engraving, but for first-rate photography and quality writing.

Not too long before this metamorphosis started, there was some parallel activity going on in some large corporations needing major image rebuilding. Prominent among them were the huge oil companies, led by the giant Standard Oil Company (NJ) now Exxon, whose image was suffering badly for a variety of reasons.

Large-scale public relations programs were begun, all designed to show the public that these companies (and this was by no means confined to big oil) were in fact dandy organizations who did much to contribute to the public weal and were not the sprawling specters that the public perceived them to be. Among the things they did was to set up tremendous photographic programs. In the case of SONJ, one such program was headed by Roy Stryker, who was known for his landmark directorship of the Farm Security Administration (FSA). Photo files were created and pictures were distributed free, with only a photo credit requested.

Fine films (i.e. *Louisiana Story* directed by pioneer Robert Flaherty) were made or sponsored, and in general the public did indeed benefit, as did the companies themselves, though to what degree is debatable.

The establishment of these excellent corporate photographic files gave impetus to smaller companies to build photographic libraries on their own industry emulating the giants. Public relations officials found that up-to-date photography from their files was not only acceptable but eagerly sought by many media editors. Moreover, these costs could be charged to annual report production and not to their own departmental operating budget. The spinoff of these practices was the back-door approach to the major magazines as sources of fine photo stories and major essays, usually free to the media. Not only were business magazines targeted this way, but many consumer publications as well.

Some of the same companies that took an exceptional interest in photography and writing also established prestigious publications of their own. They were varied and interesting and often did not relate directly to the industry the parent company was serving. They fell into the general classification of "house organs" but in reality were a far cry from the typical company publication. Outstanding examples are Standard Oil's (Exxon's) *The Lamp, DuPont* magazine, and IBM's *Think*, which reversed its earlier orientation toward people outside the company—legislators, top-level businessmen in other industries, politicians, and other "opinion makers"—and redirected its focus internally. But its intrinsic quality did not change, and *Think* and the others that have survived remain potential markets for the photojournalist. The new photographer should not ignore them, but seek them out as well as new ones. The earlier noted publications directories list them.

House Organs

Most house organs are much smaller, internal publications, and there are thousands of them. Almost any corporation with more than a couple of hundred employees has some sort of publication that reports births, deaths and marriages, softball game scores, results of bowling matches, and other items of interest to the employees and families of a particular company. For the most part these publications are not much of a market for the outside photographer, though a staffer can be kept quite busy filling the picture needs of such a publication. In isolated areas, however, the local freelance or studio photographer can find a market here, especially if there is no staff photo department at the company. These publications are by no means all dull and uninteresting; some are quite sophisticated and use photography well. They should not be ignored by the new photographer, as they are a vehicle for gaining experience, particularly as a means of learning to shoot in an industrial plant or under conditions that are less than optimum in regard to light, power, ambiance, etc. In fact, learning to shoot for company newsletters or small house organs is a good way of developing some of the prerequisites that come with the territory of the photojournalist.

From a dollar standpoint, the pay is almost insignificant. But if you can arrange to use corporate facilities such as darkrooms, lighting and power sources, and possibly even equipment, from cameras to forklifts and cars or trucks, then shooting for these publications may very well be worth the effort. And if a corporation is blessed with an attractive publication, a sheaf of pages from it would enhance the new photographer's portfolio.

Locating the Picture Buyers in Corporations

Knowing that there are thousands of markets for photographs in publications without mastheads or other identification of editorial people, how can you find the names of those who need to see your work? Photo buyers in corporations have to be searched out as carefully as their counterparts in big publication groups. With diligence you can locate them with the aid of listings of corporate officers or department heads.

How does a photographer find a photo buyer in a major industrial corporation? Start with the geographic edition of the *Standard Directory of Advertisers* (see page 23) and find the listing of those companies in your own hometown with which you are trying to make contact. As in magazine and newspaper mastheads, there is usually a top to bottom listing of major officers and often many of the minor ones as well. But instead of editors and art directors, or news editors and picture researchers, you will find comptrollers, labor relations officers, marketing directors, finance officers, product safety managers, product designers, public relations officers and many other titles. Some of the titles, particularly in the information field, can be either ambiguous or lofty or both, with many of the people hidden behind clouds of fancy names such as Director of Corporate Communications, Community Interest Director, Corporate Identity Manager, Urban Relations Counselor, etc. Don't let their titles confuse you, they are all public relations people in one form or another and are the people with whom you start.

But suppose there is no one listed in any of these fields. Which others would seem to be the obvious titles? Consider just what it is you are trying to sell. Annual report photography? Try the treasurer or secretary or finance officer of the company. Advertising or brochures? There probably is an advertising manager, or marketing director or the new products manager. None of these? See if there is an advertising agency listed, and there probably will be. If so, there should be a listing of the account executive (AE) and you can start with him. If all else fails, pick up the phone and go back to square one to ask who handles public relations or advertising.

A newer wrinkle in the production of corporate photography is the use of an outside design and production company to produce the annual report. Many large companies have long used outside public relations firms, not only to supervise the production of their annual reports, but to serve as consultants for other publications as well. The rise of specialized design houses producing only annual reports has not done the photographer coming into the market too much good, because these firms tend to build a stable of their own photographers who work for *them* rather than the parent company for whom the annual report is being produced.

What happens is that the photographer is thus insulated from actual contact with corporate management, and this is unfortunate, because when the photographer arrives at the plant, he comes in as an outsider and is not perceived as working from within management. Therefore the level of cooperation he receives from middle management is often poor and ineffectual. Another problem arises when the outside design house charges fairly stiff fees for the photographer's service but pays the photographer at lower rates. The photographer does not really know what charges are being made for his services and what the design house is actually billing, so he must be careful that the design house is not acting as both *employer and agent.* Another negative aspect of this practice is that, in order for a photographer to get the work, he often has to sign a work-made-for-hire agreement and release all future rights, which the design houses often try to exploit by sales to other picture users without further payment to the photographer.

Interview
Peter Turnley
Photographer

Peter and David Turnley are Indiana-born twins who individually and as a team are among the outstanding photojournalists of this generation. Peter, who I interviewed, spoke not only for himself but partly for David, as between the two they have collected an astounding number of journalism awards for photographs in every part of the world. They are living images of the old news photographer's dictum of *f/8 and be there!* Perhaps to me, what came through loudest and clearest was Peter's impassioned drive to *pursue* his objectives, rather than wait for them to come over the transom.

Though it was Peter I interviewed in the Black Star Agency office in New York, I came away with the feeling that I had spoken with both brothers, because, as he said during the interview, "We tend to rub off on each other and see things much the same way."

David was the 1989 winner of a Pulitzer Prize for his work appearing in the *Detroit Free Press*, and both brothers shared awards from the Overseas Press Club, World Press Photo competitions, the National Press Photographer's Association (NPPA) and the prestigious University of Missouri School of Journalism *Pictures of the Year (POY)* contest.

Peter told me, "I believe in my path as a photographer and I have no desire to be a model for anyone else. I was given a camera when I was seventeen years old and became strongly interested in photography.

"We grew up in Ft. Wayne, Indiana, where I was an intense young jock in high school and was passionate enough about athletics to think of it as a career. But I seriously injured my knee playing football and had to be hospitalized. This killed any aspirations I may have had then about becoming a professional athlete. While I was in the hospital, my parents had the good taste to give me a book of Cartier-Bresson's *Face of Asia*. I was fascinated by the photography and more than anything the way the photographs communicated all this rich excitement of their life. At seventeen I had no real strong ideas yet of what I wanted to be but, with professional athletics no longer a possibility, I began thinking more about photography.

"The guard on our football team was also the school newspaper photographer, and his huskiness and ability quickly dispelled any ideas I may have had about photography being a 'sissy' business. He taught me the rudiments of camera handling and permitted me to use the school darkroom and photo lab in general."

Turnley spoke of spending all their free time after school walking around Ft. Wayne, a typical midwestern industrial city of about 250,000, with a camera. In these walks the two discovered new aspects of their hometown. The clusters of black, Hispanic and other working-class people in inner-city neighborhoods were strange to the boys who had been reared first on a farm and later moved to a middle-class neighborhood in town. The camera became their pretext to meet people they might not have had easy access to otherwise. To Peter, the whole process of photography at that age was a passionate experience. Memories of those experiences have stayed with him and left a lasting impression. "They gave me a chance to open vistas of my own personality that I didn't know, and I devoted all of my free time during my junior and senior years and summer vacations to making photographs. David developed much the same lust for photography as I did within a few months, and quickly joined me in my explorations.

"I was lucky very early on to have had motivating and inspirational things occur. I won the National Scholastic Photography Award for my photography as a junior high school student and a few other awards as well. These were all encouraging signs that not only did I like what I was doing, but that I had a bit of talent and something to say. The award I won for National Scholastic was for a photograph of a man sitting on a porch of a wooden house. But in order to receive the award, I had to have a model release.

"David and I set off to find this man. On the day we found him on his porch, David suggested we spend a year photographing the street he lived on. Something struck him immediately about it. It was only three blocks long, the houses were similar, the people were mostly working-class whites from Appalachia. In general it was a very public place. People were always on their porches, playing ball in the street, or taking care of each other's kids. Life seemed to happen a lot in the open. We had seen Bruce Davidson's book *East 103rd Street* and were influenced by the way he used a very public place as the setting for pictures.

"We shared one Nikon F2 with a 50mm lens, and would go to this street to photograph as often as we could, after school, on weekends and holidays. We got to know the people, every house, every family. We made a practice of always giving prints to those people. They grew to enjoy seeing us coming, and one of the most exciting things after we finished a year's work on the street was that every family had a virtual album of its own. We baby-sat for their kids, went to birthday parties and did all those kinds of things. We also took a chance and submitted photographs to our high school sociology teacher as our term project rather than writing a paper. The teacher not only gave us an A+ but was very encouraging.

"In our senior year," Peter continued, "David went to New York with the pictures. I had broken my leg and could not join him, but for him it became a three-day flying carpet experience. We had made lists of all the people we knew and admired, and places we'd heard of in photography. Frankly this is something I might advise to anyone: I have never believed particularly in having someone else refer me to people I was interested in meeting. Just as when David went to New York he found the names of people he wanted to meet in the phone book and called them, I followed the same practice of calling people I had never met and expressed an interest in meeting them. If they had time, fine, if not okay. It was not because I wanted them to do anything for me, but simply because I thought they were interesting people and wanted to meet them.

"David went to Magnum first and asked if he could show his pictures to anyone. He was told to leave his portfolio but he demurred, saying he had plenty of time and would wait all day if necessary until someone could see it. Fortunately Lee Jones, Magnum's director, came by and invited him into her office. He showed her our pictures and Jones was interested enough to phone many of the people we had dreamed of seeing, including John Morris, then Picture Editor of *The New York Times*. It was a wonderful experience. We did not expect anything to come of this but were pleased to be able to make contacts. As a result of that trip, *Popular Photography* magazine's sister publication *Camera 35*, published many pages of the Fort Wayne story and a long article on the two of us."

They both went to the University of Michigan. After extensive reading on photography and photographers, Peter concluded it didn't make much sense to study photography but more sense to study almost anything else. "I realized that seeing and making photographs is, before anything else, a form of communication," he said, "and if you want to communicate you must have something to say. I had something to say, had a love for people and wanted to show that. Perhaps it was a selfish pursuit. At Michigan I concentrated on urban studies as that was the closest thing scholastically I could come up with that related to what I wanted to do, i.e., the photography of people, the way they live in cities and their social problems.

"Frankly in my freshman year I was miserable—homesick, could not understand the real use of what I was studying. When I went back to Ft. Wayne for a brief visit, I introduced myself to the city manager in the hope of finding an internship job with their Department of Urban Affairs.

"I had seen many of the FSA pictures, I was full of big ideas, and suggested that they take me on as an intern and even hopefully pay me to take photographs for them. I gave him a big spiel about doing photo stories on important problems of Fort Wayne, which they could publish or exhibit, and I was willing to commute from Ann Arbor three or four days a week.

"He went for it and gave me the job. There was a large neighborhood scheduled to be torn down for urban renewal, and the local people were up in arms about it. I did a photo story on it that was exhibited and published. At Ann Arbor I did very little photography as I was totally uninspired visually by the environment. I preferred almost not to make photographs if I wasn't excited by what I was seeing. In Fort Wayne I also met the Director of Public Relations for the Office of Urban Affairs. When she moved on to the Office of Economic Opportunity in California she wrote me proposing that I come to California during the summer months at a small stipend to do black-and-white photo essays on poverty, and OEO would publish these photographs and exhibit them in their community centers. I did, and it was a fantastic experience. I am proud of the photographs, but outside of that it was also very motivating. The process was dynamic. I felt photography wasn't only a pleasure but that it had a reason and was exactly what I believed in.

"After that summer I came to New York. John Morris introduced me to W. Eugene Smith who I had always admired. He was very encouraging. He was also honest and direct. I think all of these things are important to a young person. I then dropped out of college as I thought it useless and uninspiring. It didn't seem like a real thing to be doing as my heart was in photography. I had saved enough money to buy a plane ticket to Paris and live in a garret. I studied French at the Sorbonne and spent all of my free time walking around. I did photo stories on cafes in one district of Paris. In order to do these stories I had to spend time in the cafes and speak to the people in French. It was a great way of improving my language skill.

"Perhaps it was David's earlier visit to Paris and his letters about what he had seen and photographed and the people he met, such as Cartier-Bresson and his wife Martine Franke, that inspired me to go there.

"I also spent a lot of time at Pierre Gassman's photo lab. They printed many of Cartier-Bresson's photographs, and I met a lot of other people in the photographic world. Here I learned much photographic technique and felt that I wanted to stay and work in Europe. I returned home and finally finished college with a degree in French literature. I had almost an obsessional desire to go back to France, to work in the lab; becoming a fine printer was an important step in my professional and personal life.

"When I was home I got a job working on a highway road crew. It was really the best-paying job that an unqualified person could get. I lived with my parents and worked on the road crew, often provoking them to work overtime so we could all make more money. Eventually I went back to Paris with $20,000 which would carry me for at least a year without having to worry about finding other work.

"I had kept in touch with Gassman and when I returned to Paris he gave me a job as a printer. I worked for about six months; it was hard but interesting. My athletic ability enabled me to work in the dark for long periods of time. I think being a good printer is very athletic and I also had a chance to work with some of the best printers in the world. Besides seeing the prints of famous photographers in the trays all day long, I would spend my free time poring over their contact sheets and absorbing their images.

"During this time I would also walk around Paris with my Leica photographing whatever I could see. The great thing was that I had a place to develop and print my photographs free.

"I also discovered a one-year program for foreigners called the Institute of Political Science studying French, politics and culture that gave a degree. Even though I had a degree from Michigan in French literature and was sustaining my interest in photography, the Institute really opened me up to other things. I wasn't sure I was good enough to make a living in photography, so I thought a little more education couldn't hurt me. I found I could enroll and still work part-time in the photo lab. I did this for three years and got a Master's degree in 1981. I had three choices: either I could go to law school, join the Foreign Service, or try to work in photography.

"I had entered a number of photographic competitions, including preparation of a book dummy on Parisians. Kodak had sponsored a publishing program for young photographers, and though André Kertész was on the jury and voted for me, I came out second. As it turned out I did very badly on the law board and Foreign Service exams, ironically in English, so I concentrated on photography.

"I had become aware of Robert Doisneau's photographs and out of the blue I found his name in the phone book and called him. I showed my pictures and he must have found something he liked because he introduced me to Charles Rado, the Director of the Rapho-Guillemette Agency. Rado hired me to print photographs for books and other publications. I worked for Rapho-Guillemette Agency for four years and also began to get assignments for *TIME*, *Newsweek* and *Business Week* through their Paris bureaus as well as for French publications. I also did assignments for *The New York Times* Travel section, and though they didn't pay much, it gave me a chance to travel all over France. These assignments were good training because they made me aware of the need for meeting deadlines and delivering pictures and informational copy on time. Another part of the discipline was that you learned not only to bring back the photographs the editors wanted, but added your own concepts as well, and they all had to correspond with the journalistic criteria of the publication.

"What I found important, and it worked for me, was that I would meet journalists from different media and, because of my education in political science and interest in people and the world, I understood them and their needs. I read three papers a day and had a million ideas for stories which were not always photographic. I discovered as a journalist that they would be good stories for other papers. I got to the point where every day I was calling the Paris bureau chiefs of *TIME*, *Newsweek*, *The New York Times* and *Business Week*. Every day I had two or three stories that I thought would be good for them. In a year's time, for example, I bet I gave ten different ideas to *The New York Times* for page-two feature stories that ran, and I bet I gave fifteen to twenty stories to *Newsweek* that in one way or another, from my ideas, shaped up as a story. So I got very excited not only in the domain of taking pictures but in the whole process of journalism.

"David won a Pulitzer Prize in 1989 for his work with the *Detroit Free Press*, and I have done two books, *Beijing Spring* and *Moments of Revolution*.

"*Newsweek* sent me to the Normandy coast on the 40th anniversary of D-Day for which I made a cover and twelve pages inside. After that I became a contract photographer for them as I have been for the past seven years.

"I traveled all over the world for *Newsweek*, and covered all the revolutions in Eastern Europe in 1989. David and I were in China for two months and were there at the time of the Tienenman Square riots. I have been covering the Soviet Union regularly since Gorbachev came to power and followed him all over the world. I expect to go back shortly. I think I have the most complete individual document of Gorbachev of any Western photographer. In any event I had the good fortune to witness the entire upheaval of the Soviet Union since 1985.

"I do have a few things I would like to impart to new photographers. I was on the NPPA Flying Short Course that went to six different cities and was able to speak to about 4,000-5,000 photographers across the country. At each stop I would see many portfolios and the thing that struck me clearly was the constant questioning by young photographers of how they could be like me, how they could do what I'm doing. I was disarmed by those questions but I never felt that it was important for anyone to be like me or know why I was like I was. My response was that 'you can never teach someone because it's either clear to you or it isn't. Photography is, before anything else, a form of communication, and as such it's all about having something to say. It doesn't matter what you say, but I cannot tell you, and you cannot tell me, what to photograph.' The essential thing is that, if they are interested in photography, they have to reflect upon what they want to show other people, because it's all about their hearts and they should photograph what is important to them. No one has to be a photographer. There are a lot of other things to do in life and, beside the excitement on occasion and the seeming glamour of being a working photojournalist, the real thing is that it is also a fantastic dynamic to have the opportunity to show to so many people something that's important to you."

Chapter Three
Analyzing Specific Markets: Commercial and Advertising Photography

If you think the editorial side is complicated, try the commercial. Every letter of the alphabet could provide a classification for some form of commercial photography. In this group are audiovisual products, real estate and architectural photography. Now add public relations, passport and wedding photographs; fashion photography and display and point-of-purchase efforts — you have still only just begun to scratch the surface of all the opportunities in commercial areas.

The overlapping of editorial and commercial work became so complex and involved that the ASMP went so far as to change its name to include the broad band of advertising photographers.

Certainly their work met all other ASMP membership criteria. The only real difference was the way it was physically intended for use in publication. But the thirty-five-year-old image of the ASMP was so firmly fixed in the minds of the photographic world as that of magazine photographers, that the new complicated name was dropped and the advertising photographers remained members by interpreting the term "magazine photography" to include advertising photography in magazines. Now, in 1992, the Board of Governors has voted to change the word "magazine" to "media," so the ASMP initials are retained if approved by the membership. Stay tuned.

Complex as editorial photography is, the world of commercial photography is even more so. The editorial side is more or less limited to the familiar forms of print media plus the now growing electronic-imaging field. The commercial goes beyond the printed page or the video screen; it reaches out to three-dimensional displays, in-store windows, or point-of-purchase cutout figures on a drugstore counter. The worlds of fashion, food, still life, house furnishings and lifestyles are at once different and similar for the photographer. Each division can be broken down into minute subsections of specialization: public relations photography, product promotion, political coverage, audiovisuals for schools or commerce or just plain entertainment, TV stills, motion picture clips.

Catalogs are produced by the millions. Mail-order houses from Spiegel and Sears use first-class fashion and product photography. Chic, provocative and exquisitely printed multicolor productions emanate from Neiman-Marcus and Bloomingdales offering his-and-her's hot air balloons or other high-priced, exotic items. All of this and more is grist for the commercial photographer's mill.

Most commercial photography requires the use of a studio, and often (but not always) demands the availability of highly complex lighting equipment, although much can be accomplished with relatively simple gear. High-fashion photographs, and even many on a simpler level, are often shot on locations that are earthy, realistic and documentary in concept. Some large marketers with a great need for fashion and product photography may themselves provide studio locations and equipment and yet not employ staff photographers. In these studios a photographer can turn out a variety of photographs on subjects ranging from lingerie to ball bearings. Often banks and large advertising agencies have their own photographic departments with completely equipped studios and utilize freelancers to give them variety and a fresh approach. In forensic law and science (though this is changing because of electronic imaging), health, medicine or even biologicals, many facilities are available at law-enforcement or health-care organizations, as the average freelancer or small independent studio can ill afford electron microscopes, hi-tech computers, or other sophisticated equipment.

Public Relations and Commercial Photography: What's the Difference?

One branch of commercial photography often difficult to categorize is that broad area called public relations (PR) photography. Frequently it takes the appearance of editorial matter, yet in truth is a form of commerical photography as it is often used to promote a product, service or even the name of a personality who in turn may be selling a service. Theatrical people have as much need for public relations photography as do product managers. Corporations and their executives use photography to improve corporate images (or disguise them if necessary) and to win public acceptance in multitudinous ways. The corporate annual report has, however, been put into the editorial category of this book, where I think it rightly belongs.

What is the real difference between advertising and public relations photography? Ask thirty experts on the subject and you will get as many different answers. Internationally known architectural photographer Ezra Stoller defines publicity as everything except paid media advertising. Other professionals have other definitions. The question is reduced to basics by applying the rules of editorial usage vs. paid space. No this is not the name of a law case (though it well may become one as the issue has come before the courts and will continue to do so). Simply put, when space and/or time is purchased by a client, through an ad agency or otherwise, and material is delivered ready for printing (or airing on TV or radio), it is considered advertising. If the public relations manager or agency calls a media editor and "sells" the idea of using this material as editorial or news matter, it is considered publicity and/or public relations, and it should not be confused with paid space advertising, yet it often is. (See pages 207 and 281 on model releases.)

It would seem simple, but it's not, as there are many interpretations of the word "publicity" (see page 348). Even dictionaries differ, some holding only to the "dissemination of information" concept and others defining it as "paid advertising." The definitions we use have to be specifically oriented toward photography, so I tend to reject most dictionary definitions.

Evaluating the PR field is complex. I have talked about PR photography and its general need and use. After all, the PR agency is being hired to obtain space in the media for the clients. And just as magazine editors are interested in fresh ideas from outside sources, so major PR departments or their agencies need fresh ideas they can present to (or for) their clients in the hope of finding story space.

How to Present a Story Idea for Public Relations

When looking for new markets, what do you do when you see, hear or read of a great new machine, process, scientific breakthrough, or even a pattern or new events that point up some common nationwide problem (pollution, floods, accidents)? Do you think that perhaps you can report it in an effective way with your photographs?

At first you explore the idea by talking directly to magazine or newspaper editors by phone or memo, and you discover that while they may be interested in the subject, they are not happy about spending a lot of money on a new approach to it. Or they may not know enough about the story and would like more information in the way of pictures, copy, etc., before they commit themselves. Or they may not know enough about you to assign it. You should be able to tell by talking to them if they are really interested or not.

Don't drop it there. Find the name of the manufacturer, his PR people in or out of house, and go to see or call them, or if it's a news or public information item, check the indexes and see who has already covered the subject. In other words, research, research, research. After some effort you should be able to come up with workable information:

1. What is the subject—be it machine or situation?
2. Who would be interested in seeing publicity on it?
3. What does it do, who makes it, or what is the trend or pattern?
4. Where should it be published?
5. Why should it be published?
(All of this is simply a variant on the five *W*'s of journalism.)

If you have explored the media directly without positive results, try the back door, by dealing with the PR people. If your information and assessments are correct, you should be able to convince them that magazine X is interested in doing this story, and it might be worthwhile for them (or their client) to put up the money for you to shoot a photo essay to run in the magazine you have targeted. It is also a good idea to suggest that the PR house verify the magazine's interest by having them speak to the editor you contacted. But give just enough information to show that you've researched the story and can do the job. Keep to generalities until there is a need for detailed planning. Ideas cannot be patented or copyrighted, so you cannot protect your "idea" as such from being copied and given to someone else. Chances are, however, if you are dealing with a reputable organization, your idea will be either accepted or rejected but not stolen. If by chance it is, there is little recourse.

By proving your knowledge of the field or your expertise in the subject, and learning the policy and interests of the publication you are dealing with, you stand a pretty good chance of working your way into the assignment. Also you are demonstrating to the PR house (by inference . . . not by direct statement) that you have pipelines into that magazine that they do not have. Oh, every PR house will tell you that they can reach that magazine as easily as you can, and perhaps this is so, but the chances are their connections are with the text departments, and not the photo desks, which they rarely come in contact with. So even if this story attempt fails, they may well consider you as their seeing-eye dog to that magazine. It is also true that, if you do a fair amount of work for a corporation, and they know you also have some magazine connections, they may well hire you on that basis alone.

You can also develop some clout you may not even realize you have. I ran into a strange situation some years ago when I was doing an annual report for a large chemical company that, among other things, had developed an unusual and highly visual method of performing a manufacturing task. When I saw it (and photographed it for the company), I also thought one of the magazines I worked for frequently might be interested in the process for their "new developments" section. Indeed, I placed the picture with them for a full page of color for which they paid me their full space rate.

The PR manager of the company said to me, "I can't tell you how hard we have been trying to get into that magazine, but always have been rebuffed because they do not take 'press handouts.' How can you explain this?"

"That's easy," I said, "you've been trying to go through your text contacts. I went in the back door of the picture department and showed it directly to the art director who became excited, not because of the new process, but by the visual impact of the photograph as a 'design' item." I might have even been able to get an additional fee from the PR house for the placement, but let it go at that and charged it to "goodwill" which later paid off handsomely. I know of a colleague who frequently triples his total fees by exceptional editorial placements of his PR clients' offerings. Another side to that coin is that often my editorial clients (mainly the industrial publications) have asked me if I have seen anything newsworthy. But here too, the photographer has to use caution and not violate the security of a process that is not ready to be made public. Some of these processes may take millions of dollars to develop and bring to production.

So your secondary rights are important side benefits that you should not ignore. Exploit them to the hilt if you can. Remember that even if a PR house or their client pays you to shoot the story and a national magazine uses it, it's likely that the magazine will also voluntarily pay you a space rate for the use of the photographs. This is a right you should reserve when you shoot an editorial piece for PR use, provided you place the story directly, not the PR shop. But often you can even get that waived, if you can show that your contacts are better than theirs.

From here on it's up to you. Also by frequently offering magazines fresh ideas, they get to know you and they too can easily become a source of assignments. My experience, and that of many colleagues, indicates that these approaches are often the most promising in all fields of public relations photography.

Advertising Photography

If there is one glaring exception to the concept of presentation of ideas to a potential client, it is in photography for national advertising.

If you are on the outside looking in, particularly if you are young and just starting, the presentation of ideas to an ad agency or ad manager of a corporation will often fly like a lead balloon. Just as publications and corporate PR operations are eager for fresh approaches, the ad agencies seem to be as determinedly closed to outside thinking, which possibly says something about the staleness of some advertising photography. Why is this? The answer most frequently given is that all ad agencies have "creative directors" whose job is to come up with ideas and concepts for ads. An outside idea might appear as a threat and inference they cannot do their job.

Advertising photography is a broad term. It includes fashion and lifestyles; still lifes from food to household appliances and all manner of liquid products from alcohol to coffee and teas, anything that can be bottled, canned, frozen, sprayed or dehydrated; there are still lifes of still lifes, that is, copies of paintings and works of art and other visual works; there are architecture and construction and land and real estate to photograph. Each of these is a specialty area and yet there are common denominators outside the technology of cameras, film, processing and lighting, with other types of photography. One is the required love and desire for the field in which the photographer is specializing. There is no sense in a photographer who has neither interest in nor knowledge of clothing styles becoming a fashion photographer. One certainly can learn, to be sure, but the key word here is *interest*. The love and desire for the craft of photography and specialization in a field of interest are the watchwords for the newcomer, and nowhere is this more apparent than in the world of advertising photography.

Each specialization has its stars and there is disagreement as to what form of advertising photography pays the most. Some say fashion or personal products are the highest revenue producer; others think automotive and travel are the most remunerative. Advertising fees are usually based on a variety of cost factors such as media rates, usage, circulation, clients' advertising budgets and internal preparation charges, and while fashion is a very important part of advertising photography, it by no means dominates it, nor can it be ranked accurately as to its relative scale of importance. Gross studio billings, in still life, product and illustrative photography, are probably equivalent to fashion. Over the years advertising photography has built its stable of stars and high earners. And even though the creative director of one ad agency felt that the fashion photographer had to be "totally engrossed" in fashion, it does not seem to be the case of the advertising still life photographer, who evidently can be a lot more flexible and eclectic in his devotion to craft.

Each specialization will bring variations in methods of operation. What applies to the still life photographer does not necessarily work for the architectural specialist; the aerial photographer has many problems that the photographer behind a microscope would never understand, and vice versa. And yet it appears that even the ad agencies are becoming less interested in the specialists and more interested in the highly creative photographer who can adapt well to many genres and still have an outstanding specialty.

Insights Into the Field of Commerical Photography

Not only is the resistance to outside ideas hard to break down, but the hierarchical structure in advertising extends beyond the group heads or the creative directors. They are the supervisors of the teams that produce the ads. There are others you must ultimately reach and convince that you are the best person for the job. It is the teams of art buyers, art directors and even copywriters who are actually responsible for production of the ad including the photography, artwork, text copy and layout. When a concept is worked out, it is visualized in a layout composed of sketches, "swipes" from clippings of other ads of publications, or dummy type and photographs. This is called a composite, or "comp." From here it goes to the client, who may or may not approve. If it is not approved, the ad is reworked until approval is received and then the photographic part is sent out for execution. In some, but not all cases, execution might be the key word, because any photographer who deviates from the approved concept is invariably discouraged. In spite of statements to the contrary, it must be remembered that an ad is not generally sent out for production until it has client approval which is hard to get in a studio, after a concept has been shot.

I once attended a seminar where art directors were asked about the lack of room for photographers to move beyond the fixed layout into creativity of their own. A number of them said, "Oh, but we always allow the photographer to shoot what he wants after the original layout is done exactly as we have ordered." When another participant asked how often they use those photographs in the finished ads, the silence was deafening. (One answer to this might be found in Greg Heisler's approach . . . see page 117.)

So if ideas for advertising photography rarely are accepted from outside sources not connected with either the agency or the client directly, does this mean that the photographer should not come up with fresh ideas in which an advertiser might be interested? Certainly not. But it is far better for the photographer to get the job by concentrating on including smashing photographs in his portfolio (or "book" in ad lingo) or mailer, rather than attempt to do the thinking for the creative director or art director on how a shoot should be handled. That great photograph may well be the trigger for a whole slew of ideas from the agency on how to use this photographer's particular talent. Imagination is a commodity that is rare, but when used well can be rewarding. A friend in advertising told of one photographer who wanted to do liquor advertising. However, instead of presenting an entire ad layout, as many young photographers try to do, he went to his neighborhood bar after closing, and gathered up a great many empty liquor bottles. He washed them and then photographed them in every creative way he could. He showed those pictures to an AD on a liquor account who was stimulated enough by the beautiful imagery of empty glass bottles, to appreciate the unique approach, i.e., if one can photograph empty bottles as an art form well, why not full ones? Thus an ad idea was created, and the photographer indeed got the assignment.

Probably the most important change in the last decade in methods of acquiring photography (or any art) in advertising, has been the establishment of the art buyer as the focal point for incoming photography. Once photographers had to make personal contact with ADs, show their work and hope for the best. And before getting to see an AD, one had to hurdle the wall erected by a person generally known as the "art secretary," who, it would seem, was more interested in keeping photographers away from art directors than bringing them together.

Today it's different: Advertising agencies have merged into even bigger corporate entities than before, though there may be fewer of them. Once a big agency might have employed up to ten or fifteen art directors. Today the norm for the larger agencies can be as high as forty or more with a corresponding increase in traffic from photographers and artists seeking work.

As the number of art directors grew, the difficulties in getting to see them increased proportionately and the "art secretaries," who were essentially clerk/receptionists, frequently anointed themselves as judges of an artist's work. They usually lacked training in art or photography, and often decided, without authority to do so, whether or not a portfolio should be passed on to the art director of the account the photographer was hoping to reach.

This malaise grew alarmingly, and though many agency art directors denied it was occurring, clear proof that it was happening was obtained by the leading professional societies of artists and photographers, sometimes by methods as simple as using double-stick plastic tape to show whether a portfolio cover had even been opened.

This callousness in the agencies' handling of portfolios resulted not only in a good deal of anger being created between them and the artists, but photographers and reps were beginning to bypass many agencies, with the result that much new work was never shown, and new talents never hired. There were other abuses involved in obtaining work, not all laid at the feet of the art secretaries.

The practice of giving gifts and even worse, "kickbacks," was spreading with unscrupulous ADs demanding or hinting broadly that no work would be assigned without the commensurate showing of appreciation. Anyone sitting in the reception room of the art department of any big agency the week before Christmas, had to be especially careful not to be trampled by the rush of bearers and beaters carrying largess in the form of cases of liquor, theater tickets, and other goodies with expensive couturier labels on them. Fortunately when the odor of these practices rose high enough to reach the executive floors of several large agencies, some art directors were fired from major accounts. In at least one case, a sizable account was lost by an agency whose employees were involved in these practices.

The establishment of the art buyer system did much to stop many of these abuses, because not only was the "Berlin Wall" of art secretaries demolished, but access to art directors who *needed* to see fresh work and new talent was made easier. Moreover the art buyer was more knowledgeable about the quality of work presented and more aware of the agency's needs than the average art secretary.

Insider: Anthony Lovett, Art Buyer

Lovett is one of several art buyers at DDB Needham Worldwide, one of the most prestigious advertising agencies in New York. The agency itself is the result of the merger of two large agencies: Doyle, Dane, Bernbach, and Needham Harper Worldwide, employing over forty art directors on accounts exceeding the number of ADs.

He told me of the clear separation of functions of the art buyer and the art director (AD). The AD comes up with a concept and gets it approved by the client. The art buyer has the knowledge of talent and production that can make that concept happen and makes the assignment.

Today the art buyer resembles the magazine picture editor who makes the assignments. On magazines the AD deals essentially with the material in front of him, rarely coming in contact with the photographer and leaving the selection of talent and production to the picture editor. At the agency, the AD and the photographer work closely together but the AD usually does not have monetary power.

In the agency world, the AD usually approves the final selection of the photographers, though he is guided by the art buyer who has made preliminary selections. For instance, an AD will come to Lovett with a layout, showing a particular style that is needed. Lovett suggests who would be the best person to use. The buyers are the support group for the ADs.

Previously an AD would finish a campaign and have time to develop another one. Not so now. Today the ADs are young, right out of an art center, and though they are creative in their work, they often don't know who the important photographers are. They come to the art buyer for help and guidance on whom to hire. In the hierarchical structure the creative director guides the ADs and either accepts or rejects their concepts before sending them to the client.

Lovett went on to tell me that if new photographers do not have an agent, and most do not until they have developed a sizable body of work, they must call every art buyer in the business and make appointments to see them. It is the job of the art buyer to look for fresh talent. Many young people are too self-conscious and often shy about making approaches. It might be a tough hurdle to overcome, but it's the only way a new photographer can gain exposure. There may be several art buyers in a large agency and as a group they know what is going on. They will know if perhaps there is a *pro bono* ad to shoot inexpensively, and not very difficult to produce.

The new photographer should not immediately go out after a major campaign because it's simply not going to happen. There's too much money riding on the experience of the photographer. But there are smaller accounts, including *pro bono* ads, which pay less and will enable the photographer to get his foot in the door. These clients are more willing to use new and less experienced photographers.

DDB-Needham is a strong print agency, and heavy demands are made on them. Earlier there were fewer first-rate photographers presenting work, perhaps for some of the reasons already noted, but now competition has increased markedly as photography is very popular among young people.

Lovett prefers not to see an agent as, he says, "I love to meet the photographers directly. I think there is value in an agent because they know who to show different work to, how to market, to estimate, and have experience in problem solving. But in finality, it's the photographer who is going to do the work, and that's who I want to meet to assess his or her personality.

"In past years photographers have complained (and sometimes rightly so) that portfolios left for viewing were not looked at. Art buyers are a different breed and in a different category than the old art secretary. The art buyer now exists. I trained as an artist and I have to deal with photographers and business people.

"A great part of my job is to educate the ADs as to who was great, who is great, what the future trends are, and that's very different from the art secretary. Callous treatment of photographers never happens here because we love photography. As a Fine Arts major, I studied the history of art and the history of photography, and am aware of the importance of photography.

"We know some ADs and art buyers are careless or unfeeling about the way they treat a young photographer's work. Not so here, but photographers also have to hope for the best as there is nothing they can do to force someone to look at their book. If we make an appointment, we keep it and it's not difficult to get one. We will see every person who calls because we don't know if they could be the next greatest talent. We often see some pretty bad work, too."

There are other ways for photographers to come to the attention of the art buyer besides showing their book. [*Author's tongue-in-cheek note: Adver-*

tising, like the computer, seems to have developed a special language of its own. All photographers, artists or agents seem to fall into a new species called generically a *book*. It's not pejorative, but everyone I know in advertising seems to want to look at a *book*, not a person. Oh well.]

Mailers

Mailers are extremely important. All art buyers save the mailers they like and have a filing system for them. They have drawers full of mailers on fashion, still lifes, food, special products, etc. This is not all bad, because it becomes an imporant resource for ADs who often pore over them, though not always sure what they're after. But by scanning many mailers they often discover what they are looking for.

There are good mailers and bad mailers, and some people get carried away. All Lovett wants in a mailer is a picture, a name, an address and telephone number; no puns, no hype. He does not want to see anything in a mailer except a great picture, one that is representative of the photographer's portfolio. He is not interested in a single lucky shot, and when a portfolio comes in, they expect the consistency will match the quality of the mailer.

There is always the possibility the mailer will take precedence over an interview as there are just so many people even the most well-intentioned art buyer can see, so using the mailer may be an easier way for photographers to get through the door. But mailers are expensive, and if the photographer is expected to keep a steady supply of new work coming in, the ongoing costs of their production and distribution can be burdensome. There are some ways of short-cutting the cost of production (see page 205 on printing methods). They should be explored thoroughly for maximum effectiveness.

It is pretty safe for a photographer to leave his book with agencies using the art buyer system. Lovett assured me it will be looked at, as there is a whole new set of art buyers in the industry and that finding new talent is one of their prime functions. Once there might have been only ten art buyers in the business; now there are probably over 120 just in Manhattan alone. With this system agencies have several buyers to look after the needs of their forty-plus ADs, and they think they can cover all incoming work. Most of their important accounts use photographs.

Lovett continued, "I do not like to be bugged by a photographer but I think persistence is important. It's different here because someone is welcome to drop their book off at any time without an appointment. If they can leave it at least overnight, I will get to see it. Once seen, we like photographers to keep us up to date with mailers or tear sheets. We usually put a little handwritten note in with each return, thanking the photographer for letting us see it, and telling him what we liked or even possibly disliked about the book. So in this way we can give them a bit of direction.

"We often find promising new talent by simply going through the books and mailers. It's also very frustrating for us because there is so much talent out there that we often do not have room for. But I re-emphasize that as we can't use expensive talent on low-budget jobs. There is room for the new photographer to break in, provided he is willing to accept lower fees and perhaps spend more time on a job to balance his inexperience."

Ten years ago fees were based on a percentage of media costs, with a rule-of-thumb measurement that about 5 percent of media cost would be allocated for art purchase. This has changed drastically, partially because today agencies frequently do not know in what media an ad will run or how many insertions they will be making, and with some accounts, the impact of the regional editions. Therefore, there has to be agreement on a fixed rate for a shoot, rather than basing it on media cost. Agencies often buy material at the last minute and without any firm idea where it's going.

Fees vary widely depending on projected usage and the experience of the photographer. Rates too are based on assessment of the photographer and the space the ad will occupy unless, of course, it's a star photographer. Then it might become a horse-race.

Lovett says, "On average, a medium-level photographer shooting a full-page ad can earn a fee of between $3,500-$7,500 in consumer magazines and $2,500-$5,000 in trade advertising. Only about 25 percent of our work is trade advertising. There is no differential for regional editions here, as all of our accounts are national. Top-level photographers can average $10,000-$30,000 a day, with beginning photographers on a try-out basis earning from $1,000 to $3,500 per day. All other expenses including studio personnel are extra. Most shoots can be completed in one day; the differential between trade and consumer advertising applies even to the big names. When we buy an ad we do reserve the right to run it at any time or any place. We do not put time caps on an ad's use though occasionally we do so on agreement. We don't get too much resistance as we have a reputation for paying extremely well. We never do work-for-hire assignments. Everything we do is bought for a specific usage or bought outright at what we think are very fair rates.

"A photographer must document all his expenses carefully because we are often audited as to what we are spending on a shoot. Most photographers are reasonable in their charges but there are exceptions. I can think of two outrageous ones. One photographer who was making hundreds of thousands of dollars on a major campaign charged us for paper clips and the stationery used to bill us. Another photographer who bills in the tens of thousands of dollars, sent receipts for six rolls of toilet paper and two boxes of garbage bags when we were shooting on a beach with a model and there were no props. Or once we were doing a *pro bono* ad, which is usually an agency expense with the client paying only outside costs. We were shooting a simple head shot of a man wearing a tie. This photographer bought $400-$500 worth of ties and we felt terrible about having to pass this on to a *pro bono* client."

For re-shoots which are clearly not the photographer's fault, the agency uses different guidelines. It depends on who last approves the shot. On some accounts it's the client; on others the ADs have the last word. A re-shoot is generally paid for if the photographer is not at fault.

Lovett believes disputes can be avoided if the photographer shows the AD a Polaroid of what he is doing. Not to do that is dangerous, as I can say from experience. Some years ago (and this was just about the time that Polaroid backs became available for large cameras) I was shooting an ad campaign that took the AD and me all over the country, but with a return to the agency home office after each shoot. I saw a peculiar pattern developing. Even though the AD had crawled under the dark-cloth with me and carefully okayed the image on the ground glass, when the film came in this AD would look at the pictures and then try to beat the price down, saying, "This is not the image I wanted, so let's cut the price." I held my ground because he had seen the ground-glass image, but I also called a photographer I knew who had worked with this AD on other accounts and asked if he had had similar experiences.

"Yeah," he said, "this guy is noted for this kind of chiseling. He has tried it on every photographer he has worked with, but always backs down when you fight him on that issue. But it always makes the photographer defensive, and some of the younger ones do back down and cut the price."

On the next shoot I took along the then new Polaroid back, and instead of letting the AD check the image on the ground glass, made a Polaroid, showed it to him and said, "Is this what you want?" He said it was. I said, "Okay, initial it right now so we don't get into any arguments later." He did so sheepishly, and the rest of the account was finished in peace.

Today because there are so many systems in place, difficulties involving re-shooting, money, etc., diminish as ADs no longer deal with the money problems. They can establish a good relationship with their photographers, so by the time the shoot begins, all problems of purchase orders, prices, locations, models, etc. are buttoned up, and the shoot proceeds. That's part of the art buyers' function, to alleviate all such problems. So it's not the mess it used to be.

Lovett's agency does not like secondary rights usages even of generic photographs shot as a background, e.g., clouds, skylines, etc. But this applies only to the original photograph used in a layout, not the out-takes; they have no objection to secondary generic usage. The critical point is the ethics of the secondary use; in other words, no agency wants the secondary picture looking anything like the one they used, especially for a competing client.

DDB-Needham uses some electronic imaging, and sees nothing wrong with its use in advertising. But they do very little of it in general, except to clean up a few stray hairs on a hair spray ad or things like that. They do not use it for altering because it's expensive. They use it only for retouching.

"As for new work," Lovett says, "I, for one, do not like to look at a lot of tearsheets of what other agencies did. But if a photographer has shot mostly editorial material, and all he has are tearsheets to show his style, then naturally I look at them, but I want to see original prints also.

"What I look for are not one-shot miracles, but a point of view and mode of expression. I feel a photographer should shoot not only what he's assigned to shoot and do it well, but also what he likes to shoot and do that well. I don't like to see a lot of trendy pictures, because they won't last. I am more interested in general quality and consistency, and this will show up if the photographer shows enough of the work he likes to do.

"I suggest new photographers call every single art buyer in the business and see absolutely as many as possible. You really have to be everywhere and cover all bases. Patience too is a factor. Very often I myself will be taken with a particular photographer's work, some of it from big stars, but even so it might take two or three years before I can convince an AD to use that person.

"It is very important, and I know it can be expensive, but the photographer must leave something behind after a visit. If these items are too expensive, i.e., color prints, then he has to figure out another way of doing it more cheaply, but it must be done. (See page 108.) Because of the number of photographers who come through, I cannot remember everyone, and I need a reference point. I may not remember their face or their name but I will remember the image."

In presentations, videotape or film strips do not have much value because not every AD has a VCR handy or wants to bother finding one. Another factor, while unstated, is that like magazine editors, art buyers do not like to be locked into a fixed format of seeing work. They often like to be free to juggle prints, particularly those in story format to see how different photographs work in different relationships. Lovett prefers to see prints or large transparencies. He prefers those to 35mm slides, because while projection is very pretty to look at, agencies often do not have the equipment easily available, and often even some projection systems are not color-corrected and the viewer can be fooled on color quality.

But if a photographer wants to project his work it is advisable that he call first to see if the art buyer has the equipment available, or if it's okay for the photographer to bring a projector with him. Lovett does not mind projection and thinks other buyers feel the same way, provided it's handled well.

He also said, "I can't emphasize strongly enough that we don't want the photographer to view the art buyer or the AD as 'the enemy.' I want us to work in harmony toward a common goal. Our philosophy is that the art buyers here are the producers and we are in the middle of the entire group of account executives; photographer, crews, ADs and the client. On one hand we are the right arm of the AD and the rest of the agency, but we are also the sponsor of the photographer. We're the ones who carry their books to the ADs, saying 'look at this' and generally encourage the AD to use a particular talent."

Insider: William Taubin

Earlier, I had spoken at length with William Taubin, former Head Art Director for Doyle, Dane, Bernbach, DDB-Needham's predecessor. Taubin was unquestionably the dean of all agency art directors, winner of numerous awards for memorable campaigns, and nominated as "Art Director of the Year" for the Art Directors Club Hall of Fame in 1981. Mostly he was a thoughtful, sensitive man with deep feelings and respect for all artists. We spoke of the young photographer trying to break into advertising photography. I asked him, "How does the new photographer get started in advertising?" What he told me then is still valid today.

"It's not easy," he said. "Most photographers start by going to some sort of photography school, though I don't think that is absolutely necessary. Often a new photographer will start by getting a job as an assistant to another photographer for several years, learning the basics. Then if he has developed lots of experience and has lots of money, he opens his own studio. And of course if he is smart, he won't do it in a recessionary period such as we have now." (How visionary he was.) He went on to say, "If I were a young photographer now and had a good job in a studio, I would stay there for the present."

Taubin then was critical of the craftsmanship of many photographers, and many of his contemporaries today feel much the same. He was strong on sharpness (or deliberate fuzziness) in a photograph as an indication of craftsmanship as he felt it also means precision, and the indefinable quality called "good taste." It comes down to the photographer's knowledge of lighting, optics and film and selection of the most appropriate format. He was disturbed by a lot of young photographers who produce work in terrible taste. "Good taste," he said, "is extremely important, though hard to define. Nudity can be vulgar and in bad taste, but it can also be absolutely beautiful. A photographer's dress and appearance indicate his taste, or lack of it."

Twelve years later I went back to Doyle, Dane to find they had merged with Needham Harper Worldwide Advertising to form DDB-Needham, still a prestigious agency, and still located in the heartland of Madison Avenue. Their offices had changed, Taubin and others had retired or moved on, and, moreover, as was apparent in my discussions with Lovett, attitudes had also changed.

Lovett introduced me to Paul Guyante, a ranking AD in the agency currently working on several accounts.

Insider: Paul Guyante, Art Director

Advertising photography has changed appreciably in recent years and so have the methods by which agencies select photographers. There are over forty busy art directors in this agency, so the choice of photographers starts with the art buyer. Perhaps the parallel might be the picture editor of a magazine, especially one on the staff of a large magazine.

Guyante's primary account is Clairol, a woman's hair treatment product. He has also worked on insurance, Seagram, Celanese and others and though accounts vary, art selection procedures are much the same. On Clairol it is a beautiful image he looks for. He told me he looks everywhere: at current editorial material, at anything out there on the street, or sometimes on posters or other visual stimuli. "Many photographers do great commercial work," he went on to say, "but I never look for that kind of photographer. I look for a special point of view, one who has ideas of how he sees things, and can understand what my concept of advertising photography is."

He attended the Art Center College of Design and the Los Angeles Trade Technical College, where he also studied old-fashioned techniques of paste-up, typesetting, layouts, etc. Many of his teachers were old school too, so he learned much about craftsmanship in presentations.

He said, "Though I'm an art director in an excellent agency, I consider this is a smaller part of my overall fabric; I think of myself as a visual communicator and that's what I do with everything, even outside of the agency. I design work for myself, for friends, and have even created small furniture items.

"I have never worked on the editorial side, but I think I would love to at some time. It's where I look for new talent. I always talk to those concerned with makeup, styles, etc., to see how they use their talents editorially."

It's not hard for a photographer to get to see ADs such as Guyante. Often making a cold phone call is all that's necessary. Of course, it helps if another AD or an art buyer makes an introduction, and that too can happen if the photographer systematically builds up a list of prospective clients and keeps in touch with them. In several cases I have approached ADs who said that though they did not need anything at the moment, I should see another AD on another account . . . and then proceeded to make the introductory phone call. So, if you are seeing one person, don't be afraid to ask if he has any ideas as to who may be interested in your work, even to the point of asking him to introduce you. After all, it's the AD who makes the final choice on a job, even if actual negotiations go through the art buyer.

What is he looking for?

"I look for a good sense of design, taste, and even the grittiest, newest work which is rough and hard does have to have taste, and done in a thoughtful way. It can be provocative without being too 'over the top,' too vulgar. Oddly enough there are not as many new books presented as there used to be. Perhaps it's because there just aren't as many projects going, or possibly earlier rejections may have turned off some photographers.

"Our comps or test layouts are not very detailed. I prefer to use simple black lines on a white piece of paper just as a guide. For Clairol it will just show a head, which to me means I have to show great hair, shape and texture. What is done with it is up to the photographers. I hire them because of their points of view, and if I like what they do in figures and composition, I would love them to bring those feelings to the product and discuss them with me.

"Occasionally we use comps, or I bring in photographs from a magazine and say this is the type of styling, photography, or the graphic look that we're going to be shooting. I use these illustrations as a guide to what I want and try not to box the photographer in too tightly. I want to hire photographers who want to do something fresh and not restrict them. I want creativity.

"On Clairol there is already a preconceived notion of what we are looking for or what we have already done. I always remind photographers not to worry about previous layouts, but to concentrate on their own fresh approach. I want a wide range and the most they can get, and yet still fill my requirements."

Guyante always attends a shooting and talks with the photographers in advance so they are comfortable with his presence. He said, "I want them to feel that they are going to do something wonderful. I take an active role in the production, and have had little objection from the photographers because we have learned to work as a team. If you're creative, if you're really good at what you do, you can take whatever the concept is and make something wonderful out of it."

And that's his job too as art director; he's given rules he must follow, and the shoot has to look as if there were no rules and the production was spontaneous. Among the many ADs at DDB-Needham there is variance in procedures. But in all cases, plans or concepts have to be cleared with the client before a shoot, and work is never assigned until there is client approval. With models, initial choices are made by the photographer and AD, with final approval from the client.

Clients are always on hand also and often get into the act. Sometimes it creates a problem but most of the photographers deal with it pretty well. Guyante told me of one exceptionally accommodating photographer. He gets what he wants and appears somehow to do what the clients say they want even if they don't see eye to eye. Clients can get in the way, though, and frequently by agreement, agency or client representatives at a shoot are limited to one or two people to minimize friction.

If there are uncalled-for expenses because of expensive lunches, entertainment, etc., this is usually handled by the art buyer. Guyante said, "I never talk money with anyone involved in a shoot, leaving that to the art buyer. My job is that of creative communication. I have to get everyone working together effectively to create wonderful images.

"When photographers contact me instead of the art buyer, I ask if they have done editorial work in image beauty. If so, and if they are new, I *will* look at their work because to me it's always exciting to find someone who has not even been published yet but shows great talent.

"Also, I rarely look at commercial work but prefer to concentrate on editorial approaches and I know this cuts out a great many hopefuls. Like Lovett, I am not too happy about seeing reps as I prefer to deal with the photographers directly. I'm not against reps, but I think I can tell better from looking at the photographers' work and talking with them, whether I'm going to be comfortable with them."

There is another reason for considering whether the new photographer needs a rep. If the rep is poor, it makes the photographer look poor, and the photographer can be prejudged before his work is even seen. This is unfortunate as some reps, even if they develop an adversary relationship, often represent fine photographers. Guyante told me he sometimes has to ask himself if he wants to consider using a certain photographer if it means dealing with a rep he dislikes. If he thinks the work of the photographer is paramount, he will make exceptions.

DDB-Needham considers electronic imaging as state-of-the-art retouching. They try to shoot pictures which don't need reworking. Most of the imagery they produce is on a single piece of film. They are aware of the technology and use an excellent engraver with Scitex capability for separations.

They prefer transparencies to prints and need the first original and cleanest image the photographer can provide. They do not want second generation images and prefer to work from the original.

Older ADs have sometimes expressed apprehension about dealing with new photographers. With Guyante and his contemporaries, it's more a question of ideas, so if a new photographer has a better or more appropriate idea, he will go with the new one. It's in his search for new ideas that he looks more to the editorial approach than the commercial. He is not rigid in the scope of a photographer's work and feels if a young photographer has flexibility, he will go with him.

"Right now," he told me, "I am using a photographer who is noted for still life, but we are using him to do people. I often challenge myself by taking people from one area to another to get a fresh approach.

"I find it thrilling to work with a photographer and help create a new image. It's exciting to watch how he comes up with the concept and interprets my problems in a way I may not have thought of. I love to collaborate with the photographers, the stylists, the makeup and hair people—all that are involved. In a way it's like Hollywood and my responsibility as AD is to get all the right players together to make something wonderful. Since many of them are involved in editorial production their ideas can rub off on me."

Insider: Tana Hoban, Photographer

Connecting the advertising and the editorial worlds is a strong bridge—the photography of children, who bring an enormous emotional response to viewers. Jade Albert (see page 233) is a strong force in using children as props to buttress other advertising. Hoban uses children's portraits in a more direct way in books, magazines and products where children are the principal focus. She is widely recognized as top-rated in the advertising and editorial worlds and has produced many books for and about children.

Hoban, as a first-year student at the Moore Institute of Art and Design for Women in Philadelphia, convinced her dean she could draw better than many other students. She earned a three-year scholarship, with photography offered in the final semester, and then won the John Frederick Lewis Fellowship to paint in Europe.

Her methods have not changed over the years. She starts by finding appealing children, then photographing them over a period of several days, producing romantic, nostalgic images of little boys and girls. While her backgrounds are carefully chosen, she encourages the children to respond spontaneously to the environment. Her pictures developed a special flavor that brought her prominence. Early on, a large ad agency showed her work, which in turn led to her inclusion in a magazine article on successful women photographers. Her career mushroomed and her work began appearing in *Good Housekeeping, Ladies' Home Journal, Vogue, LIFE* and other magazines.

Hoban did just about everything right in getting new work to survive as a photographer. She did not rest on her laurels. She actively followed ad and editorial campaigns that used children and family situations. She would then track down the various art directors involved. In this way, she obtained assignments to shoot ads for baby food, children's fashions and family situations. She kept a notebook of every interview she had, what ADs said, and paid attention to their visual philosophies. She did her homework, was ready to produce, and produced well.

Advertising photography, however lucrative, is also frustrating for the photographer. Credits are rarely given in layouts and those photographers who achieve prominence do so either from successful campaigns that have caught the eye of the advertising community or from peer approval. But well-earned reputations, if maintained, can still keep the photographer functioning over many years.

As noted earlier we are concerned with those photographers who have survived economically and made substantial contributions to our craft. Frances McLaughlin Gill is one of them.

Insider: Frances McLaughlin-Gill, Fashion Photographer

Fashion photography is a branch of the art almost equally divided between commercial illustration and editorial photojournalism. Widely used editorially in fashion and other magazines, it probably receives equal if not greater billings in the advertising pages of those same magazines. There are other big outlets for fashion photographers in catalogs, brochures and point-of-purchase advertising.

Every specialty has it stars, and no star shines brighter than Frances McLaughlin-Gill, who after forty years of superb fashion photography is still producing first-rate editorial layouts and advertising campaigns.

Gill graduated from Pratt Institute and started to work first as a studio assistant. Later she joined the Condé Nast staff as a photographer for *Vogue* magazine, remaining there for twelve years until the studio closed. She then opened her own studio, and continued to produce for them under contract for another fifteen years.

She and the other photographers worked on a wide variety of subjects: still lifes, fashions, products, beauty aid, personalities, and interiors. They were directed by Alexander Liberman, *Vogue*'s legendary art director. He sharpened the photographers' skills by moving them around in various specialties. Gill says he was wonderful about encouraging all the photographers to try new approaches and new concepts in photography, but she also spoke of his insistence on photographers doing what he wanted them to do first before trying out any ideas of their own. Because of this training, she advises that photographers should always do alternate situations if possible, but never lose sight of the initial assignment. The treatment of the subject as requested has to be produced as gracefully and devotedly as possible, and then and only then, should the photographer attempt to do his own work.

Fashion is the one branch of photography in which it is virtually impossible for the photographer to work alone. Gill underlines the absolute necessity for the photographer to be able to work as part of a team, and although she thought this should be a trait of almost every kind of photographer, it is particularly true in fashion. To produce fine fashion photography one has to be able to work well with the editor, art director, makeup artists and hair stylists and, most important, the model(s). She emphasizes that the fashion photographer, in order to keep current and to stay at the peak of his craft, must work frequently and consistently as fashions themselves change so radically and rapidly.

Homework by the photographer prior to the assignment is vital to the success of the job, Gill insists. It is the responsibility of the photographer to make certain that all props are gathered, the locations scouted, even when such chores are delegated to staff. When pictures are to be made of personalities, planning ahead is mandatory, even if the photographer has to spend an extra day to find out what a person looks like, wears, and perhaps something about the ambiance of the locale where shooting will take place. Gill thinks it is hard for one to become a fashion photographer without a strong support team, especially of models. But with the need to produce in a team environment, how does the newcomer to fashion develop this when he himself is new and probably unknown?

The fashion portfolio should have photographs using the best and most experienced models available, but with four-figure rates for several hours of shooting almost the norm, how does the newcomer get samples?

Gill suggests that new photographers arrange with model agencies to make photographs of the newer models who have yet to build up large and impressive portfolios. The better model agencies make special efforts to get good books for all their models, and help them locate good photographers. Some agencies have special departments just to do this. Often photographs can be produced on a swap basis, e.g., pictures in exchange for model time.

Another source of professional models is department stores or larger specialty shops using models in fashion shows and local advertising. Garment manufacturers also employ models on a permanent basis for showroom work. These models, like their more highly paid agency counterparts, often need modeling portfolios, and it is possible that arrangements can be made to exchange services. Models in college or university art classes may be available, but they may not be "right" for fashion photography. Any models used should be of professional caliber.

Gill spoke of many young couples around — male as photographer, female as model (in a few cases vice versa) — who have a one-to-one relationship that is often useful in producing fine fashion photographs for portfolios and model books. She did not mean to overemphasize this relationship, as a big part of the fashion industry deals with men's wear, though she has suggested that some of her women photography students consider fashion photography portfolios for men on much the same basis. Most outlets for male fashion photography are in catalogs, magazines and newspaper ads, with some point-of-purchase use in stores and showrooms.

Gill stressed the importance of the model to the total photographic fashion situation, reminding us that the photographer must never lose sight of the person-to-person relationship. If too many people interfere in a studio situation, the photographer must assert his command, or the shoot will be a failure. The photographer should have his own ideas and stick to them.

As for models, Gill said that a most important role for the photographer (besides the actual shooting) is making models feel they are important. Too much handling, too much changing of costume or accessories, will tend to upset a model. (This applies to male models as well.) It's a volatile situation and it's up to the photographer to control it. The photographer must establish good rapport in order to bring out the best and most productive side of the model and everyone else on the set.

It is best for photographers *not* to do model hiring and billing. This stems partially from state laws that interpret the hiring of a model as an employment agency situation and thus tightly control commissions and fees. Another reason for the photographer to avoid billing and paying model fees is because of the large sums of money tied up in payments, often slow reimbursement and workers' compensation requirements. Personality factors sometimes are raised and occasionally an AD or client simply doesn't like the way a model looks in a photograph. Therefore, in any model hiring effort, it is important to clearly specify in the purchase order that the model or model agency will bill the client or the client's agency directly, especially if they take part in the model selection.

Gill feels that the core of any photographic effort is the actual photograph itself, so she has established her own personal criteria of five components of any good photograph, and feels that if any one is lacking, the photograph has failed: (1) skillful composition, (2) technical quality and control, (3) excellent lighting, (4) the element of chance, and (5) persisting until the right image is on film.

Insider: Patrick St. Claire, Male Model

"I'm French, trained as a lawyer in artists' rights, and planned to practice in that field. While still in law school and during a vacation I decided to try modeling. I called a few Parisian model agencies, and one told me to bring my test pictures. [French version of U.S. "book."] I did not know what they meant so I went to a photographer friend who made the tests for me. The agency liked them and I worked for them for a year in Europe.

"After finishing law school I first went to Milano and then came here in 1977 to earn quick money in modeling before returning to law practice in Europe. I signed with the Eileen Ford Agency and they have kept me so busy I never did go back. I was lucky I guess, and I work only in print medium. I feel that the amount of work available for individuals is diminishing because of the increased competition. But the total amount of work is increasing because of other print outlets, i.e., catalogs, brochures, and other direct mail publications. Women models seem to have more work than men though that gap is narrowing.

"Working with a good photographer is a team operation. And though I have input in any modeling shoot, I respect the ideas of the photographers and do not try to interfere with their concepts. Some photographers will direct the entire shoot, others will not. I have few problems with experienced photographers or agency art directors, as they often have precise ideas of what is necessary. Shooting starts with a mutual comprehension of the desired layout.

"I refer to experienced photographers. New, inexperienced ones often try to control the shooting completely even though they may not have the comprehension they should. Probably this happens when they are insecure, afraid to make mistakes, and will not accept advice from others. But after they blow one, they are receptive to the model's help. Three people are always involved in any shooting—the photographer, the model, and the agency and/or client. The model is in between and has to please both.

"In fashion photography there is a great difference in execution of ideas between Europe and America. Here the agencies look for standard catalog types to display clothes. In Europe there is more emphasis on the model—facial expression, posture, etc. One of the problems here is the money involved. With so much emphasis here on high cost, photographers are afraid to make mistakes and creativity is limited. They're afraid of losing customers.

"In Italy, for instance, there is much more freedom on the part of the model, and the photographer also has much more power. In Europe the photographer usually hires the model but here they almost never do, with that choice being left to the agency or client. I know the reasons for this but it still presents a problem. The photographer does not know what to do, the model doesn't know what to do, and frequently the agency doesn't know what to do because they all have to please the clients who often do not know what to do either.

"This creates unnecessary interference and inhibits all the participants. So if you leave the control of the shooting to one or two people you frequently will get better results. It is much easier to work that way and it is much more rewarding. Stylists do not as a rule have much input. Their roles usually are confined to the selection of clothes, products or product use.

"Frequently a new photographer will be uncertain as to what the client really wants and asks the model for assistance. Any conflict between the photographer and model vs. the agency is wrong. There should never be a confrontation, only a team operation working toward the same goal. Often problems caused by these conflicts stem from the fact that the agency art director may have two or three people with him, but the client will sometimes be represented by as many as a dozen. They feel they have to prove the value of their presence, and in order to do so, try to get into the act. The results can sometimes be disastrous. The minute you involve twenty people in the shoot instead of two there is trouble. We certainly do not need these extra people around; they do more harm than good. The model feels much closer to the photographer than to the client and the confidence they must have in each other is primary. I frequently like to work with the same photographer because we know each other, but I have no objection to working with new photographers at any time because that's the nature of the business. We have to try to establish a rapport as quickly as possible. This is something the new photographer must be aware of, and even if he is new and just beginning, he must take command and clear the location of anyone not important to the shoot. It may be hard, but if good photography is the goal, then it must be done.

"I agree somewhat with Jill Johnson's reference to her focal point being the camera and not the photographer (see below) but not entirely. The photographer is very much a personality who has to be dealt with. But it is true that the lens is what the model really pays attention to. It could be anyone behind it, as the strobes often make it difficult to see the photographer clearly. So we just focus on the lens.

"For new models and photographers alike, I think it important to avoid any social interchange with your clients. Keep everything on a businesslike level. This will prevent possible personal discomfort later."

Insider: Jill Johnson, Female Fashion Model

Jill Johnson has appeared in many U.S. magazines, but her first modeling assignment was in France while spending a "junior year abroad" as a USC student from Berkeley. She worked in Europe, but returned to New York to finish her education. On her return, she felt that while she looked "right" for the European market, she did not for the U.S. Though American, she thought she seemed "too French" or "too Italian" and wanted that "well-scrubbed American" look. To change her appearance and model look, she met with U.S. photographers. Her new look succeeded, and she began appearing in ads for a women's hair spray, cigarettes, jewelry, and fashion photography in newspapers, magazines and catalogs.

When Johnson needs new pictures, she approaches the photographer she feels can best produce what she wants. If they decide they can work together, they do so, creating what they both need for their portfolios. She confirmed model agency practices of contacting photographers to work cooperatively with new models to help prepare books. So the photographer looking for a model should consider this approach.

I was amused at Johnson's frequent references to "the camera" instead of the "photographer." She put the photographer in the same role as the director in movie or TV production, and thus her response was more to the person giving the direction than to the person holding the camera.

In discussing her role as a model, I asked her to describe her methods of work and her feelings about photographers. She emphasized how important it was to relate to the camera, saying, "You really have to block out all other elements, everything else except the shooting, because with so many people around a major ad agency shooting, if you let yourself become aware· of them, it's going to hamper you. You have to concentrate on what you are doing, what image you are portraying. Up to the shooting you have to work with everyone, but once the shooting starts, it's you and the camera alone."

I asked her if she offers input to a shooting, or if she leaves it entirely to the photographer or ADs. She plays it both ways; participating and offering input, and is pleased if her suggestions are followed, but if she senses resistance, she backs off. She doesn't attempt to steer younger photographers as she knows they are in a learning situation, just as she too went through one, and have to work out problems without help.

As for industry criticism of models not showing up on time or arriving unprepared to work, e.g., without hair and nails done, etc., she agreed that there was some truth in it and photographers are becoming increasingly concerned since it affects the shooting. She spoke of a model on a national cosmetic ad who did not show up at all and even her agency didn't know where she was. It does not happen too often, but evidently it has been happening often enough for photographers to start contemplating action through their union. Johnson assured me that she and most of her colleagues are professionals, knowing too, if complaints get back to the agencies, it hurts the models, as their agencies will stop assigning work to them.

Fashion photography has its own star system. When Johnson faces a photographer who is acting like a star, she tries to defuse the situation by keeping things light, and not bowing to pomposity or unreasonable demands. She behaves as a professional. She also acknowledges that some models develop the same "star" attitudes and then it's up to the photographer to deal with it on a level that will ensure getting good pictures.

Interview
Arnold Newman
Photographer

Arnold Newman is one of the finest portrait and still-life photographers I know. With an enviable fifty-four-year record of achievement, he is still active with portrait sittings, editorial assignments, teaching and lecturing. When he is not on assignment all over the world, his busy studio on Manhattan's West Side is buzzing with activity as he, his wife, "Gus," and assistants keep a demanding schedule of work going full steam. In recent years, he told me, he has begun to enjoy teaching more than ever, and passing his experience on to new and younger photographers.

He began as an art student, and though he doesn't feel it absolutely necessary, he considers it great training for the new photographer to have an understanding of the history of art and photography. He felt he was lucky to have had very good art teachers in basics who encouraged him to examine new and "crazy" artists of the mid-thirties — Picasso, Matisse, Braque, and others.

He started at the University of Miami. After two years he was offered a job in a Philadelphia department store making inexpensive portraits. More important, it put him in close touch with good photographer-friends Ben Somoroff, Ben Rose and Sol Mednick, young promising photographers of the time. All had studied earlier with Alexey Brodovitch, the legendary teacher, art director and graphics editor of *Harper's Bazaar*, whose influence has touched so many great contemporary photographers.

Those student days and early times were important stepping-stones for Newman and his friends. They would work all day in classrooms, studios or at outside jobs, and then spend half the night talking and exploring their whole new visual world. He feels it was one of the most exciting times of his life. Though he experimented a great deal in photography, he never lost sight of his own art outlook and training.

He came to New York in 1941 for three days to seek advice of others as to whether he should pursue photography seriously as a profession. Among them was Beaumont Newhall, Director of the Department of Photography at the Museum of Modern Art. Newhall not only enouraged Newman, but astounded him by purchasing some of his pictures for the Museum. He also sent him to famed pioneer photographer Alfred Stieglitz, who also provided considerable inspiration. In that three-day period, Newman was offered a two-man show with Ben Rose, which opened that fall and changed both their lives.

Newman returned to Florida to take a better-paying job similar to the one in Philadelphia. His salary doubled—to $30 a week, and it also helped him sharpen his executive and business skills. He earned enough to buy a Speed Graphic, received permission from his employers to set up a darkroom, and learned to process and print the photographs he made on an experimental basis. Not having the opportunity to take formal courses in photography, he began learning in a unique way, by sending contact prints to his friends in Philadelphia for critiques—while he continued to experiment.

He spent the war years in Florida, moving to New York in 1946 where he received his first assignments from *LIFE* and other magazines and participated in group shows at the Museum of Modern Art. So it would seem that Newman started at the top instead of climbing up the rungs of the ladder slowly. *Harper's Bazaar* tried to make him a fashion photographer. Not caring much for fashion, he resisted those pressures, choosing to widen his horizons with still lifes, which he loved and in which he soon became expert. He is known as much for them as for his masterful portraits.

Advertising photography, always lucrative, crooked its finger at him, and after acquiring an agent he began getting assignments. He told me that while it was always traditional in editorial photography for the photographers and editors to discuss assignments in a *vis-a-vis* situation, it rarely happened in advertising. He felt then, and still does, that the agencies always seem to limit the creative input of the photographers, who come into the picture relatively late in the planning, almost when the shooting starts. While he likes and gets along with most agency people he deals with, he also thinks the personal insecurities of others taught him to be more selective in the type of advertising work he accepts, so his need for an agent disappeared. Instead he moved into corporate work where he could command equally high fees for annual reports and executive portraits, with fewer esthetic inhibitions.

Over the years Newman has increased his income significantly through the sale of prints via the gallery route, which he finds personally satisfying. In the early 1970s when he began selling to galleries, his sales brought about $125 per print. Today the same print sells for closer to $1,000, often much higher, and he has broadened to the museum market. He just told me that he has made a substantial sale to the National Portrait Gallery, which is also circulating a nationwide exhibit of his work which first opened in Washington in April 1992. He has also produced nine books, including *One Mind's Eye* and *Artists*. His latest, *Arnold Newman's Americans*, published in 1992, is a combined effort of the National Portrait Gallery, The Smithsonian Institution and Bulfinch Press.

The mailer is an important promotional tool for the younger photographer, and Newman has had success with it, with the response far in excess of anything he had anticipated. He noted that immediate reactions are often slow, but in time bring positive results, some occurring as much as four or five years later. Newman is a strong believer in the photographer keeping his name alive and before the public.

Portraiture, Newman says, is quite different from other forms of photojournalislm because so much effort must be spent in producing a single usable photograph. While other photo assignments can frequently produce several finished pictures in one day's work, and may result in many printed pages, a single portrait or still life can take much more time and not achieve more than the one or two pages allocated in the layout. The end result must be totally satisfying to the photographer.

This is the critical issue and may not necessarily be what the client expects. When one is doing a private portrait sitting, there has to be satisfaction on the part of the person photographed, but if the portrait is of a prominent person for editorial purposes, the views of the editor and the photographer become paramount. Newman's spectacular mid-sixties portrait of the head of the Krupp works in Germany, Baron Alfried Krupp, portrayed the man in a sinister manner, which obviously made the sitter quite unhappy, but the editors were ecstatic. It has become one of Newman's most famous photographs. These are the criteria Newman operates by and why his high fees are accepted.

In discussing fees for a young portrait photographer, Newman is reluctant to have his pricing scale used as a guideline because of his extremely high professional stature, but he freely advises young photographers who approach him on practices and procedures. As for specific pricing advice, he suggests the young photographer use the well-thought-out ASMP guidelines. He commented that the beginning professional also has to carefully assess where in the "pecking order" he stands in his profession in order to arrive at appropriate fees.

He noted that in their eagerness to make sales, young photographers tend to forget the hidden costs of quality printing. Unlike editorial work, which usually results in the delivery of a single print or transparency to an editor, the portrait sitting often calls for many prints, most of which will not be used for graphic reproduction, but as "display" items, so the need for meticulous print quality is extremely important. If the young photographer does not charge enough for the sitting, or fails to charge enough for the required number of prints, he will ultimately lose money or at best make very little. He also advises the young photographer that not only must he be realistic about time spent on the sitting, but also give equal consideration to darkroom and printing time, travel time to and from a location, and even time for preshoot interviewing or preparations.

As the portrait photographer is essentially a "location" photographer, he depends a great deal on assistants, and usually the charges for them are built into his fees as part of the overall package, sometimes on a specific cost basis. Newman found early in his career there was psychological value in this practice. When assigned by an important magazine to photograph a high official or other prominent person, he would himself lose credibility if he had to be a packhorse for his equipment and set up lights. If the photographer's creativity is what is being paid for, it is a waste of money for the client to pay him large fees to be a porter or electrician.

When a photographer reaches Newman's status, and has built a file of portraits of famous people, a problem over secondary rights arises. What happens when some news magazine or other publication calls Newman and wants to use one of his photographs? Under the copyright law, if there has been no signed "work-for-hire agreement" (see chapter ten), and there usually is none in the case of a portrait sitting of a prominent personality, the photographer would have the legal right to resell that picture for publication elsewhere. But Newman treasures his personal relationships with his clients and would never under any circumstances release a photograph he made without the prior permission of that person. If the photographer expects to maintain the trust of his clients, he must scrupulously guard their privacy, even though it may mean the loss of extra revenue.

He also spoke of occasions when he has photographed situations, not people, while under corporate assignment. What happens if there is a secondary use for one of these photographs? Newman feels this is a negotiable matter and should be discussed with the client, but the client's wishes should be respected in the interest of good personal public relations.

Even though Newman does much location work, the studio is an important base for him. It is his anchor and perhaps his security blanket. For those slack periods, he told us with some gallows humor, "You have to build in the cost of a couple of nervous breakdowns." He does his best to keep his staff going with back-up printing for galleries, cataloging, contact printing, filing, etc. He also considers himself a good businessman and when he is busy and earning money, he does not rush right out and buy every electronic gadget on the market or a new sports car or stereo system whether he needs it or not.

Freelance photographers (at least some he knows) seem to have a penchant for building up lousy credit ratings, but he has always maintained the highest possible one. This too is professionalism and building the aura of reliability. His editors know from experience that, come what may, Newman will be available to deliver something exceptional, on time and to the point. This is survival at the highest level.

As a sound business procedure, he suggests that in every portrait sitting, especially those involving executives or personalities who may rise to a higher fame (or notoriety), there should be a letter of agreement as to what is being purchased and what secondary rights each party obtains. Newman feels that his clients are entitled to any use of one (or a few) pictures of each take, but when unanticipated usages come up, while the rights to use those pictures clearly rest with the client, there should also be additional remuneration to the photographer. He reserves for himself the right to use them in books, exhibits, lectures or noncompetitive media. If on occasion he gives up all rights, then he feels he should be compensated commensurately. Most professional societies recommend a fee equal to three or four times the original fee for the surrender of all rights. This is another form of keeping the photographer's work alive and having him share in the fruits of secondary usage.

Chapter Four
Building Your Portfolio: First Contacts and Presentations

The thought of making first contacts can be intimidating to new photographers. Some approach them with trepidation, others with confidence. What most new photographers fail to realize is that people need to buy photographs or photographic services as much as the photographer needs to sell them. Photo buyers would not grant interviews if it were otherwise.

The goal of the photographer is to have his work seen and accepted. All other factors are secondary, and the photographer should not try any psychological ploy or approach other than simple, no-nonsense procedures of dealing directly with those interested in seeing and possibly using his photographic abilities.

The chances are that the people you will come in contact with are experienced in their fields, perhaps are older, and maybe just a little wiser, and any attempt to con them or fool them will only result in failure of the interview. While there are some photographers who are better salesmen than craftsmen there aren't too many of them around, and it is your pictures that will prove to be the ultimate measurement. Primary to any interview or bid for work is your showcase, portfolio or, in ad lingo, your "book."

Putting a portfolio together is one of the most important things you do before entering the marketplace, and your second most important professional decision (the first being the decision to become a professional). What you present, and to whom, is paramount. It is the only way you can demonstrate to the buyer what you are capable of doing and perhaps trigger ideas for work.

Portfolios are as individual as photographers themselves. There are no fixed ways of presenting your work. It can be in the form of prints, tearsheets (pages from printed publications), and/or transparencies either for projection or light box viewers. For many years some photographers and agents have transferred all material onto slides and show it by projection from carousel trays. But there have been many changes in the way art directors or picture editors (PEs) are looking at work, and one of those changes has been a growing aversion to projection, primarily because viewers are given little choice in how material is presented. For a more amusing overview, note the comments by a tough editor on page 45, and other comments that follow.

In the late 1970s when videotape suddenly became "state of the art," photographers started putting their material on videotape or motion picture reels, complete with soundtracks. No more. The ADs and PEs haven't got room in their offices, or the time to chase down the projection gear. Yet some clients are not averse to projection, so the best advice I can give you is that you call and clear it beforehand.

Here is some general advice for selecting the material for your portfolio:

Don't show everything. Many new photographers make the mistake of including everything they have ever shot, without real thought as to whether the pictures are good, bad or indifferent. If you are just starting out, it is highly likely that your material will have a scattered effect because you are probably trying to get a foot into too many doors at once, with the result that you disperse your photographic energies. A bank of experience is required before most editors are willing to take a chance on you by giving you an assignment or starting to use you as a source of stock photography. In effect, you have to develop your own experience and prove your own creativity and/or competence.

I have interviewed many prominent editors, art buyers and art directors (see discussions with Picture Editor (PE) Michele Stephenson of *TIME* magazine and Art Buyer Tim Lovett from the DDB-Needham agency). They each have different needs, they each are constantly having to look at new work, they are both very busy doing their jobs. But when I asked what they wanted to see in the way of new work from a photographer, they were in total agreement. Simply: NOT MUCH [in the way of quantity].

They want to see enough pictures to show your capabilities, but they are more impressed with ten smashing images than fifty so-so ones. To repeat a phrase you will hear a hundred times in a hundred interviews, the people you show your pictures to are looking for a "point of view," or a style. By the time you reach a potential client, your technical ability has to be a given, and not in question.

I suggest that you build your portfolio by presenting pictures you made on your own "assignments," until such time as you can collect actual reproductions of photographs in print that will substitute for the self-assigned photographs.

Demonstrate your ability to handle an assignment. Remember that the editors or picture buyers don't want to see a lot of unconnected, unrelated photographs that merely say, "I know how to make an exposure and develop a roll of film" and nothing more. What they want to see is your ability to handle an assignment intelligently and produce a fine set of photographs from it.

Be warned about "speculation" photography. It is one thing to create your own assignments, produce the pictures, and use them either for your own portfolio or even to try to market them independently, but quite another ball game to do a "trial" assignment for a magazine that thinks they are going to get you to work for them for nothing, or owe you nothing if the "assignment" doesn't pan out.

Be appropriate: analyze the market to determine your selection. Do not approach any picture buyer without having a pretty good idea of the kind of material the organization uses. Do your homework. And don't insult the intelligence of the person you are seeking by coming unprepared or with inappropriate material.

Demonstrate the quality of your work. In assessing what to show, the experience of the photographer is vital. It is, of course, advisable to show reproductions of work already in print. If your work has not been reproduced, try quality black-and-white photographs with content that has meaning for the person to whom you are showing it, presented in a way that can be accomplished easily, quickly, and without flowery or confusing ostentation.

Guidelines for Compiling an Appropriate Portfolio

Portfolios have to be developed to the needs of the picture buyers you are going to approach. Here are some guidelines for assembling a portfolio for editorial, advertising, fashion, public relations and industrial purposes.

The Editorial Portfolio

Newspapers: The key here is an understanding of the form of journalism you are trying to practice. If it is spot news, the pictures to show are obviously news situations — fires, accidents, political occasions or celebrity interviews, sports events, homemaking or entertainment. As a beginner, you are unlikely to have many tearsheets. But local news is one medium you have a reasonably good chance of covering without formal press credentials. And while on that subject, let's talk a little about credentials and the so-called "press cards."

Unless they are specifically issued by bona fide press organizations such as newspapers, press syndication services, agencies, major wire services, or a magazine publications group, forget press cards. The use of a sticker with the word "Press" on a car is for the most part meaningless and will cut no ice with anyone in authority. Also in some cities where relationships between the working press and local police have not been of the best, a "press card" other than an official police card, can make that car the target of a host of summonses.

In most major cities, to obtain proper press accreditation, your employing paper or agency will issue a letter to the police or other security authorities, e.g. the Secret Service for presidential coverages, requesting "press courtesy" which means the issuance of an official press card. Those cards as a rule are the only ones that will be recognized and current custom seems to be a bunch of them hung over the neck of the reporters or photographers on a chain where they can readily be seen, and with different cards necessary for access to different areas. I've seen ads in photo publications for "genuine" press cards for a price. Don't waste your money: They are not worth the paper they are printed on.

Covering local press events in a small town or local area without official press credentials is easier because there are generally few local newspapers issuing press identification, and crowd control is of such limited effort that almost any medium-length telephoto lens will get you "over" the police or fire lines. In this way you can easily cover most news events that happen, and you need not be on the line to make good photographs.

These events make excellent material to build a portfolio of pictures for presentation to news editors. Frequently they can be sold on the spot to papers or publications and when reproduced, you have the added advantage of a bona fide tear sheet for your portfolio. A few sales or placements in your local paper should in time also accord you some recognition, and it is likely that local papers will eventually issue you some sort of credentials that will get you in a little closer to what is happening.

The installation of a "scanner" type radio in your car or studio will be of help in getting you to a site where something of news importance has occurred. But we must remind you that crashing police lines, developing an overinflated sense of importance and a disregard of the authorities are the quickest ways to get you tossed out or put on a permanent blacklist among police and fire officers. Also, creating a false impression of being affiliated with a particular press group can sometimes run you into serious problems, and occasionally an arrest.

Aside from spot news, there are many other photographic situations that should be covered in order to prepare portfolio material for the news world. Sports, for example, can easily be covered from the stands with long lenses.

Feature stories for papers are even easier to shoot and require even less accreditation. You pick the subject—a school, library, public building or road situation that's come under fire, or a water crisis. These items are of interest to a local paper, and how you handle the coverage of this sort of story and its presentation in your portfolio are what will make points for you.

General Magazines: The editorial world of magazines is not much different. There are many kinds. News magazines such as *TIME, FORTUNE, Newsweek*. Consumer magazines such as *Good Housekeeping, Better Homes & Gardens, Gourmet* or *Vogue* or *Sport's Illustrated*, covering homemaking, gardening, food, fashion, sports, or other specialized subjects; and the trade magazines such as *Iron Age*, or computing magazines that are focused on a specific industry or type of business. They are all very different and also very similar in their needs and methods of operation. One good method is to conceive short story plans and execute them the way you would if you were on assignment from a magazine or book publisher. They don't have to be complicated, expensive stories requiring travel, lighting or very special arrangements. Simply choose a theme you think might be of interest to the magazine you want to approach, contact the people involved to get their cooperation and shoot the story on your own, but do not give the people you are photographing the impression you are on an actual assignment. Edit it professionally. You might try laying it out with prints scaled to the layout, using the publication's page measurements.

Vary this approach, depending on whom you are planning to contact. I suggest you present more than one story. By presenting short, tight coverages on hypothetical situations in several departments, you will be able to convince the editors that you have the flexibility and skill to handle a variety of assignments within the same publication.

The same is true for rural-oriented publications. If you are in a rural area and the scene there interests you, this is where you should start cultivating your personal crop of stories.

Consumer and Trade Magazines: The same rules apply here, only the focus has to be narrower and in line with what they publish or what interests them. Again there is an infinite number of story ideas, but the important thing to remember is to study the publication closely and shoot material along those lines. We do not suggest that you copy their layouts—try to show *your* creativity by demonstrating how you would handle this story, either differently or better or both. Remember: a little humility can go a long way, so don't tell them how to run their publication.

Even a travel magazine can be approached in this manner. You don't have to be French to do a story with a French flavor. A proposed barge trip down the Rhine or Seine can be demonstrated from the decks of the Delta Queen or other excursion boat near your home.

The Advertising Portfolio

The advertising market is totally different from the editorial or public relations worlds, though their media goals are almost the same — the printed page of a magazine or newspaper, or the television screen. Not only is the advertising market totally different from most other commercial markets, but also there seem to be special ground rules about presenting portfolios and other materials. Tailor your material accordingly and consider the opinions of the agency art directors contained in this book.

Look at the work in the different media and isolate them by product. Is there any strong point of similarity in the liquor ads, the fashion layouts, the house furnishings or the material prepared for the airlines, auto companies, whatever? Study those similarities and differences. See what appeals to you. Think about how you would approach the problem. Can you do as well or better? If you think· this is the kind of work you want, then show what you can do to fill comparable spaces.

There is also a place in your portfolio for photography not directly related to a specific campaign you are targeting. This section should be tight and be well presented simply as an introductory group or one at the back of your portfolio.

There is no question that art directors want to see fresh and unusual work not directly related to what they are trying to sell to their clients, though it is often hard to get these ideas past them. There is room in a portfolio for purely experimental work, presented as such to demonstrate your own creativity to the art director. Thoughts that spring from these presentations may well lead to assignments.

The Fashion Portfolio

You do not need an expensive studio to make fine fashion photographs, nor do you need 10,000 watt/seconds of strobe capability, two assistants or a stylist. Earlier the fashion magazines were not as much interested in the picture story approach as they were in great takes of various types of clothing. But that too is changing. More and more as you thumb through the pages of the current fashion magazines, you are sometimes hard put to figure out where an editorial piece ends and an ad layout begins, because some current ad campaigns use many consecutive pages often laid out in a documentary format. Still, in many fashion magazines the closest they come to story treatments is when they cover a designer's "collection." If fashion is your interest, then talk with buyers at your local department or specialty stores to find out what is currently in vogue.

Models for fashion and theatrical shooting are relatively easy to come by. I do not recommend using your friends, spouses or siblings unless they have had some modeling experience, because they will be just as green as you. Many men and women have had some experience as professional models and most will gladly trade off a set of pictures of themselves for some of their time posing for you. Clothes can frequently be borrowed on the same exchange basis.

In making fashion photographs for portfolio use, it is wise to watch the major fashion magazines to see current *trends*. But observing a trend and being aware of it is not a license to slavishly copy it. Closely watching the kind of photography that is being published, however, will show you opportunities for creating your own visualizations and give you ideas for your own pictures.

You can find substitute backgrounds for the exotic ones that the fashion books are always pushing. Remember, it is not so much the background that is important but the foreground—the clothes on the model and how they are displayed. While it is true that a great many fashion pictures are made against rolls of seamless paper or front or rear projections of the South Sea Islands, a good many do use locations that, while not dominant, are nevertheless important. Include some location pictures in your fashion portfolio even if the locales you are using are just a local park, beach, restaurant or airport.

Above all, don't settle for one fine photo of one fine garment, but approach it from many angles. This holds true for any product photographs you are directing toward advertising. Show your ability to deal with them in a variety of ways and do not submit just one view or application.

The Public Relations Portfolio

Is it a product or situation that a public relations house wants pushed? Think about it and show how it should be handled. Picture this approach on your own and show it to the public relations house or the public relations director of the company you are seeking an interview with. However, do not forget that the main reason for public relations programs is to get *editorial* space for their clients. So in addition to those eye-catchers you show, develop some plan for media distribution that will complement the client's efforts.

Industrial and Annual Report Portfolios

Once again try to find some credible situation that you can get to and create your own concepts. There are many industrial photographs that can be made without access to a steel mill floor or the machine shops. Give thought to the end result that the corporation is trying to achieve in its annual report and try to enter by the back door. By that I mean get previous reports from banks, brokerage firms, or even call or write the company itself for copies of annual reports covering the past few years so you can understand their viewpoint. As mentioned in the guidelines for editorial work, do your homework. Learn as much about a company and its products (or services) as you can. You will make a much better impression on their PR department if they think you know a good deal about them.

I have discussed major market areas and what I feel portfolios should contain. Obviously I cannot advise you on how to approach every possible outlet for your work, but I am trying to encourage you to analyze any field that interests you, present relevant material and not inundate your viewer with nonessentials.

Portfolio Formats and Presentation

There is no single method of effectively presenting one's work. What may be good for the editorial world could be all wrong for the advertising market and vice versa. Portfolios have to be flexible and easy to change as one grows in ability, understanding and accomplishment.

Regardless of where the portfolio is directed, it should be simple, accessible and portable. Photos have to be carefully printed, clean, fresh-looking, spotted and neatly trimmed. Transparencies should be mounted in protective sleeves if they are small, such as 35mm or even 120mm formats. Larger sizes should be on lightweight cardboard mounts with the surfaces of the transparencies protected by frosted glassine or acetate.

A note of warning: Film chemists advise that some of the plastic sleeves on the market may cause chemical reactions and damage to color emulsions if the pictures are left in them for extended periods of time. (The same is true of envelopes used to store black-and-white negatives. The old kraft paper type jackets have a high sulfur content which can damage emulsions, so be sure to use a chemically inert liner for such jackets.) Be sure that the brand you are using is totally chemically inert and will have no effect on your transparencies. The better supply houses will be able to supply these materials.

Color prints or tearsheets from magazine or books should be dry mounted on thin cardboard or plastic and laminated to suitable materials. Laminating is an effective way of preserving fragile tearsheets or scarce prints before inserting them in a portfolio. Even though the dry-mounting process is not new, it is still a viable, useful and inexpensive process. Moreover, laminating materials can be bought in rolls and applied with a dry-mounting press. This will save much money for the photographer in the long run.

Portfolio Assembly

The most common portfolio format is a leather-, vinyl- or other fabric-covered volume of ring-bound envelopes of cellulose or plastic with paper inserts that can be bought at most art supply houses. The sizes range from 5″ × 7″ to newspaper-page-sized envelopes with pages as large as 18″ × 24″. They frequently are paired with large, zippered enclosures, or the ring mechanism is sometimes bound into the enclosure itself. Ring-binding mechanisms vary with the manufacturer. Some are simple holders with three snap rings; others have whole rows of shark-like teeth pretending to be snap rings, some with as many as twenty to a page. Most of the plastic holders scratch and tear easily and thus have to be handled gently, and there is no way of guaranteeing this when someone other than you is leafing through the pages. The zippered enclosures tend to sag at the bottom where the weight is and this frequently makes for a messy and difficult-to-open presentation. Nor are they cheap. A portfolio with a hard cover and ten insert sheets lists for about seventy-five dollars with extra acetate sheets costing about three to five dollars each.

I have never cared much for this type of portfolio, but one advantage they offer is that the sheets can be replaced easily and the makeup of the portfolio changed rapidly. The plastic sleeves themselves should be kept clean and free of scratches and be replaced regularly to preserve the appearance of the artwork. Because of the expense of the sheets and the constant need for replacement, some photographers have given up on this system and have substituted ring-bound laminated sheets, or even heat-sealed book-like binders that can easily be wiped off and resist scratching.

When using lightweight plastic laminates, you can also punch the edges and use vari-colored plastic binding rings or new heat-sealed binders which make, in effect, a permanent book. Spiral plastic binding requires special machines for punching and spiral application. They make for attractive presentations and you have the advantage of being able to change material easily to prepare specific portfolio presentations for specific projects. If you are reluctant to invest in plastic binding equipment or heat sealers, you can easily find a printing or binding shop in the classified pages of your phone book that will do this work inexpensively.

Another option is a strong vinyl or fabric-covered light wooden case which looks like a king-sized attache case and is large enough to accommodate larger portfolio pages plus extra materials such as mailing pieces, several annual reports and even some books. Or if you really want to show off, there are the stressed aluminum cases, some in anodized finishes that are waterproof and which can even be sat on in a crowded train or station. Their higher cost pays for itself in durability. There are many other effective designs.

Numerous other portfolio presentation materials are available. Some are called "century boxes" or "clamshells." There is a complicated French system that will combine mixed sizes of slides, transparencies and prints.

An alternative for laminated material are foam-core mounting boards that, while somewhat thicker than cardboard, are extremely light, and a large number of them can be carried in a portfolio box or attache case. The problem with foam-core is that it cannot be punched or bound, and it tends to crumble at the edges unless bound with tape. The up side of foam-core is that it is light, can be cut easily with a sharp knife or razor blade, and individually mounted photographs can be shuffled and reshuffled to follow a presentation or story line.

In photojournalism presentations where the story itself is as important as the images, the system used by the University of Missouri School of Journalism in their "Pictures of the Year" competitions is worthy of note. Here a story layout is reorganized by the photographer using lightweight mounting boards (11″ × 14″ to 14″ × 17″) as "magazine" pages. The layout is planned in story form, but instead of punching, ring mounting, or enclosing in glassine envelopes, the boards are joined accordion-style in sections of two to five boards, using hinges of two-inch aluminized binding tape ("gaffer's" tape). *After the boards are taped together*, the photographs can be dry mounted in place *over the tape hinges* and laminates or protective clear sprays can subsequently be applied. With this method the boards are kept together and in the presentation order you wish.

The board sections are easily displayed by standing them up easel style on a desk or table, or your viewers can leaf through them on a desk in what amounts to double-page spreads as they might appear in a large picture magazine. This method of display can even be used for mini-exhibits on a conference table where people can walk around and view them from all sides, as the backs of the boards can be used for other layouts. Or, since they are freestanding, a number of them can be set up simultaneously on one table.

Eight to ten of these storyboards can be carried in an attache case or portfolio box. This system gives the photographer the opportunity of displaying from ten to one hundred photographs, and the pace of exhibiting is controlled. Also it will restrain the photographers from overloading the viewer. This method is effective in showing editorial material, and can be used well in advertising.

But whatever methods of presentation are used, they must be cohesive, simple and not demanding of too much time from the viewer.

Where can you get these presentation materials? Almost any art or photo supply house will have much of it, and there are several organizations which specialize in supplying presentation as well as archival quality materials for photographers and artists. In addition to good art supply houses which can be found in most larger cities, I recommend two other sources: Light Impressions, 439 Monroe Avenue, Rochester, NY 14607, and the Maine Photographic Resource, Rockport, ME 04856. Both issue catalogs and both sell high quality materials.

Projecting Your Portfolio

As noted earlier, the once popular method of projecting 35mm photographs is falling into disfavor. Why? Because many editors do not like to be locked into screen presentations in general, preferring instead to lay a "first" exposure side by side with secondaries, to examine them all on a light table with a magnifying loupe. Many professionals worry, too, about physical projection of 35mm color transparencies and the dangers involved. While most color film manufacturers are evasive on the subject, there is no question that continued exposure to light will in time fade almost any color material. A great many photographers (and some photo agencies) therefore believe that shooting a concentrated blast of high intensity light from a projector through a transparency will hasten fading and possibly cause heat damage to the picture from the projection lamp, even if heat absorbing glasses and a cooling fan are built into the projector.

The editors of one magazine also found, when dealing with photographs of women with large areas of exposed skin, that the regular projector lamps were not color-corrected, and what appeared great on the projection room screen often failed badly in the color engraver's cameras. Hence most color transparencies for reproduction are usually viewed on table or wall viewers featuring fully color-corrected light sources. But if you still favor using projected materials in your portfolio, have good copies made for projection rather than using your originals, which should be released only for engraving.

Once an amusing incident occurred when I was ready to deliver a finished story to a veteran editor I had known and worked with for years but who had since changed magazines. I had not formally presented a story to him for some time, and when it was ready, called and said I was coming down to show it. I also asked if he had a projector at the office. He said he didn't.

"Okay," I said, "I'll bring one."

"The heck you will!" he growled.

"How come?" I asked. "Don't you want me to project my work?"

Over the line came a roar I could have heard over those 200 miles without the benefit of a phone. "I refuse to be a prisoner of the photographers!" Those photographs were examined on a light table with a magnifying glass.

This is not only true of this particular editor but of many editors who don't want to be trapped into rigid viewing formats. So bear this in mind if you are thinking about projecting a portfolio. And repeating my earlier advice, ask in advance how the editor or art director feels about projection of photographs.

This is not as critical a factor with ad agencies, who usually prefer larger format film size—from 6 cm×6 cm or 6 cm×7 cm to 8″×10″ and even 11″×14″. These formats cannot be projected except by overhead projectors or recopied back to 35mm. Even if they use 35mm, prints are often made so they can be retouched, or now with electronic imaging, retouching can be done more efficiently during the separation process.

But don't rule projection of photographs out yet, because even your best black-and-white photographs can be shown in this manner and look quite handsome indeed. One way to do this is to copy the black-and-white photographs onto 35mm Kodachrome stock which can then be projected as crisp black-and-white images on the screen. Or, using the same system, you can "create" a dummy newspaper or magazine layout with your photographs forming the picture story, and make a projection slide to show the entire page, with your photographs in scale for the story. You can also use this system to copy magazine editorial or ad layouts and avoid having to present large, or impossible to get, tearsheets of previous work. Color film works beautifully for black-and-white copying, and color background sheets add to the attractiveness of a black-and-white presentation. (Note: Many small newspapers are using color-negative film stock for superior black-and-white printing. See page 312.)

There is still a downside to leaving portfolios behind. Even considering the changes in attitudes by agency art buyers and art directors about seeing new portfolios, there are problems that still must be kept in mind.

One photographer's representative told me that she knew of materials taken from portfolios by art directors or other personnel in the art departments, not for unauthorized use, but for personal home or office decoration. These usually were prints or unusual tearsheets, and although this doesn't happen very often, it evidently has occurred enough times to warrant asking the question: How do you prevent this?

I don't know. Accusing an art director of theft is not the best way of making a friend in an agency, and other than fastening the pictures securely via the dry-mounting process or putting a little card in with the portfolio saying, "Please don't walk or spill coffee on or swipe the artwork," there is probably little you can do except look at it from the bright side. If it was so attractive as to make it worth swiping, then maybe it was that good as art material, so you quietly replace it. If it's swiped a second time, then perhaps you really have something.

Selectivity in a Portfolio

I have repeatedly remarked on the necessity for selectivity when showing a portfolio to a potential buyer. Selectivity also means not burying the buyer under a flood of pictures. Remember the adage "less is more." Not only do editors get cross-eyed after staring at hundreds of pictures in the course of a day's work, they probably begin to feel threatened by the constant barrage of images over their desks that begins to take on the appearance of a flood.

If you approach an editor with a huge number of photographs, he is going to be turned off even before he starts to go through them. But there are the other extremes too.

There was a well-known and talented photographer who was famous not only for his great photography but for his incredible ego. He was once sent abroad to do a major assignment in a foreign country with the trip sponsored by business interests in the host nation. After about six months he was asked to show his backers what he had accomplished during that first phase and he agreed. When his sponsors appeared at an elegantly catered meeting, our photographer friend, with great panache, showed just three photographs. "That," he announced, "is the overture. In a year I'll present the entire symphony!" And he did.

The new photographer is not the legend this man was, and will have to show a lot more productivity for six months' work. But the incident does demonstrate the faith this photographer had in the efficacy of just a few photographs. I am not suggesting that you limit your showing to three pictures; I am suggesting that you choose what you show wisely and sparingly and not inundate your viewers. They won't like it and probably will not like you either as a result.

Mailers for Self-Promotion: A Growing Necessity in Advertising Photography

An increasingly important marketing tool for photographers in the commercial and advertising world is the mailer. Once considered of doubtful value because of high cost, it has now become a virtual necessity for any photographer competing for advertising work. Though photographers are not running into the stone walls they once did when trying to see an art director or art buyer, the sheer increase in traffic means they must stay aware of the talent available for almost any sort of advertising photography. Art Buyer Tim Lovett's (pages 79-81) experiences are typical.

He sees as many photographers as he can, not because he is a nice guy or is sensitive to the struggles of the artist, but because he must find the best possible talent for any campaign. But there is a limit to how many people he can see, and, more important, remember who they are. What is the alternative?

One increasingly popular method of attracting the attention of picture buyers is the mailing piece, which seems to work well in advertising, but perhaps less so in the editorial or regular commercial fields. Again, because so much advertising photography involves a single photograph in a single layout, a mailer made up of smashing individual photographs is bound to attract attention. But some ADs and art buyers say they do not want to see more than one good photograph on a mailer, and this creates undue cost problems for the photographer, especially the younger ones whose finances are limited.

There are, however, some ways of reducing the costs of production but that involves co-involvement with other self-promotion efforts. For some years now there has been a rash of expensively printed books (euphemistically called creative directories) of commercial photographers' work which are distributed free to art directors, art buyers, picture editors and other professional users of photography.

Who pays for this? The photographers do by taking high-priced space ads (generally from $1,500-$2,500 per page) and illustrating them with examples of their work. How effective they really are is debatable, because for every photographer or agent who praises them, I have met an equal number who feel they are economically unproductive. However, one of the side benefits of these ad placements is that publishers will sell print overruns of the ads which can be used as mailers. At this writing there are three principle publications which dominate this market.

They are *Adweek Portfolio; American Showcase*, which also publishes a few spin-off publications more specifically targeted at corporations who might be looking for photographers for their annual reports (*Corporate Showcase*), and a more graphic arts oriented publication (*Archive*); and the *Black Book*, which is reportedly the most successful (for whom ... the publishers?) but is also the recipient of many complaints about its peculiar size and the jam-packing of some 1,000 pages.

For several years the ASMP also got into this act but ultimately gave up when its own members began grumbling that the response received did not seem worth the high cost of admission. I interject the discussion of all of these books in this discussion of mailers because of the practice of photographers using additional printed sheets for mailers.

In my interview with Eileen Togashi, a photographer's representative (see page 246), she mentioned the use of postcards as mailers which seem to have had some success. She also refers to several mailing list sources that may be worthy of a photographer's investigation (see page 248). Other photographers use privately printed brochures as mailers, as does Gregory Heisler (see page 119) who is not following the rules and is preparing a series of mailers each with six images that tell specific stories, and which he feels will be more effective than single-image pieces.

But whether one uses the creative directory method of getting mailing pieces produced or has them privately printed, is that not expensive too? Certainly, but as noted there are ways of controlling costs.

Every mail piece that is going to an ad agency or other client must be attractive, eye catching, and professionally produced. Art directors, particularly the good ones, come high, but every photographer working in advertising or editorial photography will, by the time he is ready to produce his mailer, have made some personal contacts with ADs. It is hoped that one or more of them will design the photographer's mailer at little or no cost, and possibly assist with mechanical production and printing facilities to which they usually have access. All of this can be expensive and the young photographer must determine whether he can (1) produce outstanding material, (2) afford to have it printed well and (3) actually distribute large mailings to his audience in the most cost-effective way.

Another way of producing mailing items at relatively low cost is to make a deal with a local printer who often has extra space on a printing form. (See section on printing requirements, page 206.) A "form" is a term used in printing for the actual assembly of several pages on a printing press, usually in multiples of eight pages. Depending on the actual size of the page and the capacity of the press being used, as many as thirty-two or even sixty-four pages can be printed on one side of a single sheet of paper before it is folded and cut to page size. So if you can get together with a printer who is going to run some material in four-color on a form and he has unused space because some publication may, for instance, be only six pages on an eight-page form, or thirty pages on a thirty-two page form, he probably will be perfectly happy to run a piece for you on that same run. (Be sure to check with the post office on the maximum or minimum sizes they will accept for postcards because they do vary their specifications occasionally.)

You then would have to pay only for the separations and plate-making but not the press work and probably not even the paper, as the unused paper that is trimmed off the form would normally be scrapped. An arrangement like this, and even for the original separations and engravings, can be made at even lower cost if the printer "gangs up" your transparency(s) with others when he makes up a single large separation to be cut to size later.

This way will get you quality four-color mailing pieces for as little as 20 percent of the normal costs of one prepared exclusively for you. If you are conservative in the size of your printed matter, you might come up with as many as ten or more postcards on a "wasted" section of a form that will be far more useful than the single piece you might get otherwise. One problem with this, if you want to use the postcard type of mailer, is that the paper stock the printer is using for the other job you "piggy-backed" on may not be correct for cards. If this is the case, discuss it with the printer and it still might be cheaper to rerun that form with heavier stock than preparing an entire new press make-up operation.

There is another way that might save you money if you go to the postcard route, and that's to have your mailer made up by postcard printers, as their processes are geared to smaller form sizes. Again, use caution, see samples of their work and make sure all terms of price, delivery, quality control and safe return of originals are spelled out in writing on a purchase order. (Special note: There have been some complaints of postcard manufacturers overprinting personally ordered cards for their own use. Be aware of this and be sure to include your copyright notice on any work you send for reproduction. See page 273.)

What should a mailer have in it? This is debatable and may depend on the individual taste and style of the photographer . . . not to mention his ego. There should be at least one eye-catching and distinctive photograph or perhaps even several. I have seen some complicated mailing pieces that run to several pages of beautifully reproduced material, and I have seen many single pieces that have caught the eyes of art directors to the extent that they hung them in their own offices as display pieces. But the mailer is here to stay and is often the first means of contact with a client.

Along with smashing photos it should include minimal biographical material on the photographer, credits, and most important, how to get hold of him quickly, whether by phone, fax, beeper or even telex and cable if either the photographer or the client is separated by continental divides or bodies of water.

There has to be a compelling reason why the art buyer should hire you instead of someone he already knows or has used. Geography is often a factor, as many buyers prefer to save location expenses by using local people, and this is where your new editorial contacts with local publisher's bureaus and stringers is important. Your association with a production news agency (see page 249) is vital when it comes to shooting in a specific region. More than one ad agency AD or art buyer has contacted a news agency to see if one of their regionally located photographers is available for an advertising assignment.

In spite of the more recent shift to competent photographers of general subject matter, expertise in certain fields is also useful and can be important. Are you a graduate engineer in mining, or a graduate of a school of journalism, or what studies have you completed in the arts or sciences? Any background material that can make them believe you could be more useful to them than another photographer is important. Forget the self-addressed, stamped envelope. Any art director or buyer who is interested in reaching you is not going to worry about the price of a postage stamp or telephone call. And you shouldn't either. That's the least of your costs after you have spent years in school or thousands of dollars on the purchase of equipment, not to mention some not inconsiderable sums on promotion.

Dressing Appropriately for Interviews

After devoting so much attention to effective presentation of your work, do not forget your own appearance. For the most part you are dealing with stable and probably conservative companies or business institutions. Dress is important, if for no other reason than that it may be an indication of your personal ideas of tastefulness. Some ad agency art directors have cultivated an image to make it seem that their code of dress is strictly blue jeans and denim shirts. Don't believe it. These are for the most part affectations put on by a very few. Some clients will be personally repelled by the disreputable appearance of an artist, and who needs that? There is a definite consciousness about dress even in the supposedly casual atmosphere of the "typical" ad agency.

Appearance is even more important when dealing with conventional business firms. Large manufacturers, major publishers, financial institutions, educational organizations, etc., are apt to be less receptive to the photographer who comes in with total disrespect for his surroundings. Be aware of those you are dealing with and make your photographs the only criterion of whether you get an assignment. Do not introduce other factors that may negatively influence their decisions about your work.

I suggest that men wear a business suit or at least a sports jacket or blazer, shirt and tie. For women, simple classic dresses or skirts, pants and blouses with a jacket are wise choices.

There are other appearance factors such as personal cleanliness, and even smoking, which may have some effect on the person you are trying to see. You might ask (justifiably, perhaps) what all this has to do with your photography. You are probably right, nothing, but if the buyer takes offense and a dislike to you and you aren't that strong in experience or reputation, you may never get a chance to present your work—or at least present it in a favorable atmosphere.

I am not suggesting that if you are photographing a steel-making executive you should appear in a hard hat, nor are you expected to be wearing a business suit on a mill floor. But you should pay as much attention to your personal appearance as you can, and try to avoid offending or annoying anyone whose standards may be different from yours. It may not always be possible, but at least be aware of the possibilities and think these things out. It's all part of professionalism.

Making the Actual First Contact and Presentation

I touched briefly on areas of concentration and tried to allay the fears of the new photographer in making his first contacts, presentations, or getting his first jobs. (Note: Specialization is a key, and your decision about what to do has been made by now, I trust.) For those trying the journalism track the route is well marked by precedent. Pick up the phone, introduce yourself, and ask for an appointment.

For instance, getting to see the editors of the small-town papers is comparatively easy. Simply approach them—they are usually accessible. Also, a cold mail presentation is just as dubious as a cold "walk-in" to an editorial house. But what does the new photographer do about reaching people who are some distance away from home base? What does he do about reaching people in his own area?

If at all possible, the initial contacts should be in person. This can be costly and discouraging from a logistical standpoint, and there may be a tendency to want to use the mail instead. But if you consider the amount of time and money already invested in your career, the additional cost of some personal visits should be built into your general cost of getting started.

Choose a group of market possibilities in one locale and begin by making appointments either by phone or mail. Get the names, addresses and phone numbers, from the directories listed in chapter one. Make your conversations or letters direct and to the point. Give your name and the fact that you are a photographer specializing in a certain area and that you think your work is worth seeing because it may be of use to them. For out-of-town prospects, say that you are going to be in the buyer's area for a limited period of time, and since you live a distance away you would like to have an appointment to show your portfolio and meet him during that time. That's about it. If you have a mailer or some tearsheets you can spare, by all means include them in your mail contact.

It is inadvisable to mail photographs or portfolios for the first contact, without at least talking to the prospective client. There is no sense going to the expense of preparing and shipping a presentation if the person you are addressing is not interested in seeing it, and this should be clear in your conversations.

When an out-of-town appointment is scheduled, try to arrange additional interviews with other picture buyers during the same time period given for your primary contact. Allow enough time between appointments to cover goofs in schedules others give you. If you are contacting people in a large city the most you can hope to see in any one day is four or five people—two in the morning and two or three in the afternoon.

You may not yet be at the level of the "business lunch," but if you feel you can afford it, and think it might be worthwhile to pursue this course, there is no harm in trying to take the picture user to lunch, dinner or cocktails. But I advise against it until after the first contacts are made to avoid any appearance of impropriety.

If you tell someone you are coming from out of town for the express purpose of seeing him he will probably respect this and be responsible about keeping the appointment. A few won't. Also, some picture editors and art directors set limits on the time they will spend on seeing new work and try to make you fit into their schedules. Some won't even see you at all. But these are the hazards you must face.

But for the moment, you have made an appointment. Keep it and be on time. Even if you are kept waiting for what you think is a long period, be patient. It's your work that has to be sold and you are at their mercy. Don't show your irritation and don't get angry, especially when you are finally called in for the interview.

Remember the discussion of dress. Manners, too, are important. Egos are fragile in this business, and it's very easy to feel rejected or equally easy to come on too strong. Be at ease. Be confident in your own ability and don't let personality factors intrude. Build yourself up, but do it gracefully and with tact, and don't put yourself down. It's okay to say you're the best in the world, but only if you do it with some humor. Explain as briefly as possible beforehand what the photos you are showing are all about, but then let the pictures speak for themselves.

Many years ago when I made a presentation to the picture editor of a national magazine, I started to comment aloud on the pictures as he looked at them. That in itself was all right as I kept my comments fairly brief, until we came to one particular photo and I started to say, pointing to the upper right-hand corner of the print, "Up in this direction, out of camera range, was. . . ." And that was as far as I got because the editor exploded and said,

"Dammit! Don't ever tell me *what's not* in the picture. I'm only interested in what I can see." Not only was he angry, he was right. So never talk about something in a photograph that isn't there.

Do You Leave Your Portfolio or Not?

The problems of the art buyer, AD, or picture editor, having the time to review incoming work are real. Have respect for them. What happens after you have had your interview? What do you leave behind? You have to leave something. Some ADs, art buyers or picture editors may require that you leave your portfolio with them because they may want to show it to others. Do you accede to this request?

The answer is probably yes. But remember that it's absolutely essential to retain at least one duplicate, especially if you have others to show it to while waiting for return of the presentation you have left.

In our interviews with both editorial and advertising people (see pages 11 and 79), we have discussed both the dangers and the necessity of leaving portfolios behind. Take these matters into consideration as well as presentation concerns discussed below. They should all be weighed before you make your own decision.

You should have had some business cards printed by now which you can leave. Also, some photographers have made up 3″ × 5″ index cards and even "Rolodex" file card inserts with their names and pertinent information which are useful for a secretary's file. Others leave their mailers if they have any, or extra tearsheets. Do not leave original prints, whether black and white or color, original transparencies, or any other material that is difficult, costly, or impossible to duplicate.

If you do leave your portfolio behind, it is perfectly in order to request, "Please be responsible for this and let me have it back as soon as you have shown it." Or if there is going to be a long period between showings, say, "I will be happy to send you materials at a later date when you are ready."

You should be proud of your work, and you have a right not to have it abused or disregarded. You will find this approach quite in keeping with the practices of the editorial world, and I am happy to say, the advertising world is now trying to keep pace, especially those who have replaced the unfeeling and inefficient art secretary system with the concerned art buyer. In addition, some smaller agencies (out of the mainstream of New York, Chicago, and San Francisco) have become more accessible by setting aside conference rooms for visiting photographers and artists, into which they can herd all their art directors at the same time to look over the material and meet the photographers or agents. If you use the "accordion type" portfolio described on page 104, since it is freestanding, it is easy for several people to look at a presentation simultaneously. So again, do not be afraid to ask how a portfolio will be viewed and when you may expect its return.

The sad truth is that a young or new photographer's portfolio must truly be smashing to make the average art director vary from his practice of dealing only with photographers he has already used or heard about through his associates. Confronted with this, most art directors deny it and several have proved their veracity by pointing to work assigned to photographers that I and many of my contemporaries had never heard of, who were in their twenties and who by the strength of their work gained their confidence.

I also had an experience some years ago that was quite shocking and tells a lot about the ongoing problem of "bidding" for a job (see page 235) and also the earlier noted art secretary syndrome. I was called by a major agency to make a presentation on a subject on which I was an acknowledged expert (aerial photography). I was given an appointment and arrived with what I felt was an impressive presentation that included among other things, two prize-winning books that brought me several important TV interviews and many press clippings.

Naturally, the art secretary said I should leave the portfolio. I replied, "Nope. I was called in to make the showing, and by gosh I am going to make it myself or there will be no showing." She hurriedly relayed the message to the art director who came charging down the hall full of apologies and ushered me into his office. He also called in a fellow AD and both proceeded to go through my portfolio. Both said it was exactly what they were looking for, and told me that I would be hearing from them in a few days. Curiously, I was never asked at any time about production costs, fees, expenses, page or ad rates or anything at all regarding money.

Guess what happened? Right: Nothing. After a week I phoned the art director and asked how his project was coming. "Oh," he said, "we gave it to so-and-so because his price was way under yours."

"That's interesting," I said, "since we never discussed money at all."

As it happened, I knew "so-and-so" very well, so I called him and talked to him about it. "That's weird," he said, "I already had the purchase order for the job ten days before you even went up there."

"How about your prices?" I asked. And since he knew me and had a pretty good idea what I charged, he said, "I know what your rates are, and I assure you mine were no lower—in fact, they were probably a little higher." He even sent me a photocopy of the purchase order, and it was exactly as he had stated. It was issued before my interview and his price was slightly higher than I would have bid if I had been asked.

Still puzzled by all of this, I questioned other photographers and reps who had dealings with the same agency, and finally worked it out. It seems their client had a long history of not only wanting "bids," but having their agencies see more than one photographer on any job they did. So the AD went through the charade of having other photographers come in to make presentations, knowing full well he would not be using them, as he had already made up his mind who he wanted to use. No small wonder either, why the art secretary told me to "leave my portfolio" because she too knew it would never be looked at.

How prevalent is this sort of thing? It's hard to say and harder to prove. There are certain agencies that make it a rule to have their art directors look at many portfolios at one time, preferably without the photographer present, and other agencies do this with the photographer on hand. Also under the newer guidelines as practiced by Lovett and his colleagues, I think it may be worth taking the chance of leaving your book—provided you have a duplicate for other uses and further provided that a specific deadline is made for it to be picked up and returned. In fact it may be the only way your work will be seen.

Shipping Your Portfolio

Shipping unrequested portfolios by mail puts you in virtually the same category as leaving them at a receptionist's desk or tossing them overboard at sea in a wine bottle. You have no guarantee that they will be looked at, particularly if you ship them unannounced. Yet there may be times when it is physically impossible for you to call on an art director or picture editor in person because of distance, cost or other valid reasons.

If you do decide to use the mail or other transport as a means of contact, the basic question of what to submit to what type of publication or market remains unchanged. You have to be every bit as selective (if not more so in order to keep shipping costs down) as you would in a *vis-à-vis* presentation. You can be no less organized in presenting your material than you would be when showing your work to a local client. In other words, never lose sight of the precise market you are looking for.

I suggest writing or telephoning the PE or AD of your choice and giving the same information you would be giving if you were asking for an appointment in person, but this time state clearly that you cannot come in and ask if you may send in your material. Or if you already have a prepared mailer, send it in first and then telephone for clearance to ship.

Let us assume you have received an okay to ship. How do you do it? I am reluctant to use the mail as my experiences have been discouraging insofar as the handling or tracking of photographs is concerned. I suggest outfits like United Parcel Service (UPS) for air or ground transportation, and Federal Express (FEDEX), Emery, DHL or similar services for air shipments. All of these companies will pick up, deliver to your client, pick up again, and redeliver at your order. Use good, strong, reusable containers such as those made of fiber that are often used to ship film or flat packets in interstate commerce. They are inexpensive and durable and can be reused when your pictures are returned. Both UPS and FEDEX will also provide free sturdy shipping containers ($3\frac{1}{2}'' \times 2'' \times 16''$) that can handle small portfolios or prints up to that size, mailing tubes, envelopes, preprinted waybills and even customs forms. And for international shipments they will be helpful in obtaining customs clearances abroad.

These companies also guarantee overnight service for air shipments, but they can be expensive if used indiscriminately, so don't get carried away if you open accounts with any of them. UPS ground service rates are very reasonable and reliable. All have "800" numbers for information and pick up. There are some ancillary systems for packing to avoid damage to contents, but as photographs, portfolios, books and similar materials can take a lot of shaking in travel, simple, careful packing will usually suffice.

You should prepay the shipping charges, of course, and also work out some arrangement with the shipping company, e.g., "UPS call-tag service," or make other shipping arrangements for return of your pictures. Using this procedure will ensure the safe return of your portfolio. It will also give you a record of the portfolio's receipt and dispatch, which will minimize losses. You can use this method for carousel trays, stand-up easel mounts or any of the other methods discussed for presentation.

The Interview Follow-Up

The first thing you should do to follow up on an interview is to write a note of appreciation to the art director or picture editor who took the time to see you and/or your work. If you feel you were well received and that your work impressed your audience, a note or phone call in two or three weeks' time is absolutely in order. This is the time to start sending mailers to agencies or submitting story ideas in writing to the editorial publications you have contacted, again making certain the ideas you submit are the kind of material they can use.

Start keeping a log book or card index or computer file on calls or mail presentations, including dates, whom you saw, and perhaps a small commentary on your assessment of the interview. Were your pictures really examined? Were they liked or disliked? Criticized or praised? In what way? Was there a request for more material? If so, what did you send? Anything that's germane to the interview should be noted and logged, even your reaction to the person, and perhaps the secretary's or assistant's name. If you don't record this information, a hundred interviews later you may be hard pressed to remember what happened. And it may also help to avoid the future embarrassment of forgetting that you have already seen this person.

If you produce an exceptional set of photographs for an ad or editorial layout, even for a competing client (or magazine), and can get your hands on extra prints or tear sheets, send them in to the art buyer or picture editor. Some prolific photographers have made printed forms announcing the appearance of a specific layout and offering to provide more information.

I have mentioned the use of tearsheets before as samples, but how does one go about getting them, short of buying several hundred copies of the magazine or newspapers or books in which they appeared? Most publications have a tearsheet or reprint service (for advertisers), and they will provide copies as additional runoffs if you let them *know in advance of printing* that you will want perhaps 500-1,000 (or even more) copies of a specific article or layout. Also since magazines and unsold newspapers are returnable for credit by the publishers, it is frequently possible to buy large numbers of back issues cheaply by requesting them, again in *advance*, from a publisher's circulation department.

The question of follow-up is a delicate one. Memories are short, yet you are reluctant to make a pest of yourself. Art directors and picture buyers do not object to being reminded of the photographer's existence by a flow of mailers. In fact they encourage this (see page 107). With editorial people it is easier if you have an idea or reason to call or write about other than just asking "Do you have any work for me?" Here is where the frequent flow of story suggestions or ideas fits best. Do not send in inappropriate story suggestions just to keep your name up front. But by maintaining a steady flow of good ideas, your name will be at the top of the list of those to call when a particular type of story comes up.

Handle story suggestions in a carefully planned routine. When I spot a story idea in a newspapper, magazine or even on radio or TV, I either clip it or make notes on it if it is something I feel will be of interest to any of the several magazines with whom I remain in contact. I outline the piece in a brief précis giving the basic facts, an idea of the illustrations required, the amount of time it should take to produce, and a rough travel and expense budget based on the distance from home to the location(s) involved.

If the story seems unusual and I think it will be especially tempting to an editor, I frequently spend some additional time and money on research in the way of phone calls and trips to the library, checking *Ulrich's International Periodicals Directory* (see page 23) to see who may have covered the story earlier. When I submit a story idea, I think I know enough about the subject to be able to answer any reasonable question an editor may throw at me as to its feasibility and the mechanics of producing it.

Occasionally, when I am in a remote area and see something interesting, I'll shoot a few rolls of film if it can be done without complicated arrangements or disruption of my schedule, just to show what the possibilities are, and send those along with the story idea. I don't include much in the way of photography—by no means a complete story, just enough to show what the potential is and what I am capable of doing. Sometimes it works, sometimes it doesn't, but since I run a stock picture operation as well as work actively in the assignment field, I consider that anything unsold of this nature is an addition to my stock picture collection.

Do not make these suggestions in a letter to a specific editor, but simply as a short report on your own letterhead, making several clean photocopies of the story idea. Write a personal covering letter addressed to the most appropriate editor and in it simply refer to the suggested idea, giving the publication a deadline for the acceptance of the idea. If no reply is forthcoming, or a negative one is received, then feel free to start the idea around with another editor at another magazine.

Can you send the same story simultaneously to different editors? Yes, if there is a time factor in the story itself—such as something happening that has to be covered by a certain date. But if you do send it out to more than one magazine at once, it is only fair to tell the editors you are doing so, but you are not expected to state exactly to whom it is going. The editors know from the idea content who their competition is, and it might even stimulate one of them to take prompt action on a first-come, first-served basis.

In your treatment of the story idea, you have to make it clear somehow that you are qualified to do this story as well as or even better than some other photographer, and it may be that you will get the nod simply because you first suggested a piece that might have been done anyway, but perhaps not. After all, editors do see more national news sources than you do and may well be aware of the story.

Where you have an advantage is when something happens on the local scene which has national overtones, and the local situation can be used to illustrate the piece as a microcosm of the national implications. Desirable as travel may be to you, magazines will be reluctant to send a photographer on a cross-country trek when stringers or regional staffers can put together a story to serve their national needs. But you will be recognized for initiating the idea and may draw a lot more out of it than the local shooting. Your name will become familiar, and once a fresh flow of useful ideas starts, the chances are you won't be forgotten.

Interview

Gregory Heisler

Photographer

Perhaps the brightest star on our photographic horizon today is Gregory Heisler. Not only has he earned his stripes from his clients, but the utmost respect from his peers. To them, and a long list of magazine editors and ad agency art directors, he is truly the 'photographer's photographer.' Heisler has been producing inspiring and magnificent photography which has drawn much attention since 1977, long before his work made the 1991 *TIME* magazine "Man of the Year" cover. This electronically imaged portrait of CNN's Ted Turner also incorporated over forty other images. More to the point is Heisler's own gentle personality and creative drive for innovation. Quiet, friendly and unassuming, he belies the "star" stereotype. He has never lost sight of his early struggles, basing much of his success on his liking of fine art, and an unremitting willingness to work hard.

"I am from Chicago," he told me, "and I started in high school doing yearbook pictures. I was studying to become a science major and wanted to get into the space program. I went to the University of Wisconsin, the University of Illinois, and then to RIT in Rochester. I never graduated from any place. I worked for a publisher of high school yearbooks and probably made thousands of graduation pictures. Then I got a job as an assistant and low man on the totem pole at *Playboy*. That lasted about a week.

"I was aware of Arnold Newman's photography (see page 93). He had become my idol. Before I left RIT I wrote him asking for a job as an assistant. He answered saying he thought I was too young and he didn't want the responsibility of bringing me to New York. Though he had rejected me, I was encouraged because he had responded so kindly. I even called him but he did not change his mind. I remember it was a Friday afternoon, so that weekend I went to New York and pounded on his door. He relented, tried me out the next day, and gave me the job. That was my first professional experience in New York. I worked for him for about a year making prints and then became a freelance assistant. I took full-time jobs with fashion photographers Bill King, Eric Meola, and other photographers.

"Working as an assistant benefited me tremendously. Suddenly I was on an express train. I learned more in six months than I did in my entire time in school. Working with Newman first was incredibly important and much better than in a trendy fashion studio. With Arnold it was all cigar smoke and Dektol. But he was unpretentious and hard working. He has taken a million terrific pictures, and every single one was important. He became my role model.

"In 1977 I began getting a few assignments. John Durniak at *TIME* (see page 212) gave me a small one, and also referred me to *Money* magazine. Other photographers sent me to graphic design houses for annual reports and to other editors. I was beginning to stick my toe in the water of high-level professionalism. Sean Callahan at *American Photographer* assigned me to photograph entertainers which led me to doing album jackets. Piece by piece it was snowballing and exciting.

"I was getting work from other Time Inc. magazines, and the new *LIFE* magazine when it started up. At first the jobs were small, but I was being called by them nearly every month and for bigger stories. It was a dream come true. What was great about the *LIFE* assignments was that they didn't pigeonhole you and would allow me to stretch. Once it would be a portrait, next a landscape, or a still life. They wanted to know if you had eyes. Most times you are pigeonholed. If you show fashion, you get fashion; if you show industrial you get industrial. *LIFE* was a tremendous growth period for me. I worked regularly for them on small assignments and also for other magazines. Then I did an eight-page *LIFE* story on Los Angeles Chicanos that put me on the map. I think it was my first assignment people saw as being different. It was even more important to me, because for the first time I saw it my own way, and was not imitating others.

"By now I have photographed in many areas — editorial, fashion, corporate, advertising, but I love editorial the most, as it is something I always wished to do. It keeps me fresh and I meet interesting people. It's a kick in the pants for me and it stimulates me to learn about new things, like antique dolls or radioactive dumping. These are things you may never have thought of, now you are suddenly immersed in it.

"I say to young photographers, don't worry about specialization too much. Expose yourself to as much as you can, take any assignments that come your way and work very hard on them. I don't know why it happens, but some assistants I've had, have often killed themselves for me, and yet when they went out on their own they did not seem to have that drive. They just simply were not as dedicated for themselves as they were for me.

"Perhaps this happens because they don't have the self-discipline of following through on their own. Self-discipline is very important; without it you will fail. That is one reason I do assignment work, because if I didn't *have* to be somewhere, I would dawdle, be careless of my appearance and in general be pretty lazy about it. For instance, today I was to photograph the CEO of a large company at 8:00 A.M. I got up at 5:00 to get ready, and by 8:30 the shoot was done and we were having breakfast. That's exciting and the discipline drives me.

"I think young photographers worry too much about what their style is going to be and they think maybe it should be shot grainy or with flash or available light. These are techniques, not style. I think style is something that shows up in hindsight later and you see what it has become. I would not use the word "style" for myself. I have a way that may show up as a style. My approach is to have an appropriate response to assignments, and a command of technique, so that assignments share a look, a sense of being the right thing, a sense of being seen clearly. I never do work just because it's gimmicky. I try to choose the look of a picture that seems best suited to the subject. I wouldn't try to shoot to my style; it's like trying to cram a square peg into a round hole. I don't do that, but others do. Some shoot people against white backdrops, and everything is against white backdrops.

Others shoot against a white stucco wall so everything is against a white stucco wall. Or they set up a giant sunset and use that all the time. I just think the world doesn't exist that way.

"A young photographer should remember that what he learns as an assistant in one area can be applied elsewhere. Still-life lighting can also be used with a portrait, meat loaf, or a head. On an industrial setting I may learn something to use on a CEO's portrait. There is much to be learned by keeping your eyes open.

"Photographers are constantly told to specialize. Perhaps it's a better way to make money and become successful quickly. It's also a way of becoming typed. So I avoid specialization. I don't want to be known as just a cowboy photographer or a shoe photographer. I have narrowed my work to portraiture because it's my favorite thing to do. But I still enjoy shooting other things.

"I go back to being aware of what's around you. Now electronic imaging is hot, but I have known of it since its inception and began experimenting with it. And even before I produced the *TIME* cover of CNN's Ted Turner, I had already made other covers for *TIME* using this technique. For me this is another tool with which I can express my creativity. If somebody saw the *TIME* cover and called me to do that kind of work, I would think it great and not a form of typecasting.

"A hard thing about self-promotion is that often a picture in your portfolio is already old news, even if it's the first time somebody else sees it. Or if you had done something months ago, put it in a source book or mailed it out as a poster, it may be six months or longer before you get a response. Unfortunately that's the nature of the business and you become known for making a certain kind of photograph and are often called only to repeat that style. I look for the art director or picture editor who doesn't type me. Unfortunately that doesn't happen too often and there is more of a tendency to be called to repeat what you've already done. I don't like it, but I do it anyway.

"Yet you must constantly push your versatility. If you send out portfolios that are responsive to what someone is asking for, you'll spend your entire life putting together specialized portfolios. That is even assuming you have enough pictures to accommodate so many different requests. I just send out a portfolio that I think best represents who I am and what I do. And either they get it or they don't. I don't mind because you can't please everybody.

"I use different formats for my portfolios. For corporate work I send out a carousel tray of about eighty slides, and for advertising a flat leather-bound book about 11″ × 14″, half mostly color reprints from magazines and ads, and the other half are black-and-white prints of images I like. I am beginning to send out twelve different mailers. They are thematic, each one has six images and each sequence a specific theme. We chose the thematic way because we found that people did not know what to make of a portfolio showing a variety of single images. I hope if a thinking person sees my work he will not call me to a standardized situation, but give me the opportunity to come up with something special.

"I don't mind direction from an art director on a picture. I am glad to get all the input possible *before* it comes time to shoot. I know some photographers object to clients who put in their two cents, and the photographer storms off in a huff. I'm open to anything because I feel that so often clients are not heard, are not listened to, and when they go back, their bosses yell at them. So if a client needs something important, like the screws on a machine, if they just tell me that, whatever else I do, I'll light it in such a way that the screws show up. I can still make a good picture. But once I'm ready to shoot, have all the information of what's wanted, then I like to be left alone to produce work that will make everybody happy.

"I don't agree with the widely espoused notion of giving them what they want and then doing it your way. I don't buy that. I feel that I should give them what they want better than they knew how to ask. That's like giving them your picture as their picture. Otherwise your best picture never gets shown and it's not what they were asking for. I listen to what they really want, and am a good listener. I then churn it around in my head, and make a picture I can love and still give them what they need. After all, they are paying me, I am the photographer they hire, so I give them what they want. These pictures aren't for an art gallery, they are for jobs. So I want to do the best I can to accomplish the mission.

"Even in editorial, where I get a very free hand, if the picture is supposed to say something specifically about a president or a bicycle, I give them that and still try to make a great picture. Some advertising photographs lose me in their abstract quality. I think if you need a picture of a man running fast, it should look like he's running fast, and not use some symbol for softness to illustrate cashmere clothes. I also think too many photographers alienate their clients, their subjects, their assistants, and their families, because they have ego problems. That's a shame, and doesn't have to be that way. It doesn't mean that in order to be creative you have to be a maniac. You can still be a nice person.

"I do not have news agency affiliation or a rep. I work directly from my studio for a clientele I have built up and continue building. I maintain a small stock file of personalities but it's specialized and I control its use rigidly.

"Electronic imaging is exciting. It's another medium and like having another camera format. Some pictures are better on 35mm, others better on $8'' \times 10''$, and some will be better on the computer. We can work with it in different ways. Now it's a 'special case' item. I think in five or ten years all pictures will involve computer technology. But it's still a tool to be used in many ways including as an art form. We're in the stone age now in planning lighting, shading, and color emphasis. Soon we will do it in a fraction of time on the computer.

"The important thing for photographers to realize is that digital photography will expand the creativity of the photographer, not replace it. It's the imagery conceived by the photographer that's exciting. No computer can conceive the image Arnold Newman had when he made his famous photograph of Alfried Krupp, or if only I could have made an $8'' \times 10''$ close-up of Saddam Hussein's face and looked right into his eyes, I would have given my right arm for the opportunity. So we are still dealing with the photographer's mind and not with machines. No, the computer will not replace the documentary photographer who will always be needed, but will be able to work with him side by side.

"New photographers just starting out should not only postpone career decisions, and not only learn the complete capabilities of the camera but the computer as well. They should always have knowledge of art forms, lighting, fine printing, all those special techniques that are required for great photography and then later, when they have mastered this knowledge, they can hire someone to print or light for them. Technique and vision go together and that's why the creative photographer today must be open to new ideas and learn both photographic and computer ABC's. We shouldn't be afraid to work hard. I think it's fun, and I hope I never stop.

"Up to now I have concentrated on earning a living by doing what I do best. Now maybe I want to think more about personal work. All my work then was commercial work and I make no apologies for the assignments I killed myself for. Now I'm starting to feel that there are other pictures I want to shoot, maybe not on assignment, just pictures I want to do. They might result in books or exhibitions or some other form of art expression. It will be personal in the purest sense and I hope it wil be a very effective communication with people about a specific subject. I want to do it for the pleasure of doing it. I'll still do assignments as it pays the rent and I'll still break my back working twenty-four hours a day, seven days a week producing a Ted Turner cover because I enjoy it.

"But I also want to have students to pass on to them the kind of things Arnold Newman gave me. If you take any kind of risks at all, you'll make mistakes, and I make mistakes every day but that's how you grow. And another thing I would suggest is that you take it one picture at a time. Photographers worry about their careers, my sense is to just worry about the next picture."

Chapter Five

Getting the Assignment: Determining Fees and Rates

The phone rings late one Friday afternoon. Why late Friday? Did you ever know of anything to happen in this business except at the last minute?

"This is Joe ————, director of public relations at the American Producing Company. You were in a couple of months ago and we liked your work; we'd like you to come in and talk about covering our plants for our annual report. We would like you to start at the end of next week. Are you available and can you present some sort of budget?"

So you say, "Of course. What time do you want me to come in?" You make a date for the following Monday morning and hang up in a state of euphoria.

By then it's 5:30 in the afternoon and Joe has left for the weekend.

In your excitement you didn't ask him where the plants are, how many plants there are to be covered, and other information that could have helped you plan the budget he wants Monday morning.

But all is not lost. You still have the weekend ahead of you. So you do a little scrambling. First you try to find a copy of a previous annual report. If the firm is a local company, you try the bank if it's open on Saturday, or the chamber of commerce, or a resident stockbroker, until you come up with one. In it is a listing of all the company's plants and subsidiaries, their products and the names of their corporate officers. You become familiar with the information in the annual report because it is essential to planning a budget.

The scenario can vary. It doesn't have to be a corporate annual report you are assigned to do. It can be a small editorial piece for a magazine or maybe material for a brochure for a public relations program or possibly an advertising layout to be shot on location. The essentials are the same. Any budget you prepare has to take into consideration every factor involved in the production of the photography, and you have to be able to justify your costs and fees.

Charging for Your Services

Charging for one's services can be unnerving, particularly for the new photographer. Learning to produce a realistic budget is of utmost importance, because planning a budget and negotiating its acceptance can determine whether you succeed or fail in the business of professional photography.

Fees are calculated and governed by all sorts of factors — uses, space, circulation, whether it's for editorial, public relations, annual reports or advertising — or almost every different category of photography you can mention. Knowing what to charge for a particular job involves:

- An analysis of the client's budget and needs;
- Knowing what to charge for your time or, if it's an editorial production, What the potential for space rates may be;
- And a realistic appraisal of your total costs in doing the job, including overhead.

Forty-eight years ago when the ASMP was first formed there were no guidelines, and it took several years even after the organization started to grow, before early ones were set down. Over the years they have been implemented and minimum recommended fees raised periodically to keep pace with the times and inflation. When it comes to fees, you have to decide what you think your work is worth. (You should also know what is being paid for comparable work in order to establish an equitable price.) In some editorial photography this causes no problem, as many magazines operate on a *space vs. time system*, and most photographers accept this. Space vs. time means that you are paid either for the space you achieve in layout or the time you spent producing the photographs. Most major magazines have published space rates and pay the ASMP suggested and generally accepted minimums for time spent, and if you work under these arrangements you get the higher amount when the story closes. The ASMP recommendations at this writing call for approximately $500 per day plus a certain percentage of the agreed-upon day rate for time spent in travel, making arrangements, bad weather standby, etc. This can be for one-quarter to one-half the day rates. Many magazines such as those in the Time-Life group pay about $500 per page and up to $2,500 for a cover.

Historically there has always been a squabble over the differential payment for color and black and white, and the whole question is under constant review. Photographers and their agencies want the color/black-and-white differential done away with. Ironically, today it actually costs more to process, edit from contacts and print black-and-white reproduction prints than it does to process a reversal color transparency.

Today the 35mm transparency accounts numerically for most professional color photographs, except perhaps those of food, architecture, and fashion, where the larger format is often preferred. Even here, inroads have been made by the 35mm with the development of the PC-type lenses and better film emulsions. But photographers are in conflict because, while they would like to see the differentials eliminated, they don't want to see it done at the expense of their color work. They are trying to raise the level of black-and-white prices to a par with color. This works on general assignments as more and more negative color material is used in news photography production where the editors can use either medium in their own publications. There is also a growing trend to 100 percent color. It is not working completely as yet in the stock photography market where differentials are still charged to advertisers, not only for color but also for color position in the various media. Also textbook publishers still use many pictures in black and white and they object vehemently to raising the price of black and white to the same level as color. But this too may be moot as more textbooks are being produced in color. So it is a long educational procedure for photographers to bring picture users around to their point of view.

The newest guidelines published by the ASMP indicate a variety of rates. In advertising there are other rules and procedures that have to be considered. In the appendix you will find a list of the current rates suggested by most professional groups working in this field. Whether you can live with them or not or can do better (or worse) is entirely up to you. However, what they will tell you is what is currently being paid in the marketplace.

Page Rates

Today the contemporary photographer is lucky because of the pioneering efforts of his predecessors in their professional societies. Much of the credit, too, has to be given to the major publications that use photography as a major component of their publication, and set decent standards and norms in the form of page rates. Many photographers felt then, and still do today, that many of these rates were hard-nosed guesses based on what publishers thought they could get away with, but it wasn't always the case.

In some of the earlier mass picture publications, page rates were sometimes set pretty high, only to retrogress a few years later. For example, one major publication set a rate of $300 per page for color in 1939, and that same magazine in 1992 is paying $550 per page. Another monthly paid a color cover rate of $3,500 in 1950 and in 1992 was paying $2,000.

Today, with the differential disappearing between color and black and white, it is imperative that a photographer base his fees not only on a realistic appraisal of publishing costs and profits, but also on the multiple uses of a photograph, frequently by the same houses that hired him in the first place. The photographer should always keep in mind that pictures that are assigned are often done so by editors who project future use for them within the same corporate structure. Photographs do have a life of their own ahead of them. A picture made today on the ski slopes for a sporting magazine, might well be of use to the editors of a housing magazine the same company publishes. Very often assigning magazines try to secure rights for use by their sister magazines, and while these practices may not fall under the work-made-for-hire definitions (see page 270) the projected multiple use of pictures within the "house" should be considered when establishing your price structure for assignment shooting. It is the consideration of these ideas that makes one photographer more useful to a publisher or corporate user of photography than another. It is also the *raison d'etre* in the work-for-hire controversy. So if you can convince your client that you are unique in getting your photographs (of his product, service or concept) moved into other areas, you are entitled to more money than the photographer who says, "I will do your job, pay me for it, and call me again some time."

Day Rates

The professional societies have long tried to establish minimums for day rates that would give the working photographer a realistic return for his efforts. It's a reasonable goal, but often difficult to achieve, because in the freelance world there is no assurance how many days a photographer will find work in any given year. Some photographers seem to be always working and others, equally as good technically and esthetically, seem to have a tough time making ends meet.

Much is due to luck but also much is due to how well the photographer (or the agent, if there is one) is able to sell or be sold. With current accepted day rates of $500, in order for the photographer to earn $40,000 per year on assignments, he has to work eighty days or almost a quarter of the working year. Is this realistic? If he still wants to earn that $40,000 and can only get fifty days per year, he has to ask for and get $800 per day. Can he do that? How does that compare with the competition?

One of the problems the ASMP ran into thirty-seven years ago, when they first established the "minimum day rate" formula, was that while it was helpful and a starting point for many photographers, it often became, unfortunately, the maximum — and a fixed fee for everybody. Over the years, as the cost of living increased and inflation began to take its toll, the ASMP and other groups started to raise their minimums. While the dollar numbers did increase, the percentages and comparative returns did not, and the practice of the minimum remaining the maximum continued.

When the ASMP lost its trade union status by a legislative quirk and was forced into becoming a trade association, some of the teeth they had in enforcing the minimum rate were lost, and there were indications that pricing for shooting was going to be a rat race. There did not seem to be any alternative, however. The professional photographic organizations are always quick to point out that these fees were suggested minimums and it is really up to the photographer to negotiate his own rates with his client.

But another nagging question persists — why should the young, less experienced photographer be hired at the suggested minimum when the client can get an old hand for nearly the same price? I have always had strong feelings about this issue and believe the younger photographer should *not* be discriminated against in price because of his lack of greater experience. If he has shown in his portfolio the capability of fulfilling the assignment, he should get it, all other factors being equal.

Never was this more true than in the case of the managing editor of one magazine who, in looking at a story, would have the pictures from every source laid out on the floor of his office. He walked around them and chose the pictures according to what he saw, not caring one bit about who supplied them and often not knowing who the photographer was.

Your Time — What Is It Worth?

For now photographers can operate only with the primary day rates of professional photographic associations as "hunting licenses" rather than fixed fees. What is a photographer's time worth today? The news magazines are currently paying about $500 per day for any kind of shooting, against page rates of approximately $500 for inside use and $1,500 to $2,500 for color covers. Corporate work tends to be two to three times the editorial rate. The philosophy here is that this type of shooting is frequently a once-a-year job, as in an annual report. It does not have a comparable space rate to give the photographer a chance to do better if the pictures are played more widely, in better display, and credit lines are rare if given at all. Advertising rates, as discussed previously, are frequently based on a combination of media usage, audience and space, and perhaps most important the reputation of the photographer. A double-spread national color ad today should bring from $15,000 upwards, depending upon the variables discussed by Lovett earlier (see page 82). Specialists with high degrees of scientific achievement involving extremely sophisticated equipment and knowledge may earn fees in excess of $35,000 per day, as do some top-level photographers specializing in major corporate annual report work. Skilled electronic-imaging photographers who can combine technical expertise with a highly creative sense of photography have an almost unlimited earning potential.

The ranges are wide. An agreement made in 1991 with the three major newspapers in New York and the Newspaper Guild puts minimum reporters' and photographers' salaries in a range from $1,077 per week at *The New York Times* to $928 at the *Daily News* and $826 at the *New York Post*. Other cities—Chicago, San Francisco, Denver, Pittsburgh and Philadelphia are in the $800+ class, though smaller city papers with Guild contracts such as the one in Utica, New York, drop to under $400 per week. These salaries are in addition to fringe benefits, which in some cases can be considerable in the way of health and pension plans. Private portrait sittings by highly skilled portrait photographers run from a low of $500 to a high of $4,000 per sitting and may include a number of different photographs and some rights to reproduce them in certain publications or for corporate public relations use. A studio portrait sitting by a competent but less experienced and less well-known photographer will probably not exceed one-third of these fees, however. Some of the finest and most prominent portraitists will also produce editorial portraits for top magazines at a lesser fee, usually a minimum day vs. space rate—because of the prestige and resultant publicity and because of the repeat work and secondary rights usage of many of the pictures they shoot on editorial assignments.

These fees fall into some fairly standard brackets, but rates are finally dictated by the market as well as the experience and prominence of the artists. Photographers such as the late Philippe Halsman and his contemporaries can and did command impressive fees because they were at the very highest level of artistic achievement and delivered their work with that added quality that set them apart from most others.

In the appendix you will find a list of suggested minimum fee guidelines for editorial and advertising shooting on a variety of situations. These are not "union scales" or rate fixed charges but merely recommendations by the ASMP and other professional organizations to their membership as to what should be charged as minimums for various types of work. The ASMP has always taken the position that the fees are the barest minimum a photographer should charge for his work if he wants to stay alive economically, and a reminder that these are only "floors" and not to be considered fixed prices.

Deviation From Payment Standards

Young photographers who wish to compete but simply cannot command the prices paid their seniors often ask, "How far can I deviate from the professional codes?" The answer: "As much as you want to." The codes of the ASMP are recommended for their members who, it is hoped, will uphold them. But bear in mind the ASMP also believes that to photograph or sell below these minimums means working at a loss.

What is an acceptable deviation from codes such as these? There are no hard answers, but by custom those photographers who profess to operate under these guidelines but accept a lower rate of payment may be excused if they are under a contractual relationship for a specified amount of work, or a guarantee of page space or a fixed fee for an entire package involving many days of work. Then, too, there is often the simple fact that a photographer needs the work and there may not be anyone else around whose throat is being cut by working for a lower fee.

Photographers will often find themselves faced with appeals to wait for acceptance of a project before full payment can be made. This happens frequently when material is needed for presentation use: Here there is a way of controlling it. If a buyer comes to you and says, "Look, I need certain kinds of photographs that may take a certain number of shooting days for a presentation of an idea, but I can't afford to pay the full fee unless we sell the project, so will you do it?" The answer can conscientiously be "yes" provided that, (1) a minimum "good faith" fee is paid along with all estimated expenses up front; (2) if the project is sold, the photographer will either be paid additionally or guaranteed to be the photographer on the shooting to come at guaranteed full fees, and that guarantees must be in writing; and (3) if the project fails after presentation and no further money is available, all of the photographs become the property of the photographer and any work-for-hire agreements if made are voided.

Speculation

Continuing our discussion of when it is appropriate to deviate from standard fees and rates, we encounter the concept of working "on speculation," i.e., doing the work and (theoretically) being paid later, upon acceptance. This is a practice that has damaged many a professional photographer's career and something the new photographer should understand perfectly before starting out.

The requests a freelance photographer or agency get can often seem like utter simplicity itself—for example, a group of pictures that can be "knocked off" quickly without much effort. There is a great temptation to do them on a speculative basis—producing them without an assignment and then expecting to sell them. What usually happens is that the photographer is left holding a very large bag mostly filled with empty promises and his costs from shooting the pictures. One of the situations to be wary of is the "I'll take care of you later" syndrome, when you are told that the budget is too limited for current prices for photography but if you give the editor a break now, he or she will take care of you later and the money will be made up. Somehow it never seems to happen. Though as long ago as the 1950s the ASMP reacted in anger and "outlawed" speculative photography, the practice still arises in the markets for professional photography.

Sometimes we are trapped into situations we cannot control, and even seasoned professionals are caught in painful dilemmas, by requests from people who are too low on the pecking order of some organizations to really have authority to issue such orders. This happened to me. I received a call one Friday (yep! Friday again) from a researcher at the publicity department of a large New York bank that was making a slide presentation covering different aspects of marketing and business management. She gave me a list of about twenty-five subjects, all of which had to be ready for duplicating by Monday evening for an audiovisual film strip to be presented to the bank's client Tuesday morning. I told her that I had about fifteen or sixteen of the subjects in my stock file, and as the others were outdoor items concentrated in the New York metropolitan area, I felt I could shoot the rest over the weekend. I did not request a formal assignment but a "guaranteed use" in the slide presentation. If that was acceptable, I would have all the slides ready for duplicating Monday afternoon. She was extremely grateful, and though there was no discussion of an assignment fee, she did say there was no question that they would use all twenty-five of the locations to be made on a "stock" basis. I made some rapid calculations and since the going fees per film-strip frame were in the $135 to $150 class then, the thought of a $4,000-plus fee involving two days of shooting including the stock pictures was indeed appealing.

When I got home that night I received a call from the researcher's supervisor, not only confirming the package deal, but adding two more stock subjects to the list. I was pleased and began marking map locations and gathering equipment and supplies together.

Saturday it rained unexpectedly, but Sunday was fine and I doubled up, doing two days' work in one, covering over a hundred miles of local driving throughout the traffic-ridden, fifty-mile radius of New York. I delivered the film to a lab that did Sunday night processing, collapsed in a heap at home and collected my pictures the next morning. They looked good, I edited them, worked in the stock pictures from my files, added a completed leasing memo and delivered the entire package by 10:00 A.M. as promised.

At noon the same day the package was returned, and at first glance appeared to be unopened. I called the supervisor who had confirmed the order and she calmly said, "Oh, we only used one, which is now at the duplicating lab. Thank you for your help."

I checked my returns and, sure enough, all of the pictures were back with the exception of one. I noted something else. I had inserted each group of transparencies in plastic sleeves and covered each sleeve with a caption sheet so that the photographs could not be viewed without removing the sheets. Not one single caption sheet had been lifted from the transparency protectors with the exception of the one containing the picture used. Obvious conclusion? The other pictures were *never even looked at*, let alone considered for use.

I called back and asked the supervisior about payment for my efforts. "Sorry," was the answer; "we didn't 'assign' these pictures, you have no purchase order, so we cannot pay you anything except for the use of the one picture we chose."

She continued sweetly, "Oh, by the way, the duplicating lab seems to have lost the original, so would you accept the dupe they made instead?" After a few appropriate comments (expletives deleted) because I had (1) used a good leasing memo form and (2) had protected the photographs with proper notice of copyright, I called her boss. She promptly passed the buck to her boss who took the position that, "Since you had no purchase order and, as a matter of fact, the researcher who called you didn't even have the authority to make such an offer, nor did her superior, you are simply out of luck, buddy boy!" and hung up.

I called back and told him that while it was true there was no time for a written confirmation, as it had all started on Friday night for a weekend shoot, and since such bad faith was being exercised by what I thought were honorable people at the bank, I had no recourse but to (1) apply the terms of the lost transparency clause ($1,500) in the leasing memo and (2) instigate action for *automatic* recovery for infringement of copyright for the public exhibition of photographs, i.e., the film strip (5,000 viewers at one dollar per infringement), for which by their own statement they had not issued a purchase order. There was a sudden "whoosh" of air over the phone as the big-shot bank vice president deflated quickly.

"What are you trying to do to me," he said, "get me fired?"

"I don't know about that," I said, "but I sure as hell am going to nail your hide to the wall. Maybe you think because I'm small and you're the biggest bank in New York, you can walk over me, make me run halfway around the city of New York without paying me, lose my work in addition, and can get away with it. Well, I have a hot flash for you. The Library of Congress and the Copyright Act of 1976 is bigger than you are." I then hung up.

Within ten minutes the bank vice president called back and a very rapid verbal settlement was reached in full payment of what was due. (It would seem that this would have ended the matter, but it didn't—ninety days later, not having been paid, I had to practically do battle again to receive payment.)

Any moral to all of this? You bet!

1. Issue proper leasing memos.

2. Get proper confirmations of all orders with all conditions spelled out. While a written confirmation then may have seemed unnecessary given the reputation of the bank, it obviously was required. Today with faxes and computer modems, the necessary purchase orders or confirmations of requests could have been issued instantly.

3. Learn your copyright protections. (See chapter ten.)

I have related this story in detail because there is a lot to be learned from it, and I will be discussing various aspects of it as we go on. But the primary lesson here is to avoid speculation no matter how tempting it may be.

Nonprofit Groups and Professional Courtesy

Another ploy often used by so-called nonprofit organizations—foundations, public institutions, educational groups or charities—is to approach you and ask for services for either nothing or at low cost, or for the use of stock pictures at prices bordering on the ridiculous. Their excuse always is, "We are a nonprofit organization." They forget somehow to tell you that they themselves invariably are on good salaries, the printers are being paid in full, the paper suppliers are being paid in full, the postage is being paid, and the office rent and help are also being paid at current rates. Somehow they expect the artist to accept lower prices. I handle the situation by sending them a form letter such as the one below, which politely reminds them that selling photographs is a business.

Sometimes these requests are genuine in that the groups or individuals really have no funds and you want to help. What then? Just do it as a charitable gesture and simply shoot the pictures at cost or even provide the photograph free, but don't do it at a reduced rate. By donating a free picture worth a specific amount, you can take legitimate deductions on your income

---

Memo to:

Your request for special pricing consideration has been received most sympathetically, but unfortunately we cannot respond positively. We too are a nonprofit organization. It wasn't designed that way, but that's the way it seems to work. We trust you understand.

Photography for Industry
Charles E. Rotkin, Owner & Prop.

tax if you are so inclined. And the actual tax saving may be more than what you might have received for the photograph.

Another minor but frequent occurrence is in the matter of professional courtesy. Many times I have been asked by other photographers or editors who are friends or professional acquaintances for pictures at reduced rates. I always refuse the reduced rate, but give the picture without charge. Why not accept a lower fee? Well, I feel that to do so would be to diminish the value of one's work or service and that is unacceptable to me, but I have no reluctance about giving freely to my friends and acquaintances.

The Ethics of Free Photographs

The issue of "free" photographs is complex, reaching back into the history of photography and the evolution of the professional photographer. So let us digress to address this issue, as it is something all professionals will eventually have to deal with.

Photography is probably the only form of visual communication in which amateurs outnumber professionals by such vast numbers as to be virtually uncountable. Competition to get into print is very great.

How does one get into print, especially the new professional photographer? Loaded questions such as whether the amateur or young professional should be paid as much for his time as an experienced professional, or whether space rates should be equal for all, can never be fully answered without understanding the concept of the "free" photograph.

Thirty-eight years ago the industry thought they had some answers when the ASMP established a minimum standard for a day's work. Photographers began pressuring magazines to establish space rates for the unassigned work they used. It seemed right and today is still valid. (See pages 126 and 135.)

Even before getting to the concept of what a photograph is worth, we need to make distinctions or perhaps narrow the definitions. It may not be a question of how much a photograph is worth, but how much it is worth to (1) the person who makes it or (2) the person who uses it?

Some artists feel that every image made should be seen by someone other than the image maker. If we accept this theory then the idea of the "free" photograph becomes more palatable to the professional. If we (grudgingly) admit to this, then perhaps there will be less hostility toward the new and needy photographer who sells a photograph for less than current market value in order to get started. But many look askance at the well-heeled photographer with an income from some other source who uses these give-away methods for becoming known and recognized.

The next question to be considered is: If we accept the use of a picture without charge, should the artist be expected or obliged to produce this work without compensation? Obliged, of course, is not the answer—no one should be *obliged* to do anything without compensation.

Or, consider the message. The photograph is a message, whether it concerns a social theme, a news item or a hard sell of an object or service. We seem to have no objections to leaving those messages, but the only question is, how should those messages be paid for? And by whom? Is there a universal right to know? (For free?)

I introduce these thoughts only in the hope of stimulating thinking on the part of professional photographers about what is to become of their work and how it is to be handled. In considering that output and its ultimate use, whether paid for or not, we cannot ignore the impact of the society in which we live and the role our own government has always played in the dissemination of information, from general to political propaganda or hard news.

From photography's earliest days, government has consistently played an active role and government-produced pictures were not afforded copyright protection. Even so, the earlier production of photographs for free distribution did not have too much impact on the economic lives of photographers except in a positive way. Photographers hired to shoot for the government would not have been hired at all if the government did not employ them.

One aspect of the free government photograph that does merit some discussion concerns the pictures, distributed by the White House Photography Office, of activities of the President when the photographers of the White House Press corps are excluded. There are no fees or charges made to the press associations for these pictures, nor is there any substantive feeling that the White House is taking jobs away by having their photographers cover the President. There is some unhappiness by the working press of the White House from a "freedom of press" (read: free access) viewpoint, but that is not the issue here.

An "informational" campaign was certainly behind the establishment of the famous photographic files of the Farm Security Administration (FSA) set up during Franklin Roosevelt's administration in 1935. We were in the depths of the Depression. The country was literally in upheaval since the topsoil on the farms was blowing away to become a vast "dust bowl." The poor, rural and urban, the landless and homeless began a trek across the country that assumed near-avalanche proportions, in search of a promised land. Television didn't exist, film-making was limited, and the Department of Agriculture, faced with the responsibility of bringing the plight of these Americans before the public and getting support (i.e., congressional appropriations), began using photography in a major way.

Photographers and artists were hired and put to work, among them Dorothea Lange, Jack Delano, Ben Shahn, John Vachon, Marion Post Walcott, Russell Lee, Walker Evans, Carl Mydans, Arthur Rothstein, John Collier, Jr. and others. All were gathered under the direction of a then obscure historian and archivist named Roy Emerson Stryker in the newly formed Historical Section of the Resettlement Administration later to become the FSA. In addition to the photographers in the field, complete support services were established in Washington, DC. The pictures were given free to any media that would use them. No editorial opinions were offered, as the program's directors knew the pictures would speak for themselves and underscore the tremendous need for help for those photographed. The only information provided were accurate captions, giving dates, places and a brief description of the scene photographed.

This landmark coverage became one of the great historical documents of our time. From it came many of the concepts of the great photo magazines. In fact, Mydans left the FSA to join the early *LIFE* staff. It became the proving ground for some of the best-known photographers of the period. Walker Evans joined *Fortune* and Arthur Rothstein and John Vachon went on to *Look*.

With the onset of World War II the program was absorbed by the Office of War Information and eventually disbanded. The picture files went to the Library of Congress where they are still available, open to the public (and free except for modest print charges). They are unparalleled in the history of documentary photography. Today, more than fifty years after their creation, they remain a tower of integrity in photography, and a day or longer spent now by a young photographer perusing these files would not be a day wasted but perhaps one of inspiration.

The key component of this vast program was the free photograph. This idea did not, however, die with the dismemberment of the FSA program, as Stryker went to the Standard Oil Company of New Jersey (SONJ) (formerly ESSO and now Exxon) along with many of the old FSA staff to use the same principles in the oil information business.

A new program was established, this time under private industry. The idea was the same: disseminate as much photographic information as possible without charge to the media, to tell them all about the oil business. So just as the FSA free photography became widely accepted, so did the pictures distributed by ESSO become a major facet of photo documentation. Other oil companies tried copying it, but none had the same impact. In film-making, just as the earlier government programs were responsible for the late Pare Lorentz's great documentaries, "The River," "The Plow That Broke the Plains," and others, so was ESSO to follow with Robert Flaherty's "Louisiana Story." That, too, became an American classic.

When the ESSO program phased out after World War II, Stryker moved on, this time to Pittsburgh, bringing the free photograph concept to the J & L Steel Company and the University of Pittsburgh. Both used this system of free distribution to obtain media attention for whatever messages they had to impart. By now the use of the free pictures was accepted by American business as a valid method of getting their messages across to the public. Other corporate files were established and free picture use became widespread. However, the concept of the free picture remained controversial among professionals.

Proponents took the position that it promoted the employment of photographers, but opponents felt the photographer hired to shoot for free distribution was locked into a situation over which he had little or no control. There were few or no secondary use rights available, and often the stigma of a company handout is anathema to editors and publishers who worry about editorial independence and integrity. Yet other publishers trying to project budgets for books and encyclopedias rely a good deal on the free picture. This free picture hurts the independent photographer who either depends on assignments or builds a stock file.

I spoke to a member of a photo research group which obtains free photography for textbook publishers and asked if it harmed the photographers. Her answers were partially reassuring as she felt their availability is not particularly hazardous to a photographer in highly specialized scientific, medical, or historic areas. She agreed that contemporary free photographs from chambers of commerce and convention and visitors bureaus did, indeed, impinge on the income of independent professionals. But she also justified this by citing that a photographer was hired to make these pictures. The lines become blurred here as to the real benefits to the photographer.

The story behind the abortive Federal *Docuamerica* project of the 1970s is also interesting in the context of the free picture programs. There is no question that the cultural benefits of the historic FSA programs were enormous and the photographs will forever stand as landmarks of creativity. But they were produced at a time when there was no competition to private photography and there was a downright need for these photographs.

From the end of World War II until the late 1960s there were many in the photographic world who decried the fact that contemporary America was not being photographed in any consistent way despite the efforts of the oil companies and some other corporations which may also have been self-serving. Several ideas were formulated to try to recreate a "little FSA" program that would, perhaps on a more modest scale, have the photographs made, give employment to photographers, and bring the pictures before the public. Even Dorothea Lange, in her days of declining health, voiced optimism that such a program could be started and talked with many about its possibilities.

Eventually, after several plans were proposed, a program was developed in 1970 called *Docuamerica*, to be administered by the Environmental Protection Administration (EPA). A staff was hired, photographers were called and given assignments, some running several weeks in length, to photograph a wide variety of subject material. An elaborate system of microfiche retrieval was established in cooperation with private custom color labs, and the images were released to the public free of reproduction fees. Photographers, hired at ASMP minimums, were asked to surrender all rights to the photographs to the U.S. government (as under the copyright law it seemed they were obliged to) though, as it later turned out, there were loopholes where the photographers could indeed keep some secondary rights.

But photographers began to fret when pictures began appearing in national commercial advertising that normally might bring $1,500 to $3,000 per photo, and the advertising agencies were getting them for nothing. The fretting continued and finally the ASMP took a hard stand on the matter. In a "white paper" the ASMP agreed to, and in fact encouraged, the idea of free distribution of pictures to small newspapers, magazines and other publications who could not afford to buy professional-caliber photography, but objected vehemently to the free commercial uses of the pictures. The ASMP then suggested that its membership not participate in the program unless some system of remuneration was established for commercial use.

The controversy reached cabinet-level interest in Washington but no agreement was ever reached. The program sputtered along, a few more photographers were hired, but eventually the whole project died, and its images now are gathering dust in the National Archives.

So the ethical question of the free photograph is still debated. I feel there is limited merit to the system. It is obvious that a small-town paper or low-circulation magazine, or even a limited-edition book, could never hope to spend the money required to make many photographs in the field. Yet should a publication be denied the use of them for pecuniary reasons only? Why shouldn't large corporations or the government make these pictures available? Should profit-making organizations be subsidized in this manner by the taxpayer? The danger lies in the control of distribution and the bias, if any, of the source of the photograph.

Anyone who has ever sold stock photographs through an agency or independently has, when a price is quoted, received the reply: "We don't know why you charge so much when so-and-so agency (or photographer) will do it (or sell it) for far less." These allegations are rarely true, especially when they concern well-established agencies or responsible and better known photographers, and for the most part are a ploy to beat down prices.

Where there can be deviation in prices is in the bulk sale of substantial quantities of pictures (twenty-five to fifty or more) for one particular publication. There is a tricky situation here that may put a strain on the photographer-agency relationship. On one hand an agency is in a position to supply many photographs for a single project, something it could not do if it did not have a large number of photographers in its "stable" and an equally impressive file of pictures. Yet the individual photographer's contribution to this project may result in the sale of only one or two images, so he gets very little out of the sale—way below the normal 50 percent of the regular fees. Does he accept this or not?

The agency's position is that he should, because it is simply a little extra money he otherwise would not be earning at all, and by so doing he also helps keep the agency solvent for future efforts on his behalf. But some photographers won't accept this and refuse to let their pictures go into a large pot for joint sales unless they have a high percentage of the sale and possibly a reduced commission for the agency. This is very much an individual decision and is a factor that should be taken into consideration and discussed when a photographer elects to join an agency.

Now that we've discussed many aspects of the issue of what photographs are worth and how you, the photographer, must charge for your services, let's move on to another important area, preparing a budget. Remember, Monday morning you may have a budget meeting.

Preparing a Budget

After our discussion of space vs. time rates, you should now be able to establish a budget. What should that budget include?

overhead	assistants	model time
planning	travel costs	field expenses
special needs	equipment rental	materials
processing	printing	copying

Until the photographer knows what is to be shot, where and when, what the potential weather factors are (if they are a factor at all), it will be impossible to calculate costs precisely, especially with the spectacular rise in cost of hotels, film, airline fares, car rentals and other services. About the only thing that has not risen in the same proportion has been, sadly enough, the average photographer's fee.

So, when you appear in Joe _____'s office you had better have some clear idea of what the job is really going to cost for the entire package.

Overhead

Even before you get to the point of quoting on a job, there are certain "intangible tangibles" that must be considered. Some people call it "overhead," some "general operating expenses," but call it what you will, it has to be considered part of doing business. If you are at the point where you are actively seeking work, then the chances are you have already set up your business. Wherever it is, you are going to have many costs in the way of rent, office expense, possibly lab or studio space, insurance, taxes, equipment purchases, as well as a host of other items that are not directly recoverable in your billings. You have to figure out some method of building recovery of these expenses into your job estimates, or else you are not going to be able to make the profit you need to make a living. In other words, being paid just for your time is not enough. If that is what you want, then you should be on a salaried staff job.

If you are to operate independently, you must realistically figure out what your basic overhead is or what it may come to if you can project just a few years ahead. You should also try to make an educated guess about your gross income goals. The gap between the two, projected costs *vs.* projected income goals, is the minimum amount that somehow has to be filled. It probably is too early in your career to know how busy you are going to be, although perhaps by now you are getting some inkling of how many non-revenue-producing days there can be in a year. If you can anticipate, however roughly, your annual number of shooting days, you can come up with an overhead percentage to be built into your fee schedule.

In other words, if your annual overhead from all non-billable expenses (and don't forget to include amortization of your equipment) comes to $16,000 per year, it is costing you three cents per minute just to stand still and breathe. Or putting it another way, if you are shooting at a rate of eighty working days per year, the first $200 per day of your fee goes just to pay your rent and overhead before taking out a dime for yourself. So when you start looking at the pricing schedules, you will now have a better idea of why certain fees are charged and what you have to get in order to survive, let alone earn a living.

It may be extremely difficult to allocate an accurate fixed percentage of every job you do to overhead, yet it must be worked out by some method, even if at the beginning, until you can stabilize your activity, you take arbitrary percentages and add them to your day rate or package rate. Again, being arbitrary and taking the eighty days of work I quoted earlier, an average fee of $500 per day would represent a gross income of $40,000 per year to physically run your business (and that is cutting it pretty close). Then adding 10 percent to cover overhead to the "standard" fee of $500, making it $550, becomes more realistic in terms of recovering your fixed costs.

I operate a stock photo library and from time to time employ outside sales representatives in foreign countries who work on a commission basis. I have also spent much of my working lifetime accumulating a vast library of photographs that have to be sorted, classified, mounted, captioned and filed safely and there is all the other work entailed in the maintenance of such an operation, not to mention rent of the floor space and other expenses necessary to running this file. How do I charge to recover these costs? I have to make arbitrary judgments simply for lack of realistic guidelines. When I sell certain rights to a photograph, I take 10 percent off the top of the sales price *before commissions are paid*. I do this with the hope that this more or less covers the cost of physically maintaining the file.

My accountants tell me I am probably not far off. You now know that a fee of $500 per day is not a $500 per day *profit*. And using the figures above, you will also realize that your annual overhead may indeed take nearly a third of your average day rate. If you are to survive, your budget must reflect all of these items as well as anything that is special to a particular job on which you are bidding or budgeting.

Time Planning

The only way you can estimate time for budget purposes is to find out quickly what the client wants in the way of coverage and at how many locations. You will have to build your own time schedule, estimating how long it will take you to work at each location. That should give you the minimum number of days you'll be on the location. Since nothing ever works according to schedule, particularly on an industrial or plant job, you also have to build in some additional time to account for margins of error. You have to calculate your travel time, not only to the primary location but between plants, weather factors if out-of-doors shooting is included, conferences and/or arrangement times. Be very careful in this area of time planning and take nothing for granted.

Long ago I was asked to do a major coverage of a large mining corporation with extensive properties in the Southwest. The purchasing agent of this company was responsible for "buying" photography although the selection of the photographer came through their public relations department. The purchasing agent treated the whole project with the same interest as he would buying several carloads of cement.

I was young, anxious, and didn't know any better. As the entire job required outdoor photography, I asked the PR man what to expect in the way of weather. "Oh," he said, "after February first there won't be a cloud in the sky until September first, so don't worry about it." So I didn't. I gave the client a tight (and probably over-competitive) price based on the number of days I thought the job would take, and a reasonable estimate of materials and other costs, and proceeded to the locations to shoot.

All went well until I got to the third of the four locations in southern Arizona, and it started to rain. It rained for seventeen consecutive days! The PR man said, "Don't worry, we'll adjust the whole package when you come back." So I didn't worry and waited out the rain.

When I returned the PR man said, "Gee, I am sorry but the purchasing department won't adjust the price. They said we had a delivery contract and that's the agreed-on delivery price so it has to stand."

Make your plans for shooting as tight as you wish. But remember to keep a *written* clause in your agreement for weather contingencies, strikes or any other catastrophe beyond your control that could cause delays. Depending on the time of year, the locations, prevailing weather patterns and similar factors, any price based on time alone has to be carefully thought out.

The same goes for almost any other aspect of the assignment. What about availability of plant personnel to assist? If the plant provides this help, there can be a considerable saving in your budget, and obviate the necessity of bringing help from home (see pages 140-141). What happens if a process is delayed or a machine breaks down? Be sure to clarify all of this with the client before you present your budget.

When dealing with delays in the field beyond your control, realistic measurements have to be used. It is traditional to charge from a quarter to one-half the day rate for all "nonproductive time" spent in the field, and when there are lengthy delays there can be friction over resolving the charges.

Travel time has to be considered the same way. If you can fly to a site from your own home base in an hour or two and start shooting almost immediately, do you charge for a full day of travel or a full day of shooting? In a situation like this, while the professional societies have laid down guidelines covering productivity and travel time, it might be wiser to be flexible in the pursuit of better public relations with the client. For instance, a compromise might be to charge for a half day of travel plus a half day of shooting, which should lower the first day's cost somewhat but still allow proper compensation for time. What about traveling in the evening between plants or locations? These are things that have to be considered in scheduling your travel time. There are ways of compromising with the client that will not create ill feelings, such as saving money for them by using (if available) overnight sleeping car train costs to eliminate an extra day of hotel costs, airport travel and excess baggage charges.

Field Expenses

Other considerations are field costs other than the expected ones of housing, shelter, transportation and subsistence. Are you going to need a forklift truck, or a cherry picker for shots made from high elevations, or will you have to rent an airplane or helicopter if the client wants aerials? How about ladders, props, models, set construction, electricians, plant security and personal security and safety? All of these items must be cleared *in advance*.

What about entertainment, food cost limits and bar bills? Most major magazines and publication groups which require extensive travel by their people pay a fixed per diem allowance for meals but have to throw in the towel when it comes to hotel rooms, car rentals, etc., although they try to make some effort to persuade their correspondents to find inexpensive accommodations.

An editor once mumbled at me when I left his office en route to the West Coast, "The heck with the Palace Hotel. Save money—find a friend to sleep with—it's cheaper, but don't put it on the expense account."

Company policies vary and they can also play havoc with your accounting. Tales of wild expense charges throughout the journalism world are legendary, and they vary from the cost of renting a ladder to the cost of renting a helicopter. The picture editor of one magazine called me once when I was an officer of the ASMP, and knowing that I had a wide range of friendship among his staff members, he felt free to ask a favor. He wanted to know "Why on earth would Tom Jones need a sixteen-foot ladder on a Pullman train trip between Chicago and New York?"

"Why indeed," I said. "I'll ask but I won't tell any tales out of school. If I can find out without getting Tom in trouble, I'll let you know." The editor agreed that, since the expense account in question had already been approved for payment, he was more curious than righteous about it and wanted to know the answer to this intriguing question. So did I. I called Tom and told him of the picture editor's query, adding that he didn't have to tell me, but we were both intrigued with the possibilities.

"It's no secret," he said, "You know our company has a strict rule about bar bills for the staff when entertaining is not an issue. On this assignment I put in a couple of hellishly rough days before barely making it to the train in a state of complete exhaustion. I wanted a drink—in fact several—and I was determined not to pay for them. I also knew they never questioned us on ladder rentals. So for every drink I ordered on that train trip I charged it as one foot of a ladder rental." Later I called Tom's boss, told him the story, and his response was "No objections."

Creativity, taste and ethics all play tremendous roles in the making of photographs and their ultimate delivery. And when these forces come into play there are bound to be differences of opinion and errors made. The client may not have enough visual experience to understand that ideas are not always translatable into images as one might preconceive them. Photographers, too, have to understand that what the client wants and/or needs may not agree with his own sensibilities or interpretations. This is an area where thorough discussions are mandatory and should be held in advance over every conceivable field problem that might arise.

What about unexpected costs that are a little harder to define? I once closed a story in Paris on a foggy night and had to be in London with my film by early morning. Everything was grounded, the trains were all booked, and my editors were not interested in my "problems." I did get there. It's amazing how twenty bucks worth of francs to the *Wagon-Lits* [Pullman] conductor suddenly helped find a "cancellation." But how do you bill it to your client? There are no receipts, no proof, yet it's a thoroughly legitimate charge. One way I handle this is to agree with the client *in advance* that a fixed percentage of the total expense bill will be added for intangibles such as the unexpected tipping of porters, gratuities, or other expenses.

You should discuss any special equipment needed for a job carefully with the client. Is the shooting going to require a piece of very special equipment? Is this something you should own? Can you rent it? And if so, at what cost? Or should you consider buying it and charging a rental fee for this specific use if no rental equipment of this nature is available? Take lighting equipment, for example. If you are operating even a modest-sized studio, it is likely that you have already invested several thousands of dollars in strobes or other lighting equipment.

Are you expected to tote this equipment out to East Dorten? Should you subject it to the strain of travel? Sometimes you can, sometimes not. It depends on where you are headed. If you opt to take the equipment, it might cost $200 each way for air freight alone if you are heading cross-country. Weigh that against renting the same type of equipment for, say, $50 to $100 a day for the two or three days you will be needing it, and see how it makes sense to rent the gear and charge the client for the rental.

You may own a car and probably use it for business in your neighborhood, but it is doubtful you would want to drive it or ship it cross-country for use on location, so of course you rent one and the rental is a chargeable expense. The same applies for a truck or a forklift, or even an airplane or helicopter if used for shooting. Cameras fall into this classification too. Most working photographers have a basic kit of professional equipment, but there can often be calls for very specialized gear.

Older magazines recognized this problem. In addition to paying each staff photographer an annual amortization payment in order to keep up with the basic equipment he was expected to own, their photo departments also maintained inventories of sophisticated and specialized gear for use in unusual situations where the photographer could never be expected to own such equipment. These included ultra-high-speed sports cameras with oversized film magazines, underwater rigs and housings, and cameras that could be hooked onto a missile gantry and perhaps even be destroyed by the blast-off. Ralph Morse, the "dean" of space photography, once fastened a dozen heat-activated motorized cameras to record one blast-off from the inside of a gantry. He got a sensational set of pictures but the cameras were destroyed as the rocket went by. There is much very expensive sophisticated equipment and all quite beyond the reach of even the most highly paid staffer.

So there should be no hesitation in building into your budget any specialized items that may be required on a rental basis. Sometimes the use of these rentals or "on the spot" purchases have had funny results. Because of my required mobility and the fact that I often had to be in two climate extremes almost at the same time, I have had to purchase clothing and other extras wherever I was. Once I had to go from southern Texas in summer to northern Canada two days later without a chance to hit home base. When I arrived in Canada, I bought a work coat. The magazines usually were generous about this sort of thing, but this time some cost-conscious hawkeye said, "Maybe he needs a special coat to do this job, but if he is going to keep it afterward he ought to pay for half of it." So a regulation was made to this effect and applying it for clothing seemed fair enough. However, the company from time to time ended up with some strange things when they enforced the "half interest" rule.

Once while using my own four-wheel drive vehicle in a rugged, remote area to haul a heavy load of lighting equipment, I not only broke both rear springs, which were repaired at the company's expense, but it became evident we would not get to the location unless additional "helper springs" were installed on the truck. I had this done, and then submitted my bill for them. "Oh no," said the accounting department, "If you keep them you have to pay half the cost." When I threatened to unbolt the 190-pound, grease-covered springs and put them on her desk as king-size paper weights, she quickly put the bill through for payment.

Materials, Development and Processing

In addition to obvious travel costs and other special items, there are the so called "normal costs" that have to be carefully calculated in your budget. Even the ordinary supplies you use can make a serious dent in your eventual profit if not properly planned. In your preliminary discussion with the client, find out what he is expecting in the way of a finished product. Black-and-white printing or color printing? Contact sheets, transparencies? What kind and what shape and size? All of these items are now very costly. Earlier, ADs would never accept film and processing charges because they always felt that was part of a built-in cost. It wasn't until they began to leave their offices and start spending time either in a studio or on location that they realized the amounts of film and processing used on a single job, even a simple one, could be enormous and involve staggering costs.

The prices of materials billed are a serious consideration. How do you buy and how do you sell, considering that you are neither a photo supply nor a processing business? Many professionals like to use color materials that have been pretested so that the qualities of each emulsion are known, as well as how the color ranges will relate to each other when pictures are assembled for layout. There are differences between emulsions of the same grade and ISO/ASA that may not be apparent to the naked eye. (Only your color engraver knows for sure.) So I and many of my colleagues buy large quantities of pretested emulsions (or we test certain samples ourselves) and then buy in quantity and store them in a freezer until ready for use. Invariably there will be some leakage, spoilage or waste that cannot be avoided.

How do you protect yourself? Simply by buying your supplies at trade or wholesale price and billing your client at regular list prices. There is nothing unethical about this. You will just about break even after losses due to waste, spoilage, expiration of film dates, and yet have material on hand so you can leave immediately on some fast-breaking story and not have to worry about getting a supply of film or other materials you will need.

The same goes for processing. Either you do it yourself or you farm it out. If you do it yourself, you or your lab technician's time is worth something per hour. If you farm it out, then those costs have to be paid for. Again, you should charge a modest mark-up to cover the cost of paperwork, inventories of chemicals and paper, the messenger time, lab equipment repair bills, etc. And for that matter, the carrying of the financing until you get paid. Do not feel awkward about this. It is a direct and honest way of doing business, and you can arrive at better-defined budgets without having to worry about what each item actually costs you.

Assistants and Models

Assistants and models have to be preplanned too. With the growing complexity of lighting equipment and increase in the use of large-format cameras for corporate or advertising work outside the studio, there has been a corresponding increase in the need for physical help on location. In many advertising shoots there is often a large entourage at the location — photographic assistants, models, stylists and ad agency people — and the whole affair can take on nightmarish cost proportions. But I am not talking about all that now. I am referring to the photographer who has to go into a plant or to a location and work out complex lighting or other physical situations that quite often require help and often a good deal of it. Some photographers who are well established and have generous budgets take their own assistants with them, which not only means their payrolls have to be built into the budget, but the field expenses of the support team as well. The same is frequently true for models.

In corporate (annual report), industrial, or public relations photography, I rarely bring assistants with me but insist, usually with approval of the client, that this kind of help comes from within the client's plant staff. When dealing with a manufacturing operation, I usually ask for two people, preferably one from the electrical department because a plant electrician normally is able to work anywhere in a plant and not be restricted to any one department or union jurisdiction. He will know where the electric supply sources are for your strobes or other gear and will not get you plugged into a 440V DC line instead of the 110VAC line you need. The second person I ask for is a general maintenance man who will know where to find a ladder, a dolly or hand truck, and also have unrestricted access to plant locations. The advantages of working this way are manifold. It's a lot cheaper for the client, it will give you total access to a plant, and you will have the benefit of company people with you.

When it comes to models, *some* of the above rules can be followed. If you are going to be working in a city not large enough to support a model agency and you need a model in a layout, a phone call to the fashion buyer or coordinator of the largest department store in the area will often put you on the track of someone who can fill the bill, and it will be a lot cheaper than bringing one from home base. Even having to transport models short distances may well offset the overall cost of including them as part of your entourage.

I once had an advertising assignment in a western farm state and knew I would never find a professional model within 500 miles of the location, and also knew the ad agency would never approve bringing in one from a great distance. With some reluctance I pressed a local woman into service who did not have the slightest idea of what professional modeling was about, but since she was intelligent and attractive and we were not on a fashion shoot, I took a chance and used her. She worked out satisfactorily, but that was an exception rather than the rule, and only because these particular photographs did not require close-ups or critical makeup, was I able to get away with it. Another ad in the same campaign, also shot in the West, did require using a professional model. The women's fashion buyer of the largest department store in Denver located a splendid person and I flew her by charter plane to Cheyenne, where I was shooting. She worked out fine, and the total cost was far less than it would have been to fly a model in from California, Chicago or New York.

So in budgeting you must consider these things and clarify them *in advance* with your client. There are other problems involving model hire. See pages 90-92 for more information.

Budget Format

It is the preplanning of the assignment that we are concerned with here and how much you can be specific about, especially if you have never been to a particular location before. By making up a checklist such as the sample in the appendix section of this book, you can figure out fairly accurately what you are going to spend on a job under normal circumstances. There could be many items on it that will be of no interest to you or your client, so I suggest you go over it carefully and make up your own budget form checklist on your letterhead. It can be used in many ways: (1) as a work sheet for estimating the cost of producing a job, (2) as a confirmation sheet that the client may sign to show proof of the assignment, or (3) as an itemized bill to be supported later with receipts, tickets, stubs, etc.

On the reverse side of this form are some recommended "terms and conditions." They represent an optimum set of conditions, and it is doubtful that a new and less seasoned photographer is going to be able to get a client to agree to all of them. Yet they are worth studying and drawing upon, particularly in the area of ownership and rights.

It should be emphasized that the above-mentioned optimum terms and conditions should be looked upon as goals, but practicality has to come into play also. By being too "hard-nosed" you can lose an entire job and continued relations with that client. But if the client is equally hard-nosed and over-demanding, then perhaps it might be advisable to pass up this golden opportunity and let him seek his photographer elsewhere.

What I am trying to do is establish an awareness in the new photographer that he or she is a unique person with creative abilities who must not be treated with general indifference. Respect for the artist has long been established in Europe (by law in some countries) and there are increasing efforts here to bring forth some of the same principles of the *droit de suite* (rights that follow) of an artist (see glossary).

What Is Being Bought and Sold

In dealing with clients you must be careful that all sides understand just what is being bought and sold. I discuss this here because the prices paid for a photographer's work will eventually reflect the use the client can expect from a photography project, and the photogapher, too, has to understand just what rights are being transferred after an image is created.

The most worthwhile lesson to be learned from an examination of the suggested budget form is the specification of the intended usage of the photographs. There has long been a gray area in what a purchaser thinks he is buying and what is actually being sold. Fees for the most part are determined by intended usage, and usages beyond the purpose of the assignment have to be very clearly spelled out.

The client, too, has rights and needs, and they should be respected. There should be a feeling of accommodation on the part of the photographer to make the whole assignment not only desirable, but exciting to perform.

Over the years of working in this field, I have gradually evolved a system of terms that I and most of my industrial clients have found fair and reasonable. I differentiate between editorial, advertising and industrial (or commercial) rights and establish all terms up front with my clients.

Customs of the trade have pretty much determined how editorial fees are arrived at. Advertising fees are handled differently (see page 82), and advertising rates for television are treated differently from print media, generally based on what is known as the CPM (cost per thousand) of readers of a magazine or viewers of a television program. That is why "ratings" are so important to advertisers and their agencies, and also why an experienced agent is helpful, if not downright necessary, in fee determination. But statistically the number of still photographs used in TV commercials are few and established current rates are frequently an acceptable guideline. They are not to be ignored by any means. A bigger problem occurs in pricing still photographs for advertising in regional editions of national magazines, though most large, high-budget campaigns are national in scope.

Still photographs are more apt to be used in lower-budget regional TV campaigns also. But what is a "regional" campaign? When the competition increased for the advertising dollar and television advertising began to crowd the magazines, it became important for the print advertiser to get the most out of his expenditures for media space. It did not make sense for a beer manufacturer, for instance, who marketed in only six states, to buy space in a magazine that was distributed nationally and thus pay for circulation in forty-four states that did not carry his product. Selective time buying on regional television stations could more effectively deliver a specified audience in a given region.

Therefore, the only way the print media could stay competitive was to establish regional editions. The regional is a hybrid. From an editorial viewpoint it is exactly the same nationwide or perhaps even worldwide. But the advertising is broken down by region and even by state and personal incomes, and the ad pages change with the market. *TIME* magazine, for instance, publishes many regional editions; that is, the magazine is the same editorially but the advertising content is determined by the demographic makeup of each geographical region. This is complicated and costly, but it does effectively lower the media cost to the buyer who has the need for placement in the magazine, but only in the area where he has a market. Formulas can be worked by circulation comparisons so that the use of a still photo in one layout in several regional editions of a national magazine can be a guideline in negotiating space rates. Therefore, the figures shown in the appendix of this book are only guides, since consideration has to be given to other factors: audience, insertions and usages planned—whether they are open-ended or for a specific campaign, and so on.

More recently there has been a trend toward allowing the advertising agencies to set space rates for regionals because they have better methods of determining the audience for a given ad. The agencies are not too interested in penny-pinching because their fees are usually based on a percentage of media costs.

Besides these qualifications, there is enough usage and custom to pretty well set the parameters of what an ad is worth. But the photographer should be alert to what is being asked and what he can deliver within a specified time period. Sometimes a little naiveté can help.

When I first became involved in the production of advertising photography, I was called by an agency for a job. The client said there were five locations to be covered and all the photography had to be completed in ten days. The shooting was simple, all exteriors, though some complicated prearrangements of men and equipment was necessary. My experience then was pretty much limited to editorial work, and I was familiar with current day or space rates.

When the AD asked how much I wanted for the shooting, I calculated ten days at the then ASMP minimum, and built in a 50 percent bad-weather and travel factor. As this was advertising, I knew the editortial rate was too low, so I tripled it as it would be a buy-out of all the rights to the photographs. That was the custom then, and it doesn't differ much now. I came up with a fee of $2,500 plus expenses, thinking I could easily cover the locations in the time allotted. Even so this was more than a magazine would pay for the same amount of time spent, even at going space rates, for an essay. The AD nodded, said, "Okay, pick up your purchase order on the way out," and we proceeded to discuss the assignment.

When I left, his secretary handed me *five* purchase orders for $2,500 each. The AD had been talking about the price of *each* job and, in my ignorance, I quoted $2,500 for the five locations and would have been happy to get it. No wonder he must have thought I was chintzy when I insisted on film and processing costs as extras. In this I came out with more than I expected but it might have been just as easy to interpret the meaning the other way around. So be clear in what you perceive, what the client is expecting you to do, for how much, and what the usages are going to be. And get clear purchase orders for every ad assignment you receive.

With commercial or public relations fees, you must cut across both editorial and advertising lines, because an editorial concept is frequently handled by advertising-oriented people.

My method is to work out a system with the client so he can get full value for his dollar and not compromise my ongoing rights to future earnings or usage of the materials. I always discuss negative possession, and if the client is unaware of precedents, I carefully explain that numerous legal decisions, including the new copyright law, state that a photographer, in the absence of any other agreement, does indeed own the negatives to a shooting because they are considered as *intermediate* materials and not the finished product. The primary concerns here are: Is the client getting what he is paying for? Is the photographer retaining the secondary rights he is entitled to? Actual negative possession is a big part of the answers to those questions.

Suppose the client says to you, "We have a photo department within the plant" or "We have our own system of photographic archives and we want the negatives." Do you turn down the job? Certainly not, even though it may go against your grain to give up the negatives. On the few occasions when it occurred I have compromised by shooting extra exposures or in some cases making good copy negatives or duplicate transparencies in one-of-a-kind situations and *increasing my fees to the client with his knowledge*, because of the *de facto* surrender of rights. (Even though you may have retained certain rights on paper, if you don't have copy negatives or color dupes on hand when you need them, your "secondary rights" are an illusion.)

Some clients do not understand all the ramifications of negative possession and why there may be advantages *not to have that possession*. In New York (and other states with sales tax laws) when a photograph is made for reproduction and only *rights to reproduce them* are sold, no sales tax is applicable since there is no transfer of the material. If you do a large job costing $100,000 including personnel, travel, field and laboratory charges, the transfer of negatives to the client would entail a tax of $8,750, a considerable amount when budgets are considered.

The wise client may then say, "Okay, you keep the negatives so long as we control the use of the pictures and own all of the reproduction rights." That too, can be a trap, and again you can agree in writing to restrict the use of the photographs to only noncompetitive or even non-threatening ones. It certainly would not be ethical, for example, to release any of those photographs to be used in an investigative report on the company or to use the pictures against the company to back up some EPA or OSHA (Occupational Safety Hazard Administration) complaint. No company or person wants to pay for self-incriminating matter. Also many companies want total control of their material to prevent leakage of industrial secrets, which is understandable. So there are many valid reasons why a company might want to know where their negatives are tonight.

Yet the photographer, too, has to be able to share in the "fruits of his vineyard toils." So here is where compromise can come into play. The photographer can agree that he will make the prints available for future use by the company at reasonable prices and in a reasonable amount of time. He can also restrict his use of the pictures to situations that are non-competitive or non-threatening to the company, and he can clear any borderline usages in advance, and abide by the company's decision, provided permission is not unreasonably withheld.

It must be made quite clear by the photographer that he retains the right to use these photographs for his own purposes as described above or for self-promotion. If he has agreed to release the negatives, there should be a written agreement that he too can have reasonable access to them just as promptly as the client would expect to have if he were to retain physical possession.

There are other aspects regarding the secondary use of assigned photographs that we will talk about in chapter nine. We will also deal with the whole question of copyright in that chapter, but it is important for the photographer to know at this point that the Copyright Act of 1976 clearly gives the *photographer* the copyright to anything he produces except under certain specific circumstances detailed in chapter ten.

Payment, Advances and Expenses

The last item for budget discussion is the method and schedule of payment. If you are dealing with a reputable company on a clearly defined assignment, there should be no question of prompt payment, but there is a gray area when it comes to advances and repayment of expenses. In motion picture production, where the sums are usually much greater than for still photography, it is customary for payment to be made in three parts. Usually one-third is paid on signing a contract, one-third when the shooting is finished, and the remainder when the final film negative is delivered.

In book publishing when sizable advances are considered, the custom can vary from the entire advance being delivered "up front" to a prepayment of one-half to two-thirds of the advance on the signing of the contract and the balance on delivery of the manuscript.

Still photography advances follow no formal routine. Magazines have always permitted decent advances against expenses without hesitation, and yet advertising agencies and some general business companies are reluctant to do this. I have had occasional problems when trying to apply editorial guidelines to advertising, especially when it comes to advances. Sometimes the photographer's demand for an advance is not so much a matter of getting money "up front" for out-of-pocket expenses as it is in some measure a guarantee for payment. This, then, becomes a matter of negotiation and I feel that you *must have* advances if considerable outlays are to be made for airline tickets, car rentals, hotels and meals, and other monies necessary to properly complete the job on time. I have never had any problem in obtaining out-of-pocket advances from commercial clients, though sometimes they have tempered advance cash outlays by providing airline tickes and authorizing hotel and car rental charges to be made directly to them, with which I have no argument.

I once had a dispute with an advertising art director about an advance to cover several thousand dollars' worth of airline fares and special equipment rentals. I could have charged these costs to my own credit cards, but didn't choose to do so because of the reputation his agency had begun to acquire of stretching out payments for an unconscionably long period of time.

The AD argued, "Oh, we never pay advances. How do we know we will get the pictures we need?" I responded, "You don't, but you are paying for my time. Approval of my work is not negotiable. Even if I don't bring back a single picture you like, you will still owe me for my time and expenses. Since you will have to pay anyway, why make it hard for me to make this job come out properly? After all, you hired me on the basis of what you think I can do, and statistically the chances that I will perform according to your expectations are pretty good, so cut out the nonsense and get me the $2,000 I need to get started." He did.

Getting It in Writing

With all of the above issues spelled out, the assignment is yours and you are about ready to start packing your bags, so what is left to do? A very important matter: getting *written confirmation* of all the decisions made verbally with your client. This can take the form of a purchase order, a letter of intent, a contract if the project is big enough and involves enough dollars or, in the event of a telephone agreement, a faxed memo, mailgram, telex or cable . . . anything on paper . . . outlining the specific points of agreement. Warning— unless you have dealt with a particular client before and have had no financial or other problems with him, make no move until that written confirmation is in hand.

A client once asked me why this is necessary. "After all, we are both anxious to have this project work," he said. My answer was, "Well, it will keep us both honest."

Interview

Gordon Parks

Photographer, Writer, Artist, Filmmaker

Gordon Parks comes as close to being a Renaissance man as anyone I know. Photographer, painter, filmmaker, composer, writer, dramatist, and a few other talents, are all embodied in this gentle, sensitive man. Born in Fort Scott, Kansas, and raised in Minnesota, Parks first became interested in photography while working as a dining car waiter running between St. Paul, Minnesota, and Seattle, Washington.

Parks became justifiably tired of railroads. In the evening, while the other waiters retired to the bunkhouse car, Parks would remain in the dining car to read, look at magazines, and try to get some insight into the outside world. Once, while on a stretch of lonely track, he picked up a magazine containing the work of Dorothea Lange and other Farm Security Administration (FSA) photographers.

"I became very interested in these pictures, and how they were used to depict the Depression era. Then I read Erskine Caldwell's *You Have Seen Their Faces* done with Maggie (Margaret Bourke-White), and suddenly photography became a very stimulating vehicle for me."

At that time Parks had had no photographic experience, and no desire to make a photograph. "On a Chicago layover I went to the Art Museum where I looked at some paintings. The feeling was in my blood, my psyche, whatever you call it, and that same afternoon I saw a film by Norman Ally on the sinking of the gunboat 'Panay.' When the film was over and he jumped out on the stage in a white suit, I thought that was tremendously glamorous. So when I got to Seattle, Washington, I spent my last twelve bucks on a camera in a pawnshop, an old Voigtlander Brilliant. I think I bought it for its name because it wasn't a very good camera. The same afternoon I got the camera I fell into Puget Sound trying to photograph seagulls and some firemen fished me out with a long pole, but I held onto the camera. I never took the film out because I didn't know how. The guy in the pawnshop had put it in for me.

"Back in Minneapolis I went to Eastman Kodak and asked them to take the exposed film out and develop it for me. Apparently the salt water didn't hurt it too much because when I came back, the guy at the counter asked how long I had been shooting pictures. When I said this was my first roll, he said, 'Really? Well, you have a good eye and if you keep this up we'll give you a show.' I said, 'What do you mean, a show?' He said, 'Well, we'll put your pictures in the window.' I got really busy then and in about four months Eastman Kodak gave me my first show in a store window in Minneapolis.

"This was in 1936 or 1937. It made me realize how much I wanted to *be somebody*; I wanted to get off that railway so bad and I used the camera to do it. I had thought of painting, but that was too time-consuming and too hard. I also wanted to sculpt, but that was too remote. Here I was, way out in Minnesota and already with a wife and kids, thinking it would be years before I could make any money from it. So I went for photography, and that was it.

"I got my professional start by taking pictures for an exclusive women's store called Frank Murphy's. Even though I had never made a fashion photograph before, I asked to shoot some fashions for them. Just as Mr. Murphy was kicking me out of the store his wife said, 'Frank, what does the young man want?' He told her I wanted to make fashion pictures and he had told me their work was done in New York or Chicago. I felt smaller and smaller, and was just about out the door, when the woman said, 'How do you know he can't shoot fashions, Frank?' She put some fine clothes together, got fashion models, and I double-exposed every picture but one, but she liked that one. I re-did the pictures and continued shooting until Marva Louis, Joe Louis's wife, came by, saw them and asked who had shot them. When told, she suggested I come to Chicago. I did and started making pictures of rich ladies at the behest of Marva. By then I was also doing other things on the South Side of Chicago, more documentary-type photographs."

When the Community Art Center saw his South Side pictures they encouraged Parks to apply for a Rosenwald Fellowship, even though no one had ever received one for photography. "So I applied," he said, "and I was judged by other photographers who turned me down flat, until Peter Pollack, historian and writer, said that was ridiculous." He submitted the application to a school of artists who accepted Parks for the fellowship, with every judge voting "yes."

By then Parks had met one of the FSA photographers who suggested Parks work out his fellowship at the FSA project in Washington, and put him in touch with Roy Stryker. Stryker wanted to use Parks but was reluctant to subject him to the rampant racial discrimination in Washington. (Parks learned later Stryker had told the Rosenwald people this was the only reason he hesitated to use Parks.) But the Rosenwald people evidently convinced Stryker to take Parks on, and when he came to Washington, Stryker said, "Okay, you are going to have to work out things your own way."

Stryker told him to go out and look around Washington (Stryker did this with all his photographers, directing each to learn about the area in which they would be working), and to buy a coat. So Parks walked into the most elegant department store in Washington but no one would wait on him. It was the same with the movies or restaurants. Bigotry was widespread and his anger built. He wanted to use his camera against it. One of his first pictures, of which he is still extremely proud, is a photograph of a black woman with an American flag and a mop he called "American Gothic."

Stryker was shocked, saying, "My God, you'll get us all fired!" Nonetheless both he and Parks were delighted with the picture. It was only comparatively recently that Parks, who thought the photograph had been destroyed, found it in the files, and it has become one of the most popular pictures in circulation at the Library of Congress.

On a Rosenwald stipend of $200 per month he had to sustain himself, a wife and three children. He worked out his fellowship in the first year with Stryker, and when the FSA was taken over by the Office of War Information,

Parks was hired by them. He was classified as a correspondent, and assigned to the 332nd Fighter Group, the only all-black fighter group in the segregated Army Air Corps. Among other indignities, he was kicked out of the Port of Embarkation despite clear orders from the Pentagon. Even his Commanding Officer, West Point-trained Colonel Benjamin O. Davis Jr., later to become the first black General in the U.S. Army, was of little help to Parks. But he played out his war role and returned to New York and started making the rounds. Eventually he saw Alexey Brodovitch at *Harper's Bazaar* who granted him an interview without knowing Parks was black. But when Parks appeared and assured Brodovitch that those photographs were indeed his, Brodovitch said, "I'd like to hire you but I can't because this is a Hearst Publication and they don't hire Negroes."

The friend who had brought Parks to Brodovitch's attention was rightly angered, so she sent him on to Edward Steichen at the Museum of Modern Art who was also upset. He sent Parks to see Alexander Liberman at *Vogue,* who said, "Well, I don't know how we are going to do it, but we will," and Parks started making fashion photographs for both *Glamour* and *Vogue.*

This was a great departure from the documentary style Parks had learned under Stryker, but with Stryker's encouragement he stayed in fashion because, as the latter put it, "After all, you still have to earn a living." Eventually Stryker took him on — as part of the Esso crew for Standard Oil (New Jersey), now Exxon. He tried to keep Parks out of the South as much as he could even though most of Esso's empire lay there. But there were extensive Esso coverages elsewhere and Parks was able to deal successfully with discrimination.

In 1942 when the Esso project began winding down, Parks was invited to join *LIFE* magazine's staff. There he went on general assignment duty, doing a little of everything from the front of the book to the back. He thinks in retrospect that they gave him more varied assignments than any other staffer. Some of his more memorable essays were "Harlem Gang Story," "Crime Across America" and "American Poets." He also did much fashion work early on when the fashion editor, Sally Kirkland, sent him to Paris to cover the designer collections. It was Parks's versatility that took him from fashion to documentary, to photographing crime and poverty, and back to fashion. He learned a great deal from Kirkland, but he also had to learn fashion jargon, something totally alien to him. He said there were some pretty funny moments in Paris when he was trying to tell his French models to use a little "pizazz," because that was a word Kirkland had taught him.

While this diversity may have been something that many other staffers would have liked to avoid, Parks said, "Because I am black I realized that I had to prepare myself for almost anything. It was impossible for me to accept specialization. If they said 'We need a good sports photographer' I would say, 'Well, I just happen to have one in my back pocket!' And perhaps that was the reason I did so many different things."

The watershed in Parks's career was the Flavio story. "It started," he said, "as a typical *LIFE* story on Brazil, one that contained all the usual family elements: religion, communism, and other conflicts of culture in South America." Parks found this approach uninteresting and went up to the *Favela*, a notorious slum perched on a hillside overlooking Rio de Janeiro, looking for fathers who might fit the bill. After a few desultory interviews with the aid of an interpreter, he told me, "I was sitting beside a tree on the mountaintop and saw this little boy come by with a five-gallon tin of water on his head. A beautiful child, but obviously dying of some disease. He smiled at me and I smiled back. His name was Flavio. I followed him up the steep mountainside to his shack, offering to help him carry the water, but he refused. He lived in indescribable squalor with six or seven brothers and sisters. The father was down the mountain somewhere, so I just hung around taking pictures of the scene. Eventually he returned and I explained what I was doing. Because I was so wrapped up in the story I moved out of my fancy hotel on the beach in Rio and moved into the *Favela*. I stayed for two or three days, to the consternation of my editors who had lost track of me. I went back down and cabled them, and they were sensitive enough to wire back for me to 'keep in touch and continue on the story because it sounds great! . . .' "

Parks spent nearly two months in the *Favela* with Flavio, keeping a diary all the time, and when he left, his last entry was, "Today I am leaving Flavio and he asked me if I would be coming back. I said 'yes,' but I knew I was lying and would never go back. I never want to see such poverty again in my life."

When the story ran, *LIFE* also published the diary as part of the text and letters started to pour in, insisting he go back. Readers also began sending money for Flavio — over $30,000. Parks returned and this time brought Flavio back with him to the National Jewish Hospital, National Asthma Center in Denver, where he received an education and proper medical attention. Parks followed up with another story on Flavio and later a book entitled *Flavio* (W.W. Norton, 1978), which won a best biography award. Flavio is now back in Rio with a wife, several children, a job and a decent life away from the *Favela*. Parks's involvement was so deep, it became a permanent part of his life. Besides producing great photographs and texts, he brought worldwide attention to his great sensitivity and his skill as a creative journalist who cares about what he does.

Parks is a prolific artist. He has produced thirteen books, several feature films and documentaries, and has written and directed a ballet, composing some of the music for it, as well as five piano sonatas and a symphony. He never had formal music training.

He has also painted, had his work displayed in major galleries, and was given a huge retrospective photographic exhibit at the New York Public Library. Recently an entire evening was devoted to him at New York's Cathedral of St. John the Divine, where he was surrounded by musicians, dancers and writers who performed and read his work. The huge hall was filled by friends and admirers, and attended by the Mayor of the City of New York, who let us in on a secret — Parks was a tennis partner of his. Still vigorous at eighty, he continues to work and experiment, but keeps going back to his first love, still photography, currently blending his skill as a photographer with that of a fine artist and producing new work combining paint and photography.

"Everything I have learned," he said, "I had to learn the hard way because I was so poor as a kid. I don't resent the fact that I was born poor, and I suppose if I were given my 'druthers' and someone said, 'Listen, we're going to start you over as a rich white kid and send you to Harvard or Yale, but we don't know how you are going to turn out,' I would take it anyway. I don't appreciate the scars, the buffeting around. Once I broke the blackness barrier, I refused to let my blackness impede me or become a problem. I could not work freely if I were still carrying this thing around on my back. I think what really saved me was going to Europe, where I didn't have to face the problem of racism in America every day. It freed me. I was in Paris more or less permanently in 1951 and 1952, and I covered much of Europe from there. I was able to hear the music of the masters, see the great art, and all the things I couldn't learn much about in America. The Louvre was only a block and a half from the old *LIFE* Bureau on the Place de la Concorde. I went to see the French Impressionists at least once a week. I met many writers, among them, Camus. It was a whole new opening for me over there. I had a house in the suburbs and my family with me, and when we would drive from Paris to Cannes for a vacation, I didn't have to worry where my family would sleep that night.

"I never considered becoming an expatriate. I was determined to use what I learned there and bring it back to America because I felt I was an American and my stake was here."

In discussing race and creativity, he reiterated that he is not a black artist but an artist who happens to be black. Parks talked about his novel, *Shannon*, an Irish novel. "Some of those critics," he said, "castigated me for writing on this subject, but I don't hear any complaints about a white writer writing about Nat Turner, so I can write about J.M.W. Turner, the English painter. You don't have to be a pumpkin to photograph pumpkins."

On the craftsmanship of the young photographer, Parks said, "I think they lean too much on gadgetry. They get a wide-angle lens that they know is sharp from here to there, and then proceed to shove it up your nose, get the guy's head lopsided, all in the name of photography. Many young photographers often lack concern with the true ethic of a pictorial presentation. They seem to go for the grotesque, anything that makes a picture look unusual. Maybe they feel they are not good enough to produce a good 'straight' photo, so try to attract attention by doing it another way.

"It's like some comics I know," he continued. "They think they have to use obscene language to get their audience juiced up. It really means they are not good enough comics to get laughs without using obscenity. I feel this way about some photography I see today. Too many photographers don't know what they are doing and many magazines fall in line with it too. Unfortunately some fine art directors also play the same game.

"I don't think there are enough purists around anymore," Parks said. I asked him if a *purist* could earn a living today and he said, "I don't know; it could be difficult because some editors know even less than their photographers. But if I had to start over today, I would never lend myself to anything that was not in good taste."

To Parks, the most satisfying aspect of his still photo career has been his communication with the people he photographed, less from expressing his thoughts or feelings than by permitting those whom he photographed, who had no other means of expression, to express themselves through his pictures.

He photographed the Black Panthers and said, "*LIFE* used me very well in the 1960s. They never normally sent me on black subjects just because I was black, and when the black revolution came along they tried to do the Black Muslim story without me. I had to walk a very tight line because when I was photographing the Muslims, the Panthers, and Malcolm X, I had to also prove to *them* that they could not buy me because I was black. And I had to let *LIFE* know that I had to write and photograph these pieces the way I felt about them, because my neck was on the line. So I was in a most peculiar position. I don't think that *LIFE* at first thought I was going to remain as objective on this as a reporter should be, and I was all set to prove that I could. I didn't know how I would do it, but I was determined I would. I think I survived because I shut my ears to both sides, the magazine *and* the Muslims, and reported what I saw."

He often had to defend himself at *LIFE* against editors with strong ideas, poorly articulated. He told me of one assignment in Pennsylvania where he had to photograph a miner's hands as part of a story on a "pop" singer, a miner's daughter who had just made it big. He arrived at the precise moment when the girl's father was reading a letter from her.

Parks made a strong back-lit picture of the letter with the words coming through and the dirt and grime on the miner's hands very apparent. The managing editor was unconvinced about the picture until Parks barreled in and said, "What's wrong with it? This is what you asked for plus more." The editor said, "Okay, what do you want?" Parks replied, "I want a full page." The editor said, "You got it. Now get out of my office!" But if Parks hadn't had the guts to speak up for what he thought was right about his perception of his subject matter, the picture would have been killed. And Parks's advice to the newer photographer is clear: Produce your pictures as you see them and fight if necessary for their survival.

Interview
Mary Ellen Mark
Photographer

When one turns to the table of contents of almost any major magazine
devoting space to documentary picture essays on social issues, and the name
Mary Ellen Mark is bylined, the reader can be assured before even turning
to the story, that it will be one of sensitivity and incisive reporting. Mary
Ellen Mark is one of our sharpest observers and almost any story she probes
into will reach into your heart. I talked with her in her office and photo
library (the world is her studio) in lower Manhattan. There was not much
in the way of photographic equipment visible, but what I did see was a visual
library of voluminous files on work she has already accomplished, and which
she uses to further extend her career.

She told me, "I started in photography when I received my Master of
Fine Arts degree at the University of Pennsylvania and then a scholarship
to the Annenberg School of Communication, which at that time was a more
creatively oriented school and offered degrees in photography, film-making,
TV production and writing. This was a hands-on type of academic experience. It has changed now and become very intellectual and theoretical.

"I loved photography from the moment I picked up a camera and knew
this is what I wanted to do. I loved taking pictures and being out on the
street and in contact with people I'd never met before and would never
have met if I didn't have my camera. That's what led me to becoming a
photographer.

"After I graduated I got a Fulbright Scholarship and went to Turkey to
photograph. I came to New York, printed up a portfolio and began going
around to see editors. My first break came from *Jubilee* magazine, a Catholic
publication doing in-depth reportage stories. Later I received several interesting assignments from *Look* magazine. One was on Fellini making the
Satyricon and another on a center in London dealing with young heroin
addicts. I continued working over the years primarily as a magazine photographer and doing my own projects and books. And that's where I am now,
twenty-five years later.

"I did several books. One on Mother Teresa for the Friends of Photography, others on prostitutes in Bombay (Knopf) and on runaway kids in Seattle. Other work included books on the women's ward in a mental hospital
in Oregon, and my retrospective book. These are the projects I love, because
they permit me to spend an extended period of time with groups of people
I care about, and whose lives fascinate me.

"Story ideas come from either the editors or from myself; it works both ways, but more and more now I have to search out the stories. The kind of in-depth stories I enjoy are not often done by the magazines anymore. As for books, the present economy has reduced the market for the kind of books I do because they are strong in emotional content and not always commercial projects.

"I do a lot of portraits of people, portraiture that says something intimate about them. I photograph with a point of view and a very particular approach. I like to raise questions and thoughts as to who that person is, not necessarily negative questions, but I like to get into that personality and maybe reach a secret corner of their life. I consider myself a very personal photographer. I hope my photographs reflect that.

"I have done some commercial work; I'm not against it as it can fund your personal work, and also the right advertising or commercial assignment can allow you to do great photographs—at least that is what I hope for. It would be wonderful to shoot an advertising campaign where I could do my own pictures. I think it would be great to have that kind of support as it would result in my making fine photographs that many people would see. An art director would have to have the insight to hire me because my portfolio is not recognizable as commercial.

"Basically all I want to do is make great photographs. I don't care if its for a magazine, for a book, or for an advertising client. I care about making great photographs. That's the bottom line and that's what it's all about. I just want to be given that chance.

"At present I feel the economy is affecting documentary photography because often a documentary story takes a lot of time, you have to work on a project for an extended period of time. This is money. It's not the quick take where you shoot one day and you're finished. Magazines are reluctant these days to give a lot to in-depth stories and these stories need space. Also because of the time involved, stories can be expensive.

"My strength is in working quietly and intimately with a person or group of people. I think it's very important for a photographer to realize where their strength lies and pursue that. I do not take a ritualistic approach to finding work.

"In my India circus project (which I wanted to do for twenty years) I was able to get some financing from Ray DeMoulin at Kodak, without which I would not have been able to do the project. I then hired a wonderful woman in India to do the research, make contacts and set up shooting schedules. On that project I also called some magazines and received additional help. I hope that I'll be able to do a book on the circuses. But I was able to realize a dream I had for twenty years and that is what is most important.

"For young photographers getting started now, I think there are more opportunities in commercial work than in personal documentary photography. Commercial work is tough also, but probably less so today than documentary, because the major outlets are fewer. I would still tell a young person to do their own work. I would always tell them that regardless of the times, your own personal work is very important. Ideas are good but you must show pictures that demonstrate your ability. You may come up with the greatest idea in the world but you have to be able to execute it.

"No editor, even if you have a great idea, is going to assign you unless they are sure you can do the work. I think it is a necessity to come up with twenty or thirty really solid photographs. It doesn't have to be on any project but something that proves your ability to an editor. If I were an editor I would want to see those fine pictures before I even considered that person for an assignment.

"Over the years I have had many photo essays published in a large variety of magazines. Recently, two stories for *Fortune* on rural poverty and urban poverty, and the other, about fifteen pages, for *Texas Monthly* on small-town rodeos. I have produced several pieces for *LIFE*. One on the Perkins School for the Blind and another on a homeless family living in a car in Oregon. My Indian circus pictures also appeared in *LIFE*. I did a story on young crack addicts in San Francisco for *Rolling Stone*, and the Special Olympics for *Vogue*, and other work. My photographs have also been in *The New York Times Magazine*.

"I think electronic imaging has great potential even in documentary photography because self-publishing has great potential. I am for anything that will expand the capabilities of a photographer to present new ways of showing work or develop new areas. In portraits it can be a way of expression, as an example the cover Greg Heisler (see page 117) did for *TIME*. That photograph of Ted Turner was made up of many picture elements, but it was a strong documentary image. Greg is that kind of great photographer who is always open to innovative visual expression.

"I am exploring with my husband some ideas in digital images and disks as a means of story-telling. I think there can be a form of self-publishing which may make it a little easier for photographers to get into this medium."

Fish-eye photo of middle-Manhattan (from color). Remote-operated motordrive camera on boom under helicopter skids gives unusual global horizon-to-horizon effoot, yet allows close-up of busy city center. For advertising campaign to symbolize worldwide use of the client's product. (Widely resold).

Construction workers on gate of inland waterway lock. Was used as a back cover for a magazine essay. Avoided dullness in composition by taking advantage of strong contrasting shapes and tones and using workers to add elements of scale and action. Often sold as a general construction photo.

(*Overleaf*) Railroad roundhouse at El Reno, Oklahoma. Made in 1948 from a small plane during a pipeline patrol for an oil company. With the roundhouse since razed and its old steam engines scrapped, the photograph is a graphic, historic memorial to the Age of Steam, and is now in several art museums.

Muskingum, Ohio. A lovely small-town view is set off by old trees and a placid river. Originally made in color as part of an essay on the Ohio River basin, it won a Gold Medal Award at the Washington, DC Art Director's Club and has had years of active resale.

GEM of Egypt. GEM is an acronym for a giant earth mover. Indeed it is. It took a Veri-wide camera with 100 + degree angle of view to show its 120-foot height and retain the scale of the huge tractor in the bucket. Made for an investigative expose on strip mining.

Color conversions to black and white can retain the detail and tone of a good 35mm Kodachrome. "Generational" increases in contrast are not a problem with good copy film. This stately old church and nearby houses are on the Ohio River bank below Cincinnati.

Roughnecks (oil drilling crew) on a drilling platform deep in the Louisiana swamps. A typical industrial photograph, it requires care on the part of the photographer to stay out of the way of the workers, not get hurt by flying tools, and to not fall on greasy floors.

Underground work for the industrial photographer can be hazardous to his health and to the health those around him. Here, he has to understand technical problems of shooting in high-moisture, possibly explosive conditions, and not create any problems by using unsafe photographic gear.

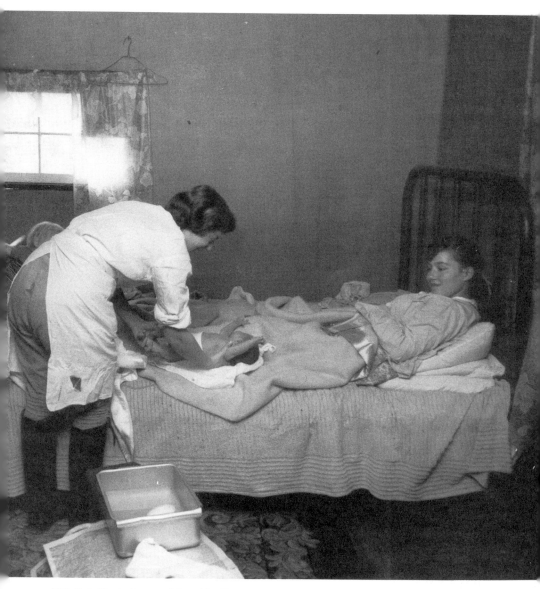

Midwife in Kentucky mountain cabin. Also an industrial photograph as it was made for a pharmaceutical corporation. It received international attention when picked up by *LIFE* magazine for a two-page spread on the Frontier Nursing Serivce, a volunteer health organization providing care for isolated families in the Appalachian Mountains. Making the photograph with a Nikon was easy compared to dealing with the hostility of the Nursing Service officials to the press because of the past behavior of another photographer.

Coils of copper tubing ready for shipment in a Midwest factory. Compounding the technical problems of producing this photograph for a corporate annual report was the fact that the client would not permit any interference in production (and rightly so) while the electricians were setting up lighting equipment. Even though slave-cell operated, high-capacity strobe units would have facilitated photography, the danger to this expensive and fragile equipment on the cluttered work floor mandated the use of large banks of flash bulbs. A view camera was used with extreme wide angle lens to maintain total sharpness throughout the image. In highly complex industrial or advertising photography such as this, it is important to take the time to make Polaroid tests, since there is no going back for reshooting if something goes wrong. Not only will these tests "proof" your images, but they also serve as checklists for inclusion of proper safety equipment where required. It is always wiser to "build" your lighting in stages by using smaller units to cover smaller areas. It is another form of painting with light. The use of high-capacity strobes here would be counterproductive. They would prevent the pinpoint detailing of corporate logos or individual worker activity. Now is the time to obtain your releases.

Rome's Colosseum from an unusual aerial perspective. So much so, that one ignorant viewer made comments on the "damage" caused by aerial bombing in World War II. [Rome was an open city.] This rarely seen approach to the ancient stadium now gives the viewer a clearer understanding of the events that took place in this arena centuries before. Making aerial photographs in Europe has always been extremely difficult, not because of technology, but deep-rooted bureaucracy, and hard-to-surrender powers of censorship that date back to the time of Hannibal's invasion of Europe. Fortunately, the reality of satellite photography has convinced many bureaucrats that these ancient monuments are not military targets, and photographers are finding new freedoms.

Wall Street photograph made from a helicopter by using a custom-built "aerial" camera with fixed focus 47mm Angulon lens on 4″ × 5″ film. By tipping the camera sharply downward, I used natural distortion inherent in a wide-angle lens to dramatize the "opening flower cluster" arrangement of tall buildings and enhance their soaring aspect. First used in *The New York Times* as a double-page ad, it has sold widely since. It was produced in 1962 and is still widely used as a symbol of New York's famous skyscrapers.

French policeman. This man's Gallic charm is evident in his visage. In travel or regional photography, one must be careful to include in the background, proper keys to the environment. Releases are unnecessary for journalistic pictures made in public places, but getting one and then sending your subject a free print will mako a new friend for you.

Bottom change, Bessemer furnace. (Now defunct.) Action documentary photographs are always exciting to make, especially when they are unplanned. I had one roll left in a twin-lens reflex and was about to replenish my film as I passed the "ballet" of the steelworkers. The action took seven minutes. I shot it with natural light and that was it.

Chapter Six
On Assignment: I

The assignment is yours, the knots have been unraveled, the purchase order has been issued, a cash advance is on the way, and you have ordered your materials. Now what?

The first thing you should do is spend time at the company office if it's a corporate job or checking previous layouts if it's an editorial or advertising assignment. The home office of the company you are covering will probably have a photo library or collection so you can see what was shot before, and how it was handled. You can also draw some conclusions about whether the company was satisfied with earlier photographers or if you were called because they were not. It may also have been evident from your earlier conversations who the previous photographers were, and if it makes any sense for you to speak with them without stirring up any uncomfortable feelings, do so. This is a delicate matter and you must use good judgment about whether to do this at all. But any information you can get about potential problems or pitfalls they may have run into would be helpful. The main thing is to find out as much as you can about what you are going to face on the location(s). Again, it's a matter of the five *W's* of journalism: What? Who? Where? When? and Why?

Travel and Housing Arrangements

How about choosing transport, housing, car rentals? This is important except in small towns where there may be little or no choice in housing and you are completely at the mercy (or graciousness) of the company you are photographing. I like to make most of my own travel arrangements if the company or client has supplied me with open-date travel tickets or travel cards.

When there is a sizable amount of equipment to be moved, I prefer to ship sturdier gear by airfreight rather than subject it to the mercy of baggage "handlers." You can also thus avoid the side effects of the airlines' bad habit of "breakfast in Chicago, dinner in Los Angeles, and your baggage in Karachi." Also there is nothing more debilitating to a case of strobe lights than a ride down a conveyor chute from a curbside check-in. It's not going to do your film any good, either, to face the increasing use of X ray in *checked baggage*.

Shipping your equipment by airfreight requires a special trip out to the airport several hours in advance of your departure, and if there are any international legs to your assignment, you will also have to arrange with customs, both here and abroad, for return of equipment and film, and find out about the import-export idiosyncrasies of the country you may be traveling to. All of this takes time, and time is what you have to allocate to these problems. If none are present, then move on.

I have also found that shipping sizable amounts of equipment by airfreight is not only cheaper for the client than shipping it as excess baggage, but also results in better handling and better insurance evaluations. You can often buy extra high insurance coverage at the airline counters, as the rate even for, say, one million dollars is very low and your equipment will get *extra special* handling. It most certainly will not be dropped down a conveyor chute and probably will be personally escorted off the airplane. You will also have a pretty good idea of what flight it will actually be on, should you and your equipment's schedule come apart.

I have no objection to the use of travel agencies, and in a smaller community they can be especially helpful because of the local and personal touch, but for the most part I have found they are not interested in handling one- or two-night reservations in hotels or motels, except for resort areas.

Because your schedule is apt to change abruptly, do your own travel bookings. Almost every major hotel and motel chain, car-rental agency and other travel organization has a toll-free (800) phone number. If you use your own charge cards to make reservations and later have to change, be sure not only to cancel but also to get a cancellation number. Otherwise you may be stuck with paying for a reservation you made and didn't keep. The same holds true with airlines, and remember too that business people traveling on short notice rarely can take advantage of reduced fare programs unless they want to go standby, which is not the way I like to travel. Always cancel rather than be a no-show. You could need that canceled seat yourself someday. I have a cardinal rule that I never travel, if I can possibly avoid it, without knowing in advance exactly where I am going to sleep, whose car-rental service I will use, and as much as possible about the city I am traveling to. One thing I do not like when traveling on assignment is surprises.

Once, when lecturing at a photographic society meeting, someone in the audience asked, "What is the first thing you do on arrival in a new city?" My answer was, "Make a reservation to leave." I wasn't kidding. When you arrive at an airport, it takes only a moment to stop by the counter of the airline you will be using on your next leg or return trip and make that critical reservation that you may or may not be able to get a few days later, particularly if it falls at the end of the week. You can always change it if your schedule changes (maybe), but at least that's out of the way and you can forget those last-minute scrambles.

Equipment and Supplies: Plan Ahead

With your travel schedule and housing arrangements set, the next step is organizing your equipment and supplies. Think carefully about what you are going to do, what you are going to need, and then add extras for emergencies. Pretend there is no camera or supply shop in the world except your own and that you are going to have to work only with what you bring from home. The only possible exception is working on location in the largest of the major cities, and supply sources there should be used sparingly. This may sound silly, but if you are as demanding of critically tested color emulsions as I am, this makes sense.

What about batteries for all purposes? Strobes? Meters? Recharging units? How about the units themselves? Have they been tested? Are they working properly? If there is any doubt in your mind about a piece of equipment continuing to function in the field, do you have a backup? What about the cameras? If you are using small cameras (35mm or 120-size), do you have extra bodies? How about convertible multifocal-length lenses for emergency use with large-format cameras? Extra film backs or carriers when that critical one jams? How about some small tools? 'Gaffer' or common one inch black camera tape? Take plenty, and from what filmmaker friends have told me, it seems half of Hollywood is held together with it. (See section on equipment.)

Marty Forscher, probably the best camera repairman in the world, has often said that a camera for professional use in the field should have two major attributes. First, it should be built like a hocky puck, and secondly, instantly repairable with a paper clip and roll of black camera tape. So far such a camera has yet to be built, so you may be called upon to make some emergency repairs in the field.

But don't try it unless you really know what you are doing. Instead, *before you leave*, telephone the manufacturers' technical representative of the major equipment you are using and ask for the names, addresses and telephone numbers of qualified repair shops nearest where you are to be based. Some manufacturers or suppliers provide special services to professionals working in the field in the way of emergency repairs, loaner lenses and other equipment, and can be generally very helpful. Chief among them is Nikon, which has established Nikon Professional Services offices in New York, Chicago, San Francisco and other cities. Contact them via their NPS toll-free number 1-800-NIKONUS (California: 1-800-231-1389), or sign up with the Kodak Professional Network, 1-800-242-2424, ext. 99. Other companies provide similar services and help at major news-gathering centers such as political conventions, Olympic events and other public functions where there is a guarantee of a huge concentration of news photographers.

Your own membership in some professional groups can be helpful in providing contacts in the field. If you are already a member of the ASMP or the NPPA, take a copy of their membership lists along with you. Not only might they be very helpful in providing some names for emergency assistance in the field, but these lists might also give you someone to have a drink or a meal with when you are tired of the motel dining room or when you've had enough of listening to the woes of the local public relations person or factory superintendent.

Getting your equipment ready for travel is something that has to be thought out carefully. Throwing everything helter-skelter into a case and shipping it off by airfreight or as excess baggage is one sure way of having trouble on location. It was bad enough in the old days when flashbulbs were used. It's worse now with strobes that won't fire, or that misfire, or are off exposure calculation. Ditto cameras and lenses. They have to be packed *very carefully*.

I have worked out a pretty good system of dealing with the X-ray problem at the security gates of the airlines. If I am shipping any sizeable amount of film and am using airfreight for the bulk of the shipment, I make sure that the major portion of the film supply goes into *one* case and that case is clearly marked *Sensitive Materials—Keep Away From Heat, Cold and Radioactive Materials!* These labels can be purchased or they can be made by a printer easily and cheaply and are well worth the price. They should be affixed to every shipping case that can contain film. Airlines as a rule do not X-ray air-cargo materials, except for some carriers that serve the Middle East and other sensitive areas, although this of course can change. When you take your shipment to the airfreight office, you can easily find out whether or not there is a possibility of X rays being used. If this is so, discuss it with the air-freight supervisors and arrange for inspection before loading so that film is not damaged in transit. Again, this is where extra high insurance coverage is helpful because your baggage will receive extra protection and personal handling by airport security personnel.

The film you carry on board and your camera bags and/or lens cases should be packed for easy inspection. Under U.S. FAA regulations you have a right to request "hand inspection" of all film materials, and that does not mean the containers will be opened and fogged. Smaller quantities should be carried in clear resealable plastic bags to facilitate handling. All film exposed or unexposed should be in either a shoulder bag or lightweight case that can go under your plane seat. No film, *exposed or unexposed*, of any sort should be left in a camera body. When you get to the security gate, under no circumstances permit the attendant to shove the bag through the X-ray scanner, regardless of assurances that the X-ray dosage is so small that it won't affect the film. To some extent this is true. One pass through the average airline scanner will not affect the film to any degree that can easily be noticed, but what the attendants never tell you (perhaps because they do not know themselves) is that X-ray radiation is *cumulative* and every time you go through a gate from one line to another and let your film pass through the machine, you pick up an additional small dose of radiation, so after three or four more passes through the X-ray machine as you change airlines, you have trouble.

Once when going through the security gate in Seattle, the young attendant tried to convince me that the X rays were minimal and harmless and she was getting quite insistent on passing my film through the machine. That is, she was until I asked her, "Are you married?" "What has that to do with anything?" she replied. "Oh, nothing really," I said, "since this machine is so harmless, but if you are planning on a family you shouldn't be hanging around that thing very long without a ten-foot pole."

I passed on, after still insisting on a hand inspection of the film, and as I walked down the corridor, I happened to turn back and look at the security section. The girl had acquired a very long stick and was busily pushing all the incoming baggage through, literally with a ten-foot pole. So don't let the airlines people mislead you. X rays *are* harmful in accumulation, and the FAA has recognized this. I have also been told without verification that these machines, on repeated use, can affect sound tapes to some degree. So if you are carrying videotapes or camcorders you might be well warned to take the same evasive action as with photographic films. With the increasing use of video disks in cameras this might be something worth investigating.

Permits

The last item of preplanning is the question of permits, if necessary, and other problems that might involve dealing with authorities. If you are going to be working on a busy street photographing buildings, traffic activity, installations of some sort, and you might have to block or step into the mainstream of traffic, be it pedestrian or motor, be prepared for it. Many municipalities will not permit a photographer to block traffic, whether it is with a tripod or a motor vehicle, unless permits are issued for this purpose. On the other hand this can be a blessing instead of a problem, because it may make your job easier.

New York City, for instance, has established a special bureau just for the purpose of encouraging the motion picture and television industries to produce films there. It is called The Mayor's Office for Film, Theater and Broadcasting, 254 West 54th Street, New York, NY 10019. Their courtesies are extended to commercial still photographers who require much the same space to work in on the public streets. All they ask of you is some proof of the assignment and enough insurance to cover any contingency that might befall the public. A simple permit has to be secured, at least a day or two in advance, in order for them to notify the police precincts involved. There are no fees nor are any gratuities expected. There are similar requirements and assistance bureaus in many large cities.

Most cities and many states have convention and visitor's bureaus or Chambers of Commerce or other official or quasi-official organizations that can brief you on the needs for such permits. Frequently they can also be helpful in making arrangements for you. There are a few other legalities that you should check before you leave for your assignment.

Are aerial photographs required as part of your job? If so, have you, or perhaps your clients, lined up an adequate aircraft and pilot? Does the pilot or flight service you are going to use have the necessary FAA waivers and required insurance for you to make the kind of pictures you need? It is quite possible that in order to make these aerials properly, the door of the aircraft is going to have to be removed. Is the flight service authorized to do this? There are very stiff FAA regulations that have to be complied with if this is going to be the case. Check this in advance so you can enjoy my "no surprises" rule.

Insurance in the Field

In chapter ten I discuss many legal points including insurance, but I would like to call your attention, in the context of the assignment, to the need for adequate liability insurance while you are in the field. What happens, for instance, if you knock over a light and damage an expensive painting in a museum? Or someone trips on a cable either on location or, for that matter, in your studio and hurts himself? What kind of insurance do you have, if any? Liability premiums for even vast amounts of coverage are quite reasonable, though sometimes the amount you may be asked to carry can seem excessive.

Once, just as I was about to photograph a huge oil refinery from the air, I was questioned by the refinery people about how much insurance I had and what would happen if the plane crashed and set fire to the refinery. I said that I normally carried $1,000,000 in general liability insurance. The oilman laughed and said, "Do you know what the replacement cost of this refinery is? Five hundred million dollars." I laughed, too, and suggested gently that he take it out of my fee if I did set fire to the place. What else could I say? On another location I had to take out a special insurance policy for $20 million to cover the sea trial of a tanker. This was a more modest demand than insuring an entire refinery, and the premium came to several hundred dollars for the half hour that I was in close proximity to the tanker. So I bought the policy and added the premium cost to my bill. There was no objection from the client.

You should carry an adequate general liability policy, and if you wish you can divide its cost over each job as part of your general expense. It may only come to a few dollars per assignment, depending on how many assignments you pro-rate the policy over and the total liability you carry. But carry something.

Once the late Bernie Hoffman was doing a story on natural gas exploration in Texas and was photographing a seismograph crew using dynamite charges in carefully spaced holes in the ground to activate the seismograph recorders. Because the terrain was dull looking, the crew agreed to move their operations to a farm that looked better and was slated for exploration later, long after the story would have closed. The farmer who owned the property agreed to let them work there, and the crew chief decided to help enhance the visuals by using extra-strong dynamite charges, adding a little water so that the blast picture would be more dramatic looking when the charge went off.

But the crew chief got carried away and put in such a strong charge that he blew the roof off the top of a natural underground canyon on the farm. It took some 200 truckloads of earth to fill the crater. All Bernie could say was, "Wait till Thompson (the Managing Editor) gets the bill for this one." Had he been a freelancer rather than a staffer, he would have needed a sizable insurance policy to cover this unpredictable event. So you can see why liability insurance is so necessary for the photographer in the field.

Safety: Personal and Public

Field pressures sometimes create unusual situations that may result in physical danger. Behavior on an assignment must always be governed by considerations of safety and avoiding personal injury. But safety for yourself is only one aspect of this; safety for those around you is just as important, perhaps even more so. While knowledge of dangerous situations has improved and most responsible companies look to employee and visitor safety, it is still the concern of the photographer to be careful and follow every possible safety regulation, even if he thinks it inhibits him.

For years I railed against wearing safety glasses, hard hats and even safety shoes on industrial or construction sites, claiming the glasses interfered with my vision, the hard hats were uncomfortable and the shoes hurt my feet. A couple of times I got downright testy when safety inspectors insisted I wear them while on their locations. More than once, due to my own ignorance (and let's admit it, arrogance), I threatened to walk off a location when they insisted on my using these items. One day when I was just about to be "invited" to leave, I got a chip of metal in one eye. That cost me two days shooting time, and when I reported back to work, I was further saved from a couple of badly smashed toes by the insistence of the safety inspector that I wear hard-toed safety shoes. After that I was more tractable and acquired my own prescription safety glasses, a hard hat and comfortable safety shoes, as well as my own coal miner's safety lamp and battery pack.

As a photographer you frequently have to set safety standards not only for yourself but for those around you. On assignment once for a magazine story on a large conglomerate that, among other things, had opened a new potash mine in Utah, I had to make pictures of the new underground operations. As I drove into the valley where the mine was located, I saw abandoned oil rigs rimming the basin, indicating we were in a depleted oil field. Scheduling had been carefully worked out. I knew the miners had just finished cutting through an underground salt bed that covered the potash deposit, and bringing out the first loads of ore would begin at the time of my arrival at the site.

Properly attired in oilskin miners' gear, hard hat, miner's safety lamp and glasses, hard-toed boots and other paraphernalia, plus explosion-proof nitrogen-filled boxes for my strobe packs and with spark-proof electric connectors, I felt ready. I descended nearly a mile in a large iron bucket suspended from a cable that was serving as a temporary mine skip (elevator), since the main head frame and hoist complex had not yet been finished. I arrived at the first working level to find a beehive of activity, only it was a scene that would have caused instant cardiac arrest to most of the toughened hardrock miners I ever knew. All around me men were smoking, using welding torches, equipment without explosion-proof motors, and open lights dangling from temporary lines without safety electrical connections. The foreman greeted me with a lit cigarette in his mouth and asked what I would like to have them do for me.

I said, "Just one thing—call the skip back down because I'm getting out of here."

"Why? What's wrong? Don't you like working underground?"

"I don't mind working here," I said, "I just don't want to die here. When was the last time you ran a gas test?"

"Oh," said the foreman, "at eight this morning."

"Well," I said, "it's now two-thirty in the afternoon. Any high school kid who studied elementary geology would know that underneath any salt bed in any oil field, depleted or otherwise, there is always a good chance of hitting gas, and you've just cut through the salt bed."

"What do you want us to do?" asked the foreman.

"Either shut down every welding torch, compressor or other non-explosion proof motor, put out every cigarette and turn off the bare bulbs, or I'm getting out of here in the next bucket," I responded.

So, in order to humor the wise guy from New York, they did all those things. I hurried through my pictures, and returned safely to the surface in about an hour. The moral of this tale? Sad to say, that mine blew up two weeks later and killed nineteen men, including the foreman.

The lesson is, when the occasion demands it, be tough. Avoiding getting hurt on the job is your responsibility too, and your responsibility to your client. If you get hurt you can't produce your story. If you don't produce the story, someone is left in the lurch.

Medical Emergencies

I have always been terrified of getting hurt or becoming ill on location. This is not because of the pain or discomfort, but because of what it can do to a working schedule and, ultimately, delivery of the job. Merely paying attention to appropriate clothing is not always good enough. While covering a roaring steel mill in the Midwest in the dead of winter, I faced, at alternate four- or five-minute intervals, fiery blasts from the 2,300 degree heat of molten steel and then the icy blasts of subzero weather when I stepped outside the confines of the furnace building. Steel workers in those days used neck-to-heel woolen overcoats made of natural wool that was spark resistant. Today they use metallic refractive fabric that will reflect heat but won't keep out the zero cold as well as the woolen coats.

Photographers in a situation like this are candidates for pneumonia or perhaps worse. But even a simple cold can make a shambles of a schedule, and an accident, however minor, can be costly in many ways. Ailments due to steel mill exposures can seem exotic, but what do you do when the Venetian blind in your hotel room comes off the wall and cuts your hand open, requiring several stitches, and you then have to hire a couple of assistants to keep you propped up somehow while you try to work? There are no answers or sure preventatives to these kinds of literally off-the-wall situations except to warn the photographer to be doubly careful of his movements and actions while in the field. Carry a small emergency first-aid kit among your personal effects, plenty of "home remedies" such as aspirin, cough medicine, insect repellent, poison ivy preventatives, and the like. And as for eyeglasses, what happens if you break or lose the pair you are wearing now?

If all this seems elementary and slightly smacking of the overindulgent mother hen, wait until something happens and you don't have what you need. Getting competent medical attention in the field can sometimes be tricky, and if required at off hours or in unusual circumstances, such as described below, be prepared for the worst because the worst sometimes happens. Make sure you have your medical or health care membership documentation, copies of prescriptions from your doctor if special medication might be called for, a spare pair of eyeglasses, or extra prescriptions for medication that can be administered by a local doctor if necessary.

I once came down with something in Salt Lake City and needed a newly developed medication not locally available. What to do? I first called my own doctor for the name of the drug and a prescription for it, then called the manufacturer to find the nearest distributor (in this case San Francisco), then arranged a complicated and expensive emergency air shipment to Salt Lake. All of this could have been avoided if I had had an extra supply of the medication in my travel kit. If this could happen in Salt Lake City, imagine the problems in what was once Yugoslavia.

There are other ways of getting hurt and requiring medical attention on location that are more difficult to project, as witness what happened to my friend Adam. He had built an enviable reputation not only as a fine photographer for one of the big magazines, but an equally impressive one as a "Casanova of the Camera." He arrived on assignment in a midwestern city once, only to find the job delayed. Having nothing better to do, he decided to look up an old girl friend who had since married a leading local orthopedic surgeon. Her husband was on duty that evening at the hospital and, as she had nothing better to do either, she decided to visit with her old friend.

Exactly what transpired is not clearly documented, but it seems that at about 2 A.M. Adam wound up on the floor of his room clutching a badly broken arm and howling for medical attention. With pain developing rapidly and panic setting in, the only doctor his friend could think of was, naturally, her husband, who agreed to come down and see to the situation. Meanwhile they concocted a story explaining that he, Adam, had fallen out of bed, broken his arm, and knowing that she had married a doctor, decided to call her for assistance. The husband bought all this but after examining the injury decided to have Adam removed to his hospital so that he could be placed under an anesthetic and have surgery. He immediately left to make preparations, saying that his wife could ride in the ambulance with Adam.

Adam's immediate thought was: "Oh God! If I go under an anesthetic and start babbling as people do, and I say the wrong thing, and this guy has a knife in his hand, I may never come out of this!"

His friend assuaged him by saying, "Yes, it's true that people talk while under anesthesia, but my husband told me that if you concentrate on a single thought before going under, the chances are any talk will be in relation to that."

So Adam said, "Let me alone, I'm concentrating." Which he did all the way to the operating room. He woke with the doctor present and looking at him with a quizzical expression on his face. "Did everything go okay, Doc?" asked Adam.

"Oh yes," was the reply, "but you were doing an awful lot of talking while I was operating on you."

"Did you understand what I was saying?"

"Yes."

"Well, for heaven's sake, Doctor, what was I saying?"

"That was the strange thing," he replied. "You kept saying over and over again: 'Adam is the best photographer in the world, Adam is the best photographer in the world!' "

Field Cooperation

Your personal approaches to people are important, and how you come across to them could have a lot to do with the cooperation you get as a photographer. One of the big business magazines used to have an unwritten internal policy that if you were sent out on a story and given the names of various people to interview or contact for assistance on the job, the story was reasonably objective and fair or even possibly laudatory. But if they told you to stay away from the plant and deal with people not connected with that corporation or operation, you knew that the story line would be a hatchet job.

Looking at it from the corporate side, if you as an executive heard that there was a team from X magazine in the area and they *did not contact* you but were asking questions about you, you would know it was time to take to the storm cellars. So, as a photographer you must know from the start if you are expected to turn up the rocks and see what crawls out from underneath, or have a straightforward approach and make the people and plant installation look as good as possible. While the investigative journalism method may be more exciting and glamorous, the chances are the other kind pays better and more often.

Field Approval

When working in editorial photography you can be put in difficult positions by people who want to see your photographs before they are printed, which of course you cannot allow. Sometimes you have to use all of the charms of a snake-oil salesman to get the person you are supposed to photograph to hold still for a portrait sitting or even allow you to photograph the situation you have been sent to do. Frequently when photographing either persons or places, those in control will ask (or demand) to see what you have produced, implying a right of refusal if you do not show the work to them for screening. How do you deal with this? Firmly. But politely and not by "dealing" at all. When it comes to editorial matters, no editor is ever going to allow prior censorship or approval, and if this becomes an issue, the chances are the assignment will be canceled, either by your editor or the client. There often is an area of compromise. If you are using Polaroid pictures for testing and you wish to show them, you can do so *if you want to*. But it must always be with the clear understanding that you are showing what you have done out of courtesy rather than for approval. Frequently the use of a Polaroid picture under these circumstances can be beneficial, but you must always reserve the right to decide what pictures are forwarded to the editor.

In factory or industrial situations I often use Polaroids as a starting point. I make a test shot, then show it to the foreman on the mill floor or the company representative who is with me, and ask if anything is out of place or if there is anything that will disclose a process secret or if an unsafe operation is being depicted. These are all legitimate reasons for showing a Polaroid, but not for the decision "we don't like this so you can't use it."

Field approval in advertising photography is always necessary in order to avoid later disputes with clients (see chapter three, page 83). Here too the Polaroid is invaluable. Frequently when I am working in the field with a large-format camera I shoot Polaroids for test purposes and knock off a few extras as gifts to the people I am photographing. Usually I do not even have to make extras, because in the course of checking exposure and lighting, I will have a couple of near-misses that will do handsomely for this purpose, and I might add, I have made many friends on the production lines this way. But even in this kind of situation you have to be careful. I know of one photographer who was extremely embarrassed because he gave an "extra" Polaroid to a local public relations man only to find the picture running the following morning in the local newspaper. So caution must be used not to break your own deadline security.

A parallel problem arose once when I shot a story for a business magazine and the company public relations man, in good faith, asked me if I minded if their own company photographer went along with me and shot some of the same situations I did for their house magazine. I had brought in large banks of lights that the local man could not have afforded to illuminate the area, and it seemed like an easy request to fill graciously. But I remembered a similar situation when a company photographer followed me around and, after I made a major effort to arrange a picture, shot the very same photo over my shoulder and beat me to my own press deadline. That company photographer, in his eagerness, released the pictures to a competing national publication that ran the photographs, and the whole nasty situation came very close to developing into a major lawsuit involving copyright and plagiarism. When using release forms, by the way, a Polaroid print can be considered "other consideration" in addition to a fee paid, if any, for the release.

So I politely refused the presence of the company photographer this time. I know of more than one occasion when the photographer assigned actually had to threaten not to shoot unless the company man was withdrawn. These things must be done tactfully but they do have to be done, and this is part of your field behavior so as not to compromise your employer.

Sometimes you run into situations where you yourself create a monster that can bite, and the bite can be nearly fatal. When New York's bicentennial

Op Sail event, a massive public celebration, took place, I sweet-talked the Navy into lending me a helicopter to cover the story and agreed to let a Navy camera corpsman come along with an express promise by the Navy public information officer (PIO) that they would not release any of his pictures until long after my deadline was past. They kept their promise, but at the last minute I suddenly found that three or four other photographers from rival news services had been given permission to join me on this same aircraft, and we were all expected to shoot simultaneoulsy from the same door position. Fortunately I was able to kill the idea although there was a lot of group kicking and screaming. I won my point with the argument that if there were four photographers all trying to shoot at the same time through the same door, two things were bound to happen: Someone—most likely the PIO himself—would be pushed out the door for setting this up, and none of the photographers would get any decent pictures at all because of the confusion and danger of everyone crowding that small open door. The Navy solved the problem by putting up four choppers instead of the one they had agreed to make available to us.

There can be other problems in getting your work done because of uncooperative personalities, and often you have to walk on eggs. A business magazine that was part of the same group that published a big news magazine assigned me to make a portrait of a man who had just been indicted in a major stock swindle case. He had already been severely treated by the sister news magazine, and I didn't think I had much of a chance of getting him to cooperate, but I called anyway for an appointment. He agreed to see me, but would not commit himself to whether he would permit me to make any pictures of him.

When I arrived, he said, "Why should I allow you to photograph me when I know not only are you probably going to blast me, but your sister magazine will probably get its hands on the pictures and murder me completely?" Good question indeed. I replied, "This is the situation. I am assigned to make these pictures and my editors *are* doing a story about this whole problem in which you are now involved. That story is going to run whether you approve of it or not. You have a number of choices: You can either cooperate, and I promise I will do the best possible job I can to make a good portrait of you. Furthermore, you may restrict the use of this photograph to this publication only, and my editors will honor that restriction and so the sister magazine will not have any right to use it. Or you can throw me out and tell me to get lost. That is your privilege. But if you do, I think I know what will happen. I will go back to New York empty-handed and then the editors will hire a stringer to hang out across the street from your office, home or club with a long lens on his camera, and the first time you pick your teeth or scratch yourself or do anything else of an uncomplimentary nature, you can be assured that is what they will run—because they *will* run something."

So the man said, "You win," and he sat for the portraits, one of which did run and it was a picture that said he was neither sinner nor saint. In my notes to the editor I did put a specific restriction on the picture for use by our magazine only, and that effectively prevented the sister magazine from using it without the sitter's specific permission. This created a furor within the company, but after I assured the editors that it was either that or nothing, they backed me up completely, and that is where the matter rested.

Not only can you expect cooperation of the client or the subject, for the most part, you probably will need it if you are working in unfamiliar territory. In addition to the usual mechanical problems of housing, regular transportation, factory assistance, etc., there are many times when you will have to depend on the people you are dealing with in the field to make appointments, do the unusual and sometimes the unexpected. Cooperation on the job by the client or subject can well make or break the assignment, and I cannot repeat too often the warning that the visiting photographer must never make a nuisance of himself, make unnecessary demands, slow up or stop production or even simply get in the way of the normal functions of the operation being covered.

Company Photographers

Another word of caution about "company photographers." In many cases the companies you are called on to deal with will have their own in-plant photo departments. This can be both a blessing and a bane. Their presence in the plant can provide emergency technical service, an extra light or last-minute supplies, but they can also cause problems for the visiting photographer in that the personal problems of the in-plant photographer may hamper or reduce the efficacy of the visitor. The plant photographer can truly resent the newcomer (and perhaps with good reason), thinking he has been by-passed when he should be doing the work. I have often tactfully told local public relations people that I do not want assistance from such in-plant people, preferring (as mentioned earlier) electricians or maintenance people to best fill my needs. But I always ask to be introduced to the staff photographers and try to make friends with them by showing them, and perhaps letting them use, new pieces of equipment or telling them about some recent technique they may not have heard of and could put to use. Mainly I make an effort to get across the idea to them that, yes, I really would like to have their help, but I know how busy they are with their own work and wouldn't want to detract from that by overloading their schedules. Thus I can feel free to call on them in case of a genuine emergency where some photographic expertise or help is needed.

You can also make friends by being helpful. I once met an in-plant man who complained bitterly that some of his electronic equipment was working erratically even though it was new. I explained that the same thing had happened to my equipment because of huge amounts of "wild" electrical energy in that area. That plant's electric steel furnaces used excessively high amperages creating electrical fields that affected sensitive equipment. By behaving in this manner, instead of acting the "big shot" who was imported over the head of the lowly company man, you can make more friends for yourself and make your job a lot easier when you are in strange surroundings.

Field Behavior

Representing Your Client

When on assignment, you are, for all practical purposes, the representative of the company that has hired you, and whatever you do or how you behave (or misbehave) will reflect on the company.

Just as you have to learn to avoid situations that might arise because of a conflict in political ideology between the client and the publisher, so too must you take care that whatever you do does not reflect adversely on the publisher or employer. In other words, you do not have the right to speak for your publisher. You cannot say to those you are photographing, "Yes, we are going to print *this* picture," or talk about *that* in the text, knowing that you have very little to say about what finally appears in print. Nor can you make any promises, minor or major, on the part of your publisher without his direct approval. You are not authorized to make policy statements about the story you may be working on, nor can you promise to honor the requests you usually get for copies of the magazine or extra prints, or anything else that requires the publisher to do, send or say something after the shooting is over.

Whenever I am asked for a copy of the article I am working on or an extra print of a story, I never make a formal promise to fulfill such requests. I do say that I will (and do) put these people's names on the list of cooperative persons, turn it over to my editors, and hope that copies will be sent. But I never guarantee this.

Frequently on an editorial assignment you are perceived as carrying the political banner of the organization for whom you are doing the story. You may have a pretty tough time dealing with this, especially if you are covering something that is politically sensitive. And by politically sensitive I am not referring solely to who is running against whom but other issues as well.

If you are doing an annual report for a public utility, particularly one that has a couple of nuclear plants, don't walk into the office or onto the plant site wearing a "no-nukes" button in your lapel. If you are photographing a mining company, forget your personal anti-strip-mining attitudes while on location. Of course, you can't and must not always hide your feelings about the subjects you are photographing, and there are some purists who say, "If you don't approve, don't take the assignment." But I suggest that when you are on someone's payroll, play it cool about your personal beliefs. If you don't, you'll more than likely be taken off the job.

Your personal behavior on the location is important. Make no demands as such but phrase your requests as politely as possible for whatever you need. If an area has to be cleaned around a machine or process, don't order it to be done but tell the supervisor or liaison person what you need. Discuss carefully with the local foremen or supervisors anything you are going to do, to see if it will create a labor or product-flow problem. Also, you may be photographing a machine operator at one moment and half an hour later have to make some portraits of the president of a multimillion dollar company. If you have to change your clothes between takes, do so. You have to be able to earn the confidence of both.

In non-industrial situations where you may be dealing with portraits of executives or other people important to your story, pay attention to their surroundings. If there are piles of papers or books or other objects that are not really needed or do nothing for the picture, ask to have them removed, but do not under any circumstances make that removal yourself.

Never forget for one minute, regardless of whom you are working for, that if you are on someone else's property, no matter what the story (unless you are clearly trespassing), you are still a guest and must always behave like one. If you are arrogant or discourteous, intentionally or otherwise, even if you get away with it, this behavior will reflect on the next photographer following you. Not only is this unprofessional conduct but, if you put yourself in the place of your colleague, think how you would feel to have doors slammed in your face or have to deal with total noncooperation because of a photographer who preceded you. Sometimes stories dealing with sensitive elements need sensitive handling. It all boils down to my deep belief that a photographer should observe and report news, not make it.

I was once asked what it is I dread on arrival at a new location. Tongue-in-cheek, I said I hated to follow too closely behind a certain famous photographer because of his reputation for leaving a trail of shattered egos and a heritage of ill will toward journalists. By a crazy coincidence, I did follow him on the next assignment I drew. It was to be shot in the same area on the same program he had covered, but for a different publication. The location was in the Appalachian Mountains in a rural area of Kentucky. I telephone our regional contact there to say I was coming down. His reply was, "Well if Mrs. So-and-so [a somewhat formidable lady who was the director of the program] hears about this, there is going to be hell to pay, and perhaps you had best not come down for a while until tempers cool." But a deadline impended and I had to press forward.

Just before I left, I received a call from the fearsome Mrs. So-and-so, who said, "If you show up in Hazard County, don't be surprised if someone takes a shot at you!" I asked why she objected to my coming to make pictures of what certainly was a worthwhile social program. She told me that my photographer friend who had preceded me had spent several weeks in the area a year earlier. She emphatically did not like the photographs that appeared, as well as their accompanying text, and most of all she didn't like the photographer because of his behavior. I never did find out how he behaved, because she hung up on me immediately, but I went down anyway and managed to get the story without attracting her attention until the deed was done and I was on my way out. No one did shoot at me, and our story ran well.

I brought it off not just because of photographic ability but by paying particular attention to the sensitivities of the people in the region in which I was working. My research also indicated that Mrs. So-and-so herself was not entirely liked by the community and I subtly used that knowledge in my approaches, making friends with certain people just for that reason. So it was most gratifying later to learn that the lady in question was grudgingly complimentary after my story appeared, and threats of future mayhem were withdrawn.

I probably could have done the story anyway, even if I had openly defied her and bulled my way through by coming in like the marines and yelling, "freedom of the press," but I chose to handle it on a low-key, almost invisible basis. I think I got a better story for it.

Relationships With Your Team

There is much more to field behavior than the points raised above. Not only are your actions with regard to those you have to photograph important, but so are your relationships with those on your team—art directors, reporters, picture researchers, public relations representatives or simply your own or hired assistants, drivers, etc., as all of them have a direct relationship to how well you perform with the camera.

Over my many years of professional photography I have had my share of conflicts both within my own team—from disagreements with writers whose perceptions were essentially nonvisual, or who had such airs of superiority that they wouldn't even consider someone else's approach to the visualization of a story—and with clients who, once away from their own home territory, felt it was their sacred duty to prove their manliness by picking up every waitress or barmaid they came across.

There are many occurrences that can delay you, inhibit you or simply make it impossible to function properly, and a lot of them stem from social or semi-social situations that arise in the field.

Until I learned better, I was at first grateful to the local public relations man or woman who invited me for drinks, dinner or other social activity after a day's shoot. It seemed infinitely more appealing than spending an evening alone in a dreary hotel room, but as I became saturated with boring tales of woe and local politics within or without the company, or with being expected to pick up checks that I could not justify for reimbursement, I became increasingly wary of accepting these invitations because invariably they would have some effect on my production the next day.

There are other situations worthy of comment that crop up primarily in advertising photography, and some of these problems have been eased by control of the shooting budgets by the larger agencies (see page 78). But with many smaller accounts the problem persists. Instead of traveling alone, the photographer shooting for an advertising layout, particularly in the fashion field, but by no means restricted to it, can often have a large entourage with him: assistants, stylists, makeup people, and most of all, from one to five people from the agency, plus a few representing the clients as well. The agency people always include ADs, sometimes copywriters, account executives and group heads. With the exception of the AD and those actually involved with the photography, the others often add very little in the way of real assistance to the project.

What they frequently manage to do is to raise the bills to such a level that the very shooting of a job becomes questionable in terms of the total expense of field production. Assignments have been canceled for this very reason, and studio pictures are frequently substituted, or drawings and sketches used instead of photography. I've run into this time and time again, and there seems to be some direct mathematical proportion in that the number of nonproductive free riders increases in direct ratio to the interest of the location. For example, on one campaign that required shooting in both New Orleans and Topeka, we had twelve supernumeraries on the New Orleans location and none at Topeka.

On some shoots I probably wouldn't mind a number of people around because it might get pretty boring without them, but when their travel charges are added to your bills or you are expected to provide fun, games and amusements for the client and friends, you can wind up "eating" the bills, as has happened to many of my friends, and it's no longer amusing. I know of one situation where the agency lost the account, and the photographer the assignment, because of the client's insistence on not only coming along when the shoot was in Europe, but on bringing some "pets" along who the agency was expected to pay for, without rebilling the client. Perhaps some big agencies with big budgets can carry on this farce, but when it happens to the individual photographer or small agency, big problems can result.

Insider: Jill Freedman, Photographer

While many photographers started in traditional ways by attending art or photography schools, getting a job as an assistant to another photographer, or chasing fire engines and police cars for small-town publications, there are others who chose more unconventional methods. Jill Freedman is a young woman with a huge talent, self-taught, who in a few years has published five books and numerous editorial pieces, and approaches photography with an awesome dediction and passion.

She made her first professional photograph when she was about twenty-six, several years after graduating as a major in sociology from the University of Pittsburgh. She told me, "I found out when my last final was, and then got the first ship leaving the country. I was away for three and a half years." She went to Israel, continental Europe, and also lived in London for a few years. When she ran out of money in Israel she became a nightclub singer, but after a while felt that even her singing was becoming "work." She packed that in, came home to the U.S. and got temporary work until she figured out what she wanted to do.

One morning she woke up and decided she wanted a camera. "I had never taken any pictures before," she said. "It came out of nowhere, but I got hold of a camera and went right out on the street and shot two rolls of film. I had them developed, I looked at them, and said, 'That's it. I'm a photographer.'

"Everyone laughed, *but that was it*. It was the only thing I really wanted to do. I had a total maniacal passion right from the beginning. I still feel that passion. Photography is a total obsession with me, and even though everyone I knew thought I was crazy, I knew better. I began looking around for some means of earning a living, and I thought advertising copywriting was something I could take seriously. I asked friends which was the best ad agency, made up some 'campaigns' for their accounts, showed them and was hired immediately. So for the next two years, every time I got paid I invested part of my salary in cameras, a darkroom or equipment.

"Only then did I start teaching myself something about photography. I didn't want to be anyone's assistant. I didn't want to be influenced by anyone. I learned technical things by reading. I got hold of some inexpensive Kodak 'how-to' manuals and a few other books on technique. I spent time at the Museum of Modern Art, studied W. Eugene Smith's prints and the work of other photographers. I went through a lot of work and looked at a lot of material—not only photographs, but paintings, sculpture, films and every other kind of art.

"After I had been shooting (and still working at the agency) for about a year or so, I went to London, made some pictures, came back and had my first show at a small gallery that was part of a photo laboratory. The day that show opened, I went to the copy chief at my agency and told him, 'I quit. From now on I am a photographer.' "

The murder of Martin Luther King had an enormous emotional impact on Freedman and she immersed herself in the civil rights movement as a photographer. After an unsuccessful attempt to get a magazine assignment, she joined the Poor People's March on Washington anyway. She marched along with hundreds of others, slept in the mud when she had to, and documented the trials, pathos and the spirit of "Resurrection City" for the next six weeks.

Still without assignment, she ran into *LIFE* reporter, John Neary, who after seeing her early contact sheets, talked her into letting him take the rest of her undeveloped film back to the *LIFE* lab. Five pictures were picked up by *LIFE*, and this was her first editorial breakthrough.

Freedman said, "I was never good at hustling for editorial work, which you have to be, and it was always touch-and-go with me. I always took it personally, which you are not supposed to do."

In 1971 her first book, *Old News-Resurrection City*, was published, and Freedman decided that photographic books were the course she wanted to follow professionally. Her fifth book, *A Time That Was/Irish Moments*, was published in 1987. Much happened between publication dates.

Since she was unable to get much advance backing on *Resurrection City*, it was equally unlikely she could do so with her next project, *Circus Days*. Publishers were unwilling to advance enough money for her to devote the time she felt necessary to such a production. Result? She hoarded her small income from odd jobs and the meager return on *Resurrection City*, borrowed a van from a friend and spent the next four years photographing and honing *Circus Days* as close to perfection as she could. In 1974 *Circus Days* was published by Harmony Press (Crown). The fine book that emerged attests to this devotion and care and, more important, firmly established her reputation and craftsmanship.

Her third book, *Firehouse* (Doubleday/1978) was presold and prepared in cooperation with Dennis Smith, a fireman-turned-author, who lent his expertise in the form of a brief text. By then she realized her need for a literary agent and secured one. Her next book, *Street Cops* (1982) was published by Harper & Row, and was also presold. With her reputation clearly established, she was able to command an advance big enough to allow her to spend the time that this book demanded.

She told me that perhaps she is her own worst enemy because of her passionate desire for perfection. But this is the only way she can work freely. She chooses her own subjects and works on them at her own pace, refining and re-refining the finished product to her standards, although she does not ignore the feelings and the advice of her editors or publishers.

Freedman functions simply enough. She usually gets an idea of what she wants to do and doesn't wait until someone tells her what he wants. Each project thus becomes a labor of love. She shot the pictures for the circus book in seven weeks of one-night stands, but it took her four years to edit, print and prepare the final manuscript. This is typical, and while it may not presage great earnings, she feels happiest and most productive in this framework. *Street Cops* took almost a year and a half to shoot and another four years for preparation, including the writing. As for her methods of preparation and work ideas, she says she usually works in different ways. With book projects she had to learn the hard way. The first two books were sold solely on the merits of the pictures. She had not made an organized plan for the book, but badgered publishers with boxes upon boxes of pictures. As she grew more experienced, she realized the necessity of "dummies" or at least some clear plans, for without careful presentation, selling was hard indeed. She feels that most editors are word oriented rather than picture conscious, and finds it is important to present them with some visual plan that can be readily understood.

Another way of working she loves, is simply to wander around and shoot pictures at random and, as she puts it, "just make pictures." She shoots almost subconsciously and it might take her years before she realizes what concept is germinating in her mind. It is not until after hundreds and hundreds of random photographs are made that Freedman begins to get the idea of what her subconscious is telling her, and a plan then evolves.

Now that she has had her fifth book published and finished the printing for a major retrospective show at a fine-arts photo gallery, she says she wants to go out and do straight assignment work, which is her first love, since she considers herself a photojournalist at heart. But assignments aren't easy to come by, and she still has to self-generate ideas and present them visually before they can become book projects or editorial material.

One strong emotional prop is her intense belief in herself as a fine photographer. She has confidence that her work is very good and in satisfying her own creative demands, knows that eventually this quality will establish itself in the minds of editors and they will assign work to her.

In her own down-to-earth style, she says, "I think things have worked out well. The one thing I have always had going for me, from the very beginning, is the feeling that if no one else liked my pictures it wouldn't have mattered because they knock me out. And if someone didn't like my pictures, it told me that they weren't very smart. Now as I look at them I realize I am doing exactly what I want to do. I'll never complain about it again, even if I have to become double-jointed and kick myself in the tail to straighten out my thinking."

She has one personal rule: never to photograph anyone who doesn't want to be photographed, except in a hard-news situation beyond her control. She has an exceptional respect for craftsmanship, though she personally is ambivalent about darkroom work. She told me of once having gone to a show and seen a print that needed spotting. She walked out because she felt the photographer had no respect for his craft. This is Freedman's way of demanding the professionalism that is so earnestly desired by photographers and editors.

Roy Rowan
Magazine Editor

It's not too often anymore that a fire horse grazing peacefully in a meadow suddenly hears the firehouse bell clanging in his mind. And though the firehouse may be miles away, and he doesn't answer fire alarms any longer, he often has the gut feeling that something is happening. Something did.

I had planned to talk with my long-time friend, Roy Rowan, whose forty-four-year track record as a journalist is very impressive. He is a good photographer, a perceptive foreign correspondent, was National Affairs Editor and Assistant Managing Editor for the weekly *LIFE*, and Senior Writer and member of the Board of Editors for *Fortune* for eight years. In addition he wrote about the *Mayaguez* affair, covered the fall of Saigon and exposed the Mafia top echelon. He spent weeks roaming New York as a homeless man for material for an incredible story for *People* magazine.

These things I knew about, and so was appreciative of the time he granted for our interview. What I did not know about then, was the pending release of probably the biggest story of his career—though that firehouse bell was still ringing. It was the cover story in *TIME* (April 27, 1992) on the blowing up of Pan Am 103 over Scotland in December 1988, killing 259 people on board, plus eleven more on the ground, and the equally poignant supporting inside, and untold, story of the air crash at Gander, Newfoundland in 1985. That apparently covered-up tragedy killed 248 American soldiers and the plane's crew of eight.

There is no question that the brilliant investigative reporting of these stories will have international repercussions. Of one thing I am certain. All journalists, as well as millions of other people, will be taking longer and harder looks at what is handed us from 1600 Pennsylvania Avenue, The Pentagon, Foggy Bottom, 10 Downing Street, Ottawa, Berlin, and the foreign offices of half a dozen other countries.

So young photojournalists or journalists-to-be looking for role models, come and meet Roy Rowan. He can tell us about honesty, dedication to craft, and his feelings about photography, below, and in chapter thirteen.

"Ever since I was eleven I knew I wanted to be a journalist. I was fortunate because there was never any indecision. The only problem was that just as I was finishing my MBA at Dartmouth College, World War II came along and I was quickly drafted. I ended up spending a short time in North Africa and a long time in New Guinea and the Philippines. After the war, I tried very hard to get a job with one of the wire services as a reporter in China. That was impossible but International News Service (INS) offered me a job as a rewrite man in Atlanta. I wouldn't do that, so I got a job in China working for the United Nations Relief and Rehabilitation Administration running their trucks in central China. We had a huge number of trucks, drivers and mechanics but because of the rugged conditions, i.e. no roads, and having to raft them over rivers, only about half of our vehicles were operative at one time.

"While I was in Central China and during the middle of the China civil war, it was a wonderful opportunity for me to freelance as a magazine writer and photographer. I knew nothing about photography but always thought I had a fairly good eye as in college I had been an artist. In 1945 when I was living in Kaifeng in Hunan Province, I went to Shanghai on a supply trip where in a Chinese bookstore I found a book by Kip Ross, then Photography Editor of the *National Geographic*, for $1.00. I also bought a Mamiya-Flex camera, a Japanese knock-off of the Rollieflex, for $25.00, so I was in business. I started shooting photographs and writing articles. On one trip I ran into a most unusual scene of 5,000 Chinese skulls lined up on a hillside in the form of an amphitheater. I shot pictures of this and wrote a little piece about it. I also had an agent in New York who had never dealt with pictures. But she sold it to *LIFE* where it wound up as a double truck. Ultimately I made about $350 ($100 a page plus some subsidiary rights). It was also distributed by the wire services all over the world. At the same time my agent was starting to sell others of my pictures to *National Geographic* for stock use at $5.00 each. *TIME* was very interested in the China civil war, and I did some stringing for them and also sold them a few pictures.

"I continued these activities and my agent seemed to be doing well in placement. Once while taking a convoy of trucks on a long trip along with the only other American, an engineer in charge of the truck maintenance, the convoy got shot up and we took a bullet through the windshield between our heads. We bailed out, and after a harrowing ride flew back to Shanghai, where we demanded protection or we would quit.

"On that same day I was in a bar and met Bill Gray, the bureau chief for Time-Life, and he suggested I apply for a job with them as their local correspondent was leaving. I went back to New York and after being turned down at *TIME*, eventually saw Joe Thorndike, the M.E., and Assistant M.E. Ed Thompson at *LIFE* who said, "You go back to China immediately where you can be our correspondent." Ironically I had also applied to the Columbia School of Journalism under the GI bill, but had been turned down. Having bypassed that two-year curriculum in learning how to be a journalist, I now was one with the biggest magazine in the world.

"So there I was back in China teamed up with Jack Birns, the *LIFE* photographer. We started to score some pretty big scoops. It was all very exciting and dangerous and we nearly got killed once in an ambush. This was all before Dienbienphu in Indochina. We did a lot of war coverage, from Burma to Manchuria and the civil war in China to the time Chang-Kai-Shek fled. Then we were evacuated to Hong-Kong. Later *LIFE* sent us both to Rome, again as a team, and we covered most of the European countries plus Yugoslavia and North Africa.

"In 1950 *LIFE* asked me to cover the war in Korea where I teamed up with *LIFE* photographers Hank Walker, Howard Sochurek and John Dominis. Carl Mydans came back too.

"After that I went back to New York. When I was about to be called up as a Reserve Officer, Ed Thompson, who was M.E. then, quickly stymied that by sending me to Bonn as bureau chief, where I also occasionally doubled as photographer. So even though I was a correspondent, writer and bureau chief, I had an active background as a photographer throughout my career at Time, Inc. By this time Thompson was beginning to rankle a bit, because he didn't like writers shooting stories and he had laid down the law. He said make up your mind—do you want to be a photographer or a reporter. I decided I really wanted to get into picture editing and management, and went back to New York in that role. But I must tell you that even today I love photography and have been shooting a few pictures for special articles for both *TIME* and *LIFE*. And a few years ago I did a ten-page color story for *Fortune*.

"From the time I came back from Europe until about 1961, I had many wonderful and far-ranging assignments, including that of bureau chief in Chicago which was the largest bureau after Washington. In time I became National Affairs Editor and an Assistant Managing Editor. By then M.E. George Hunt felt it was time to bring some fresh blood into the photo department, and for a short time I became Picture Editor. We put eight of the staff photographers out on contract and brought in some younger promising photographers. I think the first year at least, the contract photographers made more money than they did on staff, so the parting was amicable. By 1963 I became the Assistant Managing Editor for News which was an exciting period for me because we became deeply involved in the reportage of the Kennedy assassination and many other momentous events.

"I went back out to Hong Kong as *TIME* bureau chief in 1972. In 1977 I moved over to *Fortune* as a member of the Board of Editors and became a Senior Writer. I spent eight years there.

"A few last thoughts for new photographers. I think because our senses are being bombarded by all kinds of visual things, it's harder now to make an impact. I wonder also how long people are going to print on paper, and before we all carry some kind of portable video screen to read a video book or see a video newspaper.

"Also many picture editors overemphasize specialization by photographers. Perhaps they are thinking of medicine where there is so much specialization. In photography I think it is important for the photographer to be flexible and master many techniques. After all it's what you see. Your eye is what makes the picture."

Philip B. Kunhardt, Jr.

Managing Editor

The original *LIFE* magazine was conceived by Henry Luce in the 1930s, with the first edition, which appeared in 1936, featuring Margaret Bourke-White's famed photograph of the dam at Fort Peck. *LIFE* was the standard by which all photojournalism after that date was (and probably still is) measured. Ironically, according to one of its former editors, it "died because it was so successful." At its acme, its circulation reached 8,500,000 copies weekly.

It died because it had grown so large that advertising revenues, which had begun to be diverted to television advertising, did not cover the enormous cost of producing and distributing such a publication. Politics too had an influence on its demise, as it had trod mercilessly on the toes of the fat cats and political Neanderthals whether in high office or not. In their efforts to muffle the voices of criticism at *LIFE*, subtle but no less real threats of monumental postal rate increases were held over its (and other publications') head as back-door censorship. In December 1972, the then current business management (Luce had since died), possibly seeking a more prudent financial course, decided to sink the mighty flagship, even though the rest of the corporate navy (*TIME*, *Fortune*, *Sports Illustrated*, etc.) was showing a healthy profit.

But within the corporation there were stout hearts and optimists who not only felt the financial shortfall temporary, but moreover believed the world needed a publication with the stature of *LIFE*. Among them was Philip B. Kuhnhardt, Jr., an Assistant Managing Editor of the weekly *LIFE* who led the fight to keep the magazine alive. He persuaded the company to continue publishing many special editions using the *LIFE* logo and format. Even though the old weekly magazine had been abandoned, the bureaus disbanded, and staffs, fired, retired and dispersed, Kuhnhardt kept fighting. Six years later the new monthly version of *LIFE* appeared, much changed in concept, but still a strong visual presence that continues to print fine photojournalism. The first new managing editor was Phil Kuhnhardt. I talked with him about his views on photographers of today.

"I grew up in a family steeped in historical photography," he said. "My grandfather, Frederick Hill Meserve was born in 1865, the year Lincoln was assassinated. He set out in the 1890s to illustrate his father's diary of the Civil War and put together a really unbelievable collection of old photographs. He tried to collect every single image of Lincoln, put them in order, dated them and preserved them. His daughter, my mother, became very interested in that subject too. She became a Lincoln authority and wrote many articles about Lincoln. I grew up in that atmosphere and also became fascinated with photography.

"After I graduated from college in 1950 there was only one place I wanted to work, and that was *LIFE* magazine. I finally got a job as a cub reporter and have been with the company ever since. As managing editor of *LIFE*, I was asked quite often who *LIFE*'s competitors were, and I don't think *LIFE* ever had any real competitors. The biggest competitor is the memory of the old *LIFE*.

"People who grew up on the old *LIFE* were accustomed to that great breed of photographer who spent years as an apprentice and applied real dedication to learning that craft. I grew up largely in Gjon Mili's and other people's studios and watched them painstakingly get ready for an assignment, doing it with unbelievable thought and care and knowledge. They developed their own film and printed their own pictures. I don't know where you learn your craft today; that's one of the problems. You don't have many of these wonderful, dedicated craftsmen working anymore. There are obviously some very good young photographers, and they are mostly natural light, 35mm candid photographers. They are painstaking, very careful, very perceptive, very sensitive, and I think some are as good as most of the photographers of the 1940s, 1950s and 1960s. They will also be the ones who will respond most quickly to the challenge of electronic imaging."

On the subject of story suggestions presented by photographers, Kunhardt said, "Editors do look for them, but that presents some kind of problem with us, and I don't know if it is for any other magazine. A lot of photographers merely read the papers and come upon something they think might make a story and suggest it to us. That's not the kind of suggestion I want from a photographer at all, because we read the papers, too. The kind of suggestion we really want is something unique to that particular photographer that we would never know about without his suggesting it to us. The last thing we want is someone telling us 'There are going to be 10,000 boats in New York harbor this summer and I think it's going to make a terrific picture so could I have the assignment?' That's the kind of suggestion we don't want and it's hard to handle, because a lot of photographers are suggesting things all the time and just because they suggest them and we do it but do not give them the assignment, they think we have taken their idea. So it presents problems. On the other hand if he has spotted what could be a potentially good news story and comes up with an entirely different way of trying it, that's acceptable.

"I think the major problem on *LIFE* has always been that if you don't come back with a unique and beautiful or exciting and imaginative set of pictures, you have no story, and that takes great care and thought and tremendously hard work. I know how difficult it is to be a photographer and pull off a story because I've worked with so many of them. I see some people kiss off assignments so you don't want to use them again. I see some people work with enormous dedication and thought. With them it's not just when they are taking the pictures, but when they are getting ready to take the pictures, that the moment comes to decide what exactly is wanted of them, and they have to make an effort to achieve some kind of special vision. I warn people who want to become professional photographers that it's not only difficult financially, but difficult to break into in general because the whole publishing field is small and the job itself is very, *very* hard."

Chapter Seven
On Assignment: II

Fulfilling an assignment, from hard news to simple public relations or product photography, requires thought and careful procedure from the time you first arrive on location until you finally pack your camera cases and get your film off to the labs. There are no hard rules; each assignment is different and each has to be treated as an individual situation, but there are basic routines that must be followed if the assignment is to be successful.

Inspection and Establishing Contacts at the Location

You should start by checking in immediately with your local contact, either by phone on arrival if you have traveled from another city, or directly at his office or plant if it is a local assignment. If you are meeting someone at an office, announce yourself (politely) to the receptionist. And if you are kept waiting, simply wait, relaxed and without making a nuisance of yourself or showing any anger or hostility at being kept waiting.

On any kind of job involving a broad coverage, a walking tour of the entire plant or location is a must. Not only should you see those subjects that have been earmarked for photography, but you should also look at everything else around because, as the visual expert, you might well see things that the editorial contact or public relations man never considered as having photographic interest.

On one annual report assignment I went through the plant with the local public relations man, and as I walked around I made notes, keeping up a running commentary about what I would like to photograph, what I thought would make for interesting or exciting pictures, etc. At the end I noticed my client was amused, and I asked him what was so funny. "Well," he said, "you are the first visiting photographer who walked around here and told *us* what he would like to photograph and didn't say, 'What would you like us to do?'"

At first I was a bit nonplused, but my client quickly put me at ease and told me he was very pleased because it meant that I was looking at things from a fresh viewpoint. Later we sat down and discussed at length what was important to him and worked out a list combining the best of both viewpoints.

Also during the tour of a location, as you come to each department or section, you should ask to be introduced to the department head or foreman or unit supervisor and note not only their names but also their telephone extension numbers, a necessity if you have to reach someone in a hurry in some vast complex.

At the pre-shooting conferences, discuss what assistance you are going to need and, if you have not brought your own crew along, who the local assistants are going to be. It's important to confirm production schedules or the availability of the people you plan to photograph over those next few days. Will they be there, or on vacation or at some conference, seminar or lab? Until I learned to pre-check this availability, more than once I arrived only to find that our man in Chicago was actually in San Francisco that day.

It all adds up to the idea that you must work your shooting time into the operation schedule of the plant or location, and not vice versa. If you are covering a large operation, whether an industrial plant, political situation such as a convention, educational institution or anything else of sizable physical scope, and have spent the better part of the day inspecting the area and having conferences and meetings with all concerned, the chances are there is going to be very little left of that first day. But it is not wasted by any means, because it is much more important to move into an area prepared for what you are going to face than to be surprised at what you find without any opportunity to do something about it.

Now is the time to start making your immediate advance preparations. Is a certain area going to need cleaning up or possibly painting? You should also be concerned with how people are dressed and how they look. I do not expect you to demand quality street clothes for a production-line photograph, but it will probably enhance your pictures considerably if the workers on the line or the people you choose to photograph in offices or elsewhere are reasonably and neatly dressed and if the work areas are clean and tidy. These are things you should arrange before you arrive with camera in hand. It is a colossal waste of time and money to have someone scurrying around for a broom, empty a refuse bin, paint a hand-rail, or do some other chore that could have been taken care of hours earlier. Remember I am now talking about shooting a situation for a client who is paying you to make them look as good as possible. I am assuming that you are not doing a piece of investigative journalism and are not out to make your client or subjects look like fools or worse.

This attention to details applies also to editorial coverage. You probably would not be on the site if your editors did not want to produce an attractive piece of photojournalism. Even if an area is spotless when the shift or work day starts at 8:00 A.M., by 2:30 or 3:00 P.M. the place and the people may look a lot different. It is only fair that when you are on this kind of assignment you do your very best to make the operation look attractive and interesting. When photographing certain people, particularly those in the arts, their messiness and possibly sloppy environment become part of the charm of a warm and friendly photograph, and if you are doing a purely documentary approach, then you photograph it the way it is. But if you are dealing with an annual report, commercial assignment or an editorial piece for a business or consumer publication, you have to look to the details and fine points of appearance of the location and personnel.

Factories and industrial work areas are notoriously dirty and frequently unsafe, yet you are expected to make photographs that do not show this dirty or unsafe condition. It often does not take much effort to make tremendous improvements in the visual aspects of a location, and paying attention to such details will enhance your images. Just the removal of a few oily rags, a couple of lunch buckets or paper food containers, even the "girlie" calendars on the wall, will often work wonders. Sometimes the repainting of a handrail or machine protection device in the customary yellow or red warning colors will brighten an otherwise dull color picture remarkably. The pre-shooting preparations can get complicated and possibly costly to the client or subject, so you have to use good sense about such requests.

I was once assigned to cover a new oil refinery for a petroleum company that had just begun building a photo file and needed pictures to show the newness and the up-to-date quality of their installations. Arriving at the site, I found everything in pretty good condition except for three large Horton-spheres (huge, ball-shaped, spherical tanks designed to hold gases under high pressure). The forms are interesting and make for exciting visual patterns. They were finished, but unpainted, and covered with a rusty scale that, in contrast with the rest of the gleaming installation, looked simply awful.

I talked with the painting contractor about this, asking him how long it would take to paint those tanks and when he thought he might be starting. He surprised me by saying that he was planning to start that very week and that it would take three days to do them all. I suggested that he do just half a tank at a time and only from the side I was photographing. In that way he could finish the camera side of all three tanks in a day and a half, and I could wait only until those sides were painted. He agreed and went on with his task and several days later I made my pictures. The funny thing was that about ten years later I passed that refinery on a train whose tracks ran alongside it, and the backs of the tanks were still unpainted! Some of my friends and editors have teased me that I've left a series of half-painted plants all over the world, and perhaps they are right.

Cooperation on the job by the client or subject can well make or break the assignment, and I cannot repeat too often the warning that the visiting photographer must never make a nuisance of himself, make unnecessary demands, detract from production or even simply get in the way of the normal functions of the operation he is there to cover.

Preparing Your Crew

With the physical preparation of the site arranged for, the next thing to do is prepare your crew if you are using one. If you have brought your own people, there is little you need to do other than familiarize them with the location. But if you are going to use local plant personnel, arrange to brief and possibly instruct them, and the first afternoon of your arrival is the best time for this. When in the past I was using massive banks of synchronized flashbulbs that had to be changed every time an exposure was made, I would set up a mini-school right on the factory floor. Later, when I started using high-capacity strobe units, new lessons were necessary to teach the assistants how to set them up, string the power cables, hook up slave cells and strobe units, and the very special care needed to avoid knocking them over on cluttered floors and smashing expensive strobe heads. So what I still do on bigger mobile setups is to hold classes for an hour or two until the crew is used to handling the equipment safely and efficiently.

A reminder here: make sure, if you are going to be on the same location for more than a day, to get the same people back each time to avoid having to retrain a new crew each day. Determine their hours to see if there is conflict in their starting and quitting times. Make sure all bases are covered before you start using this crew. It may be pretty embarrassing for you to be photographing a shift of workers that normally quits at 4:30 in the afternoon, only to have your electrician walk off at 3:30 because he started an hour earlier and will miss his ride home.

If you are working in industrial or commercial situations and are running over from one shift to another, you may want to hold your crew over too. Can you do so without causing a labor problem? Often I have asked individual workers to work overtime, and if the company won't pay, then I do and add it to my bill. I also arrange to send them home by cab if they belong to car pools, as so many industrial workers do. These are all little things, but they can make your life a lot easier if you prepare for them.

Get Ready, Get Set, Go!

On corporate or industrial locations you should arrive at the site at least an hour before the shift starts. Your equipment should be accessible on a loading dock or wherever you are going to gain entry to the location, and a good-sized flatbed dolly should be made available to trundle your gear around. If you are working on a roving field assignment and are going to be mobile and using small hand cameras, then have everything with you, loaded, and ready to move.

Be dressed properly for the situation and, as discussed earlier, if safety gear is required for the area, *use it*! Dressing for the job is important. If you are going to be working out-of-doors in some miserable hot or cold and nasty environment, be sure your clothing will keep you comfortable and protect you and your equipment from frostbite, dust or just plain foul-ups. Pay attention to your shoes. Make certain that you are as nimble and sure-footed as the occasion demands, whether you have to climb a ladder or to the top of a car or up a tree, or scramble along a rooftop or a cliff for a decent vantage point, or have to waltz out on some highly waxed or polished floor.

Preplan how you are going to separate exposed film after each shoot so that if you have to dash off to the airport that afternoon, you won't be shipping exposed and blank film together, as I did many years ago, taking ten years off the life of the lab chief who came up with 200 blanks and thought he had somewhere run the film through the hypo instead of the developer. Also, if you are shipping daily, make sure your shipping containers are on hand and that you have everything else you need, from pre-addressed labels to light-proof boxes, packing materials, bills of lading, etc. Whatever you need, have it with you before you start shooting. And last but not least, know in advance what flight you are going to get your film on and where the airport really is and, what is more important, where at the airport to take your film.

Overcoming "Photographer's Block"

When all the pre-shooting contingencies are dealt with, it is time to move forward. Making that first picture on a new location, for myself and many colleagues, has always been a psychological hurdle. Call it stage fright, photographer's block or just plain panic—it's in all the arts in one form or another. Everyone before you has had this feeling, but as soon as you make the first exposure, it will disappear and you will settle into the routine of working and producing. Instead of worrying and stewing, think methodically and carefully about your first shooting site—what it requires, what kind of cameras, lighting, cooperation on the line or from behind a desk.

Getting People to Relax

It is possible the people you are photographing are even more nervous or uncomfortable than you. Some are simply shy in front of cameras or, because of self-consciousness, feel they have to "perform." You will find this particularly true if you are in a production area of a large plant, a very large office space or other situations where there are many people working in sight of one another. Whatever the location, your function is to put them at ease so you can photograph them in a natural and relaxed environment.

When I run into problems like this, I often try to disarm the people and put them at ease by using a little light banter, which I find often works very well. Usually in working with production or clerical personnel who are too camera conscious, getting key personnel aside and telling them that I am really interested in the situation and not the individual, and that all I want from them is to do whatever they would be doing if I were not there, is enough. If I am using Polaroids, I make a couple of tests and involve people in the photograph by asking their advice on their own appearance or something in the background. I might ask about a procedural process to get their minds off the brief "celebrity" status that making the picture affords them, and to give them a sense of participation. Or often I will joke with the production-line workers, telling them I won't compare the photographs with those in the post office as "most wanted by the FBI."

Very often you'll be all set and have your subject relaxed when some clown in the background will yell "Smile!" or "Say cheese!" or something similar, which will be just enough to distract the person you are photographing and make him feel edgy or self-conscious again. When that happens I ostentatiously stop, cut the lights and take out of my supply case a small placard which I have had previously lettered: "Assistant Director"—plus an extra cable release, and go over and hand them to the guy who opened his mouth, saying, "There is only one director on this set and that's me, but here is your union card, and you can take over if you want to." That's usually enough to cause a laugh from the others around him and cause the loud-mouth to shut up long enough for the next exposure. Once I acquired a railroad engineer's cap and was wearing it in a shop location and when a "big mouth" opened up, I walked over and offered him my hat, saying, "If you're driving this train you may as well wear the hat that goes with it." That too did the trick.

Dealing With Murphy's Law: "If Something Can Go Wrong, It Will"

Remember not to get visibly upset when things go wrong or you feel harassed or pressured. Do not rely too greatly on the latest camera or some new hotshot lighting equipment; rather, have faith in your own knowledge of the craft of photography. If a piece of equipment fails in the midst of a shoot, as it often seems to do at a critical moment, call a coffee break or send out for a round of soft drinks for the people with you. Then go calmly about repairing the equipment, if possible, or replacing it with the backup gear you should have brought along. Remember, Forscher's hockey puck camera hasn't been invented yet, so expect technical failures and learn to work around them—coolly and without panic.

Field performance is only the tip of the iceberg. What you bring back and what you ultimately deliver in the way of finished photographs are still only part of the answer to the client's needs. There are additional responsibilities that come with an assignment. Suppose you have been assigned to cover the plant operations for the annual report, or have received an assignment from a magazine to shoot an editorial piece that you may be particularly well suited to do. You did all your homework, ordered all the materials you thought you'd need, arrived at the location—and found that nothing was as planned or expected, or that the weather was lousy or that the people you were supposed to photograph just weren't around. Or for some other reason you have run into stone-wall opposition on the part of someone on the local scene who is determined to be uncooperative or downright antagonistic and may even go so far as to try to prevent you from doing what you are supposed to do. What then? Do you throw in the towel, or try somehow to get the task done? Or suppose you find you simply cannot complete the job for any number of reasons, whether your fault or not? What happens then? Do you re-shoot it? Is it possible to re-shoot it? When do you make the determination to commit yourself or your client to a large expenditure in order to get what's needed done?

This is all part of the responsibility factor between you and your client. You cannot simply say, "Well, it wasn't as they said it would be, so the heck with them, it's their fault," and go home. They might or might not pay your bills, but forget about hearing from the client again if you have this kind of reaction.

One thing you don't do is give up. If you are having trouble with someone on the local level, don't argue with him or even with his immediate superior, but get on the phone and call the person at your home office to whom you are responsible and report what the problem is, asking what *he* wants to do about it. Is the weather impossible to work around within your deadline or day-rate commitment? Again, back to the phone to tell the assigning office what's happening. Can you have more time? Should you shoot regardless of the weather? Be sure to explain to your client, if he is not knowledgeable about the reaction of film to weather, what he will be getting. In some cases, particularly editorial situations, the production of the picture is more important than whether it's a good day or a bad one. But you must let your client know what the realities are and get some answers from him about how you should proceed.

However, you cannot lay it all on the client and always ask for his advice on what to do. One of the reasons you were hired was because of your ability to solve certain problems, so work out good alternatives to offer as options to your client before you call him. How close your alternative possibilities are compared to what was originally desired should be the deciding factor in what you tell your client. Even losing an assignment because of the impossibility of photographing something that isn't there or isn't as it was expected to be is a chance you may have to take, and those are the breaks in the game. But whenever it's possible, try to communicate and discuss your problems with whoever hired you.

One of the trickiest areas to deal in is when your client has been oversold on a situation and you find it impossible to produce his bill of goods. I had a problem once with *Fortune* magazine when a writer came back with a glowing report on an impressive piece of equipment. He raved about a drying tower in a fabric mill that soared three stories through the building and had thousands of heat-drying lamps in it, and insisted that it would make a spectacular one-shot picture to illustrate the entire story. He sold the editors so convincingly that those were my instructions, one picture of this machine for a full-page lead. However, he neglected to tell us that the tower was a sealed steel box 6″ deep, 30″ wide and 150′ high and that all the lamps were *inside* the box so there was no way to insert a camera in there without melting it down. What he had seen was the inside of the box through a couple of one-inch-diameter heat-proof glass inspection ports placed a few feet apart on the tower. He did not understand the impossibility of photographing this unit as he had projected, so I ignored his request and went on to photograph other things to illustrate the story.

When I sat in on the layout conference, the writer was furious and demanded that some other photographer be sent back to photograph this great visual triumph he had discovered. Fortunately the managing editor wouldn't hear of it and simply said, "If the photographer says it's a photographic impossibility, the fact has to be accepted." And there the matter stood; he backed me up completely.

The important thing in such a case is to find other strong visual material and come back with something to equal the high expectations that were being held at the assignment desk. So while it is important that you keep in communication to discuss problems with the people who have assigned you to the project, there may be other factors which could prevent you from getting your pictures, and you have to make quick judgments and may even have to commit your client to large expenditures. Are you prepared to do this and do you have the confidence that your client will back you in your commitments?

I became involved in a tough and ultimately expensive value judgment that could have cost me my career with one magazine if the editors had not backed me in making an on-the-spot decision that normally should have been cleared with them. I was doing an off-shore oil-drilling story one cold winter day that required a big twin-engine helicopter capable of flying sixty miles over a stormy sea to the rig and bringing me back without the need to refuel. The story, on a U.S. government agency, had been cleared after many hours of conversation with them, and arrangements made for me to use the agency helicopter. I signed the waivers, and was told when to appear at their heliport, and did so.

On arrival I found that my "authorization" had been canceled and the officer in charge was suddenly "unavailable." But there was still a story to be shot, layouts to be finished, deadlines to be met, all within the next twenty-four hours. There was also a deep and violent storm moving in from the west, and I had only a few hours at the most to get everything done before being "socked in" or, worse, marooned on a rig for a couple of days. There now was also the matter of getting permission to land on the privately owned platform.

I spoke to my editor and she said to do the best I could, so I had to work it out myself. I also called the oil company, talked their public relations man into getting me permission to land, even though I had no idea whether the story was going to be a hatchet job or not. (It wasn't.) I checked the only helicopter rental operator in the area with aircraft big enough to do the job. I told the dispatcher of my needs and asked him how much it would cost.

He quoted a heart-stopping $1,100, a figure I immediately passed back to Washington. They gasped too, expecting as I did to hear a $350 to $400 rate, but said to go ahead anyway. So I dashed for the pad, and we took off with a near ninety-mile-per-hour tail wind pushing us. The pilot then came back and said that, because of the wind, we couldn't refuel on the oil rig. I had ten minutes to make my pictures as he needed full rotor power to keep the chopper on the landing pad, and the total engine time would be well over three hours, or about $3,500 in rentals.

I had been under the impression that the $1,100 figure was the total price, but it seemed it was only the hourly charge. I could have aborted the mission and headed for the nearest phone, but it was lunchtime in Washington and I knew I couldn't get hold of anyone in authority. Even if I did, there would be a meeting of a couple hours' duration before they granted the permission, and by that time we would have lost our weather anyway. So I made a decision and told the crew to go ahead, knowing that it might be my last assignment for this magazine. I had my ten minutes' shooting time on the pad (I used my motor drive), grabbed two rolls of film, climbed back into the big bird, and while we fought the gale-force wind and shuddered back, I wondered what would have happened if some new photographer had run into a situation like this. Even then I was not at all sure that I wasn't going to be asked to "eat" $2,400 of that bill. But my editors did back me and the picture editor said, "You made a value judgment, and even though we might have canceled the shoot, we accepted your decision to go ahead with it."

One sidebar to this is that my editor said she would try to bury the bill so the managing editor wouldn't see it and have a cardiac seizure, and I heard nothing more from her about it. But about a year later, I ran into the managing editor in the hallway and he said, "Oh, by the way, Charlie, I've been meaning to ask you about that helicopter bill on the offshore story."

This kind of value judgment aside, what about responsibility for production of pictures that have to be re-shot or of additional material produced because the original material is not up to snuff? When there is a failure to produce a set of acceptable pictures and the question exists of the need for a substantial amount of retakes, I feel the whole situation has to be reviewed thoroughly by both the photographer and the client.

The first question is, what happened? Who was wrong? Were you late? Did the client's people not show up? Were the models, if any, late? Or unprepared to work? Or did you shoot everything as planned and have something go wrong in the processing? Did you lose some or all of the film? Was a camera stolen at the airport? There are so many factors that can result in failure that it would be impossible to list all the possibilities. The main thing is to first find out what went wrong and then go about correcting the situation.

What happens if you travel halfway around the world, ship your film to the lab, and instead of receiving a batch of processed film, get a printed slip saying, "We're sorry, something happened, and here's a check for the replacement of the film"? This has happened to photographers over the years, though admittedly less frequently in recent times. If the assignment is over a long period of time and involves a great deal of shooting in many different localities, as occurred when I went around the world for an airline, break up your take into smaller batches and feed them to the labs piecemeal. Do this so there can be no possibility of one color processor breaking down and ruining a whole take that would be impossible to re-shoot.

Goof-Proofing Your Assignment

Are *you* goof-proof in your methods of shooting and getting your assignment finished? When shooting complicated color situations, whether on a factory floor or in a studio, you can diminish your chance of failure with the use of Polaroids or bracketing, often both, and also by using different cameras or film backs. Then splitting your takes for shipment to processing labs will be added insurance. When shooting news stories or fast-moving people or things, and there is no opportunity for test shooting, you have to do as much as you can to predetermine your needs and exposures. If you are shooting aerials of a plant or a city, don't wait until you are aloft before trying to determine your exposures. The light level of what you shoot from the air will be on the ground, so determine what it is at ground level, not by a possibly false exposure from the airplane.

Earlier I covered pretested emulsions, camera and equipment checks, and spare equipment availability. Equipment failure should never be a factor, yet unfortunately, it too often is. Usually this can be avoided by thorough testing of equipment before starting the job. But cameras can be dropped or some other piece of equipment get banged around during transit or during a shoot. If this sort of thing happens, it's your fault in the eyes of your client, and it's your responsibility to make good somehow even if it means (to use an old show-business expression) "taking a bath" by paying for the reshooting even at a great loss. Naturally there will be occasions when neither expense nor time can re-create the situation, and all you can do is hide your head and take the consequences of probably unbillable costs and fees. However, if it's not your fault or, as in the case of some advertising photography, the art director may simply not like the pictures for "esthetic" reasons, even though they may be fine technically, what do you do?

In advertising photography there are clear "re-shooting" guidelines and customs (see page 82). There are no hard rules as to what constitutes acceptance. If the photographer has clearly failed for technical reasons *within* his control and has produced no usable images at all, the responsibility for reshooting is his. But under "customs of the trade," a photographer is supposed to be given the first opportunity to do a retake before the client looks elsewhere. Yet because personal judgments are often involved, there is usually no easy agreement on what constitutes "acceptable" photographs, so it is not unusual to have to resort to arbitration.

There are formal arbitration organizations such as the American Arbitration Association as well as more trade-oriented groups like the Joint Ethics Committee (JEC), a totally voluntary organization made up of representatives of photographers, illustrators, and art directors. However, since it is voluntary, any referral to the JEC must be agreed on by all parties before it will enter the case. Although the JEC has no actual enforcement power, participants usually accept its recommendations. For further information regarding the Joint Ethics Committee, write to P.O. Box 179, Grand Central Station, New York, NY 10017.

Suppose there *is* the possibility of re-shooting a situation — a machine that hasn't gone anywhere or people who haven't left the area in which you were working or a mountain that's still in place (even Mount St. Helens kept blowing its top, for example). How do you deal with situations like these? By re-shooting at your expense if it is totally your fault, or at half fee plus expenses if it's not, but you still want to maintain good relations with the client. But use good judgment here—don't offer to spend $5,000 to recoup a $1,000 assignment. It is better to take "the bath."

Usually bills will be paid for services rendered even if the client is unhappy about what is produced. The main point is that in editorial situations there can be no option for payment on the part of the client or editor based on whether the photographs are acceptable if all the other technical standards of quality are met. Also in the editorial world a technical failure, even if it is the photographer's fault, will rarely result in nonpayment if his track record up to then has been good.

Part of the reasoning behind this philosophy is that the client's picture buyer or editor should be experienced enough to know in advance whether the photographer has the ability to produce the pictures requested, and therefore there should be no question about payment for those services even though the editor may be unhappy with the results. The presumption of knowledge on the part of the editor doesn't always work. If it turns out that the editor is untrained and not knowledgeable, disastrous results can occur. This is apt to happen more often with new picture editors whose principal training has been in fine arts rather than in photography.

A case in point: I was assigned to a story on a large pharmaceutical plant in upstate New York for a medical magazine. The picture editor herself had been a photographer of many years' standing. She had led her bosses to believe she had more knowledge than she actually had, and it was this lack of technical expertise that nearly caused me to have to reshoot an assignment that did not need reshooting. When I finished the job, I turned my film in to a commercial lab with instructions to deliver it directly to her, and from the field I left for an assignment in Georgia for another magazine. When I called her, she was in a state of near hysteria.

"Nothing is any good," she said. "Everything has a terrible bluish-white cast to it, and all has to be reshot."

There was no arguing with her at a 1,000-mile distance, and I agreed to reshoot but insisted that we meet that Saturday morning in New York with the developed film so I could see what went wrong. However, she was too agitated to wait and without telling me had already dispatched another photographer to reshoot. When I arrived back in New York and met her at her office, she threw the pictures on the light table. (I used the word "threw" because that's exactly what she did.) I looked at the pictures and couldn't find one single thing wrong. They were beautifully lit, cleanly and properly processed, and so far as I could detect, perfect in every respect including content. I must have looked at her as though she had lost her mind because she thrust the transparencies from the other photographer at me and said, "Look at these—this is what I wanted." What she wanted were pictures with a bright green cast over everything.

It finally sank in; the other photographer (and every photographer she had ever used in a similar situation) had shot 35mm film using available light, and in most cases the "available light" was from fluorescent or mercury-vapor fixtures. (I deliberately had *avoided* this situation by turning off the building lights and using big strobe units and daylight-type color film.) One would think she would have known this, having been a photographer herself, but I learned later that she had almost never shot color film on her own, nor had she known that most factory production areas are lit either by fluorescent or (even worse) mercury-vapor lighting. So when she came face-to-face with photographs correctly lit, she thought there was something wrong. I won the battle but lost the war, because I refused to reshoot. Not only did I have to threaten legal action to get paid, but I never got more work from that publication.

It is impossible to apply the same guidelines to both editorial and advertising photography, though the gap is narrowing. Unless the photographer clearly understands the requirements of the assignment and fulfills them completely, trouble lies ahead.

The Other Side of the Desk

You are a long distance from home and much of what you do depends not only on your interpretation of the assignment, but what the editor or client is looking for. These ideas are not always well defined, concepts not always clearly communicated, and other factors may come between what you shoot and what appears in print.

Gordon Parks (see page 151) tells of a battle he had with his Managing Editor over the way an important picture was treated in the layout of a story. Parks was lucky because he was able to see the layout before it went to press. And though his strong vocal objections got him thrown out of the editor's office, the editor did indeed hear what he had to say and made the changes Parks demanded.

Sometimes the battle is lost before it begins, as often the first time a photographer sees his story is when it is in print and nothing can be done except to air his feelings. On very high levels some of these arguments have ended in either the dismissal of a staff photographer, editor or writer, or dissolution of a contract. These are extreme situations and do not happen often. Most times the steam is vented by caustic telephone calls or sizzling wires. And if that person thinks their work is not being taken seriously, he or she may deem it necessary to sound off . . . if only to prevent a reprise later. But humor should be the leavening agent, and frequently a serious issue may be addressed and yet eased by a good laugh.

I was in Paris once and was appalled at the way a story I had done was mangled in layout. I guess my psyche demanded the last word (and the implied assurance that it would not happen again) so I sent the following Telex to my editor. I did not get fired as he understood my frustration and later apologized for the mishandling of the story. The wire was pure bile, but its recipient actually enjoyed it and had it posted in his office.

AFTER SEEING LAYOUT I HAVE CONSULTED WITH A LOCAL GYPSY OF MY AC-QUAINTANCE AND ORDERED ONE TWENTY DOLLAR CURSE TO BE PLACED ON YOUR HEAD STOP ASSUME THIS IS EXPENSE ACCOUNT DEDUCTIBLE STOP OF COURSE I REALLY DON'T BELIEVE IN IT BUT IF YOUR HAIR STARTS FALLING OUT, YOU DEVELOP HEARTBURN, FLATULENCE OR OTHER AILMENTS PLS KNOW ITS NOT COINCIDENTAL ENDIT ROTKIN

When to Throw in the Towel

"Acts of God" is a phrase in legal contracts from another era and can cover a multitude of difficulties. Usually these problems are less godly, more human, and in truth often reflect acts of omission rather than commission. Someone—photographer, client, or one of a dozen persons in between—has not made proper preparations or has forgotten to do something. This puts photographer and client into situations where each has little or no control, and they usually wind up at the mercy of people who could not care less about the problems or, unfortunately and too often, are downright incompetent.

This occurred when I was covering the earlier mentioned Op-Sail celebration in 1976 for *Smithsonian* magazine from a Navy helicopter. After weeks of negotiation and hours of conversation with the Navy, I boarded the chopper at the nearby naval air station (NAS) and thirty minutes later took my place in a long line of helicopters covering this marvelous and complex celebration. I was doing fine, photographing the start of the parade of tall ships up from New York's lower harbor, and just as the first vessels approached the Manhattan skyline (which was what we had been waiting for) the pilot cheerfully announced that he was pulling out of line to refuel at the Lakehurst NAS base sixty miles south. I grabbed the intercom and, using language that the FAA would have frowned on, said (expletives deleted), "What? You're supposed to have six hours' worth of fuel on this bird and we've been airborne less than an hour, and even if you came up from New Jersey you shouldn't have to pull out now."

Said the pilot, "That's true, but we have to go clear back to New Jersey again and won't have the reserve to fly much more now and still return."

"Why not refuel at the NAS in New York?" I asked.

"We can't do that," the pilot said, "because we're not cleared to draw fuel from that station."

By this time I was beginning to wonder how many different navies we have in this country. In desperation I suggested refueling at La Guardia Airport and said I would be willing to pay the cost of refueling, but the pilot said if we did that, we would have to provide fuel for the other six helicopters in the squadron. I rejected this because I had no illusions about my editor accepting a bill for 3,000 gallons of aviation fuel I didn't use . . . and particularly for the use of the "competition." The pilot was adamant about our returning to Lakehurst and pulled us out of line. We were quickly followed by the rest of the helicopters in the squadron and thus I, and thirty other working press people, missed most of the parade. I was saved only by what I had already shot, but we never made the intended gate-fold cover. So on this part of the story I was "dead" and had to throw in the towel.

This is a classic example of a lack of preparation by third parties whom you are forced to depend on though you have little recourse if they fail in their responsibilities. In these situations the chances are there usually would be no problem about being paid for your time, although some hard-nosed art directors or purchasing agents might well say, "I don't care what happened. You didn't deliver the pictures so we're not going to pay you." If you have properly protected yourself in your purchase agreement, you should be able to cover such eventualities.

Problems such as these are difficult if not impossible to anticipate, but there are other potential trouble-spots that might be more predictable and thus easier to locate. The photographer must somehow learn to be omniscient and sense impending trouble. For example, if you are sent to do a portrait and the man is not going to be on the site as planned, or the building you thought you were to photograph actually doesn't exist, or is not where you thought you were told it would be, you ought to know this ahead of time. I was once hired to cover a plant in New Mexico as part of an annual report, and *ten minutes* before I was to leave for the location I learned the plant hadn't been built yet. My client, an electrical manufacturer supplying the materials, had shipped them four years earlier and *assumed* the plant was built and running.

Once I went to Pittsburgh to cover the lighting of a night baseball game at the new Three Rivers stadium, and arrived to find that a violent rainstorm that afternoon had caused the evening game to be canceled. Try explaining this to the client (the lighting equipment supplier to the stadium) who was planning to use these pictures for his annual report closing in two days. Any delay would cost the client a fortune in lost time at the printing plant. But I also knew they had supplied similar equipment to the stadium in Cincinnati, and there was a game being played there that night also.

My emergency solution, made without consulting the client because I couldn't reach him, was to charter a plane and make some night aerials of that Cincinnati park, which was similar in appearance to the park in Pittsburgh. I was able to substitute it for what had originally been requested. Subsequently I learned that there *were* considerable structural differences that the art directors covered up by judicious placement of type overlays and a few text changes. I probably could have invoked the "Act of God" clause here, and instead of dashing off to Cincinnati, I could have repaired to the Pittsburgh Press Club bar and closed the assignment there.

Be Flexible

In planning your schedule, try to keep some flexibility in it. If you need outdoor pictures and there is a forecast of bad weather, try to get all your exteriors made before the weather changes. If you are inside and the weather suddenly turns good, be prepared to interrupt your interior work to take advantage of the favorable conditions. The same goes for other occasions. If you hear of something you may have missed in your briefings, don't be so rigid in your scheduling that you avoid taking advantage of the new situation to shoot.

Time your work carefully. For instance, if you are working in a factory with many people around you, plan to stop shooting an hour before a shift ends so you are not caught in a stampede to the locker rooms or exits. This will keep your cameras and strobe units from being knocked over. Also follow your schedule methodically so you don't have to backtrack and possibly cause further disruptions to the people involved.

If you are working in an industrial area or other crowded facility, the chances are that when it comes to meal breaks, your local contact people will suggest you lunch with them rather than eat in the company cafeteria or lunchroom. While this may be more pleasant, as most industrial cafeterias are uniformly disappointing, it's advisable to use them to save the time spent in getting in and out of a plant or office building and finding a restaurant of better quality. However, if you do decide to eat outside, avoid drinking at lunchtime, not because of morality, but so as not to inhibit your ability to function maximally when you return. Simply put, getting "bombed" at lunchtime is an automatic road to "bombing out" on the job. I have often skipped the noon meal entirely to save time, or sent out for sandwiches and coffee in order to avoid interruptions. This is particularly helpful when you have overlapping shifts on a job or when the weather is unreliable and you have to take advantage of every minute of shooting time.

Meeting Deadlines

Earlier I quipped that one of the first things I do on arrival in a new city is make a reservation to leave. This is not as flip as it sounds. Getting you and your film to its destination after a job is done is an important part of the whole performance. Deadlines can be critical, and thousands of your client's dollars, as well as your payments, may depend on whether or not you get your pictures made, processed, and delivered on time.

Editorial deadlines are considered sacred by anyone in journalism. In order for presses to roll on schedule, layouts have to be closed, prints and engravings made, type set, and a million other bits of information all locked into place at the right time and in the right position. The photographer's job of getting his pictures in on time is no small part of the total teamwork required for the makeup of any publication using photography. Deadlines are not restricted to newspapers and news magazines. Every other publication, be it a tiny neighborhood supermarket flyer, high school yearbook, or a slick annual report from a multinational company, has its schedule for printing, and in this age of satellite transmissions, plants can be located anywhere in the world . . . and often are.

Why are press closing times so sacred? The answer is not found in the romance of newsmaking but more in the hard dollars-and-cents world of advertising. An advertiser spends much money to have his commodity or service presented to a readership of guaranteed size, and if the message doesn't get out at the scheduled time, the agencies and publishers are usually stuck with penalties in the form of reduced revenues or even lawsuits for breach of contract.

Much the same holds for the production end. A magazine or newspaper is a tremendously complex enterprise, and scheduling at printing plants has to be precise. Arrangements have to be made for the size of the copy run, the amount of paper on hand, back-up press capacity for breakdowns or expansions for last-minute, fast-moving news. There are many reasons why a missed printing deadline can be enormously costly to a publisher. With one large publication group that publishes six or more large magazines, press availability has to be allocated in such a manner that each separate edition will get through the system on a precise schedule or it will affect the one that follows it. Therefore the photographer who misses his deadline, especially when a critical story is involved, is in for a hard time indeed.

The need for prompt delivery does not rest only with newspapers or magazines. It is equally important to the publisher of that routine brochure or high school yearbook. How effective is a yearbook if it comes out after graduation? Or the supermarket throwaway sheet that reaches the public after the sale is over? Apply this thinking to the corporate annual report. Corporate laws are strict about stockholders' meetings and publication of the financial data making up the heart of an annual report. The company issuing it has to rely on the graphics department of its agency or art service house, and the same necessities of magazine publishing are brought into play: engraving, makeup and typesetting—all on time. A corporation missing its publication deadline is in as much trouble as the magazine that fails to come out when scheduled. It is important for the photographer to know that what he delivers to his client is in proper condition, ready for printing, and will not require extensive additional work to get it in shape.

Photography came of age in the 1830s, but it was not until the end of the century that printed reproduction of photographs by the halftone method became commonplace. Over ensuing years basic principles of halftone engraving and printing have remained the same, though the technology has become increasingly sophisticated. Press capability to reproduce fine photography increases constantly, yet the early basics have to be kept in mind when producing photographs for reproduction.

Is it important for the photographer to understand the basics of photographic reproduction? Decidedly yes. The late Ansel Adams, unquestionably one of the great photographers of our age, and noted for his remarkably crafted images that always appeared so well in books, magazines and posters, would never submit a print for reproduction until he knew exactly what printing process would be used. Michele Stephenson, Picture Editor at *TIME* magazine (see page 11) underscored this by telling me she expects every photographer used by *TIME* to know what quality is required in every image so that it can be best reproduced by their presses.

There are three basic systems of halftone reproduction. They all begin with the halftone screen, where a photograph or other graphic art is rephotographed onto a light-sensitive plate with a halftone screen interposed between the original picture and the plate. A halftone screen is made of fine diagonal lines which break up an image into tiny dots. The "height" and position of these dots control the amount of ink used to reproduce the highlights, halftones or shadows of the photographs reproduced. How that image is then applied to the paper is embodied in one of the three systems. These are lithography (or photo-offset), photoengraving (letterpress) and intaglio (gravure). Each is an improvement over the one before and the costs naturally are commensurate.

Until recently most newspapers were printed by the letterpress method, that is, a zinc or copper engraving was made after the halftone screen produced the image on a sensitized plate; type was set in "hot metal" (lead) by the typesetting machinery; and the whole thing was locked into forms and put on the printing presses. Ink was then rolled over the forms or large drums, and the paper, coming from giant rolls, pressed against them, with the resulting images. The quality of the photograph was controlled by "resolution" of the engraving screen, or the number of dots (or lines per inch) on the plate, and the ability of the paper to hold the ink in place. Because newsprint traditionally is a soft paper and absorbs ink easily, a "coarse" (sixty to eighty lines) screen was used for newsprint, but the ink had a tendency to block up in the shadows, so the quality of newsprint photo reproduction was often poor. Deep blacks and pure whites were most difficult to print, and always have been, by traditional newspaper letterpress methods. The advantage of the letterpress system was that it was fast, and halftone engravings generally had a pretty long life so that large editions of the papers could be run without replating. On big circulation papers, duplicate drums or "stereotypes" were made so many presses could print simultaneously when press runs were in the hundreds of thousands and perhaps millions. Thus it was important that prints presented by the photographer were contrasty as the coarse screens could not separate the fine gradations of tone well. Sometimes a uniformly gray-toned print, suitable if the "grayness" were unimportant, held detail surprisingly well on newsprint.

When letterpress is used with a finer engraving screen on a better grade of paper than newsprint, reproduction quality can be superb, with full detail in the shadow areas and rich blacks and bright whites. Most of the older big picture magazines used the letterpress process, but when they died, the big presses were scrapped. Ironically as there now seems to be a shortage of this type of press capacity, the letterpress process seems doomed to follow the dodo into extinction because of the higher cost of this superb method of photo reproduction. Magazines have different problems. They usually run in smaller print runs and at a slower editorial pace than newspapers, so printers look for better quality in the paper and reproduction.

The most used process now is lithography, one of the oldest forms of art reproduction. Originally, an image was drawn on a porous stone (later on metal plates) with a greasy pencil or chalk. The water-based colors would adhere to the stone or plates except where they were repelled by the grease, then paper was applied and the image created.

In offset (photolithography) the principle is retained. The light-sensitive plate, after exposure through a screen, accepts the ink in the shadow areas and those parts of the plate which would be the highlights of the photograph reject the ink. The entire image is then transferred, or "offset," onto a rubber blanket, which in turn contacts the paper and the image is printed. This method permits the use of harder, less absorbent paper, and thus a finer engraving screen can be used with a resolution as high as 180-200 lines per inch (120 lines is a good average). Much better gradation in the halftone areas and deeper and richer blacks in the shadow areas is achieved. Technically, images printed by offset are not as sharp as photoengraving, because of the two-step transfer of image to paper. However, modern printing technology has narrowed the sharpness gap considerably, and the simplicity of the offset system and its cheaper cost make it the "hands down" winner among processes available.

Earlier I mentioned the proliferation of small-town and small-city papers. One of the main reasons for this growth has been the improvement of the offset process of photo reproduction, coupled with advances in computerized "cold type" production, which eliminates the need for the traditional "hot metal" shop at the standard newspaper. The offset process has moved into the newspaper business also, and most of the big old-line papers are modernizing their equipment to this newer printing process.

Newspapers, with their big rotary presses capable of high-speed runs from huge rolls of paper, also lend themselves to a finer type of printing called gravure (or rotogravure). Some readers may remember the old sepia-tinted weekly supplements in most Sunday editions of years past. Considering the times, the quality of reproduction of the old rotogravure sections was superb, and today many of the four-color supplements of our current Sunday papers are printed by second or third generation processes of the old rotogravure system.

In gravure printing the engraving process is reversed. The shadow areas are etched away on the plates (or drums) and these indentations are filled with the ink, and the paper literally pressed into them, which is where the term "intaglio" derives, meaning incising (or carving into) the image rather than raising it as in the relief (photoengraving) process. The quality of reproduction that can be obtained is probably the best and, under the hands of highly skilled engravers, can come very close to equaling the quality of the original photograph or artwork. Many art galleries sell "gravures" of fine photographs which are prints made by a handmade version of the gravure process.

Here, too, technology is developing and there are new methods of preparation that help cut the high cost of gravure printing. So far, quality gravure printing for the most part is restricted to the "sheet-fed" process—that is, one sheet at a time is printed on a flat press with one color at a time, so that a four-color sheet has to be handled four times before the printing is finished, with careful attention paid to registration of each color over the other.

Added to our technology has been the development of high-speed offset "web" presses. They can run enormous quantities of continuous printing from a big single roll of paper (called "the web") with incredibly fine color registration of images. Six-color webs are now common, and printing experts feel it is only a matter of time before a similar capability is established for gravure printing and the superior quality that comes from this process. For the still photographer wanting the highest quality, the gravure press using up to a 300-line engraving screen offers the best possible reproduction, but also the costliest.

Meeting Printing Requirements

Armed with the knowledge of the type of printing used, what else should the photographer be aware of when he delivers his finished product ready for reproduction? Where better quality reproduction is wanted, editors and printers prefer a rich print on matte-dried, double-weight glossy stock. To matte-dry a print it is reversed on the drying drum so the ferrotype plate will *not* come in contact with the print surface. The glossy paper stock will retain luster and capture the luminescence inherent in the print. Full matte or semi-matte papers are rarely used for reproduction because they mute the tones of the photographs, however well they pick up detail.

In sizing, the preferred practice is to deliver a print equal to or somewhat larger than the final engraving to be made. Enlargement of a print always increases grain structure, but reduction of a print to a specified size does not. So get the best-quality print you can from your negative and print it according to the printing process that will be used.

There are a few "musts" before final delivery. Spotting is one. Every enlargement, no matter how carefully printed or how dust- or scratch-free the original negative is, will inevitably show minor imperfections in the final print. These can be eliminated by "spotting," which doesn't require any great skill but rather patience. Spotting is the covering of a spot by touching up the print with tiny dabs of blended opaque ink to cover and match the general tone of the print around the blemish. The tendency to ignore this final finishing process is growing, and these uncorrected blemishes are beginning to show up in a lot of presswork, indicating equal sloppiness on the part of the printers and production supervisors. A clean, well-spotted print should be a matter of pride to the photographer and a sure sign of his sense of professionalism.

Also consider borders. Some photographers think a borderless print is more handsome, and for exhibition use perhaps it is, but when a photograph is going to a printing plant, the narrow white border on the print most enlarging easels provide, allows for a "grip" on the print in the engraving camera. It also minimizes the chances of smudges and marks on the face of the print. The white border not only serves as protection for the image, but also gives the art director space to put his cropping and sizing marks when a print is scaled for reproduction. In addition, when reproduction work is complete and the print returned to its file, the border acts as a buffer against damage and preserves the print for future use. I have also found that when a print has become quite old and worn around the edges, a later trimming of the border will give it an almost new and fresh appearance, provided it was a good print to begin with.

What about mounting? Unless a print is for exhibition use, do not mount or frame it. Mounts and frames are heavy, expensive, serve no useful purpose, and do not enhance the quality of the picture. In fact most ADs and PEs are annoyed by mounts because of the waste of space in storage and handling.

Get Releases Now

The question of releases and the necessity for them is discussed in chapter ten and applies for the most part to editorial and advertising photography. Most editorial work for annual reports or similar situations does not require the use of releases from people in on-the-job situations, especially when made with the consent of the parties. There are some corporate attorneys who feel their annual report should be so protected, so it can't hurt to obtain releases. Or, if you want to be able to put some of the outtakes into your own photographic files for other uses, it may be difficult if not impossible to get releases later from the people you have photographed. So if a release is necessary or demanded of you by the front office of your client, the time to get those releases is when you are shooting.

On page 180 I mentioned the problem I had in Kentucky where, in the course of an editorial assignment, I ran into heavy opposition by an influential woman in the community who objected to my photographing some of the local people. Technically she had no control over those I photographed, but the company lawyers felt that she might encourage nuisance lawsuits against both the company and me. Such actions, however unjustified, are costly to defend, so I went back to the Kentucky mountains, obtained "general releases" from the people I photographed and thus forestalled any suits.

Since the people you photograph on various jobs are probably not professional models and are already being paid for the activities you are photographing, payment is usually not an issue. Also, most model releases specify a minor amount of money such as one dollar or "other valuable considerations." You can give a machine worker the dollar and the test Polaroid which can be considered the "other valuable consideration." That will usually suffice. The machine worker will consider the dollar a joke but will understand that the passing of the dollar makes the transaction legal. For general editorial work, such as an annual report or a trade magazine in the field in which the worker is employed, this type of release is usually safe enough. Be sure to get the name, address and *Social Security number* of the individual. You don't have to file a report on the dollar paid, because the amount is under that required by the IRS, but if you have the opportunity to resell that photograph for a larger sum and pay the "model" an additional fee, the Social Security number will probably be needed for your IRS report. It is a good idea to make the release in duplicate, turning one copy over to your client and keeping the other for your files should an occasion for reuse arise.

Productivity

In fulfilling assignments, clients often ask questions about productivity. How long is it going to take? How much can you do in any given time? Actual conditions on the site are often unknown in advance, but yet may be controlling factors. If you are working on a commercial job with a view camera involving complicated lighting setups and you can produce five to six good photographs a day, that is good production. If you are working freely with small hand cameras, obviously your productivity rate will go up.

On one magazine essay involving about ten days in the field, with a good mix of indoor and outdoor situations, much conference and travel time between locations (all within a 200-mile radius), I turned in about fifty rolls of 35mm color film, which gave the editors more than enough material for eight pages of editorial illustration. This particular story called for a high degree of mobility, including photographing some science laboratory pictures, others from small boats and big Coast Guard cutters at night, as well as political interviews and, in general, as broad a variety of situations as one could ever expect to encounter in any story. So five rolls of film per day as an average, while it may sound low, was actually fairly good production.

The use of the motor-driven camera can be a misleading factor in assessing productivity, and *quantity* produced with a motor-driven camera is no substitute for *quality*. Except in rapid-action photography, all the motor drive does is consume large amounts of film and processing time and often does not result in any more usable pictures. It may in fact create problems of "missed" pictures because of the constant need for reloading at critical times. An editor I know once complained that she received more than twenty rolls of film for a one-column headshot. It can go the other way, too. Always provide enough material to cover the situation adequately from as many conceivable viewpoints as practical, because too little production can be just as much a shock to an editor as too much.

Picture users frequently ask, "Why do photographers shoot so much? Are they simply taking a buckshot approach in the hope that if they shoot enough pieces of film they are bound to come up with something useful?" Hardly, and while shooting twenty rolls of film for a one-column headshot is excessive, it is not unusual. Most experienced photographers do not overshoot because of uncertainty about technique. In any public or news event or even with interviews, situations change from second to second, facial expressions possibly even faster. A photographer never knows what's going to happen seconds later. Perhaps the classic example of this occurred when Dr. Abraham Zapruder, an amateur photographer, was filming the Kennedy visit to Dallas with his 8mm home movie camera simply for his own enjoyment. Had he stopped after the Kennedy limousine first entered the plaza in Dallas and said to himself, "I have enough to show the President arriving," or if he had not saved some film and kept shooting, he would not have been able to make the pictures of the assassination.

Not all situations are so newsworthy. But whatever happens, there is always the uncertainty of what can occur after you have made each exposure, and that is why most photographers keep shooting continuously on Yogi Berra's reported philosophy of "It ain't over till it's over." It can of course, be carried to excess, and the overuse of the motor drive is one way of falling into that trap. Why shoot a continuous burst of ten or twenty frames when two or three hand-tripped exposures will be just as effective?

Compared to the other costs of doing any kind of photographic coverage, the cost of film is probably the cheapest part of any assignment. But that is not to say there should be no restraint. The big problem with overshooting, aside from the cost of film and processing, is inundating the editor with images and having to assess so many in order to extract the important ones.

One of the classic yarns about all this involved a national magazine that faced a tight closing on a story of worldwide importance. To the consternation of its editors, and within a few hours of press time, they discovered they did not have an up-to-date photograph of the wife of one of the principals in the story who, it seemed, was in residence on an estate a thousand miles from New York and a hundred miles from the nearest city where there was a competent stringer. The editors frantically called him, only to learn that he was already busy for the same magazine on another part of the same story, and therefore could not make the picture. He did offer to call an old-time, retired newspaper photographer who lived near the subject, and have him hurry to shoot the much-needed picture. Meanwhile the magazine chartered a plane to pick up the film and rush it by motorcycle to their lab on arrival at the airport. When the packet was opened in the lab, there was one old-fashioned 4″ × 5″ two-sheet film holder from an old Speed Graphic inside. The lab manager opened the first compartment in the darkroom and it was *empty*. With heart thumping he flipped the holder over, and there was indeed one piece of film there. He developed it quickly and to his relief produced a usable photograph of the lady. After the panic subsided and the magazine closed, the managing editor got on the phone and roared all the way down to Tennessee, "What's the big idea of sending in only one piece of film?" Back came the calm, measured answer, "Mr. Editor, how many did you need?" So let your productivity, backed by your own confidence, fall somewhere in between and produce a good selection and variety for your clients.

Get the Facts and Get Them Right

During the process of shooting you must prepare yourself for final captions and notes. I recommend several methods of keeping track of unprocessed film. First of all, have a good spiral or ring-bound notebook that you can put in your pocket as you work but with large enough detachable pages to be useful. If you are using roll film, particularly 35mm, carry a good supply of self-stick labels with your name and address preprinted or rubber-stamped with waterproof ink that you can apply to the leader of each roll of film after you rewind it. Remember not to retract it all the way or you will lose the leader or you may peel off the label. The label will stay on all through the processing phases and will be in place with each roll as you get it back from the lab. Using these pre-numbered labels, make brief notes on corresponding pages of your notebook as to what they cover to identify each roll. If you use Kodachrome regularly, make an arrangement with your authorized Kodak dealer to set up a processing account for your Kodachrome with the nearest laboratory so that you can ship directly to the lab and the film will come directly back to you later (overnight when necessary). You will then be billed through your dealer. When you do this you will be given a preprinted supply of numbered labels that you attach to each roll of film, and the boxes will be returned with these labels intact.

The same goes for marking other forms of raw film. Use self-sticking labels that can be transferred to film protective sleeves, boxes, etc. to keep track of what you've shot and what each packet or box contains. Not only will this assist you in your caption notes, it will also enable you to double-check that everything has come back from the processing lab, or that you actually shipped everything.

Packing Up

At the end of your shooting, unload every camera body, every film holder, double-check every pocket or nook and cranny among your cases where a roll of film might have slipped; double-check the roll numbers against your pocket log, and remember now to unload that last roll of film from that last camera body you've been saving for that last great shot.

When you are through shooting, repack all your equipment, wiping clean all the greasy wires dragged across a factory floor, and collect all Polaroid and other film wrappers and dispose of them. In other words, *clean up*. Turn in any safety gear you were issued, return all props that may have been borrowed or rented, make sure your factory people return the ladders, the extra extension cords, or whatever else that is not your property, say good-bye to your field people, and head for home. If you are flying, remember to take precautions against X rays at departure gates. This is not the time for fogging the last takes.

It has always been my habit that, when I arrive back in New York, the first stop I make after leaving the airport is to deliver the film to either the commercial labs I use or to the assigning magazine's own lab or night desk. Follow the same procedure wherever you live. Get your unprocessed film to the lab before you do anything else. Then go home and relax. You've got a lot of work ahead of you.

Insider: Eddie Adams, Photographer

Eddie Adams is a Pulitzer Prize-winning photographer and a powerhouse of a performer in the world of photojournalism. He has spent most of his career with several newspapers—The Associated Press, *TIME*, *Parade*—and freelancing for many magazines.

You have seen Adams's pictures from literally all over the map. He won his Pulitzer Prize with the now-famous photograph of a Vietnamese police officer shooting a presumed guerilla in cold blood on the streets of Saigon. His self-originated essay on the plight of the Asian boat people won him the prestigious Robert Capa Gold Medal Award from the Overseas Press Club, yet he had a tough time selling the story idea to his bosses at The Associated Press. It was Adams's deeply moving story that became page-one news all over the world and triggered the acceptance of the Vietnamese and Cambodian refugees in this country. His versatility is awesome, and he is as equally at home in a studio shooting a *Penthouse* story as he is doing a major cover story in Turkey for *TIME* magazine.

How did he get started, and is there something to be learned from his experience? While still a student in junior high school in New Kensington, Pennsylvania, near Pittsburgh, he began making 16mm movies of hometown weddings. His father borrowed $150 for him, and he bought an entire studio that was going out of business, the prize possession being an old Speed Graphic. His school asked him to take still pictures of school activities covering the basketball games for the school paper, yearbook photos, etc. He began doing wedding photography, producing an entire album for about $20 to $25, and also peddled some of them to the local newspaper, the *Daily Dispatch*. When he entered high school, he was given a part-time staff job after school, which turned full-time upon graduation.

"As far as getting started is concerned," said Adams about which he still feels deeply, "my advice to anyone wanting to get into this field is to start on a very small newspaper and *not* come to New York where there are ten thousand other people to compete with. On a small newspaper you learn to make the engravings, so you also learn the printing process, and you do all your own darkroom work. Sometimes you get a chance to lay out your own picture pages, so you have a lot of control over what you do. They'll give you nice displays. It was the best learning process I ever experienced, and in all my later years I never learned more."

Adams also believes that for a career in photojournalism there are more opportunities now than ever before in local newspapers. "Pick up any of the small or even medium-sized dailies. They have more pictures, more picture pages, more picture stories than even the old *LIFE* magazine had. The newer technology they use results in excellent reproduction, and there are actually many more publications than there ever were in American publishing history. I've seen some figures stating there are nearly fifteen thousand dailies, weeklies, small magazines, and other publications using good news photography today."

Adams joined the Marine Corps, saw service as a photographer in Korea, and returned to the *Daily Dispatch*. He then moved up his career ladder to the Battle Creek, Michigan *News*, the *Philadelphia Inquirer*, and part-time on the Pittsburgh *Post Gazette*; then to The Associated Press (AP), *TIME* magazine, back to the AP, back again to *TIME*, became a contributor to *Parade*, and is still turning out great photography.

In addition to being one of the most prolific and talented news photographers I know, Adams takes particular joy in directing an annual workshop for young newspaper photographers at his farm in upstate New York. This stimulating workshop, jointly sponsored by Eastman Kodak and Nikon, uses many knowledgeable professionals as guest speakers and attracts over a hundred students every year. Some of the attending students I have talked with have come away with strong feelings of motivation and excitement about pursuing careers in news photography. The workshop is free, but students wishing to attend will have to submit a portfolio. Further information can be obtained from Adams's office at 80 Warren Street, New York, NY 10007. (Tel: 212-406-1166 or Fax: 212-732-8977.) For the young news photographer it will be a stimulating experience.

Interview

John Durniak
Editor and Picture Editor

In the world of news photography the picture editor (and occasionally other editors) was often perceived by photographers as *THE ENEMY!* Not so with John Durniak. Durniak has been one of the strongest friends of working photographers and their constant champion. So much so that the National Press Photographer's Association (NPPA) awarded him their highest honor, The Sprague Award. The NPPA called him one of the most "important influences on American photojournalism," citing him for "the highest possible ethics" and celebrating him as a "dynamic catalyst," words that ring as true today as when the award was presented. Howard Chapnick, former president of Black Star Publishing Company (see page 265) feels that Durniak revolutionized photojournalism when he became Picture Editor at *TIME* magazine, and his long background of accomplishments, before and after, attest to his continuing influence on photojournalism.

His professional life has been one of transition from photography to writing about photography and editing photography. He received a Master's degree in Journalism at the University of Iowa and while there did a picture story on students and townspeople running for a newly opened position of town coroner. *LIFE* magazine saw that essay, and a later one about the town and how it got along with the university. They were impressed enough to offer him a job as a photographer's assistant when he left Iowa. A year later he went to UPI to do TV picture scripts, and then to *Popular Photography* as a writer/photographer. He went up the ladder, and seventeen years later was its editor in chief.

His move to *TIME* magazine as picture editor brought a new consciousness about photojournalism and a heightened use of pictures. After eight years he left to become Managing Editor of the newly reconstituted *LOOK* magazine. When that rejuvenation failed, he became Picture Editor at *The New York Times* for three and a half years. After that he was a Senior Editor for Photography at *Reader's Digest* and Consulting Editor at *Parade* for another three years. Currently he's a consultant, and columnist for *The New York Times*.

"If you ask me how does a young photographer out of photojournalism school, or a freelancer, go about trying to find a job, you couldn't ask that question at a worse time in photography. The recession has really hit the media and there are more former photographers than there are photographers. The healthiest portion of photography is the newspaper and that too has been hit hard by the state of the economy, but I am optimistic about its recovery. Newspapers are using more wire service material than their own, and have cut back on staff jobs.

"*The New York Times*, for instance, has fewer photographers now than before. There are about thirty-six including the bureaus, but actually most of the bureau photography is shot by freelancers.

"But I think the newspaper is still one of the best places for a young photographer to get started. In some places he may have to start as a freelancer and work his way to a staff job. But a staff spot on a paper is a good training ground; it will provide a salary, and a photographer is often allowed to freelance while on staff. This is when they can start building their careers.

"I can give you a case history. A young woman in this area, a single mother, wanted a profession. She arranged for child care whenever she had freelance assignments for the local paper to shoot parties, traffic accidents, and other routine events. Not only did she keep busy with these jobs but she began learning at the same time. She appeared promptly, delivered the photographs immediately, and they had less trouble with her than they had in a long time. She soon was invited to join the staff which had five other photographers. She started with black and white, now is working with color and is beginning to do full-page picture stories. The photographer who starts out chasing ambulances, fire engines, police cars, and takes away a lot of the routine headache work from the other staff, can suddenly be catapulted onto the staff. And I think that's a pretty good way to go.

"I cannot give you any precise figures on what a person may earn in this kind of job but they can earn a living at it, though they may be eating a lot of salad at the beginning. Newspaper Guild starting salaries on larger metro papers can be quite respectable, but the smaller the paper, the less money they make.

"One nice thing about new photographers starting on a small paper is that they often have a great deal more freedom in how they approach a subject. Very often editors will be specific as to what they want but are not averse to photographers presenting their own afterthoughts as well. There are no two newspapers alike in the way photographers are handled. On some papers there are strong editors with a definite vision of what they want and how their paper should operate in their community. There are other papers who have taken a reporter and have said 'now you are a picture editor.'

"Some senior editor without any background in photography may have put this reporter in the position of giving assignments, mainly to make sure the right pictures go to the right desk, but they have little control of the photographers and very little knowledge of photography itself. The photographer has to feel out the situation and develop a working relationship with a strong editor. He has to do it the editor's way first and then try to top it with a better idea.

"With the weak editor you've got to be both an employee and a teacher. You have to help him learn about photography so he can be aware and actually teach him the difference between a good photograph and a bad one, technically, esthetically, and journalistically. So you're in the position of helping your boss understand what you're all about and what the medium is about. Then you have to sit down and discuss possibilities, thus taking on the responsibility of his job plus yours. You have to talk out assignments with him, talk about other options or you're going to wind up taking a simple head shot which, while it may run in the newspaper, won't be any good for him or you. You have to take the initiative if it isn't there with the editor, and pray that you can make him feel that he's doing something, so you can do more.

"A frequent problem with new photographers is overshooting. I know of situations where anxious photographers have sent in as many as thirty rolls for a simple one-column head shot, thus annoying their editors considerably. The only control, therefore, is for editors not to hire that photographer any longer.

"However, there is the opposite end of that scale where newspapers are so conscious of cost that editors with little knowledge of photography will tell a photographer exactly how many frames to shoot on a given assignment. This is the most restrictive kind of photography which in the end hurts the paper itself.

"Because of these economic conditions, photography is being restricted across the board. Editors try to reduce the number of rolls of film processed and printed so darkroom staffs can be cut. Everybody is now looking to save nickels and dimes. Newspaper circulation has dropped; TV has made inroads and many people get their news from the tube and not the papers. So we are going through a period where the papers are trying to cut costs and photography is one area that they are looking at closely.

"With magazine photography, the market is tighter but one way for a photographer to break in is to figure out how to offer his work at a lower cost. As a newcomer, if he can offer a deal to someone who thinks he's a pretty good photographer and has a lot of promise, he can break in on the basis of the price level. On the other hand he can also be ostracized and earn the antagonism of fellow photographers who he undercuts on price.

"As an editor, every one of us wants to find a photographer with a fresh approach and new vision. Unfortunately 90 percent of the portfolios we see from young people coming in are almost identical. Most new photographers have yet to develop a style. Their photographs are all over the place and if there are thirty pictures they look like they were taken by thirty different photographers. So until a photographer develops a personal style and becomes known for a specific kind of picture or an area of operation, he must do a lot of shooting.

"I never bought a portfolio in my life but I bought an awful lot of ideas. What I want to hear from somebody coming in to talk about his work and how he might work for me, are his ideas. What is it that he knows or can shoot that nobody else knows or can shoot better than someone else? If he has special entree into a world which will produce a different way of looking at ordinary things, I want to know about it. So to repeat, ideas are very important to me, and the kind of journalist he is, is more important than technique. The shooting will take care of itself if he has good ideas."

Interview
Carl Mydans
Photographer

I have often referred to that extraordinary time from the early 1930s through the late 1960s as probably the most productive period in the history of photography and photojournalism. No one with any interest in the photojournalism of that period can overlook Carl Mydans. Mydans started as a writer, a background that has stood him in good stead all through his prolific career. As a young man his interest in photography grew when he acquired his first camera, a traditional Brownie, and like many others, learned about film development and printing in his home bathroom.

He graduated from Boston University's School of Journalism, freelanced for the *Boston Post* and the *Boston Globe* newspapers for about a year and then came to New York and got a job with *The American Banker*. That was when he made what was probably the most momentous purchase of his career: a 35mm Contax with an f/1.5 lens, a fine camera and close competitor of the Leica, then coming into vogue.

Mydans used it for assignments on the paper but didn't stop there, photographing whenever he could. During one of these off-duty times he made his first important "journalistic" photograph, a picture of a man haranguing a crowd in front of the stock exchange. The man was a notorious figure who had distinguished himself by getting arrested for throwing a "stink bomb" into a ventilator shaft of the New York Stock Exchange, and forcing its closing for the first time since World War I. Mydans processed the film in his bathroom-darkoom and tried to peddle it to the wire services. He found no interest until he took it around to a competitive weekly called *TIME*. There he met Associate Editor (and picture editor) Daniel Longwell, who was becoming increasingly fascinated with the potential of the 35mm camera. Longwell became excited when he learned Mydans had made this picture with a 35mm camera, sat him down and talked with him for over an hour. As a result he took Mydans on as a freelancer for *TIME* while he still held his other job.

It was the height of the Depression. Roosevelt was President, and in Washington a photographic group was being formed called the Historical Section of the Resettlement Administration, later to become the Farm Security Administration (see page 131). The FSA director, Roy Stryker, was also aware of the 35mm camera and sent his art director to New York to seek out photographers who could handle this new and fascinating tool. He reached Longwell, who told him about this bright young man named Mydans, and

The American Banker graciously released Mydans to go to Washington to work for the soon-to-become-legendary Roy Stryker.

"Stryker," says Mydans, "was one of two men who most influenced my life. He was a historian and economist at Columbia and he brought his profound sense of history to the FSA project." It was at FSA that Mydans was to meet the other man who also had an important influence on him, and that was the FSA's art director, Charles Tudor, who moved on ahead of Mydans to become the first art director of the new *LIFE* magazine. And just as graciously as *The American Banker* released Mydans to join FSA, so did Stryker send Mydans back to join the staff of *LIFE*.

Mydans, one of the first photographers at *LIFE*, was assigned to do almost every conceivable type of story that came across the editors' desks. And it was during his early years there that he met a young staff reporter, Shelley Smith, whom he married, and often worked with as a writer-photographer team.

They roamed Europe, the United States and Southeast Asia, eventually winding up in the Philippines. After Pearl Harbor and during the fall of Corregidor, they were captured by the Japanese and interned for twenty-one months in prison camps in the Philippines and China, before being repatriated in a prisoner-of-war exchange. Mydans was reaccredited to the U.S. Armed Forces, and while photographing the liberation of Europe, received a coded tip to return to the Far East to cover the impending landings of MacArthur's forces in the Philippines. Mydans remembers arriving on D Day plus one and covering MacArthur's landing in Luzon. Actually he landed on Luzon before MacArthur because he jumped off the landing barge and raced to the beach so he could make the now famous photograph of MacArthur's promised return to the Philippines. Eventually Mydans arrived in Japan, where he photographed the effects of the bombing of Hiroshima and Nagasaki, and also became *TIME-LIFE* bureau chief in Tokyo for two years. From Tokyo he covered the first year of the Korean War, eventually returning to the U.S. to continue his career with *LIFE* until the magazine folded in 1972. But that did not mean he put his cameras away. He and Shelley went to Singapore, where they continued to photograph and write as freelancers before returning home again.

Mydans is still in close association with *TIME* as a contributing photographer. His office there is piled high with memorabilia and old and new photographs. He is still working, still writing, and has produced many books including a magnificent retrospective book, *Carl Mydans; Photojournalist* (Abrams, 1985), that used the MacArthur landing photograph on the dust jacket. Other fine books were *More than Meets the Eye* (Harper, 1959); *Violent Peace* with Shelley Mydans; *China: A Visual Adventure* with Michael Demarest (Simon & Schuster, 1979); and several children's books. He is currently working on another autobiographical book. The entire photographic world has paid tribute to his talent and leadership. In 1991 he was honored in Perpignon (France) at the *Visa Pour L'Image*, where he was cited for his "Exceptional Contribution" . . . to the world of photography, and in 1992 he received a "Lifetime Achievement" award at the 8th Annual International Center of Photography (ICP) Infinity Awards.

Thus are legends not only created but maintained, and their work is their monument. Yet Mydans is not content to rest on the "legend" role. His door is open to anyone to draw on his experience and observations of the photographic scene.

When asked to assess contemporary photography and photographers, he said, "When I talk about photography, I talk about an 'eye.' I talk about what a person who holds a camera sees through that camera, and I think there is no question that there are just as many young photographers, both men and women, who see fine pictures and create now as when we were their age. What is confusing is that in those days greater skills were needed to use the camera than today."

Mydans underscored the feelings of many of his colleagues that the proliferation of automatic cameras, motor drives and automated exposures is causing photographers to let the camera and its gadgets do their thinking for them. He is concerned that with the increase of these cameras and the thousands of photographers using them, combined with a wider selection of high-speed reversal color, and a growing use of negative color, the black-and-white photograph may well be on its way to extinction.

He thinks that younger photographers going into the market today are missing a great deal of training by failing to learn how to develop and print black-and-white photographs properly. He feels strongly that even the contemporary photographer in a hard-news situation who cannot possibly be expected to process and print, will be better at his job if he knows *how* to make prints of the best possible quality the negatives can deliver.

Mydans concluded by saying, "I think that every young photographer who is serious about becoming a fine professional should start with black and white and by doing his or her own developing and printing. The photographer should work with his images over and over again until he reaches that point where he knows his camera's lighting exposures so well, that even when he has a meter he should not have to use it. Or, at least, be in the position of knowing when a meter has failed or has given a false reading, and still produce superb exposures made by his own expertise."

This is not a throwback to provincialism by a long shot, but a plea from a master for new photographers to learn their craft well, to understand it well, and be able to extract every bit of feeling and emotion that the silver-based image is capable of producing. And, only after the basics are understood, will it be truly possible for the photographer to work totally successfully in all media, be it black and white, color or electronic imaging.

Chapter Eight
After the Assignment

Now that the job has been shot and sent to the lab, what next? How are you going to handle the developed material that will start streaming in soon? What plans have you made for it? Have you established a system for numbering, filing and retrieving? What are you going to do with all the color that's going to come back in little boxes, big boxes, envelopes or paper bags?

There are numerous methods for the initial handling of your raw material as it first comes in. I highly recommend a system that has worked well for over forty years with very little modification and is permanently expandable to fit a growing file and increasing needs of retrieval and recirculation of pictures.

Logging in Every Piece of Work

Primary to the basic system is the establishment of a method of logging in every piece of work that comes in and consigning the paperwork for it to the proper file. Over the years I have established a simple, consecutive numbering system for every job I've done. The following is my procedure for the initial logging in of raw black-and-white or color film.

When a job is assigned, I give it a file or set number and enter it into a log book, which is in the form of a heavy, bound, accounting-type ledger with replaceable pages so the entries can be typed (or entered in a computer spread-sheet format) and kept on separate sheets for each year. I then open a negative storage file with that same set number. A typical line in the logbook looks something like this:

File#	Date	Location	Client	Subject	B/W or Color Format
1222	3/31/81	Chicago	O'Hare	Airport	30-K, 32-35 E6,12-120 E6,200 4/5E6 100TX

When the lab gets the raw black-and-white stock, they develop it and hand-letter edge numbers on every frame in waterproof India ink on the *glossy side* of the film stock (on all work from 120-size upwards) with the *file number and* a consecutive negative number—e.g., 1222-2, 1222-3, etc. Each 35mm strip is cut into strips of six frames for $8'' \times 10''$ contact sheets. The 120s are also cut to fit the $8'' \times 10''$ contact format. Each strip is marked with the set number followed by M for 35mm and the roll number; no letter is used for larger stock, making sure that the factory imprint frame numbers on the 35mm are clear. So a six-frame single strip of 35mm black and white should read 1222M-1 plus the factory frame numbers for print ordering.

When the negatives are all developed and edge-marked, I have *two* sets of contact prints made, and every sheet and every frame is correctly numbered and has the number of that photograph assigned permanently. The negatives are then filed at the lab according to their assigned file numbers. As each negative is numbered individually, it is easy for the lab crew to withdraw and return one to its proper jacket for refiling after printing. If a permanent crop on a negative is desired, simply make a contact print if it is a large-format negative or make a small ($3'' \times 5''$) enlargement from a 35mm or 120; mark the crops desired in ink on the contact and paste the contact to the jacket permanently, so whoever prints the negative later will have instructions on cropping. Note that many fax machines have photo-quality duplication capabilities, some having a built-in screen to reduce contrast which makes the fax/photocopy quite legible, and thus cheap contacts for cropping indications are quickly available. Assuming we are dealing with frame #34 in black and white, your edge mark should read 1222M-1-34.

Color is treated in a similar manner. Earlier I spoke of using self-adhesive identifying labels. The numbers on these labels should correspond to your set numbers, that is, the first roll of 35mm color should in this case carry a number of 1222C-1. All Kodachrome is edge-numbered at the manufacturing plant with the month, year and frame number. Most commercial labs have numbering machines for their own mounts, and they also will probably edge-number the slides in the same way. If they do not date them, at least they will number them. If for some reason the house you use does not provide this service (or if you process your own color), you should get a small numbering machine or even a simple movable rubber stamp so that you can number your 35mm transparencies with the same system. All other color will not be numbered for the moment and if you have received the rolls uncut from the lab, leave them that way so you can retain the edge stickers that should have been transferred to the raw film prior to development. Use this system with negative color too.

Photographers just beginning to establish a photographic filing and retrieval system, and looking to stock photography as their primary activity, would do well to think seriously about installing bar-coding procedures for quick record keeping and image location. (See the Stock Photo section, pages 239-242.)

At this point you should have all your black-and-white film developed, numbered and contacted and all the color developed and numbered. If this is the system you are using, the same procedures should be followed in numbering either your 35mm work or your larger film sizes. Your subsequent contact sheets should include these numbers as well. The reasons for this basic system thus become clear. In the future when someone wants to know about print #1222M-34, you can, in just a few moments and possibly without looking at the photograph, tell when and where it was shot and what the general subject matter is without having to go through a huge numbered index to chase down the information needed about a specific print.

Using an Outside Lab

In my organization (Photography for Industry) I never have been a great believer in internal laboratory operations. In New York, where I am based, there have always been a number of first-class custom labs specializing in both black and white and color and offering related photo support services such as copying, retouching, quantity printing, etc., The kind of work I do varies widely. Sometimes there will be no lab traffic at all for days and then can come an order for 200 prints, 40 rolls or 250 sheets to be developed. To try to anticipate this kind of activity would be impossible, so I started sending my work out.

I am not suggesting that the new photographer should farm out his processing. On the contrary, most will have no choice but to handle their own black-and-white lab work either because of cost or location problems. Regardless of whether you do or do not operate your own lab, systems have to be developed to best suit your needs as well as those of maintaining an ongoing professional method of operation. Also be aware that the theory of saving money by doing your own processing is an illusion — unless you do not consider your time as money.

Preliminary Handling

Delivery of your take will vary according to the type of assignment it is. If you are doing an editorial piece for a magazine, the chances are that contact prints and negatives will be all that the editors need to proceed with the story, as most editorial publications do their own picture editing, and with the increasing use of color even contacts are becoming superfluous. If you are delivering a color story, editing out the obvious misfires, double exposures, or way-off exposures is about all you need to do for the moment. Some editors at big magazines still insist that their own staffers do the editing. Yet the two largest of the general news magazines were at direct opposites in approach. *LIFE* always had a staff to edit the raw film, and very often a story would be closed and on its way to the printing plant before the photographer even arrived back from the assignment. *LIFE*'s film editors were then led by the legendary Peggy Sergeant, who would stand in the darkroom as the film strips came out of the last wash or hung in the drying racks. She carried a railroad conductor's ticket punch in her hand and she would edge-punch each frame she wanted printed with a code for sizes. By the time the contact prints were made, the story was old hat to her and she already had ordered the enlargements. She had a fabulous eye and rarely missed. *Look*, on the other hand, being a biweekly, had more time for their closings and so kept the photographers on tap through the editing and layout stages. These were personal choices of the editors, and each had their own opinions and methods. Remember, though, that these practices were geared to getting picture news magazines out on time, with little else considered. Many of these theories overlapped and worked their way into other areas of documentary photography. When I worked for Roy Stryker on the Esso project, I would be in the field for months at a time and never saw my work until long after it was processed. If something went wrong technically, the lab crew would phone me immediately and report what they believed to be the problem, such as a shutter sticking or a light leak in the bellows or lens mount. In fact, it was pretty good discipline not to see your work until long after you were back home. You had the chance to do some editing then because your pictures were headed for a file rather than a fast-closing publication.

There have been perennial charges that photographers are their own worst editors, that they cannot judge their own work objectively and that they are too apt to equate the difficulty in obtaining a certain photograph with its ultimate importance to the story. I have never had this problem and believe that this impression was propagated by some of the photographic giants who frequently insisted on total control of their material from cropping, to printing, to layout. But you, as an emerging photographer with a large batch of photographs, will have to do a preliminary edit of the material and get the set in shape so you can present it realistically and cogently for others to make the final selection.

Where do you begin? You begin by going back to your original agreement with the client. What did he expect from you? In what form? Did you discuss prints? How many? What size? Who is going to pay for them? Over the years on noneditorial assignments I have evolved my own system, which I pass on to you for acceptance or adaptation.

After getting rid of the blanks, the over- and underexposed pictures, the ones with the light flares where you forgot to move a lamp, those you cannot save by cropping, those streaked in development (it happens), assemble the photographs into the sections where they belong. In spite of your instructions to your lab, you may well find that negatives from larger-format cameras have become separated and printed on different contact sheets without consecutive numbers. No matter—simply bring them together for comparison. I assume you've bracketed your exposures, so you must get them together, side by side, for comparison. I'm not talking about news pictures. When something newsworthy is happening, you probably are not going to get much chance to bracket. Eddie Adams certainly couldn't expect a second chance to photograph a Saigon police chief shooting a prisoner a second time. But on a commercial operation where you may even be shooting color and black and white with different cameras or with different film, magazines or backs, your final take will result in many exposures of the same situation, and so you must get them together, side by side, for comparison.

Remember that if you are not shooting to a specific layout, and you probably are not in editorial work, try to give the client alternative choices of horizontal or vertical pictures and some that can be cropped in any direction. Then boil the "selects" down to an "A" and "B" set, i.e., two or possibly three pictures per situation, depending on whether there are people in the photographs and whether expressions and movements or other factors might make one picture better than its partner.

Treat your color exactly the same way. Lay out your slides on a light table side by side. Examine them with a magnifying glass. Separate them into first and second takes (the "A" and "B" sets) and, if you are lucky, even a third pile ("C") of acceptable transparencies. The same holds true for your roll or sheet color. Lay it out on the light table or viewing box and cut the roll film apart or sort the lengths of film uncut. Put temporary numbers on the glassine protectors in red grease pencil, marking them "A," "B" or "C" to indicate choices/quality. Be sure every transparency has a glassine protector of some sort. The plastic sheets that will hold twenty 35mm cardboard mounts will be fine for the moment, but remember to choose materials that will not cause deterioration for long-term storage.

I raised the question earlier about the projection of 35mm color, but do feel that a few quick projections will not hurt the transparencies, so I often speed things up by running slides through a carousel projector with a "stack loader" for a quick appraisal of the contents of each box and to weed out the blanks and misfires. After the preliminary weeding out is accomplished, follow the recommended procedure and use light tables or viewers. However, be sure to use color-corrected light sources if you are trying to determine color quality.

Preparing Color for Delivery

Now you are ready to start numbering the larger-format color. Each transparency should be in a protective sleeve, and here is where a choice of systems has to be made. In most commercial jobs—and this involves both you and your client—it is customary to turn over to the client the first-quality original transparency so he can reproduce from it and in general keep control of it, even though the actual rights he has acquired have been previously spelled out by contract or other form of agreement. I separate top-quality original transparencies from the rest of the take and usually have either dupes, photocopies or photostats made just for reference so I know what has been turned over to the client and have a record for copyright filing. If your client has a numbering or filing system of his own, you can coordinate yours with his plan. Other clients want me to keep everything because they have neither the room nor the staff to deal with valuable transparencies. In that case I provide an alternate service, but I make a nonreproducible color contact print or machine enlargement of the original so the client can have that for his immediate reference and temporary layout use. Whatever the disposition of the work, that is, giving the originals to the client or keeping them in my files, I mount the transparency and all the other useful "dupes" in the same set, in individual die-cut mounts. I use an $8'' \times 10''$ heavy black paper folder with a die cutout for various standard transparency sizes. These can be purchased in art or photo supply houses, or made to order by paper suppliers.

I mount the transparency in a glassine envelope with a frosted back if available, then tape it inside the folder with double-sided cellophane tape, sealing the ends of the sleeves so they become dust-proof and the cover of the mount will stick tightly, preventing the transparency from being removed without authorization for copying or other uses. On the face I apply a label with whatever information is appropriate and then am ready to deliver a neatly mounted color transparency that can be easily filed and handled and, in general, survive a tremendous amount of handling without damage to the original. Some of the mounts I have are thirty-five years old, and more transparencies have faded than mounts deteriorated. These mounts last long and are ever-protective. I recommend this method highly, and when used with a colorful label, editors and picture users over the years recognize the material as being valuable and carefully packaged, and will give the work better treatment than a bunch of loose transparencies thrown into an envelope and shipped haphazardly.

At the risk of being redundant I cannot emphasis strongly enough that in order for your material to be treated with respect, you too must feel that way about your work. For handling 35mm color, I have tried many systems, none of which I am entirely happy with, but I have settled on one method after much trial and error. I file each set of mounted transparencies in small, square, plastic (chemically inert) boxes with file numbers and brief content notes on cover labels. These are stored in shallow steel cabinets such as those used to file blueprints or architect's plans. In this way I can easily locate the box I want and lay out the transparencies I am interested in retrieving and viewing on a light table. Also the work is easily replaced in the boxes and stored. For a while I used carousel trays for storage and retrieval but these became cumbersome when I had to extract individual slides to send on approval to an editor. I also had to screen them constantly, a practice now considered unsafe. The individual box system also lends itself well to the now-increasing use of bar-coding.

Each transparency should have on it the following information:

1. A reference number, regardless of what system you use.
2. Your name, address, telephone number and agency affiliation, if any.
3. A proper notice of copyright (optional but see Copyright, page 273).

The inclusion of a notice of copyright, i.e., copyright symbol © plus year plus name, is no longer mandatory under the terms of the Berne Copyright Convention which the United States joined (as of March 1, 1989), but its use is still recommended. So the habitual effort instilled in your own or your contract lab personnel at every level for proper legal protection should be continued. Each box of slides should have the set numbers, or if you are using a continuous numbering system in addition to the set and roll numbers as some photographers do, then your opening and closing numbers of each set.

When it comes to numbering the larger-format color, I use a simple consecutive numbering system, which is ultimately cross-indexed and cross-filed according to subject. I do use preprinted caption labels, but when I have them typed up I automatically include a self-carboned 3″ × 5″ index card so that all of this information is recorded at one typing. Or if you are using a PC computer now for data processing, the capabilities of the computer will save an enormous amount of time in storage and retrieval of information. Continuous-form cards up to 4″ × 6″ or "Rolodex" type cards up to 3″ × 5″ are available and can be programmed alphabetically or numerically by most word processing programs. They, and the pictures, are filed by subject in my classification system. At the same time as the captions are being made up, I start an alphabetical cross-index file by subject so that when a request is received for a certain type of activity or machine or location, the index card will show what jobs covered that subject. The important thing is to start these systems as your work comes in, not five or ten years later when you have two trunks full of unidentified transparencies without the foggiest clue as to what they are, when they were shot, and what restrictions if any apply to them. It is simple enough to do this as you prepare your material for your client as well as for yourself. So do it now.

By this time you have made your preliminary edit, had your negatives or transparencies numbered and possibly captioned, and the contact sheets made. Now what? Again see what your agreement calls for. Prints? Contacts? Original transparencies? My suggestion is that you have a few first-quality 11″ × 14″ double-weight prints made of the best of random subjects and a few 8″ × 10″ single-weight prints made of others in the set. But make no more than three or four of each size. If you have confidence in your material, you might also think about having a color print or two made, but I generally avoid this step as it is costly and usually the one you order printed is not going to be the one the client will prefer! When you have those sample prints and all the other edited material together, then it is time to get together with your client and either have a showing in his office (if it is no great distance away) or, if necessary, ship them to him by bonded carrier and ask him to call you on receipt so you can discuss them. Eventually you will come to some agreement as to what is ultimately to be printed and then you can order final prints. With some of my larger corporate clients I have also made up contact print books with occasional extra sets for scattered installations through the company empire. These assemblages are made up on preprinted portfolio sheets, bound, and sent to each plant branch headquarters where the photographs were shot. Or, as in the case of a major airline assignment, I had several copies of negative color contact print books made up for worldwide distribution so that branch offices could order duplicate color for local printing at later dates.

The important thing now is to deliver your primary effort to your client. Regardless of its ultimate form, there are a few rules that must be observed: (1) quality of selection, (2) uniformity of size or consistency in method of presentation, and (3) use of complete captions and notes, including the date the photographs were made and possibly a written report on your experience in photographing them, with any observations you have that may be helpful in using the pictures in whatever media is anticipated.

Protecting Your Negatives, Prints and Transparencies

What about the physical objects themselves? A photograph, whether in the form of a print, negative or transparency, is a unique object. When photographs are moved from place to place, change hands and ownership, are worked on, stored or otherwise handled, they can be bent, cracked, lost, have coffee spilled on them, be eaten by insects, covered with mildew, and threatened by a host of other dangers to their physical well-being. How does the photographer protect his property against these and other abuses and misuses?

To paraphrase Yogi Berra again, it's a question of *being over when it's over*, but it starts at the beginning. When a piece of film or a sheet of paper is first unwrapped, extreme care must be exercised in its handling. A film emulsion is fragile and the piece of cellulose or paper it is mounted on is not much tougher. A black-and-white or color negative, after it has been developed and edge-numbered, should be stored in a chemically inert envelope. A protective jacket or envelope on which technical information might be noted, or a contact print or photocopy affixed that indicates a permanent crop as to how that picture is always to be printed, is added. The negatives are then filed according to whatever system is used. That should be the limit of movement for that negative except for travel to and from the enlarger or contact printer. I am trying to emphasize here that you should have a policy of *never* letting a negative move beyond your control. It shouldn't be loaned out for printing by any other lab except your own in-house or contract lab. There may be a few instances when a news magazine may call for the loan of a negative for a fast, last-minute closing and they need to print it themselves. Decline *unless* a first-class print capable of being copied is available and they understand that, if the negative is lost or damaged in any way, they will have to assume full responsibility for the cost of making a perfect duplicate negative. Color negative material should be treated the same way.

Original color transparencies are a different problem. Most quality printers do not like to work from color "dupes" because most of them are not equal in quality to the original. The copying process by itself involves creating a new generation of images which invariably increases contrast. There are exceptions. Some labs and their technicians can make superb dupes that are *better* than the originals. In recent years duplicating stocks have improved to a point where the differences are minute. Duplication is important for the news agencies when there has to be a large and quick distribution of photographs requiring simultaneous worldwide distribution such as a color photograph of a presidential inauguration that ultimately made the cover of fourteen news magazines worldwide. Thus it is impossible to use originals, and the dupes used by such news agencies are of sufficient quality for good results. There are other ways of obtaining first-class dupes. Electronic-imaging duplication (see chapter twelve) has eliminated generational increases in contrast occasioned by customary film chemistry.

Captions and Notes

Over the years I have learned that a photograph without proper caption information is a useless photograph. I have already discussed technical methods of keeping track of what is on a roll of film or a box of sheet film — now is the time to make use of those notes. Many journalists who work with 35mm roll-film cameras use their camera frame counters carefully, and if they are lucky enough to be working directly with a reporter, simply calling out the opening and closing frame numbers will be enough for the reporter to keep track of what is being shot. But most young photographers do not have that luxury. They have to do this by themselves, which is why the small pocket notebook and/or the self-adhesive label on a camera back is often used to make a few important notes, and that label can be removed and attached to the roll of film quickly, particularly if a small pull-off tab is left for quick transfer.

When it comes to applying these notes to the photographs, there are various methods available. I have successfully used two systems, and they can be combined if necessary. When a job is finished, edited and ready for presentation, I make a basic line-by-line caption list showing every roll number and every frame number that is usable, either in black-and-white or in color. On this list I give as much information about the photograph that is possible to get on a single line.

Oh, there are times when this can get to be a nuisance. I remember the reaction of a photographer-friend on a major magazine who was interrupted while shooting a big fine-arts story and reassigned to photograph a Chinese fortune cookie factory for a minor play in the "back of the book." He was furious and in revenge he typed up his captions, as per custom, took them back to the cookie factory, and had each caption sliced and inserted into a Chinese fortune cookie. He stormed into his editor's office and after a few choice expletives for being taken off an important story, threw the box of cookies on the editor's desk and said, "Here are your *?#@ captions, I hope you choke reading them," and walked out. No, he wasn't fired.

My lab (and most others) always writes the actual negative number of each photograph in soft pencil on the back of each print. This will usually withstand the washing and drying process and will be readable when the print comes back. There are also waterproof markers with ink that will adhere to resin-coated papers (ask your photo dealer). For prints going immediately into a file for temporary storage this is sufficient. But for prints or other photographs going out to a client, sent on approval to an editor, or

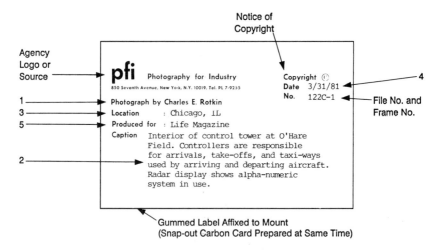

Notice of Copyright

Agency Logo or Source

pfi Photography for Industry
850 Seventh Avenue, New York, N.Y. 10019, Tel. PL 7-9255

Copyright Ⓒ — 4
Date 3/31/81
No. 122C-1

1 — Photograph by Charles E. Rotkin — File No. and Frame No.
3 — Location : Chicago, IL
5 — Produced for : Life Magazine
Caption Interior of control tower at O'Hare Field. Controllers are responsible for arrivals, take-offs, and taxi-ways used by arriving and departing aircraft. Radar display shows alpha-numeric system in use.
2 —

Gummed Label Affixed to Mount
(Snap-out Carbon Card Prepared at Same Time)

offered for possible sale or given to another person for any use, there are some "musts." Again, I repeat that you must include the five basic W's of journalism in your captions: (1) who, (2) what, (3) where, (4) when, (5) why. To these basic five I add a few extras. As an example, let us take one single photograph from my files and see what it contains and how it would be captioned if I released it for general circulation for book or magazine use. I am choosing one that was part of a set of photographs made on assignment for *LIFE* magazine in Chicago at O'Hare Airport as part of a larger general aviation story. This particular photograph did not run in the magazine, but because I retained the secondary rights, I released it to a textbook publisher who was interested in showing the inside of an airport control tower.

Who Owns the Work You Do?

The answer to this question is that, with very specific exceptions, you do. It's that simple. The Copyright Act of 1976, that went into effect on January 1, 1978, clarified a long list of vague issues regarding ownership of assigned (or, for that matter, unassigned) photography.

Up to then there was a general rule that, unless otherwise specified, whoever commissioned and paid for the work owned it. No more. The only way the assigning party can own the work you do is if (1) you are an actual employee in the full meaning of the term—that is, receiving payroll deductions, employee benefits, direct supervision by a superior; or (2) if you sign a "work-for-hire" agreement. This is a specific term used by the Copyright Office of the Library of Congress, whereby you agree that you are being employed to make certain photographs or create other graphic art and that for that period or purpose you are employed by whoever is paying you and you are indeed producing "work made for hire." It has to be in writing. It can't be an oral agreement, and it can't be implied. Many of the large magazines and publishing houses who employ photographers regularly, even though they may be freelancers or contract people, have them sign work-for-hire agreements to cover the work they are doing, and thus the employer does indeed own the work. Usually these companies recognize the value to the photographer of certain secondary rights and may specify in their agreements with the photographers that certain rights will be returned to them for other noncompetitive uses or put expiration limits on the agree-

them for other noncompetitive uses or put expiration limits on the agreements, in which case ownership reverts back to the photographer. Many of the professional societies such as the ASMP object to this and are protesting. The matter is under review by a number of publication groups. Efforts are also under way to obtain congressional revision of this clause, thus giving the artist total control of his work.

When it comes to stock photographs, or any photographs made with an oral assignment, the ownership is yours. Even a purchase order from an ad agency that says they own everything but your right arm is not valid unless you sign it or a work-for-hire agreement, or endorse the check that usurps all rights. This does not absolve you of your responsibilities for protection of your work, however. Your photographs should still carry a notice of copyright for fullest protection, although there is nothing to prevent you from granting the use of that copyright to a client for the use intended in an assignment.

It was to specifically protect the artist, and eliminate the vagueness of most purchase orders and assignment agreements made between freelancers and corporate clients, that the terminology of "one-time" rights or "all other rights reserved" was adopted. For the first time in the history of copyright law, the law seems to favor the artist over the buyer. I said *seems* to favor, because there are still some loopholes in the law that may favor the corporation and puts an undue burden on the photographer to protect himself. But I will discuss all of this in more depth when we move on to copyright matters in general. (See chapter ten.)

Record Keeping

Record keeping has always been considered a bore, and some artists and photographers consider themselves above these chores and, whenever possible, relegate them to others. But whoever does this work, it must be done accurately and uniformly so that necessary information can be found as quickly as possible.

I am not only discussing the routine keeping of records for rent, utilities, depreciation, lab and field photo supplies, personnel and the like. I am also speaking of keeping records of the jobs you do, which are the basis for the bills, captions and notes you supply your clients. Where do you keep your release forms? Your caption notes? Even your roll-film stickers after they have been removed from the processed film? Now is the time to apply your office organization system and make it work.

Earlier in this chapter I demonstrated my job logging system. Now let us continue with the example of the mythical job #1222. A file has been opened for it and there is a negative file in the lab. What goes in the office file? Everything that has to do with that job. Every note made either in the field or in the office should carry that number; every caption note, airline stub, car-rental receipt, overhead charge slip, receipts for special rentals or costs—any paper produced in relation to that job should have that number on it. Each bill or time allocation or other note should be stored in *that* file and nowhere else. Don't forget your copies of model and other releases. Include names and addresses of people who helped on the job, model agencies in that area—any information you might want to have for the future. The possibilities are truly endless, but when you need facts about this particular project you will know where to find them.

Expense Accounts

Earlier I spoke of keeping field records and entertainment records. This area, if there is an audit either by the client or by the IRS, will be the zone of most intense concentration and the cause of most headaches. You can no longer be glib, as were the correspondents in WorldWar II who, it seemed, made careers of outsmarting their magazines when it came to accountability for funds. The legendary Bob Landry, one of *LIFE* magazine's sharpest correspondents who ever flimflammed an editor, after being queried by teletype about how he managed to spend $500 on taxicabs over a certain period when he was in the Pacific Theater on an aircraft carrier, blithely wired back a deadpan explanation: "Big carrier." But that was then. These days, serious documentation is required.

As the business-management people of the major publication groups began to exercise more and more control over the costs of magazine production — and that included producing photography and writing — the rules for. record keeping got tighter and tighter, and photographers and correspondents often found it impossible to account for even the most legitimate of expenses, frequently winding up "eating" a lot of these costs themselves.This naturally led to more and more imaginative thinking, and when the IRS finally began to breathe down the neck of some of the major publication groups, open warfare was declared on the expense account. One magazine group was even forced to appoint someone in their front office to examine the expense records of not just the low-men-on-the-totem-pole who could, in theory anyway, be controlled by their editors, but also the top editors, bureau chiefs, and other executives who until then had never been questioned about what they spent on behalf of the corporation.

I got caught up in such a situation inadvertently while in Europe. Having performed an unexpected and herculean task for my bureau chief, I was, in gratitude, taken to the most expensive restaurant in Paris for a farewell lunch before returning home. The luncheon somehow grew to include others from the bureau, and my host blithely signed what had to be an astronomical check before pouring me on the boat train. Aside from a monumental hangover the next day, I thought nothing more about it until he called me shortly after he came to New York on a vacation.

"Do you know who Jane _____ is?" he asked.

I acknowledged I knew of her and her function as executive watchdog.

"Well," my friend went on, "she just called about your farewell lunch and reminded me that under current IRS rules we had to make notes about what we discussed, if the amount exceeded a certain sum [and did it ever!], so if the IRS questions us we can substantiate that business was indeed discussed. I told her I most certainly remembered the conversation, and said, 'We were talking about *you*, honey, and saying as we ordered another bottle of wine, wait till Jane gets this one!' "

So, when you take someone to lunch for business entertainment, be sure to watch your IRS Ps and Qs and substantiate your paperwork. It may cost you dearly later if you don't.

The Photographer and the IRS

What about intangibles that may be counted as money? There are no fringe benefits except those the photographer provides for himself in terms of personal pension and retirement plans (see page 355). But there are many things that the photographer does or accumulates in the course of his work that could count as income. Photographers who travel on assignment often have the opportunity to go to exotic places and locales they could never afford to visit on their own, and sometimes these assignments can be combined as business and vacation trips. On some trips family members come along, and share the adventure of the trip, or the hazards.

Combining business and pleasure trips may leave you open to IRS scrutiny, so you have to be careful about how you keep your records and allocate your costs. If your spouse or companion does indeed perform a valuable service in helping you get your pictures, there is a legitimate reason for deducting those expenses proportionately, especially if you operate as a team. I went through a pre-audit inquiry once from the IRS and was asked to explain certain deductions. The IRS man said, "According to your records, you showed a trip to Europe last year and have taken expense deductions that seem considerable. Didn't you spend any time on vacation or pleasure that some of this money can be charged to?" My reply was, "I covered eleven assignments in nine countries in twenty-eight days, drove almost 1,800 miles, flew another 3,000 miles around the continent, and rushed back to the States for a vacation with my family on an island off the coast of Massachusetts. And I have the papers to prove it, including the hotel bills for my vacation which show the date I arrived." That ended that line of inquiry and any further questions by the IRS.

I was once asked, "Is experience tax-deductible?" If you shoot on your own with the expectation of selling your work, then certainly costs incurred are tax-deductible expenses in preparing your profit and loss statement.

Earlier I mentioned that in order for a photographer to move any appreciable amounts of stock photography he must have an ongoing supply of fresh material. One way to acquire it is to shoot it either on special trips or for special projects such as books or audiovisual material. Two things become instantly apparent. One, these expenses are tax-deductible, and, two, you build your file up considerably. A single cross-country trip (by car) for shooting purposes might take a month or six weeks, cost about $4,000 to $6,000 out of pocket, and result in a couple of thousand images. If you sold just seventy-five reproduction rights in one year at an average sale of $150, you would show a gross profit of $5,000 on that set alone, and they would still be in your files for continuous use. So experience is indeed tax-deductible in this sense and can be profitable, too.

One way to augment the profits from your trip is to line up as much assignment work as you can in advance. Some photographers who travel widely to stock their files put together a map/assignment query (see appendix, page 386) showing their itinerary and send it out to every corporation they can find along the way or to editors they think might be interested in having assignments done at the locations listed. The letter suggests that they take advantage of this photograher's presence in some location of interest to them. If the photographer also gives them the opportunity to pro-rate the expenses of such a trip, it is amazing how many seem willing to spend $5,000 on assignments just to save $500 on travel expenses.

When making trips to add stock photos to your files, you must put a good deal of thought into the selection of subject matter. This may take some correspondence or consultation with editors with whom you already have established communication. If your experience has grown to the point where you are being called for special material, you might consider keeping a log on the calls you get for pictures you couldn't supply at that time and try to fill in your files with these sorts of pictures in anticipation of similar requests.

Billing

What exactly is involved in billing? What do you need in the way of supporting papers? How do you justify the sometimes strange expenses that are frequently lumped under the category of "expense accounts"? Some can be pretty staggering, some very funny, some unreal or unrealistic, some downright imcomprehensible. The stories of strange items charged back, particularly in the editorial world, are legion, and many have spilled over to the corporate side where often there is less understanding of the creativity of the artist. And as artists are creative, it follows that some of their expense accounts can be rather creative as well. Now, when you're ready to prepare your invoices, comes the moment of "truth." Your budgets and accounts had better be accurate. There are too many methods of cross-checking expense reports to leave much leeway anymore for exaggeration and account padding. Receipts are the key to everything these days, and even the Eskimo sled-dog story, variously attributed to writer Gene Fowler and/or an unidentified *LIFE* photographer, would probably have come under much closer scrutiny today. It seems that the journalist in question was faced with the need to account for several thousand dollars of advanced expense money for a trip to the far North. Even after deducting the vouchers for trains, planes, hotels, car rentals, etc., he was still shy some $500 and was hard pressed to come up with an answer to what really happened to the money. So reportedly the following items went into his expense account:

Rent of dog sled, driver and dogs	$300.
Food for sled dogs (100 lb. chopped walrus meat @ $1)	100.
Replacement of sled dog killed in accident	50.
Flowers for the bereaved bitch	50.
Total	$500.

He got away with it then, but today the accounting department would have told him that the sled probably had a charge-card machine fastened to it, and the driver a stack of preprinted dog sled rental forms, without which they wouldn't approve the expense account.

So be sure you get and retain, whenever possible, some sort of validation for expenses you wish to recover—for plane tickets and other travel expenses, hotel bills, car-rental receipts, ticket stubs, receipts for props, model hire, etc. Whatever is necessary for the job and the travel involved, you had better have some paper to justify it—or at least keep those unreceipted charges under $25, because that is what the IRS will allow in unreceipted expenses for entertainment or meals or similar costs. *A special note* regarding car rentals in this credit-card economy. Several major credit card companies have been advertising that the use of their credit cards for rental cars also covers the renter against deductibles for collision damage. This is not so in several states, including New York State. Both the credit card companies and the car rental agencies never inform the renter of this, feeling they are legally protected by tiny fine-print clauses appearing almost unreadabaly on the back of the car rental contracts given to you *after* they hand you the keys to the rental car. If you later get into an accident and think you are covered, you frequently find you are not and then become the target of collection agencies trying to recover outrageous deductibles. Photographers renting cars are warned to watch for these and other practices which, however legal, are ethically dubious, and dealing with such companies should be assiduously avoided. For example, I recently rented a car whose mirror was slightly damaged in a parking lot. Later I received an enormous bill not only for the highly inflated cost of repair of the mirror, but for the *loss of rental fees to the car renting company* while the mirror was being repaired . . . something like a week (for a mirror?). It might also be noted that this matter was referred to the Attorney General of New York State.

When it comes to billing, as you may be audited in the future and may need receipts, the accepted practice (unless otherwise specified by your particular client) is to photocopy the original receipts for your files and attach the *copies* to your bills. Check your client's own procedure on this, as it can vary from company to company. Items within the lump sums on the invoices should be listed carefully, with supporting papers attached so that the client is not faced with the chore of going through a long list of small details and can approve the bill in general. The supporting papers should give the details of the charges allowing the people in the accounting department to verify the cost of individual items. The chances are that your bill will be processed a lot faster that way because most executives will be interested only in the general aspects of the invoice, preferring to allow the finance people to check the accuracy of your columns and charges. The fees and enumerating of field expenses can be a cut-and-dried itemization, with the exception of entertainment or other unusual charges, and should pose no real problem so long as you stay within the restrictions of your agreements.

There is, however, one area that should be discussed here: billing for materials, processing, printing and other lab services. Until recently, before the wild surge in film prices, there never seemed to be any argument about the cost of materials. I am often called upon to leave town on short notice with large amounts of film and other pre-purchased supplies. And if this happens on a weekend or holiday, getting your hands on the material you need in a hurry may be a problem. So what I have always done is purchase large quantities of film and other materials in advance and keep them in a deep freeze.

Of course, when I buy in large quantities, I purchase at so-called "wholesale" prices that are considerably less than the listed retail value of a roll or box of film or other item, and when I bill for these items, I always charge the regular retail list prices. Why? For several reasons, the primary one being that I am always getting stuck with expired film and unreturnable items (although some dealers will take back unused film) and, more important today, I have to tie up large amounts of money in film and supply inventory. Therefore, I use the differential between wholesale and list price as a means of covering these losses and have never had much of a problem in justifying such charges. This is suddenly changing, however, and some purchasing agents are trying to insist that when I bill for film and materials I must send along receipts. I have refused to do so, openly citing the reason there is a difference in what I am charging and what I paid for the material. Neither would I send an invoice covering my purchase of 500 rolls when I may have used only 50 on a job. I hit a major standoff with one company on this issue that was finally resolved when I refused to supply any material at all, telling the purchasing agent to go out and buy his own film and supply me with it. The problem has persisted, however, so I always make it a point to explain the charges to my clients in advance so there will be no delay in payment.

There are discount houses that will take a roll of color film and process it far more cheaply than the quality custom lab, but I don't use them (nor should you) because there is no control over the way the material is handled and no vouching for their professional capability. Furthermore, since I am forced to establish credit lines and maintain accounts with various processing plants and labs, I have to put a percentage markup on the outside lab work, because I still have to assume all the inherent business problems.

This practice should apply as well to the photographer who does his own lab work, whether it is black-and-white or color. All of this takes time and costs money, and so must be built into the cost of a job. How do you assess what to charge a client for developing a roll of film or making a set of contacts or enlargements? The answer is to charge what the professional houses *in your region* are charging (because of possible labor differentials), and you should charge about the same, *plus* a markup for handling, because in this case you have the costs of maintaining a lab. How much of a markup do you put on these services? That's up to you. There are some nonphotographic guidelines I could offer, but these are only suggestions. Taking the wholesale versus retail film variable, for example, it would appear that a 25 percent markup is reasonable. However, you the photographer/businessman have to make that markup decision. But do not ignore it, unless money means nothing to you. Otherwise you cannot stay alive professionally.

Interview
Jade Albert
Studio Photographer

In addition to the rising firmament of journalistic photographers such as the Turnley brothers, Greg Heisler and Marilyn Bridges, the commercial world has seen comparable growth by devoted and socially aware advertising photographers, such as Jade Albert. Young, attractive, and with a remarkable *joie-de-vivre*, a trip to Albert's studio is like a breath of fresh air wafting down the dingy streets of New York's photo district. Her ebullient spirit is evident as she shows you around, her pride in accomplishments evident, and you are instantly sure that her warm welcoming attitude has been extended many times to the hundreds of children that have passed through her studio.

"I don't have a personal life though I manage to play hard and work hard so there isn't much room for anything else at present. I never thought or knew I would ever be a photographer. I am a New Yorker, I studied at Parsons School of Design, and I wanted to be an art editor at a magazine. I first went to *Glamour* magazine as an assistant art director. As an only child going to a small school, the idea of a large advertising agency was intimidating. But at a magazine I was working with only two or three people in a less pressured atmosphere. I grew up in their art department and did not know anything about the ad agency business. I was not interested in being a photographer then but was interested in graphics, design and fashion, which were all very visual.

"At *Glamour* there was a column called *Do's and Don'ts*. This was my column and once I literally saved it for the editor because when they sent a photographer out to do a beach scene, the weather was cold and unpleasant and he didn't get the picture. In the meantime I had gone to Bermuda and re-shot the pictures on my own there. When I showed them to the editor, he thought they were wonderful, but was even more amazed when I told him I had made them. I was paid extra for these pictures, in fact made more money on the pictures than my salary for the week. (While at school I took one course in photography and thought it was great.) I was so encouraged and thought it was so much fun, that on weekends I would establish a style for *Do's and Don'ts*. I was asked to take an office photograph, and then I made more and for a while I was doing both. I went on to *Harper's Bazaar* and helped redesign the magazine at double my salary.

"One day there was a crisis at *Harper's* and I was asked to substitute for the photographer who was shooting for a column called *The Love Object*. I was not writing the column but helping to put it together as a spread. I did a number of photographic sessions, had to do a lot of improvisations with lighting, and received enough encouragement from editors, friends and family to go out on my own as a photographer.

"My style has changed a great deal since I started in the mid '70s. I would like to think I have contributed to children's fashion advertising by totally bringing it around, which coincided with the time of the "yuppies." For instance, in 1986 BBDO hired me to shoot a new product, a kid's toy. The normal procedure would be to have the kid bring some clothes from home, they would use no stylist or hairdressers, or makeup people. My training at *Vogue* demanded otherwise. I used a "groomer," a stylist, and other backup people. My feelings were, why should I have this kid just say "cheese" and smile because they did this with the adult models. I think the emphasis was on the product which resulted in a heavy and lifeless photograph. I wanted to put some life into it by using texture, action, to avoid making the picture boring. I feel I made a statement there. There were so many other photographers but I didn't know my competition. There are so many people out there trying to do what I'm doing. Right now advertising is the bulk of my work.

"My bread-and-butter income is from catalogs of children's wear and products. My first major catalog was for Saks Fifth Avenue when we did not have all of these magazines for kids. We didn't have Spiegel or Sears having separate kids' catalogs. A&S stores would sometimes give two pages in their regular catalogs. The baby boom changed all that and now you have a reverse situation where the children become the prop and not the product. For example, the Michelin Tire campaign (which I did not do) uses a baby for its centerpiece. Or an insurance account I have used a photograph of a baby under a blanket to signify security. In addition, this amusing and clever campaign showed six babies' bottoms in a row with the cutline 'the bottom . . . Kempner Insurance.'

"So I think that my expertise in fashion, my feeling for children, imagination and my success in combining these elements put me ahead of much of my competition. I want to communicate and not decorate. I want it timeless, not fashion dated. I think there always is the danger of being typecast but happily in this economy thank God I'm specialized. I have defined my needs and have worked hard to be in the right place at the right time.

"I am very busy using children in all kinds of ads—for pharmaceuticals, electronics, food, toys, fashion and other products aside from fashion. In a recent pharmaceutical ad appearing in *Parents*, *Child*, *McCall's* and other magazines, I simply showed children in a bathtub.

"It is bad to be stereotyped, but if one keeps changing with the times and keeps growing, you succeed. Not long ago it seemed I was the new kid on the block, but now I'm competing with so many young people who want to do kids, I have to come up with fresh ideas and be innovative. My traffic with baby photography has increased considerably. Earlier I got a great deal of pleasure and some thrills out of my work and now it's become more of a business. I still enjoy seeing my work in the magazines but I would enjoy it more if I could spend less time on the business end.

"I do have an agent, I advertise in the *Black Book*, but much of my work still comes from word of mouth. At the beginning I didn't think mailers were very important, but I have changed my mind and realize that indeed they are because you never know when art buyers and art directors or even clients switch agencies. I did my first mailer of 2,000 last year. I think it was very personalized and generated personal promotion in the trade press. Every few months we send something out along with a sample of what I did. They have taken various forms, such as on July 4th a button (with a baby in a July 4th diaper with a little antique silk American flag), or stickers, or promotional T-shirts, each having a theme. I think in general mailers work but they are hard to measure. For instance, a year after I sent out the baby button mailer, I got a call from a Chicago agency wanting to see my book on the basis of that mailer. What happened here was that the client wanted to copy the theme of my mailer for an ad of their own so we had to re-shoot it to their specifications. Following through is what makes mailers work and I can't always do that; I have to depend on my agent. And it is my agent who has to follow through with the nitty-gritty of client contact such as telephone calls, luncheons, drinks, etc.

"I found, to my regret, that when I took time off for personal reasons and did not shoot, I lost clients as I was out of touch with them. That was when we began paying attention to our mailer. It goes to lists compiled by reading children's, shelter, and parents' magazines. I cut out every ad that I think I am qualified for or can do better.

"My promotion activities are usually confined to direct mail and I have not had much involvement with public relations efforts such as talk shows, etc. Occasionally I am asked to appear on one and am glad to do it but I concentrate on advertising promotion. Editorial publicity has its value. After *American Photographer* did a story on me I was asked by *TIME* magazine to do a cover for them. When we do get an editorial play I always get reprints and use them as part of our mailing campaign.

"When I work with an agent, I do the estimating because they do not really know what's involved in production costs, I do the billing, though the agent's responsibility is to negotiate better fees for me and do follow-ups.

"I sometimes get in trouble with the agency because I really don't care if I go over budget if that's what it takes to get the pictures I want. Then I need the agent to calm things down.

"One of the big problems today is the bidding procedure. Too often clients who go in for competitive bidding are more concerned about price than with the individuality of the photographer's work. The agencies are caught in the middle. With the art directors demanding certain qualities, and the client trying to restrict the budget, no work will go forward until the client approves an ad. It used to be that an art director would insist on a certain photographer for a particular job but now it is mandatory to obtain three bids for a client. For instance, I submitted the highest bid on a concept which the client loved. The client wanted to buy the concept but have someone else do the job because of the money problem. I felt it was my idea and my concept so in order to get the job I had to come down in price.

"That's why I need an agent—because there's a price war out there. So I have to leave it to them because I get emotional and I don't want them to think I'm a hyper bitch. It is true that money decisions are generally made by the art buyer. If an art director wants you badly enough they'll come back to you and try to help get the figures down to where the client will accept the bid. These procedures have a terrible effect on the photographers; it makes them feel like jerks when they have to come down from a submitted bid of $20,000 to $9,000 to get a job which is easily worth the higher amount.

"I think in the long run it affects their creativity when they are forced to cut corners so outrageously that they are limited as to what they can do. It gets to be such an ego thing that you say, I don't care, I want the job, it's my idea. And then the agencies realize that the job cannot be produced at the lower figure, because they've brought in so many extra people and spent so much more on food, etc., and it turns out that it costs $20,000 anyway.

"These negotiations are debilitating and I don't want to have to deal with them. I don't want to have to spend my whole day on the telephone negotiating, returning calls, etc. I just want to shoot and edit my film. That's why I depend on my agents to take this load off my back. Magazines don't need to deal with agents because there is no client to consider, but the agencies who have to deal with clients have no alternative.

"My work is different because I do my own casting as only I can know if a particular kid can do what I want done. I can't depend on casting directors to make those judgments. Sometimes I have to screen a hundred children to get three or five for a layout, and working with very small children is hard and emotionally draining. The majority of my work involves small children which is very hard but I still love it.

"As far as working conditions are concerned, and I've worked under great pressure, I have never been harassed sexually or otherwise on a job. I think it helps being a woman with maternal feelings for kids. That's a plus. I think it's a disadvantage when traveling with other women on location, because they prefer to be with men photographers at night for social reasons. There was a man photographer with us on one shoot. He also did a lot of personal service for them, such as carrying their luggage, opening doors, helping them on with their coats, massaging their egos, etc. I can't do this.

"I'm not a point-and-shoot photographer. I think my work out carefully, and even on catalog work which is highly remunerative though comparatively simple to shoot, I do not have time for socialization that is going to divert me from my work. I know this has cost me a number of accounts; I don't like it, but I can't help it. I have to feel my work, I have to work from within, and I just can't knock it out.

"It is important that I direct my work. I set the tone, and my personality is such that I have to have fun working with the kids. Lighting is very important as it creates the mood. All this develops my entire style and makes me good at what I do. It excites me and I enjoy it.

"I have no input to a job after it's finished. Some agencies will barely call you and thank you, though others are more gracious. When I'm finished with a shoot and it is edited and delivered I'm through with it. The best compliment I can get is that they call me back for another campaign."

Chapter Nine
Secondary Uses of Photographs

There is nothing in the business side of photography that will raise more hackles than secondary uses of photographs that the photographer never agreed to nor was paid for. Therefore it is extremely important to come to full agreement with the client *before you shoot* as to the exact purposes of the photographs, what options (if any) for secondary use you are granting, and what rights are being sold. So when you submit your invoices (see sample, page 380), it is of utmost importance to spell out in the invoice exactly what rights you are granting and that you insert the clause *"ALL OTHER RIGHTS RESERVED."* (This will even protect your work against uses by methods or processes that haven't been invented yet.) If you do this, there will be fewer misunderstandings about what you are charging for and what uses the client may make of these photographs.

The enactment of the Copyright Act of 1976 and subsequent modification in procedures brought about by our (U.S.) joining of the Berne Convention in 1989 (see chapter ten) were milestones in preserving secondary use rights for all artists. Not only is there a fine market for secondary uses of photographs by the photographer, but the resale of rights for stock photography has become the tail wagging the photographic dog. The first condition in reserving secondary use rights is that the photographer must organize his material in such a manner as to make it accessible to publishers or other users of photography on demand. Another important point is to remind the client, as previously noted, that you are free to use the pictures for other noncompetitive purposes but will continue to protect his interests. Also, when photographs are purchased for a specific purpose and the photographer "reserves all other rights" the only question left to consider is what to charge for those secondary rights.

The matter of rights to photographs made on assignment for advertising poses different problems (see WMFH, pages 274-276). I am not concerned with photography of products or services. As a rule, these pictures have little secondary publication value except for other trade advertising by the company that originally commissioned the photographs. Most advertising fees by comparison to editorial payments for the same type of space, are condsiderably higher—usually three to four times as much, possibly more—and rightfully so. The buyer is usually acquiring all the rights to the photographs and the option of using them as he wishes in ongoing advertising.

This attitude is now changing. Photographers are becoming more and more reluctant to give unlimited, open-ended rights to a photograph at any price, and photographers often (and by negotiation) limit use by building into agreements a cutoff point to the commercial life of a photograph. These feelings of limitation were initiated by the unhappy experiences of old movie actors, writers and directors who, in all innocence, had their copyrights usurped by the film producers without reservation, as in those days there was no television or any other foreseeable second use of old films. Later, when TV became a voracious consumer of old motion pictures for late-night reruns, the actors who were still alive (or their estates) received nothing from those enormous sales of (television) rights by the film companies to the broadcast groups.

This started happening in advertising photography as well. Some advertising photographs made on assignment were becoming classics, and used over and over limitlessly. Also, some of these pictures had a funny way of turning up in unusual places. One photograph I shot for an airline calendar on assignment suddenly turned up as an unrelated (to the airline) poster, and again as a jigsaw puzzle. Models have successfully sued advertisers for using pictures in other media and for other purposes than the releases called for, or even implied. (See page 284.)

Recalling the philosophy discussed earlier, of the artist having an ongoing share of the fruits of his own endeavors, many experienced photographers are beginning to spell out very carefully the terms of extended usage.

The importance of retention of secondary rights by advertising photographers grew to such proportions that a major stock photo agency (The Image Bank) was formed in 1974 by a number of leading advertising and editorial photographers for the main purpose of exploiting the secondary market in advertising photography. This group, composed of many of the so-called "stars" in the business, concentrated on the advertising market and some of the very highest paid editorial markets as well. They were so effective that they opened branch offices in this country and abroad. None of this could have happened if the member-photographers had not retained secondary rights to many of the advertising photographs they had originally produced on assignment.

Was it successful? At this writing, The Image Bank Agency, which grew to some sixty branches and affiliates worldwide, has been sold to the Eastman Kodak Company for a reported $29+ million dollars. Yes, the Image Bank's resale concepts plus the retention of rights by their photographers, made it very successful.

So keeping secondary rights to photographs, even advertising pictures made specifically for one client of one product or service, has become the cornerstone of the photographer's market. And he is learning how to protect these rights.

Building a File

Building a photo file is almost like digging a well—you have to start at the top rather than the bottom. In other words, you must have worked regularly to have established a decent number of photographs that are then worth trying to market. With just a handful of pictures on hand, the potential return is quite limited and it is not until you can either develop a specialization in one or more subjects, or amass a group of specializations within a general category, that these collections can begin to pay off.

Suppose you have been working in a specific area for a year or two and feel you have enough pictures (and the secondary rights) to start marketing them. How do you go about it? There are essentially two directions to take. One involves setting up a photo library, file, or collection, getting it publicized, and starting to market the pictures in an organized way, through personal sales (yourself or with salespeople), direct mail, or simply through listings in appropriate reference sources. Or you can sign with a good stock picture agency and let them do the marketing of secondary rights—or for that matter, of original rights, to as yet unsold pictures. We will discuss both in detail, starting with the independent operation.

Setting Up a Stock File System

The first step is to set up a classification and filing system that will not only deal with the present but be ever expandable, so that as you grow professionally, your file will grow with you. Then you won't be faced with the problem of being unable to find something you shot two, three, ten, or even twenty years back.

As an emeritus member of *The Picture Agency Council*, a trade organization with over 130 member picture agencies nationwide, I have spoken with many of their members who are friends as well as colleagues. I also talked with Joe Barnell, a forty-year veteran photographer with a long and successful client list of blue-chip corporations and a principal of Shostal Associates, Inc., and am in frequent contact with Jane Kinne, Vice President of the Comstock agency, now one of the largest and most respected stock picture agencies in the country. They all have strong feelings about the importance of the stock photography market and agree that it is fast replacing general assignment photography.

Barnell had spoken of one photographer in their group who started out with an independent file and established a beautifully correct stystem that worked fine—for him. He understood it, knew where the pictures were and how to find them. What he failed to do was establish a system that someone else could operate when he went off on assignment or was otherwise unavailable. Result? Utter chaos and the loss of major sales. A reminder: publishers needing pictures from outside sources seem to have a habit of waiting until the last minute before contacting a picture file, and then they have rigid deadlines, so if a picture cannot be located and shipped almost immediately, the sale will be lost. It follows, then, that a simple, workable system that is almost self-explanatory has to be developed. When it comes to classifying and cataloging photographs, it can become complicated, but it need not.

If your file grows to any considerable size over the years, i.e., perhaps in excess of 100,000 images, you might want to consider the installation of bar-coding equipment. Bar coding is becoming increasingly widespread in computerized inventory control of almost any commodity from a can of beans to high-priced champagne. More on this when we discuss stock photography sales more fully.

I started my classification program many years ago, basing it on a system used in a big government photo library and later adapted by a larger corporate collection. After much trial and error it evolved into what I now use. It breaks down into two principal categories: (1) Geographical locations that include a variety of people, occupations and ways of life, and (2) specific subjects anywhere. Thus, my master file has a section for every state in the

Union, and every one of the forty countries I have photographed. I also have a subject file that now, in addition to the United States and countries listed, covers some eighty specific subjects, industries, and processes, with room for more when needed. I have also established a simultaneous alphabetical cross-index card file which will combine and reflect all the above sectors as much as possible.

At this point it would not take too much computer time to have all data inputted to disks and photographs on CD-ROMs for wider distribution. If you go to this time and trouble — and the size (or potential) of your file should be the determining factor — do not forget the basic rule of all computer data encoding. Make regular backup copies of all computerized data. The recent disastrous fires in California that destroyed all or part of the lifetime work of a number of photographers, underscored the need for backup computer files stored separately, and when negatives and duplicate transparencies are also available, it might be wise to store them apart from the main collection.

As our business grew after World War II, so did our picture file. Our first major post-war coverage was the reconstruction of the steel industry. So our initial classifying letter "A" was given to this industry. Then, as we continued to work and photograph a great variety of subjects, we simply added letters of the alphabet for each category until we ran out of letters. We then continued with a double-letter system beginning with AA. This theoretically can go on forever.

Eventually the file began to take shape and, as the business expanded and became more specific within the "A" (steel) group, we broke that letter down into more specific categories:

A-1: Mills and furnaces (exteriors)
A-2: Mills and furnaces (interiors)
A-3: Raw Materials
A-4: Fabricating
A-5: Finished Products
A-6: Aerials
A-7: Transportation

I mentioned earlier that whenever black-and-white film is processed I always order two sets of contact prints, occasionally three if a third set is to go to a client for their permanent file. Here is the reason for this: Using the steel industry file as an example, if a particular steel mill is in Ohio, one of those contact sheets goes in the Ohio State file (Locations), and the other into the "A" (Subject) file, including the sub-letter of the subclassification. In addition, each photograph (as indicated previously) has already been numbered by set and negative number or color number, and these numbers too are merged neatly into the system. Color is not duplicated but is simply cross-referenced on the file jacket as to where the primary subject of importance in the picture is located. So a black-and-white aerial photograph of a steel mill in Cleveland would be filed under the A-6 classification, and on the jacket of the Ohio State file would be a notation that steel mills in Ohio would be found under A-6. The color would be in separate cabinets with similar sorting and cross-indexed by number and subject references. The job file has the complete set of numbered contacts.

Caption labels should be accurate and contain as much information as possible. For several decades now we have used a simple index card with a snap-out carbon that is typed simultaneously with the gummed caption label to be affixed to the jacket (see page 226). Computerization has not changed that for us, but for new files take a good look at computerization; it has made the locations of photographs and text material easier. The index card also shows the negative or color number and the file location. This system is basic to any format I use: color, black and white, contacts, or enlargements.

There are many other systems, and any system that works, is expandable and simple to follow is a good one, but you must have one if you are going to function successfully in the secondary rights area of photography.

It has been my policy never to make enlargements of photographs on speculation or for file purposes only, as it is almost impossible to predict who will want what photograph in what size or when. Over the years I have, however, accumulated many enlargements made on order and returned to us after publication. I keep them purely as reference material, because by the time they come back they are often well-worn. I file those prints using the same system, and occasionally if someone needs an enlargement in a hurry and the quality of one on hand is reasonably good, I can save time and money for my client by releasing one of those prints.

Picture Retrieval

Retrieval of pictures from such a system as this is easy enough once it is understood, but with the sizable growth of picture collections, some of them consisting of millions of pictures, there has been an ongoing search for a modern computer-operated retrieval system. Several stock picture agencies now use bar-coding for data control and some are experimenting with it for retrieval. However efficient the computer technology for logging, billing, and tracking down pictures, there is no existing electronic system I am aware of as yet that can make a judgment about a picture, pull it from the files, and get it to the client.

There have been some spectacular developments made in computerized storage and retrieval of images via CD-ROM techniques. Electronic imaging technology is going to improve this rapidly (see chapter twelve for more on EI) and the equipment for making magnificent color mural transparencies is here. Some 100,000 color images per laser disk can now be stored and retrieved rapidly. Another system involves the transfer of images to video-tape, a system already in use for making television commercials, and this too shows a remarkable potential. In both systems the images recovered are beautifully reproduced on a monitor screen, but so far there is no inexpensive "hard copy" available, though developers of this equipment anticipate this capability soon. The Scitex system can now bring a color image to the separation process in a printing plant but the cost is beyond the range of the new photographer, or almost any photographer . . . over $500,000. Kodak's Premier probably costs as much but work stations that input to main frames are within the photographer's reach and there are several different types available. See pages 322-323, and 326. By "hard copy" I mean an image that can go to an engraver for reproduction. A second and serious drawback to both systems is the high unit cost of getting a single image into the system. It is hoped that before long this problem too will be solved, but in the meantime the photographer will have to learn how to find a set of photographs, screen them down to working size and get them to the client without punching an electronic keyboard.

Just announced (April, 1992) an experimental program by the 3M Company in cooperation with four PACA member stock agencies, a new CD-ROM stock photo researching system designed to facilitate photo research by art directors and publication designers. This program will consist of a library of four CD-ROM disks, one from each agency containing about 5,000 images on each disk and related software from 3M. This is a major advance in stock photo research and the first cooperative effort between agencies in helping provide a practical searching system and library. This is somewhat different from the above mentioned 12″ platinum laser disk that can store 100,000 images, in that the laser disk is a source from one agency, whereas this CD-ROM system is expandable on an agency-by-agency basis or simpler way of updating files in a less costly manner.

Other major photo stock houses are watching this experimental program carefully, as all are faced with the problem of storing and accessing an increasing number of images that in many cases number in the millions.

Stock Sales: Getting Started

How does the beginning photographer who is operating independently start selling his pictures? The consensus of many stock picture agency people is that it will probably require a combination of many efforts to get started as a stock photo source, the principal one being specialization and the willingness to produce new and useful images frequently. Productivity here is the key. There is such a saturation of conventional images on hand now that the new photographer will most certainly have to come up with that better mousetrap or perhaps a more aromatic cheese to bait the mousetrap.

The first job is to select the market area of concentration, and the various guide books mentioned in chapter one will be a good starting place to locate the publishers or outlets you are interested in reaching. Next comes the preparation of lists of available material, but remember previous comments on how ineffective some lists are for a picture buyer, due to vagueness and lack of specific information. Then you have to consider the publication of a booklet, brochure, or mailing piece showing your picture file to the best advantage you can afford, and what you can do and offer photographically to an editor or publisher.

But again the larger agencies are already publishing elaborate four-color, magazine-sized brochures touting their wares, and several prominent agencies have had books of their work published by conventional commercial publishers.

But that's no reason to give up. The new, upcoming photographer has several advantages over his older and perhaps more staid colleagues. In order: youth, freshness of approach, ambition, not to mention hunger. Exploit it (not with a tin cup) but with a smashing mailer, outstanding exhibitions in free areas, effective publicity, original ideas and eye-catching presentations. Borrow from the experiences of the Turnley brothers (pages 68-72). Don't wait for the customer to seek you out, because if they've never heard of you they may never look for you. Find them and pound on their doors. You are not alone, make your work speak for you.

Do not by any means ignore the local level. Exploit every method you can by getting exhibits in such diverse places as a local library, chamber of commerce or tourist and visitors bureau. Somehow neighborhood banks seem to be a good place for exhibits of this type. Don't overlook community centers, school and college buildings, and any other place where there is bound to be a fair number of passersby. Ad agencies frequently have exhibition space available through their art departments. Press clubs are also a fine opportunity for exposure. Most of the clubs in the United States, as well as many of the foreign clubs, have exhibit areas, *need* pictures for exhibition on an ongoing basis, and provide an excellent audience.

It is obvious that the more people who see your work, the more will know about you as a source of photographs. Many viewers may be working in the publishing field on books, newspapers, or magazines or in ancillary industries such as printing and related services. Touch base with all local commercial art studios, as they may be designing publications and ads for advertising media and might be able to use your photographs from stock.

Getting yourself listed as a source of materials is essential and easy. Virtually all the publications in chapter one carry free listings, plus paid space ads are made available for the kind of services you offer in the way of picture files and new photography. Take advantage of the availability of such promotional listings. And if you think you can afford it, consider paid space ads in the photographers' "source books" or other trade publications in the graphics field. But once you have accomplished all of these tasks, should you sit back and wait for clients? Not unless you are wealthy and don't need the money. Running a picture file is a continuous operation. Not only do you have to maintain communications with actual or potential clients, but your file must keep growing and be constantly updated. This is true whether you operate as an independent photographer or work through an agency. Only in this way will the picture users learn that your material is fresh and up to date and keep coming back for more.

Sometimes it doesn't seem to make sense; you may believe you have covered a subject thoroughly and sit back thinking there is no need for more material, but it doesn't always work that way. For example, even though a machine or process in some industrial location is designed to last twenty years or more, you won't be able to move twenty-year-old photographs of it unless it doesn't exist anymore and thus the picture is important for its historical value.

A typical situation involved pictures of Grand Coulee, the huge Western dam built during the 1930s, and covered extensively by a photographer in 1969. He was able to sell those pictures for years until, much to his chagrin, he discovered there had been extensive renovations of the structure after he had made his photographs, so his pictures had become out of date. The only way he can move them now is to tell his client when these pictures were made. He tells his clients that there have been changes though it may well be that these changes are not important to them. However, they should still be made aware of them.

I have lost several sales because the date on the caption label indicated when the picture was made, and may not have reflected its currency. One picture editor suggested that I remove the dates from the pictures, as apparently that is what some other agencies she deals with have done. Why not indeed? I thought. But I finally decided against it, as it might compromise my copyright protection, which requires that a photograph made before March 1, 1989 (see Berne Convention pages 223 and 273) be marked with the year it was "offered for publication or first produced for publication." The loss of copyright protection is greater than the loss of an occasional specific sale. I also think it not ethical to give an editor a picture that you know is out-of-date, even if he doesn't.

Getting the Maximum Mileage out of a Photograph

Published photographs seem to improve with age and become more valuable long before they fall into the classification of historical photographs. Textbook publishers seem to be less concerned with exclusivity than ever. There is much "safe" picture use, so that the more often a picture is published, the more that photo is seen and requested. I don't remember how many times I have had requests from publishers for a photograph they had seen in a competing textbook, and were not bothered by its earlier use. If I suggested I had similar photographs from the same set, they often refused them and requested the picture they knew. That was "safe" and consequently worth more. So it follows that efforts should be made to perpetuate certain pictures in your collection for repeat business, and the photographer running a stock picture file must learn to avoid the trap of being talked into lowering the price because the picture has been used often. In the case of original color, if the transparency is lost or damaged, whoever loses it cannot take the position that it was "worn" from use and therefore has a lower value.

How do you push one photograph over another? At the outset, the photograph in any set that attracts the most attention will also probably be the best one you have in that coverage. If that photograph is published, and you can get your hands on a sizable number of tear sheets, those printed sheets not only can become a mailing piece for you but can effectively draw attention to that particular image. By limiting the choices of pictures in the group you show, you increase the statistical chances of a particular photograph being re-used.

Representation by an Agency

There are some agencies that represent hundreds of photographers and have millions of pictures in stock, and there are the small, almost custom, operations. The latter function on a much less grand scale, without the financing, capital and staff to present as effective a sales program as the larger agencies. The photographer has to make the hard choices here. The large agency will undoubtedly have more traffic, but the individual photographer's contribution may be diluted among the work of hundreds of other photographers working through the same house. The smaller agency, having fewer photographers, can pay more attention to you but may not have as many calls as the larger ones. So in actual dollar returns, working with a smaller picture agency rather than a larger one may not make much difference to the individual photographer.

Contracts: Photographers and Representatives

Most agreements between reps and photographers are cemented by formal contracts, although there are many who pride themselves on working strictly on handshake agreements. It is wisest to agree on all terms in writing before the association begins. Of prime importance to any agreement is a thorough understanding of all the problem areas involved in repping—where the troublesome parts may be and how the commissions are determined, as the percentages can vary widely. Generally, these problems can be broken down into the following categories:

1. *Identification of accounts:* "House accounts" are usually identified as

those clients the photographer already had before the association with the rep began. Most photographers do not like to pay commissions on their house accounts unless the rep takes over and services them fully and continues to bring in new work. If this occurs, the commission is usually about half what newly acquired work would bring in from an account the photographer did not previously have. Further, if the photographer has already been doing editorial work, has built a reputation in that field, and the rep takes over, it usually means a lower commission because the pay scales for editorial work are considerably less than advertising rates. Normally the advertising photographer who continues to do editorial work does so primarily for publicity from credit lines rather than the fees *per se*, so even new editorial accounts brought in by the rep are generally considered house accounts. Commissions should be paid even though some photographers feel that editorial work is all theirs. And, if maintaining editorial accounts requires help from the rep, there should be no hesitation about paying for this service. Also, as some reps get a percentage of the total business in the studio, the editorial work cannot be ignored when it comes to totaling annual activity.

"New work" is all the new business that the rep brings in. It should include reactivated old accounts that have been dormant for some time. If an old account has been dormant for at least a year and the rep succeeds in selling them on new activity, a full "new-work" commission should be paid, but the actual period of dormancy must be determined as a result of negotiation between you and your rep.

2. *Termination:* For whatever reason a contract with a rep is ended, it is generally accepted that a rep will continue to receive residual commissions for at least six months after termination of the agreement. With negotiation, this period may be extended and has in some cases been extended for as long as two years. This is a sensitive area and should be clearly spelled out in the contract. The terms and conditions may vary widely, especially if the rep has invested money in the operation. The rep under this condition may have to be considered as a full or limited partner. Usually thirty days' notice is required to cancel an agreement, and procedures for clearing up all accounts must be worked out in advance.

3. *Billings:* Normally the photographer does the billing in agreement with the rep, although occasionally the rep does the billing, especially if he or she is more established than the photographer. Here too are the seeds of discontent if either party feels that the other is "holding out" on payment of commissions or fees. In book publishing it is often the practice for the agent to do the billing, and many authors are equally unhappy over this arrangement for the same reasons. Only mutual trust permits these problems to be worked out equitably. In my office I provide the rep, agent, or photographer, if I have sold the work of another, an exact copy of the invoice as it goes to the client with every pertinent fact on it—dates, purchase order numbers, terms, etc. It is my policy to pay all commissions within five days after the client's check clears, unless there is some dispute over the amount received that may affect the rep's commission. When this occasionally happens, the rep is paid when the matter is settled. If the sum is sizable, the contract may call for the funds to be deposited in escrow until adjudication.

4. *Expenses:* As a rule, expenses are not subject to commission and care must be taken to properly account for expenses "off the top" if the job is billed on an expense-flat-fee basis. "Off the top" means all chargeables are deducted before any commissions are paid.

5. *Other charges:* What happens when a rep sells a stock picture from your files for an ad or for possible inclusion in the layout of a new shooting? This may be resolved by deducting a flat 10 percent off the top of the billing to recover partial reimbursement for the overhead of maintaining a stock file. Promotion and advertising costs must be looked at realistically. Probably the best way is to assess and share these costs on the same percentages the fees are based on. They must be discussed by the photographer and rep to determine what kind of promotion and/or advertising are needed, and whether these efforts are affordable, before such programs are initiated.

6. *The written agreement:* Most photographers and their reps operate as independent contractors and the agreements between the two should spell this out clearly so that there is no misunderstanding of the respective roles. In this way, both the photographer and the rep are protected against the actions of the other. As there will be taxes, insurance and IRS procedures to be dealt with, it is important that this independent contractor status be described in detail in writing. There are many "standard" agreements, but I have never seen one that was uniformly acceptable to all parties without negotiation. Obtain copies of rep agreements from SPAR, PACA or ASMP. Compare them, make notes on where there are differences, and iron these differences out; have an attorney draw up a simple, uncomplicated contract to be signed by both parties. Because so many contracts may involve individual interpretations, the last clause in your contract should make provision for arbitration of disputes.

Most photographer-rep agreements are based on commission on sales made. This puts a serious burden on the new rep and somewhat less on the older one who may be repping other photographers who have already built their own reputations. The ability of a young new rep to survive until the young new photographer starts getting assignments is seriously limited, and is one reason why there are probably fewer than 300 active reps in the New York area plus a handful of agencies that represent photographers and artists. Most knowledgeable people feel that it takes a year of knocking on doors and showing a photographer's work before an important return can be expected. Thus it might make sense for the photographer to pay an advance against commissions plus out-of-pocket expenses to keep the rep going for a fair trial period.

Eileen Togashi is an active photographer's representative in New York. We talked with her about her work. Her comments and experiences as a photo rep should be of interest to those seeking an agent.

Insider: Eileen Togashi, Photographer's Representative

"I've been repping commercial photographers for thirteen years. I got started as a photographer's rep because my husband wanted to be a commercial photographer in advertising, and it was a natural progression to represent him. I learned the industry by working as an office manager in a fashion photographer's studio. I worked for photographer Bill King for three years, learning the ins and outs of the business end of the studio, and my husband worked as a photo assistant for Michael O'Neill, Mike Stone and others.

"I have a B.A. in Art History from Mary Washington College in Virginia, part of the University of Virginia. I've always had a love for photography, have made many pictures, and am increasing my activity now with a view toward doing photography.

"As a rep I work with the Agency List (Red Book), *Standard Advertising Register* and other directories (see page 23). I do not present ideas to advertising agencies as they are rarely accepted. In commercial work they do not want to see campaign ideas, only what the photographer can do.

"I have represented food photographers and also tried a 'people' photographer. Her work was black-and-white portraiture for advertising. But she was new, she did not have a strong enough portfolio, and the starting-up process was too long for me so I had to drop her.

"For me (or any rep) the start-up is lengthy, a joint effort between me and the photographer. I have to see their books first, see whether I like their work, style, and if the contacts I have would work with what the photographer does. If I think the work has a marketable potential, then we continue. The photographers I have worked with have taken input from me over the years, so we really work hand in hand.

"If there is a difference of opinion we fight that out between us on a case-by-case basis. A book should always change and should never stay the same. I couldn't send the portfolio of a photographer who does cigarettes to a client who's doing cosmetics. Once we know what accounts an AD is working on, I try to bring work to him that is of direct interest.

"Mail promotion is very important (see page 107) and I do a lot of it. I take paid space in publications such as the Black Book or other similar publications. We do not take space in all of them by any means. It's just too expensive and you have to pick and choose carefully. We have dropped using most of these directories because of the high page cost and they have not brought in enough business to make it worthwhile.

"When we make up a direct mail promotion piece, we try to enlist the help of some of the ADs we are friendly with but often do the layouts ourselves. It's hard to give you an exact dollar value on what we spend annually on direct mail promotion because often there is an overlapping and continued use of previous material. A few years ago we printed a large batch of postcards and are still using them.

[Author's Note: Some have suggested 2 percent-5 percent of gross sales be allocated to advertising and promotion, but this appears insufficient for a new photographer. On gross annual sales of $50,000 this means spending between $1,000 and $2,500 per year, which will not provide much in the way of an audience. For a large studio which may gross $500,000 this would mean $10,000 to $25,000, which seems like a more realistic amount, but then again for a large studio trying to reach a larger audience, these sums do not seem realistic in terms of printing, mailing and postage, not to mention extra clerical help, design, and other promotion costs beyond the mailer.]

"We send mailers to art buyers, ADs, and account executives but we do not pay too much attention now to creative directors because we have found their response not rewarding enough. When we were sending out larger mailings in the mid '80s we included editorial directors and other publication people, but now are concentrating directly on the ad markets we feel are most responsive.

"We used to do a lot of knocking on doors but the industry has changed so much in the last few years that we have had to do more mail promotion. We stopped direct promotion for two years, and saw business plummet because the recession was hitting at the same time.

"We have now started to re-publicize with the postcards and new mail pieces. You have to keep your photographers' names alive with new people because industry changes have been so severe. Budgets have been reduced and competition has increased. People are changing by the week as accounts move from agency to agency. It's very hard to keep up with them; purchasing policies vary among the art buying departments, and the ADs switch agencies frequently. Or, account executives and ADs often leave a big agency to form their own smaller one and I don't always hear about it.

[Togashi's remarks recalled the Madison Avenue joke about an AD who told his assistant, "If my boss calls, tell him I have gone to lunch . . . and try to get his name for me."]

"So I have to work hard to maintain my lists. I'm computerized; I keep mailing lists and names of who our material goes to, clients, records of all my appointments, portfolio comings and goings, and buy new mailing lists of people who have moved around. Creative Access (415 W. Superior St. Chicago, IL 60610) and Steve Langerman (437 Elmwood Ave. Maplewood, NJ 07040) seem to have the best lists but we use Langerman the most. Since many names do not appear on either of these lists, it is important to make your own and keep them updated. You never know where a potential client will come from.

"For a long time I found repping rewarding, but now I don't know. Until the mergers of agencies started in the late 1980s, we used to know the people we dealt with, but now there is little personal contact with ADs and more with the art buyers. I've made fifty or sixty telephone calls in a single day to different ADs and sometimes never get a call back. Or when I do, I have to send the portfolio by messenger which often costs between $20 to $25 per trip, knowing full well that with certain agencies the book will often not be looked at. It's either that or having me be a high-priced messenger when I know my time can be more valuable elsewhere. It's also distressing to know that I might not get the book back for a week.

"Some agencies have changed their policies with quick reviews (see page 78), but I still have to make too many phone calls to find out if a book has been looked at and what the responses are. Until recently ADs seem to have developed the occupational hazard of being rude, impolite, and often not even looking at the work they requested. We rarely receive even an acknowledgement or a thank-you for submitting the work. Fellow reps have told me that because of the number of major agencies changing over to the art buyer system, these abuses are diminishing, and also, we now rarely come in contact with an AD until a job is assigned or has to be discussed.

"Another problem is that photographers now find themselves in a three-way bidding war. Selections are often made on a basis of price rather than ability. And we are rarely notified when another photographer is chosen even after we have spent costly time on estimating a production.

"I represent two photographers in non-competing areas. One is hard-goods tabletop, i.e. jewelry, toys, etc., and the other is a food photographer. I usually try to attend each shooting but many reps do not, and just come back for the luncheon and to socialize a bit. It seems luncheons in the studios or expensive restaurants are important, and probably at the expense of most of the photographers. But with all that, when I bring in a good account, I find it rewarding, satisfying, and profitable.

Selling Pictures to Wire Services and News Syndicates

In general the wire services and news syndicates rarely take the production of freelancers except for hard news items not covered by the regular working press. The Associated Press (AP) is a cooperative owned by the subscriber newspapers, whereas United Press International (UPI), once owned by the Scripps-Howard Newspapers, has changed hands often and at this writing its purchase by an Arab syndicate has just been announced for new distribution to the Middle East. Both services not only have their own subscribers but sell commercially to any who wish to buy their pictures. Each has its own set of photographers and uses stringers and purchases stock features. The services occasionally buy features and "stockpile" the material they buy for resale, either to their subscribers or syndication services, or to a picture researcher who walks in. When these services buy news material, it has to be delivered with speed to the nearest bureau. The participating newspapers *do not* pay for the pictures on a per-picture use basis—they pay the wire service a general fee. Whether your picture appears in one or fifty papers, you won't get any more out of it. What they offer you is what you get.

The magazine picture (production) agencies are different. There is a participation plan in the final sales, and this is where there is an opportunity to earn a great deal of money. They are more important to the photojournalist than general syndication or wire services or stock picture agencies.

Selling Pictures to Newspaper Syndicates

The newspaper syndicates are not much of a market for the freelancer either, because they use distribution systems similar to the wire services which have their own syndication. The Associated Press syndication group is called Wide World. Out of approximately 200 syndicates listed in one press guide, only about ten or fifteen really buy freelance feature material to any great extent and often specialize in a single genre, i.e. food, wine, travel, homemaking, etc. Again, the photographer has to be warned that more often than not the price received is based on a direct sale and *not* on participation by the papers that buy the syndicated material. A knowledgeable photographer will not sell blanket uses of his photographs, but can reserve certain rights such as magazine rights, book rights, foreign rights. But if he does reserve these rights he should have some idea of how he is going to market them on a timely basis. Therefore if he runs into a major newsbreak, in his eagerness to make a quick sale, he should not give all rights to a photograph without serious negotiation as to what its potentials may be for resale. The major syndication groups that might buy photographic features are: Chicago Tribune-New York News, Los Angeles Times-Washington Post, New York Times News Service, Newhouse News Services and a few others.

In general I feel that the regular wire service or syndication groups are not a good market for stock photography, except for some hard news or feature items. Be extremely careful about what rights you are granting.

Magazine News Picture Agencies (Production Agencies)

Long-time editor John Durniak (see page 212) believes that the production news agencies have really turned photojournalism around and probably saved the entire profession from withering away. These production agencies have grown in number and by now exceed the five so-called "French" agencies (because of their origin). These agencies flourish because of a get-up-and-go brand of photojournalism that has fostered the rise of many successful independent photographers. Collectively the five original agencies— Sygma Photo News Agency, Gamma-Liaison, Contact-Press Images and Sipa-Black Star (Black Star represented/distributed for Sipa in the U.S. but later separated from them), and the well-established Magnum cooperative — and the younger newer groups now account for nearly all non-staff news photographs appearing in major news magazines worldwide. Much work is also produced by direct assignment to an agency or a particular photographer they represent.

The new breed of photographers who work for these agencies have one characteristic in common that sets them apart from their predecessors, as they are not affiliated with a particular publication. David Douglas Duncan, John Vachon, Arthur Rothstein, Alfred Eisenstaedt, Robert Capa and Larry Burrows, for example, were staff members of large magazines.

These newer photographers, among them David Burnett, Eddie Adams, Douglas Kirkland, Jean-Pierre Laffont, David Hume Kennerly, Lie Heung Shing, James Nachtwey, Peter Turnley, Annie Liebovitz and others, range the world on assignments created by their own organizations, share the underwriting of the costs with the agenices, and can earn upwards of two or three times what the best-paid magazine staffer brought home. When they are on an important story that results in worldwide distribution, they can make it *very* big.

Not all the members of these groups earn six-figure incomes, but annual take-home returns range from $40,000 to $60,000 and more plus a residual income from stock sales that may equal their annual participation pay every three or four years.

The agencies move their people swiftly and operate quickly with word-of-mouth honesty. An oral promise is as good as a written one, and any failure on their part to stick to their word would travel throughout the industry like wildfire. These agencies generate a tremendous *esprit de corps*. They overcome obstacles to bring out strong, moving journalism with the highest impact. These agencies also seem to have an instinct for knowing not only what would sell but *how* to sell a story. Sometimes their instincts are better than the editors they deal with, most of whom at first passed up Jean-Pierre Laffont's fine essay on "Child Slavery Through the World." One magazine only offered a small guarantee, and with $20,000 of his own money Laffont produced an incredibly touching and sensitive story that grossed over $300,000.

Gamma-Liaison Agency said one of their best-selling stories grossed nearly $300,000 also. The other agencies have had similar successes. Each of them has its own methods of working. Some work with a handful of closely-knit photographers, others with a broad spectrum of people they can count on, scattered all over the world. The one common denominator of these agencies is a desire to maintain the traditions and styles of great journalism and the derring-do that characterized the old *LIFE* magazine and *Paris-Match*. Lucky indeed is the photographer who has the talent and freedom to become associated with any of these agencies.

Insider: Eliane Laffont

Eliane Laffont, manager of the New York office of the Sygma Photo News Agency, says that it is comparatively simple for a good photographer to join Sygma, provided they meet Sygma's criteria of photojournalism ability, youth, worldwide political sophistication and mobility. She confirmed much of Howard Chapnick's trailblazing and spoke to me of Sygma's position and their needs and handling of photography and photographers.

Laffont defines photojournalism as "information through photography," so the first requirement is that the photojournalist have the ability to secure that information on a bit of film. Youthfulness is very important, but not the only criterion to Sygma, because this agency requires that a photographer be free of complex family ties so that he is mobile enough to get up in the middle of the night, fly halfway around the world and stay on a job long enough to produce the needed pictures. This is *not* to say that Sygma discriminates on the basis of age. Far from it, because some Sygma photographers, who have been with them for as long as twenty years, have already married, raised families and lead full lives. They now concentrate on producing stories in depth that take longer to do and may not require the field rigors of hard news photography of an immediate situation. Youthfulness to Sygma also means having the flexibility to get a job done under any circumstances—the ability to sleep on a bed of stones and not require room service, expensive hotels or deluxe accommodations that could cause high cost and time delays. This could also mean moving into a poverty-stricken community to establish the necessary trust and rapport for an in-depth coverage there.

Worldly political sophistication is a must for a Sygma photographer because the world political scene is Sygma's "beat." Laffont commented on how young French students who have completed their formal education in their early twenties already know who the political leaders are around the world and have a good grasp of these leaders' politics and economics. She feels that their American counterparts unfortunately do not have a comparable knowledge of world affairs.

The last requirement is willingness to "gamble" with the agency. It is Sygma's policy to share the expenses of a story with the photographer, with those expenses coming off the top before profits are divided. As noted earlier, sometimes those profits can be high, but sometimes they are not, and occasionally both parties may lose money on a story. But the photographer has to be willing and able to bear his share.

"Given the above the rest is easy," Laffont says. "Sygma always looks for young, aggressive and talented photographers willing to make a commitment to work for the agency every day." A phone call assuring Sygma that the photographer does indeed possess all of these attributes will usually result in an interview. Laffont or an associate will look at his portfolio, discuss Sygma's method of operation, and if they feel the photographer has the talent and experience as a journalist, then there is a good chance he or she will be offered a trial period with them.

Selling to Stock Picture Agencies

The regular stock agencies which handle much of the sales of secondary rights to photographs operate on a slower and less frenetic pace than the news production agencies, and the lure of the big buck for the photographer is not there. There are substantial sales to be made, nevertheless, by photographers through these agencies and they are certainly worth exploring. But how does the new photographer get into one of these groups? It is easier than joining one of the hard-driving production news agencies such as Black Star and Sygma. But the good stock houses also have high standards of ability, ethics and procedures that must be respected if you want to work with them.

As do the production agencies, all stock picture houses need a constant flow of new and fresh material and most will be happy to see the work of new photographers. But don't swamp them. All have the dread of being inundated with images.

A dream related to me by the principal of one large stock agency says it all. She dreamed one night that for some reason every picture agency in New York had closed except hers, and when she went to work the next morning there were hundreds of trucks and drivers from UPS, FED X, and the Post Office around her door with thousands of boxes of 35mm photographs. Don't laugh. It seems this almost happened at several agencies.

Joining a Stock Picture Agency

Joe Barnell of Shostal Associates, Inc. told me what Shostal's procedure is for acquiring the work of new photographers, and their practices don't vary much from those of their competitors. He told me they are happy to find new material but it has to be done within a framework of practical operating procedures. This, he said, applies to photographers who call them, as well as those whom they may solicit on the basis of something they saw that caught their interest. From our conversations I have assembled a set of ground rules.

There are hundreds of stock pictures agencies in this country and abroad and, while their practices vary widely, many operate under the same general ground rules of quality, freshness and currency or genre specification. They are happy to see new work, and like newspapers or magazines, they need an ongoing supply of material as much as a photographer needs outlets.

The first step for any photographer who wants to approach a stock picture agency is to write or telephone and ask if they are interested in seeing his work. Do not — I repeat, *do not* — under any circumstances send in any photographs "cold." As responsible agents they will be concerned with the safety of the pictures and the cost of returning them if they don't want them.

After you have decided whom you want to contact, and have clarified in your mind or listed on a piece of paper what you have that might interest the agency, contact them and ask if they want to see your material. If they do (and most agencies do), ask for an explanation of their particular policies, then make a selection of the broadest cross-section of your pictures that fits their specifications. Pay close attention to the number of photographs the agency says it wants to see. One agency does not want to see more than one hundred the first time, another not fewer than two hundred and some many more. An agency's requirements vary with its needs, and those needs must be respected.

The material should be clean and professional in appearance and presentation. (See chapter eight on preparing captions and other information.) When you send your work, make sure you have made some preparation for its safe return at no cost to the agency. When they have seen your work and have come to some conclusion about whether they want it or not, they will contact you. If they are interested they will tell you what they want, how they want it, and other details. One sure way to get instant rejection is to bury the agency with a barrel of unsolicited work, and you can be almost certain that the only way you will get it back is *collect*. Your pictures should carry all the information discussed in chapter eight and a clear statement to the agency as to what rights you own (or don't own, for that matter), and whether you are represented by, or your pictures are with, any other agency, and under what circumstances.

Some larger agencies require a contract to be signed in advance of submission of pictures, and a few demand a fee for looking at your work to see if it's "acceptable" for them. The contract requirement is reasonable with large submissions (though not often requested) because some agencies don't want to be put in the position of editing and sorting through a mass of photographs with no assurance that a contract will be signed. If there is no agreement, the contract is nullified. Demanding a fee to simply look at your work and calling it editing is unethical and should be avoided. It is probably a scam for raising money. Some literary agents do this with young writers claiming they are providing editing service or editorial help, and this too is questionable, but in stock photography there is no excuse for this practice.

Operating an independent photo file is a tough business unless the photographer is satisfied with just occasional sales until he can build his files up to the level where the number of pictures becomes meaningful to an editor or general trade source. For this reason the photographer who wants income from secondary use of his photographs has to consider the stock photo agency and the pros and cons of belonging to one. As I wear two hats (running a small independent stock agency as well as operating as a working photographer), I look at this from both sides.

First the pro-agency side: An agency that is already established will be the natural recipient of calls for picture uses you may not be aware of or even for projects that have not been developed yet. The requests may be for books, videotape, CD-ROMs or for electronic imaging which may use multiple photographs, or perhaps even a piece of one photograph. The pictures can be for new marketing and distribution systems, or other new-fangled publishing ventures that are still only a gleam in the eye of the beholder. If you choose to go with an established, responsible and trustworthy agency, and if a good agency accepts you, you will be in good company. An agency of this type will only deal with photographers with good material, and in some cases include among their photographers many of the star names of the business. They will do the billing, the logging out of pictures under appropriate leasing memos, see that the pictures are protected, take action against anyone who abuses the images, and in general relieve you of the entire headache of marketing, handling and billing. Sounds good? It is in many cases, and I heartily recommend that qualified photographers work with qualified agencies. Ordinarily, as a member-photographer, at the end of each fiscal quarter you will receive a statement of activity and a check for the pictures sold, but agency practices vary. Some are very good, some notoriously lax.

Photographers often do not fully understand the role and duty of the picture agency and its capacity for handling their material and the paperwork it entails. The ASMP created a stock picture committee to assess complaints made by its members against some picture agencies. After joint meetings with the PACA agencies representing many ASMP photographers, it was clear that most complaints were based on ignorance by the photographers as to what picture agencies could actually do for them, and also a lack of understanding of the agencies' problems in dealing with its clients.

But the negative side of joining a picture agency must be examined. The main objections of some photographers to joining an agency are:

1. The agency takes a high commission, about 50 percent of the sales, as compared to a literary or theatrical agent's commission of 10 to 15 percent. Studio representatives' commissions are about 25 percent and ad agencies generally charge 15 to 17½ percent on media purchases. So why the difference? That lies in the amount of internal handling and paperwork that the stock picture agency has over the others.

A literary agent works with a single manuscript and there is usually a photocopy, computer disk or carbon if the original gets lost. (Not so with an original transparency.) Studio reps with lower overheads are dealing with assignments of larger dollar numbers but have fewer sales, so it requires a 25 percent fee to barely earn a living for the average rep.

The picture agency is a singular operation. It needs space to store and work with pictures, and experienced help to service requests. It also needs accessibility in high-rent business districts where publishers can reach them. Dollar amounts per sale are frequently low; a textbook sale of a single color picture for inside use currently falls somewhere in the $150 to $200 range for a quarter-page reproduction, and usually not much more than $500 to $600 for a full page. And all too often, after a picture researcher has selected fifty or a hundred pictures, none at all are bought. This is why handling costs are so high and why commissions have to be as big as they are.

2. Picture agencies generally demand a long-term period to hold the pictures in their files, currently about three to five years. Why? Because it takes much time to get pictures in and out of publishers' offices, and for picture buyers to make their selections (if any). In textbook publishing, the majority of agency traffic is notoriously slow, and it is rare that book publishers will make their selections and permit billings within the agencies' accepted time specifications. It also takes a considerable amount of time and money to catalog and list pictures in promotional materials, and agencies don't want to spend that on pictures if they are not going to have them long enough to sell them.

3. Picture agencies are frequently accused of slow payments. Taking parts (1) and (2) into consideration, the photographer can understand why this will often happen.

4. Picture agencies demand certain exclusivity with the pictures they carry from any single photographer, and the reasoning in this case is understandable. The agencies are competitive and don't want to try to sell a photograph only to find that the buyer can obtain the same, or a close duplicate, from a competing agency or directly from the photographer for less money. And it goes beyond that. There could be a rights question here; an agency does not want to be put in the position of knowing someone else is selling rights to a photograph that their agency holds, not only curtailing the agency's market, but also possibly leaving it open to a legal problem involving those rights.

Most of the better agencies don't demand total exclusivity on the entire production of a photographer's work. What they do want is exclusivity on a single subject, that is, the best pictures of any given subject, and they don't want to see some other agency peddling the same story and the same pictures by the same photographer. As to those photographs of another subject the agency doesn't take, that is an entirely different matter and most, but not all, agencies won't object to independent sales or sales by another agency of a noncompetitive type of photograph by the same photographer.

There are other complaints and other pluses but I feel that the new photographer should consider the plus factors as outweighing the minuses and go with a reliable agency if he wants his secondary sales handled by others.

Where are these agencies? There are several hundred photo agencies throughout the United States — that is, any firm or individual photographer who wants to sell photographs, either their own or those of other photographers, can call themselves a photo agency. Many are listed in their city's classified directories. Where do you find a list of these agencies and learn where their interests lie? Some of the source directories mentioned will give you a start. But the principal trade association for general stock photography is the Picture Agency Council of America (PACA) (see page 28). They publish an annual list of their member agencies, currently numbering about 130. Most important, however, is that each agency listed in their directory indicates the kind of photographs they are interested in marketing. Write or call PACA to find out the current cost of the directory and carefully study the agency listings of subject matter. (Picture Agency Council of America, Inc., % H. Armstrong Roberts, Inc., 4203 Locust St., Philadelphia, PA 19104, Tel: 215-386-6300 or FAX: 215-386-3521.)

Insider: Barbara Gottlieb, Picture Agent

"I was a photogaphy major at the Parsons School of Design, and worked two and a half years for Black Star selling photography. I loved it, and learned a lot. But a recession hit, and I worked in fourteen other jobs, the last for a now-defunct design agency with major hotel and airline accounts. I was in charge of their photo library, picture collection, and buying photography. Throughout this time my interest never flagged even though I never wished to be a photographer myself.

"Seventeen years ago when I started *The Stock Shop*, I worked from my small apartment in Brooklyn. I would come to Manhattan daily, drop off work I had prepared the night before, and spend practically the rest of the day in a phone booth calling potential clients.

"My initial task was to build a sizable library. Fortunately one of my first photographers came in with a huge amount of work. When I didn't have something I needed, I would call around and try to locate it.

"I literally did a lot of legwork; walking from publisher to publisher and other clients. I got their names from the usual directories, all of which are available in the public libraries (see page 23). We concentrate on advertising photography. There are no secrets here. Any good photographer who is willing to work hard can call any ad agency and get a list of their account art directors or art buyers.

"I did what few agents did then or now. I went out and saw people. Now my sales force does the same. I think it is very important for a photographer or his stock agent to get to know with whom they are doing business. Most are more than happy to tell you what they need in the way of photography and often commission work. Once you are on a personal basis things change. They are no longer cold, callous or impersonal.

"I run two agencies. *The Stock Shop* and *Medichrome*. *The Stock Shop* is a general-purpose agency and *Medichrome*, a subsidiary, concentrates on medical photography for use by pharmaceutical companies and research institutions in their advertising, and editorial use in health care publications. We now have some two million pictures and represent about 150 photographers. Most *Stock Shop* sales are for advertising and *Medichrome* is about 50%-50% advertising and editorial.

"How do new photographers join us? Easily, if they are good, and willing to work. We are happy to see new photographers and their photographs. They just have to call and make an appointment. We look at their portfolios and if we think their work applicable, take them on. We don't try to keep photographers out. We need fresh work to sell as much as the photographers need fresh markets. If their material is not for us, i.e., too editorial, we point them in the direction of an agency that can best use them.

"We do not need pictures that will sit in a file unsold or compete in a saturated market. If, for instance, you want to be a travel photographer, India is *not* the place to go. Everybody's got India, few people need photographs of India. We already have tons of material on India. There are few visual changes, and little advertising involving India, so since these photographs do not sell, they are of little value to us. Oh, every now and then we'll get a call for India pictures but it's less frequent than Paris, London or even New York which is constantly growing and changing.

"As for specialization, we cannot sell much of it unless the material fits well into a specific advertising campaign or advertising programs that are hot and heavy. Then we are happy to accept it.

"For a first showing by a photographer, we need at least 200 to 300 images, although we recommend they be prepared to show as many as a thousand. I don't consider that excessive. What happens is that if a young photographer comes in with just a few images on one subject, he is apt to get lost in the shuffle. He will be competing with other photographers who could be showing hundreds of photographs on themes such as life-style, travel, etc. Thus the larger the group, the larger the resource to select from. Obviously that photographer will sell better. That is not to say that if those few pictures are unusual that they won't move; they will. But quantity as well as quality is very much a consideration. While we don't limit the number of general photographers who work in one area, we obviously concentrate on those who we think have the versatility range that is generally more salable. For us these are hard choices too.

"For us, one of the more gratifying aspects is that when one of our pictures is published in *TIME* or *Newsweek*, we invariably get follow-up calls from other publishers wanting to use that same photograph. Our pleasure comes from knowing that a given picture is highly desirable. In advertising, those pleasures are not duplicated as much since we do not get credit for them, and receive fewer follow-up calls. We get a lot more money for an advertising photograph, so maybe that's our compensation.

"Our prices are pretty much what the market will bear and in advertising they are much higher than in editorial. For a full-page advertising photo that will run in consumer magazines on a limited basis, say for a year, fees of $8,000 to $10,000 are normal, even more if it's a very specialized subject and an unusual photograph. We recently sold a photograph for less than a page in space that was used by a small-sized, limited-use trade magazine for $5,000. Then they bought it again for unlimited use, also in trade magazines and we received another $5,000. And, I might add, these were not exclusive rights, because as a rule we don't sell much exclusive use. I'd rather have the option of selling it over and over again at perhaps lower fees, because the exclusivity puts a cap on the sales even though the exclusive right may seem high initially.

"Our own promotion efforts via catalogs and mailers is important. The bread and butter of our business is probably the sale of a photograph to be reproduced for one quarter of a page inside a brochure which generally costs about $350. So in order to generate enough traffic we have to do considerable mailing and advertising to our prospects. We print catalogs of photographs for both *The Stock Shop* and *Medichrome*. We're now on our third catalog. The runs were 10,000, 15,000, and the last, a more exclusive issue, another 10,000. We also take ads in *The Black Book* and other directories.

"Many agencies ask photographers to share promotion costs, and charge from $150 to $250 per picture for use in catalogs, brochures and now on CD-ROM disks. We do not charge these fees to our photographers, but if a picture sells directly from our catalogs, we add 7½ percent to our commission to help offset promotion cost. But the sale has to be the exact photograph in the catalog that was reproduced—no similars from the same set.

"Electronics play a big part with us. So far we have not installed bar coding but are looking at it seriously. Many major shops already have it but I am waiting a little longer to see what newer technology is coming out. We use computers extensively for word processing, billing data, and other paperwork but not for image retrieval. I do not believe it possible for a computer to make the same visual judgment about a photograph as a human. No agency I know is fully electronic, though an increasing number are using bar coding systems.

"Some computer experts say that using bar coding equipment for less than two million slides is a waste of time. Others disagree. I'm open to all opinions at the moment and so far reserve judgment. Bar coding is useful in the handling of transparencies for logging, billing, returns, etc. once they have been selected. This aspect interests me because it saves time. Once a slide is bar coded the code becomes a permanent license plate for the life of the slide. Electronic imaging is ahead of us. I see a great potential for it in advertising and similar use.

"I have positive feelings about the photographs coming in now. Sometimes we trigger ideas based on requests we have already received or, for that matter, anticipate. If I feel certain images have a strong sales potential we help underwrite production costs. We don't use "tip sheets" because by the time we get them distributed, they're out of date just as the news magazines have given up sending advance requests for ongoing news stories.

"The photographers must be willing and anxious to work, experimentally if necessary, and share their expertise with us. The ones that I trust and who do not have their material scattered in many places will be the ones I want to hear from. They can call at any time and I'll give them all the information I have. For instance, if some photographer is going into a hospital to make photographs, we want to talk to him and tell him what our need is immediately so that the material will get to us quickly and we'll be able to turn it around rapidly.

"Or, if a photographer is going to be shooting a family, we'd like to know about it so we can tell him what we want and can possibly market. But I remind photographers we are not hard-news oriented and will respond more slowly to requests for help in underwriting fast-breaking stories. We tend to stay with 'secure' images that are proven sellers. We are also willing to underwrite basic ecological or conservation situations that will always be in demand and for which we may not have photographs. But this comes up infrequently because with two million photographs on hand we can generally cover most requests.

"On contracts, we follow trade norms of about three years and demand exclusivity. We have no objections to a photographer working in areas we do not cover, but still want our exclusivity contract to prevent our photographer's output winding up in unexpected places. We keep a sharp eye on the ultimate use of our photographs and try to obtain as much information as possible before the sale about its use.

"We are flexible, but reserve the right of final judgment on use of a photograph or a photographer under contract to us. At times we have refused to sell photographs for campaigns we disapprove of or to anyone who wants to defame any of the products in our photographs. We do have guidelines and try to follow them impartially.

"Stock photography is a marvelous way for a photographer to make a living, and for a young photographer, a good method to get started. It's not easy but there is much personal satisfaction in making fine photographs. But the new photographer must build a sizable body of work before he is ready to go out to the marketplace. How many is problematical, though stock agents usually feel that as many as 2,000 is not pie in the sky. It is unrealistic for a new photographer to walk into any agency with only 200 images and expect to sell most of them at a couple of thousand dollars each. It just doesn't happen. In order to make a living at stock photography, it has to be a photographer's goal, not merely a side line. He has to think it through, get the help of people, and be prepared to invest time and money for materials and other expenses.

"In travel photography, for instance, the photographers have to go to places where not too many people have been before. They have to get involved with their agency, who will tell them what is hot, what is selling or even not selling. Only the agency can prevent the photographer from wasting time in producing photographs which won't sell. If they must go to places where there is a lot of traffic, then they should choose places which are always changing, like New York or London, or any other growing area.

"With a life-style photographer, the stock house is needed to assist in telling what sells, be it a family, a child, mother and child. Many of the photographers we handle are very busy, shooting like crazy and making money; perhaps the economy has something to do with it because they are listening to their agents as to what is marketable. And I think we have shaken out a lot of people who have not been serious and devoted. Yes, I think there is room for young talented photographers to earn a decent living in stock photography. In our shop more than twenty photographers are earning more than $25,000 a year in commissions.

"I feel the earning potential in stock is endless. It is possible to sell a picture for $20,000 tomorrow; it doesn't happen frequently but it does happen. That is one picture, one time. In the long run, advertising photography probably pays more than editorial photography. The rates are higher and the market is broader. There are editorial photographers who do well also; they make bulk sales and do a lot of it because they have many great pictures. They supply a textbook with twenty or thirty pictures at one time and that's a good number of photographs and the return is quite decent. In publishing we do not discount our pictures so that when the photographer makes a bulk sale he makes money. The minimum price today is about $150 for a quarter-page size inside use in a textbook. Larger uses, covers or endpapers will draw commensurately more. We restrict the electronic copying and reproduction and are very specific about what rights we sell."

Potential Payment Problem Areas

In the area of primary payment — that is, payment for the use for which the photographs were made — there is usually little argument once those ground rules are established. It is the secondary uses by the corporate or advertising client that cause the most trouble because most book and magazine publishers buy only specific rights to a photograph, and secondary uses are usually paid for according to accepted codes of the professional societies.

Before an answer can be arrived at to the question of what to charge for secondary rights, one has to know who wants those secondary rights and for what purposes. Is it the original client, or someone else? This is important because concessions may have to be made to give the original client an option for the use of the photographs he has ordered for one specific purpose — e.g., an annual report or advertising. But suppose you have been given an assignment to simply build a public relations file for a client, knowing that those pictures are going to be distributed at no cost. The only way that you can handle this is to charge enough in your original fee to cover the loss of subsequent sales.

Another area in which there can be friction is in the corporate annual report field. If a company hires a photographer to cover its plant(s) and possibly photograph the firm's executives for a specific annual report for any fiscal year, it frequently happens that not all the photographs are used, or some are repeated in the annual report for the following year. What then? If the photographer is on secure ground with his client as to what the purchase order specified, then he should politely but firmly remind the client of the agreement. If the photograph has never been used, and a new annual report, for example, is produced in a different fiscal year, the new annual report should be treated as a new publication, and because this is a new use of the photograph, the page rate should again apply. (For suggested page rates for publications other than books and magazines see appendix.) Sometimes if the secondary use is minor, as a goodwill gesture you might consider granting a re-use without fee. Otherwise, if a picture has run, and the client wants to run it again, a page-rate figure should be paid for the rerun, and if the photographer wishes to be generous in terms of personal public relations, he can look on this re-use as a secondary use and apply the same percentages of the page rates (see appendix) that book publishers do.

Though book publishers tend to buy specific rights, among some there has been a growing tendency to blur the lines of purchase. Photographers are urged to look carefully at the purchase orders they get from these houses, especially those which publish books of many different interests. They must make sure the publisher is not trying to usurp blanket rights for all their publications with a single payment.

The photographer should guard against a client's unauthorized use in national space advertising of pictures he has made for editorial or general public relations uses. In reality this seldom happens because advertising agency ADs prefer their own concepts in national ads. But it does happen when a corporation has its own internal or "house" agency. They are used to save money by reducing or eliminating agency fees. From the company's standpoint why should they have to pay additional fees for work already performed for some other use?

I have always been every careful to make these payment differentials clear to my clients and have rarely had any problems of dual usage for national advertising. I also am "generous" in allowing the clients to use these pictures at a low rate for trade advertising. This is no small matter if you consider Lovett's statement (page 82) that payment is about one-third less for trade use than for national advertising. If a major agency is paying $25,000 for a national ad, then even a one-third reduction for trade would still be a healthy fee. If this is made clear to your corporate client, then I think the lower use charge for annual report work in trade advertising will be appreciated. Circulation of trade advertising is usually limited in scope and will not reach a broad general audience. It is also possible to make special arrangements for credits in trade advertising, it may be a potential source of revenue for you from other people in the same field and also a source of good tearsheets.

One restriction on trade advertising use I insist upon, is on advertising by third parties. For example, if you have photographed a particularly interesting process in a department of a company you are working for, and they use this photograph in their annual report, that was what the picture was made for. But if you then get a call from the manufacturer of the machine you photographed for that annual report, and he wants to use it *in an ad for his company*, what is the answer? The only positive one can be (1) if your client approves and endorses any releases, and (2) payment for its use is made at standard trade ad rates, since that third party had absolutely nothing to do with your getting the original assignment. So make certain your own client understands this, because in their gesture of goodwill to the third party, your client may have given him a right to a photograph without realizing that they didn't have that right to give.

Conditions of Sale and Specific Reproduction Rights

Over the years I have evolved "condition of sale" statements which are always added to my invoices. By specifying all the options a client is buying before you start work and making sure all the options are stated in the purchase orders or memoranda of work, you will eliminate any cause for friction when you bill. Below is a sample listing of possible items that should be on the invoice forms. (See appendix for sample forms.)

RIGHTS GRANTED:

All photographs covered herein ©199- by _____ (Photographer)

1. For use in 199- Annual Report for the _____ Corporation only.
2. For internal public relations use in company printed matter of the corporation.
3. For all external public relations use by the _____ Corporation.
4. For trade advertising by the Corporation for _____ years from invoice date.
5. National Consumer Advertising options are granted subject to agreement on additional fee by the Corporation and/or their advertising agencies. *
6. Third party use excluded in any media except by agreement of the photographer and payment of additional fees by the third parties.

All other rights reserved.

* (Note: Here if desired, *and agreed upon*, you can put a time limit or requirement of addtional fee.)

This illustration is an example of the policies of most members of the ASMP and PACA. Some photographers will give a client anything he wants, some make rigid demands for payments for any use other than those originally specified. Most will fall in between, and in the final analysis, you have to set your own terms and make your own agreements. But be aware that what we have discusssed above is rapidly becoming a custom of the trade with those photographers seeking to obtain maximum mileage from their photographs. Whether you choose any or all of the items shown, the most important line after any of them is "All other rights reserved."

Retention of Negatives

The tradition of selling specific reproduction rights to editorial clients is well established, and the right of retention of negatives by the photographer has been upheld by the courts on more than one occasion. The basic legal concept here is that a negative is an intermediate stage in the production of a photograph, and, as such, is only a part of the uncompleted work or effort going into the completion of a finished product. But for all practical purposes, if you do not have the negatives, you do not have the rights, even though you may have retained them on paper.

For years many large magazines vacillated on the question of who really owned the negatives, but were clear in their assertion as to what could be done in the matter of secondary use of the photographs. It was not until the new copyright law went into effect that the rules became more sharply defined and *in the absence of a specific "work made for hire" agreement* (see page 274), you own everything.

There still remains an area of discontent when the client does not know this and subsequently tries to exercise rights he doesn't have, or accuses the photographer of selling pictures for some other use. It is in the hope of eliminating this kind of conflict that I suggest you make sure everyone concerned understands not only the legal aspects of the matter, but also the customs of the trade, which may not be clearly defined by rule of law.

I mention this now because of the importance of secondary rights to a photographer's total annual income. The concept that photographers, by retaining secondary rights can be more effectual in moving pictures than the client, can be an inducement for the company to turn the business in your direction rather than to a competitor. Why is this so?

All companies other than publishers, large or small, are engaged in the production or distribution of their primary product(s) and are not in the publication business. They recognize the need for photographs and thus commission them. After use they are pretty much disinterested in what happens to the pictures unless there is some "return" for secondary use. The word "return" here does not necessarily mean money. One return they may be looking for is the public relations value of having these photographs get into the media, and what better way than to have the photographer who makes them assure media entry by pushing hard for their secondary use. Under these circumstances the photographer would receive additional payment, but not from the client.

A book publisher I deal with regularly still comes to me for oil industry pictures even though they know the pictures are available free from the oil companies. Many publishers do not like the idea of "hand-outs" despite the appeal of the free pictures for their budgets. Also, when they request photographs directly from a company, they will usually get a highly "sanitized" set of pictures which will show the company without warts or blemishes and often without reality as well. There is also the time factor. Most picture editors will try to locate the photographers directly (even though they may be out-of-towners) rather than deal at long range with some company that has moved to the Southwest or the West. Once an editor knows of you as the source of a certain kind of picture, he will come to you and speed the selection process considerably by dealing directly. Also, if you have built a good stock file on a given industry or subject, the editors will be apt to turn to you first for a picture assignment.

Secondary Reproduction Rights Billing

Billing for reproduction rights is simpler and less complicated than billing for a shooting job, but there are some ground rules to be observed if the photographer is to protect his rights and prevent misuse. The cardinal rule is to bill for a specific use only and reserve all other rights.

Until recently there have been some pretty loose definitions of what certain rights were, and terminology was adopted that was frequently not specific enough to apply to the actual sale. Even after adoption of some of the preliminary recommendation or codes of practices and standards by the professional groups (i.e., ASMP, PACA, & ASPP), definitions were still hazy and there was little agreement as to what they really meant.

What, for instance, does the term "one-time reproduction rights" really mean? Does it mean you can print the picture just once on a single sheet of paper? Or does it mean you can print it once in one specified book, magazine, brochure, annual report, etc.? If you state on your invoice that you are selling "United States English Language" rights to reproduce a picture in a book distributed in the United States, and then get back a purchase order saying they are buying North American rights, is that the same? Of course not. Then again what are North American rights? Does that include Canada or Mexico or both?

Roberta Groves, New York Manager of the H. Armstrong Roberts Agency, a PACA member, reflected the thinking of her seventy-year-old-plus agency, and the 300 photographers they represent. She reminded me that the expression "North American rights" is terminology used by publishers and it applied to entire books rather than pictures, because books sold represent a royalty to the author who wants the widest sale possible, whereas individual pictures used do not draw royalties.

The photographer should be concerned with distribution. A "United States English Language right," means a book printed in the English language and sold in the United States. It might also include a right to distribute in Canada which could involve an additional fee. In actual practice, however, when a book is manufactured for primary distribution in the United States and is so specified in the billings, if a few copies are distributed in Canada or elsewhere, then little fuss is made about additional payments. But if there is a separate edition, printed in Canada, as the Canadian Government is pressing publishers hard for home manufacture, then the usage has to be considered as an additional right paid for accordingly. Or, you might grant a right to distribute through the English-speaking world, which would also call for an extra fee. A different grant would be a right to a publisher to lease his production to another publisher. All of these situations reflect different fee structures. So the use of the term "one-time" should be understood and be applied correctly. The terminology of rights should also be specific and include whether the rights sold are for cloth (hardcover), paper (paperback) or even certain magazine rights such as a "one-time reproduction right to appear in the issue of _____ Magazine dated _____."

Then to further confuse everyone, it is also customary to charge an additional 25 percent of the basic one-time use for additional language uses. These additional language charges are often limited to eight in addition to the primary language of publication.

When it comes to selling stock photos to advertising agencies, it gets more complicated and here the photographer must be clear in specifying in what language, in what publications the ad will appear, how many insertions are allowed, etc., or charge a fee high enough to cover any unstated publication plans. All of this must also be carefully detailed in both first discussions and final invoicing. As in the billing for a shooting job, the bottom line must be "all other rights reserved."

A Need for Change in Buyer Attitudes

There is a need for change on the part of the new picture user whose attitude is: "Why should you charge so much money for additional use of these pictures when you have already been paid for them?" This cliché died hard but it did seem to die with the maturing of picture buyers—so I thought.

Now it is being reborn again with alarming regularity, and I wonder if this is partially due to a new generation of picture editors and art editors, trying out their wings. Or perhaps some of the old ploys are being revived to use against new and younger photographers who have not been around long enough to understand the basics involved.

However it is interpreted, the answer was the same thirty years ago as it is today. When a photograph is made, it is made for a specific purpose. If it is made by a professional for a professional purpose, the chances are it has fulfilled its intended need. If a new need is created that new need has to be dealt with as a new market. In between times (and these "between times" can be anywhere from fifty minutes to fifty years) the pictures have to have a home. They have to be filed, stored, captioned, retrieved, generally kept in good condition and accessible. This costs money; it takes time (which is money) to log and "de-log" them, all of which must be charged for even though the original pictures themselves may have been made and paid for by someone else long ago.

True, computers can speed up the process of selection and the back room work, or if you use quill pens, they all still have to be amortized into your general overhead cost. So whether you have just made a set of new photographs and delivered it to the client, or have resold an existing set of pictures, there is a vast amount of handling and paperwork that must be dealt with.

In my opinion there is almost no photograph in the world that cannot be reused for some purpose other than for what it was originally produced. The trick is to bring the maker and the buyer together, and that is a job that probably consumes as much effort as the original production of the picture. It is the *raison d'etre* for the stock photo agency, the photo file, or even the lone photographer with a trunk full of unprinted photographs. I cannot overemphasize the importance of the photographer's retaining his rights and, in some cases, possibly controlling the ongoing use of his work. There could be some strong moral issues here as well. Should a photographer who is against smoking sell his photographs to a tobacco company? Or a believer in animal rights deal with a furrier? That decision is yours, but if any of these thoughts raise inner concerns, don't let morality become another word for censorship ... and I might add ... this works both ways (see the following).

Protection of the Client

While the above discussion has to do with the protection of the photographer, how about protection of the client? The client has rights too, and one of the things he is entitled to is exclusivity, or protection against misuse of his photographs. In the stampede for protection of photographers' rights, frequently the rights of the client are overlooked, *but they should not be forgotten.* If the photographer retains secondary uses to the pictures, he must be extremely careful about releasing those pictures so they cannot be picked up, used or even misused by competing publications or corporations. In industrial situations particular attention has to be paid to process security. Also, the terms of releases obtained on a client's property, or in behalf of a client, do not always give *carte blanche* rights to the photographer for other uses that can be harmful to the client, or to the model for that matter.

Questions of conscience must also be answered. If you are hired by some corporation and you find them doing something that is in serious violation of some standard of safety or environmental protection, do you blow the whistle on them? Sometimes this is called "biting the hand that feeds you." How do you handle this? If you see an industrial client dumping toxic chemicals into a river, should you photograph it, get paid for it, and then go running off to the EPA or OSHA?

The answers are a matter of conscience, and I certainly cannot make definitive judgments. But I feel that the seriousness of the violation has to be the governing factor as to whether the photographer sticks his nose into the situation or does nothing about it. I can, however, relate a few examples of behavior by other photographers who were faced with these decisions.

One freelance photographer who frequently worked for a large lumber company in the West, did indeed blow the whistle when he saw a major conservation/ecology violation, but the company did nothing to retaliate. When I asked why they continued to use him, I was told that he was the best man available for the job, and the company preferred his expertise as a photographer and took his whistle-blowing with equanimity. More than likely, however, they were pragmatic and felt the cost of the fines would not be as much as the cost of correcting the violations, including possible production loss.

In another case I know of a photographer who, when working on a job, reported a serious pollution violation by middle management directly to the company president. The company president not only thanked him but sent him a check saying the amount of the check was in acknowledgment of his consciousness-raising of higher management. This photographer also kept working. But I also know of other occasions where the photographers looked the other way in fear they would lose the accounts.

Interview
Howard Chapnick
Photography News Agency Executive

One of the strongest influences on modern-day photojournalism is Howard Chapnick, who just retired as president of Black Star Publishing Company, a pre-eminent photo news agency. Chapnick has guided and counseled literally hundreds of photographers throughout his illustrious career and helped set standards of ethics and honest journalism that have yet to be topped by any of his colleagues here or abroad.

Black Star photographers have been in the vanguard of every important news event the world over, have won Pulitzers, Overseas Press Club, World Press Photo and other awards by the bushel basket. His predecessors at Black Star were influential in charting the course of the then newly formed *LIFE* magazine. Even after Chapnick's recent retirement, the day I spoke with him I was preceded by several young photographer-hopefuls who were showing him their work and seeking his counsel.

During our interview he said, among other things, that any photographer who joined Black Star not only had to have all the technical and emotional prerequisites the company needed, but also had to be a nice person. Howard Chapnick is indeed the epitome of that requirement. He is the consummate gentleman, and a very nice person.

"Black Star was organized in 1936 but I joined it in 1941 as an assistant messenger boy," he said. "The founders were three German emigrés. Kurt S. Safranski was one of the progenitors of photojournalism. In the late 1920s he started using sequences of pictures in the *Berliner Illustrated Zeitung* (BIZ). Safranski worked closely with Kurt Korff who is often credited with influencing the early concepts of *LIFE*. Actually Safranski and Korff worked together on another magazine called *Die Dame*, which was using photographers such as Alfred Eisenstaedt, Martin Munkacsi, Dr. Eric Salomon and other German photographers doing early photographic layouts. So they were at least ten years ahead of the United States as far as photojournalism is concerned.

"The second founder, Ernest Mayer, was head of the Mauritius Agency in Germany and himself a photographic agent. The third founder, Kurt Kornfeld, was a German scientific book publisher. Safranski and Mayer were Jews, Kornfeld was only one-eighth Jewish, but violently anti-Nazi. They left Germany with whatever possessions they had, went to London first, started Black Star and came to the U.S. in 1936 to incorporate it here.

"*LIFE* was dependent in the early days on agencies like Black Star, Pix and four or five others, particularly because of their contacts with European photographers like Eisenstaedt (see page 30), Fritz Goro, Herbert Gehr, Walter Sanders and Philippe Halsman. Henry Luce's new magazine did not have many homegrown American photojournalists. They did, however, have Margaret Bourke-White, Peter Stackpole, and Tom McAvoy, who along with "Eisie" were the original four staff photographers. Carl Mydans was not one of the first four staffers, but joined very shortly after and was always considered among the starting group. *LIFE* needed more photographers to cover the world so they utilized the Black Star photographers extensively.

"*LIFE* was very important to Black Star because it represented more than 50 percent of Black Star's business, and Black Star was very important to *LIFE* because they could not put out a magazine like *LIFE* without outside photographers.

"I got into Black Star and photojournalism by accident with a summer job in 1941 after my junior year at New York University, and worked two afternoons a week during my senior year. I graduated as an accountant. I was in the United States Army during World War II for three and a half years, stationed mostly in England. I had no army photo experience. When I returned in 1946, Mr. Mayer asked me to join Black Star.

"Agencies such as Black Star, Sygma, Magnum, Contact-Press Images, Gamma, etc. are essentially production agencies in that they produce entire stories either on speculation or assignment. Or there are agencies like Woodfin Camp who are not so much assignment agencies as stock agencies specializing in special features and acquired subsidiary rights, which they market as stories or individual stock pictures to other publications here and abroad.

"Black Star's main function is not in the hard news area but in documentary photography related to the news and reflecting the world in which we live. You might say these are our philosophical roots. In addition it does much commercial work, annual reports and other types of corporate publications. It also maintains a stock library of three million photos, sells residual rights of material produced on assignment or speculation, and distributes in fifteen or sixteen foreign countries. Their work involves still photography in all its possible uses, be it a magazine assignment, book, exhibition, secondary sales to other magazines, or a combination of all of these. But our work is clearly separated from straight stock operations in which agencies take no risks or make no financial investments to create photographs.

"The situation has changed much in recent years. Many editors know that if they sit back and wait, the agencies will bring them produced material and they will not have to make assignments or other commitments except to buy rights to that material. They often pay guarantees or fees for 'first look' rights.

"There are many variables. In the old days when *LIFE* was shooting ten stories for every one they would use, they became the subsidizers and producers of great amounts of editorial material.

"The other news magazines such as *TIME, Newsweek, US News & World Report* did not do much in that area until John Durniak, as Picture Editor of *TIME*, revolutionized news photo coverages on assignment. Such work became a very important source of residual material that was then sold on the world market. *TIME* might use three or four pictures from a set, and turn the remaining material back to the photographer. Then the complex network of agencies and subagents would try to distribute the material elsewhere. In recent years, as the agencies have proliferated, the magazines now assign less than they did earlier. Now the smart editor waits to have an agency come to them with a story on the Berlin Wall, the dissolution of the Soviet Union, etc., and then buys the rights to the material.

"Black Star tries not to speculate and attempts to get advance assignments instead from *National Geographic*, *TIME*, *Newsweek*, or other magazines they feel would be interested. In this way day rates and expenses of photographers are covered, so that all the peripheral sales become profitable to the agency and the photographers.

"Also it's fair to say that more material is now produced under the aegis of the agencies and their photographers than by magazine staffs directly. A quick look at the masthead of almost any news magazine will show large editing staffs and few photographers, with the majority of the photographers listed usually working under contract rather than on staff.

"You ask what does a photographer have to do to join Black Star? As far as Black Star is concerned the door is always open. There is a popular misconception that agencies do photographers a favor by looking at their work or taking on their representation. At Black Star we didn't kid ourselves. Agencies need photographers as much as photographers need the work. But it is important to realize that the agencies do not need mediocre or merely adequate material. They need photographs that are on a higher level. It's obvious that the work of outstanding photographers sell better than that of other photographers who just happen to be in a certain place at a certain time.

"Geographic location is as important as is the quality of photography. When a photographer wants to join a first-class agency he comes in with a portfolio, and when I was at Black Star (and the policy still stands), I would look at 400 to 500 photographers' work a year. During my tenure we always saw everyone who wanted us to see them and we evaluated the work as it related to the magazine standards as we knew them. We judged work on the basis of technique, composition, spontaneity of body language, on lighting, storytelling ability, etc. I always had in my mind some eighteen different criteria and then if all the photographic capabilities were present, I wanted to be sure that the photographer was a nice human being to whom I could relate and who could relate to me so that we could have a community of interest.

"As for the format of the material they showed, I couldn't have cared less. I wanted to see pictures which stimulated my interest in work that was potentially salable. If the person happened to be a wonderful art photographer, I probably would not have been interested. Pictures do not get better because they are 16" × 20" or 30" × 40" and if photographers came in carrying the weight of the world on their shoulders I didn't want to be overwhelmed by their size. I didn't want to see pictures with music, nor did I need an explanation about every photograph. I did want to get a sense of the depth of the photographer. Did the photographer have ideas or was he just a cipher who sat there and didn't react to anything? Was the photographer an informed person who reacted to the news of the world, was curious about the world, interested in social questions and in every other aspect of the life that surrounded him or her?

"If we liked a photographer and his or her work, the procedure varied. With some photographers we started on some sort of trial basis. Specifically I can give you one example of a photographer who worked for the *Pittsburgh*

Press. I liked her work so she became a stringer photographer for us on her off days from the newspaper.

"I told her to go back and do a body of work that would be of interest to us. She did not come back for two or three years. She finally came back with a project she did on the skyscrapers of Pittsburgh and she also brought a story of a little boy that had a terrible disease called *spina bifida*, a birth defect of the spine. This was a story of a little boy who propelled himself on a skateboard and had a massive upper muscular development. I was able to sell that story to *LIFE* for eight or ten pages and sold it all over Europe. The construction photos were absolutely fantastic and they also showed her courage. I gave her a contract with a weekly draw against earnings.

"Other photographers can work on a stringer basis where Black Star does not represent them on an exclusive contract basis.

"In general a photographer earns anywhere from $20,000 to $100,000 per year or more. Black Star only has about fifteen or so photographers under contract, with hundreds more stringers.

"Photography with Black Star or any other major agency has to be a collaborative effort and the photographer must constantly stimulate the agency with ideas and material that may be produced on a speculative basis.

"If a staff photographer runs into a story in the field, Black Star does not object to his making a direct initial contact with a magazine but arrangements for payment, rights, etc. ultimately have to come from the agency. Stringers are free to make independent arrangements.

"There are the so-called 'boutique' agencies such as JB Pictures, a young dynamic agency but not a mass production one. Production agencies as we know them are generally very personalized and work very closely with their photographers. They are different from the regular stock agencies which deal for the most part in existing pictures. There is another new agency called Saba and another called Picture Group which is one of the most successful agencies operating out of the New York area. Contact Press Images and Matrix are other smaller personalized agencies that are important.

"The essential difference between the kind of work Black Star does and that of standard stock agencies is that those agencies take no risks in the production of photographs and make no investment in the production material. The production agencies usually work on assignment or on speculation based on their own strong feelings about the viability of a story. Again, this kind of speculation is different from the old kind of speculation in which an editor would say to a photographer, 'Do this story for us and if we like it we will pay you.'

"Being associated with an agency is not an automatic success story unless the photographer participates fully in applying new and productive ideas and material."

Chapter Ten
Protecting Yourself and Your Clients

Photography and the law have been in a tempestuous marriage ever since there were recordable images and litigious lawyers. Photographers and publishers, picture users, and those photographed, have often sued each other or acted in concert to sue others in all manners of actions, including invasion of privacy, libel, piracy, copyright violation, nonpayment of bills, petty larceny or grand theft, and almost any other offense against the private or public interest. In other words, the photographer is no different from any other creative artist in that he is bound, protected or abandoned by an incredible number of laws, statutes and regulations. To try to enumerate them all would be an exercise in futility. All I can do is hope to cover general points of how the photographer protects himself in the normal course of business or secures to himself what is due under the law.

The most important factor in protecting the photographer's business life is the clear spelling out of all agreements, including contracts, leasing and delivery memos, invoices and assignments of copyright. Avoid useless and complicated verbiage. I have always felt too much is written in fine print that few people ever read or want to deal with. I have seen leasing memos of several pages and contracts covering three or more pages. A good invoice, memo or letter of agreement concisely written will say it all . . . and better.

All of the above factors are an integral part of the photographer's survival and the pecking-order has to be determined by the individual. But the nature of the photographer's world has changed radically in recent years. Competition has always been fierce and will continue to be so, but the emphasis has shifted markedly.

But before getting into the tangles of copyright and the law, I want to alert photographers to the very important subject of *delivery* (or *leasing*) memos. (See samples in appendix.) Delivery memos are just that. They are detailed forms that spell out the terms under which a photograph is submitted to a publisher for consideration of use by them. These memos spell out the length of time photographs may be held; what charges will be made for the time held, research, print fees, and damages in case of loss or physical damage to the artwork and compensation for loss of future sales in that event. They also cover release availability and other conditions relating to the submission. They are usually clear and to the point. It took a long time before the publishing industry would accept these conditions, but in time most did, and still do.

However, a few publishers have set their own ground rules for looking at submissions and have refused to accept the responsibilities of caring for and protecting artists' work. Or, they have downgraded their financial responsibilities to such a point as to make any submission by a photographer an extremely hazardous condition.

How does the photographer deal with this? Most photographers or their agents I know, refuse to deal at all with these publishers and will not respond to their requests. They take the position that if a publisher will not recognize what our industry (and many courts have confirmed) thinks an unsold stock photograph is worth, then we do not wish to jeopardize the future viability of our photo collections. I suggest that new photographers consider the eventual life of their photographs as an important part of their own heritage, and not be stampeded into trying to make a sale under terms too onerous to even reasonably consider. This all goes back to the matter of personal pride of the artist in his own work.

When the big picture magazines were "hot," the photographers who contributed to them often became the role models for the younger upcoming talents. But with the demise of the big glossy stock magazines does this mean that there is neither market nor role models left?

Certainly not. There are more photographers and more outlets than ever existed in the days of the old *LIFE* and *Look*. Glamorous as working for them may have been, the fact is that between the two they employed only about fifty staff people and perhaps double that number as part-time freelancers or independent contractors. Nonstaff photographers shot on assignment, their work closely held by the publishers, and secondary use of the material was unthinkable. No more.

Today the popular magazines often have several picture editors and no staff photographers. They use many photographers, some from the production news agencies (see page 249) as well as many working under contract or guarantees. A great many pictures are also bought from stock picture agencies (see page 251). This is true also of the big European magazines. Most of their major news stories also come through news agencies from independents, some of whom are interviewed in this book.

So the primary question is, who owns the work you do? Who controls its use, or prevents its misuse? That's why establishing ownership of a photographer's work is so vital, and why I draw your attention to copyright and ownership of photographs.

Probably the most contentious phrase in the world of copyright today consists of the innocuous sounding words "Work Made for Hire" (WMFH). These words are far from the intent of the meaning of the old popular love song "Three Little Words."

Stand on the steps of the Library of Congress or at the front door of half a dozen publishers in New York and whisper "Work Made for Hire," and a dozen baseball-bat-wielding lawyers, or an equal number of photographers and artists, will come at you with blood in their eyes. In another time and place these words might have the same effect as waving a red flag at a bull, the net results being the same. Anger, confusion, and perhaps a little bit of greed. The root of these feelings is embodied in the copyright law.

Below you will find a discussion of the ramifications of copyright, including work made for hire, their good points, troublesome ones and how/why they affect you. In short, WMFH means that you have given up all your rights to a publisher, and he can do whatever he wishes with them. There is little you can do about it, especially make money from secondary sales. Since the better part of a photographer's income is going to come from secondary use, suddenly the economic viability of your professional life is at risk.

Certainly this was not the intent in the early 1960s when the Copyright Office began advising the Senate's McCarran Committee of the dire need to revise the Copyright Act that had remained virtually unchanged since 1909. For years prior to enactment there were countless meetings attended by lawyers, copyright experts, writers, artists, actors, performers and photographers, not to mention poets, sculptors, publishers and agents. Even this writer, as a former president of the ASMP, testified before the McCarran Committee on the need for changes to protect photographers, and what was required to assist the creators of copyrighted material to survive in the very rough world called publishing.

The changes and needed Congressional approvals took a very long time to accomplish. The Copyright Act of 1976 was passed effective January 1, 1978. What came out of all this discussion and Congressional action was hopefully a modernization and streamlining of an archaic system that dated back to the founding of this country. The first copyright laws were written before there were many ways of reproducing creative works. Though the printing press was already in existence, photography was not viable until the 1830s, and words such as radio, phonographs, film, television, vinyl acetate, and digitalization would have seemed to come from another planet.

Before we address the *work-for-hire* problem let's look at copyright in general. I cannot overemphasize the need for all creative artists to understand it, and not slough it off as something for the other guy.

Copyright

What Is a Copyright?

The Library of Congress's most common definition is that it is a bundle of rights that comes into being at the time of the creation of a work. A copyright is a form of ownership of a piece of property that can be bought, sold, traded, willed, inherited, donated, divided or combined with other objects to form some new entity. Yet in certain cases you must concede its "fair use" without compensation as will be discussed later.

Important to the photographer is that it is an effective method of preserving his or her rights and keeping them from being used without permission or payment *if demanded*. In the world of communications, photography is a vital tool, and a copyright in many ways resembles a patent. Almost any written or graphic works of art, literature or methods of bringing these works to the public (e.g., the printed page, electronic transmission, theatrical presentation, or a framed canvas on display) are eminently copyrightable, and should have a copyright protection.

How Long Does a Copyright Last?

Currently a copyright is for the life of the *author plus fifty years*. There are many other parts of the copyright law artists should know about, and the Copyright Office's *General Guide to the Copyright Act of 1976* has concise details that should be carefully studied. It is plainly written in non-legal terminology and will help the photographer understand those ramifications of copyright that will be of enormous help. Write to the Copyright Office, Library of Congress, Washington, D.C. 20559. Approximate cost of the guide at this writing is twenty dollars, but prices change so use their twenty-four-hour hot line (202-707-9100) for last-minute price or information and registration form changes. Also ask them to send you Kit #107 and a free publication, *Copyright Basics* (Circular #1). The Library of Congress is a remarkable institution. They do care about creative people, are interested in helping artists stay alive, maintain and preserve great picture collections and it is a facility open to everyone. Use it.

Why bother with copyright? It is your artistic expression that is at stake here and your right to harvest the fruits of your vineyard. With most photographs used in publications there seems to be little effort on the part of the printers or publishers to steal the work from the artist. Or is there?

If no copyright law existed, would there be greater use of art material in publications without payment or effort to locate the rightful owners? This is part of what makes the copyright procedure so important, even though infringements of copyright are relatively rare. Even so, there have been too many violations of common rights of ownership by others and thus a need for such laws.

Even though there have been fewer infringement cases in recent years, when they do happen they can be momentous. At this writing the U.S. Federal Appeals Court in New York has just reaffirmed a U.S. District Court decision that upheld the copyright infringement suit brought by a California photographer (Art Rogers) against a prominent New York sculptor (Jeff Koons) and his gallery (Sonnabend Gallery), not only for pirating the image Mr. Rogers had created for a postcard, but doing it in such blatant a manner as to evoke from the three-man appeals court some of the harshest comments I have ever heard from a judicial bench. Rogers had made a charming (copyrighted) photograph of a couple holding eight puppies which was widely distributed, and Koons used the image to create four sculptures that were such blatant copies that the court blasted him (and his gallery) for piracy, arrogance and avarice. The court in strong language ruled: "The copying was so deliberate as to suggest that the defendant resolved so long as they were significant players in the art business, and the copies they produced bettered the price of the copied work by a thousand to one, their piracy of a less well-known artist's work would escape being sullied by an accusation of plagiarism."

Koons in defending himself said that the copies were simply a parody (and thus protected by federal law). But the court didn't buy that, instead saying, ". . . it is not really the parody flag that the appellants are sailing under, but rather the flag of piracy." *The New York Times* reported that the court not only sent the case back to the lower court to assess damages, but also strongly suggested to Rogers that Mr. Koons's behavior was so "willful and egregious," that he might be liable for "enhanced" damages. What the final monetary award will be has yet to be determined, but I would guess there will be substantial redress for the photographer whose work was pirated.

So the question of whether it is worthwhile to protect your work or not certainly should be answered affirmatively. Yes, it is worthwhile to copyright your best work, if for no other reason than that it makes known to the world that this work is yours . . . you created it, you own it, you are proud of it, and woe unto anyone who misappropriates or misuses it.

Who Owns My Copyright?

Simply stated, you do. The original copyright law used the term "writings of an author" which made possible the copyrighting of a work by someone other than the author. The new law substitutes the phrase "original works of authorship . . ." which leaves the door open for as yet undiscovered means of communication, preserving for the author rights to his work in future media. Who, as late as 1976, gave much thought to electronic imaging or digital transmission of words or pictures? So in essence, if you created a work it is already yours unless you did it under a *work made for hire* agreement.

Copyright infringement, then and now, is a serious matter. In both versions of the law, before any suit could be brought for infringement, a copyright had to be registered. In the old act there were no time limits set as to when a work had to be registered. Today there are. In the old act a proper notice of copyright (see page 226) had to be affixed to the work or else it could fall into the public domain *if published* without notice of copyright, even if the failure to affix the notice was unintentional. It should also be noted here that there have been many cases of infringement that have not penalized the infringer if he pleaded (and proved) he was an "innocent infringer": i.e., he didn't know the gun was loaded. This is another reason why copyright notice should be clearly and firmly affixed to all works, despite the leniency granted after March 1, 1989 (see below).

What Is Publication?

Aye! There's the rub. The definition was unclear and this ambiguity prompted the Copyright Office in reports on the 1909 act to plead for the formation of a single system of copyright to promote national uniformity. Up to then the current dual system of using common law protection prior to publication and federal statute afterwards was virtually unworkable. Yet the 1976 law continued to stress the requirement of copyright notice but did ameliorate the loss factor through unintentional lack of notification. But the "publication date" is still a critical part of the copyright process and it was not until the United States joined the Berne Convention effective March 1, 1989, that the requirement of notice of copyright was dropped. But be careful here. Copyright notice is still required on work created after January 1, 1978 but before March 1, 1989, the date we joined the Berne Convention. It is only on work produced *after* March 1, 1989, that the requirement for copyright notice on all work was dropped. There are also additional benefits accruing to use of the copyright notice. It is important that photographers who want to protect their work learn as much about copyright law as they can.

To get back to publication, is that the day the photograph rolls off a printing press or when it is displayed on a shelf in a bookstore or on a TV monitor? Let us assume that you made that transparency on January 1 and suppose it sat in your file drawer unseen until you took it to the April 1 morning meeting of the editorial staff of a magazine. You handed it to the M.E. and said, "Hey, look at this beauty. Would you like to publish it and pay me $300 for its use?"

The editor says, "Let's see it," holds it up to the window or maybe the uncorrected overhead light, grunts a couple of times and passes it to the national affairs editor. The NA editor shakes his head and says, "That's a great shot, but it's not for me," and passes it to the city editor, or the sports editor, book editor and whoever else is around. They all say, "Thanks, but no thanks," and hand it back to you. No Sale. You leave crestfallen.

You then decide to copyright the photograph and get a copy of Form VA (see page 276) which asks you among other things when the photograph (work) was first published. How could it be considered published when it was never printed, is what you probably ask yourself.

The Copyright Office deems first publication was the date you *offered* the picture for sale. It doesn't matter if the editors bought it or not. Even though the requirements for a display of the copyright notice have been changed (see Berne Convention above), it is still important to use the notice of copyright on your work to call public attention to your copyright protection. The word itself derives from the Latin *publicatus* which means "to bring before the public." To underscore the above, the Copyright Office defines publication on their Form VA as follows: " 'Publication' is defined as 'the distribution of copies or phonorecords of a work to the public by sale or other transfer of ownership, or by rental, lease, or lending.' *A work is also 'published' if there has been an 'offering to distribute copies or phonorecords to a group of persons for purposes of further distribution, or public performance, or public display.'* (Emphasis added.) The statute makes clear that public display of a work 'does not of itself constitute publication,' e.g., a museum showing vs. a gallery offering a photograph for sale."

Note particularly those lines in italics because this information is critical for photographers who submit photographs for possible sale to a publisher. Copyright protection is now afforded the moment a work is created and printed notifications are reminders only. But registration is still required before a suit for copyright violation can be brought (see below). Here too is the time to consider the whole "work made for hire" problem.

What Is a Work Made for Hire?

The Copyright Office defines it as "a work prepared by an employee within the scope of his or her employment" or "a work especially ordered or commissioned for certain uses specified in the statute, but only if there is a written agreement to consider it as a "work made for hire." This sounds rather specific, and it would seem to require a written document from the client using the words "a work made for hire." So far as the terminology is concerned the definition is clear. The overriding factors are the ethics involved.

Most lawyers feel, and many courts have ruled, that these terms are definite and clear and the words "work made for hire" must be used. Not necessarily so, says another authority on copyright law, who takes the position that the terminology of a document that clearly specifies the commissioning of a specific work or project can be interpreted as a "work made for hire" agreement even if the words themselves are not used. He applied this thinking to the area which might conceivably fall under the category of "collective ownership" of a work, i.e., a situation that could arise when a client *assigns* a work.

I draw your attention to a decision recently handed down by the Supreme Court which decided in favor of the creator of the work. That case was the recent landmark Reid vs. The Committee for Non-Violence (CNV) and will probably be the yardstick against which most "work made for hire" decisions are measured in the immediate future. But some lawyers, and possibly the courts, may try to circumvent the decision with the *joint ownership* concept.

In this case Reid, a sculptor, was commissioned to make a sculpture to be erected in front of a building in New York. Aside from some general ideas about what CNV had in mind, Reid composed and created the work as he interpreted it. It was finished and installed to much acclaim and indeed met the concepts of the commission. So much so that the CNV wanted to send it on tour.

Reid refused permission for them to move it. He said the work was too fragile to be moved without damage, it might not have the same message if erected in some other location than the one for which it was created, and gave other reasons. The CNV said in effect, well we own it, we paid for it, it's our property and we'll move it if we want to. That's when the case went to court.

Briefly, the Court found for Reid, citing several of the criteria listed below including direction and control of the artist (or rather lack of it), purpose of the work, and the absence of any "work made for hire" agreement.

Under the Copyright Act, the only way the assigning party can own the work you do is if (1) you are an actual employee and creating the work is the purpose of your employment, and you are subject to payroll deductions, receive employee benefits, and there is direct supervision by a superior; or (2) if you sign a "work made for hire" agreement.

This is a *specific term* used by the Copyright Office of the Library of Congress whereby you agree that you are being employed to make certain photographs (or create other art) and that for that period or purpose you are employed by whoever is paying you to produce a "work made for hire." It has to be in writing. It can't be an oral agreement, and it can't be implied. Yet some unconvinced art buyers and users often attempt to evade this clearly written ruling by applying subterfuges.

The main ploy is claiming joint ownership of a work, taking the position that since you were told to make the work to their exact specifications, those specifications constitute "direction." Under a joint ownership doctrine a joint or collective owner can create all sorts of havoc with royalty payments and secondary use fees, or use the work in areas the photographer objects to, sometimes violently.

So be careful with what you sign, and don't depend totally on the use of the words "work made for hire" as the decisive factor in determining whether your agreement is valid or not. Artists or other creators of literary works who are employees of the United States Government are exempted from copyright privileges if the work they produce is part of their job, but, curiously, their work can be copyrighted abroad.

Many of the large magazines and publishing houses who employ freelancers regularly demand they "voluntarily" sign work-for-hire agreements to cover the work they are doing, and if they do the employer does indeed own the work. Of course we all understand what the word "voluntarily" really means.

Some publishers have a benign attitude about this and say they recognize the value to the photographer of his secondary rights. They may even specify in their agreements that certain rights will be returned for noncompetitive uses or put expiration limits on the agreements, in which case ownership reverts to the photographer. It might also be noted that even WMFH agreements expire after seventy-five years, so if you are in no hurry perhaps you can bypass this problem.

Unfortunately the WMFH agreement is often a stratagem and an acquisitive power play. Many companies know well that the hungry photographer needs the immediate work and is unable to resist the power of corporate giants. They then re-use the pictures in other publications of theirs, or sell and resell those photographs to different publishers and advertisers without any benefit to the photographers.

Many of the professional societies, such as the ASMP and Graphic Arts Guild, several unions of artists and writers, trade associations of creative workers, and thousands of independent creators object to this and are fighting hard to eliminate the WMFH clause from the copyright act entirely. Several bills have been introduced in Congress but without positive results as yet. But the subject is under continuous review and the battle goes on to obtain Congressional revision and give the artist total control of his work.

This is not going to be easy, and even those who are strongly protective of photographers' rights, such as Attorney E. Gabriel Perle, formerly Vice President for Law at Time, Inc. and a leading authority on publishing law, feel that the entire WMFH question may not be settled for years to come. Perle believes that more court study is needed, but also hopes that the question will be moot in ten or fifteen years even if new anti-WMFH legislation is not passed.

When I asked him why he felt that way, he said that by then photographers would have learned many of the ground rules of protecting themselves and their work, and would be in a position through use of the copyright law to maximize the value and use of their works.

But Perle was more troubled about the legal implications of electronic imaging than he was about WMFH, because of the greater opportunity to use and disseminate copyrighted material in new images made from collections of other images or manipulation of a single image, and the ease of obtaining them. He too hoped that existing copyright law would be the controlling factor, but again felt more court study was needed.

Registering a Copyright

This is very simple. You need to obtain a copy of Form VA from the United States Copyright Office, Library of Congress, Washington, D.C. 20559. (If you are transferring the copyright to someone else, or you are trying to register a copyright for a work made by someone else, you will need a Certificate of Transfer or an Assignment of Copyright form. Some post offices carry these forms.) Fill out Form VA or GR/CP (for group coverage), enclose two copies of the photograph if published, one if unpublished, and write a check for twenty dollars to the Registrar of Copyright. Make sure *your name* is on the check. All forms should be followed precisely. Complete instructions are on each form. Fill in every space that applies to you and your work. The law specifies the use of the "best edition" of work that has been published before registration with the Copyright Office for "deposit purposes" (i.e., filing). But what is "the best edition"? For a photograph, the Copyright Office will accept several different forms as "the best edition." The Copyright Office's *preferences* are as follows:

1. *The most widely distributed edition*: This can be tricky; I ran into a problem with the Copyright Office recently in the matter of registration of a photograph made on a 35mm color slide. Knowing that the slide is a positive photograph, I thought I was being helpful to the Copyright Office by enclosing Type C prints from the slide for copyright registration, as I had

been distributing both 35mm slide copies and C prints. This started a chain reaction, however, requiring a lot of discussion with them before the matter was resolved. Was a Type C print the best edition of the slide? I thought so but the Copyright Office had its doubts. However, it was eventually accepted by them as a "best edition of the work," since Type C prints were accepted by my clients, and the copyright was subsequently issued. If you are using 35mm slides as your normal method of distribution of your work, the Copyright Office will accept high-quality "dupes."

2. Next in preference is an $8'' \times 10''$ glossy print. The Copyright Office will accept other sizes or finishes if necessary, but they must be of "best quality" to meet their needs.

3. They also prefer unmounted prints to mounted ones for space-saving reasons and, if possible, archival quality rather than the average photographic paper.

But twenty dollars per registration? Isn't that a lot of money considering how many images a photographer takes in the course of a year? To register all of them would be practically impossible and costly beyond belief. But this is not quite as bad as it sounds as you can register large groups of images for a single fee. (See page 279.)

The new (1976) law was a great improvement on the old (1909) law. There were distinct gains, but also losses. The main gain was the automatic ownership of the work by an author the moment it is created. The new law also changed the concept of authorship. The terminology was important. The 1909 law spoke of "original works of authorship" without defining who had the right to those original works. The 1976 law was more specific by substituting a definition of authorship as the work of an author fixed in a tangible means of expression. The main losses were in the creation of the WMFH morass, the fixed time in which the author was required to register a work, and the loss of automatic penalties (statutory damages) to the infringer, some of which could be very stiff indeed.

I know because I tangled with a publisher who bought a copyright-protected photograph from me for a one-time use in a brochure, and several months later ran it as a two-page spread ad in forty Sunday newspaper supplements nationwide without telling me or negotiating a fee. The old law protected me since that publisher was *automatically* liable for a $1.00 penalty per infringement, with the Library of Congress considering each printed image an infringement (with a $5,000 limitation per publication for infringements). But even so, 200,000 infringements at one dollar each is not exactly peanuts. The new law would protect me but only as far as I could prove "damages," and what sort of "damages" could I prove under those circumstances? No, I did not press the $200,000 penalty, but came to an amicable settlement which was 100 percent more than I would have received if my picture was not under copyright protection. But both laws require registration before any action for damages can take place.

Now the Copyright Law requires the photograph to be registered within three months of the date of first publication in order to be eligible for statutory damages or counsel fees. If the photographer does not register his photograph within this period, he does not lose all rights to protection, but judges may be expected to award considerably smaller amounts in case of infringements. Also if a photograph was published before March 1, 1989, and it was not registered for five years after publication, the Copyright Office will probably refuse to accept a later copyright, taking the position that your copyright expired and the photograph falls into the public domain.

One way of getting competent legal help in this area, particularly for impecunious photographers and artists, is a pro bono group called the Volunteer Lawyers for the Arts at 1285 Avenue of the Americas, New York, NY 10019 (Tel: 212-977-9270). They will not collect bills for you but advise you of your options and help you if they can. But in all fairness, since they are a volunteer group, they do need time to handle matters and if you need their services, patience is important in your dealings with them.

What Else Is "New" in the New Copyright Law?

The 1909 law listed fourteen categories, including photography, and the 1976 law added seven more that did not exist earlier. So while photography is well rooted in copyright law, it's up to the photographer to implement it by exercising his right of copyright. In the 1909 law the protection of artists was subservient to publishers' interests and the artist remained the low figure on the creative totem pole. Witness the rulings that those who paid for or commissioned a work were the rightful owners of the copyright in absence of other agreements. The new law takes almost the opposite position, i.e., in the *absence of* a specific agreement in writing, such as a WMFH agreement, *the artist* owns his work completely and irrevocably.

Awards can be made for (1) proven damages by infringement, or (2) if elected by the copyright holder, statutory damages which can range from $500 to $20,000, with awards up to $100,000 in the case of willful infringement. However, with so much of this left to the judge's discretion, filing for infringement in the federal courts can be expensive and uncertain.

I have mentioned "publication" and "publication with notice" which are critical terms in copyright language. When the term "publication with notice" is used, it means the physical notation on the photograph of a copyright notice. This traditionally requires the symbol © of copyright, the word Copyright, or the abbreviation "Cpa.," along with the name of the owner of the copyright, and the year of first publication. In the United States, any one of the above is legal and acceptable. However, only the symbol © is accepted internationally. These notices, in the case of photographs, must be applied where they can be easily seen on the photograph. In the case of a black-and-white or color print, they can be on the edge or the back of the photograph, or on a transparency or a permanent slide mount.

When you deliver a work for printing, you should demand, as part of your agreement, an assignment of copyright *back to you* if the work was copyrighted in the publication's name. Routinely in book publishing the publisher secures the copyright to a work, but *your contract* with the publisher should have a clause in it clearly stating that the publisher will secure the copyright *in your name*. This is important, so examine your contracts and galleys carefully to make sure this clause is in place.

Because it is quite clear that photographs offered for sale or use by a publisher are considered "published," it is important that every photograph so offered be submitted with one of the recommended delivery or leasing memos (see appendix) with all details of use and rights properly described and acknowledged.

One of the biggest sources of trouble in the copyright laws is the "fair use" interpretation. "Fair use" up to the 1976 change in the law was never clearly spelled out but evolved as a custom to be defined later by the courts.

The new regulation did, for the first time, define it (see below) and we quote the Copyright Office Guide as to their specifications of "fair use."

1. "The purpose and character of the use, including whether such use is of a commercial nature or is for nonprofit educational purposes;
2. "The amount and substantiality of the portion used in relation to the copyrighted work as a whole;
3. "The nature of the copyrighted work;
4. "The effect of the use upon the potential market for or value of the copyrighted work."

Terminology aside, what "fair use" really means is the right of people who do not own the copyrighted material to use it in their own work in a limited, non-competitive way. One way of looking at it is to measure whether by using your work without compensation you are competing with yourself.

But the real measurement of fair use also has to be based on the way your work is being used. For example, some years ago a TV network filmed a guided tour of the White House. During the filming the cameras paused for a moment on a painting on the wall and then moved on. The artist whose painting appeared on camera claimed infringement. Was he supported by the courts? No, because the fair-use principle was applied here as the network was able to prove that whether the painting was there or not they would have been doing that documentary in exactly the same way. This was considered fair use.

So be prepared for occasional unauthorized use of your work and make sure that if you claim infringement the user is not protected by fair use.

The section on the photographer's library lists books and other publications with more specific information on the copyright laws and how they may apply to you. Read them carefully and do not relegate copyright law to something that is for others.

Registering Large Groups of Photographs

Individual registration of photographs can be costly, yet some photographers want protection of virtually their total output. I do not believe the registration of every picture you produce is necessary. Good editing of your original takes should cut down the number of images you register to manageable numbers. But even so how do you accomplish it without going broke at twenty dollars per image? There are different ways of lowering the cost of copyrighting photographs. The Copyright Office is flexible and reasonable in their requirement for registering large groups of photographs (use Form GR/CP) and there are guidelines to be followed:

1. The materials to be deposited (i.e., the unpublished photographs you wish to have protected by copyright) should be arranged in an orderly way.
2. They should be grouped under a single general title such as "The Collected Photographs of _____, © 199__.'
3. All photographs submitted in this manner must have been created by the same person.

Pin up a large number of photographs on a wall, making sure they are flat and do not curl. On an $8' \times 12'$ wall you can get up to 172 $8'' \times 10''$s or almost 700 $4'' \times 5''$ contact prints. Shoot one clear black-and-white picture with an $8'' \times 10''$ camera if you have one, or on as big a film size as you can, and make two sharp, clear $8'' \times 10''$s of this group. Register this single photograph for the twenty-dollar fee, send one print for unpublished images along with completed copyright forms, and you're covered. To register groups of published photographs in periodicals, pin them up in the same way organized by month of publication (but only those covering a twelve-month calendar period), shoot and send two prints with forms VA and GR/CP and the twenty-dollar fee. The necessity for this additional copyright protection of work already published in periodicals is that though material so published may carry the copyright notice of the publisher, that copyright extends only to the way it was used in the publication, e.g., that page may not be copied, but if the individual photograph is used elsewhere, it may be difficult to prove copyright unless the photograph is protected individually. This exact situation once happened to me when a photograph I had sold for editorial use in a food trade magazine, was indeed stolen (by copying from the printed page) by a stove manufacturer who not only copied the photograph from the editorial use without permission, but then used that photo in an ad for his product in the very same magazine some months later. However, since the original photograph had already been copyrighted, the infringement was spotted and the advertiser paid a very large settlement.

This method is technically acceptable by the Copyright Office if every image to be copyrighted is clear, sharp, flat and readable. A better system is to bind large numbers of photographs in book form. You don't need a bookbinder for this; any simple method of fastening the pages of photographs securely together will be accepted for the single twenty-dollar group registration fee. However, you must follow an organized and acceptable format. You can use bound contact sheets, keeping all the black and whites together, and color contacts or 35mm dupes in another group. You can group the 35mms in countless pages of sleeves, or make up color contacts if you use negative color. The deposit materials must be the same size in all cases. Transparencies have to be 35mm mounted either in cardboard or plastic, *not in glass* mounts. Contact sheets or other deposit copies should not be less than $3'' \times 3''$ in size and not over $9'' \times 10''$, but $8'' \times 10''$ is preferable.

With color you can also supply color photocopies such as the $8'' \times 10''$ photocopies of 35mm slides that are now available at a reasonable cost from retail copy centers. The great advantage of group picture registration is that once registered, you do not have to register again when individual photographs are published later. To sum up, the general use of copyright by the photographer is highly advisable and is an element of the defense of your rights. It can also be an important weapon in protecting your financial and legal rights and interests. Although somewhat complicated, it is by no means an insurmountable task and can normally provide simple protection for the photographer without the services of a lawyer.

But remember, when there is need for a lawsuit for copyright infringement, or using the copyright law to protect your rights, engaging an attorney knowledgeable in copyright matters is advisable. The very act of copyrighting your work should inhibit most potential infringers.

One last thought on copyright litigation. The procedures for filing, registering and receiving notification by the Copyright Office can take a long time. Considering the volume that office has to deal with (frequently hundreds of applications are received in one day in many classifications), it's amazing how quickly, in general, applications are processed. But when litigation looms and the copyright has to be registered before suit can be filed, the normal time it takes to process a copyright claim can seem quite lengthy, and may seriously slow down the adjudication process. The Copyright Office has a procedure for expediting the registration when speed is essential. They do, however, request that you not apply for "expedited handling" unless absolutely necessary, as it really does disrupt the orderly function of the Copyright Office. It's also expensive, so give the expedition process a second thought. "Is this trip (to Washington) really necessary?"

Releases

Next to copyright, probably one of the most misunderstood areas of interest to the photographer is the entire subject of model releases, building releases, invasion of privacy and libel. There are some general rules and some specifics and both are subject to variations. In general, when covering a news event or item of public interest such as might be published in a newspaper, magazine or television program, model releases are always considered unnecessary. When photographs are used for advertising or "trade," usually for the sale of a commodity or service, releases are necessary.

There are blurred lines of definition because a magazine or newspaper that publishes photographs is presumed to be publishing newsworthy items in the public interest. But if the photographs used are designed to encourage the sale of the magazine or newspaper, does that make the newspaper or magazine an item of trade? Probably, if the publication is being produced with an eye toward making a profit. So again taking into consideration the cross-over problems, let us look at the whole release question in general, and the incredible case of *Arrington vs. The New York Times* (see below).

Photographers and users of photography have always had to walk a tightrope when it comes to publishing freedom, the Constitutional guarantees of the First Amendment notwithstanding. Just as we thought that all bases had been covered as far as releases were concerned, a new threat arose to that freedom which sent chills throughout the entire nonadvertising publishing industry.

The case threatened the very existence of every freelance photographer and photo agency doing business in the state of New York. And since New York is the seat of most American publishing, it was a serious threat indeed. In the opinion of a number of leading attorneys in the publishing field, it produced one of the most bizarre, unclear and confusing decisions ever handed down in a publishing case.

Briefly, a prominent news photo agency was assigned by the Sunday *New York Times Magazine* to produce editorial photographs for a story on middle-class black people. They did so and one of its photographers made a photograph of a black businessman walking in the street carrying an attaché case. No release was obtained, and in fact the photographer did not even know who the man was, since the photo was made with a long lens on a crowded public street. It was used as the cover. There was no identification of the person and no pejorative remarks of any sort were made in the captions or the text.

The man in the photograph sued the *Times*, the photo agency and the photographer for a huge sum, claiming an invasion of privacy even though he was on a public street at the time he was photographed. When the case went to trial, *The New York Times* was separated from the suit under the

First Amendment of the Constitution (which includes the Freedom of Press clause) but then came the "zinger." The judge and subsequent appellate courts found for Arrington. They ruled that the photographer and his agency, by selling the right to reproduce that photograph, sold it for the "purpose of trade," thus putting it in the same category as an advertising photograph used in the sale of some object or service. And the use of a photograph for the "purpose of trade" *does* require a release.

Under all established procedures, mere publishing of a photograph made in a public place and in a news context by a bona-fide press organization, did not require a release. Yet the judge ruled that such a photograph made by a freelance photographer for the same purpose would require a release. Nor would the judge clarify why the same photograph, if made by a staff photographer of the *Times* and used by them in this situation, would *not* require a release.

The implications of this ruling if allowed to stand were tremendous. Theoretically anyone who attended a football game, perhaps with the "wrong" person, and was inadvertently photographed seated in the stands by a freelance photographer using a 2000mm lens focused on the fifty-yard line, would be able to sue for invasion of privacy. Yet if the same image was made by a staff photographer and then published, there would be no such right. This ruling struck terror in the hearts of all photography suppliers and users, and could be interpreted as applying to artists' work appearing in publication. One prominent editor in a burst of gallows humor, referring to the Freedom of Press statutes, said, "There goes the neighborhood."

For once there was unanimity between the majority of the professional journalistic societies and major news and broadcast organizations. They had a common hope of overturning this strange decision, which if unreversed could put every photo agency out of business and shut off a large part of the supply of photographs used by the major publications. Ad hoc committees were formed, money was raised to fund legal appeals to the Supreme Court, and hysteria reigned.

Fortunately cooler and wiser legal minds convinced the ad hoc committee that even if the huge sums necessary to pursue an appeal to the Supreme Court were raised, there was no assurance that they would reverse the lower federal court. In fact, statistics on such reversals were not encouraging. The law firm suggested other approaches which were then pursued.

The end to this cliff-hanger tale came when a bill was passed by the New York State legislature exempting the sale of rights for news photography from the "item of trade" concept. But since it was not retroactive, defendants in the Arrington case were still stuck with the judgment. I have since been told that Arrington dropped his claim.

Before the matter was resolved, and this took a considerable amount of time, the ASMP attorneys suggested that a special clause be added to all delivery memos and invoices to protect photographers from being judged as co-defendants to any suit against publishers using their photographs. It read: "Client will indemnify Photographer against any and all claims and expenses, including reasonable attorney's fees, arising out of the use of any photograph(s) unless a model or other release was specified to exist, in writing, by Photographer. Unless so specified, no release exists. Client will also indemnify Photographer against any and all claims and expenses, including reasonable attorney's fees, arising out of the use of any photograph(s) that exceeds that granted by any releases provided by Photographer." (A rubber stamp will do fine.)

So while the necessity for this clause is moot in New York State, it is a good idea to use it anyway because not all states have adopted the provisions of the New York legislative changes to the general business law which was used in the Arrington case.

What Is a Release?

A release is exactly what the word implies. It *releases* the photographer or his agency from liability for the use of the photograph in whatever item of trade or communication the picture is used. A release is always needed when there is an advertising or commercial use of the pictures, and a release is generally not needed when news value is the purpose, especially if the picture is made in a generally accessible public place. Also, as discussed previously in the editorial situation in Kentucky, where there was clearly no advertising or trade intention for the use of the pictures, releases may be obtained in order to avoid legal harassment by a third party.

What constitutes invasion of privacy is a most frequently misinterpreted issue. How does one define permission to use a photograph of a person or a building? How many times has a camera been pointed at someone who says he will sue for "libel" if the picture is used? Remarks like this should not be given a second thought. Libel means making a statement that is untrue and thus damaging to someone's character or reputation. If you poked a camera under the window shade of someone's apartment and made a photograph of the people in the room, that would most certainly be invasion of privacy, but if you photographed some man in a theater or nightclub and it turned out that the woman with him was not his wife, you have not committed either a libelous action or an invasion of privacy. If you used the photograph in a news item, there still would be no course of action for those photographed . . . if they were photographed in a public place, involved in a public event. If the photograph of someone at a nightclub table taking a drink was used as an ad for a certain brand of liquor, that would be an invasion of his privacy requiring a release, but not libel, so long as you didn't alter any facts. But you would be responsible for using the photograph without permission. If you trespassed into a situation, that would be invasion of privacy and a release would be required, but if you were in a public place or even in a private area with permission to be there, it would not be trespassing.

The intent of the use is critical, however vague the lines of definition are. I mentioned earlier that if a photograph of a person is used in an advertisement, a release must be obtained for the use of that photograph in that manner. Yet even this comes into conflict in some cases with the "fair-use" principle (see pages 278-279). In a well-known case, a photographer for a national magazine made a picture while on private property, a resort, and without specific permission of the property owner or the person photographed. It was a picture of a woman lying under a palm tree at a beach some distance from the camera. The simple travel-type photograph was meant to illustrate an article on this resort area. When published, the particular picture was printed very small, about 3″ × 3″, and with no possible identification of the woman or the resort. Simultaneously an ad was prepared by the publisher's ad agency, touting the article and using this photograph, but in the ad the picture was enlarged to almost a full newspaper page size. When blown up, it appeared that the woman was a known movie star. Her agent sued, claiming the use of her picture for advertising (an item of trade) in the magazine was an invasion of privacy.

The case was dismissed on the "fair-use" basis; that is, the photographer did not know who the person was and that picture would have been made at that beach anyway and published whether there was anyone in the picture or not. No identification of the woman was made, and there was no attempt to capitalize on the fact that she was a famous personality. So if you get in trouble inadvertently, have your attorney examine the issues closely to see if the fair use concept can be applied.

In selecting a proper model release (see the appendices of this book for samples), you must consider a number of things. There has been litigation concerning advertising photographs when the model or photographer has charged that the pictures published were not for the uses intended at the time they were made. In one well-publicized incident, a model posed for an advertising photograph reading a book in bed. The client was a publisher and the picture was intended to stimulate the sale of books. There was no problem or litigation with the ad that was produced.

However, the picture was subsequently sold to a bed sheet manufacturer and, with some suggestive overtones added to the copy, was used to promote the sale of sheets. The model objected, sued, and won her case on invasion of privacy grounds, because the second ad portrayed her in a derogatory manner. She won her case even though she had signed a "broad-form" release giving the photographer and agent the right to "use the photographs for any purpose." The court ruled that it was clear that the model in this case did not intend to allow her photograph to be used in this suggestive manner and felt the ad did cast her in an unfavorable light.

Releases can be written precisely to protect the photographer against this kind of negative reaction, and if you feel you are getting into situations like this, it might be wise to talk with a publishing attorney to determine what your model releases cover in the way of secondary sales. If you are doing a straightforward piece of photography, even though secondary sales are contemplated, you should have little to worry about. But even though everything you have done is legal and correct, you will often have no control over what some third party may have in mind. You should protect yourself by specifying that the reproduction rights are sold *without release rights* to the secondary buyer and that you will be held harmless in any action incurred that may arise due to the buyer's use of the photograph.

Funny things happen too, except they may not be so funny with the principals involved. With the expertise on releases a matter of routine knowledge to advertising agencies, one wonders how a major agency got in deep trouble by using an unreleased photograph of a recognizably famous chef in an ad (in Europe) for a popular hamburger chain. The chef didn't like it, and at this writing it is before a court in the Netherlands.

I also know of an author who, when assembling a book under contract to a major publisher, purchased publication rights for a photograph he wanted to use editorially. The photographer granted a general release for editorial rights and also included "publicity rights." The picture was used, fully credited, and there was no complaint from anyone. Unfortunately, the publisher then ran an ad for the book, using this picture among others. The photographer demanded more money for the use in the ad, not from the publisher but from the author.

He in good faith asked the publisher for this money but the publisher refused, claiming that the "publicity rights"granted in the release were the "same as advertising" and that they would not pay an additional sum.

The photographer threatened to sue the author, who consulted his lawyer. The latter reaffirmed the long-accepted trade custom, that publicity and advertising are *not* the same, and are *not* interchangeable, and suggested that the author refuse to pay the photographer, further suggesting the photographer seek redress from the publisher directly, since the author had nothing to do with the publishing of the ad. It is also well-accepted trade practice that in *any* publication it is the publisher who is responsible for the content of the publication, not the editors or authors. However, the photographer refused to deal with the publisher, and continued to harass the author, even though he had no legal responsibility in the matter. But in order to avoid the cost and nuisance of defending a lawsuit, the author eventually paid the photographer out of his own pocket.

The whole mess could have been easily avoided if either one or two options had been exercised by the author. If the release had been written more clearly in the first place to permit advertising use of the photograph, the photographer would not have been able to demand an additional fee, and would have probably been most happy to see his picture used in a promotion that might have brought additional work to him. Failing that, if an extra fee had been stipulated for advertising use, the publisher would probably not have used the photograph in the ad at all as he had several hundred others of equal quality to choose from without extra fee. Furthermore, if the author had stood his ground, he could easily have been separated from the case, as he obviously was not the publisher of the ad. Using the first option would have been infinitely easier and simpler. Be aware of this kind of nuisance claim and be certain that releases are drawn accurately and clearly.

Building releases can be tricky, and there is no real body of law on whether they can be demanded except in advertising use. Even here the rulings are unclear and can often be protected by "fair use." I had a curious situation develop when a prominent photographer (and friend) leased one of my aerial photographs of a section of a city in which a well-known building was pictured among thousands of others. The other photographer was doing an ad for an elevator-manufacturing company that had supplied the elevators for that building, and my photograph was used as part of a composite photo prepared by the second photographer, who incorporated the exterior of the building. When the ad ran, I received an irate phone call from the building owners, who threatened to sue me and the other photographer for including their building in the ad. I defused the problem by pointing out that I had not prepared the ad and furthermore that the use of a picture of their building in a mass of other buildings made in a public area would not be interpreted as improper, especially as I had made the photograph long before the ad was even conceived. So you see, photographers can be embroiled in situations not of their making and for which they should not bear any responsibility.

What is the situation involving private property in an ad? This has to be dealt with carefully, and probably a good part of any legal action will depend on the words used in the text. The mere showing of a building in a public place without comment cannot be considered either libel or an invasion of privacy by the photographer. It is up to the producers of the ad to obtain the necessary building releases and assume responsibility for the ad copy.

Interiors of a privately owned building might present other problems, but logic dictates that you would not be inside a private building without permission to make photographs for advertising purposes. If you sneaked into someone's property to make photographs without permission for editorial use and were caught in the act, the legal problem might be one of trespass and invasion of privacy, but probably not if you shot the building from across the street or from an airplane.

The same goes for other private property photographed for advertising. Use standard property releases and also remember that the new copyright law will protect you because you own everything you shoot except WMFH or those images with secondary use restrictions. You need not seek permission to use a photograph you made from whoever commissioned you, except that it might be good public relations to ensure that the secondary use of a photograph is non-competitive with the commissioning party.

This is not restricted only to advertising use. The whole area of libel and invasion of privacy extends across a broad area of photography including the editorial world. It even involves free photographs distributed by a government agency if the persons in the photographs object to the editorial context of their use. Once during FSA days, a photographer made a picture of a poor family in the doorway of their cabin in a poverty-stricken area of the deep South. The caption, written by the photographer and affixed to the print, simply gave the date and location and was limited to a statement of the essential facts, "Farm family in the doorway of their home in west Texas." The picture was used by a magazine in an editorial attack on the very same government program that provided the photograph. The magazine caption added pejorative comments about the family and clearly offered editorial opinions. The family sued the magazine, the government agency, and the photographer. The latter two were quickly separated from the case because they hadn't said anything in the way of editorializing about the family, and viewers could form whatever opinions they wanted from the picture. There was clearly no libel or invasion of privacy. The magazine did have the responsibility for what they said editorially about the picture, and for their subjective remarks about the family, and the publication was held responsible for its comments.

So even if a release has been signed, a release itself does not carry the right to abuse, degrade or otherwise subject anyone to ridicule or cast them in any other unfavorable light. This question arose with the publication of some historic documentary photographs that clearly identified some families as having been poverty-stricken when the government agency made those photographs fifty years ago. The question now is, does the publisher have the legal right to publish photographs that the subjects might now consider degrading because their status may have changed over the fifty-year period? This has not yet been resolved in the courts but it does present a perplexing question of ethics to be considered by the photographer who may attempt to market pictures of this nature.

Trespassing for the purpose of making unauthorized photographs presents certain legal questions that at best are confusing. There is no question in the minds of some attorneys that photographing on private property without the permission of the owner is an invasion of privacy even if the premises are open to the public, as a restaurant or shop might be. One attorney suggested that photographing the owner of a shop on the street in front of his building, if the building is clearly recognizable, might also be considered an invasion of privacy, even if an editorial purpose rather than advertising is intended.

First Amendment rights of freedom of the press do not negate the rights of personal privacy within the confines of one's private property, and news photographers should be aware of this. When a TV or a photographic crew practicing the new form of "journalism by confrontation" descends on a businessman suddenly and without warning in the hope that he will become flustered and say or do something improper, it has been held to be an invasion of privacy by a court in New York. Does this concept protect against the use of a long lens to shoot onto private property from a public way? Probably not, but it's still a gray area. While there may be some justification for using this kind of photograph in news journalism, there is no justification whatsoever for using pictures made under these conditions for advertising or trade purposes.

So it is back to basics here. It is the intent as to how a photograph is to be used that must be the deciding factor on releases. How you handle the legal questions arising from these intentions is the critical concern. The release is a protective device, but it is not foolproof or all-encompassing.

One final thought. When a minor is involved in a photograph, the signature of the minor is usually worthless. Therefore it is imperative to have any releases involving minors signed by their parents or legal guardians.

Insurance and the Photographer's Other Responsibilities

What is the photographer responsible for? Like any businessman, he has to cover all the aspects of doing business in his own state. In addition to dealing properly with copyright and model releases, he may also be liable for special actions resulting in physical damage to property, getting hurt on the job or creating some condition where someone else gets hurt. Much of this boils down to what kind of insurance the photographer carries.

Under most state business laws he has to carry insurance on his staff, if any, liability for any damage he may incur in the course of doing his job and proper insurance on the equipment or property he borrows or rents or uses on location. Under other laws he may or may not have to contribute to various state and federal unemployment insurance, medical insurance, disability and worker's compensation programs. In my small shop in New York in 1992, I pay about $5,000 a year for all forms of insurance, from camera floaters to general liability policies to cover accidents, such as when I cracked the plastic bubble on a helicopter or a tool that fell out of a window. This does *not* cover my personal auto insurance but does include commercial vehicles such as trucks, platform equipment, station wagons, location trucks and so forth, rented and used on the job. Regarding car and truck rentals, read the fine print on the back of rental contracts. You may think you are covered by credit card insurance, but often you are not.

In addition to the standard business policies mentioned above, there are several coverages peculiar to photography that you should consider:

Camera insurance: "Floaters" or "all-risk" or "marine floaters," as they are variously described, protect the photographer against loss or damage of his equipment, wherever it may be at the time of loss. The most common is the policy that will pay you a stipulated amount for your lost, stolen or damaged equipment. The amounts are based on equipment costs or replacement value. These values must be constantly updated to take into account such factors as inflation, wear and tear, and the availability of replacements, whether new or used. Photographers should keep a careful eye on the market value of their equipment. For example, one series of Leica camera manufactured in 1965 and long out of production now commands a price of five to six times the original cost, not because it is a collector's item, but because in the eyes of some photographers a comparable camera has never been manufactured. So if that camera is lost, and the photographer feels he may die a slow death without it, he may have to pay through the nose to replace it. Insurance policies should reflect those increased values rather than simple depreciation deducted for age, wear and tear. Note that some companies retain the option of replacing lost equipment, and you must be careful of what you accept as part of your contract with an insurance company. Not all lenses or cameras are alike in quality, even if they are of similar manufacture, and in your contract for coverage, if the insurance company retains the option of replacement, insist on a proviso that the replacement must be of equal quality to the item lost. Lens quality and camera construction and operation can be checked by any first-rate camera repair facility. My camera floaters in 1992 cost slightly under 4 percent per $1,000 of valuation, so a photographer with about $10,000 worth of equipment would be paying approximately $375 to $400 per year.

If you are running your own studio or processing operation, special equipment should be insured. Water processing, refrigeraton, filtering equipment, temperature and humidity controls and other systems should be itemized on the policy. They can all be protected through standard fire, theft and casualty coverages, but special equipment should be carefully itemized.

Film and Negative Insurance (on the job). The movie industry some years ago developed a "raw stock" insurance program that protects producers from accidents during field production or actual damage to the exposed raw stock (film). The ASMP, in conjunction with an insurance underwriter, has developed a five-point program for still photographers called PHOTOPAC that has similar if not all the protections of the raw stock policy. Note, however, that some of the elements may be covered by other policies the photographer has, so if you opt for the PHOTOPAC, be sure to double check your other coverages.

The basic elements of PHOTOPAC are:

1. Equipment: usual camera floater-type insurance.
2. Props, sets, wardrobe: protects against accidental damage but not against theft.
3. Extra expenses due to delays caused by accidents on the set.
4. Property damage liability: standard third-party damage liability also protects against lawsuits by third parties damaged.
5. Negative film, faulty stock, camera and processing problems: does not cover photographer's goofs, but almost everything else.

Negative or Transparency Insurance (Valuable Papers Coverage). This is tougher to cover and most photographers don't bother with it because premium costs are high and the individual return per lost image is low. The only protection one can buy that makes sense is large-scale coverage on an entire collection of work, i.e., as much as a million-dollar policy on a collection of 50,000 negatives or transparencies. Each individual negative or image would be worth only $20 in this case (for insurance purposes only), and the loss of a single picture or even a few would not be important enough financially to justify filing a claim. However, if you had the entire collection covered, even with a deductible for partial loss, and your entire studio burned or was largely destroyed by a disaster, then a blanket policy on your lifetime collection of work would at least give you some means of attempting to rebuild your files.

The safest way to protect photographs that have to leave your studio is for the client to assume the risks involved, as specified in your leasing memo, and his responsibility is automatic if he retains the pictures under the requirements of the memo. Most publishers and printers carry a form of "valuable paper insurance" that specifically covers lost or damaged artwork. Therefore if they do lose your material, regardless of how they respond to you, your leasing memo is a valid contract with them for the safety of the photographs and it is highly likely that they are insured against loss. As for damages to someone else's property, the multi-peril policies mentioned below will cover most situations. Make sure your policy specifies that your general liability policy will cover the property of others for any reason. Otherwise, in the event of a claim, the insurance company may take the position that they will protect you only if your negligence is involved. If you do damage or lose someone else's property and there is no negligence on your part, they may be off the hook and you can get stuck. So be sure you cover *all bases* with your broker when you discuss these policies.

Liability Insurance. Can the photographer be sued? If you are a staffer, your employer assumes the risk for any damage you create in the field. If you are a freelancer, that's another story, and you must be adequately protected—and you must also protect your client.

What kind of special insurance do you need? This will vary from state to state and will also depend on what kind of photography you are doing. If it is general commercial work that may take you to a couple of dozen plant locations in the course of a year and may include some high-risk areas, probably the best form of insurance you can carry is something generally known in the insurance trade as a "special multi-peril" policy. This sort of policy is not very expensive and the one I carry covers me for up to $1,000,000 of general liability, plus a number of other coverages ranging from my own office equipment to medical payments and other losses. This particular policy cost me about $500 per year in 1992. Of course, the premiums will vary with the total coverages requested, but I have found that $1,000,000 is a highly acceptable amount of protection. If I need something special for a particular job (such as covering a sea trial of a $50,000,000 tanker), I purchase special insurance and add it to my general expense for the job. But operating normally, I do not anticipate doing more than $1,000,000 worth of damage to anything on any job I am on, and short of setting fire to a multi-million-dollar oil refinery I feel I am covered for most eventualities. But you never can tell.

Once, just before taking off to make aerial photographs of a huge oil refinery for an annual report, the plant superintendent stopped me to ask how much insurance coverage I had. I told him I had taken out a special $20 million dollar policy, but he snorted and said, "Twenty million? That's nothing. If you set fire to this refinery it would cost $500 million to replace it." All I could answer was, "Well, in that case take it out of my salary at $50 per week." But I did promise to stay on the perimeter of the plant (which is where I had planned to shoot from anyway) and took off.

When I apply for a street permit to shoot in a public place, the city agency usually accepts the $1,000,000 policy as adequate coverage against most situations. If you feel that is not enough coverage, discuss it with your broker.

There are a few other policies you might consider holding. If you do a lot of aerial photography (as I do), you should have the same policy offered to professional pilots or anyone else in commercial aviation who has to fly often in nonscheduled aircraft. This policy is important if you fly on government aircraft for nonmilitary purposes, as in order to fly on those planes you usually must sign a waiver absolving the government of responsibility.

I was once scheduled to fly on a government plane and had signed all the necessary waivers. Yet my authorization to fly was cancelled at the last minute. Why? I was given unsatisfactory answers but finally one official told me that probably the government couldn't make the waiver stick and was really afraid of its liability in case of an accident. So the easiest way to get out of the dilemma was to cancel the flight authorization altogether. Keep this in mind when dealing with government or private air transportation and double-check your own protection.

Health and Accident Insurance. Other policies worth considering are health and accident policies. Sometimes it is difficult for the freelancer to get adequate coverage at reasonable rates, but if you are a member of professional groups such as the ASMP or NPPA your membership makes you eligible for protection at group rates. For the freelancer, disability policies are very important, since if you get hurt on the job you will not have any sick leave or worker's compensation to protect you and your family. So get the best possible coverage you can find, and remember that in the case of membership in professional organizations, the savings you make in group policies may very well offset your membership costs in the organizations.

The question of coverage for employees in the field should also be studied. If you have a staff in a studio or even in the field, your employees are usually covered by your regular workers' compensation policy. But if you go out to some area away from home base and hire someone to act as an assistant, gofer or chauffeur, and he or she gets hurt on the job, what then? Under most state laws you would be liable if you did not have proper worker's compensation unless you could prove the "independent contractor" status of the person you use. But you can't always get away with calling everyone you hire an "independent contractor" if they work with you on a regular basis. If you hire someone who operates under your direction, you are an employer and the worker's compensation boards will not consider it any other way. The only way casual help can be legally considered independent contractors is if they are engaged only on this basis. If they have their own letterheads, invoice for their services, have a local base of business, and conform to the general business practices of their own state, they will be considered so.

How do you, as a sometime employer of a driver, electrician or stylist, protect them (and yourself)? The simplest and most direct way is to take out a temporary policy to cover the period of employment, and either terminate it when the job is over or try to work out a permanent arrangement through your broker to give you credit for the unused term of the policy until you next need help and reinstate it. Do not under any circumstance attempt to hire anyone in the field without proper protection, because if he gets hurt you will be, too. Also, by clearly establishing the independent contractor status, if it does exist, you are also protected against damage suits and embarrassing questions by the IRS because you failed to make the proper deductions and make quarterly employee payments to the IRS. With the proliferation of pension funds for even occasional labor, as in the movie industry, the status of anyone you hire must be clear.

Other Insurance. What else can the photographer be liable for other than normal business pitfalls? The specifics of photography can always open doors to trouble when pictures are not produced according to plan. Failure of delivery of verbal promises for space in publications, given when the photographer convinced his client he could do the work but did not do so, is lamentable but not actionable. Under the new copyright laws, liability for the photographer who makes secondary use of a photograph diminishes, as he already owns what he produces, and if the pictures are used improperly, the responsibility is the publisher's.

The mere act of *making a photograph* (or just pointing a camera at something) regardless of how it is used later, is in itself not illegal. (After all, you may have forgotten to put film in the camera or cock the shutter.) Only its *use may be actionable*. Even photographing in highly classified military areas does not automatically become a crime if the photographs are never developed, which might occur when unprocessed films are confiscated. An examination of most military or security regulations will show that the terminology they usually use involves the *dissemination* of unauthorized photographs. Nor does merely erecting a sign by some overzealous patriot prohibit photography and make the taking of pictures a crime. In order for such a sign to have any legal meaning, some legal statute or ordinance must be passed by an authority with jurisdiction in the matter.

While the photographer has to pay attention to and obey the laws of the country or community, he should stand on his own rights and not bow to any threats of legal harassment or police intimidation that prevent him from making or using the pictures he is legally entitled to produce. This may be easier said than done. The NPPA's *Press Photographer* frequently reports confrontation incidents between working press and local law enforcement officials at the scene of a crime, accident, or other newsworthy event. Some of these confrontations have become pretty nasty, occasionally resulting in violence and arrests. Fortunately they are diminishing because the courts have become more and more responsive to the First Amendment guarantees regarding freedom of the press, and more law enforcement officials are indeed beginning to accept these dicta.

These are the hard ways of securing one's rights. There are other methods less taxing. A reporter and I were working on an investigative journalism story on a matter of public interest (i.e., news), when we were stopped and harassed by the local police, who while not actually charging us with any offense as far as "illegal" photography was concerned, were obviously instructed to discourage us from working. Things were getting pretty sticky until the reporter reached into his pocket, extracted a small card he evidently carried just for this purpose, on which was printed the First Amendment to the Constitution of the United States, and proceeded to read it to the cops. Dumb amazement was the main reaction by the two police officers. Finally one of them shook his head, reached for his patrol car radio and called his superior. "Hey chief," he said, "we stopped those guys from _____ magazine like you told us to, but one is reading us the First Amendment to the Constitution about freedom of the press. What do we do now?" Back came the answer, "Leave those nuts alone and get the hell out of there!" The "nuts" proceeded with shooting the pictures they were sent after.

Collection

What about collecting money that is due you? Most reputable companies will pay within standard periods, such as thirty days after invoice date. Yet during a time of high interest rates, some companies with a poor cash flow will try to delay payments. Other clients, particularly some old-line advertising agencies, are notoriously slow with payment. They invariably plead that they have to bill and collect from their clients first before they can pay their suppliers, often extending payment of the photographer from 90 to 120 days. I refuse to accept this because for the most part it's untrue, as most large agencies are funded strongly enough to pay their suppliers promptly. So I pressure the accounting departments of companies that are more than sixty days in arrears. Dealing with the accounting departments (accounts payable section) is often more productive than trying to get an art director or art buyer to approve payment, especially if a purchase order has been issued — and it should be in all advertising and commercial work.

As any small businessman will attest, many large companies, particularly banks, are almost avaricious in charging high interest and late fees when your payments are slow, but when you turn around and apply the same tactics to them their howls are frequently monumental. I had to fight my way to the top of the corporate heap at one bank before I could find a responsive official and tell him that they had to pay interest or pay in full within thirty days for photographs I had made for them. He finally agreed to payment in full.

This type of activity is time-consuming and frustrating and does not make for good relations between photographer and client, but it must be done or *you* may suffer a fatal cash-flow problem. I recommend that you incorporate in your invoice form a statement that interest of 1 to 1½ percent per month will be charged on accounts thirty days or more in arrears. Some companies and the U.S. government, given an option of a tiny discount for payment within ten days, will often exercise it. I once billed the U.S. government five dollars for a print, and tongue-in-cheek offered a one percent (ten-day) discount. On the ninth day after billing, I received a check for $4.95.

Just as you feel it is the duty of companies to pay you promptly, you cannot disregard your responsibility for paying your suppliers equally promptly. If your accounts receivable are slow, you may be placed in the embarrassing position of having to stall payment to your suppliers.

Probably the least painful way of maintaining business credit ratings is to borrow on short-term notes from your local bank, pay your own accounts promptly, and repay the notes when the receivables come in. This is the same procedure followed by many large corporations. Interest rates, high or low, have to be built into the general cost of overhead for doing business. Avoid, if possible, using bank cards for credit as at this writing they average 18-20 percent interest compared with current commercial interest rates of about half that or less.

There is no truly economical way of getting around this problem. There are some companies (factors) who will buy your receivables, but usually their discount rate is so high that it is much wiser to borrow from a bank to cover your bills. You will find that, high as current short-term interest rates are, the factoring companies cost even more.

Studios in fixed locations depending on walk-in traffic for portraits and other commercial work may find a partial answer to slow collections in the bank credit-card system. Again this means paying the bank a percentage of your sales, but it may be cheaper to do this and have a steady cash flow than to be stuck with extremely slow payers or even nonpayers. I say partially as customers may not purchase *anything* with a bank card because the interest charged is currently so outrageous that it frequently nullifies the advantages of a sale price on any commodity. The bank-card system will not work with corporate customers and most certainly not in locations where there are no walk-in customers.

With this traffic you have to depend on other methods for keeping your bills moving. Since much photo work involves the reproduction of pictures, even the copyright system can be of help if the amount due you is substantial. The use of your photograph with subsequent non-payment is an infringement of copyright. There are substantial penalties for infringement, and if *willful* infringement can be proven (and *willful nonpayment* is one form), the penalties become quite severe. A problem here is that the amount of money due has to be considerable in order to make a federal infringement case plausible and worth pursuing through the courts. Also actual damages have to be proven before a federal judge can make a determination, and he can reserve his decision on a substantial redress. But the use of the copyright law should not be ruled out, and when and if the occasion arises it should be discussed thoroughly with your attorney to see if it makes sense to go this route. Remember, though, that mere nonpayment may not be considered "serious damage" by some federal judges, but the threat of copyright infringement may be sufficient to make the client pay promptly.

Another way of collecting what is due you, involves turning over your account to a collection agency. But like the factoring companies, a collection agency's fees are apt to be quite high, and there is nothing that will arouse the anger of a client, even if he is by now an ex-client, more than a call from a collection agency. But desperate needs sometime require desperate action. Even so, you should consider the costs of the collection process, and the ill-will generated, before you choose the collection agency route.

Short of a full-scale lawsuit when the dollar numbers are high, pressing of claims in small-claims courts is often quite feasible. The amounts covered by these state courts vary from state to state, and average $1,500 to $2,000 limits. There are a few booby traps to watch for. The theory behind small-claims court is that the claimant should not be forced to use (and pay) a lawyer for collection of a relatively small amount of money. In actuality it often doesn't work that way, because if you are suing a corporation in small-claims court and that defendant is represented by a lawyer, the judge may make it quite clear that you as the plaintiff had better be represented by a lawyer as well! So there goes your saving of lawyer's fees, particularly if you lose the case. Also, even securing a judgment in a small-claims court does not necessarily guarantee that payment will be made because enforcing the judgment, if there is failure to pay, can also be a time-consuming and costly effort. Still, if your claim is near the limit and you are dealing with an individual rather than a corporation, it may very well be worthwhile taking your case through the small-claims courts. Many states do provide for night sessions and the costs are minimal. So don't shrug this off without investigating its feasibility.

There are some other ways of collecting money due you. If you are a member of a credit reporting service (for which you pay an annual fee) such as Dun & Bradstreet, reporting unpaid bills to them will eventually affect the credit ratings of the companies concerned and may spur them to clean up their acts. If you are a member of a professional group, the group itself may have some machinery for expediting claims for its members or, if nothing else, a reporting system that will advise about deadbeat experiences other members may have had with a particular client.

Whatever method of collection you use, the basics are that your paperwork must be in order and the terms of sales or sales of rights have to be clear and indisputable.

Other Legal Protection of Your Work

If the movement of a negative is restricted, the chances of harm coming to it are minimized, so with decent care in handling there need be little worry about loss of an irreplaceable black-and-white negative or color photograph or color negative. It is when the original color has to start moving in the stock picture market that troubles start and multiply.

When stock picture traffic first began to grow, photographers and agencies were pretty casual about securing physical protection for their images. However, as the markets expanded and business increased, the number of transparencies lost or damaged began to multiply alarmingly. The casual attitude toward the safeguarding of photographs began to change when users were getting sued for large amounts. At this time the leasing or delivery memo began to take better form and became the transmittal vehicle for the movement of photographs between photographer and user, or agency and user. As the problems increased, some of these memos became tougher and tougher in an effort to stem the rising tide of abuses. Even the transportation companies became involved because as photographs began to move between cities the responsibilities of the carriers became more important. It took long, hard years before trade customs were established to determine the value of unsold photographs, conditions to be met before a photographer released them to a potential user, and the user's responsibilities for safeguarding and return of valuable images. Only after numerous court cases were won by photographers or agencies were certan norms established as to what a picture is worth, even when sent to a potential client without guarantee or assurance of its use. Also critical was the determination of what a photograph that *may never have been used or seen* was worth.

That issue was legally resolved in a landmark decision in 1949 (Lake vs. Railway Express Agency [REA] 98 NY Sup. II 202 NY Supreme Court). This was exciting for photographers and gave them a solid basis in establishing the value of their pictures, seen or unseen. In brief, a transportation company (REA) lost some forty machine-processed, and never seen by anyone, color photographs. The shipment was insured for $5,000, and when Lake, the photographer, claimed the amount, REA said that the amount was simply a limitation of liability on the shipment and he would have to prove the pictures were worth $5,000. This was a tough one because no one knew how many good exposures he had out of the forty-odd pieces of film he had shipped. But Lake pressed on.

At the trial the judge ruled that Lake was an established professional, and his earlier sales records indicated he could expect to sell about 45 percent of those pictures; he thus awarded him about $4,800 for the set, or about $266 each. In 1949 that was no insignificant amount of money. Today, lawyers advise against using this case as a yardstick for dollar amounts for lost photographs because a judge might use those 1949 prices, which would be inappropriate today. But the principle was established and this ruling was never upset.

Thus, a value for an unsold (and in this case unseen) image was established. Photographers and agencies became more adept in handling and evaluating materials, and they now clearly stipulate a dollar amount on the resale value of lost photographs. Note the term "stipulate" here, because in legalese it means that both sides accept as fact that this is the value of the photograph. There were earlier legal pitfalls in the terminology used in some of the leasing or delivery memos. For a long time after basic values were established, some memos stated that the client would be responsible for a *minimum of* or *up to* X dollars for the loss of a transparency. "Not legal," claimed the more knowledgeable lawyers. A client has to know what he may be liable for, so the responsibility for a fixed sum as to the value of a photograph has to be stipulated before a claim can be made for its loss.

There have been many court cases decided in favor of the photographers for lost transparencies and other photographic material, and as of this writing about $1,500 seems to be an average amount stipulated for the value of unsold rights. This is something the photographer should pay attention to in preparing his own leasing memos. At no time have I ever put a fixed value on the loss of *a piece of film itself*. When an original is lost, what the photographer is claiming is for reimbursement against the loss of *resale* income or, if we refer to the REA decision, what the judge felt was what the photographer could *expect to sell* in the years to come. The principle has stood the test of time and is a solid base for evaluating unsold rights of a photograph.

Interview
Ezra Stoller
Architectural Photographer

The star-studded system of contemporary photography has many beacons attesting to the brilliance and accomplishment of the leaders of every branch of our craft. There are great names in fashion, portraits, documentaries, news and myriad other specialties, and if the star in each group moves on, he or she is quickly replaced. That's the name of the game, but with one exception—Ezra Stoller. And though Stoller has racked up his 8″ × 10″s, and talented new people have arrived, I know of none who have reached his stature and prominence.

I immediately hear howls of protest, and the names of others are thrust before me, but I am not convinced. Maybe it's because I have known Ezra Stoller almost all my working life, have seen his photographs reproduced in the finest architectural and general magazines, and perhaps because the ASMP honored him with a *Lifetime Achievement Award*. He has taught at Harvard, been awarded an Honorary Membership in the American Institute of Architects (AIA), produced one book, *Modern Architecture*/Abrams (1990), and is working on another for photographers and architects. So I put Stoller at the top of the world's architectural photographers, and perhaps that too is as it should be.

Stoller grew up in architecture, studied it, lived it and has breathed it all his life. He took his degree in Industrial Design because he did not want to spend another year studying when he was already working as an architectural photographer. He learned the language of architecture and worked with architects, and although he was deeply interested, he really didn't think he would be a great architect himself. He said he remembered making the rounds of architectural offices where there were whole drafting lots full of empty drawing tables with no one designing new buildings. By then he concluded that he was more of an architectural journalist than a working architect.

He became so involved in his work that at his peak he was doing some 130 assignments a year—a staggering amount of work then or now. It may account for the broadness of his shoulders, developed perhaps by toting an 8″ × 10″ camera to the far corners of the world. He found working with the world's great architects infinitely more rewarding than slaving over a drawing board.

He said, "I couldn't have these feelings if I were involved in any other kind of photography. I could never be a portrait photographer because, though I am interested in people, I could never have the necessary objectivity and would forget all about the camera in my dealings with them. In architecture I have a fine sense of space, a thorough understanding of construction, and it still turns me on.

"And even when my feet began hurting at three in the afternoon, if I was on an exciting job, I'd continue working and was often amazed at how much I could turn out in a day. I learned a little jargon in school, but mostly I learned on the job, and architects began to appreciate that I took their work seriously. Architecture, like any art form, is a language.

"It's hard to separate the economics and business aspects from the esthetics and very early on I worked out a system where I could work for architects who couldn't pay much money but who needed my kind of photography. Production expenses, already horrendous, would often mount higher with weather delays. A system had to be worked out to distribute costs among all the users of photography, not just the architects who could not carry this load. So they paid for what they used, the record and exhibition rights, and the bare expenses."

Stoller got into the journalistic aspects of his craft from the very beginning, when he formed a close friendship with famed graphic designer Will Burton. When Burton became art director at *Fortune*, he brought Stoller with him. He continued to produce fine photography for them that led him into industrial assignments, pharmaceuticals, and other work.

There is similarity in the way an architect plans a building and a photographer faces his problems, and Stoller's knowledge of architectural planning led to his expertise in architectural photography. He said, "In all my work, the same architectural approach prevails because there is a strong cross discipline here. The discipline is that first you have to state the problem, and if you state it well and clearly you are already halfway home." He applies this thinking to the way he photographs. Stoller does not photograph on impulse; but carefully plans what he wishes to say. His pictures are well thought out before he takes a camera from its case.

I asked him if he talked with architects before shooting. He said, "I really don't like to beforehand because they always want to talk about their buildings. Explaining their buildings is like explaining your photographs. If you have to explain them there is not much point to them.

"On the other hand," he said, "since I am educated in and responsive to architecture, I understand it, know what to do, and what the architect is trying to say. If the building in actuality isn't too good (and after all, some jobs don't come out well) at least I know what to hide behind a tree or a bush. Above all, I am committed to what the architect is doing. I am not documenting a construction job nor am I interested in the space the editors give me, since there is little to be gained.

"Also, by understanding what the architect is putting into a building, I can, by judicious use of light, angles and lenses, uncover some things he may have given up on, and I am able to bring them out photographically."

He cited with pride a telegram he once received from Frank Lloyd Wright, who called him a "wizard" for having successfully photographed a job that Wright found disappointing. But because Stoller knew and understood what Wright was attempting architecturally and was sympathetic to those ideas, he could bring out the best features of a building and play down the less successful things.

Stoller was critical of photographers who are more concerned with their photographs than the buildings in front of the camera. In other words, he feels more often photographers are interested in making the photographs than being concerned with what the architect was attempting to say in his design. Stoller has always been aware of the spatial aspects of a building as a structure and what his photography can do for it.

He feels fortunate he began his career at the time modern architecture was coming into its own. He was trained in the classic Beaux Arts school of architecture, where "eclecticism" was the key word—that is, making effective use of things that have been done before. In architecture this is particularly true, and he feels that the whole mode has almost come full circle during his career lifetime. He defines eclecticism in architecture as "reassessing the best of the past and reworking it.

"As it applies to the architect, so must it apply to the architectural photographer. Functionalism is the key to any building. It has to express what it is doing, how it is built, and show the honest use of materials. The same things happened in photography with Edward Weston. Before his time photographers went to great lengths to produce misty scenes on bromide prints with canvas textures to imitate painting. Weston dealt with the realism of photography, and everything was in terms of the photographic medium. He wasn't trying to imitate painting."

Stoller thinks architectural photography is one of the most demanding disciplines in the photographic world. He also discussed technique, and he has strong feelings about photographers who become so caught up in "technique" that they use it to cover their own deficiencies in interpretive photography. To Stoller, photography is a tool whose main function is to document ideas. The architect's ideas are spatial concepts.

Despite his pessimism about the quality of architectural photography, Stoller feels there will always be a market for it and a chance for the good photographer to earn a decent living because buildings are still being built and architects still need photographs of them. But he warns the new photographer not to expect too much in the way of a fine showcase for his wares. He also reminds newcomers that in spite of their talent, especially if they rise a cut above the competition, there will always be someone willing to work more cheaply, so they must be on guard against loss of integrity by competitive price cutting. Stoller firmly believes the public will respect principle and quality and be willing to pay for it even in a declining market.

As for education, when he started there were only two or three schools that adequately prepared architectural photographers. He is appalled that with all the photo schools, seminars and workshops around, the proportion of fine architectural photographers hasn't risen appreciably. Part of the reason, he feels, is in the fact that new photographers won't use or don't know how to use the view camera, and even though the perspective control (PC) lenses for the 35mm camera have helped somewhat, they still cannot do the job. Stoller thinks it is terribly hard to make a good architectural photograph with the 35mm camera, and the unsatisfactory results are glaringly obvious. He says, "The smaller the camera, the tougher it is to shoot a job." He knows high operating costs are driving the $8'' \times 10''$ camera out of the architectural market because, "Who can afford to shoot and process 100 sheets of $8'' \times 10''$ color film per day, modest production for the good architectural photographer, at current prices? And if the photographer is using Polaroids as well, add another 30 percent to the daily material costs. So we have had to go to the smaller camera. There are $2\frac{1}{4}'' \times 2\frac{3}{4}''$ view cameras still being made that retain the swings and tilts, and reduce operating costs considerably but still give the architectural photographer a chance to produce decent work. The $4'' \times 5''$ monorail view camera with a 120/220 roll-film back may be even better, because the quality and variety of roll films, and ease of handling (no film holders to load, unload or pick up dust) all work in the photographer's favor." Stoller finds that though the smaller camera works quite well, it is still hard to operate, and those trained to compose their photographs critically on the ground glass of the large camera may find the smaller format restrictive.

In expressing his philosophy, he said, "In architectural photography almost more than in any other field, you have to have total control of your pictures, and retain the rights so that you can resell them. In this way you spread the cost between the architect and everyone else interested in using those pictures. And it's how the architectural photographer makes his money. But don't have any illusions about it. Maintaining an architectural file is not something that takes care of itself and runs unassisted."

The sale of architectural photography does not depend on the photographer or agent, but on the architect, who spreads the word that pictures of the building he designed are available from the photographer. This is where the original agreement with the architect becomes important, and the photographer must make certain that the architect understands what rights are granted to him. If he doesn't, the architect, in his eagerness to have his building seen in the architectural, construction or real estate pages, will try to give the pictures away, which is not profitable for the photographer. It is incumbent on the photographer to make certain that all the architect can say is, "All I own are record and exhibition rights to these pictures. I cannot sell them or authorize their reproduction. You have to contact the photographer for any other use."

So the architect, not the building owner, who seldom is involved until the structure is occupied, and not the editor, is the primary client of the photographer. If the building owner has commissioned the photographer, then he pays a fee commensurate with the contemplated use.

Architectural photography is usually divided into three pay scales:

1. *Record and exhibition*: This is usually the lowest cost (for the architect) and entitles him only to prints for record and exhibition. The photographer owns the negatives and other subsidiary rights and usually charges a day rate plus expenses.

2. *Publicity rate*: (Usually charged for commercial buildings.) This includes publicity rights for the person to whom the pictures have been sold. Publicity is *everything but paid media advertising*. Stoller was very carful to define these rights as belonging to those who commissioned the photos and excluding any third party who may have an interest in the building or its components. Special rights can be granted, as Stoller did for a professional association to which an architect belonged. He granted the association an option to use one of the photographs of a building the architect designed only if that architect won a prize in a forthcoming competition. Stoller granted this right on that contingency basis.

What Stoller is clearly telling new photographers in architecture, as well as other disciplines, is to always specify and clearly state what rights are being bought and sold.

Reflecting on the new copyright law and the "work-for-hire" agreements that are now bones of contention (see chapter ten), Stoller said he has no problem with WMFH as he does not accept such agreements and refuses to make photographs for any client that demands them. When I asked him if he recommended that new architectural photographers refuse to sign them, he laughed and said, "I recommend that no photographer sign a work-for-hire agreement except in an 'all rights' situation for which he is paid an appropriate fee." So much for that.

3. *All rights*: Stoller said there is a third scale that is simply called "all rights." If the client pays enough, he can buy any rights he wants and do whatever he wants with the photographs. But Stoller keeps possession of the original negatives. He reaffirmed his feeling that an "all-rights" agreement is work for hire. Stoller has no quarrel with this since presumably the client is paying enough to cover any potential loss of secondary sales.

When producing editorial photography on direct assignment from a magazine or other publication, Stoller works on a day rate that he says can be quite reasonable and modest, but also charges a page rate in addition when the photographs appear.

I asked him if a magazine will normally accept this, as the trade custom is to pay either space or time rates (whichever is higher), but not both. He said it was rough to uphold initially but he usually worked it out by charging a very low day rate (usually the ASMP suggested minimum). His magazines accept this because they know they are getting the best in the field and the total price becomes a bargain. I asked Stoller if he felt that the younger and less prominent photographers could command this pricing structure. He said he thought so if they charged a very low day rate as a floor for their work and relied on their skill and ability to raise the final price to a fair and equitable one.

He also pointed out that architectural photography is usually assigned a specific space in a magazine and unless the photographer fails abysmally or the printing plant burns down, the chances are the photographs will be used.

Chapter 11

Basic Equipment for the Professional

Putting together a kit of basic equipment depends so much on a photographer's area of specialization that listing recommended equipment is difficult. I refer not only to the photojournalist and the commercial studio operator but also to the in-house corporate and industrial photographer.

Equipment for the photojournalist has to be portable. Probably the most useful single invention for the traveling photojournalist is the small folding hand cart that can carry up to 150 pounds through airport corridors or tight location areas.

To properly equip the new photographer for a broad range of capability on a professional level in 1992 involves a minimum capital investment of about $7,500 for field equipment, possibly more if other equipment is needed for a studio.

Going beyond the 35mm system is essential if you accept the assessments of the leading editors we have interviewed on craftsmanship in architectural, fine arts and industrial photography, or general studio work. There are other formats that are more closely geared to specialized areas, but before plunging into them the photographer should evaluate his interest for this work and decide if those special cameras are worth their very high cost. In this group are extra-wide-angle cameras (excess of 120 degrees with some claiming a full 360-degree coverage). They can do wonders but are also "gimmicks" that must be used sparingly. Editors become bored, as they have with the fish-eyes and panoramics.

Two, possibly three different formats are basic. A 35mm system is mandatory, backed up by view camera capability, preferably a 4″ × 5″ monorail system with appropriate swings, lenses and accessories to save money over the larger 5″ × 7″ and 8″ × 10″ studio cameras. Medium-format 120/220 roll film size is optional in either 2¼″ × 2¼″ square (6cm × 6cm) single-lens reflex or the so-called "perfect" format 2¼″ × 2¾″ (6cm × 7cm), in either single-lens reflex or rangefinder types. Later, if need requires and budget allows, you could invest in such specialty cameras as the "superwide" or underwater varieties. Underwater equipment is mentioned here not for actual underwater use *per se* but for tough environmental applications. On several occasions I have used underwater cameras deep in waist-high water in coal mines and oil field swamps.

Insider: Ralph Morse

To assess the basic field equipment kit for the new professional I asked the advice of Ralph Morse, a veteran thirty-year staffer with the old *LIFE* magazine, who still maintains connections with his former parent group of publications. Morse was noted for his coverage of the space program for *LIFE*. Over the years he has developed an amazing faculty for getting his equipment to work in some of the toughest places, such as inside a space gantry used for blast-offs where he was still able to retrieve unburned film. One rumor Morse denied was that when the astronauts first landed on the moon, he was already there to cover their arrival. He is probably the most peripatetic photographer I ever met, and he reaffirmed my thinking that simplicity of equipment must be the touchstone for the emerging professional. He agreed that a wise selection of basic equipment has to be an early priority not merely because of cost but also for reliability and dependability.

"I think," he said, "the new professional should avoid the over-highly complicated automatic cameras that are guaranteed to do everything but make up your bed in a hotel room or cook a meal for you. Not only are they very expensive, but nearly impossible to service. Some are in the repair shop more often than on location.

"My own survival kit includes three 35mm bodies, seven lenses with focal lengths of 17mm, 24mm, 35mm, 85mm, 105mm, 200mm and 300mm, and a minimum of one motor drive. I recommend two motor drives if the photographer expects to do much remote work, but I caution on their overuse (see page 9). I do not recommend the use of zoom lenses for the initiate because if a zoom is substituted, for example, for three standard-lengths lenses and it is dropped on a concrete floor, not one lens is out of service but three. Other specialty lenses such as the fish-eye, or extra-long focal lengths from 400mm to 2,000mm up can come later in the professional's career.

"As a second system the $4'' \times 5''$ variable-swing monorail view camera is best. To start, three or four lenses: the 90mm wide-angle, 135mm, and 200mm are necessary. As the sophistication and skill of the new photographer grows, an expansion of his lens inventory to include the wider-angled 65mm and perhaps a few convertible lenses that increase working focal lengths to 400mm or 500mm, is a good idea. Ten cut film holders, a roll film adapter, and a Polaroid back should complete this kit.

"I am ambivalent about medium format cameras only because of the cost vs. use factor. Even though I use almost any system because of the variety of photography I do, I rarely use my own medium format single lens reflex cameras. Square ($2\frac{1}{4}'' \times 2\frac{1}{4}''$) film sizes are popular in fashion studios, but most finished photographs are cropped into rectangular shapes for publication anyway. Thus the 35mm should be absolutely adequate for handheld use, and when the superiority of 35mm Kodachrome over most 120 film (Kodachrome 64 [Daylight] Professional is available in 120) is considered, the need for the square format declines."

As the photographer's experience grows he can begin to think more about specific camera equipment, including the addition of medum format cameras. One of the best uses for the mid-size 6×7cm camera is for aerial photography. The negatives, four times larger than 35mm, are more desirable because of increased detail required over large areas, and the use of a studio camera would be impractical. Today the best aerial camera is the 6×7cm along with near rigid body, pistol-grip handles, interchangeable lenses and film backs. If you can find a used Konica Press (or U.S. labeled Omega) grab it, as it is an ideal aerial camera. It can also be used successfully for sports or other action photography. Wide-angle lenses, macro lenses, bellows extenders and the underwater rigs can all come later when there is more money to spend and clearer work direction.

Morse takes the same approach with portable lighting—simplicity. He recommends two or three portable flood lamps that are nothing more than plain sockets and variably shaped reflectors with socket extenders for possible flash bulb use. Alligator-type clamps or even ordinary sockets with reflector-type photofloods will often do as adequate a job as some of those nifty halogen rigs all neatly stowed in a fancy case, costing $1,000 and up for the set. Two or three eight-foot lightweight folding stands that can be weighted with anything lying around will also cover most situations. Larger ones (to a sixteen-foot lift) are still available for under $100. Only when the young photographer has reached the high billing stage should he think of eighteen-foot rollaway stands costing about $300 each. Steel movie light stands are useful, but much heavier.

Discussing reflectors above, I mentioned a bulb extender for possible use with flashbulbs. Flashbulbs? Didn't they go out of date with the horse-cars? One #2-type flashbulb will give out about the same light as 25 pounds of strobe gear, and it will take about thirty-five to fifty pounds of strobe equipment to equal the light emitted by one #3-type bulb. When you have to light a large industrial area, it's a lot easier and cheaper to string up eight to ten large flashbulbs than to "mule-train" the equivalent amount of electronic gear that is easily knocked over, with the resultant smashing of $300 flash tubes. Flashbulbs can all be fired in sync by a variety of low-cost boosters and adapters on the market.

It seems ironic that on the sixtieth anniversary of the invention of the flashbulb, two of the three major U.S. manufacturers of large bulbs have discontinued them, but Sylvania is still marketing a line and at this writing is continuing production. So don't be afraid to use flashbulbs for quick, cheap and efficient lighting. They are light in weight and their cost can usually be billed as part of your operating expenses, whereas the cost of your own strobes is a capital investment that is hard to recover on a per-job basis. Nor is there any cost for transporting flashbulbs once they have been used.

And a warning to those who have never used big bulbs before. Be very careful how you load them, making sure all electrical circuits are disconnected. If a big one goes off in your hand while you are inserting it in the holder, you won't die, but you will sure wish you had.

When acquiring strobe lights, think about the output and don't "overpower" yourself as well as your budget. I recommend the small 200-watt/second (battery/AC pack) strobe units with or without thyristor controls or dedicated capability. Dedication is an internal sensor built in to the camera body which controls shutter/aperture settings while nondedicated (thyristor) units require manual settings of the lens aperture. The output of the newer models are impressive indeed and that, coupled with highly increased film speeds in both black and white and color, make photography workable in a wide variety of poor light situations. The young photographer's mind should still be agile enough at this stage in his life to figure out exposures by guide numbers and leave the complete automation to those having more money or those covering hard news who may have to follow some VIP around through a variety of lighting situations and distances.

As for the larger studio or industrial strobe equipment, I think that when the need for that stage has been reached, two or possibly three 2500-4000 watt/second AC-powered strobe packs with extra heads, umbrellas and slave cells will cover most situations requiring additional light in a fair-sized studio or even in the field. Strobe units are getting lighter and better, with some delivering a thumping 6,000 w/s of power and others can be ganged up to give the sun a lot of competition.

All of the above plus a good sturdy tripod and perhaps a low-boy, one or two good meters, including a strobe or color meter if possible, should give the photographer a good base to grow on. Again caution is advised. Don't go hog-wild on new gear. Some highly advertised equipment is obsolete before you even unpack it, or if not outmoded has been superseded by more efficient models made by the same company.

When it comes to moving this equipment, Morse carries the three 35mm bodies and their lenses in one sturdy foam-filled aluminum case that he can hand-carry on board an airplane and stow under his seat. Everything else, including film, extra-length lenses and lighting gear he ships via airfreight and thus (in the United States) avoids subjecting the film to X-ray contamination. As for shipping large quantities of film, rather than carrying it Morse prefers shipping it, maintaining that if your fresh roll film is lost in travel you can always buy more at the drugstore.

The camera bag market has proliferated like couturier-designed clothes, and a variety of soft nylon, reinforced and padded bags with individual nesting compartments for lens and camera bodies overwhelm you whenever you walk through a supply house or camera store. Think carefully about ease of handling, airplane stowage and general protection, as I have yet to see a decent photograph made by a manufacturer's label on a camera bag.

As for buying used equipment, I don't unless it is a specialty item with a good reputation that can be thoroughly tested before purchase. If and when I buy a used camera or lens, I try to buy it from the original owner to get some idea of how the camera has been handled. If you find a piece of equipment that looks okay, have it tested and examined by an expert and make sure your sale is subject to its passing all tests. Lenses, unless they were abused or the coatings have deteriorated, don't wear out; diaphragms, as a rule, can be kept in working order; shutters and release mechanisms can be maintained in good repair. Electronic components are different. A thorough technical appraisal must be made before a purchase is completed.

Insider: Marty Forscher, Camera Equipment and Repair Consultant

For five decades New York-based Marty Forscher with his Professional Camera Repair Service in the heart of Manhattan's jewelry district has probably been the strongest backstop of the working photojournalist, and unarguably the best camera repairman anywhere. He is known for his great track record of innovative adaptations and repairs to some of the most complicated photographic equipment ever made. He designed and produced the Polaroid back for the 35mm camera and has been a worldwide consultant to manufacturers, photographers and photographic organizations. I have known him for years and often spoken with him at length about durability, repair and maintenance of all photographic equipment.

When I last saw him he had just sold his shop to his employees who are maintaining his tradition, and was headed for the ski slopes. He agrees with Morse about the need for a professional photographer to keep his equipment down to the simplest minimum. Citing a few of the biggest photographic names of our time—Duncan, Cartier-Bresson, Haas, et al,—he said, "The common denominator among all those guys is that they used very basic equipment, mechanical in nature when they had a choice, rather than electronic. Many of them don't have meters on their cameras. There are points to be made on behalf of each type of equipment, but the primary concern is that equipment has to be dependable. There is a direct relationship between simplicity and dependability.

"I am not opposed to technological growth," he continued, "but I find that with high-tech growth there comes a certain amount of dependency. One measurement I use to identify the professional is his familiarity with his equipment and his procedure in making a photograph. In this age of highly sophisticated technology, photographers often allow the instrument to override their own judgment, and that's wrong. Sure it makes sense to base your exposures on meter readings, but protect yourself; never doubt your judgment and give your pictures the benefit of making a few exposures predicated on your judgment. Usually you will find that *you* are right."

As for professional equipment he considers trouble-free, Forscher said, "Traditionally over the years the 35mm mechanical cameras like the M series Leicas, the Nikon Fs and F2s and the Canon F1 have been the backbone of the professional photographer's working gear. They are no longer produced, but those experienced professionals who have them are still using them. Some have had their mechanical components replaced by electronic functions. But a lot of new electronic cameras have mechanical override capability, so if the electronic functions fail, the camera is still operable at the higher shutter speeds. Cameras with a combination of both make the most sense to me."

As for view cameras, Forscher says that some of the older and most reliable ones still being produced—Linhofs, Sinars, etc., represent a standard of excellence that the photographer can rely on.

Forscher continued, "You can lay out guidelines and parameters about equipment, but the important thing to know is that you cannot live with only one camera. If you have a need for one camera, you must own two; if you have a need for two (for color and black and white), you should have three."

Forscher spoke of a photographer on a job shooting black and white and color, whose color camera jammed. "He came in and screamed at me. I just looked him in the eye and said, 'You're a professional photographer and you are not prepared to go on an assignment.' I also said, 'You can't possibly go out without the minimum of equipment, and if you need to shoot both black and white and color and you have only two cameras, you are not prepared.' You have to be prepared for the worst and from where I stand the worst always happens."

When asked where the biggest source of trouble is in the field, Forscher said, "Rough handling. But I don't want to be judgmental about this since I've seen professional photographers at work and I know it can be a very rough business. You have to understand the environment in which you work and have to take as many precautions as possible. I find that a lot of professional photographers are not adequately equipped. They are out in the field ill-prepared. They often go to Rome or Cairo or Bombay and if I or my counterpart is not around, they become frantic and phone for help. I tell them to call the biggest newspaper in town or the news bureau of press organizations like AP, the National Geographic stringers, Time-Life, etc., and see if they can get some answers."

Forscher thinks it best to hand-carry cameras on board aircraft, or at least the bodies and meters if not the lenses. The bodies are the most vulnerable and they too suffer from "jet syndrome." That is, when you put cameras on an airplane they're exposed to high-frequency vibrations and very often the screws vibrate and sometimes fall out. Every photographer should carry a set of small screwdrivers and tweezers as part of his travel kit, and every now and then, when he is sitting around a hotel room, he should check for loose screws, possibly back them out a turn or two (*do not take them out*) and put a dab of nail polish on the threads. That will lock them down permanently. Also be careful of batteries. They should *never be left in a camera*. The little batteries such as are used in electronic circuits sometimes explode after being subjected to the stress of flying, and if they will do that out in the open, think of what would happen if the explosion took place in a camera body. *Professionalism is more than being able to create a fine photograph; it also means arriving on the job with dependable equipment in the best possible condition.*

Considering the reality of working in the field, I want to add a few choice items based on my experience:

1. Never let a camera lie around in the sun without protection over the lens. The lens is a light-gathering instrument and can focus enough of the hot sun's rays to drill a hole through a titanium shutter.

2. Never leave a camera, light meter or other sensitive equipment in the glove compartment of a car or locked in a trunk in hot weather. Temperatures in these compartments can reach nearly 200 degrees and melt film and ruin batteries and electrical circuits. Also, unattended equipment is temptation for thieves. The late David Eisendrath, a well-known and innovative photographer-writer, advised that a vinyl covered locking steel cable, such as the type used for locking automobile hoods or bicycles, can often be slipped quickly through the handles of camera cases, securely lashing them together while you wait for a taxi at an airport, thus foiling the grab-and-run thieves. You can also loop these cables through the metal parts of bed frames, radiators or bathroom fixtures in hotels to inhibit theft.

3. Always carry a small kit of pocket tools, including jeweler's screwdrivers, pliers and especially a good loupe that will stay in your eye socket, or at least have a headband for it so that you can use both hands to make minor repairs. Two of the most important items I carry in my emergency kit are rolls of tape: standard "gaffer's" type plus extra rolls of black, light-proof paper camera tape available in all photo supply stores, that can be used to make a quick patch on a cloth curtain shutter (and still roll with the spindles) or seal up a cracked camera body. Include a couple of small rolls of light-weight bell wire for emergency flash or strobe hookups, some tripod conversion screws and one "vise-grip" type plier with a swivel ballhead fastened to one of the handles. This can make a marvelous and rough temporary tripod, light or prop holder. It can be clamped onto the back of a chair, a water pipe or almost anything else the jaws can span. Be careful, however, to protect the surface of whatever you clamp onto, to avoid marring it.

Rentals and Other Supplementary Equipment

It is necessary for the new photographer to assemble, for as low a cost as possible, a reliable kit of cameras, accessories and supporting equipment. There will be times, however, when you have a big lighting job and find it impractical to carry enough lighting equipment with you or don't have enough hands around to operate it; or when that specialty camera you thought you would never need is suddenly called for.

What is the answer? Rentals. There is no shortage of strobe and other lighting equipment for rental in almost every major city in the country, and if you are in doubt, a call to the manufacturers or distributors of the equipment you want will quickly uncover someone near you who has it for rent. I suggest you not go out and invest thousands of dollars in lighting or specialized equipment if you can rent it. Renting also means no maintenance or cartage headache. When you rent lighting equipment locally, you know it's going to work, or if it conks out, the rental organization is usually available to fix it or replace it. You can probably rent enough strobe equipment locally to light up a huge public hall for less money than it would cost to airfreight and deliver the same equipment from your studio, or if you are traveling to a remote place where there is no possibility of renting, then renting and shipping by air from the nearest major city would also probably be less expensive than dragging it from home base.

The same applies for cameras. If you need something very specialized, it is likely that as a professional you can either borrow it from the manufacturer's representative at no cost or rent it reasonably from professional houses specializing in camera rentals throughout the country. How do you locate them? Many are listed in the classified pages of local telephone books. In the newer photographer's reference books there are all sorts of listings for equipment rentals. A call to the nearest professional colleague in whatever organization you belong to will also probably give you a lead toward who has what you need wherever you are. Get in the habit of stuffing your ASMP or NPPA membership list into your camera case. Besides having the name of someone around to have a drink with, it may be extremely valuable for finding local assistance. Membership in manufacturers' professional groups, Nikon, Kodak, Olympus, etc., will also put you in touch with hard-to-find unusual equipment or facilitate quick field repairs.

A few years ago I needed the use of a super-wide-angle camera. To buy a new one would have cost $1,500. I did not think I would need it again for another year but I was convinced that it was the best camera for this particular job. I found the name of the U.S. distributor in the pages of a photographic magazine, called him and arranged to borrow one. In a half hour it was on its way to me by air and I was using it within six hours on a location 2,000 miles away. Rental pays.

Rental fees for specialized equipment are part of any job, and when billing for expenses you are expected to include them. This practice is not confined to commercial work but extends to every photographer who works on assignment and for that matter to every staffer on the payroll of a publication or corporation. When you are hired as a photographer, it's your talent that is being hired. It's not an extension of the "have gun will travel" philosophy. A craftsman is expected to bring his tools, but there are limits to his investment or ability to tote them. The new photographer should not hesitate to add these items to rental bills as specific expenses. It is customary for a client to pay for the use of extraordinary equipment.

Other rentals that the client will pay for are odd-ball items like a cherry picker or a rising scaffold. Do you need a high-lift platform, and the local public utility or sign factory doesn't have a bosun's chair or a snorkel truck? Try the airport caterer, whose trucks usually have high-lift platforms so they can roll food carts to the galleys of a 747, which stand thirty feet off the ground. The possibilities are infinite, but the thing to remember is that rental of extraordinary equipment is quite an ordinary procedure.

Setting Up a Good Home Base

Your home base will say much about the way you conduct your affairs. You do not want to do business with some publication or client that looks like it won't make it through the end of the month, nor do you want to give others the impression that *your* business is unstable or disorderly. Any visual impressions you make on any of your clients will be those created by you, i.e., the external appearance of your office, studio or darkroom. These tangible indications express your ability to run an efficient, well-managed operation.

Do you need an office, studio or darkroom? That depends on the kind of work you will be doing. For photojournalists the answer is probably "no" for a darkroom or studio. The business side of things can probably be taken care of in your house or apartment, with a typewriter, or a PC computer with a good-sized hard drive and legible printer, filing cabinet and a few other pieces of office equipment. Some simply rent desk space in commercial buildings; even a store front has possibilities if the rent is cheap enough, or perhaps you can share space. Photographers planning to move into commercial work will need a studio, however, as well as some kind of office.

Do you need a darkroom? If you follow Arnold Drapkin's dictum (see page 10) that the photojournalist should know how to develop and print superbly (not merely adequately), you'll find that the best way to learn is in your own lab. You can take all the courses you want at the best technically oriented schools, but the final test will come in your own darkroom. After spending hours and hours on tough printing, you may begin to appreciate the craftsmanship of the W. Eugene Smiths and other masters.

I am referring to black-and-white processing and printing because even though you should know how to process and print color, most professionals feel it is unnecessary to own a color-capable lab. There are some excellent small color-processing kits, but the necessity for computer-controlled chemistry, the heart of the modern color-processing lab, is beyond the means and even the practicality of the beginning professional. This limitation extends to the active photographer who does a reasonable volume of color work. But "reasonable" is a debatable word. A journalist who goes out for three days and shoots twenty rolls each day may think he is producing a lot, but chemicals for even sixty rolls will barely "wet" the inside of the tanks of the larger professional color labs. One major color lab in New York has a capability of running hundreds of rolls of film an hour, all precisely computer controlled for chemistry, temperature, replenishers and all other aspects of finely tuned processing. Several authorities are convinced that even the most skilled and careful home processor of color materials cannot do a job comparable to any of the big commercial processors.

The use of a color lab for professional work extends to other related services, and in the end it is wisest for the new professional to establish a good working relationship with the nearest well-equipped and competent color lab and let them do the fine processing required. With modern communications the most remotely located photographer in any of the fifty states is but a few hours away from a professional custom lab.

Black-and-white processing and printing present other problems. In spite of the wider use of color in news and general interest and specialized magazines, there is still a substantial amount of black-and-white photography being used, and editors are rightfully demanding the highest print quality. Also, many news publications, from newspapers to magazines, need the prints almost immediately, as they publish more frequently and have shorter "closing" times. So, does the new photographer need a black-and-white lab? Perhaps. Again, it depends on the circumstances of the individual. If you fit any or all of the following qualifications, you should have your own up-to-date black-and-white processing lab:

1. Location. You are more than twenty-five miles from a quality black-and-white custom lab or the local lab cannot provide immediate service.

2. You are working for a newspaper or other news-gathering organization and do *not have access to the lab at their plant*. Ditto if you are doing public relations or other corporate work and the company for whom you are working does not have lab capability or other equipment and facilities you need.

3. You are working on the local level, including walk-in trade and institutional or political clients, or as a stringer for a variety of publications.

4. You like to experiment and get the most out of your negatives and are generally dissatisfied with the work turned out by the commercial outfits.

There are other influencing factors, including start-up costs, maintenance and the need for keeping the darkroom up-to-date. Growing technology in black-and-white as well as color processing makes it almost mandatory that the photographer stay current not only with his equipment but on new processing methods and techniques.

From the outset of this book, I planned to avoid any discussion of highly technical processes or procedures, leaving that for the technical experts, but I mention chromogenic technology to illustrate the problems of keeping up with the market and the high cost of remaining contemporary. Chromogenic films are a breed of black-and-white film processed in "C-41" color chemistry and then printed normally. According to some experts this system produces superior sharpness, tonal gradation, and every other feature sought in black-and-white photography. It also appears to be particularly good with very large blowups of 40" × 60" or larger, and some experts are championing a changeover to this system, while others are ambivalent. I do not recommend any particular brand of film or type of processing but mention this only to demonstrate to the new photographer that he must be aware not only of new products and processes, but of the necessity of considering the costs of such changeovers.

There is a growing trend for using negative color stock for black and white in small newspapers. But in order to use it effectively it also requires a color chemistry, and on newspapers, even small ones, speed is essential. We assume you are not equipped for digital transmission yet. So a lab with this color chemistry capability is just as essential as one for black and white. Therefore, I feel it is important for the new photographer to establish a good relationship with the technical representative of each of the major film, chemical and equipment suppliers in his area. Most of them are only an "800" number phone call away, and when a problem arises they are only too happy to help. Since these services are free you should not hesitate to use them. Make a point of having this information handy so you can use it when the occasion arises. Don't wait for a crisis. When you are in the process of installing new equipment or a new chemistry system, discuss your new installation with the experts.

When you decide to go with one system or one distributor, you will find a lot of technical doors opening for you, from the planning of darkrooms to water systems and filtration, even silver recovery if the volume of your work suggests it might be appropriate.

The Basic Darkroom

I had spoken on this subject with the late Ralph Baum, founder and president of Modern Age Photographic Services, one of New York's oldest and finest custom processing firms, and just reaffirmed my conversations about the basic darkroom with Elizabeth Cunningham, an acknowledged specialist in the lab equipment field. The essentials of their recommendations are that a basic installation, costing approximately $10,000 (1992), a capital investment, should act as the springboard for an efficient, modest-sized black-and-white lab and give you the option of doing limited color processing and printing. The basics should include the following equipment:

1. A good sink, minimum size 42″ × 60″, with direct drain so maximum washing systems can be used. Also an extra drain outlet if installation of a silver recovery unit is planned. Baum also recommended a second, smaller sink with a separate drain for smaller-scale temperature control.

2. Four 16″ × 20″ trays, or perhaps smaller ones to conserve chemicals.

3. A temperature-controlled filtered water system with mixing valves, easy-to-grip faucets and a large visible thermometer.

4. Nikkor-type stainless-steel developing rolls and tanks with capabilities of two to ten rolls. (Installation of large, deep tanks is not recommended until volume is over forty rolls per day.)

5. Conventional hard-rubber tanks for sheet film. Recommended film carriers are standard stainless-steel holders, four to a hanger.

6. A good condenser-type enlarger with flexible capability (35mm to 4″ × 5″) and with a cold light (for sharper black-and-white images) or color-corrected light source. Some portrait photographers suggest diffusion-type heads to soften lighting, but the choice has to be yours. If larger negatives are anticipated, perhaps a used 8″ × 10″ enlarger can be acquired. A modern computerized 8″ × 10″ enlarger is very expensive. Also, critical focusing equipment and a small hand level to check alignment of easels is useful.

7. A contact printing system — either a standard contact printer or a large piece of optically clear plate glass for contacting with the enlarger.

8. Professional-quality safe lights and foot-switch-operated white lights over final fixing bath, and if possible, an electrical interlock to prevent white light when paper supply is unprotected.

9. Washing equipment with a substantial water supply close to normal processing temperature. May be installed in a non-dark area with a print drop slot in the wall of the darkroom.

10. A work table of sufficient size, at least 28″ from walls to provide access to all sides.

11. A small paper cutter.

12. A film dryer. A homemade one constructed of a steel clothes-storage cabinet with a small, well-filtered warm-air blower at the base to circulate warmed air at low speed can be made at low cost. Be extra careful of heater controls. Install full thermostatic protection to avoid melt-down of emulsions. Hair dryers can be a good heat/forced air source, but check on the asbestos insulation used in older models.

13. A print dryer. With resin-coated papers, mechanical dryers are becoming obsolete. Some photographers still prefer heated chrome dryers that can be used for either ferrotyping or matte drying.

14. Ventilation for temperature, humidity and dust control. With increasing concern about toxicity of film-processing chemicals, some reading of current literature on the subject is a good idea. Several publications are worthy of note: *Making Darkrooms Saferooms*/NPPA, *Overexposure: Health Hazards in Photography*/Susan Shaw, The Friends of Photography, and *Ventilation, A Practical Guide*/Nancy Clark, et al, Center for Safety in the Arts.

15. A slide copier or negative-duplicating equipment, handling 35mm to 8″ × 10″ transparencies and larger opaque material on a copy stand. They need not be in "dark" area.

16. Small items: chamois cloths, compressed-air sprayers, static-reducing compounds, rubber gloves and tongs, brushes and spotting colors, and a clean area for mixing and storing chemicals.

17. A refrigerator, for substantial film and paper stock supplies. (Long-range film storage should be in a freezer at 0 degrees or lower.)

Equipping a Studio

The new professional photographer must make the hard choice of whether he needs a studio in the first place. In many larger U.S. cities there are fully equipped studios for rent. Quite often the owners of these installations have extended periods of "downtime" due to lack of business or being out on location and are only too glad to rent their space on a daily or even longer basis. So do not eliminate the possibility of renting an existing studio rather than taking on the burden of trying to equip and maintain your own. Professional publications, such as the *Photo District News* published in New York, often have listings of both local and out-of-town studios, darkroom space for rent, used equipment for sale and other services.

However, if you decide to go the studio route, what do you really need? Again, Cunningham and others recommend that a modern, fully equipped studio have the capability of strobe or other artificial lighting such as quartz or even common tungsten. Perhaps a source of natural light from a large skylight, or the new roof "bubbles," might be useful if available. Also required is the usual collection of scrims, flats, overhead banks, spots, booms, dollies, extra cables, and overhead cable carriers. Add your tripods, tables, and all other supporting gear, filters, gelatins, studio lights, transformers, etc., and the total bare bones cost will probably come close to $15,000 (in 1992) considering that the list price today of just a 2000-watt/second Norman strobe unit is about $1,300.

There is other equipment that belongs in either the studio or lab: opaque copying devices in addtion to transparency duplicators, dry mounting presses and binding equipment. All of this is becoming increasingly more useful to the studio, lab or agency that has to send many copies of a single transparency to a news service or other distribution organization, or distribute multiple portfolio materials. Some agencies are even now considering the installation of color Xerox 35mm duplicators, or laser desk-top publishing capability so that nonreproducible reference prints from transparencies can be airmailed, modemed or faxed world-wide for not much more than the price of digital transmitting (or airmailing). All this and more has to go into a studio/lab operation, and acquiring all the equipment and constructing the actual space can be very costly in both time and money.

This does not take into consideration electronic-imaging equipment which I feel is still a long step away from the new photographer equipping a full service laboratory. It might be re-noted that duplicating of color via the digital electronic-imaging systems does not add generational increases. For additional information on electronic imaging see chapter thirteen.

Insider: Ken Lieberman, Color Laboratory Owner

Ken Lieberman, who has been a color processor for as long as I can remember, and whose specialty is color processing and printing for many of the top-flight professionals, spoke not only of technical matters, but more important, of his concerns about photographers and their needs.

"Ten or fifteen years ago," he said, "color photographs and black and white were shot on their respective stocks and processed acccordingly. Today, while this separation of films still occurs, there has been a tremendous shift by news photographers to use negative color processed in C41 or E6 chemistry and then producing either black-and-white or color prints from the color negative. A black-and-white photograph printed on Panalure paper has a remarkable range that is well suited for small offset presses. Also even the bigger publications are making this shift in film stocks because of the increased flexibility for the photographer and the advantage of going either way for those publications which are also printing color.

"The reason for this is the tremendous exposure latitude and the added advantage of taking that color negative and doing almost anything you want with it within size limitations. But I wouldn't want to take a color negative and make a print larger than 16″ × 20″ and expect full range. This usage is for news photography essentially, but in the commercial side we must look at the final objective of the photographer. If he wants a large color print I immediately say, shoot transparency film, the bigger the better. Since most photographers are now using 35mm, there is a wide range of excellent transparency stock such as Kodachrome or Fujichrome. I can take the slide and make an 8″ × 10″ color negative and the sky's the limit as to final print size. But if the print requirement is 11″ × 14″ or smaller, then by all means stay with the color negative.

"The startling change in recent years has been in the film speeds. Negative color is about 1600 without pushing and I want to remind photographers that when film is pushed there is an inherent loss of quality, so the old axiom of the slower the film the better the quality still stands. That is not to say that to get the best quality one should use only larger film sizes. Irving Penn, one of the world's most renowned photographers, shoots everything from 35mm Kodachrome to 8″ × 10″ sheet film, and it's all beautiful.

"The quality of color printing has improved from 'C' prints and their equivalent to dye transfers. Even the old Carbro process is coming back in a new form. I still favor the dye transfer for the best quality, and the principal purpose of the refined Carbro process is for archival use. Dye transfers are not archival except for the separations made prior to combining the colors. So the photographer who needs quality color printing does not have to look far for it.

"A lab like ours is not concerned about electronic imaging at present as the bulk of our business comes from the exhibit end of color processing and printing for individual photographers or publishers. Also we deal only with professionals who are busy and don't want to get involved with the technology of color processing and printing equipment, which now costs from $10,000 to $15,000 to install for a small laboratory. It makes more sense for them to send their work out to a quality lab. This is true even for photographers who work a long distance from a quality lab. Modern air transportation companies such as Federal Express and UPS can deliver overnight service to or from any lab in the country, so the photographer is no longer isolated.

"Video photography, where a digitalized image in a 35mm camera back can be transmitted over a phone line, is here, but is not in widespread use yet. Several experimental prototypes are being tested but the hardware and software involved are still big buck items. So we do not see a major move to videography very soon. But the possibilities of transmitting a full-color story from a remote area by phone and satellite quickly are mind-boggling.

"Though the ethics controversy over digital imaging does not involve us, we do have concerns about protection of copyright when large numbers of prints are ordered by ad agencies or other users of photography. If we receive an order for an unusual number of prints we always check back with the photographer to make sure that he is aware of the multiple print order. This is to protect him against unauthorized distribution of his work which can easily happen when many pictures are sent out simultaneously.

"While there have been great technical improvements over the years in film and film chemistry, cameras, lenses and other equipment, I feel the professional photographer needs a personal service laboratory for high-quality work, and has to build a relationship of trust with that lab. This is the lifeline for a photographer's existence and should always be so."

Support Personnel

If you have a lab, do you need a staff? If so, *how* do you acquire one? The acquisition of support personnel may require progressive steps beginning with the self-employed photographer functioning as his own lab chief, technician and studio assistant. But if you have gone beyond the beginning stages and are now generating enough business to require help in the lab, whom do you hire and what should you expect from them?

Availability of help will vary with the community. In New York there seems to be a chronic shortage of good lab people compared with the number of labs that are around. Printers and other highly skilled technicians are always in demand, but general assistants may outnumber the available jobs. We think it unrealistic to expect the beginning pro to be able to employ more than one person, at least for the first few years, though some of the bigger and more established studios employ as many as twenty persons. If the photographer gets involved in electronic imaging, then a whole new set of skills is needed, possibly beyond the capability of the photographer.

When the new photographer starts to look for a staff, he should turn to talented younger people who want to be photographers and utilize their desire, knowledge and love of the medium. There is a real advantage to hiring smart beginners to work for you. You probably will not have to correct any bad habits or practices an older and presumably more experienced person might have already developed and brought with him. But do not forget older people. They may not have the agility to jump over a tipped piece of equipment, but their experience, sagacity and age may indeed keep that piece of equipment from tipping in the first place. As for handicapped workers, remember too that darkrooms or photo labs do not require any unusual mobility or special manual dexterity.

For office help, while you probably will need someone with standard office skills—typing, computer word-processing, telephoning, filing, etc.,—it might be wise to find somebody who also has a background in art or art history or who at least has a feeling for graphics. Such a person will be of inestimable value in selecting, editing and generally working with photographs. In New York and other states, there are programs of "cooperative education" on both the high school and college levels that provide students part-time work in some specialty relating to your work. They will work eagerly and devotedly for you as part of their training program. The advantage to you is that there is either very low or no cost, depending on the program. The disadvantage is mainly one of short-term duration geared to the length of the school year.

Other part-time help should not be overlooked, either. But whomever you do hire, do it on a straightforward, systematic and professional basis. Follow all local regulations insofar as working conditions, taxes, insurance and other benefits are concerned. If your business begins to flourish and it looks as if you are going to need permanent help, don't think it is too early to look into medical insurance plans and, even though it may seem light years away, employee retirement and pension plans, including your own (see page 355). When the business person is young and first starting out, all these things seem to belong on another planet. They don't. They are all part of the way a professional organizes a lasting career and stays alive professionally long enough to enjoy it.

Organizing, Managing and Protecting Your Home Base

As for organizing and managing your office, the simpler the system you put in, the easier it is to manage. What *kind* of picture filing and retrieval plan you select is not particularly important as long as you select a good plan and stick with it, making sure it is self-expanding so you don't have to reorganize your entire system every few years. (See page 239.)

Safeguarding Negatives and Transparencies

The physical protection of your work must be an objective that you have developed early in your professional career. Although I am not talking about classification systems *per se*, the physical protection system must be a type that will be compatible with your basic filing and retrieval system because every image should be well protected at all times. Perhaps you feel you are not yet ready for fireproof and fire-retardant safes—not many of us are—but you should at least consider them; some commercial labs and big corporate picture collections indeed use these storage methods. Black-and-white negatives of different sizes should all work together in a compatible system. Negatives should all be kept in sturdy steel files. For many years I have successfully used standard 4″×6″ steel card file drawers (many are stackable) with the center divider removed to accommodate full-length #10 envelopes of negative strips.

Storage of negatives and transparencies is important. Not only are their containers important, but humidity and the tendency of emulsions to mold are critical factors to consider in planning their preservation. The cabinets should be in a well-ventilated room, and they too should be ventilated with small two-inch grilles inserted in the upper and lower back part of the cabinet, such as are used by carpenters for eave vents in house construction. Or you could invest in a dehumidifier or consider continuous air conditioning, especially if you are in a high-humidity environment.

Fire control and other preservation tactics are also necessary. Don't store your negatives or transparencies *in an area where a pipe could burst* or rain water flood the cabinets, for example. You might consider raising your cabinets off the floor on shipping pallets and covering them with waterproof material. I have obtained many pallets free from lumberyards or warehousing operations which normally throw them away. I doubt that even a heavily insulated fireproof cabinet will keep the heat of a major fire from damaging emulsions; however, an adequately protected steel cabinet will probably save your negatives from sprinkler damage.

Security systems also should be considered. It is unlikely that your negatives or transparencies will be stolen, but cabinets should be kept locked. Rigid security against general theft should be considered. With the nationwide increase in crime and the near impossibility of getting adequate burglary or casualty insurance in some areas, casual attitudes about the safeguarding of your capital investment must be abandoned in view of pragmatism. If your premises are frequently unattended at night or on weekends, a secure burglar-alarm system should be installed. There are several types of systems available, and if you live in a small community with a fairly efficient and mobile police force, the silent alarm may be the best since it will call for assistance quickly and the chances of catching the intruders are relatively good. In larger and more heavily crime-ridden areas, audible alarms that can be hooked into police systems would probably be better.

It is necessary to secure an efficient, well designed security system. With the increasing incidence of false alarms caused by inferior units, many police departments are now charging owners for those calls, or, even worse, ignoring the calls. So if you have invested $10,000-$15,000 or more in lab, studio and office equipment, the question of protecting your investment is a matter that you must consider. Also, your insurance rates will be lower with added protection. A good photocell-activated system covering about 2,000 square feet with two automatic dialers, one for police and the other for your residence, can be installed for about $2,000, depending on its complexity.

Some of your thinking on this subject should carry over to your transportation methods as well. Thefts from cars are a continuing problem. Audible burglar alarms for cars are becoming useless as so many police departments ignore them. You might prefer rugged steering wheel or transmission locks, but anti-theft devices for cars are a must. I use an electronic power cut-off system that prevents "hot-wiring." Some insurance companies allow a lower rate if these devices are installed, though the dollar reductions are minuscule. I think the best insurance is never to leave unattended equipment in autos. Consider the ingenuity of the photographer who had a heavy safe welded inside the trunk of his car and placed his cameras in the safe.

Interview

Arthur Rothstein

Photographer

Photojournalism is a lot more than hard news photography, as I once pointed out to a young documentary photographer who had been photographing social conditions in Nepal under a university grant and who was confused about the precise definition of her work. I explained that a twenty-page essay in *National Geographic* or *LIFE* that takes six months to shoot is just as much a part of photojournalism as a photo coverage of a fire or a hurricane. Documentary photography as practiced by Lewis Hine or Jacob Reis, and honed to a fine art by the Farm Security Administration (FSA) photographers, is also very much a part of photojournalism.

Arthur Rothstein, a forty-year friend and colleague, who, sadly, died in 1985, started as a documentary photographer with the FSA, went on to be a photographer and technical director of photography for *Look* magazine, and later an editor at *Parade* magazine. He was the classic example of how a photographer evolves through various opportunities in the photography world.

"I was a photographer and a member of the Camera Club at Stuyvesant High School in New York City," he told me. "I went to Columbia College and founded the Camera Club there. The photography I did in my junior and senior years helped pay my tuition. It was there that I met faculty members Rexford Tugwell and Roy Stryker. Tugwell was a professor and Stryker an instructor in the economics department, and I got to know them well. Tugwell became a member of President Roosevelt's 'Brain Trust,' becoming his Undersecretary of Agriculture and head of the Resettlement Administration (RA), later renamed the Farm Security Administration. Tugwell brought Roy Stryker in to direct their Historical Section.

"Stryker loved the use of photographs and in his work at Columbia got to know Lewis Hine and became familiar with Jacob Reis's work. He used photographs from many sources and became knowledgeable as a picture researcher. When he came to Washington he persuaded Tugwell to let him produce a historical record of the RA in photographs. Not knowing anything about photography and aware I was a science and chemistry major who was also a good photographer, he asked me if I would work with him in Washington.

"As soon as I graduated in June 1935, I became the first photographer hired by the RA. That was the beginning of my career, but not my original aim. I had no intention of being a photographer but had planned to study medicine or get my Ph.D. in chemistry to go into biological research. It was the height of the Depression. My folks didn't have much money, and I didn't know where I would get the money for tuition or to sustain myself. So when this job came along it was a fantastic opportunity and I thought I would make enough money to go back to school.

"In those days it was a very good job. I got thirty dollars a week, two cents a mile for the use of my car, and five dollars a day for food and lodging. My first job was to set up the lab. Nobody knew much about 35mm film—that was a totally new concept. I was a pioneer Leica user and when I set up the FSA lab, I also recruited lab technicians who knew how to use a Leitz 35mm enlarger. We also had good printers for the larger negatives, and by October I was ready to go out on assignment.

"My first assignment was to photograph the people being resettled in the Blue Ridge Mountains of Virginia, and I photographed them mainly with a Leica camera and got some of my best pictures. From that point on, I traveled the country, and one of the most famous pictures in my whole life was made very early in my career.

"It was the dust storm photograph, and it put me at a great advantage, because some photographers go through their entire careers and don't make any famous pictures at all. Other photographers make their most famous pictures at the end of their careers. I made mine in the spring of 1936, and it was widely published, much appreciated and highly regarded.

"So after barely starting work I had become a famous photographer, and it became impossible for me to drop this profession. I stayed with it and I've been a photographer ever since. I don't regret it. It has been a very rewarding and satisfying life and I think that I have done some good with my photographs. I have benefited from being a photographer in many ways. I think because I was a photographer I was healthier, both mentally and physically. It was the best thing that ever happened to me. I stayed with Stryker for five years.

"In 1940 I joined the staff of *Look* magazine, which was ony three years old. But World War II came along and I went into the Army and OCS, Officer Candidate School. From there I went overseas as a photographic officer, serving in China, Burma and India. At the end of the war I was the photographic officer for the China theater and was stationed in Shanghai. I earned three battle stars, some medals, and I took a big convoy, as its commander, over the Burma road. I had a lot of adventures and fortunately I survived everything—being shot at, and a variety of diseases, some of them pretty bad. I was in Shanghai in 1946 when the U.N. was mounting a relief effort there, and they needed someone to document their activities. I resigned my commission and worked for them for a short time, which was a good experience.

"I came back to New York in 1946 and was offered two jobs, one on staff for *LIFE*, and a chance to return to *Look* magazine by Dan Mich, who said that if I came back to *Look* I would soon be director of photography. With *LIFE* I knew I would be one of thirty-six photographers, and though it was tempting to work for *LIFE*, which was bigger and more prestigious, I went back to *Look*. It was a good move, and I was able to build up a staff of fine photographers, many still my good friends who have become successful. I stayed with *Look* until it folded in 1971. After that I worked on some special projects and then became an associate editor at *Parade*, where I am picture editor and can also do photography."

He told me *Parade* had its limitations as far as space was concerned, but the limitation was more than made up for by its immense circulation, the largest in the world — 22 million every week at that time. No other publication has that kind of circulation, and one picture in *Parade* was seen by millions and millions of people.

When I asked Rothstein what he liked and what he didn't like about photography, as compared with twenty years earlier, he replied, "I think twenty years does not go back far enough. Let's take the period of the 1940s to 1960s. Then there were fewer photographers. Photography was not easy — professional photography of any kind was, and is, hard to do. You had to be extremely skilled and knowledgeable to be a good photographer, but now technology has created cameras and equipment that make it very easy to take pictures. This is not to say it has become easier to know what to photograph, or easier to know when to release the shutter. Productivity has increased and it's also technically possible to take more pictures in a short time. As a result we now have many photographers without strong training or high skills. Of course it still requires a certain amount of talent, but mainly it's a matter of dedication and desire to be a photographer, and if I say, 'I'm going to be a photographer,' there's little to prevent it. So if many photographers compete with each other, there are fewer stars.

"In the early days there were big names, the stars, the well-known photographers. This caste system was nurtured by the big picture magaines, which were great showcases. Today there are few left. There are fine magazines that publish photographs well — *Smithsonian*, *National Geographic*, and a few others — but they have neither the large format or frequency. The new monthly *LIFE* has a small circulation, and while it's well printed and is a fine showcase, it isn't a news publication, so it has certain limitations.

"Photographers today have to resort to other ways of having their work seen and having their pictures appreciated as creative efforts. They are going in heavily for books, and there are more picture books being produced now than ever before. Some are self-published or vanity-press-type publications. While it's wonderful to have picture books produced, few make a lot of money from them, and few books have been lucky enough to return the cost to the publisher. Another showcase is exhibiting in galleries and museums. Photography has become a fine art and is being collected for investment, so it's possible for the photographer to make some money out of it. Portfolios or individual pictures can be sold, and it's wonderful to see that a photographer in his or her own lifetime can benefit financially from photographs being considered a collectible fine art. However, there are only a few hundred photographers in this magic group. I don't know how you break into it. I don't even know how I got into it. I know I benefit from it because my work is wanted by museums, it's collected, and the auction prices of my photographs keep going up. But I also think of Edward Weston, who died in the 1950s, and he was very happy to sell anybody one of his prints for ten bucks, though Ansel Adams has benefited handsomely from his sales. But poor Edward Weston died in poverty."

I had asked Rothstein to comment on craftsmanship and he said there is a general sloppiness, but doesn't think the photographer is entirely to blame. He thought the responsibility lies with the editors, picture editors and art directors who do not demand more. "Most," he said, "are not sufficiently knowledgeable themselves to know good quality. There is a classic definition of the art director who knows what he wants but doesn't know what it is.

That's what we have today. We also have a lot of young typographical experts from art and design schools who know nothing about photography.

"For too many users of photography, it is an embellishment, or a decoration. The way photographs are treated with lack of respect is an indication of that. Where these practices are prevalent, they make the photographer feel disgusted and not inclined to a high level of craftsmanship. Yet modern technology and techniques make it possible to produce photographs that are better than those of the past.

"Some suggest a photographer consider specialization, although I have never specialized — in fact, when people ask me what my specialty is, I always say 'versatility.' I think photographers should decide whether they want to specialize or whether they want to be versatile. I'm very proud of the fact that I can do any kind of photography. I approach every assignment with enthusiasm. It makes little difference whether I am photographing something for an ad or editorial use; or even somebody's birthday or wedding. Whatever the assignments are, I come to them all with the same degree of quality and professionalism. I think that this is the only approach to be considered by the photographer.

"Another thing I think about is that many photographers start out today with the concept that they are artists. I never considered myself an artist. Some people *think* that my photographs are works of art, and I'm delighted if they do. I have always thought of myself as a photographer performing a useful service or a function of some kind, but never art. I don't believe in photography as art for art's sake. I do believe in photography as art for humanity's sake. I think that those photographers who become fine arts photographers are missing out on some of the satisfactions of producing pictures that can influence public opinion, inform or entertain people. I also think they are missing out on an added dimension in photography. It's a universal language that's easily understood by people all over the world. It's a great way to communicate."

Chapter Twelve
Electronic Imaging and the Retirement of the CPA

Considering that over half of America's workers are concerned in one way or another with information dissemination and its management, we have to take a sharp look at digital technology. From the great governmental mainframes holding IRS data, social security and motor vehicle records, and perhaps much more personal information than we wish, to the 20 million plus home computers, this technology touches every American in the country. Digitalization is used to price a can of beans in the supermarket; give you a bum credit report because some incompetent information manager has inputted wrong, biased or misleading information about you; or possibly charge you interest on money you don't owe. It affects you every time you get on an airplane, train or bus. At the hospital you are no longer a person, but a byte, a blip on a piece of magnetic tape.

The newest terminology in photography is "electronic imaging" (EI) and "digitalization" of images. Both mean the same, both are new buzzwords in our lexicon. "Retirement of the CPA" announced in the title of this chapter does not mean your accountant is now living in a grass hut in Tahiti, but simply that photographic images can now be altered electronically in such a way that detection is almost impossible. The old methods of retouching by Cutting, Pasting and Airbrushing are on the way out in initial image alteration, though these techniques are still used after an image has been changed in the final assembly of an ad or poster (see pages 321 and 323).

Although electronic imaging has been with us now on an operational level for at least ten years, most photographers as well as the lay public have given it little thought. They paid scant attention to images they saw in publications that had been altered, subtly or otherwise. But then one incident occurred that, while not serious by itself, opened a whole can of worms as to the ethics and journalistic use of the medium.

A few years ago the *National Geographic* magazine commissioned a picture story on Egypt. The photographer did a splendid job, as most *NG* photographers do. The story was laid out, and the cover photograph selected was a fine one of the Pyramids. There was only one problem: The picture did not fit the rigid design format for the cover and the editors wanted to use the image in the largest way possible, given the limited page size of the magazine. Their solution was to literally move one of the Pyramids slightly to the left, which did not destroy the visual impact or beauty of the photograph, and for the most part no reader acknowledged being aware of the move. That is, until some Egyptologist looking at the cover photograph sensed that something was "wrong" even though he apparently knew nothing about electronic imaging or its use in this cover photograph. Then the storm broke and the photojournalism world was thrown into a turmoil. The ethical discussions over this move have been ongoing.

John Durniak, a nationally known picture editor (see pages 212-214), in discussing electronic imaging, cited the 1991 *TIME* magazine "Man of the Year" cover photograph by Gregory Heisler which was produced with this new technology. Heisler, he feels, is one of the finest photojournalists on the contemporary scene, and Durniak paid him high praise for using this new system of imagery so well.

He also said, "I think we'll see two phases of electronic photography go into higher gear. One will be in the transmission of the electronic imagery. With major news events such as presidential conventions or Olympic Games, photographers will make images on standard film, process them quickly, and transmit them electronically to their newspapers, magazines or TV stations within one hour of the actual shooting.

"There is also a new digital form of still photography. Kodak's digital back attached to a 35mm Nikon encompasses this objective, which makes it very easy to shoot an image and transmit that image immediately by telephone line without any darkroom processing. This system, already developed, is expensive and currently costs around $25,000 or $30,000 to install, so I don't see widespread use immediately. Eventually, of course, the prices will come down and the system will be more widely used. This is the camera that produces the best quality so far. There are other cameras of this nature, but they are not yet portable and can only be used in a studio. They are gigantic. I can also see situations very shortly where photographers can be hooked up to telephone lines by wire (or satellite), take the pictures and almost instantly transmit them to their papers where the editing will be done. This is further down the line and hasn't occurred yet but it's coming. I do not see video replacing film immediately but see the two mediums working side by side. Until digital beats film in quality I see no replacement.

"Electronic photography has been around a long time. The reason it did not take over the field earlier is that the quality of the electronic image was not as good as standard film produces. So far there is nothing electronically that matches the quality of film, and the amount of information film can capture. So Eastman Kodak, while they have entered the photo imaging business in a big way, are also improving standard films by making them faster, more color responsive to the scene, and more accurate in the way they interpret images. Kodak and Fuji are now coming out with the best film we have ever seen, even while the revolution in electronics is going on."

Electronic imaging can do more than retouch a photograph, move a pyramid, remove a few telephone wires, delete smoke from a factory chimney or stray hairs or blemishes on a model's face. Electronic imaging permits the components from many photographs to be combined into one single image, or parts of one photograph may be moved around within the frame lines of a single photograph to create an entirely new image.

How does it work? How is it now possible to take bits and pieces of any photograph and move them around within the image frame or even add parts of other photographs? With electronic imaging computers one can screen one or more images on a VDT (video display terminal), a computerese name for a TV color monitor. The operator can, as Durniak said, "replace one person's head with another's, substitute a camel for a cow or put spots on a dog that didn't have any spots, and create new images that never existed before." In other words, it's an electronic extension of the cut, paste and airbrush technique. The time is rapidly approaching when photographers, in order to stay current in their field, must be as computer friendly as they are with cameras and lenses. This is not to say that the new photographers have to rush out and spend a half million dollars on an electronic imaging mainframe or even a more modestly priced work station, but they should start learning the capabilities of these new tools and how they can best be used to expand their own creativity.

Not wishing to get into technical details I was not sure I understood too well myself, I went to Atlanta to speak with Bill Simenko, president of Meteor Photo, who knows as much about the technology of electronic imaging as anyone in the business. He gave me the overview I think we all need to properly understand the process. He was for many years a Kodak TSR (technical sales representative) and later regional sales manager for sixteen states. He worked closely with Ray DeMoulin, then head of their Professional Products Division, and currently Director of the Center for Creative Imaging (see page 324). Meteor Photo is one of the largest electronic imaging and color processing laboratories in the world, with two impressive high-tech plants, one in Atlanta and one in Troy, Michigan, near Detroit. They are involved with the Premier system in concert with batteries of other EI equipment.

"Originally," Simenko told me, "we were all looking at Premier as a means of doing make-ready prior to going to murals and the uses of photography other than photo-offset. The Kodak Premier system is different from Scitex-Visionary because it is not directed at offset printing. There are, however, many similarities in the use of a scanner, the way they image, use work stations to manipulate the image, change color, and import other images. The differences between the two systems is that Scitex and their competitors, Hell and Crossfield, were all designed for the graphic arts industry to prepare material for separation at the printing plant level so they can come up with the four basic colors, i.e., cyan, magenta, yellow, black (CMYK), needed in printing. Premier does not 'write it' out as CMYK but as RGB which is the conventional red, green and blue and what you get are not separations but photographic images, either 8″ × 10″ color negatives or transparencies from which prints or murals can be made. If those new images are to be published later, then separations can be made by the printing plant.

"The electronic imaging process starts when a photograph is placed into a work station of an EI computer. The photograph is scanned and the elements of the image are broken up into tiny bits of electronic information called pixels (a contraction of the words 'picture elements') and stored electronically on a CD-ROM disk that is similar to the new audio disks which are used for sound recordings. The pixel is merely the dot part of an image that makes up a 'raster file' which in turn is a combination of pixels.

"The operator can then take these pixels and move them around to formulate new images or combine them with other groups of pixels that form images on another piece of film. Does this frighten you? It shouldn't, because you should look on these new electronic marvels as new tools that will help you to expand your thinking, and enable you to create photographic images. Never lose sight of the fact that no computer can think for you. It can enhance, implement and bring to fruition what you have conceived in your mind. If it cannot mix your creative juices, it will allow you to use them in ways no one thought possible a decade ago.

"The difference again is that Premier is always at the highest resolution. The Scitex and the others can give you different resolutions (scans) but the printing industry does not require such high resolution. Another difference is that the pixels created try to simulate the grains of silver halide so photographically it looks like it's an original. In many respects if you do not put a microscope on it or enlarge it sufficiently you can be completely misled into believing that you are looking at an original transparency.

"Premier can import different formats, different film types and make them all look the same whereas in other systems they stand out as different formats and different film types. One of the great pluses of electronic imaging is that because the new images are created digitally, an unlimited number of identical copies can be made without generational changes in contrast or color.

"These new technologies are driving everybody absolutely crazy because they are so complicated. You can start out with a PC image or an image that has been put into a Macintosh, you can manipulate it there, you can output it now on a Canon CLC-500 laser copier, or as we do in Troy, onto a bubble-jet printer and make a 30″ color print in six minutes. That's the new world."

Simenko further added, "One of the things we are working very hard at now is to convince the art directors, and there are a lot of them in Atlanta and Troy, the designers, and the buyers of photography of the differences between the two systems. We don't want to have a war because that's detrimental to everybody. What we're trying to get them to do is understand that the Premier systems have secondary uses of the photography aside from the making of separations for printed ads in magazines or newspapers. Our uses are strong in point of purchase or for high quality murals. That huge backlighted transparency you saw in the Atlanta airport, which we made, was put together from one 4″ × 5″ and two 35mm transparencies. Electronic imaging does not stand alone. After a digitalized transparency is produced the make-up of large murals or prints is all done by conventional methods."

He continued, "That's the reason we have artists in our own art department. We need their artistic knowledge to finish the work on a digitalized image. They are artists, not electronic technicians, and they can put together images in the old way. You can teach an artist how to run a computer but it is difficult for the computer technician to function as a creative artist.

"In addition to the two systems, Scitex-Visionary and Kodak's Premier, computer hardware, software, and camera manufacturers such as Macintosh, Apple, Nikon, Canon and others have all developed astounding new supporting equipment that has to be critical in turning the world of photography around. Other programs such as Adobe, Barco, Dicomed, and others, all become vital components and I am sure only the surface of technology has been scratched. We are not surprised at the ability to reconstitute images. This has been around for a long time. What is surprising is how easy it is to do this with computer technology. The equipment is all computer-based, requiring a high degree of skill in its operation and is very expensive — far too expensive for the individual photographer to ever hope to acquire, except for the basic work station as mentioned below."

I teach a college-level course to photographers in New York on many of the subjects covered in this book. Recently a young, talented art student interested in commercial art joined the class and became fascinated with the potentials of EI as it applied to her field. At the end of the session she told me that, while this new world interested her, she was frightened of computers and did not think she could cope with them. She is not alone. I have heard these same fears expressed by other new and talented artists. I was delighted to hear her express herself openly because it gave me the opportunity to go into my song-and-dance routine to calm her and assure her how *unimportant it is to be able to operate* an electronic imaging computer.

What *is important* is an understanding *of what can be done with it,* no more or less proportionately than the difference between being unable to make a good print and knowing a bad one when you see it. There are plenty of good printers around who can be hired to produce the print quality you want. Extend that same philosophy to modern color processing which is highly computerized. After all, how many photographers today process their own color film or make color prints? Very few, considering the number of photographers at work.

So ability to operate the computer is less important than your knowledge of what can be done with it. Computer work stations are becoming ever more numerous along with the technical personnel to operate them, and although you are not looking for work in that field, their proliferation can be useful to you in accomplishing what you desire graphically. Also, as more work stations are made it should not be too long before the cost of a work station is comparable to the cost of a common desktop PC.

When the subject of electronic imaging arises, especially among professional photographers with long experience in using conventional films, one of the first fears expressed is whether EI technology will replace conventional film. Pictures are composed only in your mind and within the frame of your viewfinder. So for the foreseeable future the silver-based image you form in your camera with conventional film will not be replaced by magnetic tape, but the ability of moving these images, or components of them, will be enhanced and expedited electronically by hardware already in place or still to come. But wanting to dig deeper, I caught up with Ray DeMoulin (see page 322). He was frank and open, but he also surprised me by his strong concerns over the ethics of electronic imaging and its impact on copyright (see chapter ten) rather than the technical side.

DeMoulin said, "Electronic imaging is not going to replace the silver halide image. Film is going to be the input medium forever, if you want something to come out that is of the highest quality in the end. Perhaps I can simplify this by giving you the motion picture analogy. Let me just change that to the professional photographer. He sees the same technology coming into his arena as the videotape. This is not going to do anything but add a piece of technology that he needs to look at and work with and bring into his business, and then decide when he needs visual imaging and when he wants to go to conventional films. It's going to be different for each photographer. The photographer should not have fears of having to install $50,000 worth of lab equipment or digital cameras. My feeling is that these photographers would do better by keeping their cameras, storing their film in the refrigerator, and being ready to go at a moment's notice.

"There is no substantive difference in electronic imaging and silver imaging photography. With conventional film there have always been technical problems of developing, dodging, burning, vignetting, correcting a print, etc. Those same problems exist in EI photography except that they are easier to deal with mechanically. If the total number of problems increase, it's because there will be many more photographers using EI technology when they become computer literate and do not have to go into the darkroom to move the pixels around."

As discussed in chapter ten (legal issues) and partially in chapter thirteen (education), one of the critical problems requiring addressing is the need for education, which in turn raises ethical questions, not technical ones. It would appear that we may have to look to the courts for definitive answers on copyright, usage and reusage. DeMoulin, Simenko, and others too, feel strongly that the industry itself must sponsor heavy debate on who owns the copyright of a manipulated, changed, or enhanced image.

Heisler, in his *TIME* cover, used thirty or forty images (all with proper permissions), but each of those images had a copyright. Now a collage of all of these images exists as a single photograph. There is nothing wrong with this, but it opens an area for debate concerning the copyright of the new image, including what, if any, limitations were put on Heisler's collage of forty different images. As Heisler told me, these particular images all came from CNN, whom the cover story was about, but what kind of copyright snakepit would Heisler have found himself in if each of those forty images came from forty individual sources? Or, if he sold that composite photograph to some other publication, as normally might be his right, would permission have to be obtained from the owner of each image that appears in the collage of photographs? It's not easy to find answers now and it may get worse later. But that's the way it's going to be, and those rules of copyright in place today will probably prevail.

It does not look like an insurmountable problem now, but in the future with the proliferation of EI photos, we will have a harder time controlling them and it's going to take court litigation to provide concrete guidelines. We already know the courts are going to have worries about making decisions on evidence that may have been manufactured with altered images. It is one of the most interesting photographic questions we have today.

DeMoulin added, "There might be ways to prevent these conflicts. As an old research and development person in the film area, I'm wondering if we can't find an electronic lock on an image that says you can't take that image through a computer and change things without somehow revealing that there have been changes. I am also worried about the ease of duplicating many images without generational increases and still not violate the copyright.

"Since I am not in the imaging business I don't have to worry about the copyright violation of this nature, but as a teacher I think it is a vital issue to bring up for debate, and how one person might protect himself versus another. Technology ought to prevail in some way and give us help to prevent unauthorized use by providing invisible but fail-safe electronic keys to protect the copyright holder. We have tried for years to work out such a system on paper coatings to prevent unauthorized copying but it has not worked.

"Videotape does have a mechanism that will indicate whether or not it's an original version or a copied one. So we need to explore the technology of electronic imaging further. So far we have been so involved with its initial development that we have not been able to pay too much attention to these later requirements. I'm sure it will come."

For this book I interviewed many photographers, editors, picture agents, art directors and art buyers, electronic experts, laboratory people and others. Their opinions of EI were divided, and their feelings revealing.

Former Senior Writer and member of the Board of Editors of *Fortune* and former Assistant Managing Editor of *LIFE* magazine, Roy Rowan (see page 185) said, "As for electronic imaging in documentary photography, I think that anything that has impact and conveys an idea that creates a mood is good. After all, if you just want to see events as they unfold, you can probably watch them on television.

"I know that some editors think there is no room for electronic imaging in honest reporting because it distorts the scene, but I disagree with that. I don't believe you have to be precisely faithful in that way in constructing an image. You act more like an artist by creating the atmosphere that will convey the message, and if you can convey a very good message that's fine. The *National Geographic* picture of the pyramids was different. That was rigging a picture and it's not what I'm talking about. I'm talking about creating the atmosphere that projects a message beyond the straight photograph. After all, photographers have always conceived moods with lighting or shadows. The lighting we often see is not the lighting that exists naturally in many pictures. But the photographer can provide lighting in any way that accentuates what he wants. I don't think the moving of the pyramid was a great crime, but if you apply photo imaging to the Zapruder film of the Kennedy assassination you're screwing around with history."

Casey Allen, (see his discussion on education, page 353), also said, "Computers for use in photography are complex as well as expensive. A complete paintbox installation such as the Barco Creator can cost half a million dollars. For most photographers, this is too costly to own. Already, computer service shops to which photographers can bring their work are opening around the United States. Photographers don't have to become experts with these wizard machines but they must learn enough about them so they can talk intelligently with the operators. Paintbox operators say that the large majority of these photographers—out of ignorance—utilize less than ten percent of the computer's potential. Too many photographers use the computers for tasks that could be performed just as well in their own darkrooms. The computer takes less time but that time can cost $500 an hour. Photographers must learn to use the computers for improving their concepts rather than just routine, run-of-the-mill retouching.

"There has been a good deal of talk about the ethics of using computer technology to alter pictures. The cover photograph for the book *A Day in the Life of America,* for instance, was converted from a horizontal to a vertical, the cowboy was moved closer to the tree and a moon was added.

"People seem to forget that photographs have been combined, retouched, cropped, dodged and burned-in since photography was invented. News magazines and newspapers have even been known to occasionally leave out certain parts of photographs for editorial reasons. The difference with computers is that when alterations are done electronically, there is absolutely no way to detect the changes. Once you move into pixels, all pixels look alike.

"Some concerned editors and photographers are now careful to identify any photographs that have been altered by computers. There will always be people, however, who are not concerned with ethics, who always take advantage for personal gain. The courts already have recognized the computer's ability to modify or change reality; in a number of cases, the use of audio or visual recorded material has been strictly limited as evidence.

"In the last ten years, economics and computers have forced broad changes in photography. The day of the star photographer is rapidly passing. There are few clients left who will pay $10,000 to $15,000 for a 'name.' Stock houses now have tens of millions of images for clients to pick from, including shots from the 'name' photographers. And the price is right.

"Paintbox computer artists are beginning to take over many of the creative functions from the photographers. These artists work directly with the photographic images on the computer screen. Under the direction of the client and art director they are able to go from original conception to separations, often in just one session. A few photography schools are already working on budgets to include these computers in their curriculum. Photographic perspectives of the twenty-first century will have a far different viewpoint from those of the twentieth."

But the problems posed by the comparatively minor action of *National Geographic* will not go away. They may continue to haunt us for a long time. "Was this move ethical?" asked many people. "Did this destroy the assumed honesty of photojournalism?" Asked a lawyer, "Who is going to believe a photograph submitted as evidence in court?" An art director said that for advertising and commercial use it is a splendid way of combining many ingredients to cook up an advertising photographic stew. And since advertising is not documentary journalism, he saw nothing wrong with it. Yet even in that context there was disagreement.

A recent ad for a manufacturer of blue jeans reproduced some old FSA photographs of farm workers wearing jeans alongside contemporary models wearing the same type of clothing as casual wear. In this case there was no alteration of the original image, but it would not have been hard to do so. And since those original photographs were in the public domain, there could be no claim of copyright infringement. But the question persists: Would this be overstepping the lines of ethics by altering a strong documentary photograph to conform with the desires of a marketing person in industry. I also remember the revulsion expressed by some people (and long before electronic imaging) over an ad, also for jeans, which showed Adam, one of the principle figures in Michelangelo's painting on the ceiling of the Sistine Chapel, also dressed in jeans. Oh, well. Technology changes, but bad taste still exists, and electronic imaging just makes it easier for it to be exhibited.

So you can see we are having a more difficult time coping with the ethics of electronic imaging than the technology. There is a strong division of opinion on how and where this new system of electronic imaging should be used. Many journalists I have spoken with are apprehensive. Others are not and look to it as a fine opportunity to create great new images of vital importance without disturbing the integrity of a news situation.

We know now that with electronic imaging it is comparatively easy to change or manipulate images. So while there may be a danger of its use in forensic law because it can discourage the use of photographs as evidence, on the other hand there are wonderful and useful applications of this graphic science; it can enable photographers, artists or art directors to create entirely new images from existing ones without having to go out in the field and shoot them. It can help art directors change the shape of a photograph to fit a precise layout without altering its editorial content appreciably. So it's possible to change a photograph easily and make it look like the real thing. In the old days you could easily spot the alterations, now you can't.

Earlier, Simenko had said, "Technology aside, when we are talking of documentary photography or news reporting I feel there is no place for digital imaging where you can manipulate the components of a photograph. That has to be pure. For everything we do for ourselves and send out as promotional material we clearly state that the image was digitally manipulated. As for *National Geographic,* I too think they were wrong. I don't think you can take the real world and change it and then present it as the real world. Commercially digital imaging is fine. In one way or another images have been manipulated forever."

There are additional ethical problems that even non-editorial people have with manipulation, or for that matter with mass printing in conventional laboratory practices. As did DeMoulin earlier, both Simenko and conventional color processor Ken Lieberman (see page 312) expressed concerns that extended over into copyright protection for photographers and artists whose laboratory work they may be dealing with. If an image is being used for commercial application as art or a thing of beauty, Simenko feels he has no problems with it. He worries about his responsibility when the image is used to misrepresent facts. He worries about copyright infringement and does everything possible to protect copyright holders. It's more than being a serious problem in his lab; it should be of very high ethical concern to all laboratory operators. Simenko went on to say, "I think we are closely approaching an impasse in the ethics of photojournalism and the use of photo imaging because I don't know how you can ever determine if an image is manipulated. When you look at conventional photography you can pretty much determine if something has been manipulated.

"I think future photographers are going to need the capability and understanding of both electronic and conventional chemistry systems, and learn to make them work together. I think they are going to have to learn to handle a computer just as well as they handle a camera. Heisler, who understands both systems, has become a great photographer because of his expanded knowledge. I think he is truly the photographer's photographer."

Eric Meola, who has already built an enormous reputation as a studio photographer, is reaching newer heights by his application of the digital process. He now works with every conceivable format, multiple images, or different films and has come up with incredible images. These artists are going to be at the cutting edge of all of this new technology because they can see how it will work in their futures. And I think the future of any photographer is going to be in using both disciplines.

Where does electronic imaging fit in to the education of a photographer? Ben Fernandez, Chairman of the Department of Photography at Parson's School of Design and the New School (see page 366), has definite feelings about electronic imaging in education.

He told me in part, "I do have mixed feelings about electronic imaging. As a journalist and documentary photographer I will not get involved with it. As a teacher I have to because the students have to know of the technology. I deliberately close my mind to it because of my fear of the seductiveness of the computer to control or manipulate my ethical attitude. So even if I do not practice it, I know its theory. I cannot allow myself to change an image and then try to pan it off as a real thing. That's the problem.

"The rationale of using the computer to clean up images, to remove and move things around so that we 'get what we want' is not strong enough for me. We can still get what we want on film with conventional methods without resorting to practices which may be suspect as far as authenticity is concerned. This is the ethics of what we teach and the student must make his choice in which direction to go."

We have discussed here as minimally as possible the technology of electronic imaging and have quoted several prominent admirers and occasional detractors of the field on their use or non-use of the medium, particularly in the world of photojournalism and advertising. But there is more to it.

What else is within the scope of EI? If Eastman Kodak Company is to be believed—a great deal. They have established The Center for Creative Imaging in Camden, Maine (Tel: 1-800-428-7400) under the direction of Raymond DeMoulin (see page 322). The Center is a school devoted to electronic imaging, staffed by professionals and visiting experts.

We are not touting this particular institution (nor discouraging attendance either) but a glance at their curriculum points to many possibilities for the use of this phenomenal medium. New worlds are being opened in all manner of graphics, text, video and sound, and all in a common language. Some of the course titles are tantalizing, and include "Imaging Tools and Techniques," "Making Imaging Decisions in Business," "Teaching Creative Imaging," "Special Effects Imaging," "Pixels and Silver, Photographers and Dentists," "Self-Publishing Photographic Books" and a host of others. Call the Center for a catalog, it may open new vistas for you.

How do we use these new tools effectively other than in moving pyramids, eliminating stray hairs in portraits, or making masterful composites of many images for a magazine cover? Electronic imaging is one of those rare mediums that is so multifaceted that it is open to an enormous variety of communicators, perhaps in fields yet to be invented. Those interested in magazine and newspaper illustration in general use it to expound a visual idea with clarity and perhaps elegance. EI can deal with drawings, photographs, text as blocks and the software and hardware necessary for desktop publishing.

Desktop publishing? What's that? It's a method of publishing that does not require the use of a large printing press or printing company, but uses fairly simple computer installations. In desktop publishing you combine the elements of writing, photography, art and type composition in simple, inexpensive ways to prepare publications that run in size from one page to fifty or more. There are many software programs geared to your own desires and specific needs. Some are sophisticated and some simple. Take your choice. Desktop publishing is essentially a small operation. It can be handled by a single person, though it's by no means that limited.

So far much of this discussion has revolved around individual photographers, editors, and technical people, all trying to bring new vision to the communicators. How do artists, photographers, art directors, designers and illustrators learn to live with each other professionally and use their individual capabilities in cross-over techniques to achieve a common goal? With electronic imaging. Do you want to make an illustrated map, or engineering drawings that can project a three-dimensional finished object, be it building, boat or boot? Are you a textile designer and need inexpensive ways of seeing what your product will look like?

If you walk into the city room of nearly every newspaper in the country the first thing you notice is the absence of noise of typewriters and hysterical editors trying to emulate scenes from *The Front Page,* a play and film from a book on newspaper life in Chicago in the 1920s. Instead you will see banks of computer terminals and hear words like Atex-Rennaisance, or Adobe Photoshop, Barco, bandied about, and rarely hear anything in the way of machines, typewriters and phones ringing. Why?

Because even as I write this chapter, I am looking at a twenty-eight page, full-sized newspaper called *Electronic Times.* It is lavishly illustrated with color and black-and-white photographs, and written, photographed and published by professionals participating in the Electronic Still Workshop of the National Press Photographer's Association in September 1991. Considering the entire issue was put together under conditions not dissimilar to that of a daily newspaper with electronic components supplied by some twenty-one vendors of equipment and systems, it is a staggering look at the future of electronic journalism in the newspaper world.

In photographic book publishing, electronic imaging is becoming a principal player. Keeping in mind Casey Allen's commentary about the cover used on *A Day in the Life of America,* I talked with Rick Smolan, a former photography contributor to many magazines including *LIFE, Fortune, National Geographic,* and *Newsweek.* Smolan and his partner David Cohen conceived the entire *Day in the Life of (Country)* book series that has been a sensational success, selling in editions of six figures on many different countries and popular subjects, e.g., Christmas and baseball.

Smolan said, "Electronic imaging has made everyone sensitive to the propriety and honesty of how images are perceived by the reader. Credibility of photography is the most important thing we have. If we damage the credibility of photography then we're in trouble. Short of that, everyone looks for a rule. I can't give you the ultimate rule, because it never works. For every ultimate rule there's a wonderful and practical exception.

"For example, the *Louisville Courier Journal* published about twelve years ago an ethics manual on how to handle things in the newspaper, including such things as telling the staff they will accept no free Cokes, sandwiches in the press box; politicians would not be permitted to give political writers a bottle of bourbon at Christmas; and many other things which were unacceptable. Then they got to what was actually published in the newspaper, saying that any time there's a commercial sponsorship of an event, you will drop the name of the sponsor and substitute the name of the city in which the event took place. So if the Virginia Slims Tennis Classic was being played in Charlotte the event had to be referred to as the Charlotte Tennis Classic. So they followed the rule book exactly until three months later the Buick Open was played in Pontiac, Michigan, so you can't have an ultimate rule."

The computers, their terminals, mainframes and electronic imaging work stations are now capable of handling all the work of reporters, photographers, editors, type directors and composers (type, not music . . . though that's with us too) long before being sent down to the printing plant.

There is also a bright future in electronic imaging in the nonprofessional field. For a long time the Camcorder and related hardware had professional applications, but now the Camcorder is very much a consumer item and can be bought in any electronic shop at pretty low prices. DeMoulin thinks the digital still camera will ultimately penetrate the market and possibly get to a point where you can put a hundred or two images on a disk and play it back at home on your video monitor. I agree with him. The horizon is tantalizing and I am sure we are not chasing a pot of gold at the end of a rainbow.

So the new photographer just getting started should be able to take his artistic capabilities and enhance them with computer technology. I see a great future for photographers, not necessarily of the Heisler, Meola or Newman level, but those who can bring their craft to a state of comfortable economic viability. The future is here . . . it's still wide open for people with open minds and open eyes and, oh boy, it *is* working.

Interview
Berenice Abbott
Photographer

I have always had a special regard for Berenice Abbott, who began to work as a photographer in the 1920s. And as I write, I sorrowfully read her nearly full-page obituary in *The New York Times* telling of her death at age 93. I am sad, because somehow I thought she would be with us forever, a sturdy monument to our craft. Berenice Abbott consistently produced landmark photography covering a wide range of subject matter from portraits to splendid views of great cities, and even macrophotography of objects and physical phenomena. When she was over eighty, she had the vigor and stamina to get into a car in New York during a snowstorm and drive back alone to northern Maine, where she lived and worked. And again her indomitable spirit rose when she came to New York in 1989 for the opening of her huge retrospective exhibition at the New York Public Library. She was late for the starting ceremony because she decided to shop at a department store first for something more appropriate to wear, appearing in a new fur jacket.

My personal admiration for her stems from the fact that she was my only formal teacher of photography. She began teaching at the New School for Social Research in 1935, and indeed established the photographic program there. My two semesters of study with her during the 1940s laid the groundwork for my own professional career. When I first started to study and work with her I asked a mutual friend to tell me something about her. I was told, "She's a hellion on technique, and if you try to cut corners she'll have your head—so watch out!" So I salute her for this along with her devotion and insistence upon quality and creativity, and her long loving friendship. This was all part of her unyeilding commitment to craftsmanship and professionalism, and anyone who spoke with her up to the time of her death, would verify that her strength was still apparent.

Abbott was a student at Ohio State University until World War I interfered and she left her studies. She went to New York, taking with her a desire to become a journalist, though she later chose to be a sculptor. She led what she called a "desperate existence," doing odd jobs of any sort for sheer survival, including a try at debt collection, at which she did not do well. After three years of such work, she went to Paris and got a job with Man Ray, the American Surrealist. Man Ray was experimenting with photograms, but earning a living with conventional portrait work. She worked in Man Ray's darkroom finishing his prints. Abbott worked with Man Ray for three years during the 1920s and with his encouragement set up a small studio of her own in Paris, where she concentrated on the artists and writers of her community.

She made evocative portraits of James Joyce, Janet Flanner and Jean Cocteau, as well as other notable artists and writers of the time. Portraiture was then (and probably still is) a word-of-mouth business, and she began building a clientele by referrals. Starting with a 5″×7″ glass-plate view camera, she graduated to an early reflex camera and her reputation for making fine portraits with it grew quickly. When I asked her what she charged for portraits in those days, she made a point of saying that she charged whatever May Ray charged, because she did not want to compete with him on a price basis. She said it was hard to recall, but it seem she was getting about 1,000 francs per sitting, which would have been about thirty to forty U.S. dollars.

At first, she said, she felt a little guilty about competing with Man Ray as he had taught her all she knew about photography, but when people began coming to her because they liked her work on its own merits, she discarded these qualms.

She had begun to do well in Paris, but when she returned to the United States for a abrief visit, she was overwhelmed by the spectacle of New York and felt she had to photograph and live there. She closed her Paris studio and arrived in New York, just a few months before the Wall Street crash of 1929 and the onset of the Great Depression. She did not think the crash would affect her as she had no money invested (nor did she have any money at all). She simply did not realized how it would affect everyone in the country, portrait photographers included. But as she had just opened her studio, she plugged away and concentrated on personal portraiture as she had in Paris. And as in Paris, more by word of mouth than anything else, referrals came in New York too, and she slowly acquired a following.

Her first editorial assignments were for *Fortune* magazine in 1930-31, when she made a series of portraits for them. When the appeared, requests for her to do editorial work began to come in. She got her assignments then, as photogarphers still do today, by showing her work to editors and being persistent about it. True, there was not the competition there is today, and she was well aware of it when we talked. Nevertheless, she thought the principles are still the same: in order to become known, your work must be seen, and if you see enough people and your talent is persuasive, your chances of getting work are good, though by no means automatic.

Abbott was also fortunate enough to participate from 1935-38 in the now-famous Federal Artists Project, a Depression-born program initiated by Franklin D. Roosevelt that gave artists, writers and other creative people a chance to earn a living. She felt lucky to be part of it, and it was during this period she produced many fine photographs that appeared in her book, *Changing New York* which even today stands as a classic. Her direct, well-crafted photographs of New York's tenement and row houses, skyscrapers, and the city at night, are both memorable as art and historically significant. She had other books published. *Berenice Abbott — American PHotographer*, by Hank O'Neal, with an introduction by John Canaday (McGraw-Hill/1982).

Abbott had always been interested inscience, and when her "New York period" had run its course, she tried to get into scientific work. As a woman, she found most doors closed to her, though in 1958 she did join an educational project in Cambridge to make scientific photographs for a high school science textbook. The images she produced, while masterpieces of detail and clarity, also demonstrated here eye for fine art and were published in

1960 in a highly acclaimed textbook called *Health*. She also began taking on more commercial work.

When I spoke to her about her early career priorities, Abbott explained that she loved photography first, and that she would photograph whatever work she could get in almost any field in which she felt competent. She told me that she never felt "precious" about her photography, that she had always loved it in its many forms, and that she would continue to do so.

Abbott sought work by traditional methods: she made up portfolios, went around and showed them to editors, did some teaching, and gradually began building up a reputation that brought her more into commercial work. This gave her a chance to make a living and also to experiment with the things that fascinated her, such as developing new processes to improve scientific photography because ordinary photograhic methods didn't seem good enough at that time for the work she wanted to do. She felt the photographic equipment available to her at the time was limited, and began designing her own cameras, tripods and lighting equipment, including an innovative spring-loaded pole for mounting lights now known as a "cat pole."

Her insatiable curiosity about the world around her also led to her discovery of an almost unknown Parisian photographer named Eugene Atget, who she met in Paris in 1925. Atget had carved a small niche for himself with his photography of local buildings, monuments and artifacts reflecting the culture of Paris, which he sold to artists, historians and publishers. When he died in 1927 in near obscurity, Abbott sought his work out and rescued some 8,000 prints and close to 1,500 glass-plate negatives. She brought them with her to New York in 1929 where they became the focus of exhibitions, print sales and books of Atget's work, and brought fame to him. Eventually Atget's work was acquired by New York's Museum of Modern Art where they remain a permanent part of the museum's collection.

I asked Abbott about her feelings concering craftsmanship, and ofher satisfaction (or lack of it) with the images she sees. Her answer was, as always, direct: "I haven't seen too many images that have impressed me!" When asked what she looks for and doesn't often find in contemporary photographs, she told me, "Significant subject matter, carried out with technical skill." She felt that this combination is lacking in photography today, except for the possible exception of spurts photography and some photojournalislm, which caught her fancy when she was active.

She was disgusted with the quality of most photographic prints she saw, and felt far too few photographers took the time to learn to make excellent prints of their work. As for having someone else print a photographer's work, she admits that it was hard for her to find a printer who met her personal printing standards, though she recognized that many photographers often need to have their work printed by outside printers.

On photographic education, she disagreed with educators who emphasize an art background to the detriment of technical training. Technical training, she thought, must not be neglected. She felt it important to have an artistic sense, but was worried that young photographers who began by studying painting, may become self-conscious about the medium. This could be detrimental to their general training as a photographer. "Self-conscious artiness is fatal," she said, "but it certainly would not hurt to study composition in general."

It was her opinion that too many photographers have become human rubber stamps in that they repeat themselves and tend to photograph the same things. Abbott felt they were passing up the realities of life around them in favor of imitations of other mediums. "Many photographers don't see and think enough," she commented.

When I used the word "abstraction" referring to photographic work, she became quite vehement and said, "Abstraction in photography is ridiculous, and is only an imitation of painting. We stopped imitating painters a hundred years ago, so to imitate them in this day and age is laughable."

I asked her then if she had any gems of wisdom for the young photographer today, and she said, "None. They should just go out and photograph and stop talking about it. That's the only way they are going to find themselves. They can't do it in their heads—they have to go out and do it in the camera and get it on film."

Chapter Thirteen

Capitalizing on — and Expanding — Your New Reputation

Photography As a Fine Art

Exhibits, galleries, and fine arts publications — this is a truly difficult area as far as making money for the new photographer is concerned, but by no means should it be ruled out completely, for there are striking opportunities in this field. More than the financial gain, however, the use of photography as an art form has opened that door to untold numbers of people who have strong desires to create images but may lack the craftsmanship needed to draw, or the dexterity to paint, weave or carve.

There has been a tremendous increase in the gallery sales of fine arts photography because of the proliferation of photo galleries devoting themselves exclusively to this art form. In New York thirty years ago there were perhaps one or two galleries that were art galleries by definition, and handled fine arts photography as a sideline. Recently many important photographic galleries have opened and some well-established art galleries have added photographic departments. There are now probably thirty or more in New York alone and another 250 scattered across the country, not to mention major cities abroad. But is this a good market for the newcomer?

Probably not, unless the photographer is very avant-garde and has come a long way very fast. In order to be hung in a major gallery, a solid reputation resulting from years of effort is required. The work of the late Ansel Adams, long considered the dean of American photography, can now command $5,000 for a print at a gallery, and his estate is represented by several different galleries. At an art auction one of his prints of "Moonrise Over Hernandez" sold for $47,000 and reportedly resold privately for $70,000.

Gordon Parks (see page 146), the noted photographer, had a show in New York where some of his color abstractions in print form sold for $6,000. Richard Avedon, the well-known fashion photographer, has sold some of his prints for a reported $10,000. In the last few years, the twin Starn brothers have sold avant-garde photo collages for as high as $75,000.

Lesser-known names in the smaller galleries can do fairly well. Marjorie Neikrug, who runs a fine gallery in New York (see page 343), has a constant parade of well-known and lesser-known photograpers on view, as well as an extensive collection of historic photographs and artifacts. Many of her print sales are in the $400 to $500 range but can go as high as $25,000. The art gallery market is not restricted to New York. There are galleries in Chicago,

Texas and California, all selling from the highest to the lowest ranges quoted above. Where are they concentrated? When painting was the principal interest of the art galleries, they were centered for the most part in Manhattan's East 57th Street (and above) area. But then several things happened.

Young and developing artists needed large studios to work in and the only viable spaces left were in the old, run-down and largely deserted factory district of the lower west side *south of Houston* street. These enterprising artists grabbed them for studio space, and in many cases converted them (often illegally) to living quarters as well. Hence Soho was born. Many upper-east-side galleries followed them as their own rents skyrocketed, and the newly born photography galleries joined them. The streets in Soho are now cheek-by-jowl with galleries, cafes and other gathering places. And because of the allure of the artistic ambience, Soho also drew many who were not artists or concerned with the art market, but often had sizable incomes. Result? Many artists were driven out and relocated to even drearier areas, such as Noho and Tribeca (all geographic acronyms of lower Manhattan). But a thriving art market has grown, and it has its counterparts in San Francisco's Union Street and elsewhere.

Museums that buy and sell constantly are a big market for the photographic galleries. There are some curious stories about museum acquisitions (via some galleries) that are reminiscent of the yarn about the wholesale grocer who peddled a carload of spoiled sardines through several levels of commerce and remarked, when someone protested that they weren't fit to eat, "Of course not; they are only for buying and selling."

True or not, gallery sales, or even exhibits with direct sales, can lead to other things, primarily getting the photographer's name to the public. Gallery exhibits invariably require posters, and there are some that are almost as much in demand as prints, in the same manner as posters of art exhibitions are in themselves a form of collectible art.

But in order for photographers to become known as art photographers they have to crack what can seem to be a Chinese Wall. This is not due to indifference on the part of gallery owners or curators, because they too, as well as their art buyer or picture editor counterparts, want to see an ongoing supply of fresh and new material. Sadly, many photographers, particularly the younger ones, do not have good fine art training and thus are more vulnerable to the clichés in imagery.

Exposure to fine art (or photography) in a setting conducive to easy and relaxed viewing, while common in Europe, never seemed to take hold here. Cafes in Paris, Rome and other centers of culture always had room for art on their walls and were places where artists, writers and musicians could gather and share a common ground. This bothered many people here, and in particular Helen Gee. She speaks from long experience as a curator of fine arts photogaphy but not as a current gallery owner.

Insider: Helen Gee, Curator of Photography and Art Consultant

"I became interested in photography in the early 1950s after seeing exhibitions at the Museum of Modern Art. I decided to study photography and took a course with Alexey Brodovitch, the famous Art Director of *Harper's Bazaar*. But I dropped it when I found it was too design-oriented.

"Next I studied with Lisette Model, whose work I had seen and admired. I was her first student in her first class, which she held in her home before joining the faculty of The New School. Afterwards I studied with Sid Grossman, a difficult though inspiring teacher. He rarely looked at a student's work, yet he could set you afire through sheer talk alone, provided you survived his three-hour monologues.

"I was a color transparency retoucher, raising a child alone, and always very, very busy. But I felt the need to do something creative, so I went on photographing whenever I found time. Then one day, while photographing a street festival on New York's lower East Side, I hit on the idea of combining a photography gallery with a coffeehouse, giving photographers a place to exhibit and a place to meet. There had never been a gallery devoted exclusively to photography and I thought it was time there was one. There were not enough collectors to support a gallery so it was up to espresso and cappuccino and good things to eat to keep it going.

"Coffeehouses were becoming the rage. The idea of sitting at a table sipping coffee, reading newspapers, meeting friends, as they did in the cafes in Paris, was catching on in New York. This one would have an added attraction, a separate gallery with fine photographs on the walls. The only place where you could see exhibitions of photography at that time was at the Museum of Modern Art. And so *Limelight* was created.

"*Limelight* existed for seven years. Over this period I held more than seventy exhibitions, covering a wide spectrum of approaches and styles. I showed documentary photography, photojournalism and what we refer to today as 'fine art photography.' What I tried to do was show *good* photography and not push any particular approach. Among the exhibitors were Ansel Adams, Lisette Model, Robert Frank, Eugene Atget, Brassai, Berenice Abbott, Edward Weston, W. Eugene Smith, Arnold Newman and Julia Margaret Cameron. I also showed the work of lesser-known photographers, and put on several group shows.

"Prices were low. An Ansel Adams was thirty-five dollars, a Robert Frank, twenty-five dollars, a Paul Strand, a whopping $125. But the dollar had a different value then. The subway was a nickel, coffee a dime—except at *Limelight* where it was fifty cents and up—so most of the photographs seemed expensive at the time. A couple of shows nearly sold out, but generally there were few sales. The audience, however, was enormous. Each exhibition was seen by over 5,000 people and besides reviews in *The New York Times*, they received excellent press notice elsewhere.

"After closing the gallery in 1961, I became an art consultant and built collections for many corporations. But most were not ready to accept photography as an art, and I provided them mostly with paintings. However, this has changed, and corporations make up a good part of the photography market today.

"Are galleries a good market for photographers today? Some have made a good deal of money but generally it is very difficult. Even those photographers who are selling well depend on commercial work for a living. While painters can command prices in the upper thousands, photographers can expect much less, usually less than $2,000. And once the gallery commission is deducted, which is usually about 50 perecent, even selling out a show does not mean big bucks. Ironically the big money is in vintage photography, that is, photographs that were printed around the time the picture was taken, and preferably by the photographer. The more rare the photograph, the higher the price for even an old print.

"There are, of course, exceptions. A few photographers, working within the context of the art world, and drawing on art world ideas, have made all sorts of money. I recently brought some of my students in my critique class at Parsons/New School to a major New York art gallery where they saw work—in this case, the Starn twins—*priced at $50,000 to $75,000.* They were impressed with the prices, but not with the work.

"As for photo murals, I see no viable market, though I have been told of new technologies for producing them with electronic imaging equipment which have reduced their manufacturing cost considerably, so that might help stimulate sales.

"In organizing exhibitions, I look for the work of young photographers, creativity being the criteria. The original eye is rare. Most work is derivative. It is probably more difficult to arrive at a personal style than in any other medium. The camera can be used promiscuously, and the very ease of taking pictures results in a glut of images. Editors and photography dealers have often to wade through mounds of material to find something fresh.

"Let's face it, the grant money is gone. Photographers are facing a difficult time. Sadly, there are more photographers than there are accounts. The best they can hope for is to be able to make a living and to do their personal work on the side. By personal work, I don't mean pictures of family and friends, but work that is personally expressive. One is naturally much freer when not working for a client but there are some photographers, though they are the exceptions, who are given the freedom to work creatively even while doing commerical work.

"Photographers handle this in different ways. Some will not shoot unless they are being paid, while others, such as Elliott Erwitt, always have a camera handy, whenever and wherever they are. The late Gary Winogrand never seemed to stop shooting, whatever the circumstances. He left many hundreds of rolls of film that he had not gotten around to developing.

"In past decades, photographers worked with an eye to the magazines; now they work with an eye on the galleries. Both are equally deadly. In order to work well one must work from one's own sensibility, with an eye to doing good work.

"Forget for a moment the *size* of the art market. The question is: How do your photographers work their way in? There is no way except the old-fashioned way, pounding on doors and hoping one will open. It is very hard as many galleries, having already developed a roster of exhibitors, are not eager to look at new work.

"While certain prices seem to have gone through the roof, they have often been generated by publicity or controversy, such as in the case of Warhol or Mapplethorpe. I don't think the Mapplethorpe controversy had the chilling effect on creativity that a lot of people thought it would. But what it did was double the price of the photographs, in line with the old adage of burning books in Boston.

"But the art market is fickle. What may be 'in' today may be out tomorrow. So the best thing to do is create good work, and forget the vagaries of the marketplace."

Somewhere among the complex of museum directors, gallery owners, curators, art consultants, historians and educators, are the critics. Often because of the long deadlines of their publications, their opinions do not appear in print until a show has closed or moved to another city. Does this reduce their validity? No, because the post-exhibit criticism may well influence the future output of an artist.

Insider: Allan D. Coleman, Critic

"My background is in literature and writing. I became interested in photography as a 'looker' at pictures in the mid-1960s, and also as a result of reading theoretical work on mass-media communication by William Ivins and Marshall McLuhan. I was doing some freelance writing and, while not formally trained in the visual arts, I was interested in them. In 1967 I realized that not much photography criticism was being written for a general audience, so in 1968 I started doing it.

"Earlier markets for photography criticism were narrow and confined to a few major publications like *The New York Times* (for whom I wrote some years ago), a few syndicates and photography magazines, but it has broadened and changed over the past twenty-five years. I now write a column for the *New York Observer*, a weekly general-audience newspaper, and have published in virtually all the U.S. photo magazines, as well as in many smaller journals here and abroad.

"There is a market for the young photographer in fine arts photography. But while there are many outlets for such work, there are also many young photographers trying to get into them. I think not many are making a living off their fine arts work, so many teach, which keeps them fed and still allows them time to pursue fine arts work. Others do applied photography; some find ways of marketing their imagery in galleries, books, posters, postcards and print sales.

"After seeing a great number of photographers' books, I think many younger photographers are not being well published. If a young photographer has developed special areas of interest that match popular tastes, then the subject matter may be the driving force behind commercial publication, rather than the photographer's personal vision. This is not to say that it doesn't matter how good the photographer is, but rather that the subject of a commercially published book takes precedence over photographic style. Thus a fine art book by a young photographer may very well be published. Also, it's occasionally viable to self-publish. If costs are controlled carefully, there may be a real, however small, market for such a book.

"Getting a self-published book out can enhance the artist's credibility. Attitudes toward what was once called the vanity press have changed considerably in recent years; this approach to publishing is not denigrated as much as before (see page 58). Many excellent and important books have been produced this way, such as the work of Ralph Gibson. His first two books were self-published under his own imprint, Lustrum Press, and received enough attention to enable him to publish other photographers' work. There are other self-published books which, while not considered classics, are substantial, and it is wrong to assume that they were published out of 'vanity'.

"If some photographic books are vanity productions, one must also consider the fact that most commercial publishers do not have a very sophisticated awareness of contemporary photography; thus this may be the only way a photographer can see his work in print.

"Co-publishing is terrific if one can find a publisher to share the cost of production and distribution. However, many photographers and artists are not producing books commercial publishers can understand. Also, publishers are not interested in producing expensive books that can at best sell only 2,000 to 3,000 copies, which translates into a loss for them.

"The art market for photographers has other possibilities beyond book and gallery sales, but these will probably generate more visibility than money. They give you 'calling cards' which you present to people to enhance your credibility. The gallery is a useful outlet through which to merchandise your work and it's wonderful to have someone else do that for you, if your work is salable. The private collector is another outlet for one's work.

"I think the young photographer should be strategizing a long-term plan which would start with the exposure of his or her work to colleagues and the community in which he or she lives (see page 14). There is also a wide international network of photo magazines specializing in fine art photography. Some of these are low-budget, some less so. They include *Camera International* (France), *European Photography* (Germany), *Creative Camera* and *Ten-8* (England). Here there are *Photo Metro* San Francisco, *The Center Quarterly* (Woodstock), *The Photo Review* (Philadelphia). There are many serious publications which serve as showcases for photographers. Collectors do not read popular photographic magazines, which are mostly technically-oriented, and aimed mainly at amateur photographers.

"The best way for a young photographer to get exposure in the fine arts world is to be aware of and possibly attend the national and international photography festivals such as Mois de la Photo (Paris), Mois de la Photo (Montreal), Houston FotoFest, the Arles Festival (France), and the various biennials in Spain, Greece and elsewhere in Europe, Latin America, the U.S. and Japan. Traveling to these events are the movers and shakers·in fine art photography from all over the world. You can think of it as photography's 'permanent floating crap game.' One component of all of them is an environment in which these movers and shakers actually look at portfolios. At Houston FotoFest, one can pay a registration fee, take a ticket and get a twenty-minute shot at showing one's work to someone who's reviewing portfolios, which includes curators, collectors, editors, publishers, and sometimes even critics. These are smaller versions of the big art expos, but at those one usually doesn't have situations where the galleries are reviewing portfolios.

"I don't think it's the job of the critic to suggest to artists how they should go about conceptualizing their work, or working out their relationship with the market. I rarely go to openings as a reviewer as that is no way to properly view an exhibition. I attend them for social reasons, restricting my viewing to a time when I can concentrate on the imagery. I review a mix of what is being shown at major institutions, commercial and noncommercial, galleries and offbeat locales. I make it a point to look at work not only by artists I am familiar with but also at a percentage of those unfamiliar to me. I try to address a variety of different styles. It's also necessary to juggle the dates the exhibit is opening and when the publication I review for is closing.

"There are no simple answers to how to get a critic to a show, but once there I look for something more than just a few 'good shots.' I work on the assumption that anybody reasonably skilled with a camera can always make a few; if not, they should hang up their cameras. The ability of the photographer to construct larger statements rather than single images is certainly something I look for. Does this person have an actual idea here? Do they pursue the idea in some interesting way? Do they develop the issue or theme, show some concern—whether it's a formal concern, or a subject-based concern? I look for something which goes beyond the single image to some larger idea.

"The best way for a young photographer to organize his portfolio would be to think in terms of an exhibit's contents rather than techniques. That's why I advise bringing a coherent, unified portfolio to those people you're asking to look at your work objectively, so they can then assess whether you can develop an idea, rather than having good images scattered all over the place. I look for an appropriate craft level; beyond that my tastes are eclectic. I look for the best of all kinds of work they can do but I don't favor landscapes, portraitures, reportage, the grotesque, or anything else.

"Photojournalists rarely wind up in galleries and gallery photographers are seldom photojournalists. Nowadays photojournalists' work occurs in a fragmented arena in which people are not encouraged to develop genuine photo essays or stories but instead provide strong single images. There are few W. Eugene Smiths or David Douglas Duncans. Some contemporaries, like Sebastiao Salgado manage to cross over between fields and do a creditable job in both. He has a remarkable sense of how to craft a theatrical and sumptuous image that makes it very powerful on the wall as well as on the printed page.

"The market is not criticism-driven; it is almost the reverse. Criticism, and to a certain extent even historianship, can be market-driven. About fifteen years ago, for the very first time, the work of Carleton E. Watkins, a Western landscape photographer of the nineteenth century, came on the market in a big way and a couple of albums of his albumen prints sold at auction for $100,000. At that time, just about any book on the history of photography would rarely mention Watkins, or at most give him a footnote. Within a year there were major monographs and scholarly articles about him, and he became a reference point for people. Why? Because someone paid $100,000 for some of his work.

"So I tend to think that the market for the currently high-priced moderns was not made by the critics, but by the galleries, who knew people who collected art and were interested in photography, people who would collect photography if in some ways it resembled the art they liked, and pay well for it. One type of collector, for instance, likes 'big art'—I mean this literally and physically—big prints, and it got so that people were buying photography on a per-foot basis, as you might with large canvases.

"I would say that the young or emerging photographer would be wise to consider the art market as a peripheral one. I don't think it is useful to think of it just as a market; but it might be an arena, a field of ideas in which the photographer feels his work belongs. Then the smartest strategy would be to view an involvement in art photography as a long-term project. The proper developmental steps to go through would be first to build a local audience; then to develop an expanded audience, through the wide network of alternative galleries, i.e., college galleries, art institute galleries, artists' space; and then making your work familiar abroad, becoming aware of those kinds of presentation spaces outside this country, and also trying to place your work in some of the smaller magazines.

"I'm against young artists renting space to exhibit their own work, because I don't believe artists should have to pay for their own exhibits. I am certainly opposed to what is now known as the '$15 show' where you send in some slides and a check, a juror picks three, and they're hung in a group show. Photographers think that such a mention might look good on their resumes, but they only look good on resumes to someone who knows nothing about the field. I get lots of resumes in the mail, and I can identify those '$15 shows' and the sponsoring institution. When I get a resume which lists fifty or sixty of those shows, there's a kind of pathos to it. On the other hand there are many institutions that exhibit work but do not require the artist to pay. They may not sell much of your work, but they show it to a good audience. There are also many other places to show one's work that are off the beaten track, such as hospitals, senior citizens' homes, schools and libraries. There are all kinds of places around the country that are happy to show work, and in many cases will treat it respectfully.

"The new photographer should build a genuine audience first, and get a sense of what it means to exhibit. The 'perk' might not be sales, but the exhibitor hosting an opening where you would get to meet people who *look at* your photographs — just ordinary people off the street, who might provide you with feedback, which I think is a rare thing for most artists. This is not feedback from a critic, but the authentic response of the average person. I think that's invaluable; and if local critics respond, and they are apt to in a smaller community, then this too is valuable and it gives you a track record as an exhibiting artist.

"It is very expensive to mount a major institutional one-man show. When I hear of an unknown twenty-five-year-old without a track record, without previous acknowledgement, suddenly appearing in a major exhibit space, I realize the 'fix' is in, either financially, or else the curator has decided he or she wants to be a kingmaker. These shows do not interest me. I am interested in work that comes up through the ranks; I think that's the healthiest relationship one can have to one's work. It's to create an appropriate dynamic for your work within yourself and within your relationship to the field.

"In this country there is no peer pressure on publishers to publish work that is worthy. That is beginning to change a little. When a photographer wins an important achievement award or fellowship and comes before the public eye, occasionally a publisher may pick up on it and publish that work. This is the lunacy of the market, and it's exclusive to photography.

"The entry into the art market for photographers depends on a long-term commitment to your vision, a concern that will withstand a possible lack of interest; the photographer is probably in trouble if he or she doesn't have the strength to deal with this. The fine arts field is overpopulated; there are probably more fine arts photographers than the world can support financially. So you're a little fish in a big pond that's full of little fish. But art photography is not a young person's medium. A photographer needs a maturing period. If you were to take any famous photographer and look at his work before he reached the age of thirty, you probably wouldn't see much that's worthwhile.

"I want to make clear that it's not the job of the artist to please critics or conform his or her work to the tastes of critics. That way madness lies. Criticism is feedback, criticism is opinion. It may be more or less knowledgeable opinion, useful feedback, but that's what it is — it's not the word of God. It's just the response of somebody who looked at it and, ideally, said what they thought of it in a clear language the artist can understand.

"What does the professional artist do with feedback from critics and the audience? It seems to me he should attend to it, because the professional artist is not merely concerned with self-expression, but with communication. The question of who one is communicating with is negotiable but the only way you're going to find out if you've communicated is by listening to the feedback. I believe that self-expression is infallible. No one can tell you that you have not expressed yourself. It seems to me that what the critic does best is to analyze and specify the communication that the artist is trying to convey. The critic is trying to find ways of saying whether, and how, that communication succeeds or fails."

Marjorie Neikrug is a gallery owner who concentrates on photography as a fine art, and she has not fled to Soho, but maintains a fine small gallery on New York's upper east side.

Insider: Marjorie Neikrug, Owner, Neikrug Galleries

Marjorie Neikrug started her gallery in 1970 and has the oldest photography gallery in the U.S. showing only photography and ephemerals. With a Fine Arts background, she spent two years at Sarah Lawrence College, painted, 'pulled' lithographs, and owned a Pre-Columbian gallery. She has designed many shows for collectors and museums, and is a tested, certified senior appraiser for photography and fine art. She is also a member of the American Society of Appraisers and the Appraisers Association of America.

I spoke with her in terms of new photographers entering the gallery market and she responded candidly.

"For a young photographer who wants to 'enter' a gallery, he has to do his homework and know which galleries are appropriate for his work. Then he must start knocking on doors, make phone calls, ring bells and finally come in to show his work. At first when we began to see new photographers, they seemed more concerned about printing than content, and I began seeing a wide range of images. Some were good, some less so.

"Although they print beautifully, unfortunately they seem unconcerned as to what they print. We're having a difficult time dealing with it, because it often lacks dimension. They have little or no background in fine arts, and really have little esthetic understanding, so it's all very sad.

"I look for content, esthetic value, good printing, and the interpretation of what is photographed. I also look for depth and meaning in a photograph. Very few have that. Now they are going in different directions and using trick photography—computer imaging, or other processes. I don't mind it; I like it because it's innovative, but they haven't studied as they should. I'm not talking about everybody who comes through here, but out of the twenty or thirty portfolios we look at monthly, only a few have the qualities we look for. Just as in painting, where there has been a lot of copying (of style) of the masters, in modern photography too there has been copying of the master photographers such as Elliot Porter, André Kertesz and Gene Smith. The new work tries to emulate it but it doesn't work very well.

"Perhaps this lack of content is a reflection of their own lives which in their struggle to survive in tough times shuts off the vistas of what's around them. So instead of coming in with fresh approaches, they say, 'Oh, what the hell,' and imitate the work of the famous photographers of the 1930s and 1940s and even through the 1960s. Much of it was protest photography of the Vietnam period, but I haven't seen much protest photography today. We are getting a lot of nudes, perhaps influenced by our own *Rated X* exhibits which have been running for fifteen years.

"We see little originality, even in the nudes, and because the body is so gorgeous, photographers should be able to do better with it. But they are not, and until they learn how to draw with light they won't do much better. I have a love for images and they have a power to affect me emotionally.

"Much of our sales are to other galleries, museums and institutions, but many photographs are purchased for personal use such as home decoration. I am often asked, which kind of photographs can one live with as decoration?

Speaking for myself, I have many photographs at home, mostly black and white, although I have some color. I like great beauty, I like reportage. I want scenics, landscapes, beautiful flowers. I love living with photographs.

"The photographs we take in for individual sale should have an understanding of the present and possibly of the past. I want to see what's in somebody's guts. There is a difference between choices selected for museums and by individuals. Different curators also look for different things; the Metropolitan Museum of Art looks for the past and the Museum of Modern Art looks for the present. Public buildings such as hospitals look for work that is cheerful, upbeat, and tells a story. Corporations often look for historic pictures such as the FSA, which has a great deal of emotional content and a sense of history.

"Recently we exhibited the work of FSA photographers. It was attended to a great extent by young people who had never heard of the FSA. Their reaction was amazing. They were really excited, realizing that this was history, and it did a lot of good because these young people learned about the problems of that period. While these are historic pictures, for these viewers they were new statements and I think many of them went away with profound impressions of our past.

"A new photographer's portfolio does not have to have many pictures. They should almost be a teasing sample of what he has. They should be bits and pieces of his work. The photographs should be neat and clean and the photographers pleased with what they are showing. Photographers can bring their portfolios in at present on Fridays; we will look at them and have them ready to return the next day. If we find something worthwhile, we will talk further with the photographer.

"By experience I can pretty well judge the quality of a photographer's work after seeing only four or five images. It is not necessary to deluge us with huge quantities of work. I don't like to look at transparencies as they are cumbersome and time-consuming to handle, but I will if necessary. It's easier for me to judge prints, or even contact prints, as that is what we're going to work from in choosing images to show.

"Most new photographers need seasoning, and we hope they realize a growth period is needed between the first and second scheduled presentations of their work. We also hope that when they leave here after their first showing they will leave feeling good, they will have optimism, will go on with their work, and take time to improve on it.

"I always try to find something good about a photographer's work and encourage them to come back. And when they have ripened we will give them a show. When we tell a photographer to come back in a year, we are not trying to rebuff them, but help them understand that we would not ask them to come back if we did not feel good about their work in the first place. We hope the prospect of indeed having a show later will encourage and stimulate them. Most do come back in a year, sometimes longer, but they all come back and we have given shows to many.

"I always enjoy encouraging new photographers, seeing them develop and return. Very often when they come back and are accepted, we will put them in a group show and thus they will have their foot in the door. I'm not afraid to give a new photographer a show; it makes me feel good.

"For us it is also a long, arduous and time-consuming task to make the public aware of the quality of a new photographer's work. Very often we put their work in our racks so that when people come in for scheduled exhibitions they also can browse through them and see other work.

"When a photographer is given a show, and his work is offered for sale, we take a 50 percent commission. We ask the photographer to participate in the expense of the invitations and to present their first-rate prints, mounted, matted, and ready for hanging. We do the framing and the hanging without the photographer present, but afterwards if they want to switch some pictures around this is fine with us. But I like to get the show up first and then adjust it if necessary. Exhibits run for six weeks and we limit them to about six per year.

"To repeat, initial presentations are very important. It tells me what the photographers think of themselves and offers me a clue as to what they are doing in their work. I have to feel their excitement.

"I am often amused by the differences among photographers; sometimes when they come in to present their work they are also interested in what is already hanging in the gallery. I appreciate that, for it tells me they are interested in what other people are doing. Others march in, drop off their work, and march out and do not seem to have the slightest interest in what we are showing currently. This also tells me something. When that happens I know their work will not be profound. I don't know if this happens because they are shy, and they shouldn't be shy, or if they are simply not interested in other photographers' work."

Beyond the Private Galleries: Institutions and Museums

If the private gallery is a potential sales market for the beginning photographer, it also has its limitations. Much satisfaction comes from recognition, or the pleasure received from knowing that your photograph is being seen (or purchased) for its artistic value and not, as one old newspaperman once told me, used to simply prop two columns of type apart in a printing form.

Sales by a gallery are an important, if not a primary, source of income for many photographers . . . particularly those who do not actively pursue journalism careers or specialize in studio work. Yet many important commercial and journalistic photographers are in major institutional galleries, e.g., Avedon, Parks, Penn, Smith, et al. In private galleries their sales can command four- or five-figure dollar amounts, but the institutional (nonprofit) exposure is often more important to them.

Most gallery operators were trained as fine art dealers, curators, lawyers and in other occupations, none of which required any professional handling of a camera. One outstanding exception is Cornell Capa, former *LIFE* staff photographer, brother of famed war correspondent-photographer Robert Capa, and now Executive Director of the International Center of Photography in New York. The Center not only mounts important photographic exhibitions, but provides many other services as a center of photographic learning and as a photography museum.

Of the several institutions that in whole or part are devoted to photography, The International Center of Photography (ICP) on New York City's "Museum Row" on upper Fifth Avenue, and its new branch in the Kodak Building in midtown Manhattan, is pre-eminent. In eighteen years it has achieved the miraculous position of being the primary "House of Photography" in the world. Dreamed of, conceived by, and directed by Capa, it has fought its way through the tightest of budgets with limited grants, not enough public funding, and far too little active support from the very photographers it is trying to help in order to achieve its prominent position.

ICP is a vital insitution fully devoted to galleries, classrooms, workshops, bookstores, and meeting rooms, staffed by some fifty people not including volunteers, teaching staff and part-time employees, all dedicated to making this the primary center of photography anywhere.

ICP does have galleries and exhibit space and indeed shows many photographers who are new and relatively unknown. But like so many other institutions of a similar or near similar nature, they are swamped with requests for exhibits that they cannot possibly handle. In its caring way, however, it at least has set up machinery for dealing with the hopefuls, both new and old, who want to achieve recognition of their photography. This does not mean that anyone who secures an "audience" is going to have a show. Far from it. Only a tiny percentage of them can be accommodated, but many have been pointed in other directions, to other institutions which could use their material, and to additional classes and workshops within the ICP to broaden their concepts and interests in photography. Many have had their work published because of leads given them by staff of the ICP and, because of new directions, have rechanneled their photographic efforts. It has a sensitive reviewing staff, currently directed by Mrs. Ruth Lester, formerly contributions editor at *LIFE* magazine for many years.They are responsive and caring, so that an appointment made by phone or letter will usually result in an interview, and often some pretty solid advice about the next move to be made in that person's photographic life.

However, failure on the part of the photographer to achieve any actual exhibit support from ICP is not a reason to lose interest in this organization. Membership in the ICP by all professional photographers, new or old, regardless of where they live, is important and useful because it keeps them in touch with the photographic community, and aware of artistic trends and developments through its exhibits, bookshops and traveling shows. There are other institutions in other parts of the country that provide some of the same services, but they usually are part of larger museums or universities with photographic departments, and are not wholly devoted to photography, with the exception of the George Eastman House in Rochester.

Non-Gallery Exhibits

Exhibits can lead to sales, even if not held in commercial art galleries. Frequently photographers can get free exhibit space in other areas, such as a press club, bank lobby, community center or recreational building. I know of one exhibition program of waterproofed photographs held out-of-doors in a major public park that brought a good response to the participating photographers. Many advertising agencies make exhibition space available to upcoming photographers because they want their ADs to see fresh materials. It doesn't always produce work, but frequently has done so.

There is also a growing market for corporate art photography. Years ago the great corporate photographic files were frequent sources for employment of working photographers. At one time the Standard Oil of New Jersey picture project was a model for many smaller companies employing as many as thirty photographers. That file has been closed with its collection of prints and negatives transferred to the University of Louisville, which is doing an excellent job of making the pictures available. Most other corporate clones no longer exist or are so parochial, they have little objective value.

Working in the creative arts is different from other jobs in that you do not leave your work behind you when you walk out the door. Photography becomes part of your very existence, and many of your personal pleasures from photography will come from finding outlets to show your work. Exhibitions, other public showings, gallery sales, can all enhance your income.

Critic Al Coleman (see page 339) talked about important art shows, their value, the importance of being exhibited, and publications that function in this market. For the most part Coleman was referring to fine arts photography and its eventual marketing.

Some younger and less experienced photographers do not feel secure enough to face the hard world of national and international competition among museums, galleries and large-scale art festivals. For these artists there are simpler and less costly methods of making one's work available to the general public. They are generally grouped under the loose umbrella of arts and crafts shows, mall shows, street fairs, church fairs. The arrangements are similar. As an exhibitor you rent a table or booth and display your wares: in this case, well printed black-and-white or color photographs of any subject you think people might like to purchase for home or office display. They should be clean, nicely matted and attractive.

Some private exhibitors have said the return can be quite remunerative. One photographer claims a profit averaging $1,200 per exhibiting weekend. Another photographer appearing to be making a living from direct print sales to the public, states he grosses approximately $50,000 for the period of May through mid-October. *The Guilfoyle Report*, published by Ann Guilfoyle (see page 59), recently reported that one (unnamed) photographer showed earnings of $250,000 a year and reported sales at The Ann Arbor Street Fair alone of $25,000. This does not happen to all exhibitors, and the report went on to cite others who earned less money and still others who became discouraged and gave up on this method of marketing. Other photographers operating in this market often deal with local galleries and act as suppliers for their market.

This is all certainly worth considering. According to the *Guilfoyle Report* print sizes vary from 5" × 7" to 16" × 20" with a variety of mats and mounting. Mounting can be simple matted mounting board, foam-core, or even more expensively mounted and shrink-wrapped around hardboard. Prices range from $20 to $350. Some photographers offer landscape, collages, C-Prints, dye transfers, almost any format and any design. Glass/Plexiglas framing for this kind of market is not always advised because of the expense, but some enterprising marketers invest in the necessary equipment and labor because they see a potential profit in frames and mounts. Still others make deals with local frame shops to have samples and prices available. Cute animals and pretty landscapes seem to do well. Many buyers at annual shows are repeat buyers, but one question persists. Do buyers at these street shows have the ability to distinguish between good photography and "kitsch" art which they seem to buy in huge quantities? So far there are no definitive answers, but there is no question also, that sales of good prints of good photography have increased a great deal.

Where are these fairs? There is a thriving business promoting them with many boosters both local and national. Some publish accurate directories, some less so. Most prominent is the annual *Harris-Rhodes* list ($40 p/a) POB 142 LaVetta, CO 81055 (Tel: 719-742-3146), or from Sunshine Arts Magazine, 1700 Longwood Drive, Longwood, FL 32750 (Tel: 407-323-5927).

In some larger urban areas classified phone books list exhibitors and producers of street fairs, and exhibitions and flea markets.

Display and Exhibits — The Personal Side

There are many other ways of securing space for your photographs. Personal exhibitions that can be moved throughout the area where you live for display in public and private institutions not only will provide a great deal of satisfaction but will publicize your name until a recognition level is reached that will start paying dividends. Even donating photographs to charity or public service auctions can be a good source of personal publicity. When these pictures are auctioned off your name and your work will come before a very large audience.

Personal exhibit programs can be expensive but can also be charged as legitimate promotion costs. I know photographers who organize well-designed traveling exhibitions of their work, reserve public meeting rooms in major hotels around the country, and invite every art director, picture buyer, museum curator and director, and anyone else possibly interested in their photographs to an opening cocktail party. Everyone likes "openings" — especially when there is an open bar — and a good publicity program can usually result in substantial local press coverage. One small photographic cooperative operation such as described above had a total production, transportation and publicity cost of about $6,000 that brought in work assignments or picture sales totaling over $40,000.

Public speakers bureaus and booking organizations will often book photographers (those who have interesting material or are well-known) for lecture and slide tours before all sorts of private, institutional and service club audiences. The fees are satisfactory, considering that little more is needed than a projector, a reasonable stage presence, and interesting pictures.

Traveling Shows

Traveling shows, like a personal portfolio, require careful thinking and selectivity of material, and their design and construction are critical factors. A show, just as a portfolio, should have a theme, as it is the deciding factor as to where the show is exhibited and under whose auspices. The most critical decision in planning a traveling show is whether it will travel by itself and be hung, or set up, by others at the destination, or whether the photographers, agent or anyone else will travel with the unit and do that work.

The traveling print show is an excellent method for any photographer to reach a wide audience. The initial costs may seem high, but if the show is well-constructed and scheduled for considerable movement, it should amortize its cost over several years.

Slide shows can also be assembled as single- or multiple-projector arrangements with appropriate mixing and dissolving equipment, which can be rented at a reasonable cost. This type of exhibit requires a protected environment, but the rental of space such as an office building lobby can be obtained cheaply, and there are usually building personnel around to protect the installation.

Capitalizing on One's New Reputation

Resting on one's laurels is not the way to get ahead. Photography is a graphic art that requires the photographer to keep his name in the public eye or he will be quickly forgotten. After the exhibits and traveling shows are completed, the listings printed, the mailings mailed, then what? It is up to the photographer to seek out some ongoing method of maintaining himself in the public eye. TV talk shows or local news broadcasts are not beyond the reach of the newcomer, and the photographer should never forget what has been repeated here often; any media which uses large amounts of visual material has a great need for new supplies of it.

With the generally widespread use of cable-TV there is an even greater demand for illustrated material. The current edition of *Literary Market Place* (see page 23) lists sixty-five TV broadcast companies that might well be interested in your color slides or even black-and-white photographs. Ditto book reviewing programs also listed in *LMP*. If you have just produced a photographic book, and think it's a worthy effort, then this too is a wide open market, occasionally a recurring one with the same broadcast group. When a book of mine was featured once on a national TV "morning" program, I was happy of course but thought, well, that's that. I was even more pleased when the show's booking desk called two months later to ask me to come back with more photographs from the same book.

Grants and Other Funding for Photographers

Small but satisfying sources of limited income for photographers are grants from government and private foundations. I stress the words *small* and *limited* because those are the operative words. In spite of literally thousands of photographers who apply each year for Guggenheims, National Endowment for the Arts (NEA/Visual Artists) Fellowships from $5,000 to $20,000 annually, and grants from The National Endowment for the Humanities (NEH), as well as smaller groups, the total number of recipients annually is miniscule, estimated to be fewer than 500. But there are more grant programs around than one would believe. In addition to those noted above there is the W. Eugene Smith grant of $15,000 sponsored by Nikon; the World Press Photo grant of 5,000 Dutch Guilders (currently worth $2,500 U.S.); the Oscar Barnack grant from Leitz (10,000 Guilders); and many more including Pulitzer Prizes ($3,000). And every state in the union has some sort of State Art Agency grant. Probably the best and most comprehensive sources of information on all grants, photographic or otherwise can be obtained from The Foundation Center at 79 Fifth Avenue, New York, N.Y. 10003; The Visual Studies Workshop's listing called "Etc" in the back of each issue of their publication *Afterimage*, 31 Prince Street, Rochester, NY 14607; and a newsletter from the New York Foundation for the Arts Inc., Suite 600, 5 Beekman Street, New York, NY 10038. There are other grants, some sponsored by educational and commerical photographic organizations, and with some diligent searching you might well turn up some organization that is willing to contribute to your professional welfare.

Continuing Your Photographic Education

One of the obvious places to find a new audience is in teaching, as there is an ever-growing demand for photographic education (see below). Teaching should not be left to those who simply have had academic preparation as their groundwork. Several well-known photographers have begun to spend more and more time teaching. I am often startled at the amount of work that comes back to them through their students, many in small workshop situations but some through larger and more formal academic outlets. Many of the students are not photographers but want to learn about photography to broaden their own professional skills.

These students may be in the process of becoming public relations people, art directors, picture editors or buyers, and even movie producers. So if in the course of their instruction they meet a teacher who is knowledgeable about the craft they are seeking to learn, what better place to turn the need when it arises but to this same person who has already demonstrated his knowledge of the field?

Many local publications in your area might welcome a photography column from you for little or perhaps even no cost for a few trial issues (although if the column should take hold and prove popular you should be paid for it). This would be a fine way for you to sharpen your photographic image and keep you in the public eye.

In photography, the question of education, whether primary, advanced or continuing, is vexing because there are so few real measurements of its value to the budding photographer. Nevertheless, many young photographers feel a need for more formalized instruction to fill gaps in their repertoires. Some want to branch out and teach photography, which usually will require a degree for qualification. There appears to be as much need for refresher courses or new education for established photographers, as there is for younger professionals (or professionals-to-be). The problem is what to study and where.

There are many settings in which the photographer may advance his or her knowledge. Over one-hundred institutions of higher education in this country teach photography or photojournalism, and their curriculums are as varied as their locations. In addition, there are literally hundreds of workshops, short courses and summer-vacation programs from Maine to San Diego, not to mention thousands of local community centers, church groups and high schools at which photographic instruction is offered. Care is needed in choosing a course, however.

The Workshop Vs. the College Degree

If the comments of Thompson and Drapkin about the lack of craftsmanship in current photographers' work are to be accepted, it follows that the new photographer should look seriously at the "holes" in his training or think about what he didn't study when at school rather than what he did. If he agrees that something is missing in his training and that he should do something about it, what direction does he follow? Go back to school and do it all over again? Hardly. Study on his own with a series of good basic books? Perhaps. (I recommend some later in this chapter.)

But what about the self-taught professional who suddenly realizes that perhaps his self-teaching or experience wasn't good enough or whose education fell by the wayside while he was just trying to survive and run his own operation, or who has had little contact with his peers? If time and money permit, this professional might take specific courses in some special technique of interest. For this person, the older, traditional schools of photography might be the best bet, as many offer courses not leading to a degree or certification for teaching. Art Director Paul Guyante (page 85) commented that not only had he studied at the Art Center College of Design in Pasadena, but had also attended the Los Angeles Trade Technical College where he had learned basic and perhaps old-fashioned techniques of paste-up, typesetting and layout. Or the photographer might take electronic imaging seriously enough to enroll for special courses in Parsons/New School or the more expensive and more comprehensive programs at Kodak's Center for Creative imaging in Camden, Maine.

I questioned several graduates of a well-known school that offered a three-year accredited program leading to a degree and discovered that in the course of that three-year curriculum there had been one session devoted to the view camera, one on lighting and a couple on the high technology of electronic circuits in cameras, but nothing whatsoever on the business side of photography. There were a lot of discussions on ethics, on photography as a fine art and on printing, but not much more.

Any discussion of photographic education for the new or older photographer may be — pardon the pun — academmic, since most such photographers probably feel they have absorbed as much instruction as they can hold, whether it was in a workshop, a seminar or a college-level course.

Within the academic system there has often been controversy about teaching methods and curricula. Thus the student, new or old, should consider carefully the many options available, including some conventional academic training or the newer methods such as suggested by Cornell Capa and Ben Fernandez. Both have proved themselves in the field, but have moved beyond active shooting into teaching or gallery or museum operations. Critics of fine arts photography who also teach have a place in the education system since much of their published opinion has a direct bearing on exhibitions of photography in galleries and museums.

Learning photography with a view toward running a commercial studio or becoming a photojournalist is one thing; teaching photography for one's living is something else. It could be an interesting outlet for established photographers and might also be the economic salvation of many. Unfortunately, too many photographers who have worked hard to establish careers and reputations have seen themselves bypassed for academic positions. This is because traditionally there seems to have been little room for the teaching of "practical" or "applied" photography at the college level by qualified, formerly working photographers or editors. There is a curious history to this situation that is deeply tied in with fine arts photography. Let us look more closely at the relationships between academia and fine arts photography.

According to a recent survey there are only about seventy-five institutions of higher learning in the United States offering degree programs in photography. Almost all of them operate through their fine arts departments and ultimately grant Bachelor or Master of Fine Arts degrees. A few journalism schools are also granting bachelors or masters degrees in science for some technically oriented students in communications photography. I know of no doctoral progams in still photography except in the fine arts programs. One hopes that in time this will change. It also appears that there are only about 90,000 students in the United States enrolled in these BFA or MFA degree or credit programs. Only a tiny percentage will go on to doctoral studies.

One interesting spinoff from this fine arts training is that these very students have become the heart of the market for fine arts photography by acquiring a taste for still photography as a fine arts collectible. It would also appear that the majority of the photographers who supply fine arts photography to the 200 + U.S. galleries that market it are, for the most part, the instructors in the BFA and MFA programs. The protective blanket of their academic salaries and tenure ensures that they will not have to deal with the day-by-day exigencies of covering fires or politicians or producing layouts or commercial work. Most BFA and MFA photography instructors are members of the Society for Photographic Education (SPE), a professional group whose membership is restricted for the most part to teachers of photography.

Much of the funding for photography degree programs comes through the college level programs funded by grants from the National Endowment for the Arts. Individual photographer's grants also came from such sources, but many are rapidly being cut back, and individual grants programs, though still funded, are frequently extended over a two-year period, effectively reducing the available amount by 50 percent.

The market for fine art photography has softened considerably due to national economic problems. Several prestigious galleries are in financial trouble and need serious infusions of major capital to stay alive. Print sales have dropped considerably. Annual returns to the photographers from gallery sales have in some cases not exceeded a few hundred dollars, and this is not enough to provide impetus either for the photographer or the gallery.

Recognition of these problems was apparent at one meeting of the SPE where requests by students for more "practical" courses prompted the SPE to schedule talks about such mundane things as "survival" and other subjects geared to bringing the photographer a more direct financial return. Hence there may be new opportunities for the experienced "practical" photographer to turn to teaching courses to enhance his earnings.

The absence of degrees held by the "applied" photography teacher has not been solved as yet, though there are two routes that he may follow to qualify. One is for the photographer to accept adjunct professorships. The other, though more time-consuming and costly, is for those experienced photographers who already have a degree in almost any discipline to return to the teaching institutions and acquire a higher degree that will give them the credentials needed to teach in institutions of advanced learning.

Cornell Capa explained reasons for other new directions in photographic teaching. He spoke of the role of the International Center for Photography in influencing social awareness of the photographic student.

"Photographers, like many artists," he says, "are solitary beings. In the mid-1930s when I and many of my contemporaries belonged to one of the first magazine-oriented photo agencies called Pix, photographers wrapped themselves in secrecy regarding their work. A radical change took place with the formation of cooperative agencies such as Magnum, the now-defunct Scope, and others. These agencies gave photographers a chance to see their colleagues' work with little danger of piracy. By the early 1970s we saw a rash of workshops, seminars and schools that brought photographers into the educational scene.

"All kinds of things started to happen when photographers began to discuss their work and share it with others. What we were seeing up to then were only the professional photographers who were working for publications. But gradually they were outnumbered by many young people, a heavy preponderance of them women, who began studying photography and teaching it as a profession. At that time there were no galleries that sold photographs and very few people who bought them. It wasn't until the 1970s that the market expanded, that galleries were formed, and that photographers began to make superb prints for sale. These prints became one-of-a-kind collectible objects, and that uniqueness extended to Polaroid prints."

Capa also spoke of the opportunities for SPE members to make fine arts photography under almost ideal economic conditions (so much for the concept of the starving artist). He agreed that most of the successful fine arts photographers are within the halls of academia. But he did not play down the importance of the qualified, nonacademically trained professional who can earn substantial fees by lecturing in workshops, seminars and non-credit teaching institutions. Capa feels that a qualified professional teaching these courses can earn between $10,000 and $16,000 a year on a part-time basis, not counting his normal sales channels. A full-time teacher should do as well as a tenured BFA in a formal institution.

I asked Capa if many of the 140 or more lecturers he has used at ICP in the past eight years for his weekend workshops and seminars have had to cancel their appearances due to work conflicts. He said that ICP has had to cancel only a handful of lectures because of time conflicts, and for these, fortunately, the center was able to substitute other qualified people. There is no doubt that the experienced freelancer who wants to build a lecture/seminar income has to be careful about accepting conflicting shooting commitments, but often, when a conflict does occur, the photographer and institution can find mutually acceptable solutions or substitutes.

On the subject of the training and planning necessary to succeed, Capa talked with great admiration about Douglas Faulkner, an extremely successful and versatile photographer who makes a specialty of nature and underwater photography. "Faulkner loves the water," said Capa, "loves being underwater and trains himself to explore the world he is vitally interested in. He has learned as much as there is to be learned from reading and studying what this underwater world is about. He has obtained, created and built the equipment he thinks he needs to get those pictures, which are more beautiful than the naked eye can see because photography often makes the invisible visible. His work demands that he be in the right place at the right time and, most important, have an idea of what he is pursuing.

"But whether it's under water, in the air, or on the street, it is the same. The photographer must be able to distinguish those things that are to be photographed from those that are not. A certain amount of excellence and quality of mind are necessary, otherwise the photographer is a 'one-shot person'—he may become known for the one shot that brought him fame. But he won't be able to repeat it."

Capa quoted Edward Steichen who, when asked by a younger photographer, "How come the same lucky accidents seem to happen to the same photogaphers?" answered, "No chance!" The photographer may have had the skill to produce the "lucky shot," but he can do it only once. Good photographs made *repeatedly* are not "lucky shots," but are the result of the *skill* of the photographer.

Insider: Casey Allen, Educator

I talked with Casey Allen who began shooting professionally in New York City in the late 1940s. He taught photography for twenty-five years at New York University where he was an adjunct professor; he also taught at the School of Visual Arts. In the 1970s he was the host and producer of his own show, *In and Out of Focus*, over WNYC-TV31. His column, "Behind the Scenes, is currently appearing in *Studio Photography*. Allen, like many educators, is as much concerned with current photography education as he is with educating the photographer in the use of electronic imaging in pursuing his profession. The first part of our discussion begins below, but because of Allen's interest in this medium we have included his other comments in the section on electronic imaging (chapter twelve).

"One of the first things a young photographer should learn is that talent is not the most important ingredient for success. Business know-how is number one, salesmanship is second and talent is third. There are many photographers out there with mediocre talent who are successful because they have business know-how and are bang-up salespeople.

"With the dramatic increase in the number of photographers over the past ten years, business savvy is a vital skill. New York City alone attracts more than 1,000 graduates from photography school programs each year. The biggest complaint by many of these graduates is that they aren't prepared for the business realities of professional photography.

"A few of the schools give short business courses for one or two semesters. That just doesn't cut it anymore in our economy. Overheads are increasing, mergers and bankruptcies have reduced potential markets, and there's always the federal tax mess in Washington. It's a business jungle out there.

"Some of the schools are already paying attention to the problem. They're among the ones that I believe have the best photography programs in the United States: Art Center College of Design in Pasadena; Brooks Institute in Santa Barbara; Boston University; University of Missouri School of Journalism; Rochester Institute of Technology; Syracuse University.

"Photography schools cannot turn out complete photographers. The rest has to be learned on the job. There are no shortcuts. An apprentice period is almost mandatory. Anyone interested in becoming a fashion photographer, for instance, should first become an assistant to an established fashion photographer. The best place for aspiring photojournalists to get a start is on a small-town newspaper. Art photographers just seem to evolve, many of them coming from the ranks of photography teachers. An interesting note: some of the best "art" photography is now being done by professional photographers on commercial assignments.

"Computers in the last ten years have revolutionized photography: automatic aperture, automatic shutter, automatic focus, selective automatic exposure. In fact, automatic cameras themselves are competing with the professionals. Where a company used to hire a professional photographer for a job, the employer now hands an employee a point-and-shoot camera. Unfortunately, a large part of the viewing public doesn't see the difference in these employee shots; sometimes there isn't that much difference.

"There have been some arguments in photographic and publishing circles that the computer interferes with the creative process. Photographers such as Jay Maisel, Greg Heisler and Eric Meola have already showed us that this is simply not true. Computers are an aid to creativity, not a hindrance. Computer imaging allows the photographer to expand his imagination and explore new techniques that were previously impossible."

The high cost of personal ownership of electronic imaging equipment (i.e., the photographer's own work station) should not deter the student from learning how to use it and work with it. Eventually it is hoped electronic imaging (see chapter thirteen) will become part of the photographer's "tool box." However, books on the history and craft of photography are still the basis of the photographer's education.

Insider: Don Underwood, Financial Planner

"I was born in Oklahoma and spent my early professional days on several daily and weekly newspapers working as a sports reporter, general reporter, police reporter, and even as managing editor before joining *LIFE* magazine. For the next ten years I was with them as a correspondent in Miami and Chicago, Bureau Chief in Dallas, Assistant Editor and an Associate Editor in New York. From there I went to the University of Utah as an Associate Professor of Journalism, before returning to New York to work for Merrill Lynch in their advertising department. I am now Vice President of Retirement Plans Department — and area I've been specializing in for the last twenty years.

"Even though I am now far removed from day-by-day professional dealings with photographers and artists, I have always been concerned with their economic welfare and have assisted many of them in planning their economic futures. The days of the photographer being a staff member of a large publishing corporation and participating in all their side benefits of accident/health insurance, sick leave pay, and vacation pay, are gone. The photographic world today is made up of freelancers who often experience feast or famine.True, there are a handful of photographers, particularly in advertising, who enjoy a six-figure income, but the majority of new photographers and even modestly established photographers earn far less.

"My first bit of advice to these upcoming craftsmen is, 'Do not depend on the kindness of a stranger.' What I'm saying is that the photographer must learn to take financial care of himself from the moment he starts practicing his craft. Ultimately, his Social Security will not be enough, and in studies I have seen on the aging of Americans, people are living much longer than before. The young will be paying for the old, and what happens when there are more old than young? The young photographer has a long way to go before he reaches the Social Security level, but there appears to be a time ahead in the 21st century when Social Security may run out. If that were to happen, what would the photographer (or anyone else) retiring then do? So we come back to the need for establishing a personal form of Social Security. Even now some senators are estimating that early in the 21st century payroll taxes could eat up to 35 percent of one's income. Right now two-thirds of the nation are paying more in payroll taxes than they are in income taxes. Recently, a British commentator, speaking about Social Security noted that 'Americans have devised an extraordinary scheme whereby their grandfathers are mugging their young.' Let me outline a five-point plan for a young photographer to follow:

1. You have got to put money away as you make it. If you're making hay while the sun is shining, yo also need to save while the sun is shining.
2. You *are* going to have to save more. Since you're living longer, you have to worry about your assets being gone before you're gone.
3. Put money away systematically; don't wait until the end of the year to put whatever money is left into the savings account. Budget for savings just as you budget for a car or for house payments.
4. Save 'tax advantaged.' If you can have an Individual Retirement Account get it; that's a fine, small tax advantage. If you are making enough money to have a Keogh plan, get it. That's an even better tax advantage. The Keogh plans are for the unincorporated business man

as well as those incorporated. Under certain circumstances you can put up to $30,000 a year away in this manner. Let me differentiate between the IRA and Keogh plans. In the IRA anybody who has earned income can contribute to that plan up to $2,000 a year. And if you are not covered by any other kind of plan, you can take it as a total tax deduction. The difference between the two plans is that the IRA only allows you to put away $2,000 a year whereas the Keogh plan lets you put up to 10 or 15 percent of your earned income to a total of $30,000 a year. There are two versions: a money-purchase plan or a profit-sharing plan. So if your income is in a six-figure plus bracket, you certainly would want to go into a Keogh plan. But if your income is between $30,000 and $50,000, always take that first $2,000 and put that into the IRA and then go into the Keogh plan as far as you can. My reason for emphasizing both of these plans is that both have tax implications. They are part of the 'save tax advantaged' program we just mentioned.

5. Save smarter. This means that instead of earning 4 or 5 percent in a savings account, try to earn 6 or 7 percent or more. Don't go crazy, don't speculate, but be a little more aggressive by investing in equities—that is, the stock market. Investing in equities is the only way to beat the erosion of your assets by inflation. For the past sixty years stocks have shown a markedly superior income to bonds and money market funds—about three to one. When inflation comes back (and it does periodically), equity funds have consistently shown a parallel growth. In other words, you should always try to top the inflation rate by your equity growth by about 2 or 3 percent. If today inflation is around 3 percent, your equity income should be about 3 or 4 percent higher. If you don't stay ahead of that inflation rate you are actually losing ground.

"I am simply telling the photographer to think ahead. The glory years may be great but they don't last forever. It's true that the creative person will tend to ignore the hard numbers of economic life but if he has a friend who is an accountant or a broker or a lawyer who is knowledgeable in investment, he should seek advice from him. He should not go it alone without regard to the realities of the hard world. Such a person will help him find good rates and, if they are professionals, will probably charge him for the advice. If they don't charge an arm and a leg, it's worth it. I repeat, ask for advice from professionals.

"In the course of all this, keep good records, particularly if you're freelancing, because IRS frequently casts a beady eye on the self-employed and audits can come often. Also, when you are preparing your taxes it is a good time to make your financial plans for the coming year. Tax time is the first quarter of a given year and the best time to do your financial budgeting. And don't treat budgeting like it's a New Year's Eve resolution. Pay attention to it—your future fiscal sanity depends on it.

"Another way of looking at this is to consider the 'yuppies'—the young upwardly mobile people. They have made money and their incomes have increased but they often haven't been in one place long enough to accrue vested interests in pension plans. So now there comes a time when they wake up—and they're in trouble. If the rising photographer is actually earning the bulk of his income from work other than photography, he might well consider using his income as a photographer for savings purposes and thus build some savings. Eventually, if he becomes a full-time professional photographer, he will have a solid footing established.

"I want to have photographers — particularly those in the 'sandwich' generation — avoid having to face what I call the triple squeeze: (1) You may be in your forites or fifties and are for the first time facing up to putting money away for retirement for yourself. (2) You may have married late or had children late and now are faced with getting your kids through school. It's always incredibly costly. If they are in their upper student years, going into their masters or doctorates, you still have to help them. (3) While you have the burdens of planning for your own retirement and your children's growth, you may also be faced with parenting your parents.

"Don't be squeezed. Start saving early."

The Photographer's Library

As do many other artists, the photographer frequently works alone as when he is composing a photograph or solving some technical problem, even though he may be physically surrounded by people. If he is covering hard news he has little time for conversation either with colleagues or whomever he is covering. If he is working in a factory he cannot spend much time in conversation about his craft with a man on a lathe or a crane operator. And if he is photographing nature or the out-of-doors, there is usually nobody with him. So much of his knowledge will come from books, from looking at other photographs and from observing how they are used. The most reasonable answers to problems are in the photographer's own library. True, there are many photographers who can visit local museums, a photo center, press club or a well-stocked library, but there are also many who do not have such access. Therefore, the photographer needs to establish a small but basic library of nontechnical books to help round out his concepts on photography and to see what other photographers have done before him and not, as Arnold Drapkin says, charge into a picture buyer's office to announce the re-invention of the wheel or show some photographs that are copies of photographic work already produced by someone else.

Some of the things the photographer can learn from this primary collection of books will be drawn from the experience, the trials and tribulations of photographers of historic photographs or contemporary colleagues. Good books can make the new photographer's path easier and perhaps make him a better photographer.

(Note: Books, particularly those with a graphic arts orientation, are highly perishable. If they do not become instant classics or are more technically oriented and therefore able to stay alive because of library reorders or college bookstore traffic, they often die a sad death by a tumbrel-type trip to a recycling plant or the remainder tables. If you [or your book dealer] do not know whether a book is available, the "bible" of every bookstore, a huge volume called *Books in Print* (BIP) published by R.R. Bowker, will tell you if the book you are looking for is still being published. If it is your book dealer should be able to get it for you.)

There is a bookstore in New York that specializes in out-of-print photographic titles: *A Photographers' Place*, 133 Mercer Street, New York, NY 10013. Also, mail-order houses carry many out-of-print books, or will try to find them for you. They usually publish catalogs or occasional newsprint journals which list large numbers of out-of-print (O/P) books on photography and other visual arts. Among them are:

Neikrug Photographica Gallery, 224 E. 68th St., New York, NY 10021. Photographica and books.
Fred & Elizabeth Pajerski, 225 W. 25th St., 5K, New York, NY 10001.
John S. Craig, P.O. Box 1637, Torrington, CT 06790. Old manuals, antique cameras, old books.
Kingston & Rose, P.O. Box 233 Cambridge, MA 02238. Twentieth-century books, journals.
Albert Morse, 30 Miller Ave., Mill Valley, CA 94941. O/P Twentieth-century books.
Witkin Gallery, 415 W. Broadway, New York, NY 10012. O/Ps and used, rare books.
Strand Book Store, 828 Broadway, New York, NY 10012. A browser's heaven, over a million books of all genres, illustrated and text.

The history of photography is fascinating because it has moved so fast in so few years. In the 150-plus years since the development of the first permanently fixed image, not only has photography become a multi-billion-dollar business, but a communication system for millions all over the world. The following books comprise a small library that will give the photographer a capsulated history of his art, some of the accomplishments and the landmarks of achievement, and also a look at what his contemporaries are doing. If you have a deep interest in the history of your craft, these books should find a permanent place on your bookshelf, along with others of your own choosing:

The History of Photography by Beaumont Newhall/The Museum of Modern Art, originally distributed by Doubleday and now available from Little, Brown & Co. First published in 1949 as the result of a Guggenheim grant and revised in 1964 and 1982. It was updated recently, and is a classic.

An exquisitely beautiful book is *Fox Talbot and the Invention of Photography* by Gail Buckland, published by David Godine, Boston (1980). Buckland's treatment of Talbot's pioneering effort in the development of a permanent image is sympathetic and sensitive. Seventy pages of well-produced photographs of Talbot's early work make this a "must" for anyone interested in the earliest history of the permanent image. There is also much to be learned of Talbot's experiences not only in the development of his processes but how he fared in the marketing of his work. Buckland, a superb researcher and curator, is active in the United States and England. She also produced another important book on photography, which is:

First Photographs by Gail Buckland. Macmillan Publishing Co. (1980). This handsome picture book contains over 200 "first photographs" in such diverse categories as animals, art, government, history, explorations, labor, transportation, war and peace and dozens of other subjects covered by photography from its first development in the 1830s to the present. It includes the real "first photograph" of the flag raising at Iwo Jima, not Joe Rosenthal's historic and well-publicized picture that was actually a re-enactment of a photograph made several hours earlier by Marine Sgt. (Navy) Photographer Louis R. Lowery. Such is the stuff that Buckland's book is made of, and because of its historic accuracy, this volume deserves a permanent place in the contemporary photographer's book collection.

In a similar but much more contemporary vein is *Great News Photographs and the Stories Behind Them* by John Faber, first published by Thomas Nelson & Co. in 1960 and revised, updated and republished by Dover Press in 1978. John Faber just told me he is now updating it, so look for it soon.

Faber, a long-time observer of news photography and unofficial historian for Photographic Administrators Inc., a trade organization known as the PAI, has done a splendid job in amassing many historic news photographs covering numerous events from 1855 to 1978 and the new edition will bring us even closer. Faber takes us from Roger Fenton's early Crimean War coverage through the turn of the century, the turbulent periods between two World Wars, and disasters including the Hindenburg explosion, the bombings in Wall Street, the sinking of the liner *Vestris*, and many other pictorial and newsworthy events. The equipment used then was a far cry from modern cameras, and these pictures will teach important lessons to younger photographers who have never heard of anything larger than a 35mm.

Other books on your bookshelf falling somewhere between Buckland's historic volumes and Faber's collection of classic news pictures should be:

The Eyes of Time, Bullfinch, 1989
Eyewitness to War, Smithsonian Institution, 1989, a marvelous work of Daguerreotypes of the Mexican War
Origins of Photography, Helmut Gershenheim/Thames & Hudson, 1983
The Camera & Its Images, Arthur Goldsmith/Ridge Press/Newsweek Books, 1979. This beautifully produced volume covers the development of the camera and photographic work from the early nineteenth century to the present. It pays homage not only to the early pioneers but to the current photographic greats as well. It is a fine bridge between the past and the present in photography.
The Daguerreotype, Smithsonian, 1992
Art of Photography, Yale University Press, 1989
Legacy of Light (on Polaroid), Knopf, 1987

Also in a more recent vein try to find copies of:

Era of Exploration, Winston Naef
Art of Fixing a Shadow, Little, Brown
Photography Until Now, John Sarkowski. MOMA & Bullfinch Press
World History of Photography, Rosenblum/Abbeville (now in paperback)
Masterpieces of Photography, from George Eastman House/Abbeville
Laura Gilpin, An Enduring Grace, Sandweiss/Univ. of Texas
Decisive Moment, Henri Cartler-Bresson/Simon & Schuster
Diary of Light, Andre Kertesz/Aperture
Walker Evans, American Photographer, MOMA/Little, Brown
Puerto Rico Mio, Jack Delano/Smithsonian
Passage, Irving Penn/Calloway-Knopf
Women Photographers, Sullivan/Abrams
Remembrances, Eisenstaedt/Bullfinch/Little, Brown
Flowers, Mapplethorpe/Bullfinch
LIFE-World War II, Kunhardt/Little, Brown
Ndbele/African Art, Margaret Courtney-Clarke/Rizzoli
African Canvas, Margaret Courtney-Clarke/Rizzoli
The above two books by Courtney-Clarke are spectacularly beautiful and create a magnificent bridge between art photography and social documentation.
Quiet Light, Sexton/Bullfinch/Little, Brown
Powerful Days, Civil Rights Photographs, Charles Moore
I Dream a World, 75 Black Women Who Changed America, Brian Lanker
Moments of Revolution, David & Peter Turnley
Beijing Spring, David & Peter Turnley
(The last four books are all from Stewart, Tabori, Chang/Publishers.)

Books on Contemporary Photography

Turning to the more current news gatherers, two books of merit on a more individual level are:

Photojournalism: The Professional's Approach, 2nd Ed. by Ken Kobre. Focal Press/1991. Kobre, an active freelance news photographer with a long list of newspaper and magazine credits, now teaches at San Francisco State University. The book includes a wide selection of fine photojournalism by working newsmen and newswomen, as well as some excellent step-by-step details in preplanning and executing, finishing and laying out magazine and newspaper stories. Extremely useful to the young photographer specializing in photojournalism.

Dave Kennerly's *Shooter*/Newsweek Books 1980, is probably out of print by now, but an excellent book to have if you can find a copy of it. It is an autobiographical tale of his rise and emergence as a fine photojournalist who eventually was appointed President Ford's personal photographer in the White House. Kennerly has now returned to active news photography and is based in California, where he covers a wide variety of political and other types of newsworthy stories. This is an easygoing tale of his experiences, particularly where he rubbed lens covers against the elbows of Washington VIPs, and some of his stories are amusing. But many, such as his adventures as a combat photographer in Vietnam, are less so. Kennerly's book is, in its way, an interesting diary reflecting the spirit of the modern photojournalist, especially if there are political overtones to his coverage.

The National Press Photographers Association publishes annual volumes called *Photojournalism* (by year), a selection of the national NPPA photojournalism awards entries, which in turn cover the major events of the year by members of the NPPA. These are excellent and handsome volumes and show the best in newspaper photojournalism for the year of publication. Currently they are distributed by *Running Press* of Philadelphia.

Books on the Development of Documentary Photography

Earlier books, particularly those reflecting the development of documentary photography, have important historic value and are still first-rate reference sources. Most are O/P, but if the eagle-eyed browser should spot a copy of any of the following titles in a used bookstore he should grab it:

The Best of Life, Time-Life Books, 1973.
The Compassionate Photographer by Larry Burrows, Time-Life Books, 1972.
Self Portrait by David Douglas Duncan, Abrams, 1969.
War Without Heroes by David Douglas Duncan, Harper & Row, 1970.
The Eye of Eisenstaedt by Alfred Eisenstaedt, Viking Press, 1969.
Witness to Our Time by Alfred Eisenstaedt, Viking Press, 1966.
Words and Pictures by Wilson Hicks, Harper Brothers, 1952.
More Than Meets the Eye by Carl Mydans, Harper Brothers, 1954.
The Picture History of Photography by Peter Pollack, Abrams, 1958./Revised
In This Proud Land by Roy E. Stryker and Nancy Wood, NY Graphic Society, Ltd.
A Vision Shared by Hank O'Neal, St. Martin's Press, 1976.
The Concerned Photographer Vols. I & II, Cornell Capa, Viking, 1968, 1972.
Industry and the Photographic Image by Jack Hurley, Eastman House/Dover, 1981.

This list represents a small sampling of the many fine and informative picture books, both in and out of print, which the young photographer who takes his work seriously should make an effort to obtain.

Books on Marketing and Law for the Photographer

There are other titles that belong on the photographer's bookshelf which deal more with marketing and business efforts and are good reference works. There is some overlapping among them, particularly in the three books dealing with copyright and the law, yet each seems to have covered points that the other two do not go into in much detail. For additional reading, I recommend the following books:

Selling Your Photography by Arie Kopelman and Tad Crawford. St. Martin's Press, 1980. This is a book written by two practicing lawyers. Kopelman was Executive Director of the ASMP for five years and Crawford active as general counsel for the Graphic Artists Guild, a trade organization of commerical artists.

Photography: What's the Law? by Robert M. Cavallo & Nancy Wolff. Crown Publishers, revised edition. Cavallo & Wolff are active as attorneys in the photography field and Cavallo is former general counsel to the ASMP.

These two books reflect on the various associations the writers have had with the ASMP and its members, and both go into depth on the legal aspects of photography, although the Kopelman-Crawford book goes further into general marketing and business of photography than the Cavallo book. Both deal with copyright and contracts involving photography. You should own one or the other, or both if you can afford them.

The Copyright Book, A Practical Guide by William S. Strong. MIT Press, 1990. This book deals strictly with general copyright matters, including photography. It is also useful for the photographer because he can easily see how other aspects of the copyright law apply to nonphotographic work, and if his efforts should take him out of the world of photography into writing, filmmaking, or any other area, this book will give him a solid grasp of copyright in all its aspects.

ASMP Monographs and White Papers; Special publications. Prices shown are for members and nonmembers:

Valuation of Lost Transparencies, $12.00/14.95
Copyright Guide for Photographers, $3.95/4.95
Legal Guide for Visual Artists, $13.55/16.95
Overexposure: Health Hazards in Photography, $15.15/18.95

Books on Writing for Photographers

With more and more photographers producing text pieces for their photographs, as well as captions, the new photographer should have a good dictionary and a good thesaurus at hand. Several PC word-processing programs have a dictionary and thesaurus built into the program. Also there are programs on disks that will help you with billing, data processing and inventory control. Check your local software house. There are many resources available and your bookstore will provide comparative material.

Three other books on writing are important. A slim volume by William Strunk, Jr., called *Elements of Style*, was written in 1935 and later revised with an introduction by E.B. White, Jr., in 1959. It is a classic and is reprinted constantly in inexpensive paperback editions. *Elements of Style* has become the night-table companion for insomniac writers who seek to learn to use language clearly, concisely and effectively. They much prefer to read it and re-read it constantly instead of becoming glassy-eyed prisoners of late-night TV reruns. I know of one prolific writer with a lifetime of experience who told me he buys a half dozen copies at once and scatters them throughout his house so he can pick one up and read it wherever he is at any time. He never seems to tire of it, finding freshness each time he reads it. This short book is a must for all who want — or are called upon — to write.

Many press organizations publish internally what they call "style books." They are usually for their own employees and contributors, delineating the way that a particular company uses words, titles, abbreviations, etc., and in general offering considerable guidance. Most style books are restricted in circulation to the staffs of their respective companies, but several are generally available in bookstores. I recommend *The New York Times Manual of Style and Usage*/NY Times Books, (with frequent updates) or an older publication called *Chicago Manual of Style*/University of Chicago Press. These three books should give the young photographer some insight into the language he uses when filing his copy or detailing captions for publication.

Books on the Aesthetics of Photography

The vast number of photographic books being published makes it impossible to include everything, but we'd like to point out a few unusual books:

Susan Sontag's controversial essay *On Photography*, originally published by Delta Books, Dell Publishing Company (1980), from earlier writings published by Farrar, Straus & Giroux, and now published by Doubleday, is a philosophical analysis of photography as perceived by Sontag. It has been both applauded and attacked by the photographic world. The contemporary photographer who is concerned with the sociological perception of photography will find it interesting reading. I disagree with Sontag on many issues she raises, but these are my own subjective judgments.

Vicki Goldberg, writer and photo critic (for *The New York Times*, *American Photo*, and other publications), has written several excellent books of importance to the photographic community and the general public. One work is a collection of other photographic writing she edited, called *Photography in Print*, originally issued by Simon & Schuster and now reprinted in paper by the University of New Mexico Press ($17.95). She has also written an incisive biography on Margaret Bourke-White (Harper & Row), and *Photographs That Changed Our Lives* (Abbeville Press, $39.95).

Another important book that is harder to categorize is *Documenting America*/University of California Press. This overview of the Farm Security Administration Photographic Project (paperback $24.95) is an extremely valuable reference to the historic FSA project. It has the Library of Congress numbers available for print service for scholars and historians.

In trying to build a photo library, one must remember that it is an open-ended process. There are always new books coming out and many desirable ones quickly go out of print. The photographer who wants to keep his thinking current should not only carefully read the book review columns in the various photo magazines, but also keep a watchful eye on the major literary review publications of the larger and more influential newspapers in his area. Ironically, most photographic supply stores do not stock many books, except for a few "how-to's" claiming that heavy normal sales traffic precludes allocation of much counter space to the display of books. The photographer has to get the books he wants in regular bookstores or perhaps by mail. Collecting photographic books should be an ongoing habit and money should be allocated for the purchase of new books just as surely as one allocates general overhead expenses.

Benedict J. Fernandez

Educator and Photographer

Ben Fernandez, Chairman of the Department of Photography at both Parson's School of Design and the New School for Social Research in New York and one of the brightest names in contemporary photography, had an unlikely beginning to his career. New York born and "street wise" in his youth, he put in two years at Columbia University as a physical education major. He made the swimming team and helped to support himself by working nights at a photo lab, but gave up school to become an operating engineer at the Brooklyn Navy Yard. He developed a further interest in photography, bought a third-hand Leica and joined a New Jersey camera club. The Navy was phasing out the yard and offered him the option of moving to California or Hawaii as an operating engineer or being retrained in some other capacity. He expected to be taught computer programming, but to his amazement they offered to retrain him as a ladies' hairdresser.

After a few choice and explicit descriptions of where the Navy could put their hairdressing program, he made photography his profession. Through a friend, he met Alexey Brodovitch, *Harper's Bazaar*'s famed Art Director and teacher, who accepted Fernandez as a student in his workshop.

Brodovitch's art direction was breathtaking and innovative, and his photographers' workshops were famous and influential in the development of many great photographers, among them Arnold Newman, Ben Somoroff, Ben Rose and Richard Avedon.

Fernandez's first major newspaper appearance came in 1966 when *The New York Times* ran his pictures of a draft-card burning. His photographs began getting published more frequently during the next six months and he felt he had really arrived when he had a *New York Times Magazine* color cover of an anti-Vietnam War demonstration. Da Capo Press/1968 published his book called *In Opposition: The Right of Dissent in America in the 1960s*. In that same month, George Eastman House in Rochester exhibited his photographs in a show called "Conscience, the Ultimate Weapon: The Role of Dissent in America in the 1960s." It became one of their longest-running exhibitions.

As an educator, Fernandez is a strong believer in photography as a tool for social communication. He prides himself on being one jump ahead of trends because, as he as said, "By the time it became fashionable to photograph dissent in America, I was already beyond that and ready to move on to something else." He did not leave dissent photography because it was no longer needed, but felt that it would survive without him, and turned to political action photography rather than political dissent.

Fernandez also became close to the Kennedy family in a curious way. Like many other beginning photographers he eked out part of his livelihood by photographing weddings. One, at New York's Plaza Hotel, was attended by Robert Kennedy. Fernandez, refusing to act the "paparazzo," did not make any pictures of him or other celebrities present, relying, he says, on his own good taste not to encroach on the personal lives of these people. Evidently Kennedy became aware of the photographer who did not invade his privacy. As a result, Fernandez was invited to photograph the Communion of one of the Kennedy children. He also met other Kennedy family members and became involved with the civil rights movement. He met and became friendly with Dr. Martin Luther King, covering much of King's civil rights work and eventually producing a book with him called *Trumpets in Freedom* for a Canadian publisher.

Fernandez won a Guggenheim Fellowship in 1970, several NEA grants, and operated a commercial studio in New York for about six years. But photographic education interested him, and he started a novel free school for ghetto children that had its headquarters in the basement of the Public Theater. "Combating the Mental Poverty" became the theme of his educational project, knowing that in order for children to combat it they needed education. Photography, he felt, was an important educational tool. The only charge for his courses was the agreement by some of the students that they would teach successive classes of children entering the program.

Education is now his main activity; his dual chairmanships in two prestigious schools give him the opportunity to develop photography as an educational method. He strongly believes that a socially aware photographer will be a better commercial photographer. This is the keystone of his educational philosophy, and he anticipates many of his students will go on to fine careers in photography within this humanistic framework.

His unconventional approach to photographic education is far different from most schools and colleges. In his earthy way he compares photography to a social visit to a friend's house, saying, "When you visit someone, you don't come without a present." Pursuing this further, he adds, "When you come to photography, you don't come empty-handed either. If you do, you'll get empty pictures. You have to bring something with you. You must have a point of view, a position, something to say. Photography is not a field in which you can develop something out of nothing. A camera just sits there, like a pencil. It does nothing without a thought. If you have no thoughts you are not going to be a photographer. If you want to be a photographer, you have to start having something to say.

"That means you need some sort of education," he continues, "because education helps you to formulate and condense ideas so that you can then relate to something. In photography you want to amplify that something. You want other people to understand it, and thus you start developing what I call a 'visual vocabulary.' With a pencil, you have to learn your ABCs. With a camera, you have to learn the basics, too: composition, color balance and so on. In that respect, photography is no different from any other sort of learning."

Primary to any photographic education, Fernandez thinks, is the need to spend at least two academic years learning all there is to know about film, cameras and optics, as well as the many ways of extracting the fullest photographic image from any shooting. Color must be included, and with the advent of electronically produced images, the student should also learn what image-producing problems have to be dealt with in that medium. There are many ways of learning the technology of photography, he thinks, but the key to all of them is thorough grounding in knowledge of the capabilities of cameras, lenses, film, tape, and now the relevant computer hardware and software. Without this understanding, all efforts to produce new and fine photography will fail. The bottom-line question Fernandez asks is, "Will the student be able to speak visually?"

He cautions, though, that the student should never be so carried away by technique that he loses sight of his objective. Fernandez has seen too many young photographers get so caught up in technique that they lose the emotional impact of making good images. The photographer has to walk the thin line between technique and creativity. Fernandez thinks it is unimportant how many ways a photographer knows of doing something so long as he knows the best way. He should be able to use his knowledge without being confused. Thus he must know, for instance, *the qualities and capabilities* of the wide-angle lens, the view camera or any other special tool that has to be used in select circumstances. Today a knowledge of electronic imaging must be added to the list. In addition to the two years spent on the above, another year is required to learn other mechanical needs of photography.

"What I get nervous about," he adds, "is the student who gets so caught up in the theory of an idea that he never executes it! And that's the part that's frightening. Every job is a learning experience and each time he should come back a little wiser. Come to the job with knowledge, but expect to leave it with more. And don't come with just enough to make yourself look like a fool. You don't need to embarrass yourself or your client." But he cautions against the student accepting too much from the manufacturer. Fernandez warns about having a machine do the thinking rather than the photographer. This is where every bit of personal knowledge should come into play in order to create the best possible photography.

"It's the false notion that pictures are made easily. Automation tends to make so many images look alike, have the sameness (and dullness) to them. The photographer caught in this trap is one who does not experiment with lighting, motion, exposure, and thus does not bring anything new to the problem. This is where these minimum years learning the craft of photography are so important."

Fernandez worries, too, about the direction he sees photography taking today. Knowing virtually nothing about art, young photographers are choosing the camera to produce an art form quickly, with little or no effort. The result, he says, is banality and dullness and, even worse, outright copying of someone else's style. When an important photographer has a museum show, Fernandez frequently sees many "knock-offs" of that exhibitor's style. Those photographers were looking for a rapid success without understanding the art form involved. He also feels that the young photographer today is being taken advantage of, thus fostering the illusion that photography is easy and that, in order to earn big bucks, one need not have to "learn or bring too much with him." He blames much of this on manufacturers who want to make photography look painless.

Fernandez tells his students that if it is monetary success they are looking for, they may be disappointed. He reminds them that for every highly successful Richard Avedon, Arnold Newman, Gregory Heisler, or Irving Penn, there are probably thousands of photographers who will never produce anything remotely resembling that body of work. But, he says, "If a photographer has what I call the "L" *(for longevity)* factor, he will probably make some fine photographs in his time." But he then adds, "The photographer must also have *chutzpah*, and if he doesn't have it, he will never make it."

Fernandez approves of continuing education for the photographer because any new education is a plus factor, especially if the photographer needs to know something about a new phase of photography. He is also concerned about the photographer's commitment to improving his skills or point of view and to photography in general.

He looks for students or other hopefuls who are capable of making decisions and want to explore themselves with the camera. They are the ones who will make good photographers, because they are curious, and they work with their cameras to satisfy their curiosity. As a byproduct of all this they can look at their "curiosity" and enjoy it vicariously. So his main thrust is for photographers to develop a point of view, and he feels that education is probably the most practical way to do it.

"I have always felt that having a point of view is extremely important. It is doubly so in this new era of electronic imaging. At the New School we have acquired new equipment such as a Premier main frame and software which permits image manipulation. (See chapter twelve for fuller discussion of the technology of electronic imaging and its equipment.)

"So what you are hearing is that I am no longer a photographer in the classic sense but a computer 'nerd.' I am rebelling against this, but as an educator I know that it is very important that our students have the opportunity to deal with it. I am not changing my position on photographic education but what I'm doing is pointing out to people that the computer has now made photography easier and more accessible.

"Another way of looking at it is that when some painters saw photography they said painting was dead. Painting as we knew it when it was recording the image of somebody had to take a background seat. Then we got the Impressionists, we got the photographers, we got a whole new kind of expression in painting. Well, I think EI is going to give us the opportunity to use photography in ways we have never been able to before.

"What is going to happen is that now we're going to produce photographic illustrations as never before, and improve news and historical photography. We're going to see a resurgence of some of the older crafts of personal photography such as fine papermaking, excellent printing, and dye transfers. Even the old and magnificent Carbro prints are coming back in a new form. These are craft and art procedures which will never go away."

With this new technology Fernandez thinks photography now has a chance to become a true art form in itself and not derivative of an earlier genre. Therefore he thinks it important that students be aware of what they're doing and what is being done, and that they know how to deal with all the topics of illustration in photography, journalism, etc. "We now are able to take computer technology and mix it with the new art procedures above. Previously a student had to go through all sorts of complicated calculations to get proper exposures, filtration, etc. to produce a good color print or separation. Now all he has to do is feed his material into a computer, scan the image, and decide what kind of photograph he wants to make. The computer can take over from there and technically there will be fewer problems. This new technology will not do away with film chemistry but will make the computer an electronic assistant to the photographer in producing better images.

"From an educational viewpoint, I want to emphasize that EI is not killing conventional image making. Creativity is still very much the guiding impetus and we don't want our students to forget it. At a recent workshop a number of prominent speakers inferred that photography as we know it is dead and being replaced by the new toys. This is not true.

"Electronic imaging only accentuates the age-old problem of cropping, retouching, airbrushing, etc. but it doesn't alter anything. It simply makes it easier for the editor, the art director or graphic designer to change things around to what he wants rather than what the photographer took. The photographer, if he wants to be true, still has to make the photograph as he sees it. It is still the photographer's responsibility to create the image. Many fine photographers today are doing that with the aid of electronic imaging. At the Maine workshop recently I saw some big name photographers working until two or three o'clock in the morning composing and recomposing their own images.

"But for its stance in photographic education today, I feel it's not in a very good place, because people become involved in the manipulation of images. Others are caught up with the idea of fine art, which you cannot criticize, because only the artist knows what he means. Then you have the problem of the photojournalist who has to make a judgment call on whether or not the editors are going to manipulate the picture as they wish it to appear or as he perceives it.

"This is a good time in the sense that there are many opportunities to teach people the ethics, the values and the necessity for honest photography. For the artist and illustrator it's great. But for the journalist's ethics it is wrong. And there are a few more truths. I think the teachers are too young yet; we have older teachers who are not avant-garde enough and understanding. Education in photography is still a broad subject. For example, there are Ph.D.s in photo chemistry, lenses, and optics. But in photography so far all you can get is a Ph.D. in Fine Arts. We have not defined a Ph.D. in photography as yet. I think EI is going to help us do that. But I think it's going to be another ten years before we can come to an understanding of what it is and how we're going to teach other disciplines along with it. And right now because of the craziness of so many choices, I doubt if our teachers can fully deal with it yet.

"In summation I wish to add that we have unparalleled opportunities with EI. Let us not drag the old into the new, but explore the new for what it is. And we will continue with our standard procedures in photography.

"I came to photography because I suffered from dyslexia and was unable to communicate with the written word. I learned a visual vocabulary and I learned how to analyze images. Now I have a greater opportunity with EI to make my visual language more astute. As a witness I have to only tell the truth. My vocabulary is only what it is. As a storyteller the electronic image gives me greater license."

Author's late note: As this edition closes and is catapulted to the print (summer of 1992) it has just been announced that Fernandez was awarded a Fulbright Grant (fellowship) for a lengthy study of the effect of photography on politics in Europe. Bravo Ben! We all await your return and your findings.

Appendix

Pricing Your Work

Overview to Pricing Stock Photography

Pricing one's work is often analogous to the old joke, "How do you get rescued from a desert island?" Answer: "Start making a Martini at 5:00 P.M. You can be certain that someone will shortly show up to tell you how to do it differently."

In chapter five we discussed how to properly price work and how to get an adequate return on stock photographs. I suggest you reread this section carefully because there are no hard rules about pricing and no rigid guidelines. Photography does not exist in a vacuum untouched by the world around it. As in any other craft or trade, prices are subject to the age-old laws of supply and demand—except in the arts, where there are the added dimensions of content and artistic merit. A photograph, as we have often said, is a unique object. It is not merely a piece of film, tape or glass (in the same commodity category as cellulose, magnetic tape or plate glass) but a created image that simply uses these materials as a carrier. What is bought and sold is the image, not the carrier. The photographer (and the client as well) must never lose sight of that fact.

In the field of photography, many experienced professionals often consider the exposure meter as little more than a "hunting license," and unfailingly rely on their own instincts as to whether an indicated exposure is correct or not. The same can be said of the charts, tables and lists that will follow. They are "hunting licenses," guesses, and combined averages of surveys by several professional societies. They are also the result of many years of consultation with practitioners in the field as to what is being paid. Most established and secure photographers will show you their invoices. They know that their sales depend on the unique quality of their work, and do not worry over the threat of underpricing by an over-anxious beginner. There are exceptions, but the average prices reflected below are reasonably accurate. Remember, ad nauseum perhaps, that these are estimates. It is up to you, the photographer, to establish your worth.

Color photography, even in newspapers, has increased, and there is a concerted effort to bring black-and-white photography to an equal pricing plane with color. But we have to be realistic. The market for color stock photography in small town papers is small, but its use in books, published locally or nationwide, is on the rise. More and more previously black-and-white textbooks are adding color, some are now all color.

I believe the book market is the most accessible to new photographers.

It has developed enough trade experience to have established acceptable standards for the use of stock photography. In most textbook publishing, up to 40,000 copies is considered a normal printing. Press runs in substantial excess of that number should be considered when pricing. One thing you must ascertain is the size of the edition for which your work is being purchased. Most book production people will tell you the truth if you ask them. Your invoice should reflect these terms. Occasionally, a publisher will run additional printings with the aggregate run exceeding 40,000. Unless they advise you of this, it is often difficult to know when to bill for excess printing. When you negotiate your pricing schedules, your questions about the press run should be enough of a warning that you are aware of these parameters, that most reputable publishers will not try to play games with you. Generally, encyclopedias are printed in editions larger than 40,000, and should be priced accordingly. Unfortunately, not as many encyclopedias are being published as once were, so the market is more limited.

Head shots of authors should be treated differently than text material, and paid for either on a portrait-sitting basis, or as a percentage of the charges allocated for front covers, back covers or end flaps.

Magazines, Newspapers and Television

Magazines

Space used:	¼ pg.	½ pg.	¾ pg.	Full pg.	Dbl. pg.	Cover
Circulation:						
1-3 million	$500	600	750	1000	2000	1500–3000+
500M-1 mill.	$400	500	650	750	1400	1000+
250M-500M	$300	400	500	600	1200	750+
100M-250M	$250	350	450	550	1000	600+
Under 100M	$200	250	350	450	900	400+

Sunday Supplements
(Owned by publication, not purchased elsewhere)

Space used:	¼ pg.	½ pg.	¾ pg.	Full pg.	Dbl. pg.	Cover
Circulation:						
3 million+	$450	600	750	1000	1800	1500+
1-3 million	$350	500	600	850	1500	1000+
Under 1 mill.		400	500	750	1400	750-1000

Daily Newspapers

Space used:	¼ pg.	½ pg.	¾ pg.	Full pg.	Dbl. pg.
Circulation:					
+300,000	$300	350	400	750	1000
−300,000	$200				

TV Editorial Use (As news items)

National	$400	Regional	300	Local TV	150
National cable	$300	Regional cable	200		

Note: Many print and TV press groups are members of syndicated services which permit use of their material by other syndicate members. Be certain you specify that the rights you are granting do not include syndication rights without additional payment . . . and know what those payments are. This is important when unexpected hard-news situations arise and the photographer, in his eagerness to sell the photograph, may not realize its full resale potential.

Educational Film Strips

For single image use in 1500 units or less, $150-175. For multiple images, negotiate.

Miscellaneous Uses

In greeting cards, exhibit prints, educational study prints, puzzles, murals or new unspecified uses. These all should be considered on a case-by-case basis, but use the above guidelines for circulation, size and intended use as the determining price factors.

Textbooks

Space used:	¼ pg.	½ pg.	¾ pg.	Full pg.	Dbl. pg.	Cover
Press runs:						
– 40,000	$250	350	425	500	1000	1500-2500
+ 40,000	Increase all above by 20%. (Negotiate for printed h/c.)					

Encyclopedias

Press runs:

– 40,000 unlikely, use + 40,000 above.

Trade Books

Trade books use few single photographs by individual photographers except for covers, end flaps or author head shots. Negotiate use, but not less than comparable textbook rates. If photographers supply photographs for whole sections or chapters or inserts, negotiation is necessary to determine the relative importance of text/illustration.

Paperbacks (Trade)

Trade paperbacks often use the same book bodies as hard cover books. List prices are lower but unit sales should be higher. It is unlikely a trade paperback will be printed in small runs. Prices should be negotiated with that factor in mind.

Other Considerations in Textbook Pricing

In textbooks, whole sections are often begun with a "unit opener" distinct from a chapter head or frontispiece, and should command the following proportional rates:

¼ page or less	50% of cover fee if used as a unit opener		
½ " " "	60%	"	"	"
¾ " " "	70%	"	"	"

Revisions. What is a revision? There is little agreement on what constitutes a revision. A survey of textbook editors and picture suppliers has resulted in a two part definition, i.e., minor and major revisions.

Minor revision. If there have been some changes in text, without design changes in the placement or size of a photograph, these are minor revisions and no new fee is applicable.

Major revision. If the photograph is relocated in the body of text or changed in size (which would make it difficult for children using both editions in a classroom to follow the pagination as directed by teachers) this would be a major revision and subject to a 75 percent charge of the current space rates.

Warning. A new *edition* of a book is not merely an additional printing of an existing book. A new edition usually is a major revision incorporating design changes that probably involve picture sizing and placement.

Second warning. Regarding reuse by the same publisher in a different book. If, for instance, a publisher wants to use a picture purchased for a physics textbook in a new book on mathematics, this is a *new work* and should be priced at the new book rate. If the publisher wants to use the existing film from the old book, that's permissible; it will save them money on production cost, thus making the repurchase more attractive. And it will save time and effort for you, in rehandling the original transparency. No new laboratory charges or print fees are applicable here.

For multiple language rights, see Foreign Language Rights and World Rights in the Glossary.

Corporate Annual Reports and House Organs

In spite of the many detailed charts of prices for stock photography in these classifications, few are actually followed. Most of these publications are inwardly directed toward their own operations, products or services. Most photography used here is assigned, often as large packages or by day rates. When individual stock photographs are sold to these publications, price recommendations for magazine or regional publications of similar content and distribution should be followed.

Record Albums and Tape Package Covers

It is difficult to determine average prices paid because of the great variety of source material. Typical current prices paid for album/cassette covers by established production companies are in the $500 to $1,500 range if produced on assignment or purchased as stock. Wraparound covers and small photos on album back covers are often included in total price, as are enclosures (program notes, promotions for other albums etc.). If a reduced payment sale is made for test purposes, be sure to *specify on your invoice* that full payment will be made if the test is successful, i.e., the album is marketed. In this particular medium it might also be a good idea to remind the buyer (tactfully) that use of a copyright image without agreed payment is an infringement of copyright.

Advertising Rates in Magazines, Television and Newspapers

Most general consumer magazines, especially those with large circulation, do not use much stock photography from the regular stock houses. They use the news production agencies that are more apt to have photographs of personalities, politicians and other public figures. Consumer magazines often use color photographs from stock sources in non-news capacities, i.e., food, fashion, housing, lifestyles, travel, and usually follow established page rates that parallel textbook page rates above. *Special note:* Since most advertising material is prepared directly for the printing process, part of your price negotiations might include a substantial (and free or at low cost) press overrun of attractive ads to be used as mailers. The time to talk with publisher's offices or agency production people about this is well before a layout goes to press.

Consumer Magazines (Advertising average reported prices)
National

Space used:	¼ pg.	½ pg.	¾ pg.	Full pg.	Dbl. pg.	Back cover
Circulation:						
3 million +	$1500	1800	2500	3000	6000	5000
1-3 million	$1000	1250	1500	1800	3600	3000
500M-1 mill.	$ 750	1000	1250	1500	2500	2000
Under 500M	$ 600	750	800	1000	2000	1800

Above are for single insertions.
For multiple insertions:
1-3, base rate + 20%.
4-10, base rate + 50%.
10 +; negotiate, but apply time
 cap if necessary.

Additional rights with time caps:
Total buy-outs = 5× the base price.
One yr. unlimited use, base plus 200%.
One yr. exclusive use, base plus 125%.

Regional

Space used:	¼ pg.	½ pg.	¾ pg.	Full pg.	Dbl. pg.	Dust Jct.W/A
Circulation:						
3 million +	$900	1100	1500	1800	3600	3000
1-3 million	$600	750	900	1100	2200	1800
500M-1 mill.	$450	600	750	900	1500	1100

For multiple insertions, use percentage formula for national advertising (above).

Local Advertising

Several professional organizations suggest fixed percentages of regional rates, but practicality tells us that for the most part small local publications simply do not have budgets set as strictly as the larger regional and national publications. Use the regional scales suggested above with at least a 25 percent reduction in base rates as a negotiation base. Its also unlikely that small local advertisers will be reaching circulation figures in excess of 100,000. For multiple insertions in local advertising the percentage rates above can be followed.

Trade Magazines

Trade magazines are an important part of the magazine publishing world and probably have as many pages of advertising (if not more in some specialized magazines) as their consumer-oriented counterparts. Since they are usually targeted at a special interest audience, circulation is lower, though there are some exceptions. Many major business magazine editors cringe when the term "trade" is thrust upon them, but it is accurate, if one considers that their trade is "trade and commerce."

Estimates of trade ad prices vary and much often depends on the very special nature of the commodity or service advertised. At this writing art buyers at major advertising agencies say they pay about one-third less for trade advertising assignment photography than they do for consumer photography, and that includes the big stars. Since trade figures are so diversified, with many trade magazines being printed away from the mainstream of the larger publishing companies, it is logical to expect that their allocations for stock photography in trade advertising will follow the same pattern. So expect a one-third reduction of comparable space rates. Additional payment for multiple insertions, buy-outs, or extended use still apply.

Newspaper Page Advertising

Newspapers can be a source of revenue for stock photography in advertising, but, again, with the exception of the large major city dailies, circulation is well under the average of the standard consumer magazine. Most newspapers are targeted at a local market, with only a few such as *The New York Times*, *The Washington Post*, *USA Today* and the *Wall Street Journal (WSJ)* vying for national readership. Ironically, the WSJ does not use editorial photographs and only a few in scattered ads, so it does not seem to be an encouraging market. Much of the photography used in newspaper advertising is for national accounts such as airline, automotive, travel and bankcard advertising. These ads are usually produced by major agencies, though often by branch offices in the home city of the advertisers. In chapter thirteen where we discuss electronic imaging, please note that Meteor Photo, the preeminent company in the country, has its plants in Atlanta and Detroit. Why? Because that is where the agencies that use their services are located. And though Meteor and their client agencies are dealing with color, those agencies also produce other advertising, including black-and-white newspaper advertising. Some photographs used in newspaper advertising are produced for local department or other service stores, food chains, and petroleum products.

Prices for newspaper stock photos for newspaper ads have to be adaptable, often on an edition-by-edition basis. If suburban editions are published, they must consider their local audience. Remember, here the contact point has to be the local or regional branch of the advertising agency that is making up the ad, not the newspapers themselves. Below are listed some general guidelines, but even more important is the flexibility required to deal with local needs and budgets.

Space used:	¼ pg.	½ pg.	¾ pg.	Full pg.	Special insert
Circulation:					
+450,000					
1st ins.	$600	750	1000	1500	2000
Additional insertions:					
1-2, base plus 10%					
4-9, base plus 7.5%					
10+, base plus 5%					

Continuous run or suburban editions negotiable.
250M-400M, reduce base by 15% all categories.
50M-250M, reduce base by 25% all categories.
Follow magazine guidelines for buyouts or extended time caps.

Brochures of Special Printed Publications and Flyers

These special publications should be treated on a case-by-case basis because of size variation, press runs, test runs and mass mailings.

Space used:	¼ pg.	½ pg.	¾ pg.	Full pg.	Dbl. pg.	Cover
Press runs:						
+ 1,000,000	$600	750	900	1200	2000	2000-2500

500M-1 million	less 10% all levels
250M-500M	less 12% all levels
150M-250M	less 15% all levels
20M-50M	less 20% all levels
Under 20M	less 25% all levels

Wrap-around covers: Plus 75% of full cover.
Back cover: 75% of front cover.
Inside covers: Front, 65%; back, 50% of front cover rate.
Reuse: Negotiate, but not less than 75% of original base fees.
Reissue: For new campaign or sales program with minor alterations, 75%-100% added.

Television Commercials

The use of still photography for TV commercials is widening, but the growth area appears to be in regional and local programming, especially for UHF or cable systems. Compared to the enormous overall costs of mainstream network programming, prices of stock photographs are minor outlays and agencies are usually generous with their fee structure. When a product photograph is needed, the agencies will often use out-takes from studio assignments. One exception is travel, where photographs of exotic backgrounds are used either with, or instead of, an advertiser's product. When a stock photograph of a location is purchased for these purposes, the agencies may superimpose models or products either by front or rear projection systems, or electronic imaging, and then re-copyright the new image. Be certain your invoice shows your clear retention of rights to the image you have sold and prohibits third-party use.

Most TV commercials are purchased in cycles usually lasting thirteen weeks, or purchased for two, thirteen-week cycles. Images are shown briefly, often for only a few seconds. But these short exposure times may also affect the prices advertisers are willing to pay. To them a three-second exposure on a 30-second commercial may not be worth as much as 10- to 15-second exposure on a 45- to 60-second commercial, so some haggling can be expected. But this market should not be ignored. One caveat: Be aware of the practice of re-editing the second thirteen-week segment and re-using your photograph in a different version. This is really a new commercial and should be paid for accordingly. Also be sure to double-check your agreements on so-called "wild-card" or random uses that are inserted randomly in "lead-in" programming.

Circulation:	1st 13 week	Two 13 week cycles
National network	$800-1500	1200-2000
National cable	$700-1250	1000-1500
Regional/cable	$500-750	750-1250
Local cable	$250-500	400-900

Internal (house) testing: Flat fee $300-500.
Additional cycles: Base price plus 25%.
Multi-use in same commercial: Negotiate,
  but not less than 50% of base price.

Commercial Packaging of Products

Variable depending on size of illustration, distribution.
Should be negotiated with agency or design house handling point-of-purchase sales.

Distribution:	Small spot	Main illus.	Full illus.
Regional	$350-500	750-1000	1500-2500
Local product	$200-300	400-600	500-750

Test mock-up: Flat fee not less 250.
Reuse: 75% of base fees.

Billboards

Outdoor billboard displays are usually large and exposure can run from three months to a year. Board sizes are usually designated by sheets, i.e., a 24-sheet is a large full-size commonly used board. This market is declining because of environmental objections to billboard display. Earlier published price reports may no longer be realistic. Fees are usually based by the number of displays and may vary by city, state, regional or national locations. Purchases are handled by the ad agency on the account, though sometimes by the billboard companies, who are identified on the boards.

Locations	3 mos.	6 mos.	9 mos.	1 year
City (up to 12)	$ 700	800	1000	1200
State (12-40)	$ 800	1000	1500	1750+
Region (up to 100)	$1000	1500	2000	2750+
National (100+loc)	$1750	2250	2500	3000+

Point of Purchase (Counter/rack displays)

Rates for these products should be comparable to general packaging fees. They are frequently controlled by agency or design houses. Room for negotiation here is based on distribution, where displayed, and size of display.

Posters, Postcards and Calendars

These are used for many purposes: theater/film/art announcements, promotion of products and services, or simply as decoration. The photographer should determine usage and base price on the correct category. Poster sizes usually run from 8″ × 11″ to 30″ × 40″ or even larger, and runs can be from a few hundred to a million or more. All of these factors must be considered. The comparable use tables herein should be guidelines. Calendars have a variety of shapes, formats and illustration content. All above factors of distribution, size and runs must be considered before pricing work. Material for this medium should be sold only to organizations with verifiable sales records.

Presentation, Test Layout, Artist's Reference and Art Rendering.

These are all low budget items and simply have to be negotiated. Fees can range from $100 to $500. It should be made clear that if the test design or presentation does "sell," then the fee should be charged as for a final product.

All forms shown in this appendix that are credited to the ASMP are used by kind permission of the American Society of Magazine Photographers. It should be noted that any agreements shown herein are only *suggested* ones, based on ASMP's extensive experience. However, the Society renders no legal opinion concerning their application. Individual modifications are encouraged for specific circumstances. Other suggested forms from either Charles E. Rotkin or Photography for Industry are offered in the same manner. Please feel free to adjust the terminology to your needs.

Stock Photography Delivery Memo

STOCK PHOTOGRAPHY DELIVERY MEMO

TO:

PHONE NO:

ORDERED BY:
CLIENT:

DATE:
SHIPMENT NO:

PROJECT:
OUR JOB NO:

YOUR P.O. NO.:
YOUR JOB NO.:

PHOTOGRAPHS TO BE RETURNED BY:

QTY.	ORIG. (O) DUPL. (D)	FORMAT	PHOTOGRAPH SUBJECT/ID NO.	VALUE (IF OTHER THAN $1,500/ITEM) IN EVENT OF LOSS/DAMAGE

_____ TOTAL COLOR
_____ TOTAL B&W

CHECK COUNT AND ACKNOWLEDGE BY SIGNING AND RETURNING ONE COPY. COUNT SHALL BE CONSIDERED ACCURATE AND QUALITY DEEMED SATISFACTORY FOR REPRODUCTION IF SAID COPY IS NOT IMMEDIATELY RECEIVED BY RETURN MAIL WITH ALL EXCEPTIONS DULY NOTED. PHOTOGRAPHS MUST BE RETURNED BY REGISTERED MAIL, AIR COURIER OR OTHER BONDED MESSENGER WHICH PROVIDES PROOF OF RETURN.

SUBJECT TO ALL TERMS AND CONDITIONS ABOVE AND ON REVERSE SIDE

Acknowledged and Accepted: _____

Please sign here   *Date*

S1-90

TERMS & CONDITIONS

[1] "Photograph(s)" means all photographic material furnished by Photographer hereunder, whether transparencies, negatives, prints or otherwise.

[2] After 14 days, the following holding fees are charged until return: Five Dollars ($5.00) per week per color transparency and One Dollar ($1.00) per week per print.

[3] Submission is for examination only. Photographs may not be reproduced, copied, projected, or used in any way without (a) express written permission on Photographer's invoice stating the rights granted and the terms thereof and (b) payment of said invoice. The reasonable and stipulated fee for any other use shall be three times Photographer's normal fee for such usage.

[4] Client assumes insurer's liability (a) to indemnify Photographer for loss, damage, or misuse of any photographs and (b) to return all photographs prepaid, fully insured, safe and undamaged, by bonded messenger, air freight, or registered mail. Client assumes full liability for its principals, employees, agents, affiliates, successors and assigns (including without limitation messengers and freelance researchers) for any loss, damage, or misuse of the photographs.

[5] Reimbursement by Client for loss or damage of each original transparency shall be in the amount of One Thousand Five Hundred Dollars ($1,500), or such other amount set forth next to said item on the front hereof. Reimbursement by Client for loss or damage of each other item shall be in the amount set forth next to said item on the front hereof. Photographer and Client agree that said amount represents the fair and reasonable value of each item, and that Photographer would not sell all rights to such item for less than said amount.

[6] Photographer's copyright notice" © [YEAR OF FIRST PUBLICATION] [PHOTOGRAPHER'S NAME]" must accompany each use as an adjacent credit line. Invoice amount will be tripled if said credit is not provided.

[7] Client may not assign or transfer this agreement, or any rights granted hereunder. This agreement binds and inures to the benefit of Photographer, Client, Client's principals, employees, agents and affiliates and their respective heirs legal representatives, successors and assigns. Client and its principals, employees, agents and affiliates are jointly and severally liable for the performance of all payment and other obligations hereunder. No amendment or waiver of any terms is binding unless set forth in writing and signed by the parties. This agreement incorporates by reference Article 2 of the Uniform Commercial Code, and the Copyright Act of 1976, as amended.

[8] Except as provided in [9] below any dispute regarding this agreement shall be arbitrated in [PHOTOGRAPHER'S CITY AND STATE] under rules of the American Arbitration Association and the laws of [STATE OF ARBITRATION]. Any dispute involving $_____ [LIMIT OF LOCAL SMALL CLAIMS COURT] or less may be submitted without arbitration to any court having jurisdiction thereof. Client shall pay all arbitration and court costs, reasonable legal fees, and expenses, and legal interest on any award or judgment in favor of Photographer.

[9] Client hereby expressly consents to the jurisdiction of the federal courts with respect to claims by photographer under the Copyright Act of 1976, as amended.

[10] Client will not make or permit any alterations, additions, or subtractions in respect of the photographs, including without limitation any digitalization or synthesization of the photographs, alone or with any other material, by use of computer or other electronic means or any other method or means now or hereafter known.

[11] Client will indemnify and defend Photographer against all claims, liability, damages, costs, and expenses, including reasonable legal fees and expenses, arising out of any use of any photographs for which no release was furnished by Photographer, or any photographs which are altered by Client. Unless so furnished, no release exists.

Courtesy: ASMP

Photograph Delivery Memo

PFI Photography for Industry
1697 Broadway, New York, N.Y. 10019
(212) PLaza 7-9255 Cable: PHOTOINDUS

MEMBER IPACA
PICTURE AGENCY COUNCIL OF AMERICA, INC

YOUR ATTENTION PLEASE!

NO: _____

DATE: _____

WE WOULD APPRECIATE YOUR PAYING
SPECIAL ATTENTION TO PARAGRAPH 3
ON THE REVERSE OF THIS FORM. These
fees will be charged unless you contact us
in ADVANCE of the expiration date of the
free period and request an extension of time.

TO: _____

No. PFI	DESCRIPTION

BLACK AND WHITE
Contact Prints
Series Nos. Description

BLACK AND WHITE ENLARGEMENTS
Series Size Finish Description

Courtesy: Charles E. Rotkin, Photography for Industry

Photograph Delivery Memo (cont.)

PFI   Photography for Industry
1697 Broadway, New York, N.Y. 10019
(212) PLaza 7-9255   Cable: PHOTOINDUS

PICTURE AGENCY COUNCIL OF AMERICA, INC.

TO: **PHOTOGRAPH DELIVERY MEMO**

1) IN THE EVENT THAT ANY OF THE COLOR PHOTOGRAPHS LISTED HEREIN ARE
LOST, OR DESTROYED BEYOND REPAIR BY YOU, YOUR AGENTS, ASSIGNEES OR
CARRIERS, YOU SHALL PAY TO ME and/or PHOTOGRAPHY FOR INDUSTRY THE
SUM OF $1500 FOR EACH SUCH PHOTOGRAPH, AND THE SUM OF $3000 FOR ANY
COLOR AERIAL PHOTOGRAPH PRODUCED OUTSIDE OF THE UNITED STATES. SUCH
PAYMENT TO BE MADE WITHIN 60 DAYS OF THE TIME OF SUCH LOSS.

IT IS FURTHER AGREED THAT IF DAMAGED PHOTOGRAPHS ARE NOT REPAIRED
TO MY REASONABLE SATISFACTION WITHIN 30 DAYS OF DAMAGE, THEN PAY-
MENT FOR SAME SHALL BE MADE IN THE SAME MANNER AS A LOST PHOTOGRAPH.
THIS MEMORANDUM (AND THE PHOTOGRAPHS ENUMERATED HEREIN) IS NOT
CONSIDERED A BAILMENT AND IS SPECIFICALLY CONDITIONED ON THE FACT
THAT THESE ENUMERATED PHOTOGRAPHS ARE RETURNED SAFELY TO US
IN THE SAME CONDITION AS RECEIVED FROM US.

2) In the event litigation is commenced by us against you to collect any amount due
hereunder, you agree to pay us our reasonable legal fees, no less than $500.00
plus any disbursements incurred by us in connection with such litigation.

3) A MINIMUM HOLDING FEE OF $_____ will be billed on material held longer than
FOURTEEN DAYS except where PFI is given a guarantee of usage at a mutually
agreeable fee or where other specific arrangements are made in writing at the time
of delivery of these photographs. AFTER FOURTEEN DAYS an additional charge of
$1.50 per day per photograph will be made until the photographs are returned to us.

4) A SERVICE CHARGE OF $_____ will be billed on material requested but not used
unless prior arrangements are made to waive this charge.

5) DAMAGES to transparency mounts caused by re-labeling or mis-handling will be
charged at the rate of $10.00 per mount. Damage to black and white prints caused
by mis-handling will be charged at the rate of $5.00 per contact sheet and $15.00
per 8" x 10" enlargement. Damage to color prints, color screens or other graphic
materials will be charged for commensurately. In the event that a transparency is
lost after engraving, then all separations both continuous tone and screened and all
other related graphic arts materials shall be turned over to us by you and/or your
printers and engravers and shall become our property at no cost to us whatsoever.

6) REPRODUCTION RIGHTS GRANTED: Only those reproduction rights which are specifically invoiced are granted. All other rights are reserved. No promotional or
advertising rights are granted when pictures are released for editorial use including
reproductions of covers or dust jackets for promotional purposes. Any copyrights
secured for these transparencies shall be reassigned to us.

7) MODEL RELEASES: No model releases or other releases exist unless such existence is specified by PFI. Licensee shall idemnify PFI against any and all such claims
arising out of the use of any photographs unless the existence of such releases is noted.

8) DELIVERY AND RETENTION OF THE LISTED ITEMS FOR LONGER THAN 24 HOURS
SHALL CONSTITUTE YOUR ACCEPTANCE OF THE WITHIN TERMS.

ACCEPTED BY_____AS AGENT FOR _____

Courtesy: Charles E. Rotkin, Photography for Industry

Invoice

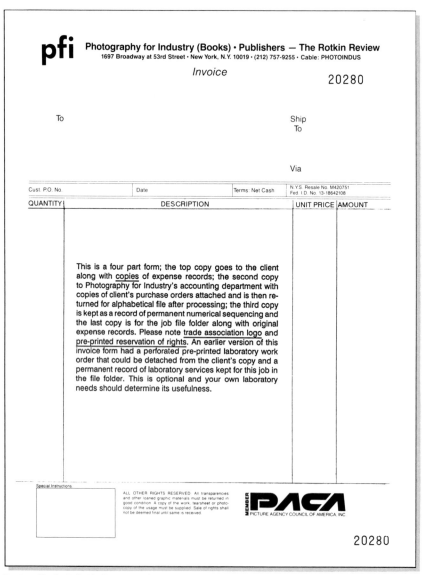

pfi Photography for Industry (Books) • Publishers — The Rotkin Review
1697 Broadway at 53rd Street • New York, N.Y. 10019 • (212) 757-9255 • Cable: PHOTOINDUS

Invoice

20280

To

Ship
To

Via

Cust. P.O. No.	Date	Terms: Net Cash	N.Y.S. Resale No. M420751 Fed. I.D. No. 13-18642108
QUANTITY	DESCRIPTION		UNIT PRICE AMOUNT

This is a four part form; the top copy goes to the client along with copies of expense records; the second copy to Photography for Industry's accounting department with copies of client's purchase orders attached and is then returned for alphabetical file after processing; the third copy is kept as a record of permanent numerical sequencing and the last copy is for the job file folder along with original expense records. Please note trade association logo and pre-printed reservation of rights. An earlier version of this invoice form had a perforated pre-printed laboratory work order that could be detached from the client's copy and a permanent record of laboratory services kept for this job in the file folder. This is optional and your own laboratory needs should determine its usefulness.

Special Instructions

ALL OTHER RIGHTS RESERVED. All transparencies and other loaned graphic materials must be returned in good condition. A copy of the work, tearsheet or photocopy of the usage must be supplied. Sale of rights shall not be deemed final until same is received.

MEMBER **PACA**
PICTURE AGENCY COUNCIL OF AMERICA, INC.

20280

Courtesy: Charles E. Rotkin, Photography for Industry

Release

ADULT RELEASE

In consideration of my engagement as a model, and for other good and valuable consideration herein acknowledged as received, I hereby grant to _____ ("Photographer"), his/her heirs, legal representatives and assigns, those for whom Photographer is acting, and those acting with his/her authority and permission, the irrevocable and unrestricted right and permission to copyright, in his/her own name or otherwise, and use, re-use, publish, and re-publish photographic portraits or pictures of me or in which I may be included, in whole or in part, or composite or distorted in character or form, without restriction as to changes or alterations, in conjunction with my own or a fictitious name, or reproductions thereof in color or otherwise, made through any medium at his/her studios or elsewhere, and in any and all media now or hereafter known for illustration, promotion, art, editorial, advertising, trade, or any other purpose whatsoever. I also consent to the use of any printed matter in conjunction therewith.

I hereby waive any right that I may have to inspect or approve the finished product or products and the advertising copy or other matter that may be used in connection therewith or the use to which it may be applied.

I hereby release, discharge and agree to save harmless Photographer, his/her heirs, legal representatives and assigns, and all persons acting under his/her permission or authority or those for whom he/she is acting, from any liability by virtue of any blurring, distortion, alteration, optical illusion, or use in composite form, whether intentional or otherwise, that may occur or be produced in the taking of said picture or in any subsequent processing thereof, as well as any publication thereof, including without limitation any claims for libel or invasion of privacy.

I hereby warrant that I am of full age and have the right to contract in my own name. I have read the above authorization, release, and agreement, prior to its execution, and I am fully familiar with the contents thereof. This release shall be binding upon me and my heirs, legal representatives, and assigns.

_____   _____
DATE   NAME

_____   _____
WITNESS   ADDRESS

Courtesy: ASMP

Release

SIMPLIFIED ADULT RELEASE

For valuable consideration received, I hereby grant to _____ ("Photographer") the absolute and irrevocable right and unrestricted permission in respect of photographic portraits or pictures that he/she had taken of me or in which I may be included with others, to copyright the same, in his/her own name or otherwise; to use, re-use, publish, and re-publish the same in whole or in part, individually or in conjunction with other photographs, and in conjunction with any printed matter, in any and all media now or hereafter known, and for any purpose whatsoever, for illustration, promotion, art, editorial, advertising and trade, or any other purpose whatsoever without restriction as to alteration; and to use my name in connection therewith if he/she so chooses.

I hereby release and discharge Photographer from any and all claims and demands arising out of or in connection with the use of the photographs, including without limitation any and all claims for libel or invasion of privacy.

This authorization and release shall also inure to the benefit of the heirs, legal representatives, licensees, and assigns of Photographer, as well as the person(s) for whom he/she took the photographs.

I am of full age and have the right to contract in my own name. I have read the foregoing and fully understand the contents thereof. This release shall be binding upon me and my heirs, legal representatives, and assigns.

_____
DATE

_____
WITNESS

_____
NAME

_____

_____
ADDRESS

Courtesy: ASMP

Release

MINOR RELEASE

In consideration of the engagement as a model of the minor named below, and for other good and valuable consideration herein acknowledged as received, upon the terms hereinafter stated, I hereby grant to _____ ("Photographer"), his/her legal representatives and assigns, those for whom Photographer is acting, and those acting with his/her authority and permission, the absolute right and permission to copyright and use, re-use, publish, and re-publish photographic portraits or pictures of the minor or in which the minor may be included, in whole or in part, or composite or distorted in character or form, without restriction as to changes or alterations from time to time, in conjunction with the minor's own or a fictitious name, or reproductions thereof in color or otherwise, made through any medium at his/her studios or elsewhere, and in any and all media now or hereafter known, for art, advertising, trade, or any other purpose whatsoever. I also consent to the use of any printed matter in conjunction therewith.

I hereby waive any right that I or the minor may have to inspect or approve the finished product or products or the advertising copy or printed matter that may be used in connection therewith or the use to which it may be applied.

I hereby release, discharge, and agree to save harmless Photographer, his/her legal representatives or assigns, and all persons acting under his/her permission or authority or those for whom he/she is acting, from any liability by virtue of any blurring, distortion, alteration, optical illusion, or use in composite form, whether intentional or otherwise, that may occur or be produced in the taking of said picture or in any subsequent processing thereof, as well as any publication thereof, including without limitation any claims for libel or invasion of privacy.

I hereby warrant that I am of full age and have every right to contract for the minor in the above regard. I state further that I have read the above authorization, release, and agreement, prior to its execution, and that I am fully familiar with the contents thereof. This release shall be binding upon me and my heirs, legal representatives, and assigns.

_____
DATE

_____   _____
(MINOR'S NAME)   (FATHER) (MOTHER) (GUARDIAN)

_____   _____
(MINOR'S ADDRESS)   (ADDRESS)

_____
(WITNESS)

Courtesy: ASMP

Release

RELEASE

For valuable consideration received, I hereby grant to _____ ("Photographer") and his/her legal representatives and assigns, the irrevocable and unrestricted right to use and publish photographs of me, or in which I may be included, for editorial, trade, advertising and any other purpose and in any manner and medium; to alter the same without restriction; and to copyright the same. I hereby release Photographer and his/her legal representatives and assigns from all claims and liability relating to said photographs.

Name (Print) _____   Date _____

Signature _____   Phone _____

Address _____

City _____   State_____   Zip_____

If Minor, Signature of Parent/Guardian _____

Witness _____

Courtesy: ASMP

Release

PROPERTY RELEASE

For good and valuable consideration herein acknowledged as received, the undersigned, being the legal owner of, or having the right to permit the taking and use of photographs of, certain property designated as _____, does grant to _____ ("Photographer"), his/her heirs, legal representatives, agents, and assigns the full rights to use such photographs and copyright same, in advertising, trade, or for any purpose.

The undersigned also consents to the use of any printed matter in conjunction therewith.

The undersigned hereby waives any right that he/she/it may have to inspect or approve the finished product or products, or the advertising copy or printed matter that may be used in connection therewith, or the use to which it may be applied.

The undersigned hereby releases, discharges, and agrees to save harmless Photographer, his/her heirs, legal representatives, and assigns, and all persons acting under his/her permission or authority, or those for whom he/she is acting, from any liability by virtue of any blurring, distortion, alteration, optical illusion, or use in composite form, whether intentional or otherwise, that may occur or be produced in the taking of said picture or in any subsequent processing thereof, as well as any publication thereof, even though it may subject me to ridicule, scandal, reproach, scorn, and indignity.

The undersigned hereby warrants that he/she is of full age and has every right to contract in his/her own name in the above regard. The undersigned states further that he/she has read the above authorization, release, and agreement, prior to its execution, and that he/she is fully familiar with the contents thereof. If the undersigned is signing as an agent or employee of a firm or corporation, the undersigned warrants that he/she is fully authorized to do so. This release shall be binding upon the undersigned and his/her/its heirs, legal representatives, successors, and assigns.

_____
DATE

_____
(WITNESS)

_____
(NAME)

_____

_____

_____
(ADDRESS)

Courtesy: ASMP

Map/Assignment Query

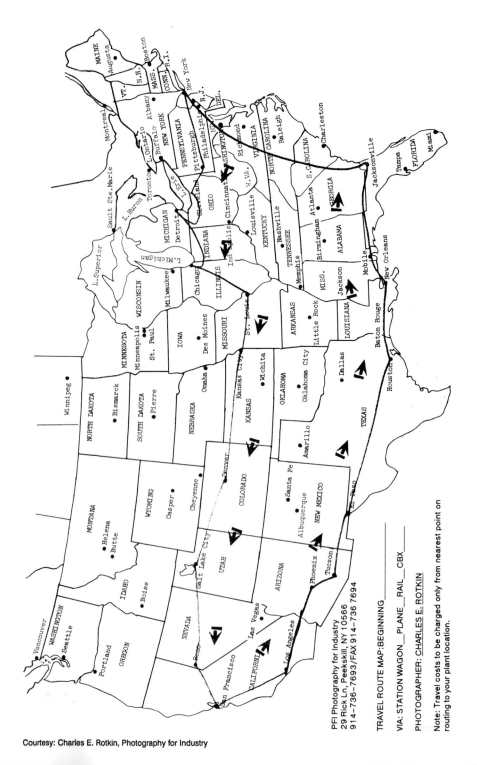

PFI Photography for Industry
29 Rick Ln, Peekskill, NY 10566
914-736-7693/FAX 914-736 7694

TRAVEL ROUTE MAP:BEGINNING _____

VIA: STATION WAGON__ PLANE__ RAIL__ CBX _____

PHOTOGRAPHER: CHARLES E. ROTKIN

Note: Travel costs to be charged only from nearest point on routing to your plant location.

Glossary

Access Fee. Fee paid to a museum or other institution for right to inspect acquisitions for possible reproduction rights.

AD. Abbreviation for Art Director.

Advance. Payment made to a photographer in advance of final billings.

Advertising Use. Use of photographs in paid space advertising.

Agency, Stock. See Stock Agency.

All Rights Agreement. Sale of all rights/copyright.

Annual Report. Annual financial statement by a publicly owned corporation.

Approval, On. Clients may ask to hold pictures pending purchase.

Archival. Free as possible from chemicals causing premature aging.

Archive. Photo library dealing in historical photography or artwork.

Art Buyer. Advertising agency person who purchases photography and art.

Art Director. Designer responsible for layouts in editorial or advertising use.

Art Reference. Use of photographs/art as a source of technical information.

Artwork. Whatever is not text or type in graphic arts production.

ASMP. The American Society of Magazine Photographers.

Assembly. Group of pictures used as one illustration.

Assignment (of Rights). Transfer of rights from one user to another.

Audiovisual (AV). Mixture of sound and visual images for projection.

Bleed. When an illustration reaches any or all edges of a print.

Brochure. Advertising pamphlet or booklet usually for business or promotion.

Buy-Out. Sale of all rights. Hidden trap in a work-for-hire agreement.

Caption. Title or explanation of a photo.

CD-ROM. Computer or audio disks used for sound/music/electronic imaging data storage. Acronym for Compact Disk-Read Only Memory.

Client. This is your customer. Be nice!

Camera-ready Copy. Material ready for reproduction in offset printing.

Canadian Rights. Rights to reprint and sell published material in Canada.

Closings. The times set for the last bits of material to go into any publication before including artwork.

Co-Publishing. Publishing arrangement whereby an author and publisher (possibly a book packager) share costs of production, distribution, etc. of a book and the profits.

Cold Type. Type not made by the hot metal process. Now computer generated and composed directly on film. Also used for handmade presentations or portfolios. Can be purchased in art supply stores in various type fonts.

Column. A width measure image of type on a page.

Composite. Multi-image print showing proposed layout of all elements.

Comp. An abbreviation for the term "composite." Used in advertising.

Conversion. Black-and-white image made from color or vice versa.

Copyright. Legal ownership in a work(s) to protect it from unauthorized use.

Corporate Industrial Photography. Photographs made for corporate industrial client.

Credit Line. Identification of producer or supplier of illustration or copy.

Cycle. Period of time for repeat use of work (e.g., TV shows or commercials).

Delivery Memo. List of photographs submitted with conditions of usage.

Demographics. A market analysis of an area by income, population, spending or other criteria.

Distribution Rights. Various rights to print a photograph in publications.

Double-Truck. A term used for a photograph covering two full, facing pages.

Droit-De-Suite. French phrase meaning rights that follow. Protection of artists in Europe, particularly for artists receiving a percentage of ongoing sales of their work.

Dummy. Mock-up of a publication, often with dummy type and photostats.

Duotone. Printing a halftone in two colors from a one-color original.

Dust Jacket. Paper cover for hardcover books. May use photographs.

Edition (of a Book). This is an often disputed term, and can mean different things, such as press runs, uses by ADs for comps, or distribution where copy or art layouts change.

Editorial Use. Use of a photograph other than in advertising or promotion.

Electronic Imaging. Using computers to move (or remove) elements of a photograph(s) to create new images or color separations. Used for retouching.

Endpapers. Illustrated, usually double-page spreads at the very beginning or end of a hardcover book.

ENG (Electronic News Gathering). A form of videotaping for broadcast use. Now used in digital backs of (hand-held) still cameras for electronic transmission of images to publication plants.

Exclusive Rights. Sole grant of nontransferable rights to client.

Filmstrip. Individual images and/or words on film for projection.

First Publication Rights. See First Rights.

First Rights. First-time right to reproduce a photograph in any medium.

Flat Fee. Single fee for all or specific rights.

Flyer. Usually a single printed sheet or fold-over, often used for advertising.

Foreign Language Rights. Rights to publish a book (originally published in the U.S.) in a foreign language.

Frontispiece. Illustration used facing title page of book.

Gang-Up. Used to group images together to make one single set of separations that will be cut up and used separately in printing.

Gatefold. Multiple page foldout.

Generational Increase. In customary film chemistry, contrast usually increases with copying step. Does not occur in digital (electronic) copying.

Gofer. An errand runner, usually meaning "go fer this" or "go fer that."

Gravure. Using intaglio plates (reverse dots) for quality print reproduction.

Gutter. Part of book or magazine where the pages meet in the binding.

Halftone. Printing plate made with a screen to control ink flow over image.

Hardcover. Book binding where the case (cover) is made of firm material.

Holding fee. Charge for holding work beyond time stated in delivery memo.

Hot Metal. Typesetting using molten lead characters (Linotype process).

House Account. Photographer's account without commission due on fees.

Imprint. Publishing term for identification (and address) of a publisher.

In-House. Term indicating origin of a work prepared by sponsor, not agency.

Insertion. Placement of an ad in a periodical.

Invoice. Bill for services, expenses, rights, and licenses of work.

Keystoning. A "keystone" shape to a print (or transparency) occurs when copying a painting or other flat artwork if the camera lens is not set at the center of the painting and the film planes of the copying camera are not exactly parallel to the painting being copied.

Kodak Premier. Electronic imaging system used to make new transparencies or prints.

Leasing Memo (Delivery memo). A form used by photographers or stock photo agencies enumerating terms and conditions of photo/art submission.

Letterpress Printing. A form of printing where the image is engraved on a metal block, then inserted and printed on a press. Superior reproduction often results, but high expense limits its use.

License of Rights. Legal term for a grant of specified rights for a publication.

Mainframe. Central computer hardware with large storage and memory capacity. Remote work stations can be linked to a central mainframe unit.

Matte. Nonglossy surface.

Mechanical. Preparation of material to be photographed for an offset printing plate.

Monitor. The video display terminal (VDT) of a computer or television set.

Motor Drive. Electrically operated film advancing/rewinding components in a camera.

Multi-Image. Several images shown at the same time in print or by projection.

Multiple Rights. Licensing of a photograph for use in more than one market.

Non-Exclusive Rights. Grant of rights for a photograph. May be used elsewhere.

North American Rights. Publication rights limited to the U.S. and Canada.

Offset Printing. The most popular form of publication printing. The inked images are "offset" or transferred to a rubber blanket on a press and the paper pressed against the blanket. A modern version of the lithography process.

Onetime Rights. Right to reproduce a photograph once, in one publication.

Out-Take. Usually refers to extra or similar images from a shooting session.

PACA. See Picture Agency Council.

Page Rate. Payments for work per page in a publication based on space used.

Paperback. Softcover books, usually intended for mass distribution.

Pasteup. See Mechanical.

Picture Agency Council (PACA). A trade group of stock photo agencies.

Picture Editor. Person who analyzes/assigns/buys photographs.

Picture Researcher. Expert in locating visual material, may do prior edit.

Pixel. Data (acronym for picture element) used in electronic imaging.

Press Runs. In book publishing, usually the number of sheets run on a press, or copies of an entire publication.

Printings. The number of times the same book is run without changes.

Progressive Proof. Progressive color proofs show the step-by-step progression of color inking. Color bars are standard color tones on a proof sheet to be used with comparisons of actual printing.

Promotional Rights. Right(s) to use a photograph to promote a specific person, place, not to be confused with advertising (paid space rights). Be careful on uses of a magazine cover (with your photograph) to promote publication.

Proof, Photographer's. A test sheet of work, usually a contact print.

Proof, Printer's. Part of reproduction process; test submitted for approval.

Quarterly Report. Corporate financial and progress statement.

Reflective Copy. Opaque (as opposed to transparent) artwork; shown by reflected or overhead projector.

Rejects. Different from out-takes or similars in that they are usually of inferior quality and should not be offered for submission.

Releases. Written permission to publish, utilize, or offer for sale a likeness of a person, place or thing.

Reprint. Additional print run with no change of editorial content.

Reproduction. Transfer of photographic image via a printing process.

Reproduction Quality. Quality of reproduction in printing process.

Revisions. In book publishing, when the book is restructured. Re-use of photographs may require additional payment if changes are significant.

Royalties. A system of payments by publishers to authors. Usually based on a percentage of sales.

Scitex-Visionary. An electronic imaging computer system primarily used to make color separations in the graphic arts industry.

Screen Engravings. Used in half-tone reproduction of photographs or artwork. A fine screen is interposed between copy and sensitized materials to break up images into dot patterns to assure even flow of ink over highlights/halftones.

Secondary Rights. All rights to a photograph that exist after primary rights have been disposed of.

Separations. Separating the primary colors of a photograph so that they may be printed in successive applications to register in complete color. Normally four colors are used, but six colors are available for high quality.

Software. Computer data storage material required to run computers.

Spread. See Double-Truck.

Stock. See Stock Agency.

Stock Agency. A photo library containing the work of many photographers (or artists) that can be leased for reproduction in any suitable media.

Syndication Service. News and photo organizations which distribute existing stories (or single photos) to other publications. Some syndication groups are owned by the parent press company of publication.

Tearsheet. A page from a publication using a photograph (or writing).

Trade Books. Books sold "to the trade," that is, through regular book stores.

Transparencies. Photographic images, usually positive, on film to be viewed through transmitted light.

VDT. Video display terminal. See Monitor.

Work Stations. Remote computer installations where basic electronic imaging procedures are performed and then transmitted electronically to mainframes for production.

World Rights/Multiple Languages. Rights to publish worldwide.

Index